Clinton Heylin is recognized all over the world as a leading authority on Bob Dylan. He was co-founder of *Wanted Man*, the British magazine dedicated to studying Dylan's life and work, and for a number of years edited the news section of its quarterly magazine, the *Telegraph*. He published his highly praised biography, *Dylan: Behind the Shades*, in 1991 (reissued in Penguin in 2001) and followed it in 1996 with an equally well-received account of Dylan's recording career, *Dylan: Behind Closed Doors*, which was nominated in the USA for the prestigious Ralph J. Gleason Award for music books. His other books include *Day by Day: A Life in Stolen Moments*; *From the Velvets to the Voidoids*, a history of American Punk; *The Great White Wonders*, an in-depth history of bootlegging; *No More Sad Refrains*, a biography of Sandy Denny; and *Can You Feel the Silence?*, a biography of Van Morrison. Brought up in Manchester, he now lives in Somerset.

Clinton Heylin

BOB DYLAN:

Behind the Shades

Take Two

PENGUIN BOOKS

Original dedication: *For Jill, 'the girl with me behind the shades'*
Dedication to new edition: *To John Green, Anthea Joseph,
Howie Wyeth and Allen Ginsberg, peace in the end*

PENGUIN BOOKS

Published by the Penguin Group
Penguin Books Ltd, 80 Strand, London WC2R 0RL, England
Penguin Putnam Inc., 375 Hudson Street, New York, New York 10014, USA
Penguin Books Australia Ltd, 250 Camberwell Road, Camberwell, Victoria 3124, Australia
Penguin Books Canada Ltd, 10 Alcorn Avenue, Toronto, Ontario, Canada M4V 3B2
Penguin Books India (P) Ltd, 11 Community Centre, Panchsheel Park, New Delhi – 110 017, India
Penguin Books (NZ) Ltd, Cnr Rosedale and Airborne Roads, Albany, Auckland, New Zealand
Penguin Books (South Africa) (Pty) Ltd, 24 Sturdee Avenue, Rosebank 2196, South Africa

Penguin Books Ltd, Registered Offices: 80 Strand, London WC2R 0RL, England

www.penguin.com

First published by Viking 2000
Published in Penguin Books 2001

7

Copyright © Clinton Heylin, 2000
All rights reserved

The moral right of the author has been asserted

Set in Monotype Bembo
Typeset by Rowland Phototypesetting Ltd, Bury St Edmunds, Suffolk
Printed in England by Clays Ltd, St Ives plc

Contents

A Preface in the Past Tense (1990)

In the beginning was Scaduto. It was 1971. For five long years Bob Dylan had maintained a public profile that Howard Hughes would have been proud of. Anthony Scaduto's was the first serious biography of the man, at a time when there was little information about his roots, his early life, and his dreams of fame. It dutifully recorded his small-town youth in Hibbing, his year in Minneapolis, and his early days in New York. By 1965, Dylan had outgrown the former friends Scaduto had talked to, and in the final section of his book Scaduto's previously racy style, bereft of any major sources except Dylan's own rewriting of his history in cagey interviews with the author, dissipated into song analysis and speculation.

It was another fifteen years before the publication of the second serious Dylan biography. In that time Dylan had reached the peak of his commercial success, released perhaps his most perfect album, converted to born-again Christianity and embarked on a series of tours all exceeding in scope his mid-sixties touring activities. On September 29, 1986—the twenty-fifth anniversary of his famous original endorsement of Dylan in the *New York Times*—Robert Shelton published his own, long-awaited biography of his old friend.

Shelton's plans for a book had been first mentioned in the summer of 1966. The volume had been two decades in the making. Not surprisingly, given the level of expectation, it was a profound disappointment. He barely advanced the story beyond Dylan's fabled 1966 motorcycle accident, and much of the chunky tome was filled with pat song analysis and cuttings-file outtakes. Though he filled important gaps in Scaduto's narrative of the early years, Shelton did Dylan a great disservice by interring him in the period he had already spent twenty years trying to live down.

Since Shelton's book there has been one pretender to the title of serious Dylan biographer. In the fall of 1988, Bob Spitz, author of a previous book on the 1969 Woodstock Festival, published a biography as expansive as Shelton's and as racy as Scaduto's. Yet, despite conducting many original interviews, Spitz did not advance Dylan's story. His interviewees were mostly the familiar names used by Scaduto and Shelton, and his Goldmanesque approach, excruciating prose style, dubious sense of Dylan's history, and—yet again—virtual exclusion of Dylan's post-accident career resulted in what one reviewer described appositely as 'a thick, petrified, one-pound hunk of wood-fibre.'

Now Bob Dylan is fifty. It is twenty-five years since he fell off his motorcycle in Woodstock. Yet the history of those twenty-five years remains untold. Two-thirds of this book is devoted to Dylan's post-accident career. It is my intent to show the full sweep of his life to date, and his post-accident years actually represent five-sixths of his entire recording career.

Of course Dylan's rise to fame is an important part of his story and the first section of *Behind the Shades* deals with the well-documented pre-accident years. Though Scaduto and Shelton have given good coverage to this period, I have tried to explore a particular thread which I find weaving in and out of Scaduto and Shelton, but rarely overtly: What made Dylan so different from his contemporaries in Hibbing, in Minneapolis, in Greenwich Village, and among the pop-music icons of the mid-sixties? Why did he continue to grow when others, equally well regarded, stagnated? The ability constantly to reinvent who Bob Dylan was, and is, remains the primary characteristic of his art. It is the way he unleashes new works. The process may be subtler now, but it remains apparent. In the early and mid-sixties it actually seemed as if Dylan had no control over his chameleon changes, they proceeded at such a frantic pace. It is likely that Dylan never really knew in those days how close he was to the precipice.

How Dylan has coped with the legacy of those amphetamine years is an equally remarkable story. Like another 'would-be genius,' Orson Welles, he is generally thought to have created his masterpiece, the *Blonde on Blonde* album, before he was even twenty-five, and then spent the next twenty-five years twisting in the wind, determined to assert himself as an abidingly creative artist. But, unlike Welles, he did manage to surpass that youthful masterpiece with the remarkable *Blood on the Tracks,* and came close twice more during his so-named religious period.

If the motorcycle accident represents an obvious demarcation point in Dylan's career, his religious conversion has been the other major break with his past. That his post-conversion career has been detailed in a total of less than thirty pages by both Spitz and Shelton does a grave injustice to a major period of Dylan's ever-changing career. Though this period reads as a catalogue of missed chances and poor judgment, the last decade is the story of a very personal battle to construct a worldview that retains his faith in both God and humanity. The struggle has led to its fair share of great Dylan songs. Yet if the story in Part Two of *Behind the Shades* in no way parallels Orson Welles's post-*Kane* career, Part Three's narrative is rather similar in its repeated hints of revival, the promise of masterpieces often unfulfilled or rendered minor by lack of discipline, or the neophobic impulses of others, though the release of *Oh Mercy* and *Under the Red Sky* enables a tinge of optimism to color the final pages of my book.

Dylan's perennial reinventions of himself led me to structure this book around each new guise that he has taken upon himself. In most cases a chapter revolves around a major work or tour introducing a new Dylan (e.g. *Another Side, Blood on the Tracks, Tarantula, Renaldo and Clara,* the Rolling Thunder tours). It is a convenient form to use but it is only a convenience, perhaps the dominant color in my patchwork, but there will be more besides.

Dylan's career could as easily be divided by his geography. Certain chapters fit neatly into the geographic notion, coinciding with artistic periods as well. Thus his 1960 apprenticeship in Minneapolis marks an obvious divide. His fleeing New York for Durango, and finally settling in Malibu, again marked an important change; while his 'retreat' (1966–69) is often referred to as his Woodstock Period (a slight misnomer, given that he had been spending most of his free time there since 1964). Certain albums have been the product of Dylan's geography. Most of *Another Side* was written in Greece in May 1964, 'the Basement tapes' was written and recorded in Woodstock, *New Morning* was the first product of his return to New York City at the end of 1969, and *Blood on the Tracks* was largely composed during a summer on his Minnesota farm, as was *Street Legal*.

A credible biography is a bringing together of such strands. It draws from all and distills down to a point of view. With a living artist the picture can never be complete. This book can only be a signpost along the way. Dylan also presents a difficult subject because he has trusted people and they have repaid him accordingly. Many of the most important people in his life have refused to talk about their relationship with him. The voices of his wife Sara Dylan, his ex-manager the late Albert Grossman, and his confidants Victor Maymudes and Bobby Neuwirth are largely absent from this book. Fortunately, most of his important musical collaborators have been less recalcitrant.

Dylan himself cooperated with both Scaduto and Shelton in the composition of their books, freely giving interviews and in Shelton's case suggesting people he should contact. Yet in both cases there was a price to pay. Though neither book could be described as authorized, Dylan exerted his influence upon both. Inevitably this led to a slightly sanitized portrait of the man, particularly in Shelton's book. Spitz, predictably, went to the other extreme and chronicled each and every tale of anyone who had a chip on his shoulder and a grudge to bear. Dylan, like most biographical subjects, is not looking for an accurate portrayal. To quote Orson Welles, 'I don't want any description of me to be accurate, I want it to be flattering. I don't think people who have to sing for their supper ever like to be described truthfully, not in print anyway.'

Dylan's voice, though freely represented in this book, is not the voice of a man presenting an authorized portrait of himself, save perhaps in the few instances where I have drawn from his comments in the *Biograph* booklet. (Note: Though many of the *Biograph* quotes there come from Cameron Crowe's interviews with him, Dylan also appended his own written additions.) His words have been selected from over two hundred interviews he has given in the last thirty years, from raps he has given at concerts in his more gregarious days, from bio-poems he has written. It is one of the great myths of Dylan lore that his interviews are invariably a stream of put-ons and put-downs. In fact at certain points in his life, notably in 1978 and 1985, he has been very keen to talk about his past in a surprisingly frank and honest manner. Readers will find Dylan's voice represented here on a far greater scale than in previous biographies, but without a concomitant personal influence upon the finished product.

Many of the sources I interviewed did not offer their version of Dylan for this book, though certainly they were aware they were contributing to a detailed chronicling of his career. Most of the original interviews quoted were conducted over the last nine years, intended for and published in *The Telegraph*, the journal of Wanted Man, the Bob Dylan Information Office. The majority of these were conducted by myself or John Bauldie, my co-founder of Wanted Man and editor of *The Telegraph*. I consider the use of this archive of exclusive interviews to be one of the book's strengths. People treat the idea of talking to a biographer quite differently from that of talking on behalf of what could be referred to as a cross between a very high quality fanzine and a critical quarterly.

The use of this impressive archive of interviews, I believe, enables a far more accurate portrait than the one that would have resulted from the guarded interviews I might have obtained in the guise of biographer. I trust I have performed no disservice to those who freely gave of their time for the purpose of being interviewed about Dylan, and I hope they will share my belief that the result is considerably fairer and more accurate than previous Dylan biographies have been.

I have tried to give each commentator his own voice, rather than provide a secondhand paraphrase of what has been said. I trust the reader will feel a sense of Dylan's many-sided self through his verbatim recollections and the recollections of those around him, a feeling that for me rarely comes through in other accounts of him. Needless to say I have tried to document what I believe really happened, but the reader must be aware that there is much myth-building at stake here, and that Dylan's friends and collaborators revel in that process as much as the man himself does. For each brick I pull down, there may well be another put in its place.

Finally I should like to comment on the viewpoint from which this book was written. I hope that readers will find *Behind the Shades* an invigorating mixture of original research, cuttings-file hopping, and skeptical but informed commentary. What will readily be apparent from the book is that I believe that Dylan is (not 'was') an artistic genius. Though popular art forms have produced few such geniuses, scarcely a handful in the sixty years of mass communication introduced by the talkie era (my own selection, in case you may be curious, totals only four: Fred Astaire, Orson Welles, Bob Dylan, and Jimi Hendrix), the notion that popular art cannot, by its nature, produce them is absurd.

Though a reader who does not share my appraisal of Dylan will still find his story a fascinating one, he will find it hard not to notice an abiding faith in the quality of Dylan's work. This does not mean that I am wholly, or indeed largely, uncritical of Dylan. Indeed, the way that he has (mis)used his talents at points in his career is dealt with at length in *Behind the Shades*. Still, those who are looking for an exposé of a fraudulent sixties icon will be sadly disappointed. After all, 'To live outside the law you must be honest.'

Clinton Heylin
August 1990

A Preface in the Present Tense (1999)

'Every great man nowadays has his disciples, and it is usually Judas who writes the biography.'

—*Oscar Wilde, 1887*

Having departed from my 1991 biography, *Dylan: Behind the Shades,* with a parting shot—'No book is ever finished, only abandoned . . .'— I find myself back on the holy slow train, trying to decide if Judas or Peter should be my preferred role this time around. Or perhaps I am to play Paul, a man of strong opinions and fixed views, whose 'version' of his philosopher-king colored posterity's view more than any interpreter of the tablets who had known their author firsthand?

After all, as I am forever reminded, I have never actually met the man around whom I have spun so many of my musings. And if one has not met one's biographical subject, how—the subtext goes—can one hope to know him, let alone explain or reveal him to unknowing eyes? Well, that's Richard Ellmann on the scrapheap. But it is a surprisingly pervasive view that firsthand acquaintance should take precedence over critical judgment, historical perspective, and a thirst for making sense of the whole picture. Would Sara Dylan, even if she could assuredly put the intimate in biography, be capable of writing something that gave a sense of her former husband's importance, let alone the self-publicity machine known as Susan Ross, an ex-girlfriend from the late eighties, who recently wrote, in her pitch to publishers for a 'revealing memoir' of the man:

Since none of the previous authors have spent time with him or even knew him, they are hard-pressed to draw accurate conclusions about Dylan. Their information is so speculative and limited, at best, that even in recent books, none of them mention (or know) that Dylan has been married three times or has eight children. None of these authors know why and how he married his wives, whether they were pregnant at the time, what his feelings on abortion are, and whether he married for love or because his accountant said alimony is tax-deductible.

Ms. Ross is evidently as unaware of the difference between a memoir and a biography as she is of the fact that Dylan has only seven children. As for Dylan's views on abortion, one suspects that they changed between the time that he cajoled his then-girlfriend, Suze Rotolo, into having one in 1963, and when Kurt Loder questioned him about the subject in 1984 ('If the woman wants to take that upon herself, I figure that's her business'). Likewise, knowing information is one thing, dispensing information another. Knowing of at least one of Dylan's children by one of his eighties backing singers back in 1991, I nevertheless chose to respect their right to privacy. I decided that it had no obvious bearing on the relationship between the man and his art—unlike, that is, his relationship with the lady in question—and would unnecessarily draw the man's ire.

Ross's grand assumption still presupposes that all the people I have interviewed about Dylan, and whose interviews with and about Dylan I have assimilated, have shown themselves to have insights about the man above and beyond anything I myself might be able to construct. It presupposes that the man who wrote the songs is the man I might meet in a bar one windswept night when he feels like baring his soul and I feel like listening—voilà, Interview with an Icon.

Peter Guralnick addresses the general question in the 'Author's Note' to the second volume of his Elvis Presley biography, *Careless Love*, and smartly concludes, 'At some point, you simply have to believe that by immersing yourself in the subject you have earned your own perspective.' Guralnick, by his own admission, has 'spent eleven years with Elvis,' writing and researching his two volumes. Ditto with Mr. D, except I now get to reevaluate most everything I wrote first time around. My revisit affords the reader both 'whitewashed golden calf' and 'incendiary atomic musical firebrand loner who conquered the western world' (Dylan's own assessment of Guralnick's Elvis). The curve of Dylan's career—in my hands, at least—resembles not the parabolic symmetry of Guralnick's Elvis. But then, the finishing end in Dylan's case is (God willing) not yet at hand, and therefore certain forms of information remain taboo.

Ms. Ross herself made a great deal of the 'fact' that Dylan married twice in the eighties—and generated something of a stir when the story reached the press, after her failure to elicit a publisher's advance excised her from whichever part of Dylan's inner circle she'd previously inhabited. One suspects that she has only Dylan's word that he married the two mothers of his three youngest children. But if the price of 'knowing' Dylan is 'believing' Dylan, then surely someone who has been on the receiving end of his duplicity should recognize when an unnecessary toll is being exacted.

Dylan has equally delighted in taking in a biographer or two in his time. Shelton showed a willing credulity when Dylan spun his now-famous yarn about living as a hustler when he first came to New York:

I shucked everybody when I came to New York. I played cute . . . I have a friend . . . He's a junkie now. We came to New York together . . . We hung out on 43rd St., and hustled for two months . . . I got the ride here in December 1960. I came down to the Village in February . . . And I had the guitar. I didn't have any place to stay, but it was easy for me. People took me in.

It is one of my favourite Dylan yarns, for a couple of reasons. One, the idea of this nineteen-year-old schmuck from nowheresville hanging out on 43rd (I thought it was 53rd, but gabba gabba hey), hustling, is too beautiful to pass up. Two, that the people who bought into the story wanted to buy into it, and Dylan knew that he was telling them what they wanted to hear. For Shelton was not alone. Dylan also told proximate versions to the Australian poet Adrian Rawlins and to sidekick Victor Maymudes around the same time—in 1966, when he presumably hit upon it—and evidently convinced them it was so. Maymudes told the tale as truth to one of Dylan's girlfriends in 1987; Rawlins insisted on its veracity to me in 1994.

Now it so happens that the story does tell us an awful lot about Dylan—more than any example of 'truthfulness' he might have chosen to reveal about his early days in New York. It reveals a fixation with Arthur Rimbaud—whose famed conceit, *le dérèglement de tous les sens*, he was living in 1966—so strong that this 'thief of fire' appropriated the legend of young Arthur's subsistence hustling, on his arrival in Paris, into his own mythopoeic biography.

As the same biographer who wrote, in my 1990 preface, that a credible biography 'distills down to a point of view,' I perhaps part ways with

Guralnick. Guralnick, in the painful details of Elvis's actual physical collapse, assumes a reportage style that deliberately avoids asking the question that nags at me, and which I suspect Dylan—who was profoundly affected by Presley's death—would also like to ask: Does it have to be this way? In 1999 I feel surer about my own judgments regarding Dylan-the-artist than I did in 1990, and tell it as I see it. Caveat emptor.

To establish the relationship between that artist and the man, I have again relied on the firsthand verbatim recollections of as many voices as were willing to share their thoughts (some 240 souls). Their perspectives on the relationship between the creative act and the creator necessarily shaped mine, though not at the expense, I trust, of my own perceptions. The more perceptive 'insiders' invariably raised their own questions, like Cesar Diaz, who spent five years in almost daily proximity to Dylan and who told me:

I think the greatest masterpiece he has ever pulled off is the fact that he can make people believe that part of him is involved in the writing of those songs. To me each song is a play, a script, and he'll be that guy from the song for that moment but [then] he'll change back to Bob. People make the mistake to think that he's the guy that sings 'The Times They Are A-Changin'.' [But] the guy that wrote [that song] only existed for that moment, for that righteous thought. It took me a while to realize that. But he actually convinces you that yes, it is me who is talking to you and I'm being sincere about it . . . he is able to convince you that it is him at that point when he is singing the song, when in reality he's just singing a song and just playing. So he can never answer questions [like], 'How do you feel when you sing "Forever Young"?' He cannot put himself in that position. He already did once when he wrote the song.

This is a devastating denial of those who equate the artist with the man, and at a number of levels it has the ring of truth (to invoke Wilde again, 'Man is least himself when he talks in his own person. Give him a mask and he will tell the truth'). But then, the man known to Cesar Diaz between 1988 and 1993 was most certainly not the man who wrote 'The Times They Are A-Changin'' or 'Forever Young.' That Diaz should pick, as an example of a 'righteous thought,' a song of which Dylan told Tony Glover, as the first draft sat at his typewriter, 'It seems to be what people want,' perhaps suggests that he isn't even the one that 'convince[s] you that it is him' in the moment that the thought is sprung.

Cesar's voice—the voice of a man who has 'nothing left to lose'— echoes through all that is to come, not as a statement but as one especially loaded question: is Dylan only/ever 'that guy from the song for that moment . . . for that righteous thought,' and, if so, who is he most of the time? Having hopefully moved on from the question I asked nine years ago—How much do the works reflect the man?—in *Behind the Shades—Take Two* I presume to document a constant, unresolvable conflict between man and artist.

In this, I seem to have been left increasingly alone, save for Dave Engel's remarkably thorough research into Dylan's childhood and family history. Though there remain as many pseudo-academics purporting to interpret the man's work as ever, and he retains his share of advocates in the media for whom he can always bring it back home, the past decade has been a depressing period for those who thought that the building blocks were in place for any number of serious analyses of the man/artist. The cynic in me might even suggest that as Dylan has sunk into parody as a performer, so many of his enthusiasts—at least those determined to write that all is fine in the world as long as His Bobness can remember his lines—have assumed an equally parodic view of his work and significance.

I believe that the toll Dylan's pursuit of his artistry has had on his twin-self stands in starker relief now, in 1999—when his muse has deserted him, it seems definitively—than in 1990, when a reinvigorated Dylan, still looking for revelation, was reveling in his tightest touring band, his strongest collection (*Oh Mercy!*) and his most commercial project (*The Traveling Wilburys*) in a decade.

But then my view of the nature of popular genius has changed. Of the figures I picked as examples in my previous preface, neither Astaire nor Welles managed to sustain their genius beyond their forties. I have come to believe that there is a co-relationship between the artist and his chosen medium that works against maintaining an artist's urge for innovation (publishers, please note, this is a book proposal in code), whether maverick or mainstreamer, and have added this context accordingly.

Any comparison between mavericks oiling the very coilsprings of mass-produced artistry—and yet railing against the technology, promotion, and surface values that give mass marketing its impetus, dynamics, and purpose—is particularly choice when it comes to Dylan because, like perhaps only Orson Welles this century, he was blessed with two forms of genius that, though outwardly compatible, were (and are) in fact constantly at war with each other. In both cases, it was often easier, creatively and financially, to play the performer—and as actor and singer, they generally both conveyed (more than) a sliver of genius in their appointed roles—than the auteur. But then Welles the actor was always a finer actor when directed by his greater genius, just as Dylan has always been a greater singer when expressing his own words of wisdom.

Directed by some inner calling, Welles was twenty-six when he made *Citizen Kane,* forty-two when he made *Touch of Evil,* forty-nine when he made *Chimes at Midnight;* Dylan, twenty-four when he made *Blonde on Blonde,* forty-two when he made *Infidels,* and forty-eight when he made *Oh Mercy!* Welles then spent a frustrating thirty years wrapped up in ill-conceived and unfinished projects, intercut with endless award ceremonies and plaudits from those who, as Truffaut eloquently put it, 'owe him everything.' The bit parts kept coming. Sometimes his presence, even in cameo, would so dominate a film that it would still be remembered as 'a Welles film' (in *The Third Man,* he's in frame for all of ten minutes—care to name the director? Lead role?). But even the parts eventually dried up, reliant as he was on the beneficence of those whose function his towering presence denied—the producers.

Dylan has been able to commit himself to 'what it is I do' in a way that Welles could not. And, as a performer, interpreter, and singer, his glory days have not always coincided with periods of songwriting genius. Indeed, he has been able to sustain the performing side of his craft into his early fifties, notably at the November 1993 Supper Club shows and some truly powerful shows in the spring of 1995, but he has increasingly sought to pursue this aspect of his artistry—the lesser talent—at the expense of his greater genius (I personally ascribe 1961–62, 1966, 1975–76, 1979–81, and 1987–92 as the great performing eras, as opposed to the songwriting peaks of 1962–67, 1974–83, and 1989–90).

Though Dylan is the pre-eminent popular artist of the century, and displays a greater capacity for surprising detractors and converts than any contemporary, I personally doubt that another quantum leap remains. That Dylan himself no longer believes he has yet to paint his masterpiece seems borne out by recent comments made to counterbalance the suspiciously effusive greeting given his Grammy Award–winning album *Time out of Mind,* a work constructed by proxy, built on sand. The burden of being Bob Dylan has broken more than the man's back. The dissolution of his worldview, his romantic attachments to women unworthy of the moniker Muse, the failure of artistic resolve brought on by his chronic indiscipline, and a frustrating disregard for extracting the most from that dying voice within, makes for a quite different portrait from that of the fifty-year-old Bob Dylan. But then I am still writing about a moving target. May he yet rage against the dying of the light!

Clinton Heylin

August 1999

Part One
Busy Being Born

1941–55: In My Younger Days

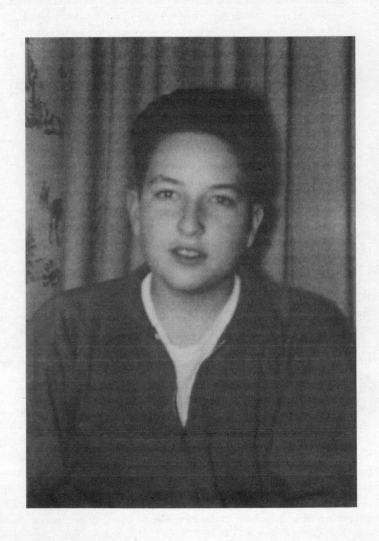

1

My country is the Minnesota–North Dakota territory / that's where
I was born an learned how t walk an / it's where I was raised an went
to school . . . my / youth was spent wildly among the snowy hills
an / sky blue lakes, willow fields an abandoned open / pit mines. contrary t rumors, I am very proud of / where I'm from an also of the
many blood streams that / run in my roots.

—*Bob Dylan, 1963*

You can change your name / but you can't run away from yourself.

—*Bob Dylan, 1967*

At a 1986 press conference a middle-aged, slightly wizened rock 'n' roller
insisted, 'I'm only Bob Dylan when I have to be.' Asked who he was the
rest of the time, he replied, 'Myself.' His creator, forty-five-year-old
Robert Allen Zimmerman, had been a mere nineteen when he had
reinvented himself as Bob Dylan: just three years older than the Arthur
Rimbaud who wrote to his old teacher, Georges Izambard, in May 1871
and proclaimed, *'Je suis un autre';* barely three years younger than his
maternal grandfather, Benjamin David Solemovitz, when, in 1906, he
took off from Connor's Point, Wisconsin, to rematerialize three years
later working as a clerk for a fellow Jew, Abraham Friedman, in Hibbing,
Minnesota, henceforth to be known simply as Ben Stone.

Back in Connor's Point, Stone had had a sister named Ida, a year
younger, by all accounts a pretty little thing. That is, until September 24,
1906, when a young Scotsman named John Young shot poor little Ida
down, before blowing his own brains out with a .32 revolver. Young
had been living in rooms adjoining the Solemovitzes' for three years and
had become more than friendly with Ida. But Young had refused to
recognize the ostracism that would have resulted had Ida chosen to marry
outside her faith. According to the *Superior Telegram,* 'Young was madly
infatuated with the girl . . . a difference of opinion is apparent as to
whether the girl reciprocated his love.' Her father, Sam, refused to
countenance the possibility that his baby girl might have died for love.

Ben, who was close to his sister and devastated by her death, undoubtedly knew better.

Leaving the family behind in Wisconsin, Solemovitz chose to reinvent himself seventy-five miles north, in Hibbing, at the heart of Minnesota's Iron Range, a scabrous landscape shaped by intensive strip-mining that created both the largest man-made pit and the largest slag heap in the world. Founded by the adventurer Frank Hibbing in 1892, after he had cleared a road west from Mountain Iron, Hibbing was erected near to the spot where he had apparently awoken one crisp winter morn and uttered the immortal phrase, 'I believe there is iron under me—my bones feel rusty.'

By the time Ben Stone had found employment with Abraham Friedman, the boomtown had already acquired eighty-eight hundred citizens, sewers, a municipal lighting plant, a fire department, and the largest grade-school building north of the Twin Cities, Minneapolis and St. Paul. However, by 1921 the mining companies found that Frank Hibbing had not erected the town near to the best ore but directly on top of it, and the whole town, houses and all, had to be moved on rollers to the suburb of Alice, leaving street signs and tracks from the old Hibbing behind. Living on the edge of such a surreal wasteland was bound to affect anyone, particularly those for whom the Moving of Hibbing was merely local folklore.

Bob Dylan: I ran into a girl [one time] . . . She said I was a strange person and she told me why. She said, 'You were born in a certain area where the ground is metallic.' [1980]

Ben Stone had been just five in 1888, when his parents, Robert ('Sabse') and Bessie Solemovitz, abandoned the plains of Lithuania for the promise of Superior, Wisconsin. Though Stone left Superior behind in 1906, his heart and the heart of his family remained behind. When he died in May 1945 he chose to be buried in Superior, even though he and his wife, Florence—who had also lived in Superior when she had first arrived in America from Lithuania—had lived in Hibbing for nearly four decades. Their four children, and their grandchildren, all still lived in Hibbing save for their eldest daughter, Beatrice, who lived in Duluth with her husband Abraham Zimmerman and their four-year-old son, Robert. Whether 'Beatty' brought her son to the funeral of his maternal grandfather has not been recorded. Whatever the case, Florence Stone, née Edelstein, now found herself a widow at the age of fifty-three.

Florence Edelstein had been the eldest of ten children, the whole clan being presided over by Florence's imposing father, Benjamin Harold Edelstein, a salesman from Kovno who had arrived in Hibbing from Superior, aged thirty-six, with his wife, Lybba, and his then six children in 1906, shortly before young Ben Stone hit town. Once established in Hibbing, 'BH' abandoned selling furniture and stoves and entered the entertainment business, purchasing the first of four Edelstein theaters, the Victory. As vaudeville gave way to the dependable escapism flickering off the movie screen, Edelstein expanded his operations to include the Gopher on Howard, the State, also on Howard, and the Homer on 1st. That a town of just eighteen thousand could support four cinemas in the forties suggests just how central the images conveyed from Hollywood became to postwar middle America.

Beatrice R. Stone was the second of Ben and Florence's four children. Born three years after her brother Vernon, on June 16, 1915, she was a vivacious child and a devoted member of a large, and seemingly ever expanding, family unit. Though Hibbing would always be a curious place to grow up a Jew—the town was largely given over to Slavic Catholics and Nordic Lutherans—Beatty's large family cocooned her. Hibbing offered few dating opportunities to the single Jewish girl—it was to the bright lights of Duluth, a town that among its hundred thousand citizens boasted some two thousand Jews, that the brash, recently graduated seventeen-year-old turned.

Ethel Crystal: We knew that all the worthwhile Jewish boys were in Duluth. To us, Duluth was a great big beautiful city with a large Jewish population, three or four synagogues to depend on, and plenty of people like us there to meet.

It was there, at a New Year's Eve party to welcome in 1933, that she met Abraham H. Zimmerman, another first-generation American Jew, with four years on Beatty and a job with Standard Oil. The fifth of six children by Zigman and Anna Zimmerman, who had emigrated from Odessa to Duluth in 1906 during the great Eastern European exodus, the shy Abe was bowled over by this feisty young Jewess. In his quiet, steady way he began a long-distance courtship, which ended in June 1934, when Abraham and Beatrice were married.

The newlyweds were always going to choose Duluth over Hibbing, particularly given Abe's steady promotion through the Standard Oil ranks, and they seem to have led a contented existence through the first twelve years of marriage, twice punctuated by the birth of baby boys: Robert Allen—his Hebrew name Shabtai Zisel ben Avraham—at five past nine on the evening of May 24, 1941, in St. Mary's Hospital, a roll down the hill from their Duluth tenement; and David Benjamin, born in February 1946, also at St. Mary's Hospital.

Though Beatty's family remained ensconced in Hibbing, the young couple were part of a large clan of Duluth Zimmermans, comprising four uncles, one aunt, a dozen cousins, and one grandmother (Zigman had died in 1936). As Dylan himself truthfully recalled, 'My grandmother had about seventeen kids on the one side, and on the other side about thirteen kids. So there was always a lot of family-type people around,' as well as the aforesaid thriving Jewish community. A survey of the Jews in Duluth by Joseph Papo, conducted the year Dylan was born, counted 2,633 Jews in 827 family units, a third of whom were foreign born, four-fifths of those coming from Russia and Lithuania. Most were white-collar employees or owners of small businesses. According to Papo,

There is no serious, open anti-Semitism in the community and the relationship with the non-Jews is friendly. During the Brotherhood Week, the Temple Men's Club arranges a special meeting to which the members invite non-Jewish men.

And yet, despite the calm insularity of the Duluth Jews, a year after the birth of their second son the Zimmermans returned to Hibbing. Young Robert was nearly six when the decision was made, by which time the striking view of Lake Superior from their house on the hill was well enough lodged in his psyche that he recalled it in the opening couplet to the 1973 song 'Never Say Goodbye': 'Twilight on the frozen lake / North wind about to break.' According to Beatty, 'We moved back because that was my home town.' In truth, it was a response to a serious family crisis. Shortly after David's birth, Abraham Zimmerman was struck down by polio. Though he stayed in the hospital just a week, recuperation was slow and painful, and the option of returning to Standard Oil receded with each month spent at home.

Bob Dylan: My father was a very active man, but he was stricken very early by an attack of polio. The illness put an end to all his dreams . . . When we moved from the north of the country, two of his brothers, who were electrical fitters, opened a shop and they took him with them, so that he could mind the shop. [1978]

The grand opening of Hibbing's newly refurbished appliance store, Micka Electrics, took place on June 6, 1947. Abraham's older brothers,

Maurice and Paul, had made him secretary-treasurer, initially unsure of how much responsibility he could take on. If 'the illness put an end to all [Abraham's] dreams,' the move to Hibbing, while returning a delighted Beatty to her family fold, also gave their elder son a whole new landscape on which to graft his visions. Though he would later gasp for release from its suffocating conformity, to a young kid Hibbing could also be a wildly romantic place, with a sense of specialness that never left him.

Bob Dylan: I had some amazing projections when I was a kid . . . They were a feeling of wonder . . . [I] grew up in a place so foreign that you had to be there to picture it. [1978]

Bill Marinac: From Bob's house to my house was a huge, abandoned iron-ore dump. Just below the dump was what we called the Willows—it was just willow weed—very thick and very high. It was like a forest for us . . . We kids used to camp out there and play there. This was our fort and clubhouse, it was our area. Of course, with ducks and all the woods, you couldn't help but be close to nature. If you took a hike within ten minutes from home, you were in the woods. If you wanted to go fishing, that was within a half-hour from home.

But the Hibbing to which Beatty Zimmerman returned with her spouse and offspring in 1947 was coming to the end of its useful life. The need for iron to keep the Allied armies on the march had kept Hibbing economically buoyant through the latter half of the Second World War, but even the president of Oliver Iron Mining admitted to the Hibbing Chamber of Commerce the same year that 'the greatest of all iron-ore mines is nearing [its] end.' Young Robert would grow up in a town where every industrial dispute, and there were several through the fifties, would bring the local economy to a standstill, and where every miner had a store of stories from the old days if anyone had a mind to listen. And listening was what Bobby already did best.

Because of the suddenness of the move, and a temporary postwar shortage of accommodation, Abe and his family were initially obliged to join Beatty's recently widowed mother, Florence, in one of the four 'Alice Apartments,' at 2323 3rd Avenue East, just south of Alice School. To make ends meet Beatty returned to work—as a clerk at Feldman's. More so even than in Duluth, Bobby Zimmerman now found himself enveloped by relatives. Within walking distance of Bobby's house at 7th Avenue East and 25th Street was Uncle Maurice, at 2620 3rd Avenue West. Grandma Anna Zimmerman had also left Duluth, and was now living with Maurice. Uncle Paul Zimmerman lived at 3505 3rd Avenue West. And that was just the Zimmermans. Great-uncles Julius, Samuel, and Max Edelstein remained in Hibbing, as did uncles Vernon and Lewis and aunt Irene, whilst his great-aunts Goldie Rutstein and Rose Deutsch lived barely twenty miles west in Virginia, Minnesota. The redoubtable BH, in his seventy-seventh year, continued to preside over the whole clan. Despite the protection such a large family afforded, Bobby still encountered his first bout of anti-Semitism at this time.

Larry Furlong: The kids used to tease Bob, sometimes. They would call him Bobby Zennerman because it was so difficult to pronounce Zimmerman. He didn't like that . . . His feelings could be hurt easily. He often went home pouting.

The Jewish community in Hibbing in the late forties and fifties remained a small enclave, a minority in an essentially distrustful Catholic infrastructure. The response of the Jews was to look to the larger town of Duluth not only for cultural activities but for religious guidance. An indication of the problems of being a Jew in the North Country came about the time Robert Zimmerman's bar mitzvah was due.

Bob Dylan: The town didn't have a rabbi. Suddenly a rabbi showed up under strange circumstances for only a year. He and his wife got off the bus in the middle of winter. He showed up just in time for me to learn this stuff. He was an old man from Brooklyn who had a white beard and wore a black hat and black clothes. They put him upstairs above the café, which was the local hangout. It was a rock & roll café where I used to hang out. [1985]

Needless to say, the L & B Café on Howard Street was not a rock & roll café in the winter of 1954, when young Bobby was undertaking instruction in Hebrew from Rabbi Reuben Maier in his rooms above the café, and the shy twelve-year-old was hardly at a stage where he was 'hanging out.' His bar mitzvah was as effusive and extravagant as the proud mother. At the evening proceedings that concluded Bobby's bar mitzvah, in the ballroom of the Androy Hotel, four hundred invited guests beamed their beneficence down upon the boy-become-man. Many of the four hundred had come from Duluth and Superior, some even from the Twin Cities, to celebrate another man among them.

At this stage, Bobby continued to play the dutiful son. In public situations he seems to have confined himself to refining his powers of observation. A shy kid among the enforced hubbub of Hibbing High

School, he had begun to jot things down, not poetry exactly—Robert Shelton's biography details just two early poems, written at the age of ten, on Mother's Day and Father's Day respectively—just 'things,' a few observations to be revisited. When talking to TV host Les Crane in 1965, Dylan was at pains to separate these early scribblings from later songwriting impulses:

Bob Dylan: Well, I started writing a long time ago. You know how you write, you write these insane things down when you really don't know what else to do. That's when I started writing. [Now] when I started writing songs—that's a different story. I started writing songs after I heard Hank Williams. [1965]

Hank Williams, country's foremost singer-songwriter of the postwar era, was not the first to tug at Bobby's heartstrings, but he was indicative of two important strands coming together: a nascent interest in music with a certain authentic twang that superseded technical considerations, and a fascination with those who died young, preferably at the height of their powers. Dylan himself recently rewrote the path by which he arrived at Hank Williams, suggesting that it was Johnnie Ray who first piqued his interest in the sounds coming out of the family radio.

Bob Dylan: Johnnie Ray . . . was popular and we knew he was different . . . He was an anomaly . . . After that, I started listening to country music . . . We used to get the Grand Ole Opry. [1997]

Dylan has surely mixed up his names. The singer most likely to have touched Bob as early as the year of his bar mitzvah (Ray's main period of chart success being 1956–58) would have been Johnnie Ace, who had several Top 10 hits on the R&B charts in 1953–54, including the gorgeous 'Never Let Me Go' (rendered in equally exquisite fashion by Dylan himself, twenty-one years later, on the Rolling Thunder Revue). Ace learned the true meaning of losing a bet when he blew his brains out playing Russian roulette backstage at a concert on Christmas Day, 1954.

Via the hugely popular Opry radio show, Bobby learned the songs of 'Hank Williams, Hank Snow, Hank Perry—all kinda Hanks!' The Williams legend—dead drunk (literally) in the backseat of a car on the way to a gig in Canton, Ohio, on New Year's Day, 1953, at the age of twenty-nine—was already being fueled by other country singers. But the particular album that struck him hardest at this time was by another

Hank, the very much alive Hank Snow. The songs themselves, though, were drawn exclusively from the repertoire of a man who died eight years before Bobby was even born—the Blue Yodeler himself, Jimmie Rodgers.

Bob Dylan: When I was growing up I had a record called *Hank Snow Sings Jimmie Rodgers*. . . The songs were different than the norm. They had more of an individual nature and an elevated conscience, and I could tell that these songs were from a different period of time. I was drawn to their power. [1997]

Though Rodgers's death was considerably less romantic than those of Ace and Williams—he died of chronic tuberculosis before his thirty-sixth birthday—he may well have inspired Bobby Zimmerman's first attempt at songwriting. Though we have no exact date for the composition in question, 'The Drunkard's Son' is signed Bobby Zimmerman and, remarkably, appears to draw directly on a Jimmie Rodgers song, 'A Drunkard's Child,' from which it takes its form and opening lines, 'My father is a drunkard, my mother is dead / And I am just an orphan child, no place to lay my head.' The lyrics spin a tale in classic country-tearjerker form, even down to the mawkish coda: 'I'm hiding with Jesus who I'll always be by / And my mother, who I love oh so well.' That a recently bar-mitzvahed Jew should be both aspiring to hide 'with Jesus' and envisioning a fatherless heaven perhaps suggests that Robert was already looking beyond his roots, and especially his own particular version of patriarchal authority. Or is that reading a tad too much into an adolescent pastiche of a country ballad?

If Hank Williams and Jimmie Rodgers gave the young Zimmerman a sound to call his own, James Dean, who appeared in 1955 in *Rebel Without a Cause*, dispensed the fury. The sense of a time bomb barely contained seemed directly to mirror the sense of isolation of a million teens. At this stage, Robert Zimmerman was just one more.

Bill Marinac: The two of us went to *Rebel Without a Cause* a couple of times. And he kept going. I think he went at least four times. He was one of the first to get a red jacket like James Dean. That was a good film, it made a really big impact on us. I think it was the times. Maybe you had to be there, in a small town in the fifties.

Bob Dylan: [I liked James Dean for the] same reason you like anybody, I guess. You see something of yourself in them. [1987]

In September 1955, James Dean was killed in an automobile accident near Paso Robles in California. He wasn't even twenty-five. Closer to home, Anna Zimmerman had died of arteriosclerosis in April 1955, and the young Bobby most certainly attended his grandparent's funeral, held at Duluth's Tifereth Israel cemetery. The young Robert, though, was already becoming inured to death, not because of any particular death in his extended family but because, as he famously told Chris Welles of *Life* magazine in 1964, 'I was born with death around me. I was raised in a town that was dying.'

As he entered the adolescent terrain, the physiological changes he was going through became fused with a dramatic change in the American psyche, foretold in a new language seemingly indecipherable to those not coursing with hormones: *Awopbopaloobop alopbamboom!*

1955–59: The Golden Chord

2

The reason I can stay so single-minded about my music is because it affected me at an early age in a very, very powerful way and it's all that affected me. It's all that ever remained true for me . . . And I'm very glad that this particular music reached me when it did because frankly, if it hadn't, I don't know what would have become of me. I come from a very isolated part of America.

—*Bob Dylan, 1997*

If the quiet, reliable Robert Zimmerman was already sliding toward apostasy when Dean drove his Porsche off the road, hearing a certain rock & roll record on the radio the following month set him into free fall. Like many contemporaries in smalltown US of A, young Robert's connection with the new music was initially through radio stations, which late at night beamed coded messages to the young at heart, as if each three-minute single comprised a series of semaphore signals across enemy lines.

Bill Marinac: I had a big old Zenith radio in my basement. My dad had an antenna hooked up to the TV antenna . . . [Bob's] dad had a hookup like that in their house. Our parents were very understanding.

The epiphanous moment probably came when Pat Cadigan, or, to give him his preferred moniker, Pat the Cat, spun a new Specialty single on his WDSM show, beamed out of Duluth at 710 on the dial. With five thousand watts of power to play with, Pat the Cat began spinning singles for young Minnesotans sometime in 1955. One night in October 1955 he put on Specialty 561—'Tutti Frutti' by Little Richard. Nik Cohn conveyed the overwhelming impact of hearing that record for the first time in his seminal *Pop in the Beginning:* 'At one throw it taught me everything I ever need to know about pop. The message went: "Tutti frutti all rootie . . . awopbopaloobop alopbamboom."' Or, as Lou Reed later put it, 'When I heard [it] on the radio, [it] encompassed everything that was missing from my world.' Recorded September 14, 1955, 'Tutti Frutti' was released a month later, hightailing it to number seventeen on the pop charts—though, representative of the chasm opening up between those who liked 'the real stuff' and those who liked 'to hear the words', Pat Boone's antiseptic copy climbed a further five places up the charts. If Boone had known what the song was *really* about—anal sex—he might just have stuck to more saccharine fare.

'Little' Richard Penniman: One song which would really tear the house down was 'Tutti Frutti.' The lyrics were kind of vulgar, 'Tutti Frutti, good booty, if it don't fit don't force it, you can grease it, make it easy.' White people, it always cracked 'em up, but black people didn't like it that much. They liked the blues.

If young Robert wasn't quite ready to become a back-door man, Little Richard's lacquered example was enough to inspire him to resume pounding the Gulbranson spinet piano that had been sitting in the Zimmerman living room ever since his father had picked it up wholesale, hoping that his two sons might display some musical promise. David, who quickly learned his scales, loved his piano lessons, but the elder son quit after a single 'lesson' with cousin Harriet Rutstein. That was before he heard Little Richard, and he decided further lessons, this time under the guidance of one Clarabelle Hamilton, were in order.

Though Dylan has claimed to have played guitar from the age of twelve, the piano was in fact his first instrument. It would not be until 1957 that he would begin playing the guitar, his school chum Monte Edwardson showing him the basics. Even his piano lessons did not turn him into the accomplished player that his younger brother soon became. His music teacher at school recalls the contrasting sight the two Zimmermans cut at the keys:

Val Petersen: When Bobby played the piano he would stand and really pound it. But when David played, he sat and played very nicely.

However, even as a raw fourteen-year-old with hardly any formal training, and even less patience, Bobby compensated with an all-encompassing determination to master the instrument well enough to emulate his newest and most vital hero. That such an unschooled soul was already an original seems to have been lost on the locals. It was most certainly lost on his despairing father.

Pat Mestek: I remember going into his father's store. There was an old piano in the back and I had the idea Bobby was supposed to be stacking shelves, or sweeping or something. But he would be pounding on that piano, making his own melodies. And his father would say, 'Don't make so much noise!'

Abraham, in unison with the majority of middle America, undoubtedly presumed that this infatuation was a passing whim, along with the 'jungle' music now assailing the airwaves. However, a year passed and still Bobby was pounding the home piano to pieces. Unbeknownst to his father, he had already conceived of a need for Hibbing's first homegrown rock & roll band. So, in the fall of 1956, sufficiently sure of himself on the piano, Robert approached a trio of players in the high school band, asking if they would be interested in putting a band together to play something other than polkas.

Larry Fabbro: None of us had ever heard the music he wanted us to play. Chuck and I were into jazz; Bill Marinac learned the string bass from a Yugoslavian folk-dance group in the area.

The band—given the name the Shadow Blasters by Bob—consisted of Zimmerman on piano, his old chum Bill Marinac on bass, Larry Fabbro on guitar, and Chuck Nara on drum and cymbal. The months of rehearsals devolved down to a single gig of note, but its impact seems to have stayed with Dylan and his contemporaries through all the simple years. The student council at Hibbing High had arranged a variety show for April 5, 1957, and announced that a local jazz 'quintet,' including Larry Fabbro, would perform. According to the school newspaper, the *Hi-Times*, 'Surprise numbers are also on the program, and there are rumors concerning a sensational novelty number which at the moment is top secret.'

John Bucklen: He got up there . . . in this talent programme at school . . . came out onstage with some bass player and drummer, I can't remember who they were, and he started singing in his Little Richard style, screaming, pounding the piano, and my first impression was that of embarrassment, because the little community of Hibbing, Minnesota, way up there, was unaccustomed to such a performance.

The news was out all over school. Legend has it the performance ended with Bobby breaking the piano pedal. He was even sporting a Little Richard-style bouffant, something he maintained long enough for his 1957 yearbook photo to record the change. That it was the quiet Zimmerman lad who had undergone this metamorphosis gave at least one classmate a whole new slant on his fellow pupil. John Bucklen was stunned that anyone else at the school was on the same wavelength. He recalls the younger Bobby as the kind who 'had the new clothes, shirts buttoned to the top, hair nice and combed . . . kind of nerdy, I guess.' The new Bobby, on the other hand, was willing to change into that performer self on request.

George Haben: He would get up [at school] and do songs—imitating Elvis and so on—and it was hilarious! To hear this wild singing coming out of a boy who kept to himself, [who] was really very quiet.

But the Shadow Blasters was never going to amount to anything beyond a 'sensational novelty number,' and now that Bobby had had his first taste of public performing he decided he liked that person up there onstage. If it had taken him eighteen months to realize Little Richard live, he did not wait to form his second band. The Golden Chords was to be a trio—piano, guitar, drums—and this time Bobby did a little market research.

John Bucklen: Monte Edwardson was the only decent rock guitar player around, so Bob sort of latched on to him. Leroy Hoikkala wasn't a very good drummer but he could keep time, so Bob got him too. He was anxious to get anything together that could complement his music.

Hoikkala recalls that even the sixteen-year-old Bob Zimmerman was looking to apply 'his own version' of rock & roll to his original sources.

Leroy Hoikkala: He was interested mostly in Little Richard . . . But he did a little bit of everything, improvising a lot . . . He'd sit down at the piano and play some of the most fantastic chords I'd ever heard . . . He'd hear a song and make up his own version of it.

Using the piano to channel ideas to his collaborators, Bob provided the trio with its idiosyncratic impetus. The Chords would last in this guise until the late spring of 1958. They even began to play regularly at Van Feldt's snack bar and a small barbecue joint called Collier's on Sunday afternoons. By 1957, rock & roll had assumed bona fide teenage-revolt status. Even if some of Hibbing's teenagers realized the Golden Chords were no great shakes, they were still the one and only rock & roll combo they had. Dylan himself fondly recalled these carefree days in 1986, with something approaching nostalgia.

Bob Dylan: We were just the loudest band around ... What we were doing, there wasn't anyone else around doing. [The music scene] was mostly horn kind of stuff, jazz—there was one other band in town with trumpet, bass, guitar, and drums. [1986]

Having established a small following among contemporaries, Bobby was anxious to return to Hibbing High with his new band in tow. The coronation of the homecoming queen, one Shelby Clevenstine, on Thursday, February 6, 1958, afforded him such an opportunity. Scheduled for the afternoon was a brand of entertainment assembled by the Pep Club: a magic show, a skit by Hibbing High School cheerleaders, plus a 'local rock & roll instrumental group and several vocal selections.' It was the 'vocal selections' by the Golden Chords that got to the kids. The entire student body of eighteen hundred assembled in the highly ornate high school auditorium at two in the afternoon. Bobby had put microphones in the piano, in front of the guitar amps and bass drum, and three at his side for his vocals. The sound was LOUD. And this time it was no novelty number, but some authentic rock & roll hollers. If the afternoon set was raucous, the evening show in front of kids, disapproving teachers *and* parents was hardly toned down, despite the principal's instruction to cut the house mikes.

Adult disapproval was not long in manifesting itself. When it was announced, in March 1958, that the annual high school student-council talent show was to be held in the high school auditorium, the school administration also took the opportunity to inform any students performing that they would be liable for any *further* damage to equipment—namely the grand piano! If Bob had gained enough performing experience not to stomp the piano pedal until it snapped, he was not going to be given the opportunity to prove it this time around. He was not asked to perform. The Chords had also been denied their 'rightful' place at the Winter Frolic Queen Coronation, an event staged by the Chamber of Commerce. Though they had undoubtedly won over a crowd of 250 kids at the Little Theater auditions in the Memorial Building, the judges decided the winner of the Carnival Talent Contest was some no-talent, no-hope pantomime artist. At least he was quiet.

Not to be denied, Zimmerman teamed up with a disc jockey and reserved the Hibbing Armory, and then commenced to drive around town in a convertible, advertising through a rented loudspeaker. A fifty-cent ticket gained admission to a 'Rock & Roll Hop for Teenagers.' Your favorite hundred top records 'plus intermission entertainment by

Hibbing's own GOLDEN CHORDS featuring Monte Edwardson, Leroy Hoikkala and Bobby Zimmerman.' It was an audacious move, and a raised digit to the high school student council.

At the same time as Robert discovered rock & roll, he came to realize that girls had their uses. His friends witnessed the performing Zimmerman now taking over, and found a willingness to fall flat on his face worked as much offstage as on.

John Bucklen: If he wanted to talk to somebody, he wouldn't be shy about going up and talking with them . . . He had a kind of quiet manner about him like he was shy . . . [But] he was bold.

Freudians would doubtless revel in evidence that Bobby's tastes in women manifested themselves early and endured. The man who recorded 'I Want My Milk' in 1961, and populated his one major celluloid effort with cleavages galore, liked 'em 'plump and large-breasted,' to use Shelton's choice phrase, from way back when.

John Bucklen: As far as girls were concerned, Bob seemed to have a thing for girls who were top-heavy . . . I was going through my old high school yearbook recently, and they were all fat and big-breasted . . . He was going with these girls while he was with Echo [Helstrom], and it sort of tore her up a bit. She used to call me up and start crying.

So sixteen-year-old Bobby Zimmerman was not intimidated by 'goyrls,' liked them with a bit on top, and was a two-timer from the start—patterns to be repeated. Further fuel for the psychobabble brigade comes from a little game he used to play with his friend Bucklen, the victims of which were usually girls. The game was called Glissendorf and it was an impromptu word game with no purpose other than to confuse some innocent third party:

— *I see it's raining.*
— *It isn't raining.*
— *You say it isn't? Okay, if you wanna be difficult, it isn't. So let's move on. What's the next first thing to come to your mind?*
— *The what?*
— *The what? Just what I thought. I won! You won!*
— *I don't understand.*
— *That's exactly right. You don't understand. You don't understand.*

After one particular round of Glissendorf, one girl started crying and Bucklen began to think that maybe this was a tad cruel. Zimmerman, though, was all for carrying on.

John Bucklen: He was a master of the put-on . . . and he hasn't changed . . . There was a current of hostility [there].

The hostility coursing through Robert was largely directed at figures of authority, notably his reliably staid, but increasingly bewildered father, Abraham. Robert's penchant for 'top-heavy' girls was not about to concern his dad, but he also tended to prefer girls from the 'wrong side of the tracks.'

David Zimmerman: Bobby always went with the daughters of miners, farmers, and workers in Hibbing.

Though some pseudo-romantic, Steinbeckian picture—reflected in that formative effort 'The Drunkard's Son'—was bound up with Bobby's fascination for those who had to scratch and scrape a subsistence, it was also guaranteed to infuriate his father. That both Bobby's best friend, John Bucklen, and his high school sweetheart, Echo, came from 'trailer trash' backgrounds was no coincidence. Echo Helstrom, a young blonde whom he dated throughout the summer and fall of 1957 and into 1958, was the most long-standing of his Hibbing girlfriends. Not surprisingly, the initial connection was 'that rock & roll music.'

Echo Helstrom: I met him . . . at the L & B Café in Hibbing. That was back at the beginning of our eleventh-grade year, 1957 . . . he was always so well dressed and quiet, I had him pegged for a goody-goody . . . I mentioned [the song] 'Maybellene' [to him] . . . '"Maybellene"!' he screamed. '"Maybellene" by Chuck Berry? You bet I've heard it!' . . . And on and on about Chuck Berry, Fats Domino, Little Richard, Jimmy Reed— Bob thought he was fabulous, the best!

Echo and Bobby quickly became the devoted couple. Echo even enjoyed seeing Bobby rehearse and play with the Golden Chords, though she shared the embarrassment of her friends when they got booed.

Echo Helstrom: Bob was pretty serious about his band and they practiced a lot. It was all a blues sound then . . . Bob sang and played the piano, and he used to practice with the band in garages around the neighborhood.

Nobody liked their music much, least of all Bob's voice . . . [and] in the big auditoriums people would laugh and hoot at Bob.

Though he was genuinely smitten by Echo, Bobby still took off for Camp Herzl in the summer of 1958, to work on new ways of impressing the girls. Bobby had been attending Camp Herzl throughout his teens, but it was a newly confident Zimmerman who hit camp that year. There was one girl in particular he was interested in at camp, a sharp-tongued but pretty blonde, Judy Rubin, later to be an important lady in his life, though at this point theirs seems to have been an innocent enough friendship. Rubin excepted, he now seemed to perceive Camp Herzl as just another audience to impress.

Steve Friedman: It's somewhere about a hundred miles south [of Duluth], a co-ed Jewish summer camp . . . He was the star of the camp. He used to sing just like Jerry Lee Lewis, a dazzling imitation. He'd play a piano while standing up.

If Echo was seemingly content to await Bobby's return, his band did not prove so obliging. Whatever Zimmerman's own belief that he was the Chords' motivating force, in the North Country a good guitarist like Monte Edwardson was at far more of a premium than a lead vocalist with eccentric delivery and a somewhat startling manner. After another failed talent contest in May, Edwardson and Hoikkala were approached by two junior college students, Jim Propotnick and Ron Taddei, who convinced them to dump the frontman and form a four-piece, the Rockets. They even went as far as to record a single at Kay Bank studio in Minneapolis. On Bob's return, he found an article proclaiming a new act, the Sensational Young Rockets, in the local paper. It had evidently not occurred to him that Monte and Leroy might be less committed to the Golden Chords than himself. Twenty-five years later it still stuck in his throat.

Bob Dylan: Lead singers would always come in and take my bands, because they would have connections, like maybe their fathers would know somebody, so they could get a job in the neighboring town at the pavilion for a Sunday picnic or something. And I'd lose my band. [1984]

As far as is known, Monte and Leroy were the only Hibbing musicians who ever dispensed with Bobby's services—and he may not have shared the view that they had done him a favor—but the loss of the Chords pushed him to pick up the guitar. No damn guitar picker was gonna walk out on him again! Now seventeen, Bobby had convinced his father to buy him a motorcycle in order that he might maintain at least one vestige of the Brando–Dean perimeters-of-society outlaw persona. It also allowed him to make regular runs of seventy miles to Duluth, where he began working on his guitar-playing with his cousin, Stevie Goldberg. Sometimes the two of them would visit another Jewish kid, Dan Kossoff, in Superior, Wisconsin, and the three of them would strum back and forth, showing each other chord progressions.

In double-quick time he also found a band in Duluth he could front. The Satin Tones—'a very ironic name for the kind of music they played,' according to Bucklen—became something of a local success, playing one song on a local TV station in Superior, Wisconsin (just over the border from Duluth), and recording a session for Duluth radio. In Hibbing, though, they continued to play second fiddle to the Rockets. With another cousin, Bill Morris, on drums, Marsh Shamblott on piano, Dennis Nylen on string bass, and Bobby now on guitar and vocals, the Satin Tones may have represented a change in direction, but Bobby experienced a familiar sensation when they played the St. Louis County Fair in Hibbing that September—the sound of boos and demands to turn it down. Bob remained, as ever, unfazed, increasingly sure of what he wanted. Described as 'giving a wild, "Elvis" rendition' of some rocker by the local paper, the Satin Tones faced off against Bob's old sidekicks, the Rockets, who had the sense to stick to crowd-pleasing covers.

Rehearsing on weekends in Hibbing, the Satin Tones campaigned unsuccessfully for high school dance gigs until another offer came Bob's way. Ironically, it came from the Rockets, who were now in need of a new singer/rhythm guitarist, as Ron Taddei was now on his way to college. Bobby succeeded in talking Edwardson into letting him front the boys again. Retaining the name the Rockets, they played the Airport Bar, the Moose Hall, and Hibbing youth center, Bobby alternating on guitar and piano. However, the Rockets were about getting gigs, playing what people wanted to hear, and securing rebookings. With Bobby, it was back to the old days of pushing the volume, the choice of material, and the intensity of the performance beyond what paying audiences felt comfortable with, and once again Monte and Leroy decided to dispense with Bobby Zimmerman's services and return to their staple diet of Bill Haley and Buddy Holly covers.

The Rockets' wasn't the only rejection slip he received that fall. Bobby had been pushing Echo's trusting nature to the limit for some time. If he felt that he could continue to blow his plums and still return to Echo in

Hibbing, he was also pushing his luck. In the first semester of his final year at high school, Echo gave him back the ID bracelet he had given her the previous summer.

Echo Helstrom: He began taking off every weekend, going down to Minneapolis or St. Paul—to listen to music, he said, but I knew he was seeing other girls as well.

That she did it in front of his schoolmates seems to have stung more than the gesture itself. If confrontation suited his artistic bent fine, in real life it was something he always abhorred. Another pattern waiting to be stitched.

Zimmerman had indeed been taking every opportunity to hitchhike or ride down to Minneapolis and St. Paul, to check out the action there. His regular trips to Duluth and Superior, where he could always rely on a hospitable relative nearby, had convinced him just how far removed from the center of, well, anything, Hibbing continued to be. Dylan would later tell a somewhat embroidered version of his first exposure to live rhythm & blues—some cover band playing Little Willie John's 1956 hit, 'Fever,' in a bingo parlor. Save for the undoubted substitution of Detroit for Superior (or Duluth), and the fact that he must have been at least fifteen, the story has the ring of truth.

Bob Dylan: One of the great lakes is called Lake Superior . . . across the lake is a town called Detroit, and I happened to go to Detroit once when I was about twelve or so, with a friend of mine. We had relatives there. I can't remember how it happened, but I found myself in a pool-hall parlor, where people were coming to eat all day and play bingo all night, and there was a dance band in the back . . . Anyway, this was my first time face-to-face with rhythm & blues. [1980]

The experience appears to have suffused Bobby with an ongoing need to repeat the experience. It didn't take him long from the acquisition of his first driver's license at sixteen to realize that Minneapolis and St. Paul were where he needed to be. Looking always to escape down Highway 61 whenever opportunities arose, Bobby would hunt down the places where live rhythm & blues could be found.

Steve Friedman: Sometimes we'd hitchhike down to St. Paul, stay in a lousy hotel, and look for live music . . . rock, rhythm & blues—Bob was very into black music.

In Minneapolis Bob could be whoever he wanted to be. John Bucklen, his best friend and only male confidant through the final two years of school, traveled with him one time and saw the first halting steps toward a new persona: Bob, the Put-On Artist.

John Bucklen: When I went down with him once, we went to a black neighborhood where he introduced me to some black kids our age that he knew . . . I stayed at my aunt's house. He stayed at his cousin's house. That was in Highland Village, a suburb of St. Paul, maybe the summer of '59 . . . We sort of snowed the people down there that Bob was down to cut a record . . . and I was his bass player. That impressed a lot of people. We went to parties. Bob would sit there playing the piano and impressing people with how talented he was.

His fascination with black singers seems to have been an extension of his interest in those who lived on the edge of the safe, sound world he had been born to himself. If his tastes in rock & roll remained eclectic, a bias for more down-and-dirty, R&B-influenced sounds began to emerge, fostered by Bucklen's discovery of a new radio show being beamed from Little Rock, Arkansas, and sponsored by a mail-order outfit called Stan's Rockin' Record Shop.

John Bucklen: About that time, I hooked up with the late-night radio: KTHS, Little Rock, Arkansas—Brother Gatemouth, Stan's Rockin' Record Shop Review. The name of the program was No Name Jive. He'd play nothing but good blues music. Chuck Willis, early Chuck Berry, Ray Charles, some older blues—maybe sneak in a Lightnin' Hopkins or Blind Lemon Jefferson. I told Bob about it. We ordered a lot of records from Stan's Rockin' Record Shop . . . 'Send for this,' Brother Gatemouth said, 'I'll send you my picture.' We thought he was a black guy, but when we got the picture we found out he was a half-bald white guy.

Playing everything from the likes of B. B. King and Jimmy Witherspoon to Otis Rush, Magic Sam, Buddy Guy, and Betty Everett, Stan Lewis, a.k.a. Brother Gatemouth, via the records he mailed to them COD, gave Bucklen and Zimmerman one man's overview of R&B. But there was still something otherworldly about a show beamed out of Arkansas. The boys craved a more direct, hands-on crash course in the roots of rock & roll. Again it was Bucklen's perseverance with the dial on his radio set that revealed a guy playing rare R&B out of Virginia, Minnesota, three times as close as Duluth, and twice as real.

John Bucklen: You have the Iron Range and all of a sudden something happens that doesn't fit . . . a guy who had a show in Virginia, Minnesota. He called himself Jim Dandy . . . a black guy who played good, what we called rare rhythm & blues about an hour a night on WHLB. . . Bob and I had to find out about this guy so we went to visit him. We spent many hours talking with him . . . He lived in a third-floor apartment of this old house. We had to climb up all these stairs . . . He had a lot of records. He was a jazz fan. He said, 'I like blues. I like rock music. But there's no depth to it like jazz.' . . . He was good for us. It was like going to a guru. You'd sit with legs crossed listening to this guy talk . . . just a black guy whose soul was in the right place. As far as I knew, the only black guy within fifty miles.

Bucklen sat and listened as raptly as Bob, but it was that driving beat that spun his particular wheels. All that stuff Dandy spouted about the blues he skipped over in his mind, pushing him to play some more of those rhythm & blues 78s. Bobby, though, was taking it all in. He knew that there was something underlying even electric-blues masters like Howlin' Wolf and Muddy Waters, something that dare not speak its name. He was also beginning to forsake the piano. Perhaps the salutary lesson that the Rockets had given him (twice) had pushed him away from forming bands and toward some way of making it alone. The first step was befriending his guitar.

Bill Marinac: In '59 he started dabbling in [acoustic music] very seriously. We had a jam together, just the two of us, in his house. At that time, he did it on electric guitar. We were talking about . . . [what] if somebody could write lyrics with some social meaning, and could do that in a rock vein. He was already into it.

Dandy's course of recommended listening seems to have somehow skipped over one key figure in the history of popular song, a man who provided the crucial link between twelve bars and modal scales. Born Huddie Ledbetter, but universally known as Lead Belly (two words), he was discovered on a Library of Congress field-recording trip by Alan Lomax. Having spent much of his adult life in prison, Lead Belly was forty-eight when Lomax rescued this remarkable repository of tradition from obscurity, and generously assigned half of Lead Belly's music publishing to himself. Which of the many recordings Lead Belly made in the last decade of his life the young Dylan first heard has not been noted, though Bucklen dates the occasion of this particular epiphany to the summer of 1959.

John Bucklen: Just after he'd left high school but before he left for Minnesota he called me on the telephone, as he'd done so many times before, and he said, 'I've discovered something great! You've just got to come over here!' . . . One of his relatives had given him some rare Lead Belly records, old 78s, and he was flabbergasted by them . . . He thought it was [all] great. I thought, this isn't great—it's okay.

Songs like 'Irene,' 'Good Morning Blues,' and 'In the Pines' had an otherworldly quality that Bobby had probably only previously heard in such distilled form in the songs of Jimmie Rodgers.

If Bucklen is correct about the date of their phone conversation, Bobby's discovery of Lead Belly almost certainly came after he suffered his most crushing expulsion from the world of rock & roll combos. In the summer of 1959 Robert Zimmerman was staying with relatives in Fargo, North Dakota, working as a busboy/dishwasher at the Red Apple Café, when he was introduced as a piano player of some note to Bill Velline, the elder brother of Bobby Vee, in Sam Paper's Recordland store.

Bobby Vee and the Shadows had secured their big break the night Buddy Holly's plane went down on the way to a gig in Mason City, Iowa, on February 3, 1959. The Shadows' bassist had convinced the promoter to book them as Holly's replacement (Bob Zimmerman had been one of the fortunate few who caught Holly's penultimate performance at the Duluth Armory, later insisting that it seemed 'as if there was a halo around Buddy's head' that night). Having hitched themselves to the Midwest circuit, on June 1, 1959, Bobby Vee and the Shadows cut four songs for the SOMA label, including the self-written 'Suzy Baby,' which was soon to become the first of a string of hits for Vee that would last until the Beatles rendered him redundant. Meanwhile, Vee had decided that they were in need of a piano player to play some Jerry Lee Lewis tunes.

Bobby Vee: There was just a rhythm section at that time, and [we thought by adding a piano] we would probably have the ultimate rock & roll band. So we asked around the Fargo area and a friend of ours suggested a guy that had been staying at his house and working at a café as a busboy. So my brother met with him and they went over to the radio station to use the piano. He sort of plonked around a bit and played 'Whole Lot of Shakin'' in the key of C . . . He told my brother that he'd played with Conway Twitty, so he didn't even want to audition the guy and he got the job. He was kind of a scruffy little guy, but he was really into it, loved to rock & roll. He was pretty limited by what he could play . . . He liked to do hand claps, like Gene Vincent and the Bluecaps, who had two guys who were hand-clappers. He would come up [to my mike] and do that every now and then and then scurry back to the piano. He wanted us to use the stage name of Elston Gunn for him. We went out and played a couple of small jobs in North Fargo, then . . . since we didn't have a piano, and weren't in a position where we wanted to buy one and lug a piano around with us . . . decided to work as a four-piece band again. We told him that we'd decided not to use a piano . . . He was a bit disappointed at the time.

Devastated, more like. It is interesting that Vee should recall Bobby Zimmerman—the 'scruffy little guy'—requesting a stage name, and that that stage name should be Elston Gunn, a name Bob had been using since at least the previous summer, when he had put together a short-lived post-Chords combo, Elston Gunn and the Rock Boppers. Elston Gunn was also, almost certainly, the name that had come to him when he ran around to Echo Helstrom's place that summer to tell her his new stage name (she would later insist that it was Bob Dylan that he came up with).

His experience with Vee may well have been the death knell of his rock & roll dreams, though he would continue to play the rock & roll aspirant when it suited him throughout his time at college. His discovery of Lead Belly both reinforced his need for a new direction and pointed him down a different highway.

Of course, the most abiding question—only partially answered by Bob's tenure with Vee in Fargo, after working at a café—was where had he been all summer? When he returned to Hibbing and his old pal Bucklen phoned, asking how and where he'd been, he told one of his great big whopping lies.

John Bucklen: Bob went off one summer for quite a while . . . I was downtown one day and I saw Abe Zimmerman and I said, 'How's Bobby?' He said, 'Oh, he's home now.' So I called and I said, 'Whatcha been doin', Bob?' And he said, 'Well, I've been recording for this record label by the name of Bobby Vee.'

When Robert Shelton traveled to Hibbing to interview Dylan's family in 1968 for his biography, he also inquired of Dylan's parents where young Robert had been all that summer. They also told an untruth, placing their son in Denver, Colorado, a year before he was there. There can be little doubt that Beatty and Abe knew Bob had not been in Denver in the summer of 1959, the year before he went to college, rather than at a time when he had flown the coop for good and was barely in touch with his folks, and yet Beatty told Shelton unequivocally, 'The minute Bobby graduated, he was off to Central City, Colorado.' A motive for Bob's lie to Bucklen is obvious enough—he wanted to associate himself with Bobby Vee, Recording Artist—but what incentive would Mrs. Zimmerman have to lie? Possibly that her son was somewhere else, somewhere she didn't want anyone, least of all a biographer, to know he had been.

According to a psychiatrist who was there at the time, the young Robert spent some time at what has been described as a 'country club reform school' in Pennsylvania in the late fifties. Deveraux had a reputation for dealing with 'difficult' adolescents and, at considerable expense, young Robert was apparently sent to the school in the summer of 1959. The sort of money required to send him there can only have come from the ultra-Orthodox patriarch, B. H. Edelstein, who must have been in agreement with his father that such a short, sharp shock was in order. It is not known how long Robert was in Pennsylvania, but it seems likely that he drew upon the experience when writing about the somewhat stricter regime of a pukka reform school in the 1963 composition 'Walls of Redwing.' Interestingly, Dylan once told Al Aronowitz that he'd served time at the Redwing Reformatory, perhaps another example of him telling some autobiographical truth in code.

Such action on Abe's part suggests not only a father at the end of his tether, but some irremediable breakdown between Abraham and Robert. Abraham had always been unhappy about his son's taste in friends and girlfriends.

John Bucklen: His father, who was very stoic, always looked at you kind of, what the hell are you doing here? That's the feeling I got.

That said, Abraham had extended his elder son a certain amount of slack, buying him first two and then four wheels, though his bemusement at the changes in his beloved son grew with each passing year of adolescence. He also despaired of the slide from academic excellence that had neatly coincided with the onset of rock & roll bedlam. From the sixth to eighth grades, i.e., from 1952 to 1955, the young Bobby had regularly appeared on the school honor rolls, invariably sharing the pedestal with Dennis Wichman and Laura Wilcox. Then came the change. As he slid off the honor roll three times between 1956 and 1958, even his usually supportive mother chided him. Robert, though, was now beyond his parents' command and snapped back, 'The honor roll isn't everything.' To his parents, though, it was, and Bobby seems to have made some effort to respond, since he did make the senior honor roll in 1959 along with Wichman and Wilcox (though on graduation he would not receive a pin, which required four appearances on the roll in a single school year).

Much has been, and should be, made of Dylan's rejection of his family name. It has been interpreted as a deliberate rejection of his religious identity, though he would have been hard pressed to disguise his physical appearance. Far more plausible is that he was making a grand gesture, denying that he was his father's son. By the time Dylan got to Minneapolis in the fall of 1959, he barely spoke of his father, and when he did, as one Minneapolis friend noted to Scaduto, he would go 'on about how he couldn't stand his father, and [make] veiled hints that maybe his father wasn't too nice.' Bonnie Beecher, the 'real' Girl from the North Country, specifically recalls in the early months of 1960 'there [being] some conflict about his father wanting him to use the name Zimmerman and Dylan refusing to use the name.' Some occasion the previous summer had turned the gap between Dylan and his father into a chasm that would not be edged shut until after the motorcycle accident—even if, much to Bob's chagrin, he would continue to be financially dependent upon Abe for some time yet.

Of course, the flight from Hibbing was not just about turning his back on his father. There was Hibbing itself. If his flight took place in stages, it was not the stages of a perpetual runaway painted in his 1963 bio-poem 'My Life in a Stolen Moment,' but a man-child spreading his wings, slowly but surely, to encompass first Duluth, then Superior, then Fargo— as far-flung from his father as he could yet be!—until finally Minneapolis and St. Paul beckoned.

His musical farewell to Hibbing and the high school came the spring of 1959, when he performed at the annual Jacket Jamboree in the school auditorium, a mere two years after his startling debut performance there. This time he gave an almost ersatz version of the singing rebel as he performed 'As Time Goes By' and 'Swing, Dad, Swing' with Bill Marinac on string bass, John Bucklen on guitar, and—the first evidence of a love for backing singers—Fran Matosich, Kathy Dasovic and Mary Defonso on backing vocals. On June 5, 1959, Robert Zimmerman graduated from Hibbing High School. His ambition, according to the yearbook: 'To join Little Richard.' Such an ambition would have to wait. He had managed to duck beneath the academic wire, securing a place at the University of Minneapolis, making his parents happy that their son was going to further his education, and making himself happy that, come September, he would be getting the hell out of Hibbing.

Minneapolis was both excitingly new and comfortingly familiar. Not only had he spent many weekends in his final high school year visiting the state capital, and had the inevitable cousins and aunts in nearby St. Paul to call upon in times of need, but he knew a small coterie of fellow North Country Jews also bound to be freshmen at UMinn, including Larry Kegan, a lifelong friend, who had become permanently wheelchair-bound after damaging his spine diving into a pond at camp the previous summer. Beatty would even later tell Shelton that Kegan's accident 'must have had something to do with Bobby's career . . . That was a real tragedy in Bobby's life.' As for Hibbing, one imagines, as Bobby pulled onto Highway 53, past Duluth, and onto Highway 61, he didn't look back.

Bob Dylan: I left where I'm from because there's nothing there . . . When I left there, I knew one thing: I had to get out of there and not come back. Just from my senses, I knew there was something more than Walt Disney movies. [1965]

Bob Dylan: I'm not the only one that left there and traveled around . . . everybody left there. I don't really know of anybody that stayed there. [1965]

1960: SAMmy Bound for Glory

3

John Bucklen: Bob kind of surprised me when he went to college . . . He came back to Hibbing . . . just before the Christmas vacation. He had an old acoustic guitar . . . and he didn't have any neatness to the way he combed his hair, which was unusual, 'cause he used to be fastidious about that . . . He played me this folk song and said, 'Man, this is the thing—folk music!' I think [it] was 'Golden Vanity' . . . He said, 'Down there when I play, my name is Dylan.' . . . He said it was after Dylan Thomas, spelled D-y-l-a-n.

It's a long, long way from Lead Belly to 'The Golden Vanity,' a sixteenth-century ballad first collected in Pepys's broadside song collection under the title 'Sir Walter Raleigh sailing in the Low-lands: Shewing how the famous ship called the Sweet Trinity was taken by a false gally, and how it was again restored by the craft of a little sea-boy, who sunk the galley.' 'The Golden Vanity,' No. 286 in the Child canon of *English & Scottish Popular Ballads,* was not a song acquired from Lead Belly. Nor was it a song featured by the woman to whom Dylan subsequently attributed his conversion to folk—Odetta. And yet it certainly struck a chord with Bob, remaining in his set as late as October 4, 1961 (and then receiving a welcome in the fall of 1991 for a few shows). Dylan, in the *Biograph* notes, says he learned the song from a well-known Minneapolis folkie.

Bob Dylan: [Sometimes I was] part of a duo with 'Spider' John Koerner, who played mostly ballads and Josh White type blues. He knew more songs than I did. 'Whoa Boys Can't Ya Line 'M', 'John Hardy,' 'Golden Vanity,' I learned all those from him. [1985]

But according to Koerner, they did not meet until the new year, when they ended up swopping folk songs on the loading bay outside the university chemistry building, by which time Elston Gunn was truly dead and buried. Young Robert doesn't seem to have paused unduly between setting himself up at the Sigma Alpha Mu fraternity house and heading for campus coffeehouse the Ten O'Clock Scholar to try for a gig as a guitarist-singer. Its owner, David Lee, had recently started using folksingers to entertain the customers, though payment was not one of the perks on offer, simply the opportunity to play to people.

David Lee says that, when he asked Robert Allen Zimmerman his name, he replied, 'Bob Dylan.' Dylan himself said, in 1971, 'It just came to me as I was standing there in the Scholar.' But it seems inconceivable that Bob would not have thought long and hard about who he might like to be and we know he had displayed an early penchant for stage names. That Bucklen should recall Dylan telling him back in December 1959 that he took the new surname from Dylan Thomas is significant. Dylan has always insisted in interviews that this was not the case and constructed a scenario, usually involving gambling uncles named Dillon, to explain away the name. Dave Whitaker, who first met Bob in the spring of 1960, recalls him saying that 'Dylan was his mother's name, and that he had taken it because . . . he didn't want to be known by his father's name.' In truth, it is hard to see where, save his Welsh namesake, the name could have sprung from in October 1959.

If 'Bob Dylan' was a self-conscious attempt to reinvent himself as anything but a Zimmerman, the fact that he was from the very start a folksinger clearly took many who had known him in his Elston Gunn days by surprise. That the change to acoustic folk was as sudden and spectacular as the chronology suggests it was, Dylan has attributed to one woman, Odetta Holmes Felious Gorden, a classically trained singer who began singing in Broadway productions in the late forties before arriving at her real roots in 1956 with her powerful debut for the Tradition label, *Odetta Sings Ballads and Blues*. Whatever the immediate significance of his new name, the metamorphosis into 'Bob Dylan' began with the purchase of the first Tradition album by this husky, full-throated maîtresse of folk. The album had an immediate effect.

Bob Dylan: The first thing that turned me on to folksinging was Odetta. I heard a record of hers in a record store, back when you could listen to records there in the store. That was in '58 or something like that. Right then and there, I went out and traded my electric guitar and amplifier for an acoustical guitar, a flat-top Gibson. [Her first album was] just something vital and personal. I learned all the songs . . . Anyway, from Odetta, I went to Harry Belafonte, the Kingston Trio, little by little uncovering more as I went along. Finally, I was doing nothing but Carter Family and Jesse Fuller songs. [1978]

Sure enough, the adenoidal young folksinger was soon inflicting much of *Odetta Sings Ballads and Blues* on the caffeine-charged audience at the Scholar—'Jack o' Diamonds,' 'Muleskinner Blues,' and 'Another Man Done Gone' were staples of his Minneapolis repertoire—and he would already have been conversant with some of the more country-crossed folk material championed by the likes of the Carter Family or the Monroe

Brothers. The Kingston Trio, who had actually topped the charts in 1958 with a traditional Appalachian murder ballad, 'Tom Dooley'—instigating, some have insisted, the whole folk revival—would have been inescapable at this point. But Dylan's repertoire would have been limited by his inexperience with the acoustic guitar, which he had only begun to play early in 1959. He was playing no harmonica, and was singing in a sweet, rich voice that sounded like a cross between a country twang and the more saccharine kind of folksinging popularized by the Kingston Trio.

But whither 'The Golden Vanity'? This was surely a song only 'real' folksingers sang, and Dylan had yet to fall in with the Minneapolis minor-key folkies, or to consume records of traditional singers at a startling rate. Could it be a song he had heard back in Hibbing? Perhaps he had attended the recital by Richard Dyer-Bennet at the National Guard Armory in 1957, where Dyer-Bennet undoubtedly performed the song. Perhaps that's how he thought folk songs should be sung, in a concert-trained manner, with the words clearly formed. His new friends in the Twin Cities were soon snapping him out of that!

Clearly Dylan knew he had latched onto something with an undertow beyond anything he had yet encountered. Rock & roll, R&B, electric blues—he was having none of them. Well, not at the Scholar, anyway. When it suited, he would happily regale anyone who would listen with stories of his days on the road with Bobby Vee. When the renowned folksinger Cynthia Gooding came to Minneapolis that fall, he couldn't resist insisting on his rock & roll credentials, something she good-naturedly reminded him about on a radio show in 1962:

Cynthia Gooding: I first heard [you] . . . I think three years ago in Minneapolis and at that time you were thinking of being a rock & roll singer . . . you were studying.
Bob Dylan: I was making pretend I was going to school out there—I'd just come in from South Dakota . . . from Sioux Falls.

Already Dylan was fast covering his North Country tracks, if not his rock & roll past. At the fraternity house he would also entertain his fellow Sammies, as and when he felt the need to be on their good side. A frat brother and friend from Camp Herzl recalls:

Jerry Waldman: He was quiet . . . [except when] he played the piano and everybody would gather around and we'd sing rock & roll songs.

The likes of Waldman and Larry Kegan were not the only habitués of Camp Herzl to find themselves in Minneapolis that fall. Much to Bobby's delight, Judy Rubin was also in town. Young Bob had had a considerable crush on Judy at camp, and throughout his first semester he launched a series of charm attacks, in an attempt to become 'serious' with her. Though Judy attended his gigs at the Scholar, shouting requests and generally encouraging him, she was never in love with him. Judy was also the kind of girl who respected her parents' views. She would not have dreamed of going against their wishes—Dylan would later go so far as to call her 'the pawn of her parents'—and a Jew who denied the good Jewish name with which he was born was hardly going to top their list of suitable suitors.

Judy Rubin: My parents didn't like him, neither did a lot of my friends, and there were too many things, including drugs, that separated us.

In April 1963 Dylan would jokingly suggest that his rejection by Judy set his ethnic awareness back many years. In fact, he was still writing about Judy—and how he hated her parents with all his heart—as late as May 1964, though it was probably the ongoing interference of another mother, Mary Rotolo, that recharged this particular memory bank. He was clearly profoundly affected, saying that 'Judy broke his little out of high school heart,' and in a remarkable unpublished poem written early in December 1963, Dylan recalled his first Christmas in Minneapolis:

'ring ring her ma answers/her ma hates me/snobby sort . . . wants the best for her daughter/society bitch/bitch of a mother . . . talks down at me when she knows/it's me callin.'

This poem corresponds very closely with events that Christmas, as related to biographer Bob Spitz by Judy Rubin herself. According to Dylan, he could 'never once' get through the door when Judy's parents were in. It was a miserable Christmas vacation, and yet he endured most of it in Minneapolis, preferring to visit Hibbing fleetingly to show Bucklen 'The Golden Vanity' before sharing in a family feast and taking off again, in his mind's eye standing on the highway trying to flag a ride but probably, in truth, as a passenger in his father's car. On her return to Minneapolis, Judy finally confessed that she had fallen in love with someone else, and though she offered to stay friends, Bob was not about to take up that option.

In fact, by the spring of 1960, Dylan may have come to feel that he was losing his touch where women were concerned. The next girl to whom he turned, hoping to assuage some of his frayed feelings, managed to do something even more hurtful—Gretel Hoffman promptly married a guy she'd met at a party she attended with Dylan. When she met him on the street and told him the news, he came up with the sort of response that would have made even his amphetamine-fueled '65 self proud: 'Call me when you get divorced.'

This time, though, they did stay good friends. Indeed, Gretel's new husband, Dave Whitaker, would become Dylan's second great mentor. However, Gretel and Bob would never again be as close as they had been in those winter months of 1960. Though never romantically involved, it is easy to see how Dylan considered Gretel 'his girl.' Between January and March they would get together every single day at the Scholar.

Gretel Hoffman: We did nothing but soak up all the city's culture and talk about books and music.

Gretel shared Dylan's fascination with folk music, introducing him to an old brothel song about a prostitute dying from syphilis looking back on her days in 'The House of the Rising Sun.' She also shared his love of Odetta. As with Echo before her, Gretel found that the way to something more cerebral than a roll in the hay with Bob was through music.

So it was, too, with the third woman he met in Minneapolis who knew how to break his heart—Bonnie Beecher, Dylan's Girl from the North Country and first muse. According to Beecher, they had first met prior to Dylan's induction into Sigma Alpha Mu, in which case Bob had already scouted out the Scholar prior to attending university, for it was here that Bonnie overheard two young lads, Bob and Harvey Abrams, discussing some decidedly obscure blues singers.

Bonnie Beecher: I didn't know anybody else who knew who Cat Iron was, or Sleepy John Estes, so I perked up my ears and turned around and I started to join [in] the conversation.

Like Dylan, Bonnie was ostensibly attending university. Such was the mothering instinct that she, and many others, had for the young tyke that she ended up being kicked out of her sorority house for associating with such dissolute company. Yet she continued to take him under her wing.

Bonnie Beecher: No one would let him even play for dinner. I ended up shoplifting for him, stealing food from my sorority house.

Though the sisters were largely immune to Dylan's charms, one other member of Beecher's sorority, a banker's daughter by the name of Cynthia Fincher, was equally intrigued by Dylan. Though they were not ever an item, Fincher liked to play banjo, and in the fall of 1960 they would often play together at the Purple Onion pizza parlor. It is her voice that can be heard on the so-called First Minneapolis Tape from September 1960, berating him for not playing the songs she wanted him to.

The amount of mothering that Dylan inspired became something of a running joke among his male friends in Minneapolis. If his front was sometimes wondrous to behold, beneath it was someone who could be sweet and charming. When he recognized a common bond, he seemed to have no problem endearing himself to girls *and* their mothers, uptight society bitches excepted. With Ellen Baker, another girlfriend from his Minneapolis days, Dylan's charm worked on both generations, and he regularly used the Bakers' house as a rather comfortable stopover between the rooming houses that passed for off-campus accommodation. He seemed remarkably self-aware for a nineteen-year-old when it came to charming women, but he was not unduly selective when it came to satisfying his more basic urges.

Ellen Baker: Bob was funny about his women. At first he seemed very shy, sort of scared . . . but it didn't take long before you found out a good deal of that was an act. Bob was surprisingly amorous, and undiscriminating! He'd see a girl on the street or at a party, and it didn't matter what she looked like or who he was with, if he was in *that mood*.

Evidently he was interested in experiencing as much of life as a nineteen-year-old would-be beatnik, fresh from the backwaters of Hibbing, could. Nor did he restrict his sexual adventures to the equally inexperienced girls he noticed while playing at coffeehouses or parties. One brief liaison in Chicago at the end of 1960 clearly left an indelible mark.

Bob Dylan: I met this woman in [a] bar. She picked me up. It was horrible. I felt used. I was about nineteen and she was, well, she was old. Really old. God, it's all coming back to me. I'll never forget her red hair . . . She was big. I thought she had a lot of experience. I'm not going to tell you her name. Even if I could remember it . . . She was wearing a print dress. And a girdle. She made love to me, did it all. I just walked into her room and stood there with my eyes hanging out. She lived in just one room, with a closet, a sink, and a window which looked out over the street. She had a dresser with a mirror on top that you can tilt whichever way you want, and a bed with a mattress that sagged clear to the floor in the middle . . . That woman was sixty years old and she had filed down her teeth! [1978]

Save for acts of immediate gratification, sordid or otherwise, Dylan confined himself to friendships with women who were interested in his type of music. Both Bonnie Beecher and Ellen Baker were very support-ive of Dylan the music maker, both sharing an abiding interest in folk and blues. In Ellen's case, as a useful adjunct to the accommodation, Dylan soon learned that her father had an unsurpassed collection of folk-music literature and vinyl, to which he was allowed open access.

Ellen Baker: He hardly ever seemed to have a place to live. But he liked our house just fine . . . Besides having both my mother and me charmed and a free place to stay, he had my father's huge collection of bound folk music to peruse . . . my father was quite a collector. He had old manuscripts, sheet music, and folk magazines . . . We'd harmonize old tunes from my father's old records, and songs that were the type Bob was doing then. Not the bluesy stuff he picked up later, but traditional things, sort of A-minorish folky.

The songs he sang at the Ten O'Clock Scholar may have suggested someone with little more than a dilettante's knowledge of folk music, but Dylan could be a fast learner, particularly when it was something that seemed to satisfy some basic craving for authenticity and depth. He soon realized that folk music was a form whose secrets had been debated for over three hundred years with no resolution in sight, a combination of oral literature, popular philosophy, melodies bathed in the anonymity of centuries, and a fusion of classical European forms of cadence that in the New World had been forcibly mingled with the blues. He set out in search of the most authentic replications of what he would later appositely describe as 'the only true, valid death you can feel today.' Bonnie, in particular, was witness to an almost pathological interest in getting back to the source of each recording he heard.

Bonnie Beecher: I would go off and find a record—a collection of old blues stuff with a bunch of different artists on—bring it back to Minnesota and we would play it through.

Harvey Abrams: Dylan was the purest of the pure. He had to get the oldest record and, if possible, the Library of Congress record[ing].

He also quickly developed an instinct for the songs most imbued with that 'only true valid death' on any folk record he seemed to hear. Paul Nelson—who was co-editing Minneapolis's low-budget answer to *Sing Out*, the *Little Sandy Review*, at the time—recalls stumbling on evidence of how acute Dylan's instincts were:

Paul Nelson: He had left his songbook [here] once, where he wrote down songs he was interested in singing. We had a lot of traditional records, and invariably he would pick the best song from [a] record. He would seem . . . [to] be uncanny.

Shrewd as his choices of songs to cover were, even in 1960, one would be hard-pressed to find evidence in Dylan's early recordings of the man who would transform popular music irrevocably over the next five years. And yet the earliest tape of Bob Dylan, a twenty-seven-song session recorded by a fan at her sister's St. Paul apartment—the so-called St. Paul tape—does feature two songs that reappeared ten years later at the *Self Portrait* sessions, 'Saro Jane' and Paul Clayton's 'Gotta Travel On'; one song that appeared thirty-three years later, on *World Gone Wrong*, 'Delia'; as well as four Woody Guthrie songs—'Pastures of Plenty,' 'This Land Is Your Land,' 'The Great Historical Bum,' and 'Columbus Stockade Blues'—and two songs that would provide the necessary spark for two early Dylan originals: 'The Two Sisters,' the prototype for 'Percy's Song,' and the equally traditional 'Go Way From My Window.' Dylan ducked out of playing 'House of the Rising Sun' that night, though it was requested, as well as Ewan MacColl's 'Go Down You Murderers,' perhaps the most powerful songs in his nascent repertoire.

The St. Paul tape had been made at the request of Terri Wallace, who regularly attended Dylan's gigs at the Ten O'Clock Scholar in the spring of 1960. It was Terri who suggested in May that Dylan should consider playing the Purple Onion in St. Paul as well as, or in preference to, the Ten O'Clock Scholar. When Dylan asked to be paid at the Scholar—as he was now actually bringing some business in—he was refused, and the Purple Onion became his venue of choice.

Terri Wallace: I met Bob Dylan at the Ten O'Clock Scholar when some friends and I decided that we wanted to try something different . . . this was during the days when espresso coffee places were the big rage . . . He just reminded me of a little choirboy, he had such a cute little cherub face . . . I remember a pair of brown corduroy pants that he wore almost all the time, and I know that he wasn't real concerned with his appearance . . . he had worn them so often he had a rip in the crotch . . . [But] he was looking for other places to sing.

If this first known Dylan recording—the only pre-Denver recording certainly extant—shows a familiar-enough repertoire for a young folk revival singer, what might throw most fans conversant with the New York Dylan would be the voice. On 'The Two Sisters,' the classic Child ballad, collected that year in Alan Lomax's *Folk Songs of North America,* he can be heard singing in a strangely sweet tone, 'I'll be true to my luuurve.' The unfamiliarity of this voice even led one intellectually challenged Dylan collector to make the unfounded (and subsequently disproven) allegation that the tape was a fake. Everyone who knew Dylan at this time has commented on his voice, how different it was from what it later became. Spider John Koerner, with whom he started playing in January 1960, describes it as 'a pretty voice.' It was this sweet voice which first impressed Terri Wallace.

Terri Wallace: He had . . . the most beautiful voice . . . I really thought he had a good singing voice. Which I might add was something of a disappointment after he became well known, and I heard the voice that made him famous . . . It was so different from the voice that I had first heard coming out of him.

There is one performance of particular significance on the St. Paul tape, an innocuous enough minor-key blues tune, given the title 'Twenty-One Years Old' on the tape. It just happens to coincide with John Bucklen's description of one of Dylan's earliest folk compositions, 'One-Eyed Jacks'. In it the singer affects the world-weariness of a fifty-year-old bluesman. The affectation was to endure through at least the first album.

John Bucklen: As his folk music love and involvement grew, so did his hair and his style. He had a list of about a hundred songs that he had written, and some of them were really great. I remember one that he did . . . I'm the only one who knows it apart from him, I think . . . It goes: 'I'm twenty years old, there's twenty years gone, don't you see me cryin', don't you see me dyin', I'll never reach twenty-one.' Another verse is: 'The Queen of his Diamonds and the Jack of his Knave, won't you dig my grave with a silver spade, and forget my name.' It was one of those tragic things that was appropriate for the time, a backwoods blues folk song.

Though little more than a compendium of commonplace blues images, and like-as-not introduced as traditional at the Scholar, 'One-Eyed Jacks'—and other such lost 'original' Dylan ditties as 'Greyhound Blues,' 'Blackjack Blues,' and a rewrite of 'Every Time I Hear the Spirit'—set Bob apart from his Dinkytown contemporaries.

Spider John Koerner: The thing I remember about Dylan was occasionally he'd write a song. I don't remember anything about [the songs] 'cept some of them were really nice and clean, and had bite to them, [but] none of the others of us were [really] doing that.

The other characteristic that set Dylan apart was that he was deadly serious about what he was doing, and where it was gonna take him. At the start of the spring semester he went from part-time student to full-time folksinger. From day one, he had been made to feel extremely uncomfortable by his brothers in the Sigma Alpha Mu fraternity house.

Rich Cohen: He was sort of considered a freak, but the actives weren't any tougher on him than on any of the other[s] . . . I was one of those people asked to shape Zimmerman up—[to] make grades, wear the right clothes, and fit in. I failed.

Steve Bard: He looked like a fifteen-year-old high school kid, who hadn't matured much. Frankly . . . he was the kind of kid you always picked on in high school.

SAM was a rather conventional Jewish lodge. Bob was reluctant to contribute to fraternity life, and did not enjoy the jibes of those brothers who knew of his nighttime activities down at the Scholar. If the brothers considered him a 'freak,' he was not an entirely passive victim of their disapprobation.

Jerry Waldman: In college, my most vivid memory of him was during the first quarter of school when we had to put on a skit for the actives. Bobby and Bernie Paul and I wrote the music, making fun of the brothers.

Dylan's departure from the fraternity house was the end of his formal education. He would be self-taught from now on. Though he continued to attend lectures intermittently, he was immersing himself more and more in the bohemian lifestyle of his new, hipper friends, even if he had yet to inform his parents of his abdication.

Ellen Baker: Bob was serious about his schoolwork for a while. At the very start. He tried very hard, but it wasn't him. He finally decided he just wanted to play the guitar and party.

Not that Dylan hadn't tried to combine the two lifestyles, just that the result was never in doubt. One incident related by Bonnie Beecher illustrates a Dylan who—having loosened the bonds around him in high-tailing it to Minneapolis—was determined to test Blake's dictum about 'the road of excess' firsthand. The anecdote shows a remarkably self-assured girl.

Bonnie Beecher: I was walking to the building where I had my final and I noticed a crowd standing around. Sure enough, Dylan was lying in the middle of the street and [he was] just a mess, you know. He had thrown up and he was passed out on the street . . . And I remember thinking, 'I could just keep walking . . . I don't have to go in there and say I know this person' . . . But I took a big sigh, knew I was going to be late for my test, and dammit, I went in and picked him up. He was barely conscious. I had this ludicrous drunk hanging on me, covered in vomit! I walked him into the ladies' room, cleaned him up. I wanted to take him home, but he said, 'Naw! I have to be at the music building!'

By this point he had assuredly met Dave Whitaker, a trenchant and galvanizing influence on him. Dylan would later say that one day he was 'on this side' and that, after meeting Whitaker, 'suddenly I was on that side.' Along with Bonnie Beecher, Harvey Abrams, Gretel Hoffman, and Hugh Brown, Whitaker began to reshape Dylan's worldview. Dylan, writing in the fall of 1963, pointedly contrasted his new friends with the fraternity brothers he'd left behind:

Bob Dylan: I'd fell in with a new kind a people there in Minneapolis. I was going t new kinds a parties an thinkin new kinds a things . . . I read into what I was doing an saw myself romantically breakin off all ties with all things of the established order although I'd never really been accepted by that order anyway . . . what I saw connected with the fraternity house summed up the whole established world.

Of course, one of the things that separated the 'new kind a people' from 'the established order' was their penchant for popping pills, smoking weed, and quaffing a carafe or two of Chateau le Plonk. Though Dylan was not about to shy away from his share of illegal substances, it was drinking that gave him the bravado to come on to women and to conquer his stage fright. Dave Whitaker's role in the transformation of Dylan into the Dinkytown equivalent of a hipster managed to be simultaneously deleterious and enlightening. Bob started staying up all night, reading books Whitaker recommended—everything from Sartre to the beats— and rap-talking, glass in hand, until dawn.

Dave Whitaker: There was a black club we used to go to, and all of these prostitutes were sitting there, and you'd come in and there'd be these guys playing the blues. And using drugs. Drugs were coming in. The truckers were using bennies and we used to take four or five and we'd go on for two or three days at a time, drinking beer, playing guitar, and going from scene to scene . . . He used to get really fucking drunk, we all did. But he would always play that guitar. When he couldn't even stand up . . . he would stand up and play that guitar.

Dylan's instincts were already working overtime, trying to figure out where he needed to go to round out his education. This time around he did not come up with the East Coast but rather Denver, Colorado. Why Dylan *actually* went to Denver in the summer of '60 will in all likelihood continue to be a mystery. It was hardly a local excursion from Minnesota, being some 920 miles from home. However, he had doubtless 'often dreamed of going West . . . always vaguely planning and never taking off,' when those words, on the first page of one book Whitaker held in particularly high esteem, leapt off the page. Jack Kerouac's fictionalized account of his adventures *On the Road* with Neal Cassady, something of a sensation on its hardback publication in 1957, had begun with the Kerouac character (Sal Paradise) hunting down 'western kinsman of the sun' Dean Moriarty in Denver, Colorado. Whether Dylan saw Denver, like Sal Paradise, 'looming ahead of me like the Promised Land, way out there beneath the stars, across the prairie of Iowa and the plains of Nebraska,' his own later account of the trip portrayed it as a response less to 'hear[ing] a new call and see[ing] a new horizon' than to the offer of a floor and a gig.

Bob Dylan: [When] I hitchhiked to Denver I think I went there because I knew a girl whose floor I could sleep on . . . I stayed around Denver for a while, but there was only one coffeehouse, and they wouldn't give me a job. But then I met a stripper who worked at a bar called the Gilded Garter, and she bought me some clothes and got me a job playing 'Muleskinner Blues' between strip acts. [1978]

Considering the leap of faith involved in such a trek, it seems surprising that Dylan would have taken the promise of a 'floor I could sleep on' on trust. And he apparently had enough money on him to hole up at the Salvation Army hostel, conveniently located next to Denver's premier folk club, for a few days. The Exodus was a prestigious gig in the folk world, the Denver equivalent to New York's Gerde's or Cambridge's Club 47. That year saw the release of an entire album celebrating the rostrum of regulars at the Exodus, *Folk Festival at the Exodus*, featuring the likes of Ed McCurdy, Don Crawfurd, and a twenty-year-old Judy Collins, whose five songs on the album include her take on 'This Land Is Your Land.' It would have been something of a coup if Dylan *had* been allowed to play there. He was not.

Though Dylan hung out at the Exodus, soaking up folksinging on a whole other level, his own playing ambitions were directed at the Satire, Denver's home away from home for second-string folkies. One Walt Conley was then playing at the Satire. Conley's account (in Spitz's biography) has Dylan arriving at the Satire telling Conley that an ex-girlfriend from Minneapolis had suggested he look him up. Again according to Conley, Dylan auditioned unsuccessfully at the Satire, and subsequently crashed at his house for three weeks, until Conley managed to get rid of him by getting him a gig out of town, at a place called the Gilded Garter in Central City. Within a week Dylan had apparently left the Gilded Garter, having stolen twenty dollars from the owner, and returned to Denver.

Not only does this bear little resemblance to Dylan's 1978 account of his time in Central City, it leaves several questions unanswered: like, how could Conley have known Dylan was a competent piano player? That was what the Gilded Garter actually required, it being a touristy, honky-tonk joint. Dylan would have played guitar and sung at the Satire, tending to confine his piano playing to occasions when it impressed girls. In fact, the only matter Dylan and Conley seem to agree on was that the Gilded Garter gig did not last very long. In October 1961 Dylan told Izzy Young that it lasted a week and a half. He told Shelton, more plausibly, in 1966, that it lasted 'a few weeks.'

Bob Dylan: I played for twenty minutes, strippers worked for forty minutes with a rock & roll band. I'd play for twenty minutes again. Never stopped.

One night I was about ready to strip myself. Worst place I ever played.
[1961]

And yet on two separate occasions, in February 1964 and March 1966,
Dylan couldn't resist taking his traveling companions to see the joint he
played in the summer of 1960.

Corroboration for much of Dylan's version comes from Kevin Krown,
a local folksinger he met in Denver. Krown told Scaduto that he met
Dylan while 'he was playing piano in this Central City joint' and that
'he was living with this stripper down the road.' If he was living with a
stripper—as both Dylan and Krown contend—it seems surprising that
he played the burlesque house for only ten days, particularly as his
Minneapolis friends say he was gone most of the summer. And, despite
Conley's insistence that Dylan stayed at his house for three weeks, it is
difficult to see how Dylan could have survived for that long without a
job. According to Krown, Dylan came to Denver having already been
offered the job at the Gilded Garter. This may be less romantic, but it
makes a helluva lot more sense than the 'promise of a floor' story. It
would also explain why Dylan felt he could take time out for a few days
beforehand to check into a cheap hotel and check out the local folk
scene. Krown's portrait of Dylan certainly contrasts dramatically with
the permanently broke man Conley has sought to paint.

Kevin Krown: In those days he had the money, he was the one doing the
buying. He had a job and a few dollars and I was broke. He actually gave
me a couple of bucks when I was ready to start hitching again.

In all likelihood, Conley's portrait was colored by two actions characteristic of Dylan at this time: first, a willingness to take permanent loan
of record collections—in this case Conley's, on leaving Denver; and
second, they apparently fell out over a girl they were both chasing,
perhaps the very same Gilded Garter stripper.

Conley's unwitting generosity was not confined to his record collection. When Dylan returned to Minneapolis, he had also acquired a song
from Conley that had the jump on most of the material he'd been playing
thus far. It was called 'The Klan' and, though it did not survive the
transition to New York folkie, it signaled another change in Dylan as a
performer and vocalist, as well as reaffirming his unerring instinct for
taking the best of what other folksingers had to offer—in this case a
single song.

Dave Whitaker: The difference had actually happened before . . . going to New York. He came back [from Denver] with a difference in accent. He spoke differently. He was more sure of himself, really. He had gone to Denver to the Exodus, and he came back with one song that he used to play, that was entirely a new level in show business, called 'The Klan.' It was a surrealistic poem . . . someone wrote it and gave it to him.

Conley's 'The Klan' was one manifestation of the change Denver induced. Another came as a result of nights spent inside the Exodus watching one of the great unsung bluesmen of the era, Jesse 'Lone Cat' Fuller. Now sixty-four years old, Fuller was still out there, reminding the fortunate few of the times he hung out with Lead Belly, playing the likes of '99 Years and One Dark Day,' 'Fables Ain't Nothing but Doggone Lies,' and his one virtual standard, 'San Francisco Bay Blues,' always with his twelve-string guitar and harmonica, placed in a metal neck brace for him to blow between verses. This style of playing, by the summer of 1960 quite unorthodox, clearly intrigued Dylan.

Though a couple of sources have suggested that Dylan played harmonica from his early days in Minneapolis, there is no evidence he adopted the instrument until after his return from Denver, when at least one close friend recalls his all-consuming determination to learn to play the damn thing.

Bonnie Beecher: I got him his first harmonica holder at Schmidt's Music Shop. He would come over to the sorority house . . . and he'd play this harmonica, which he didn't know how to play! And my friends would come in and they would just go, 'Uurgh! Who is this geek?' . . . I wanted him to play guitar, which he could play well and which I knew would impress them, but he just wasn't having any of it. He was saying, 'Naw, I wanna get this—hwang! WHwaongg!' I was mortified, but he didn't give a shit.

The connection with Fuller is no mere happenstance. Dylan told Izzy Young in October 1961 that he 'met Jesse Fuller in Denver at the Exodus . . . Jesse was playing downstairs and upstairs was Don Crawfurd.' He later told Robert Shelton that he had 'quizzed Fuller' about playing harmonica using a rack. He was already soaking up tricks of the trade in time-honored fashion—the folk process—among people who believed copyright was reserved for the wholly original:

Bob Dylan: If somebody played the guitar, that's who you went to see. You didn't necessarily go to meet them, you just went . . . to watch them, listen to them, and if possible, learn how to do something . . . And usually at that time it was quite a selfish type of thing . . . It wasn't necessarily a song; it was technique and style . . . I certainly spent a lot of hours just trying to do what other people had been doing. [1968]

The standard version of Dylan-as-chameleon states that, at this point, having returned safe and sound to Minneapolis, he transformed himself into an acolyte of Woody Guthrie. Not that he didn't already know Guthrie's more famous songs, four of which feature on the May 1960 St. Paul tape, but his obsessive personality had not as yet latched onto the charismatic example of Woodrow Wilson Guthrie. Within a matter of weeks of returning from Denver, having developed dramatically as a performer, he would begin to sound like a disciple of the absent Woody. Shortly afterward, he began to play the harmonica using a metal neck brace. The combination of Guthrie mannerisms and the mouth harp in its brace would, within six months, become a trademark. Dylan's adoption of the Guthrie persona seems to have come so soon after his return that some old friends thought it was an affectation he had developed in Colorado.

Bonnie Beecher: He came back talking with a real thick Oklahoma accent and wearing a cowboy hat and boots. He was into Woody Guthrie in a big, big way . . . At the time it seemed ludicrous and pretentious and foolish, but now I see it as allowing a greater Bob Dylan to come out.

In fact, Beecher's 'cowboy hat and boots' suggest more of a homage to Woody's Jewish 'son,' Elliott Charles Adnopoz, a.k.a. Ramblin' Jack Elliott, rather than to Woody himself. Indeed, it would appear that Dylan's initial vision of Guthrie was a highly Elliottized version of the man. (Elliott had spent half a dozen years in the fifties following Woody around, soaking up all he could as his folk apprenticeship.)

Dylan was greatly aided in his education by the fortuitous acquisition of Elliott's recordings for the English folk label Topic in the late fifties. Elliott's first album for Topic comprised a tribute to Guthrie. Entitled *Talking Woody Guthrie*, it totaled ten Guthrie originals, of which '1913 Massacre' was soon both a powerful addition to Dylan's repertoire and the source of Dylan's first composition of note.

Jack Elliott: Bonnie Beecher said [to me], 'Bob used to play all your records before he came to New York. He was fond of your voice, and he listened to your records and picked up your style.'

These Topic ten-inchers, though, were damnably difficult to find stateside. Exclusively English in origin, owners of these recordings almost constituted a secret society. Acquisition was a mysterious process. Dylan first heard these recordings at *Little Sandy Review* HQ, co-editor Jon Pankake's apartment. The speed and accuracy with which he proceeded to become the person he heard on the Topic records was little short of astounding. Pankake recalls someone who 'seemed to be very hungry for songs and music . . . I played a Texas chain-gang song from an Alan Lomax [album] for him. Then I offered to play him another song from a record, possibly by Peggy Seeger. He said that he was more interested in learning and hearing directly from people.' Of course, with Jack Elliott he had no choice but to learn his sound from record.

Paul Nelson: He came over to us because we had the magazine and he wanted us to promote concerts, and we didn't really want to . . . I know we played him the first Jack Elliott record he ever heard . . . They were sent from England, 'cause they were on Topic and no one else had them . . . Also probably, not certainly, the first Folkways *Anthology [of American Folk Music]*. . . And when we played him the Elliott stuff he came back in a day, or two at the most, and . . . from being a crooner basically, nothing special— he [had been] singing Josh White and Belafonte songs and Odetta songs and wasn't writing anything—he came back and sounded like he did on the first Columbia record. He had this whole style down that quickly, and that was impressive. He did what it took Elliott ten, fifteen years in two days, and it was really convincing.

Dylan, though, was not content to reconstruct himself without the Elliott Topic albums to hand at all times, and he set out to acquire them by the most direct method available, presumably not envisaging a time when he might be hung as a thief.

Paul Nelson: They were just gone and we sorta knew who had 'em because Dylan was interested in those, and we knew that if we found Dylan that would clinch it. Because the Jack Elliott records were in there, and he couldn't have stolen them from anybody else. We tracked him down through Tony [Glover] and we had like five [addresses], one address would lead to another . . . and there were a lot of people looking for him for various reasons. Finally [we found out where] he was staying, at a place like two blocks from where we were staying, and we went over there one night, and Jon had this huge bowling pin and Jon is six foot three and he was going to do his John Wayne impersonation with the bowling pin . . . Dylan came in and Jon waved the bowling pin around. He had no intention of hitting him but Dylan didn't know that at the time. And they played this out. First he denied it and then said, No, he did have them, and [so] it went on. Jon'd be angry for five minutes and then Dylan'd sorta seemed to realize . . . he wasn't gonna get clobbered by the pin. After ten minutes, Jon would go through the scene again and Dylan would go through the scene again and it'd be the same ending; and it went on for about an hour like that, and it got comic. I knew nothing was going to happen. Everyone was playing the same role but with less and less conviction. I remember Dylan being very cool about the whole thing, even when he thought he might get hit.

Jon Pankake: Tony [Glover], who had been spending time with Bob around the time, said he expressed some surprise at seeing certain records at Bob's, including some English records by Jack Elliott that had not been issued over here . . . They were all very good records. He had very good taste. There was also some Woody Guthrie stuff . . . I wasn't really that angry but I wanted to be sure he got the message . . . The funny thing is that I didn't feel that there was anything malicious about his stealing the records. I think he believed that he needed them more than I did. But I felt that it expressed a certain amount of contempt for me personally.

Dylan's highly selective tastes in folk were already apparent in the albums he appropriated, which included Elizabeth Cotten's *Negro Folk Songs and Tunes* and Mike Seeger's *Mountain Music—Bluegrass Style*. Nelson's account stands in marked contrast to the hysterical tale, told by Watt Conley to Spitz, of Dylan tossing albums out of his bedroom window to dispose of goods stolen from Conley and his roommate. Though more magnanimous than Conley, Pankake never really forgave Dylan.

Around this time Dylan also borrowed, this time with the owner's blessing, Dave Whitaker's copy of Guthrie's romanticized account of life on the road, *Bound for Glory*. Whitaker was regularly recommending books for him to read, books that never appeared on any university curriculum at the time. One book that affected Dylan greatly was Jack Kerouac's *Mexico City Blues*. Allen Ginsberg's *Howl* was another favored text. But neither of these, and nothing else, struck Dylan in quite the same way *Bound for Glory* did, nor gave him the requisite new persona.

Dave Whitaker: My role, as far as Bob was concerned, is that I taught him to read, turning him onto the world of books . . . For him reading had always been a painful process, outside of his existence. He told me in

Oakland, in 1978 . . . 'I never thought of reading books until I met you.'
I'd say, 'Bob, you've got to read this,' and he'd read it . . . I gave him *Bound
for Glory*, which is the story of these folksingers and how you could earn
your living going from place to place, [Woody] and Cisco Houston, playing
these songs and taking a collection . . . And for days Bob carried it around,
and he read it, and he came to me and said, 'Come on, Dave, I want to
show you something.' And he went and picked up his guitar and he had
memorized 'Tom Joad' . . . it's a twenty-minute song! . . . Bob did have
this marvelous ability to hear a song once and commit it totally to memory.

It was a very specific version of Guthrie in which he now cloaked
himself. What really appealed to Dylan was the heroic figure Guthrie
portrayed in *Bound for Glory*, one 'of these folksingers [who knew] how
you could earn your living going from place to place,' not the husk of a
man hospitalized in 1952 with Huntington's chorea, an irreversible
degenerative disease that would take fifteen years to kill the man whose
guitar had killed fascists. The wisecracking folk poet who wrote 'This
Land Is Your Land' (complete with anti-patriotic verse), 'Pastures of
Plenty,' and 'Grand Coulee Dam,' auteur of the talking blues form,
a loose, almost free-verse, song shape with an easy, cascading tune
and an extended melody line that permitted every verse to end with a
suitably weighted verbal riposte, was the figure he sought to emulate. It
was with a series of talking blues that Dylan first began to affect an
Oklahoma twang to his voice. And that twang became more and more
pronounced as he immersed himself totally in Guthrie's *oeuvre* and
projected character.

The second-earliest recording of Dylan, normally referred to as the
first Minneapolis tape, shows the first stage of the 'Guthrie phase' of
Dylan's development. Probably recorded at the beginning of September,
it features a Dylan who had discovered the *Bound for Glory* Guthrie and
the talking blues, but not seemingly how to play the harmonica. There
are four talking blues on the tape, three by Guthrie and one improvised
by Dylan about his roommate Hugh Brown, 'the laziest man in town,'
who is so indolent that, even when it is raining on his bed, he won't get
up and close the window. Also on the tape was Fuller's 'San Francisco
Bay Blues,' seemingly learned from Elliott's second Topic album rather
than Fuller, since neither it, nor any of the other cuts, features 'the first
white performer to combine the Sonny Terry harmonica with the
Woody Guthrie guitar,' to use Harvey Abrams's choice description of a
Dylan soon to evolve.

Through the fall of 1960 Dylan worked at his harmonica playing.

Though he still played the Purple Onion, he had another regular gig in St. Paul, at the Bastille, which had fewer of the distractions that made the pizza parlor such a hard gig. Sometimes he would play with Cynthia Fincher, who accompanied on banjo; sometimes he would play with Dave 'Tony' Glover, who had only gradually come to consider him a worthy enough musical companion. Glover and his partner, Dave Ray, were highly respected musicians on the local scene. Dylan had first met Tony Glover, an important influence who pushed him to look beyond Minneapolis, in May, at a party held by the recently married Gretel Whitaker. Though it wouldn't be until after Denver that he and Glover became buddies, Glover even then made a mental note of Dylan, who refused to continue playing at the party until certain people stopped talking and began listening. Glover noticed Dylan's insatiable thirst to learn, that incredible way he had of soaking up influences, styles, tunes.

Glover chooses to underplay his role in Dylan's development. And yet he not only provided some much-needed tutoring on the mouth harp, but recollects that Dylan originally had a chord harmonica, that is to say one that can be played in a number of different keys. Though suitable for certain types of traditional music, this harmonica type was not of much use when playing the blues, where you were required to bend notes. It also required a higher degree of musical expertise than the conventional blues harmonica. Glover suggested Dylan change to a single-key harmonica, à la the great Sonny Terry, and showed him how to play 'cross-harp,' where the harp player plays in a different key from the one the harmonica is tuned to.

The pace of Dylan's development as a harmonica player proved truly remarkable. More than any other instrument, the harmonica would always seem tailored to his musical ideas, and it remains the only 'lead' instrument he can play with any confidence. Within days of reaching New York in January 1961 he was already competent enough to secure a regular gig as a harmonica accompanist for Fred Neil (a wonderful Fred McDarrah photo from the Café Wha in February captures a cloth-capped Dylan, mouth harp cupped, playing along with Karen Dalton and Neil). As Beecher recognized, it was his capacity to genuinely not 'give a shit' about the opinions of others that made him a nigh-on perfect example of the self-taught musician. If not everyone in Minneapolis noticed a man on the move, when his old friend from Hibbing, Bill Marinac, visited him that fall he was surprised how far his ex-rock & rolling buddy had come.

Bill Marinac: After he went down to the university, he had an acoustic and his harmonica. We got together and jammed again. He'd started to write some music. It was really tender, a lot of very good blues, a lot of things about growing up.

Marinac was not the only one impressed by Dylan's development. In the fall of 1960 Rolf Cahn came to Minneapolis. A renowned guitarist with albums on Moe Asch's Folkways label, Cahn apparently informed a few friends on his departure that Dylan was 'the most talented guy around.' Odetta also came to Minneapolis that fall, and again Dylan received the commendation of a noteworthy folk performer.

Bonnie Beecher: I remember Cynthia Fincher coming running over to my house saying, 'She said that Dylan has real talent and he can make it!'

Such plaudits no doubt reinforced Dylan's intuitive faith in his own abilities and the suitability of the path he had chosen. Yet when he announced to his friends in early December that he had decided to head for New York to find the great Guthrie, he was met with derision by those on the Minneapolis folk scene apt to complain of the ingratitude of one about to rise above them.

Stanley Gottlieb: When he told us he was going to New York, we thought he was crazy. We said, 'You can't make it here; how the fuck are you gonna make it there?'

In fact, Dylan *had* 'made it' in Minneapolis, having become some kind of big fish in a fair-to-middling pond. Unfortunately the pond was one thousand and five hundred miles from New York, and he had no intention of being there when it froze over. He doubtless took solace from the knowledge that many of his peers regarded him a noteworthy performer—save perhaps for his love of Guthrie covers, which could be a little wearing at times—but he could make no further headway in the North Country. Many who would later disparage the 1960 Dylan had seen a lot of him in the spring and early summer, far less of him in the fall, as he honed his art away from the campus nexus, in Minneapolis's twin city, St. Paul. They had not seen the startling pace at which he had developed as a performer since his return from Denver. Dylan wisely trusted his instincts, and as long as he continued to do so his development as a popular artist was assured.

Bob Dylan: I'd learned as much as I could and used up all my options . . . When I arrived in Minneapolis it had seemed like a big city or a big town. When I left it was like some rural outpost. [1985]

Unfortunately, even with his consummate skill at acquiring floors (or ladies' beds) on which to lay his head, the young Dylan was going to need some help from home if he was going to make it all the way to New York. According to his uncle, his parents were already aware of his quitting college—and had come to terms with it—when he returned to Hibbing, cap in hand.

Maurice Zimmerman: Bobby was . . . independent—like when he quit school. Came home from Minneapolis and told his parents he wanted to go to New York, to try and make it on his own. Didn't want any help, just took enough money from his father to get east.

Abraham recalled it differently, requiring a concession from his son whereby 'he could have one year to do as he pleased, and if at the end of that year we were not satisfied with his progress, he'd go back to school.' Presumably, it never occurred to Dylan that he might just find himself, a year down the line, still no further down the road to fame and fortune. Whatever his thoughts, a respectfully shorn son took the money and ran.

Bonnie Beecher: It was an unexpected trip he had to make up to Hibbing and he wanted me to cut his hair real short, real short so that [they] 'won't know that I wear long hair.' He kept saying, 'Shorter! Shorter! Get rid of the sideburns!' Then in the door come Dave Morton, Johnny Koerner, and Harvey Abrams. They looked at him and said, 'Oh my God, you look terrible!' . . . [and] he went and wrote that song, 'Bonnie, why'd you cut my hair? Now I can't go nowhere!'

'Bonnie, Why'd You Cut My Hair?' was one of a number of comical, semi-improvised throwaways Dylan had begun composing (he reprised it one last time on the May 1961 'Party Tape') but, as he headed out of Minneapolis, Dylan also began writing another song for Beecher, a song in which he tried to remember the good times. 'Song to Bonny,' just like the later 'Song to Woody,' took as its tune Guthrie's '1913 Massacre,' a favorite of both Bonnie and Bob. Some time after Dylan arrived in Chicago, he played Kevin Krown his new song, Krown later becoming convinced that he had been played 'Song to Woody' back in December 1960.

The resemblance between the two songs was not merely musical. Addressing in the first person both Bonnie and Woody, in the former he tells Bonnie, 'I think that you know what I am doing and where I must go,' whereas in 'Song to Woody' he does not presume to tell Woody anything, because 'I know that you know.' 'Song to Bonny' is also littered with folk-song commonplaces, for example, 'Springtime's a-comin'' and the grass'll turn green.' More significantly, he changes a familiar traditional opening from 'My parents raised me tenderly' to 'My mother raised me tenderly.' Evidently the son of the father was still not in a mood to forgive.

How much Dylan's trip to New York was bound up with visiting Woody Guthrie remains unclear. According to Whitaker, Dylan set out for New York on a whim, after being up all night and attempting to phone Guthrie at Greystone Hospital near Morristown, New Jersey, where he was confined as Huntington's chorea slowly wasted his body away. The fact that Dylan visited Hibbing first makes it clear that the trip was no such whim. Though Dylan clearly realized that going to New York would provide him with an opportunity to visit Guthrie, it would have been an uncharacteristic display of naïveté on his part if he had really traveled fifteen hundred miles east primarily to see Guthrie.

Scaduto is the only previous biographer to have chronicled Dylan's trip from Minneapolis to New York accurately. Spitz was simply lousy on his history, claiming that Dylan headed straight from Denver to New York, a claim denied by a mountain of evidence. Shelton accepted Dylan's even more implausible claim that he'd arrived in New York in December 1960 and spent two months in Times Square hustling as a male prostitute, evidence merely of his desire to reinvent his past long after stories of running away as a child and joining the circus had been revealed as a sham. In fact, his convoluted journey to New York is well documented, not least by himself.

Bob Dylan: I went to Chicago first and stayed there. Then I went up to Wisconsin, which was more or less the same general scene as it was at the school in Minnesota. And from there I went to New York. That was quite a trip. Another guitar player and myself got a ride with a young couple from the campus whose parents were from Brooklyn. They were going there and wanted some more drivers, so we just drove. [1978]

However, Madison does not lie directly between Chicago and New York—it's between Chicago and Minneapolis, on Highway 94. And yet, neither Dylan nor Scaduto are mistaken. Having arrived in Chicago around Christmas, Dylan looked up Kevin Krown, who had returned to Chicago from Denver, and crashed at Krown's place for a couple of days before moving in with a girl (or perhaps it was the sixty-year-old red-haired woman he later claimed he slept with in Chicago). At this point, he seems to have become disheartened, abandoning his original plan and deciding to head back north. Hitchhiking as far as Madison, whose campus had an active folk scene, Dylan wrote to the Whitakers informing them of his change of mind. Madison, though, provided enough opportunities for an itinerant folksinger like Bob to convince him to stick around.

Marshall Brickman: Eric Weissberg and I roomed together. Our apartment was the place where all the folksingers wound up. We were the underground railroad. One day this guy, Bob Zimmerman, came through town on his way from Minnesota [sic]. He had a brown suit and tie and played sort of blues on the piano.

Brickman and Weissberg were considerably harder to charm than other young Madison folkniks. Dylan quickly attached himself to another local boy, Danny Kalb, an adept blues guitarist, with whom he proceeded to play at a local coffeehouse.

Danny Kalb: Dylan was sort of a strange person when I first met him. He was the first guy who had marijuana in his mitten . . . He took out his guitar and he started playing some Woody Guthrie songs. Bob seemed like a repository of songs, from this sort of generalized left-wing people's songbook . . . He was nothing out of the ordinary. I knew a lot of people like that— even myself . . . I believe that Bob played with me . . . on harmonica, at the Pad, a little beatnik coffeehouse, very small . . . I used to sit on top of the piano there and play blues . . . I'd got my version of 'Poor Lazarus' from Dave Van Ronk and I shared it with [Dylan] in the kitchen of Fred Underhill's house in Madison.

Dylan may have shared songs and a piano with Kalb, but his faith in his musical powers seems to have been undermined by the competition he encountered playing at parties and coffeehouses in Chicago and Madison. Perhaps Kalb's assessment—'he was nothing out of the ordinary'—had even impinged on Dylan's mental armor. It was Fred Underhill who saved Dylan a few blushes, and handed him the opportunity of fulfilling his destiny, when he told him about a friend of his who was heading to New York and needed a couple of relief drivers to share driving duties. Underhill was up for the jaunt and being from Williamstown, New Jersey, presumably knew all about Greystone, Guthrie's living mausoleum. So, with his newfound friend to hold his metaphoric hand, Dylan found himself agreeing to complete the journey east as originally planned. Underhill apparently did not feel it his duty to apprise their main driver, one Dave Berger, of the young Dylan's Woody fixation.

1961: Hard Times in New York Town

4

We drove straight through without stopping, which was typically what we did. He was singing all the way—it was annoying, that weird monotonic kind of style with Woody's twang. It was a pain in the ass. As we got into New Jersey, I finally told him, 'Shut the fuck up.'

—*Dave Berger*

Bob Dylan and Fred Underhill arrived in a freezing cold Manhattan on or around January 24, 1961, being dropped off uptown by an exasperated Berger. Dylan recalled two feet of snow covering the ground. Fred and he may have intended to walk the fifty blocks down to the Village— after all, this was New York, money was tight, and they had a lot to take in—but when they realized just how cold it was, they hopped a subway. In the released recording of 'Talkin' New York,' on his first album, Dylan would claim that he took 'a rockin', reelin', rollin' ride' straight down to the West Village. In the original draft of the song he says he 'rode the subway for a couple of days.'

Whatever the truth, they eventually hit upon the Café Wha, a fairly seedy 'basket house', a place where singers passed the basket. It was Tuesday, hootenanny night, and anyone was allowed to get up on stage and sing a couple of songs. Dylan would later claim that the audience 'flipped,' though it seems unlikely that a large, appreciative crowd would have congregated at the Wha on such a bitterly cold weekday night. The owner of the Wha, Manny Roth, though, must have heard something, because Dylan was soon playing there in the afternoons. After his brief set that night, Roth told the few Village stalwarts in attendance that Bob and Fred were looking for a place to crash for the night.

Bob Dylan: My buddy and I . . . picked out this fellow who was with a girl. Then my buddy says to me, 'He doesn't look so hot . . . He looks pretty gay.' And I said, 'He looks OK'—and anyway, he was with a girl. And so we went up[town] with him. And the girl got off at 34th Street, and we got off at 42nd Street! Well, we went in a bar before we went to find this place to stay, and we met his [gentleman] friend 'Dora.' 'Dora' was his friend who stayed with him. Both of us looked [at each other], and ran out of the bar. [1961]

Perhaps it was at this point that Fred and Bob chose to ride the subway for a couple of days. At least the subways had heating, and they *had* arrived smack in the middle of what Dylan later called the 'coldest winter in seventeen years,' actually the worst in twenty-eight. But in all likelihood, however much they *thought* about running out of the bar, they took a chance and spent a warm if worrying night with Dora and his friend.

That first week in New York, Dylan did the rounds of the many folk joints in the Village. The first weekend he turned up at Izzy Young's Folklore Center, a small shop with an impressive assortment of 'folk' fare on vinyl and in print, as well as assorted acoustic instruments. It also had a back room in which folkies regularly congregated, to talk and sing. That first Sunday morning, Dylan was to be heard in the back running through 'Muleskinner Blues' on one of Izzy's autoharps. J. R. Goddard, of the *Village Voice*, was an early convert.

J. R. Goddard: People looked on in amusement as he began hopping around a bit. He was funny to watch, and anybody with half an ear could tell he [already] had a unique style.

But before that, probably the first thing Dylan did when he arose on Wednesday the 25th was to travel out to New Jersey, to the daunting Greystone Hospital, to visit Woody Guthrie. Woody had told the Gleasons that he 'picked Greystone because it was the prettiest damn booby hatch I came across . . . so I fixed it so that I'd get arrested and sent there.' In truth Greystone picked him, at a time when he was running out of options. Diagnosed with a hereditary, degenerative disease of the central nervous system, and having seen his mother die of the very same disease, he was by his own admission 'scared witless.' By the time Dylan found him, Guthrie knew he was destined to be permanently interred in Greystone, save for weekend sabbaticals in East Orange, at the home of Sidsel and Bob Gleason. In his first year in New York, Dylan visited Woody often, and all those who accompanied him have spoken of the rapport that clearly existed between the elder statesman of folk and his not-so-apparent heir.

John Hammond, Jr.: I had a car and I would drive him to Brooklyn [New Jersey], to the hospital, to see Woody Guthrie. Woody really liked Bob, and Bob really liked Woody. [In fact] he idolized him. Woody was not well at all. He had spasms and I felt uncomfortable seeing him in such pain, but Bob was really mellow and real calm, and I was very impressed with Bob's ability to handle that whole thing. He played Woody's tunes for Woody, and some of his own.

After meeting Guthrie for the first time, Dylan barely waited till he made it back to the Village before he penned a postcard to the Whitakers saying, 'I know Woody . . . I know him and met him and saw him and sang to him . . . Goddamn.' Such, though, was Bob's burgeoning reputation as a teller of tall tales that few back in Dinkytown believed him. When Bonnie Beecher visited a few months later he insisted on taking her to Greystone to meet the great man.

Bonnie Beecher: I think he took me to meet Woody Guthrie in the hospital mainly because he wanted me to go back to Minnesota and tell Harvey Abrams, Hugh Brown, and Red Nelson . . . that he really was a friend of Woody's. Which he was! . . . Woody was in the insane asylum section with all these creepy people . . . He played 'Hard Travelin',' but it was hard for him to hold the guitar because he had these spastic movements . . . And then Dylan played 'Pastures of Plenty' . . . And Woody loved Dylan, loved Dylan doing his songs.

Woody Guthrie was permitted by the hospital to spend each weekend at the Gleasons', where he could be made to feel comfortable in the company of old friends. Congregated there would be figures like Alan Lomax, Pete Seeger, Ralph Rinzler, and Ramblin' Jack Elliott. Dylan, also, managed to secure an early invite to the Gleason gatherings. Indeed, he was there the first Sunday in February 1961 when Cisco Houston, Woody's oldest and dearest friend, and a fine traditional singer in his own right, said his goodbyes and sang for Woody one last time. Dying of stomach cancer, Cisco was going back home to California, where he died on April 29, 1961.

Though initially daunted by such company, Dylan's exuberant self-confidence soon flowered and within a couple of weeks he was self-consciously joining in the conversation, though he rarely played for the assembled throng. At the same time, he had ingratiated himself with the Gleasons and, when he had nothing pending in the Village, would often stay over in East Orange for a few days at a time.

Peter MacKenzie: It was at the Gleasons where Bobby would practice by singing into the tape recorder, learning how to use a microphone. He and

Kevin made [a] tape one day. Kevin sent out several copies of those recordings . . . trying to drum up interest in him.

The tape in question seems to have been made one afternoon in February. The first known recording of Dylan playing guitar *and* harmonica, the seven-song tape opens with a favorite of Krown's, 'San Francisco Bay Blues,' and concludes with a long-forgotten country hit from 1940, Lulu Belle and Scotty's 'Remember Me (When the Candle Lights Are Gleaming).' The songs in between, though, drew entirely from Guthrie's established repertoire, including 'Pastures of Plenty,' 'Jesse James,' and Guthrie's take on 'Gypsy Davey.'

If this was indeed intended to be Dylan's first audition tape (of sorts), it suggested someone self-consciously walking in Guthrie's shadow. However, for anyone conversant with Dylan's Minneapolis sets, it also suggested someone who had digested Guthrie's songs and style at a bewildering rate. Dylan had been blessed with a remarkable ear for song. As Sid Gleason observed, 'He'd go maybe twice through a record and he'd have all the words copied, and chord progressions [too].'

Sid Gleason may have been one more matriarch to charm, but Dylan had no shortage of opportunities to work on his orphan-boy act in the Village. And, as the early photos bear out, he cut quite a figure at the time.

Eve MacKenzie: The first time [my husband and I] met Bobby was in February 1961, after a Jack Elliott concert at the Carnegie Recital Hall. At that concert was Marjorie Guthrie . . . [who] invited us down to hear Cisco Houston at Gerde's that night . . . Anyway, there was this young fellow sitting on a bench to the left of me, wearing this little corduroy hat, very quiet, smoking one cigarette after another, leg jerking up and down, in a black winter overcoat down to his ankles, with the collar turned up. He reminded me of a character out of a Charles Dickens novel. Marjorie introduced him to us as a young folksinger from New Mexico named Bob Dylan . . . Bobby was looking over at the table [of sandwiches], but not saying anything. He looked hungry . . . so I offered him one of our sandwiches and said, Eat! It's free . . . You never saw a sandwich disappear so fast in your life.

During his first few months in New York, Dylan made considerable use of the maternal instincts he seemed to engender in otherwise sane women, and which he had already refined in Minneapolis.

Liam Clancy: Dylan had this image of the lost waif, and all the girls wanted to mother him—he made out like a bandit!

A certain lack of discrimination and a mock shyness that soon revealed a considerable libido proved to be a potent combination in the Village, where the more bohemian girls found previously unsuspected maternal desires being brought out by this chubby, boyish Huck Finn character. He delighted in showing off his prowess to his male friends, most of whom were more bashful (or maybe more discriminating) than Dylan.

Mark Spoelstra: He had a lot of nerve with girls. More than I did. Chasing them, coming on to them, not being intimidated—man, Dylan was remarkable.

Dylan was not used to being without a lady companion for any length of time, and the pattern continued in the Village. Within a week or two of his arrival, he had moved in with a beautiful, bright dancer named Avril, who had fallen deeply in love with him. With a base in the city and a home away from home in New Jersey, he had organized his affairs well. Now he could concentrate on making a reputation as a New York folksinger.

He had soon scouted out those places in the Village where anyone with a guitar could get up and play. Initially his only real opportunities were at the basket houses, where acts played without actual payment, relying upon donations from the crowd at the end of their set. There were numerous such establishments in the Village at this time, like the Figaro, the Commons, and the Wha. Greenwich Village was the epicenter of a buzzing folk revival.

At the beginning of February, Dylan was playing regularly at the Commons, Café Wha, and even the Gaslight. More upmarket establishments like the Limelight, the Village Gate, and Gerde's Folk City remained as yet inaccessible, save for Gerde's Monday hootenanny night, when amateur talent endeavored to impress club owner Mike Porco enough to secure a paying gig. Meanwhile, Dylan supplemented his meager earnings by playing harmonica at the Café Wha, his first stop in the Village that Tuesday in January.

Bob Dylan: I worked for Manny [Roth] all afternoons, from twelve till eight. I worked the day shift back then . . . It stayed open from eleven in the morning until four in the morning and there was constantly something happening on the stage . . . You never really did get popular there, 'cause people never knew who you were. Nobody was billed on the outside . . . You passed the basket . . . That's why I started wearing hats. It was just a nonstop flow of people, usually they were tourists who were looking for beatniks in the Village. There'd be maybe five groups that played there. I used to play with a guy called Fred Neil . . . He would play mostly the types of songs that Josh White might sing. I would play harmonica for him, and then once in a while get to sing a song . . . when he was taking a break or something. It was his show, he would be on for about half an hour, then a conga player would get on . . . And then this girl [presumably Karen Dalton] . . . used to play sweet Southern Mountain Appalachian ballads, with electric guitar and a small amplifier . . . Then there'd be a comedian, then an impersonator. And that'd be the whole show, and this whole unit would go around nonstop. And you got fed there, which was actually the best thing about the place. [1984]

Dylan would later suggest, somewhat caustically, that he was 'blowin' his lungs out for a dollar a day.' Certainly it was hard work for little pay—but it *was* experience and it allowed him to join a growing band of authentic young troubadours wandering the streets of the Village. When he wrote to the Whitakers at the beginning of February he told them he was playing the Commons, where 'people clap for me.' However, his Minneapolis friends might have had trouble recognizing the man singing at the Wha. Not only had that hokey Okie accent become even more pronounced, but in the Village he was considered first and foremost a harmonica player. The man who had made that awful racket at Bonnie's sorority barely five months earlier had quickly discovered a natural aptitude for the instrument. He had also, seemingly unconsciously, developed a way of playing that set him apart from his Village contemporaries.

Bob Dylan: This sounds a little vague, but sometimes, like most of the time, I would blow out on the harmonica because everybody sucks in. The proper way to play is like Little Walter or Sonny Boy Williamson would play—which would be to cross it—and I found myself blowing out more because nobody was doing that . . . And that's what defined that harmonica and guitar sound, which I hadn't heard until that point. I just stumbled on it one day. [1978]

Dylan himself readily admits that there were some conscious influences involved in the style of harmonica playing he now adopted. Jesse Fuller may have been the first performer who impressed him live, but by now he would have heard Sonny Terry's harp accompaniment to some of Woody's and Lead Belly's recordings, if not his classic albums with Brownie McGhee on Prestige. Nor did he forget the music he had heard in Hibbing and Minneapolis, notably that reedy sound his old hero Jimmy Reed had managed to get on his records.

Bob Dylan: Jimmy Reed blew out instead of sucking in on [the harmonica]. He had his own style of playing—he'd play like three notes, sometimes the whole solo would be like three notes. [1989]

In those first few months Dylan was developing at such a pace that the chronology has become twisted by inconsistent and unreliable recollections by contemporaries, many with agendas of their own. Some ex–Village folkies have Dylan writing prodigiously a year before it was true. Others omit his days as a harmonica accompanist, or forget the occasions when he played piano at Gerde's hootenannies. The Dylan who was not even twenty was still trying styles on, seeing which ones fit.

Something, though, had clicked since he'd arrived in New York. In less than three months he secured a support slot to John Lee Hooker for a two-week residency at Gerde's Folk City. Though Dylan was doubtless conversant with his earlier, electric R&B recordings for Modern Records, Hooker had recently reverted to a solo acoustic format, issuing *The Folk Blues of John Lee Hooker* on Riverside in 1959, the beginning of a lucrative new career as a folk-blues artist. Dylan spent the week before he began support duties, from the fourth to the tenth of April, watching Hooker work his charm on a packed-out Gerde's, and honing his own set down to the five-song maximum afforded support acts.

The two songs he was sure he wanted to incorporate into each night's set were a new arrangement of 'House of the Rising Sun' taught to him by Dave Van Ronk, and the first song he had written on his arrival in New York, 'Song to Woody.' If it seemed impertinent to some that he should lift the tune for his affecting tribute from one of Guthrie's own efforts, there can be little doubting the sincerity of this particular song. On giving his handwritten manuscript to the Gleasons, he wrote at the bottom of the sheet: 'Written by Bob Dylan in Mills Bar on Bleeker Street in New York City on the 14th day of February, for Woody Guthrie.' If the prototype for 'Song to Woody,' 'Song to Bonny,' concluded with a folk cliché, this time Dylan introduced a newfound sense of equivocation. After glorifying those who 'come with the dust,' Dylan refuses to express any desire for 'some hard travelin' too.' His trip from Minneapolis to New York, via Chicago and Madison, had perhaps taught him the true meaning of 'hard travelin'.'

And yet, barely had the Gerde's residency run its course before Dylan was retracing his steps back to the North Country. If he was looking to be gone with the wind, the sort of confrontation he hated most seems to have precipitated a prompt departure.

Mark Spoelstra: Avril was really in love with Dylan but he was intimidated by her honesty and directness . . . I walked in on them in a restaurant when Avril was breaking up with Bob . . . All she wanted was honesty. She was very intense about it. And Bob just kind of played the James Dean thing— very quiet, reserved, and cool, like he couldn't have cared less. The next day he left her a note and simply disappeared.

Though Spoelstra's take on the café confrontation was of a couple breaking up, this was clearly not Avril's intent. She was just trying to get Bob to be a little more upfront with her—which was tantamount to breaking up in Bob's book. Whatever the note to Avril said, it evidently didn't reveal where he was bound. Avril turned up at Eve MacKenzie's door in a state, crying, 'He's gone! He just picked himself up and he left. I didn't know he wasn't coming back.' In fact, he had returned to Minneapolis. That he hadn't planned such a trip is confirmed in a postcard, dated April 28, to his parents, in which he states, 'I don't know if I can come home then (or when I expect to now).' He also informs them he is making a hundred bucks a week(!) and has 'already played the top place in New York for folk music.'

Minneapolis provided Dylan with the first real opportunity to gauge how far he had progressed in those six months. Those who had envisaged a humbled Bob coming home were in for a shock, as were those who felt he might have toned down his Guthrie fixation.

Jon Pankake: He was pretty much transformed by the time he got back to town. I stayed to hear him at the hoot and, musically, he was just potential. His guitar was shockingly out of tune. He started to mumble something about Woody's guitar always going out of tune . . . I thought he was terrible but I was fascinated by him. When he had been here, he had been as inhibited as the rest of us but now he was howling and bobbing up and down. He picked up his freedom before he had gotten his technique.

The two 'party tapes' from Dylan's stay in Minneapolis show an artist who had been daily a-growin' while his North Country friends had been content to pass time. Though nine Guthrie songs punctuate the couple of dozen items recorded, it is Dylan's reworkings of Rabbit Brown's 'James Alley Blues,' the traditional Scottish ballad 'The Trees They Do Grow So High,' and the death ballads 'Pretty Polly' and 'Railroad Boy' that provide the better signposts to a new Dylan.

How he changed so quickly from Guthrie clone to genuine interpreter, capable of powerful harmonica playing and marvelously expressive singing, can never be definitively nailed down. Dylan himself was mystified by the process. When he attempted to write a book two years later, his initial intention was to base it around his arrival in New York, when he 'has come to the end of one road, knows there's another road there, but doesn't exactly know where it is.' Though the tapes show us the stages in the transition, they fail to explicate it. That said, they suggest a more gradual change than those achieved by Robert Johnson when he sold his soul to the devil, or Rimbaud when he discovered absinthe and buggery. Perhaps, as Paris unleashed Rimbaud's muse, it was New York itself that released Dylan's.

Only on leaving town that May, though, did he write his first New York song, 'Talkin' New York,' which was sketched out as he awaited a lift on the New Jersey Turnpike. As with 'Song to Woody,' it was adapted from one of Guthrie's musical templates. He stopped off in Madison, again, on his way back from Minneapolis, staying with a girl named Ann Lauderbach who—aside from being involved in a poetry group at the university—had provided Dylan with a crash pad when he had passed through town the previous December. At Avril's insistence, Kevin Krown had tracked him down to Madison, but Bob seemed in no hurry to come back to New York, and Avril finally gave up waiting, taking off west. Right on time to be too late, Dylan returned east, expecting his rent-paying girlfriend to still be awaiting.

Peter MacKenzie: [But] Avril had to leave the apartment. So she came to live with my parents for a couple of weeks. Then her brother [or] mother got sick. She had to leave for San Francisco. When she left, Bobby came back and he wasn't sure what to do 'cause she had closed up the apartment, left town, and he was coming to the house to say, Hi, what's happening, and basically found out she wasn't there. There he was with his guitar over his shoulder and his little suitcase which only had one pair of underwear in it and my mother asked him if he had a place to stay, 'cause it was like two in the morning. He said, No, no, I'll find a place. He never asked to stay . . . [but] there are some people, when you're sitting across the room, they have a way of asking that, after you offer to do something for them, they can disclaim they ever asked for anything. And he just stayed.

In classic Dylan fashion, he now seems to have been overcome with remorse, and insisted on calling Avril so he could sing her a song he had just written for her, 'California Brown-Eyed Baby,' set to the tune of Guthrie's 'Columbus Stockade.' In the final verse he advises the ubiquitous 'boys' not to ramble, but to stay in their hometown, get a girl who loves them, 'and settle down.' Perhaps for the first time he was writing for an audience, in this case of one. He was certainly not writing *from* himself.

Eve MacKenzie: He was insisting on using the telephone. 'I'm gonna call her!' And I tried to stop him. He said he'd call collect, and I said no, that [Avril] was a poor girl and she couldn't afford to take a call collect . . . But he did call her—maybe it was the next day—and she took the call. And he said, 'I have a song for you.' And he sang 'California Brown-Eyed Baby.' I held the phone for him, he sang it, and everybody cried. It was the first time we'd heard him sing one of his own songs.

The few songs he'd written at this point were mostly talking blues in the Guthrie vein. It was a form that allowed full rein for his mordant wit and that way he had with folk phrasing. Initially they were more extensions of his storytelling than songs in themselves. And yet they proved extremely popular. 'Talkin' New York' was a sardonic depiction of his early weeks in the Village. 'Talkin' Hava Nagila Blues' mercilessly parodied the type of folk song repeatedly requested by weekend tourists. 'Talkin' Bear Mountain Picnic Massacre Blues,' perhaps the finest of his early talking blues, was a hilarious résumé of a boat trip to Bear Mountain which had been oversold because of counterfeit tickets.

Aside from his talking blues, which were always ripe for interpolations and asides, Dylan had also developed the knack of telling long, rambling monologues, often disjointed yet combining almost a rap poet's sense of rhythm with a self-conscious, down-home patois. Indicative of his ability to slip between rap and song was an astonishing version of 'Black Cross,' a spoken monologue he'd learned from a Lord Buckley record that told the story of a poor black farmer, Hezekiah Jones, who is hung by white racists for being well-read.

Jack Nissenson: He was always an incredible storyteller. He was distant . . . onstage, very into his own thing, but he could do these long, long monologues, with no point, and no punch line—except they kept you in hysterics. Same when you talked to him. He either told you a story, or he said, 'Yeah? Is that right?' as if what you were telling him was the most amazing thing he'd ever heard.

Arthur Kretchmer: Onstage he was essentially a funny character. Maybe that isn't what he intended to be, but the audience reaction was one of laughing, not at but with Dylan. I recall him standing up there looking behind the curtains for the words to his next song, or cracking up about something which he was mumbling to himself. He was natural and loose, a real country character, and that is what everybody loved about him . . . Sometimes he would play piano, or tell a funny story, or just clown around for a few minutes.

If he was already an original on stage, he was still relying on songs from yesteryear for his repertoire. However, in the summer of 1961, as Dylan settled into his new home at the MacKenzies, he really started to apply himself to the craft of songwriting. Initially, these efforts were not intended for public performance, they were exercises to see if he had it in him to become another Guthrie, surely the extent of this folk poet's ambitions.

Eve MacKenzie: Bob's routine at this time would be that he would come home . . . three or four in the morning . . . sit down at the table, close the doors and start writing. And then he would go to sleep until noon. Then I would prepare breakfast. I always made him breakfast.

Thanks to Eve and Mac's sense of these writings' historical worth and Dylan's devil-may-care attitude toward them, the manuscripts of many of these formative efforts have survived, songs with great titles like 'Preacher's Folly' and 'Died for a Dollar,' comprising line after line of derivative drivel. If, in 'Colorado Blues,' he wrote something semi-autobiographical, disparaging Denver and Central City and wishing he was back 'in the good ol' USA,' most of these early songs placed Dylan in a milieu he had never known, and can barely have even read about. One has him playing a Second World War soldier addicted to morphine ('Dope Fiend Robber'); another has him playing a seaman dying of syphilis penning a final letter to his sweetheart, nobly informing her, 'I've got that ol siff and I'll not bring it home dear to you.' The one song that could be described as vaguely topical was 'Down at Washington Square,' which dealt with the occasion one Sunday in early April when

the busking folkies protested en masse against residents' attempts to ban
their weekly gatherings.

One of the primary appeals of his understanding, undemanding landlady, Eve MacKenzie, was that she never asked where he had been if he
went missing for a few days. Even after less than six months in New
York and one long trip 'home,' his ramblin' shoes couldn't stay in one
place too long. At the beginning of May, before his trip to Minnesota,
he'd headed up to an obscure folk festival held at a hotel in Branford,
Connecticut, with Mark Spoelstra. There he met Bobby Neuwirth,
destined to become his regular sidekick in the amphetamine years, and
jammed with a Boston folksinger named Robert L. Jones.

In June he visited the self-same Robert L. Jones in Cambridge,
Massachusetts, home of the famous Club 47, where he was introduced
by Jones to Eric Von Schmidt. He would return to Cambridge in August,
again hooking up with Von Schmidt, and this time he would meet
folksinger Carolyn Hester and her husband Richard Farina, finally get
to play at the Club 47 (at Hester's invitation), and be invited to play harp
on the forthcoming sessions for Hester's debut album for Columbia. Not
that Dylan was looking to the Cambridge scene to further his ambitions;
the real appeal of that scene was the lack of political directives attached
to the art of folksinging.

Eric Von Schmidt: One of the things that separated the Boston-Cambridge
group was our devotion to the roots people, the folk elements and not the
political usages of these songs. We just loved the music . . . Just recently I
heard a quote from Pete Seeger where he said, 'It isn't whether the song is
good, it's will it do good.' That was about as far from the way we looked at
a song as you can get . . . unless you were trying to break some little lady or
if you were looking for a place to spend the night, that probably was the
closest thing to using a song to achieve an end.

Now here were sentiments Dylan could embrace—and embrace them
he did. Looking back, it is easy to forget how divided the early sixties
folk scene had already become. The New York scene was initially
dominated by those who championed the traditional, 'purist' approach
to folk song, wherein a song acquired worth by its origins and 'authenticity,' or a politically appropriate attitude, rather than by any intrinsic
melodic or lyrical power.

Bob Dylan: Folk music was very split up . . . You know, many people
didn't want to hear it if you couldn't play the song exactly the way that

Aunt Molly Jackson played it. I just kind of blazed my way through all that kind of stuff. [1984]

One of the ways Dylan blazed his way through was to put himself inside the song, as blues musicians like John Lee Hooker and the Reverend Gary Davis were wont to do. Trad Folk, founded on an academic construct based on field recordings of largely geriatric singers of questionable pitch, insisted on 'genuinely classic impersonality.' The position was summarized best by the late Professor Bertrand Bronson:

The dominant impression conveyed by a good folk song sung in the best traditional style is . . . one of genuinely classic impersonality. . . . They are sustained and made far more impressive by . . . the characteristic singing, which is of an incantatory masklike aloofness that apparently makes no concessions to ordinary fluctuations of human sympathy or excitement, nor shows any awareness of audience, but tacitly acknowledges . . . the strangely abstract, impersonal law of tradition.

The irony is that almost nobody sang folk songs in their original modal forms, and as such the notion of authenticity was by and large bound by little more than instrumentation. The fact is that even if B. F. Shelton's 1927 recording of 'Pretty Polly' conveyed 'genuinely classic impersonality' and Dock Boggs's 1927 recording did not, no folk revivalist considered Boggs, most of whose 78 rpm recordings he sang to order, to be anything other than an authentic traditional singer. His credentials were the banjo he played, the poverty and obscurity he lived in, and the weal and woe he sang about.

Dylan's take on the synthesis he managed to achieve has changed over the years. In December 1961, he told Robert Shelton, 'I really couldn't decide which I liked the best, country or blues. So I suppose I ended up by becoming a mixture of Hank Williams and Woody Guthrie.' But one would be hard pressed to find much of Hank Williams's spirit on his debut album. He would later admit to a more eclectic synthesis, observing that he 'crossed Sonny Terry with the Stanley Brothers with Roscoe Holscomb with Big Bill Broonzy with Woody Guthrie.' But even this was less than half the picture. Perhaps he was being deliberately coy, insisting that his fusion came solely from artists steeped in tradition. As bluegrass pioneer Peter Stampfel recognized, other equally real roots showed through in the way he put the songs across:

Peter Stampfel: He was doing all traditional songs, but it was his approach!

His singing style and phrasing were stone rhythm & blues—he fitted the two styles together perfectly, clear as a bell.

As a result, Dylan divided opinion in folk's circles-within-circles more than any Greenwich Village newcomer since the Kingston Trio kicked off the debate by putting the second folk revival into gear. Bruce Langhorne, the most in-demand guitarist at New York folk sessions through the first half of the decade, encapsulates the extremes of opinion Dylan engendered when he says, 'People either liked him or they hated him. A lot of people who were more into the traditional folk performers thought that he was [just] another Woody Guthrie imitator, and a lot of people didn't like the fact that he didn't have a crystal clear voice, and talked his way through a lot of his songs. But a lot of people liked his charisma and his stage presence.' Nor were all champions of traditional singing doing the ostrich. The New Lost City Ramblers' John Cohen recognized the validity of what Dylan was doing, even if he himself went down the path lit by Bronson:

John Cohen: Once you get into that area of folk music, there is an incredible richness. Most people in our world have lost touch with that. They don't know how to listen to old ballads. I think Bob does . . . The path I followed led me to attempt to sing like those old singers did. Bob heard much of that same old music, and took from it what he needed. He had the feeling, and made his own interpretation of it.

No matter how much he 'blazed . . . through all that stuff,' Dylan could not escape the comparisons people drew, or the disdain his music sometimes generated. When he spoke to Izzy Young in October he tried to insist that 'folk music' was just a name and that he sang 'a lot of old jazz songs, sentimental cowboy songs, Top 40 hit parade stuff . . . old blues and Texas songs,' whatever the last category might be. He also insisted that what he did was not 'Folk music' but rather 'folk music.' If their huge and immediate popularity had made the issue of the Kingston Trio's lack of authenticity moot, the early Dylan still remained part of the madding crowd. Friends recall a singer who could prove a most adept house clearer when the time came for club owners to shift those last few recalcitrant customers.

Happy Traum: Before he made his first album he was even rougher sounding and more off pitch, and he didn't tune his guitar . . . We used to play in a place called Gerde's Folk City . . . we would let him come in and

do some songs for the late show . . . He'd start playing and if there were ten
people in the audience, five people would get up and walk out.

Dylan also found it hard to secure gigs out of town, where his unique
approach to performing made him an unknown quantity. Club owners
prepared to book him for the sheer joy of seeing him play were heavily
outnumbered by those who would go to any lengths to keep him out.
Terri Thal, Dave Van Ronk's girlfriend (and later his wife), took on the
responsibility of managing Dylan part-time, aided and abetted by Kevin
Krown. She succeeded in obtaining a booking at the Café Lena, in
Saratoga Springs, and Lena Spencer, the owner, loved his performance—
but there was much heckling from the audience the night he debuted.
In despair, Thal convinced Krown to make a tape of Bob playing his set
at the Gaslight Café.

Terri Thal: We made a tape of Bob, and I took it up to Springfield,
Massachusetts, where Carolyn Hester and Richard Farina were playing. The
guy who ran that club flipped. We really did a selling job. We went to
Boston and I tried to get Manny Greenhill to do a concert with Dave and
Bobby, and he turned me down. I went to Cambridge's top folk club, Club
47, and a couple of other places, and they all turned me down. Nobody
wanted him.

Despite its failure to generate out-of-town gigs, the six-song recording,
the so-called first Gaslight tape, gave a good idea of the point at which
Dylan had arrived by September 1961. It features three Dylan originals—
'Song to Woody', the best of his talking blues, 'Talkin' Bear Mountain',
and 'Man on the Street'—as well as a ludicrous duet with Van Ronk on
Guthrie's 'Car Car' and his own arrangements of two traditional songs.
Apparently two of Dylan's supporters, Carla Rotolo and Sybil Weinberger, even tried to get legendary Columbia producer John Hammond
to listen to the tape, without success. However, eight days later Dylan
found himself sitting in the same room as Hammond, who was perhaps
wondering why the name Bob Dylan rang a bell. The circumstances by
which these two men—separated by a couple of generations but
bound by a common love of authenticity—came together is tangled up
indeed.

One of the two traditional songs featured on that Gaslight 'audition'
tape had only recently entered the Dylan repertoire. It was a plaintive
number called 'He Was a Friend of Mine,' and he had acquired it from
newfound friend Eric Von Schmidt having only just returned from his

second trip to Cambridge, where he had spent a rewarding afternoon with the talented Von Schmidt.

Eric Von Schmidt: Dylan came up . . . it was Huck Finn hat time, before his first record . . . When we got to my apartment he wasn't much interested in playing; he wanted to listen. So I played 'He Was a Friend of Mine', 'Wasn't That a Mighty Storm,' 'Baby Let Me Lay It on You,' 'Acne,' and a couple of others. It [sure] was something the way he was soaking up material in those days . . . [but] he wasn't at that time quite able to handle material that related to the blues, and he was still feeling around for a way to do that.

At this stage in his development Dylan was prepared to cop material from just about anybody. He soaked up an enormous amount just by sitting and listening to contemporaries like Von Schmidt, Mark Spoelstra, Dave Van Ronk, and Carolyn Hester in clubs, coffeehouses, and apartments. The ear that had impressed Paul Nelson in Minneapolis and Sidsel Gleason in East Orange also seemed remarkable to the folksingers of New York and Boston.

Liam Clancy: The only thing I can compare him with was blotting paper. He soaked everything up. He had this immense curiosity; he was totally blank, and ready to suck up everything that came within his range.

Later, Dylan would come in for a good deal of stick for the way he appropriated not only other singers' best songs, but often their actual arrangements. Obligations arising from moral debts may not have been always served once he learned the actual ins and outs of music publishing. But in his first year in New York he was as much a part of the folk process as his fellow scramblers. Hence the open admission of his debt to Von Schmidt on the Columbia recording of 'Baby, Let Me Follow You Down'; or the acknowledgment on Ian and Sylvia's debut platter that their version of 'C. C. Rider' 'was arrived at in the course of a long afternoon session with Bob Dylan last summer'; or Dylan donating an old blues tune he'd learned from Dave Van Ronk to Carolyn Hester one August afternoon in Boston, for use on her forthcoming recording session at Columbia. This was the folk process, and had been since, say, Scottish minstrels in the Middle Ages adapted Danish and Breton ballads to their native tongue. No one yet knew how much money a Dylan rendition of a traditional arrangement by a Paul Clayton, or a Jean Ritchie, or a Dave Van Ronk, might actually generate. And when you ain't got nothing . . .

Part of what set Dylan apart was a streak of ambition as wide as the Mesabi Range. At twenty, the idea that there might be a price to pay was still blowing in the wind. Hence, starting in June, he began to work on persuading Robert Shelton, the *New York Times* folk critic, to review one of his gigs. In July he phoned Shelton to tell him he was playing a week at the Gaslight, but Shelton considered that strictly small-time. At the end of July, he received a small but favorable mention in Shelton's review of an all-day hootenanny at the Riverside Church, at which he performed a four-song set, also his first radio broadcast since his Hibbing days (WRVR-FM broadcast the entire day's proceedings). Finally, at the end of September, he convinced Shelton to come down and see the first night of his second Gerde's Folk City residency, still in the support slot, this time to the Greenbriar Boys.

By this time, Shelton was already providing him with a place to rehearse and open access to his own folk-music collection. Shelton also acted as a useful barometer, indicating when he thought Dylan was working up something truly original, and when he was simply regurgitating old values already reiterated a thousand times by more authentic troubadours than a middle-class ex-college student from Minnesota.

Robert Shelton: We used to knock around listening to music together, and that period was interesting because Dylan was listening to every bit of music he could hear. He walked around with his ears hanging out, eager to follow whatever was going on in folk music. He'd come over to my house and play piano, and listen to records.

When Shelton's review finally appeared, it was no whim on his part. He had been musing about how best to introduce Dylan for some weeks before his September 29, 1961, review. Shelton's first and most famous review was extraordinary because it gave a young, promising *support act* at Gerde's a three-column headline—'Bob Dylan: A Distinctive Stylist'—a photo no less, and four paragraphs, which concluded with the prescient claim that 'Mr. Dylan [may be] vague about his antecedents . . . but it matters less where he has been than where he is going, and that would seem to be straight up.' As Shelton himself would later admit, 'The layout, the picture, and the headline trumpeted Dylan even louder than [the] story.'

Most other Village folkies had previously been unaware of how much Shelton thought of Dylan. Dylan, though, was greatly concerned about what Shelton thought, and when *Little Sandy Review* editors Jon Pankake and Paul Nelson came to a hootenanny at Gerde's in the fall of 1961, he apparently visibly blanched on seeing them, and turned to Shelton and said, 'Don't talk to those guys, they'll tell you all sorts of stories about me. Don't listen to them.' As the *New York Times* folk critic, Shelton couldn't be anything but a figure of considerable influence downtown. Support on this scale inevitably caused some animosity toward Dylan in the Village.

Liam Clancy: [Shelton], more than anyone, was responsible for Bob Dylan. He pushed and pushed and pushed. He thought Bobby Dylan was a tremendous poet. [Even when] he . . . made a very folkie record . . . with John Hammond that wasn't doing anything . . . Shelton kept pushing.

Suze Rotolo, Dylan's girlfriend at the time, remembers them being told about the review by Shelton, and Bobby raced down to the corner store to buy a stack of copies, one of which he surely sent back to his family in Hibbing, proof that he had fulfilled his side of the deal he'd struck with his father. Subsequently Shelton almost became Dylan's unpaid press officer, writing the sleeve notes for his first album, giving him glowing reviews for his October 1962 appearance at the Town Hall with the Travelin' Hootenanny, his solo performance there in April 1963, his guest appearance with Joan Baez at Forest Hills in August of the same year, and his triumphant Carnegie Hall gig in October. A possibly jaundiced Izzy Young insists that Shelton's articles were always first vetted by a small coterie of advisers.

Izzy Young: At the time, [Dylan] was living at Dave Van Ronk's house, and playing at Bob Shelton's house a lot. That's when I got to know him and that's when I became part of the little mafia around Bob Dylan . . . Bob Shelton was the main mafia. He'd write an article in the *Times* about him being in Mike Porco's place and I'd read the article beforehand, and Dave Van Ronk would read the article beforehand, and we would approve it. And then it would be put in the paper.

Even Dylan was caught out by the enthusiastic, almost triumphal tone of that first review in September 1961. Shelton's review was a welcome endorsement when Dylan needed it most. Though John Hammond subsequently claimed that he signed Dylan to Columbia before he had even read Shelton's review, Shelton recollects in *No Direction Home* that Dylan told him, the night after the review was published, about seeing John Hammond that afternoon and being offered a five-year contract with Columbia. The standard story, which Shelton reiterates in his biography, has it that Dylan attended the first Columbia session for Carolyn Hester's new album, held the day the *New York Times* review ran, and Hammond was so impressed by his 'authentic' look and his harp playing that he offered to sign Bobby without even hearing him sing.

Even for a man who later signed Bruce Springsteen thinking he was an acoustic singer-songwriter who'd swallowed a dictionary, signing a folksinger based on his harp playing and his hat wouldn't have been so much trusting to instinct as operating by radar. In truth, there are few convincing aspects to this account of Dylan's Columbia signing. Hammond's decision genuinely seems to have been unaffected by Shelton's review, even though the review certainly made it easier for the wily old producer to get his whim endorsed by the upper echelons of Columbia A&R.

What we don't know is whether the proselytizing of Carla Rotolo and Terri Thal, combined with his son's endorsement, had already impinged on Hammond's consciousness when he first met Dylan. He had certainly already been told about Dylan by his son, John Hammond, Jr., who it seemed recognized real talent as well as his father.

John Hammond, Jr.: I was not that close with my father, but I do remember having told my father about this guy that was in New York playing at Gerde's, and at other coffeehouses, and that this guy was really good.

We do know John Hammond, Sr., first met Dylan in mid-September at a rehearsal session for Carolyn Hester's first Columbia album, Dylan having been invited by Hester to provide harmonica accompaniment when he was hanging out in Cambridge that August. The rehearsal was held at Ned O'Gorman's apartment on West 10th Street. At the rehearsal, Dylan showed more than an unaffected mastery of the harmonica. He must have run through 'Come Back Baby,' which he had introduced to Hester only the previous month, and Hammond was impressed enough to want to hear more.

Carolyn Hester: At the end of the session in Ned O'Gorman's apartment, I'm sure that Bob had realized that he was going to have a chance to get to know Mr. Hammond.

Despite the oft-repeated story that he offered him a contract on the spot, Hammond subsequently insisted that he *did* audition Dylan. In fact, Eve MacKenzie, with whom Dylan continued to reside, specifically recalls him returning from the practice with Hester and saying to her that John Hammond came by, heard Bobby sing, and said to him, 'Come and see me. I think you have something.' Eve also recalls that Dylan asked her to keep this secret at the time.

John Hammond: When I first saw Bob Dylan, it was at a rehearsal of Carolyn Hester's down on West 10th Street and he had on his cap . . . this was before he opened at Gerde's Folk City . . . I liked what I heard of him there so much I asked him to come up to the studio. I didn't know that he did much singing, *but I knew that he wrote*. So I asked him to come up and I heard some of the things that he did, and I signed him on the spot.

What Hammond certainly did not do was organize a proper audition tape—the records at Columbia confirm this. This suggests that Hammond was either scared of his bosses *actually* hearing Dylan sing, or that he was testing an organization he had only recently re-joined to see if they still had faith in his judgment. Or both. Whichever way it came down, it was a shrewd move on Hammond's part. Hammond's recollection also fits in with Shelton's assertion that Dylan had already agreed to sign with Columbia by the night of the 29th (though it still required the rubber stamp from upstairs). Not that Shelton's endorsement wasn't the talk of the session that afternoon, or that Hester and her then-husband Richard Farina weren't willing champions of the cause.

Carolyn Hester: When . . . we were actually in the studio, Dylan had had his own featured gig at Folk City and Robert Shelton had written the now-famous review, which was so laudatory, and Richard [Farina] and I had our own copy of it, and we took it with us to the session, and it was our copy of the review that John Hammond read. We were actually pushing it off on him.

But Hammond had already decided to sign Dylan—not that it involved a huge risk on his part. The contract that was sent to Dylan, care of Mikki Issacson, on October 26, 1961, was a typically unilateral recording industry contract that gave the company five-yearly options to purchase 'your services at recording sessions at our studios, at mutually agreeable times, for the purpose of making phonograph records,' the results of which 'shall be entirely our property, free from any claims whatsoever by you.' In exchange, they gave Dylan a measly 2 percent royalty on whatever they elected to release, and no guarantees that they would continue the relationship beyond his first album. It was a contract signed by someone who had seized an opportunity, without considering the benefit of due representation.

Despite his comment in his autobiography that he 'knew that [Dylan] wrote,' Hammond undoubtedly signed him as a performer. Save for 'Song to Woody,' Dylan had no really strong original material at this point. Deciding which songs from the common pool of folk songs he should record for his first album now became Dylan's main conundrum, occupying him right up to the actual sessions themselves in November. There was still time to go through a few record collections and find some obscure songs to make his own.

Perhaps the best archive he had direct access to belonged to Carla Rotolo, the dark-haired older sister of his new girlfriend, a seventeen-year-old golden beauty named Suze. Suze had regularly attended Dylan's gigs during his first spring in New York—ever since he'd played his first paying gig at the University Folk Society in early April—though more as a companion for the love-struck Sue Zuckerman than as a devotee of his work. Suze herself first met Dylan at the post-Riverside Church bash in July, and Zuckerman quickly found herself excluded from the picture as Dylan directed all his attention at the busty beauty by her side. In a matter of weeks Suze and Dylan became a regular Village fixture and he found himself flung into his first serious romance since his days in Minneapolis.

Carla was more of a fan of Dylan's music than her sister. She regularly sang his praises to Shelton and, along with Sybil Weinberger, tried to tout Dylan's crude audition tape around the record labels. She also had an occupation of great interest to the folklorist in Dylan. She worked for Alan Lomax, a man ever mindful of his credentials as the premier living folklorist in America. Lomax had published *Folk Songs of North America* the previous year, after years of working on similar folk-song anthologies with his father, John, and Dylan had clearly been through the book with an otherwise unused comb (a scrap of paper among the MacKenzie manuscripts has a whole set of numbers that tally with songs in Lomax). Dylan could go round to Carla's, or Lomax's, and listen to recordings from the collection. After all, he couldn't read music, so even if he learned the words, he still needed to hear a tune in order to play any of the old songs. Through the years Dylan has continued to acknowledge the debt he owed to Lomax, if not Carla, only recently referring to Alan as 'one of those who unlocked the secrets of this kind of music.'

From such a resource he was able to hear original field recordings Alan's father, John, had made ever since the day in 1904 when, across the Brazos river from Texas A&M College, he heard a lady called Dink sing her song, called simply 'Dink's Song' in *Folksong USA*. Though every line came from another song, another place, the overall effect led Carl Sandburg to 'compare them to the best fragments of Sappho.' Dylan transformed such songs, but they also transformed him.

If Carla encouraged Dylan's musical education, his personal growth was now bound up with her underage sister, Suze, who provided some much-needed stability, even if their romance was accelerating at a pace that remained touching only as long as they remained equal partners in the relationship. Carla's endorsement of Dylan certainly held no sway with Suze's mother, who distrusted the young whippersnapper from the start.

Mary Rotolo: He told me so many lies right away, and while my daughters and their friends didn't seem to notice, they were stories that were highly suspect . . . beyond belief to an older woman.

Suze temporarily subdued Dylan's raging polygamy, and he finally prevailed upon her to move in with him in December, a major commitment for both of them, particularly as she had not yet reached eighteen, the age of legal consent. But at last, with the small advance he'd garnered from Columbia, he could afford his own place and, when he wanted to be, he could be real insistent. With a steady relationship, the respect of his peers, and an increasing repertoire of songs, both original and traditional, it would seem that Dylan's career was already living up to Shelton's billing. However, a particularly disastrous concert uptown at the beginning of November reminded him that there really was no success like failure.

Part of the problem was that those willing to attach themselves to this comet were not necessarily the ones best equipped to ride its tail. Izzy Young had been befriended by Dylan back when he needed every friend he could get, but his interest in Dylan the artist had not really been piqued until he read the Shelton review, reinforced by a comment the wily entrepreneur Albert Grossman had made to him the second week in October, which Izzy thought worthy of comment in his journals: 'I think Dylan can make it.' Suddenly Young was taking him up to Moe Asch at Folkways Records—who had turned Dylan down flat back in the spring, when Dylan would have signed a contract with anyone, even the notorious Asch—and suggesting a feature in *Sing Out*. Young then arranged for him to make his first studio radio appearance, on Oscar Brand's WNYC show *Folksong Festival*, even if Young's recollection of the session—two of his own songs on a piano!—doesn't tally with the recently unearthed tape.

Izzy Young: I had a reputation in New York that I didn't call up people every day to say, 'Hey, this guy's great.' It was very few times. So I called up Oscar Brand. 'Listen, there's this guy in my store, he writes really good songs, you should really listen to him.' He said, 'Okay, send him over.' So I went over to his studio, which was in the Village at the time, and he sang two songs . . . his own songs, and he was mumbling. I was very embarrassed and Oscar was embarrassed. But . . . he put him on the radio.

In fact, Dylan's performance was exemplary, ripping through his arrangement of Guthrie's 'Sally Gal,' complete with whooping harmonica riffs, and the traditional 'Girl I Left Behind,' which he couldn't resist insisting he had learned from a farmer named Wilbur. Brand also gave an important promotional plug for the forthcoming concert at the two-hundred-seat Carnegie Recital Hall (part of the Carnegie Hall complex). Young arranged to book the hall, print up the programs, and attempt to sell the hundred tickets required to break even. Unfortunately, only fifty-three people attended the November 4 concert, and many of these were Dylan's friends, and therefore from his personal supply of freebies.

In particular, Young was baffled by the non-appearance of Shelton, but there was no way Shelton could have reviewed another Dylan set six weeks after his 'jet-propelled push.' The performance—the first half of which has been circulating for many years among collectors—is more than a little hesitant. Dylan's confidence seems to have been so depleted that he resurrected Guthrie's '1913 Massacre' rather than play his own 'Song to Woody.' The raps between songs are also hardly the free-wheelin', rambling monologues he was famous for at Gerde's, as Dylan struggles to find a punchline to each impromptu remark. Indeed, his self-deprecating introduction to 'Black Girl (in the Pines),' one of the few songs held over from his September Gerde's sets, suggests just how out on a limb he felt he had gone:

Come pretty prepared tonight. This is a new list. I used to have one on my guitar about a month ago. That was no good. Figured I'd get a good list. So I went around . . . to other guitar players—sorta looked on their list and copied down songs on mine. [Pause] Some of these I don't know so good.

His search for new songs was not really about finding material for an unreviewed gig to fifty-three largely familiar faces, but putting together a set of tunes he could record for Columbia that would—in toto—be seen as some kind of statement, setting him apart from his contemporaries, the best of whom were also scrambling to present their own repertoires on album. Dave Van Ronk had just recorded his third album for Folkways; Ramblin' Jack Elliott his second for Prestige. Much of the Carnegie set was clearly intended as a trial run for the album, though just three songs definitely made it to the sessions, 'Pretty Peggy-O,' 'Gospel Plow,' and 'Fixin' to Die.' At Carla's apartment on Perry Street, Dylan continued to trawl his way through her collection, picking potential songs, discussing selections, changing the list from day to day.

Carla Rotolo: He spent most of his time listening to my records, days and nights. He studied the Folkways *Anthology of American Folk Music*, the singing of Ewan MacColl and A. L. Lloyd, Rabbit Brown's guitar, Guthrie, of course, and blues . . . his record was in the planning stages. We were all concerned about what songs Dylan was going to do. I clearly remember talking about it.

On one piece of paper he scratched one of his angular guitar drawings and wrote, in capital letters, THE GREAT DIVIDE, a Guthrie song he had been performing at Gerde's, and perhaps a working title for the forthcoming album. Underneath he wrote two sets of song titles, with numbers alongside:

1. The Cuckoo [Is a Pretty Bird]
2. Snow White Dove [a.k.a. Railroad Boy]
3. [Will the] Circle Be Unbroken
4. Pretty Polly
5. On My Journey Home
6. [Man of] Constant Sorrow
7. [The] Great Divide

1. Trying to Get Home [!]
2. Highway 51 [Blues]
3. [The] Battleship of Maine
4. [The] Lady of Carlyle [sic]

Not resembling any set he was known to be performing at the time, this list of songs includes four songs (2, 3, 4, and 6 in the first column) found on the May 1961 party tapes, a couple of favorites from Gerde's 'The Cuckoo' and 'The Great Divide'—and some four songs for which no Dylan recording/performance is known from this period. The two broadside ballads, 'The Battleship of Maine' and 'The Lady of Carlisle,' would have been quite daunting performances with which to close an album, if that was his intent (though Dylan managed a seemingly impromptu word-perfect 'Lady of Carlisle' in Australia in April 1992). The emphasis on ballads of British origin (column 1: 1, 2, 4; column 2:

3 and 4) would also have been quite a statement in itself. As it is, just two songs from these early jottings made it to the sessions (and the album): 'Man of Constant Sorrow' and 'Highway 51 Blues.'

What is interesting about the list is the lack of any originals, and inclusion of a solitary song by Woody. Dylan was clearly determined to disavow the Guthrie mantle he had so cherished barely six months earlier. In a copy of the Guthrie songbook, *California to the New York Island,* marked 'the property of Bob Dylan,' can be found an introduction by Pete Seeger, a section of which had been highlighted by Dylan for inward digestion:

Beware of trying to imitate Woody's singing too closely—it will sound fake and phoney.
1. Don't try and imitate his accent.
2. Don't try and imitate his flat vocal quality.
3. In short, be yourself.
What any singer can learn from Woody's method of performance are such things as this:
1. A matter-of-fact, unmelodramatic, understatement throughout.
2. Simplicity above all—and getting the words out clearly. They are the most important part of the song.
3. Irregularity.

This last perhaps needs explanation: to avoid a sing-song effect, from repeating the same simple melody many times, Woody, like all American ballad singers, held out long notes in unexpected places, although his guitar strumming maintained an even tempo. Thus no two verses sounded alike. Extra beats were often added to measures.

Dylan learned this lesson well. In December, when he recorded his third Minneapolis tape, the only Guthrie songs among the twenty-six titles were 'Ramblin' Blues,' his own adaptation of 'Sally Don't You Grieve' ('Sally Gal'), and Guthrie's obscure quartet of VD songs. 'Ramblin' Blues' would also be the only Guthrie song recorded for the first album. It would not make the final cut.

That first album, called simply *Bob Dylan,* was recorded over just two three-hour afternoon sessions, November 20 and 22, at a reputed cost of $402. And yet Hammond would later suggest that Dylan was something of a nightmare to work with.

John Hammond: Bobby popped every *p,* hissed every *s,* and habitually wandered off mike. Even more frustrating, he refused to learn from his mistakes. It occurred to me at the time that I'd never worked with anyone so undisciplined before.

Perhaps Hammond expected to complete the album in a single afternoon! As it is, Dylan managed to cut seventeen complete songs, more than an album's worth, in a couple of afternoons, suggesting quite remarkable discipline. If both Hammond and Dylan later dismissed the results, Hammond seemed perfectly happy with what he had at the time. Suze Rotolo, after sitting patiently through both sessions, occasionally loaning Dylan her lipstick holder for use as a substitute bottleneck, wrote to her friend Sue Zuckerman at college, claiming 'John Hammond . . . completely flipped. I swear, if Dylan vomited into the microphone, Hammond would say, "Great, Bob, but try it again with harmony."' Dylan's own assessment of the sessions was concise:

Bob Dylan: I just played the guitar and harmonica and sang those songs and that was it. Mr. Hammond asked me if I wanted to sing any of them over again and I said no. I can't see myself singing the same song twice in a row. [1962]

Allowing for a little Dylanesque exaggeration, that's a pretty fair summary of the sessions. Five of the album tracks really were cut in single takes ('Baby Let Me Follow You Down,' 'In My Time of Dyin',' 'Gospel Plow,' 'Highway 51 Blues,' and 'Freight Train Blues'), while 'Song to Woody' made the grade after just one false start. Dylan also cut the last four songs in single takes, without respite, concluding with the most extraordinary performance of the sessions, as demonically driven as anything Robert Johnson put out in his name, a rendition of the sixteenth-century Scottish ballad 'The Dæmon Lover,' a.k.a. 'The House Carpenter.' Introduced as a tale of 'a ghost come back from out in the sea, come to take his bride away from the house carpenter,' Dylan conjures up every banshee that ever wailed 'all for the sake of thee.' Why he chose to record such a favorite in folk circles, having not played the song in any documented performance, giving it such a powerful reinterpretation, and still omitted it from his lucky thirteen, is the first of many mysterious calls in the man's recorded output.

It was probably during that second session that he was introduced to a young Columbia publicist whom Hammond had recently taken under his wing.

Billy James: I wrote these publicity bios . . . I guess because I had some knowledge of music as a fan, John Hammond . . . would invite me to his recording sessions . . . I got a call from John, in his patrician way, 'Billy, I have a young man up here in the recording studio and I think you might be interested.' This was [at] 799 7th Avenue . . . and I was immediately taken with him, I was flabbergasted, I had never heard a skinny little white young kid sounding like an eighty-year-old black man before and doing it with that sureness and intensity, and that unswerving understanding of who he was, and what he wanted to do.

Yet Dylan quickly grew dissatisfied with the results achieved over the two afternoon sessions. As early as the following month, he told Shelton, who was pseudonymously composing the sleeve notes, that the notes were better than the record. They were not. However, his decision to incorporate so many songs new to his repertoire—just two of the covers and both originals on *Bob Dylan* had been in his club set in September— meant that this was an album of songs he had not really lived with. When Dylan described the songs to Hammond as 'some stuff I've written, some stuff I've discovered, some stuff I stole,' there is an implied casualness to the choices made. Evidently he had yet to understand the importance of delivering on record. Or perhaps the problem had been one of trying to second-guess his audience, such as it was.

The Dylan on *Bob Dylan* was not yet ready to stamp his authority upon his listeners. The night after he completed the album, he was at the MacKenzies' sharing a Thanksgiving meal with Eve, Mac, their son Peter, and Suze, afterwards playing an informal set for his friends. Once again, though, he found himself having to deal with someone convinced he had a better idea of who Bob Dylan should be.

Peter MacKenzie: Halfway through 'Baby Let Me Follow You Down,' Kevin Krown walked in and he immediately stopped singing, and . . . they started chatting. At that point Kevin took over the entire proceedings and you can hear it [on the tape], the dialogue between the two of them, where he basically tells Bob what to sing, [and] how to sing it. Bob had his own agenda and here's Kevin telling him, 'I want you to do this song, I want you to do that song—hey, make the people happy.' He really didn't want to do that, but he couldn't really squirm out of it. The two big songs that he wound up doing, that Kevin was really pushing for, were 'San Francisco Bay' and 'House of the Rising Sun,' which was his signature piece at that time.

Krown and Dylan went back further than New York, and that made their friendship unique. They also were constantly constructing verbal jousts for each other. Krown, who hated peace and quiet, knew how to goad Dylan. As Eve MacKenzie put it, he 'really taxed Bobby's brain. But he really liked that at the time. They matched each other in [a] battle of wits [and] Kevin was one of the few people who could hold his own with Bob.' Dylan, though, was not so sure he wanted to 'make people happy.' The failure of *Bob Dylan* would convince him that he should have more faith in his own instincts and less in others, no matter how close or sincere. It was a hard-won lesson.

Evidence of how quickly Dylan moved beyond these songs was provided a month to the day after the final session for his debut album. Having selected thirteen songs for his recorded debut, he proceeded to perform twice as many at Bonnie Beecher's apartment in Minneapolis on December 22, Tony Glover recording them on a reel-to-reel tape recorder. The legendary so-called Minneapolis hotel tape provided a far more diverse selection of songs, and illustrated Dylan's harmonica and guitar work to much greater effect. As an illustration of how quickly he outgrew the hastily assembled material chosen for the Columbia set, there are only four songs from his month-old album on the hotel tape.

Glover recalls a Dylan who had gone from being a run-of-the-mill kind of player and singer into a really dynamic picker and performer; doing bottleneck blues and playing some pretty damn fine cross-harp. He had also written a few songs, and seemed to have Woody Guthrie down to a T. Sitting on Bonnie's bed as he polished off a bottle of Jim Beam, Dylan was putting some real drive into these folk and blues songs. Glover vividly recalls the sheer energy of Dylan, and the incessant tapping of his feet on song after song. The tape was done in a single night over two and a half hours, pretty much straight through.

Perhaps inevitably, given the informality of the occasion, there are at least half a dozen moments on the hotel tape that transcend anything on *Bob Dylan:* the 'Black Cross' monologue; the bottleneck playing on 'Baby Please Don't Go'; singing the pants off of the old washerwoman on 'Dink's Song'; the pentecostal fury of 'Wade in the Water'; 'Stealin',' turned inside out and upside down till it's stealing back to its good ol' used to be; and, finally, a remarkable rewrite of the traditional 'Nine Hundred Miles' where Dylan transcends his source material for the very first time. It is hard not to see 'I Was Young When I Left Home' as a message to Mom: 'I used to tell my ma some time / when I'd see them ridin' blinds / gonna make me a home out in the wind.' And make a home out in the wind he had. Even if he *had* come home for Christmas. In the new year he would take notions he'd acquired over a two-year apprenticeship in traditional song and make them his own.

1962–63: Songs of Innocence

5

I just wanted a song to sing, and there came a certain point where I couldn't sing anything. So I had to write what I wanted to sing 'cause nobody else was writing what I wanted to sing. I couldn't find it anywhere. If I could I probably would have never started writing.

—*Bob Dylan, 1984*

As has been documented, Dylan had been writing his own songs since his Hibbing days. However, the bridge from the purely imitative to something original had only been crossed a couple of times up to the time he entered Columbia's portals. 'Song to Woody' was certainly a statement of intent, and 'Man on the Street' had a point of view all its own, but Dylan remained essentially a folk revivalist of repute.

'I Was Young When I Left Home' also tapped into some mysterious spirit. Even though it was quickly discarded as a song, not even making the publishing demos he cut the following month, it gave Dylan an all-important clue as to how he might mold traditional melodies and sensibility to his own worldview. The following month he wrote another remarkable song of remembrance. Originally called 'Reminiscence Blues,' it would be copyrighted as 'Ballad for a Friend.' In six three-line verses he wrote his first song about the North Country, with its 'lakes and streams and minds so free,' a eulogy to a friend he heard had been left dead by a diesel truck 'on a Utah road.' The three lines of each verse are resolutely understated. The sense of loss, reflected by the fractured nature of the information received and the memories set off, is highlighted by the guitar's solitary lead on each verse's wordless final line.

'Ballad for a Friend' was one of seven original songs recorded the second week of January. In an attempt to raise some funds for Dylan between the recording and release of his debut album, John Hammond had arranged a music publishing deal with Leeds Music. All seven were to be included in his first songbook, *Bob Dylan Himself*, accompanied by five arrangements of traditional songs from the first album (the songbook was finally published in 1965). The demo tape mostly collected songs from 1961 that he wished to preserve: 'Talkin' Bear Mountain,' 'Man on the Street,' 'Hard Times in New York Town,' and an unabashed rewrite of Robert Johnson's 'Crossroads,' 'Standing on the Highway.' However, a pair of freshly penned originals found Dylan tackling potentially rewarding genres, the reminiscence blues of 'Ballad for a Friend' and the outlaw blues of 'Ramblin' Gamblin' Willie.'

A minor song, both in terms of its craft and its performance, the Leeds Music 'Ramblin' Gamblin' Willie' was the first in a long line of Dylan songs celebrating those outside society. Willie is the supreme Robin Hood figure, spreading 'his money far and wide, to help the sick and poor.' He meets his death when he is gunned down after being dealt the dead man's hand—aces backed with eights. The song ends with a clumsy moralistic verse, informing the listener 'the moral of the story is very plain to see,' gamble and you'll end up like Willie—a most peculiar conclusion to draw from the previous portrayal of Willie's glorious exploits.

If semi-autobiographical 'songs of nostalgia' had so far resulted in Dylan's best work, it was not the route he chose to travel at this time. Whatever political consciousness had been instilled by time spent with the Whitakers or the Van Ronks, his songs of 'protest' to date, such as they were, were about little men in the grip of an uncaring system— 'Man on the Street,' 'Hard Times in New York Town'—or tales of man's exploitation of man, like 'Talkin' Bear Mountain Picnic Massacre Blues.' This was about to change.

At the end of January, Dylan wrote the first of what for two years would be a steady flow of contemporary protest songs. Despite her subsequent disavowals, it can be no coincidence that such songs started to flow from Dylan's pen shortly after moving into his West 4th Street apartment with Suze. Suze came from a family with a strong left-wing bias, and at the tender age of seventeen she was stuffing envelopes at the headquarters of the Congress of Racial Equality (CORE).

On February 23, 1962, Dylan was due to appear on the bill of a CORE benefit at City College. On January 29 he played the MacKenzies a song he had written especially for the occasion; and on February 1 he walked into Izzy Young's Folklore Center and did the same for Young. The song was called 'The Death of Emmett Till.' It was hardly a topical song, given that Till's murder was a notorious race killing that took place in Money, Mississippi, back in August 1955. 'The Death of Emmett Till' was more a murder ballad in the style of 'Omie Wise' and 'Pretty Polly,' particularly in its graphic description of the way two brothers dragged Till from his great uncle's house, pistol-whipped him, shot him in the head and then, with a length of barbed wire, tied a heavy cotton-gin fan around his neck, and threw his body in the Tallahatchie River. His crime? Daring to flirt with one of the brother's wives in a local grocery store, after Till had boasted to some black friends of his white girlfriend back home in Chicago. Again, Dylan couldn't get a handle on what he was trying to say at song's end, merely enjoining his listeners to 'make this great country of ours a greater place to live.' Hallelujah. Yet, when he played the song live on Cynthia Gooding's radio show the following week, she exclaimed at song's end, 'It's one of the greatest contemporary ballads I've ever heard . . . It's got some lines in it that make you stop breathing!'—perhaps a comment on the quality of the competition.

It seems unlikely that Dylan would not have been conscious of the profound influence Suze was having on him. He would later tell Shelton that Suze 'was into this equality-freedom thing long before I was. I checked the songs out with her.' She was considerably better read, her sister had access to the most impressive archive of American folk music anywhere in the world, and her views on valid expressions of protest provided him with valuable feedback. At least one of his surrogate mothers worried about the scope of Suze's influence.

Eve MacKenzie: Suze . . . wanted him to go Pete Seeger's way. She wanted Bobby to be involved in civil rights, and all the radical causes Seeger was involved in. Suze was very much with the cause . . . She influenced Bobby considerably that way.

In fact, Seeger had been observing the young man's growth from his days at the Gleasons'. And, as the man who warned of the dangers of slavishly imitating Woody, Seeger that winter conceived, with Agnes 'Sis' Cunningham, of a magazine that would publish only contemporary folk songs. It was to be called *Broadside*. The emphasis of the magazine well reflected its title, publishing the modern equivalent of the penny broadsides that moralized on current events in the seventeenth and eighteenth centuries. In the very first issue, Cunningham stated their aim loud and clear: '*Broadside* may never publish a song that could be called a "folk song". But many of our best folk songs were topical songs at their inception.'

Pete Seeger: I took him up to *Broadside* magazine and introduced him to Sis Cunningham, and *Broadside* was the first magazine that published Bob.

Dylan had apparently already been told about the magazine by Gil Turner, over some *vin ordinaire* at McGowan's, but Seeger was particularly interested in what Dylan could do with a talking blues to give it a topical bent. And so, at his first meeting with Cunningham, Dylan played them a brand-new talking blues about the John Birch Society. Its wry humor barely concealed a scathing portrayal of the right-wingers, making it ideal fodder for *Broadside*. 'Talkin' John Birch Society Blues' appeared in the magazine's very first issue, late in February 1962. For the remainder of 1962 and through 1963, he would be *Broadside*'s most regular contributor, and it would be the first outlet for such important Dylan songs as 'Blowin' in the Wind' and 'Masters of War.'

'Talkin' John Birch Society Blues' may have been one more satirical monologue, but it was closely followed by 'Let Me Die in My Footsteps,' the best of Dylan's early protest songs. He talked to journalist Nat Hentoff at great length about the genesis of 'Let Me Die in My Footsteps,' a song about the building of fallout shelters, and one of his overlooked gems from this period (it was finally released on *The Bootleg Series Vols. 1–3*):

Bob Dylan: I was going through some town . . . and they were making this bomb shelter right outside of town, one of these sort of Coliseum-type things and there were construction workers and everything. I was there for about an hour, just looking at them build, and I just wrote the song in my head back then, but I carried it with me for two years until I finally wrote it down. As I watched them building, it struck me sort of funny that they would concentrate so much on digging a hole underground when there were so many other things they should do in life. If nothing else, they could look at the sky, and walk around and live a little bit, instead of doing this immoral thing. [1963]

A return to the incisiveness of 'Song to Woody,' 'Let Me Die in My Footsteps' placed a topical preoccupation—the threat of nuclear war— inside a universal theme—'learning to live, 'stead of learning to die.' Though it would become a hostage to obscurity with the advent of 'Blowin' in the Wind,' 'Let Me Die in My Footsteps' may well be Dylan's first masterpiece.

The night after he played the song to Izzy Young, Dylan wrote a companion piece to 'Emmett Till' after watching a PBS documentary on TV. 'The Ballad of Donald White' was based on Bonnie Dobson's version of 'The Ballad of Peter Amberley,' a song composed in 1881 by John Calhoun. Dylan even used certain lines wholesale from the original, no longer applied to a young lad killed in a lumberjack accident but to a boy killer who 'murdered someone 'cause he couldn't find no room in life.' 'Donald White' temporarily returned Dylan to the status of broadside hack, though Cunningham and Seeger loved it, asking him to play it on a WBAI *Broadside* radio special in June.

It was around this time that the legend of Dylan's prolific nature began to gather pace. Certainly 'Emmett Till,' 'Talkin' John Birch,' 'Let Me Die in My Footsteps,' and 'Donald White' in less than a month was quite an outpouring from such a fledgling songsmith. Evidently there was some basis to the stories.

Bob Dylan: I wrote wherever I happened to be. Sometimes I'd spend a whole day sitting at a corner table in a coffeehouse, just writing whatever came into my head . . . just anything. I'd look at people for hours and I'd make up things about them, or I'd think, what kind of song would they like to hear, and I'd make one up. [1965]

Dylan, at this point, was more than happy to feed a myth that led to him being described in *Sing Out*, at year's end, as 'the most prolific young songwriter in America today.' When Pete Seeger asked him during the WBAI radio show in June about all the songs he had written, an almost bashful Bob reeled out the story for all its worth:

Bob Dylan: Sometimes I go for about two weeks without making up a song—well, the songs I sing. I might go for two weeks without writing those songs. I write a lot of stuff, in fact I wrote five songs last night, but I gave all the papers away. It was in a place called the Bitter End . . . But I don't sit around with the newspapers, like a lot of people do, and pick out something to write . . . about. [1962]

Part of Dylan's coyness stemmed from an awareness that what he was doing was almost the folk equivalent of 'modernizing' popular classics. Talking to Gil Turner, who interviewed him for the knowledgeable readers of *Sing Out* in the summer of 1962, he avoided terms like 'write' or 'compose,' insisting that 'the songs are [already] there . . . I just put them down on paper.' Certainly, as Turner himself dryly observed, 'the tune [is] almost always being borrowed or adapted from one he has heard somewhere, usually a traditional one.' Not that the twenty-one-year-old Dylan wasn't more than happy to acknowledge his influences. Talking about 'The Ballad of Emmett Till' on her radio show *Folksinger's Choice,* he good-humoredly admitted to Cynthia Gooding that he 'stole the melody.'

Bob Dylan: I stole the melody from Len Chandler, he's a folksinger. He uses a lot of funny chords when he plays. He always wants me to use some of these chords, he keeps trying to teach me new chords all the time. He played me this one, said, 'Don't those chords sound nice.' I said, 'They sure do,' and so I stole it, I stole the whole thing. [1962]

'Emmett Till,' though, wasn't about to make anyone rich. As Dylan later admitted, it was 'a bullshit song.' On the other hand, the song he penned at the beginning of April, backstage at a Gerde's hootenanny, was going to make him very rich. Thankfully, Dylan's arrangement of an anonymous slave's cry for emancipation, 'No More Auction Block,' a.k.a. 'Many Thousands Gone,' seems to have been wholly his own, and this original folk song was genuinely from the common store of American balladry, having been collected as early as 1867.

Ironically, the plaudits that 'Blowin' in the Wind' quickly accumulated (save from Dave Van Ronk, who told Dylan it was 'incredibly dumb') gave him cause to pause. He did not wish to attract the single epithet of 'protest singer.' He considered it limiting, fiercely resisting even this early attempt to categorize him. In April, at a performance at Gerde's Folk City—before the song had even been published on the cover of the sixth issue of *Broadside,* or acquired a middle verse— 'Blowin' in the Wind' was being prefaced by a disclaimer: 'This here ain't a protest song or anything like that, 'cause I don't write protest songs . . . I'm just writing it as something to be said, for somebody, by somebody.'

It would be some months before Dylan would write another topical song of note. This did not mean that Dylan backpedaled on his newfound political consciousness, simply that he was once again preoccupied with songs of remembrance, not for a lost youth but for a lost love. When Gil Turner interviewed him for *Sing Out* that summer, Dylan was still championing the legion for whom popular song was capable of sign-posting change.

Bob Dylan: I don't have to be anybody like those guys up on Broadway that're always writin' about 'I'm hot for you and you're hot for me ooka dooka dicka dee.' There's other things in the world besides love and sex that're important, too. People shouldn't turn their backs on 'em just because they ain't pretty to look at. How is the world ever gonna get any better if we're afraid to look at these things? [1962]

He also knew that he was capable of more than a handful of questions. It is debatable whether Dylan ever rated 'Blowin' in the Wind' an important song. It was omitted from his landmark Town Hall debut in

April 1963, and his London concert debut in May 1964. Indeed, on the evidence of the second Gaslight tape, it had been dropped from his set by September 1962. According to John Hammond, Sr., there was even a point when Dylan was considering omitting the song from his second album, *The Freewheelin' Bob Dylan*. In 1966 he recalled the time when 'everyone started calling me a genius . . . [but] I still hadn't written what I wanted to . . . I was never satisfied with "Blowin' in the Wind." I wrote that in ten minutes.'

If Dylan perceived the song as just another notch in his belt, there was one man who envisaged a whole lot more. That man was Albert Grossman. Another son of Russian Jewish immigrants, Grossman had opened Chicago's premier folk club, the Gate of Horn, in 1957, pro-gressed to managing Odetta the following year, and co-produced the first Newport Folk Festival in 1959. As ruthless in business as Colonel Tom Parker, Grossman had another side. He was concerned with selling authenticity and, as Peter Yarrow told Fred Goodman, 'the difference between something that was bullshit and something that was brilliance was to other people just a shade of gray. But to him it was absolute black and white.'

Grossman had been content to watch Dylan work through the amateur management skills of Terri Thal, Kevin Krown, and Izzy Young, all the while taking notes. In July 1961, when Dylan debuted at the Gaslight, Grossman was there at his usual table in the rear. In October 1961, when Young asked what he thought of Dylan, Grossman told him that he 'has a . . . chance of making it.' He refrained from adding, 'But not with you.' Grossman knew where the real money lay—in music publishing—and Dylan had yet to come across as a songwriter of real insight. Until 'Blowin' in the Wind,' that is.

Grossman's initial interest was not the singer, but the song. In the spring of 1962, he had been introduced to Hermann Starr, the head of Warner's music publishing operation, by his old friend Artie Mogull and, between them, they cooked up a deal by which Grossman 'would receive 50% of the publisher's net profits from the publishing of every performing artist whom he attracted to Witmark [Music].' What this meant was that it was in Grossman's interest to cut the worst possible deal for any artist he introduced to Witmark—say, 50–50—because he stood to gain half of what Witmark took from the deal. No way could he extract a similar amount from an artist, even one he managed.

Unfortunately, even though Mogull now dangled a thirty-thousand-dollar advance in front of Dylan for a three-year contract with Witmark, there was a serious spanner gumming up the works: Dylan already had a music publisher, as of January 5, 1962, when he had signed a contract with Duchess Music. Thankfully, he hadn't as yet demoed or copyrighted 'Blowin' in the Wind,' though its publication in the May issue of *Broadside* qualified as copyright-by-publication, making it technically the property of Duchess Music. Legend has it that Grossman gave Dylan a thousand bucks and told him to go around to Duchess and buy the contract back. Apparently unused to the whiff of mendacity, an assistant at Duchess checked Dylan's publishing sales, saw a lot of zeros, and gave him his contract back, consigning *Bob Dylan Himself* to the back burner.

On July 12, 1962, Dylan signed a new publishing deal with Witmark Music and immediately cut a demo of 'Blowin' in the Wind' in their small recording room on the fifth floor of 488 Madison Avenue. It was registered for copyright to M. Witmark & Sons on July 30, 1962. Dylan would continue to demo his songs onto a mono 7½-inch-per-second reel-to-reel for the next eighteen months, eventually recording around forty publishing demos for the Witmark operation. According to the engineer at these sessions, Ivan Augenblink, the music arrangers on the same floor would ask him to shut the studio door when Dylan came in, lest his idiosyncratic vocals disturb their delicate sensibilities.

For brokering the deal between Dylan and Witmark, Grossman stood to make 25 percent from Dylan's Witmark catalogue in perpetuity. Dylan, though, had evidently sparked Grossman's interest, and on August 20, 1962, Grossman also became Dylan's manager, adding another 20 percent share 'on all other income received *under contracts then in place* and those entered into while under Grossman's management'; as well as 25 percent 'on all incomes received by the Artist from recordings or motion pictures.' Thus, Dylan was set to receive 40 percent of his music publishing for writing the songs, while Grossman was making 35 percent (half of Witmark's 50 percent and a fifth of Dylan's 50 percent) for arranging to have them administered. A quarter of all his recording income was also quite a hefty commission, given that Dylan had already secured a recording contract (hence the 'contracts then in place' clause in the agreement). But then, Grossman never suffered doubt about his self-worth.

Martin Carthy: There was a story that Odetta had come to the end of her contract and he said to her, 'Okay, you've come to the end of your contract. Now this year you could make approximately $100,000 and your agent could take twenty percent, but if you come with me, I'll make you $250,000 and take fifty percent.'

That the twenty-one-year-old North Country boy was beguiled by the flashing dollar sign Grossman proffered is evidenced by his handling of contract 'negotiations.' When Grossman approached Dylan about managing him, Dylan sounded out a couple of trusted friends as to the man's credentials. Though pretty much everyone told him to be wary— 'Grossman's a damn good manager, but don't sign the standard seven-year contract, leave yourself a get-out clause'—Dylan still signed up for the full seven years, by which time he would be, as the plaintiff in the Dylan–Grossman suit in the eighties put it, 'a superstar, having written and performed . . . some of the great favorites of popular music.' It was to prove an expensive decision, on both a personal and a professional level.

When Dylan conducted his straw poll about Grossman, he encountered no shortage of opinions. Albert Grossman was a man about whom everyone seemingly had a point of view. Even the idea of associating with the likes of Grossman was seen by some as tainting Dylan; others saw it as incontrovertible proof of an intent, all along, to succeed. Not surprisingly, it was primarily Dylan's contemporaries who resented Grossman. They knew that Dylan was being groomed for success, and for each of his detractors, one can still find someone who believes Grossman to be the main reason that Dylan grew into an international phenomenon.

Peter Yarrow: Albert was a man of unusual tastes and a different kind of insight into music. He was concerned first and foremost with authenticity. Did the music have real substance, value, and honesty? But he was also concerned with having impact and influence in the larger world, the heartland. It was a very rare combination . . . There never would have been a Peter, Paul and Mary, there never would have been a Bob Dylan who could have survived and made it without Albert Grossman. Personally, artistically, and in a business sense, Albert Grossman was the sole reason Bob Dylan made it.

Yarrow is undoubtedly right when he says that, without Grossman, there would have been no Peter, Paul and Mary – this may yet be stopping him getting through the Pearly Gates. But Dylan's career had a momentum all its own in the early to mid-sixties. Even if Grossman was an important stabilizing factor during the increasingly fraught rise to fame, there is no evidence that he interfered in Dylan's musical direction on any significant level (his two contributions in the studio appear to have been to convince Dylan to record 'Mixed Up Confusion' with a Dixieland band and to record 'Desolation Row' with a full electric band—the results being buried without ceremony in both cases). The young Dylan, though, undoubtedly needed an older, wiser head at times.

D. A. Pennebaker: I think Albert was one of the few people that saw Dylan's worth very early on, and played it absolutely without equivocation or any kind of compromise. He refused to let him go on any rinky-dink TV shows, refused to let Columbia do bullshit things with him . . . And Dylan in his early stages required that kind of handling—'cause Dylan himself would go off at spurious tangents.

Grossman's impact was certainly immediate. In August, on Grossman's advice, Robert Zimmerman legally changed his name to Bob Dylan. In November, Grossman began a concerted campaign to remove John Hammond, Sr., from Dylan's field of influence. After all, Hammond was the other music-biz figure Dylan placed his trust in. He was also the man who had convinced Dylan to sign a contract with Columbia, apparently without legal advice, and Grossman most definitely wanted his artist out of *that* contract, and preferably snug-as-a-bug with Peter, Paul and Mary on Warners. To paraphrase Ron Decline, Grossman wanted to protect Dylan from, well, people like himself.

John Hammond: While he was doing his second album for us, he came up to me and asked me about Albert Grossman. He said that Albert Grossman . . . wanted to sign him and what did I think. I said we'd been on the board of the Newport Festival together and I thought I could work with him. I found out later I couldn't . . . Grossman's first idea was to combine Dylan with a Dixieland band!

Hammond Snr. was not the only Hammond family member for whom the Dylan–Grossman alliance signaled the end of a friendship and the beginning of a 'new' Dylan:

John Hammond, Jr.: Before he met Albert, Bob was really accessible. Then Grossman began creating a mystique of exclusiveness. He secluded him away up in Woodstock and that changed Bob . . . I lost a lot of my feelings for him that I had when he was just a regular guy.

Of course, it will always be difficult to disentangle the changes wrought by ever-increasing pressures from the imposition of Grossman's paranoiac worldview on Dylan. That said, those who had known Dylan best, pre-alliance, seem in little doubt about the dynamic and its origin. Kevin

Krown noted that he grew 'very aloof after Grossman got to him,' and, like Hammond, Jr., Krown passed quickly from confidant to acquaintance once Dylan crossed that particular divide.

Not that Grossman's influence on Dylan was entirely without reciprocation. The 'new' Grossman began to wear his hair long, dress casually, and generally assume a Buddha-like countenance, save when his artist's integrity was up for negotiation—even integrity having its price in the Grossman credo. For the next four years, Grossman would be Dylan's father figure, best buddy, and business manager rolled into one. He taught Dylan the virtues of acquired mystique and, in return, was allowed a glimpse of the wheel on which Dylan's genius was then bound. Perhaps the final judgment of the relationship lies with Al Aronowitz, a would-be journalist who, under Grossman's careful gaze, took self-imposed sabbaticals in Dylan's company:

Al Aronowitz: Bob and Albert weren't cut from the same cloth but from the same stone wall . . . When I asked Albert how he happened to team up with Dylan, he told me: 'We were both waiting for the same bus.'

Grossman had hopped aboard when Dylan was most susceptible. Abandoned that June by the love of his life, Suze Rotolo, who was spending the summer in Italy, Dylan found himself temporarily rudderless. That Suze was a talented artist in her own right, and that as a painter she could learn an enormous amount from a few months in Europe, did not impinge on his sense of loss one jot. His own pain was his only concern. She sailed for Italy on the eighth of June. Dylan was pining by the ninth, all thoughts of topical songs, studio sessions, and song publishing flung from his mind.

Eve MacKenzie: He was very angry with [Suze] . . . when she went off to Italy for a while. She wanted to study her art. She was an artist. And I told him that night when he came here for dinner, when she was gone, that he shouldn't be angry, that he had to understand that she was only going for a short while and that she'd be back. He was quiet. He didn't answer.

A month and a day after Suze sailed away in the morning, Dylan was back in Columbia's Studio A, on the seventh floor of '799,' recording material for a second album. Though the first two sessions had taken place back in April, it was with this session that he began cutting the album in earnest. Reflective of his state of mind at the time was the album's original working title, *Bob Dylan's Blues,* culled from a song cut at the July session. Dylan stuck largely to this theme throughout the afternoon.

Dylan had his own blues to document. 'Quit Your Lowdown Ways' castigates a woman in the tone of a righteous preacher seeking to save a fallen woman—for himself. 'Down the Highway' stacks one conventional blues image on another, conjuring up one long, lonesome tone. The most directly autobiographical of his early blues compositions, it depicts a true love taking his heart in a suitcase 'all the way to Italy.' 'Worried Blues,' though originally reflective of someone else's pain, defies its unknown author to lay claim to it; while 'Honey Just Allow Me One More Chance' gives a name check and a half-share to the long-dead Henry Thomas, whose 1928 recording of the 1890s 'coon song' 'Honey, Won't You Allow Me One More Chance' purported to be its source. However, Thomas's original provided no more than a song title and a notion, which Dylan turned into a personal plea to an absent lover to allow him 'one more chance to get along with you.' It is a vocal tour de force and, along with 'Quit Your Lowdown Ways,' showed a Dylan prepared to make light of his own blues by using the form itself. It also showed a man who could now transcend his sources at will.

He had already shown a willingness to embrace the spirit of the blues, and a certain flair for amalgamating its unique imagery from disparate sources, at his first Columbia sessions of the year, on April 24–25. The versions of 'Corrina, Corrina,' 'Milk Cow Blues,' and 'Rocks and Gravel' at these sessions illustrate an increasing inventiveness with the form. In the case of 'Corrina, Corrina,' he used very little of the traditional song, 'Corrina,' abandoning its common-meter ballad structure in favor of a twelve-bar blues, and then liberally borrowing whole sections of the song's imagery from Robert Johnson, the great delta blues singer who had begun to exert a hold on Dylan's imagination in the early months of 1962.

When he debuted 'Corrina, Corrina' at Gerde's in mid-April, whole verses had been interpolated from Johnson's 'Stones in My Passway,' '32.20 Blues,' and 'Me and the Devil Blues.' 'Milk Cow Blues' also owed more to Johnson's 'Milkcow Calf Blues' than Kokomo Arnold's original (from which Dylan proceeded to take the opening verse of 'Quit Your Lowdown Ways'). Also slipped into Dylan's live set that summer were versions of 'Ramblin' on My Mind' and 'Kindhearted Woman.' All of these songs appeared on Columbia's 1961 collection of Johnson recordings, the seminal *King of the Delta Blues Singers*.

Somebody at Columbia, presumably either Hammond Snr. or Don Law, both of whom had had a hand in the Johnson reissue, had given

Dylan a copy of the album at the turn of the year. Its impact seems to have been immediate and profound. The following month Dylan informed Izzy Young he was writing a song called 'The Death of Robert Johnson.' For somebody as death-obsessed as the young Dylan, a major part of Johnson's appeal was bound to be the mystique surrounding early death, at the age of twenty-seven (or maybe twenty-six), poisoned (or was it stabbed?) by a jealous woman (or her husband), having made 'just twenty-nine of the greatest blues recordings ever.' At this point, Dylan needed to feel that was all it took—just twenty-nine recordings. He must have been aware how precarious his tenure as a Columbia recording artist looked set to be.

Bob Dylan, released in March 1962, had sold very poorly—supposedly a mere five thousand copies in the first year. Fortunately for Dylan, who had been cruelly dubbed Hammond's Folly within the organization, Hammond's own reputation became bound up with his own. Even if Hammond had not been so inclined, he was now required to get behind Dylan with all his might, to ensure that Columbia elected to take up their option. Dylan would be saved from demotion to the likes of Prestige, who had expressed an interest in taking over his recording career, not because of his transition into a powerful interpreter of the blues, but because of the songs he now began to pen himself. At the July session, 'Blowin' in the Wind,' cut in three takes, proved that Hammond's happy knack of signing talents before they reached full bloom remained intact.

Having organized his affairs, and secured his immediate future with Witmark, Grossman, and Columbia, Dylan took off for Minneapolis at the beginning of August. He hoped the familiar landscape, friends, and family might take his mind off of Suze. But nothing seemed to work. Stuck in Minneapolis with his blues again, he found nobody who even knew the 'fortune teller of his soul' well enough to share some of his loss. Recording a third 'home' session for Tony Glover's thirsty recorder, this time at the home of the Whitakers, he prefaced one new song by admitting that, 'My girl, she's in Europe right now. She sailed on a boat over there. She'll be back September 1st, and till she's back, I'll never go home.' And it really seems like Bob meant it. The song he was fiddling with, but had not yet realized, had been written one particular sleepless night, as he refused to lie in his bed 'once again' until 'my own true love is waiting.' Perhaps it was the very same night he had phoned the Van Ronks.

Dave Van Ronk: I remember we got a phone call from him at four or five o'clock in the morning. Terri picked it up. Bobby said he was standing in a phone booth some place in Minneapolis. It was nineteen degrees below zero and he was crying, 'I want Suze.'

'Tomorrow Is a Long Time' dealt with a whole set of emotions that Dylan had previously only confronted in secondhand form. Perhaps only now was he able to approach his anguish with sufficient perspective to write about it in the first person. As it is, 'Tomorrow Is a Long Time' was written when tomorrow still offered some hope of relief. As he'd told Glover's recorder, Suze had been due to return on or around Labor Day. However, shortly before she was due to return home, she broke the news to Dylan that she had decided to stay in Italy indefinitely.

Dylan was devastated, and this time the song he wrote was 'a statement that maybe you can say to make yourself feel better . . . as if you were talking to yourself.' As longing and loss became colored by an inner anger, he took a melody folksinger Paul Clayton had taught him, and wrote about a girl who 'wasted his precious time.' If 'Tomorrow Is a Long Time' was Dylan's first great song of hurt, 'Don't Think Twice, It's All Right' was his first great put-down song. Adopting Clayton's jaunty, devil-may-care lilt, the lines that depart from tradition suggest a subtext of real hurt—'she wanted my soul,' an absurd request had she not already acquired his heart.

Having gotten some feelings out of his system, Dylan once again attuned his ears to the world at large. His sense of a world going wrong was made manifest in September when, with the Cuban missile crisis looming and tension-filled talk reverberating around the coffeehouses, he wrote a song that catalogued a world peopled by worried souls, a world where 'black is the color and none is the number.' According to John Cohen, he wrote 'A Hard Rain's A-Gonna Fall' originally as a poem, only later putting it to song.

John Cohen: In September 1962 Bob had shown me the words to 'Hard Rain.' The text to 'Hard Rain' was a big change from rock & roll music or blues or country songs, which I kind of connected him with. I said, 'Bob, if you are going to do that kind of thing you should look at Rimbaud and Verlaine.'

Given that it took its verse pattern and melody line from the Child ballad 'Lord Randall,' it's unlikely that Dylan ever intended simply to recite the words of 'Hard Rain'—particularly as the last verse insists, 'I'll know my song well before I start singing.' At least one Village habitué vividly recalls the night Dylan first sang the song at the Gaslight.

Peter Blankfield: He put out these pieces of loose-leaf paper ripped out of a spiral notebook. And he starts singing ['Hard Rain'] . . . He finished singing it, and no one could say anything. The length of it, the episodic sense of it. Every line kept building and bursting.

Within a matter of days, Dylan found himself playing the Carnegie Hall for real, part of a hootenanny organized by Pete Seeger. He decided to premier his new song to the largest audience of his career, as part of a set extended to twenty minutes to cater for it.

Pete Seeger: Once again they had too many people on the program and I had to announce to all the singers, 'Folks, you're gonna be limited to three songs. No more. 'Cause we each have ten minutes apiece and no more.' And Bob raised his hand, and said, 'What am I supposed to do? One of my songs is ten minutes long.'

Seeger was so knocked out he appropriated the song for his own set. Inevitably the hard rain Dylan referred to in the song was taken by many to be nuclear fallout, even as its author went to great pains to point out that the song had a broader sweep, a wider meaning, one appropriate before, during, and after the Cuban missile crisis. This hard rain had more in common with the biblical apocalypse than bombs falling through the air.

Bob Dylan: It's not atomic rain, it's not fallout rain . . . I [just] mean some sort of end that's just got to happen. [1963]

Bob Dylan: I wrote it at the time of the Cuban crisis. I was in Bleecker Street in New York. We just hung around at night—people sat around wondering if it was the end, and so did I. Would one o'clock the next day ever come? . . . It was a song of desperation. What could we do? Could we control men on the verge of wiping us out? The words came fast, very fast. It was a song of terror. Line after line after line, trying to capture the feeling of nothingness. [1965]

How a twenty-one-year-old Dylan encapsulated the magic and mystery of a five-hundred-year-old ballad, the deep dark truths of Dante, and the apocalyptic symbolism of the French poets and the beats into six and a half minutes of sheer terror, appositely 'captur[ing] the feeling of nothingness' borne by those living on the brink, can never be realized by cold literary analysis, the tautologies of historical incidence, or even by mere biography. But 'Hard Rain' was certainly a summation of whole strands of poetry and song, in a way that 'Blowin' in the Wind' was not. It also suggested that such a talent was never going to be contained by something as self-referential and exclusive as the folk revival.

If 'A Hard Rain's A-Gonna Fall' was a sidewinding return to topical song, it led to a series of more mundane protests against the folly of man: the crass 'John Brown' now reads like one of those songs Dylan condensed down to a single line in 'Hard Rain' ('the executioner's face is always well-hidden'); while the grim tale of a father killing his starving family, 'The Ballad of Hollis Brown,' was one more 'tragic tale of independence and free will' culled from the folk idiom. Though he would record the latter for his second album, it would have to await a 1963 rerecording before it became a component of official product. On the other hand, 'John Brown' wouldn't even be recorded for *The Freewheelin' Bob Dylan* (or its successor). It had seemingly been earmarked for *Broadside*, on paper *and* vinyl, appearing as a mistakes-and-all recording by 'Blind Boy Grunt' on Folkways' July 1963 compilation *Broadside Ballads*.

Part of the problem was that Dylan had stockpiled a daunting number of songs for his second album (he would end up recording thirty-seven different songs), and still he refrained from laying down Columbia takes of the likes of 'Ballad for a Friend,' 'Tomorrow Is a Long Time,' 'Long Ago Far Away,' or 'Long Time Gone'—all songs consigned to a virtual existence as publisher's demos. Dylan clearly had his reasons for refraining from cutting these songs for Columbia, ones unrelated to their actual merit.

All four certainly had the edge on the knockabout rockabilly pastiche he spent three whole sessions that October and November trying to get down on Columbia tape. 'Mixed Up Confusion,' issued as a no-hope 45 in the Christmas rush, would later be seen as indubitable evidence of this folkie's undiminished love of rock & roll. Sounding like an outtake from one of those fabled mid-fifties Sun sessions, 'Mixed Up Confusion' sank without trace, deleting its way into serious collectability. Though nobody seems to wish to take credit for this piece of lateral thinking, it was apparently Hammond who had the idea of putting Dylan together with a studio band.

Bruce Langhorne: John Hammond put the whole thing together [but] his orientation was jazz, y'know, so he figured if you put two musicians together, they'll figure out something to play . . . [Dylan] was actually doing some very interesting things with guitar, he was playing some very interesting changes. He wasn't a virtuoso guitarist, but he had some very creative ideas.

Dylan finally stormed out of the third session, only returning when assurances came that fourteen takes of 'Mixed Up Confusion' were enough. With all the musicians, save Langhorne, paid scale and sent packing, Dylan got back on the program with a gorgeous rendition of 'Don't Think Twice, It's All Right' that might just have illustrated how good a guitarist Dylan had become, save that it's Langhorne who provides the faultless accompaniment. Whatever 'very interesting things with guitar' Dylan was coming up with, they were evidently best expressed by a virtuoso like Langhorne. Langhorne and Dylan also got to practice playing together on a lovely 'Hollis Brown,' though it would be another two and a half years before they would share a Columbia studio again. Dylan's audience was not quite ready for another 'Mixed Up Confusion,' even one with content.

Dylan, though, was determined to press on and finish his second album. Three weeks later, on December 6, 1962, he arrived at Columbia for his seventh session of the year. Three songs from that session made the final cut on *Freewheelin'*, each one a first take. Dylan's extraordinary ability to focus in the studio was now almost his to command at will. Thus when he wrapped the three-hour session up with the epic 'A Hard Rain's A-Gonna Fall,' one take was all it took. Likewise 'I Shall Be Free,' Dylan's shameless rewrite of Lead Belly's 'We Shall Be Free,' was a first take—even if Dylan couldn't resist a couple more goes before admitting that number one was best. But it was Dylan's one-take's-all-I-need dispatch of 'Oxford Town,' his sardonic view of current events at the University of Mississippi, that astonished Hammond, who can be heard on the master reel exclaiming at song's end, 'Don't tell me that's all?'

It was presumably this session at which Hammond and John Court, Al Grossman's partner, went at it hammer-and-tongs and Court was ordered out of the studio by Hammond. According to Court, 'He didn't stop [Bob] for mistakes, feeling, mood, or anything. He just kept the tape rolling, and every once in a while looked up over the magazine to say, "Okay, are you through, Bob? Is that it?"' And yet the actual session tape shows that Hammond was as incredulous as the other onlookers at how easily Dylan was working through the songs *he* intended to record, even if Hammond had something of a reputation for letting his artists sink or swim.

Billy James: John . . . could be reading *The Nation* or *The Republic* or the *New York Times* while the session was going on . . . I can't tell you precisely what hands-on meant with John.

Whatever the future held, it looked like Hammond had at least overseen an album that delivered on the promise half hinted at on *Bob Dylan*. Dylan left town twelve days later, equally convinced that his second album was under wraps. He was about to complete the final part of his not-so-formal degree in folk music, making his first trip to England, the font of all Anglo-American folk tradition. Albert Grossman had somehow managed to persuade the BBC to pay his airfare to London to play a small part in a BBC drama called *Madhouse on Castle Street*.

Dylan flew to London Airport around the 18th, a couple of weeks ahead of filming duties (actual filming was scheduled for December 30), planning to explore London and immerse himself in its folk scene. Odetta, also on Grossman's roster, was already in London with Albert when Dylan checked in at the Mayfair, off Piccadilly—the BBC's choice—checked out of the Mayfair, and checked in at the more homely Cumberland Hotel, by Marble Arch. If Dylan had gotten on with his life after Suze's verbal bombshell, even venturing into other yielding arms for the first time, he was still besotted with Suze and devoutly wished to be reconciled. Ironically, as he headed for Europe, Suze was returning home. She had set sail from Italy on December 13, arriving home five days later, around about the time Dylan was standing outside a club on London's Cromwell Road. Tuesday nights were Troubadour nights and, as the most renowned English folk club of its day, the Troubadour was the obvious starting point for Dylan that winter evening.

Anthea Joseph: The day before he turned up I had been in Collet's record shop . . . And I got the latest copy of *Sing Out* that they had, in which was the first Shelton interview [sic] with Dylan and I read it and thought, this sounds interesting . . . The following day . . . there I was [at the Troubadour] . . . and these feet came down the stairs, cowboy boots, which in those days were rather unusual, and jeans, which were also fairly unusual. Then the jacket. Then this face. Then the hat. He had the hat on . . . He trundled up to my cubbyhole and started shoving money at me and said, 'I'm looking for Anthea. Can I come in please?' And I said, 'Well, I'm Anthea'—and the penny dropped—and I said, 'You're Bob Dylan, aren't you?' And he said, 'Yes.' I said, 'Well, you can have your money back provided you sing for us.'

It had been Pete Seeger who'd suggested Dylan look up Anthea, who ran the Troubadour on Tuesday nights. Having made his first important contact on the English folk scene, he soon made his second. At some point in the evening, Martin Carthy arrived to check out the evening's fare. Carthy, one of a new band of English folksingers then emerging, was about the same age as Dylan, and more than willing to accept a new face on the scene. Carthy soon struck up a strong friendship with Dylan, who crashed on Martin and Dorothy Carthy's floor after the BBC money ran out.

Martin Carthy: He was in England for about three months [sic] . . . We'd see each other at the various clubs there were. There was the King & Queen, there was the Troubadour, there was the Ballads & Blues on a Saturday night, at the Roundhouse pub down on Wardour Street . . . His time in England was actually crucial to his development. If you listen to *Freewheelin'*, most of which was made before he came to England, and you listen to the next album after that, which is *Times They Are A-Changin'*, there's an enormous difference in the way he's singing, in the sort of tunes he's singing, the way he's putting words together . . . Bob Dylan's a piece of blotting paper when it comes to listening to tunes. If he doesn't learn the tune, he learns the idea of the tune and he can do something like it. It had a colossal effect on him.

Carthy himself had a profound influence on Dylan, introducing him to traditional English variants of songs he only knew from Appalachian derivatives. By the end of 1962 Dylan had become something of a walking encyclopedia on American folk music, from which all of his knowledge of English folk music came. Not that he didn't delight in singing English ballads, but usually in the form in which they had been transposed to America. A Gaslight recording from two months earlier has him performing the likes of 'Barbara Allen,' 'Handsome Molly,' and 'The Cuckoo Is a Pretty Bird,' even if the last of these was based upon Clarence Ashley's highly idiosyncratic reinterpretation. He now found another surface he had as yet only skimmed.

Bob Dylan: I ran into some people in England who really knew those [traditional English] songs. Martin Carthy, another guy named Nigel Davenport [sic]. Martin Carthy's incredible. I learned a lot of stuff from Martin. [1984]

When Carthy played him songs from his own repertoire, Dylan, ever the sponge, was soon working on his first adaptations of authentic English folk songs. Two songs certainly introduced to him by Carthy were 'Scarborough Fair' and 'Lady Franklin's Lament.' Carthy's arrangement of 'Scarborough Fair' provided him with the basic melody for two of his most beautiful love songs, 'Girl from the North Country' and 'Boots of Spanish Leather.' If 'Scarborough Fair' gave these songs 'the idea of the tune,' 'Bob Dylan's Dream' owed 'Lady Franklin's Lament' a more wholesale debt. The whole 'dream . . . I thought was true' aspect Dylan derived from a ballad memorializing Lady Franklin's dream of finding her husband, the Arctic explorer Sir John Franklin—who had vanished into the Arctic wastes on an expedition in 1845—alive and well, a dream dashed by an 1859 expedition that found a stone cairn on King William Island detailing his death.

As Dylan has indicated, Carthy was not the only English folksinger from whom he acquired a whole new take on English folk tradition. A good friend of Carthy's was Bob Davenport, who also befriended Dylan. Though Davenport's influence is less apparent than Carthy's, Dylan wrote at least half a dozen songs based directly on English folk songs, either during his stay in England or shortly after his return to America. A couple of these may well have been prompted by versions he heard from Davenport.

It seems to have been an extraordinarily fertile period for Dylan. Certainly written at this time was 'Masters of War,' a scathing attack on warmongers based on Jean Ritchie's arrangement of 'Nottamun Town.' Who or what prompted Dylan to recall Ritchie's version of an English riddle song—which he undoubtedly already knew from Ritchie's original—has never been confirmed. However, the song was singularly absent from the Witmark demos Dylan cut a couple of days before his trip to England. Recalled by both Joseph and Carthy as featuring in his club sets in England, it was certainly introduced to his New York friends in January 1963 as a song he had written in England. Ritchie later asserted her copyright of the arrangement, and a one-off settlement was made by Dylan. 'Only a Hobo,' a superior reworking of the earlier 'Man on the Street' that took as its source the 'Poor Miner's Lament,' also appears to have become part of Dylan's intellectual baggage upon his return to America.

But the most evidently English song Dylan wrote on or before his return to America was called 'Liverpool Gal,' another song based on a British ballad made popular by the energizing aspects of American tradition, in this instance 'When First unto This Country.' Seemingly autobiographical, the song tells of a brief affair with a Scouse lady he met standing by the Thames, feeling all alone and homesick. The presumably autobiographical aspect of the song most likely explains its omission from his repertoire, save for a home tape made by Glover in July. Despite being written when his relationship with Suze appeared to be at an end, its subject matter would not have sat well with her.

Another love song written at the time was 'Fare Thee Well,' a straightforward reworking of 'The Leaving of Liverpool.' The Clancys have claimed that Dylan lifted his arrangement directly from theirs, and he unquestionably knew the Clancys' version from his time in New York. However, all evidence indicates that Dylan relearned the song from Scottish folksinger Nigel Denver, the third important influence from his time in London (and the person he conflated in his mind with Bob Davenport). Carthy certainly recalls Dylan regularly requesting Denver to sing 'The Leaving of Liverpool.'

'The Leaving of Liverpool' was not the only song in Denver's repertoire that intrigued Dylan. According to Jim McLean, there was another song Denver sang, Dominic Behan's 'The Patriot Game,' that Dylan took a particular interest in. Within three months he had adapted not only the tune but the whole theme of the song, 'With God on Our Side' becoming Dylan's most precise debunking of the God and Country ethos.

Jim McLean: [Dylan asked me], 'What does it mean, Patriot Game?' . . . I explained—probably lectured him—about Dr. Johnson, who's one of Dominic [Behan]'s favourite writers, and that's where Dominic picked up [the] saying: 'Patriotism is the last refuge of a scoundrel.'

However, unlike Carthy and Davenport, Denver never became friendly with Dylan. Indeed, one evening late in December, Denver finally had enough of this Yankee upstart and told him exactly what he thought of his credentials as a folksinger.

Anthea Joseph: They had a row. It was [over] the fact he considered Bob couldn't sing his way out of a paper bag, couldn't play a guitar, and couldn't play a harp, and that Nigel was infinitely better.

Perhaps Dylan's most legendary performance that winter in London came a couple of days before his contretemps with Denver, when he went along with Anthea Joseph to the Singers' Club. Part of Denver's fierce resentment of Dylan stemmed from the fact that he wrote his own songs, and Denver was a dyed-in-the-wool purist when it came to folk music, whereas Carthy and Davenport were prepared to accept Dylan as a troubadour who utilized—but was not mired in—the folk tradition. Dylan knew the type. But if the Village had had its fair share of purists, in London the purest of the pure could still be found, people for whom even Appalachian variants were a trifle sullied. Their home was the Singers' Club, run by Ewan MacColl and Peggy Seeger.

Anthea Joseph: I took him to the Singers' Club. Bert Lloyd was there and I walked into the bar with Bob, clutching guitar, and we went up to the bar, bought a drink, and Bert knew about Dylan and I introduced them. So Bert then introduced him to Ewan and Ewan sort of looked at the guitar and we all trailed upstairs. The first half of the Singers' Club was deadly serious—no floor singers in the first half, not ever—and the audience by this time had begun to recognize [Bob]. Not because of any publicity but because the word had got out. So the muttering was, 'Bob Dylan's here, Bob Dylan's here.' They kept on looking at him and Bob was getting the giggles . . . And we went downstairs at half time, had another jar, went back upstairs, and it was getting people off the floor, and there was no way they could say no. He had to be got up! . . . [Of course] he wasn't trad. And it was *distinctly* traditional . . . He did 'Masters of War' and 'Ballad of Hollis Brown,' which goes on forever with the chorus and [there were] many extra verses. When you got up off the floor your maximum was five minutes really. [Dylan did] twenty! And he did it on purpose. I'm sure of it. Absolutely sure of it. And brought the house down.

That Dylan chose to perform two 'original' songs whose melodic sources were hoary old British ballads, 'Pretty Polly' and the surreal modality of 'Nottamun Town,' must have particularly stuck in MacColl's gravelly throat. He never forgave the uppity upstart and would later write several vitriolic articles dismissing Dylan's work, but by then Dylan had long progressed beyond the metaphors at the end of MacColl's particular tunnel.

If Dylan dispensed with MacColl by relying on his ever-refining skills as a songwriter, his response to Denver was more classically brattish. Needless to say, he had not appreciated Denver's concisely expressed opinion of his musical chops, and on New Year's Day 1963 he proceeded to show what he thought of Mr. Denver at the King & Queen pub, a venue where, according to Carthy at least, Dylan had previously been accorded a good reception.

Ron Gould: The featured guest that night was . . . Nigel Denver—a Scottish Nationalist, fiercely patriotic. He was singing an unaccompanied Scottish ballad, nice and quiet, when Dylan came in and stood at the back of the audience. Straight away he began to create a disturbance, talking very,

very loudly, saying 'What's all this fuckin' shit?' or something of that nature, really nasty. 'What's going on? Where's the drinks? How do you get a drink here?' And this went on all through the song, with people in the audience telling him to be quiet. Nobody knew who he was. Then Nigel said, 'I don't know if you realize it but we allow the performers to perform, during which time the audience keeps quiet.' And Dylan looked up and said, 'I don't fuckin' have to keep quiet. I'm Bob Dylan.' Which really enamoured him with the audience!

Anthea Joseph: He was drunk . . . And so was Nigel—again . . . And he *was* awfully bad that night.

Having got that off his chest, Dylan completed his inconsequential role in the equally inconsequential BBC play and took off for Italy for a few days, Odetta tagging along for the ride. He would later tell Scaduto that he had gone there in the expectation of tracking Suze down in Perugia. If he was really unaware of Suze's departure, as the trip implies, it suggests a couple who had all but stopped conversing. It was in Italy that he worked up Carthy's 'Scarborough Fair' into 'Girl from the North Country' and an embryonic 'Boots of Spanish Leather.' If the former was Dylan's second song to Bonnie, the inspiration for the latter was never in doubt: 'She says, I don't know when / I'll be coming back again / It depends on how I'm feeling.' On his return to London he had the good grace to play Carthy the former.

Martin Carthy: When he came back [from Italy], he'd written 'Girl from the North Country'; he came down to the Troubadour and said, 'Hey, here's "Scarborough Fair,"' and he started playing this thing.

Dylan's failure to find Suze in Italy seems to have brought a whole set of emotions to the surface. This time, though, he found solace in the company of a couple of American friends going through similar shit themselves. Eric Von Schmidt and Richard Farina were both doing the London waltz under the pretext of cutting an album for Dobell's.

Eric Von Schmidt: Dick was breaking up with his wife; I was breaking up with my wife; and, probably, Bob was breaking up with . . . Suze.

Richard Farina and Carolyn Hester were about to be history, and he was as keen as Dylan to not remember what he was drinking to forget. Dylan, exposed to British beer for the first time, had already shown the mean streak he could display when he downed a few too many. In the company of fellow strangers he showed a mellower side, though again Nigel Denver would ultimately be on the receiving end of a sozzled Bob. Roped into providing some harmonica accompaniment for the album Richard Farina and Eric Von Schmidt were recording at Dobell's, Dylan arrived at the session with a carrier bag full of beer. A loose session was on the cards. Offered a bottle of Guinness, he took a swig, exclaimed, 'My God, what's this?!' and emptied the remainder of the bottle on the floor. By the evening Dylan, Von Schmidt, and Farina had been at the juicer for half a day. Having completed the session, they headed down to the Troubadour one last time (Dylan and Von Schmidt were going home in two days).

Anthea Joseph: They all turned up about eleven o'clock, absolutely out of their gourds except for Ethan Singer, the fiddle player. Ethan was straight as a die and very embarrassed by this collection of bozos that he was looking after . . . The Troubadour has—you can't call it a stage—a platform. [It's] less than a foot. [Dylan] was falling off it. And finally I supplied him with a stool and said, 'You'd better sing sitting down 'cause otherwise you're gonna hurt yourself.'

In the middle of Dylan's impromptu set Nigel Denver arrived at the club, fully expecting to sing with Judy Silvers, the scheduled act that night, who had already performed her first (and as it turned out last) set. Denver began heckling Dylan from the floor, but Dylan was too wasted to care, and no matter how much Denver taunted Dylan, he refused to acknowledge Denver's existence. Denver finally stormed out of the club. As Von Schmidt later commented, 'Dylan [just] wouldn't let him exist.'

Dylan had not only refused to let Denver exist in person. His very presence in London that winter was an open challenge to Denver and his kind to revise their view of folk music or be lost in the flood. Dylan's visit had given a new dimension to his writing. He returned to New York prepared to concentrate on reworking all traditional forms. For the foreseeable, it would be exclusively Bob Dylan songs that his audiences would hear, even if some of those melodies attached to his 'chains of flashing images' still sounded mightily familiar.

1963: While the Establishment Burns

6

Folk songs showed me the way / they showed me that songs can say somethin human.

—Bob Dylan, 1963

Even though the change in him after his trip to London may not have been as dramatic as, say, his return from Denver in 1960, his friends noticed a new dynamism in Dylan. He no longer seemed content just to write songs and sing them. He seemed to be looking for a purpose that transcended mere song. In 1965, when he was the king of folk-rock, and determined to be dismissive of past conceits, he would tell commentator after commentator that he began writing protest songs in order to jump into a scene about to happen. Many commentators have dismissed this as a rewriting of history by Dylan, arguing that the sincerity betrayed by songs like 'Only a Pawn in Their Game' and 'Masters of War' belies such claims.

The 'finger-pointin'' songs, at least those Dylan wrote between January 1962 and June 1963, were undoubtedly genuine expressions of frustration and anger at the neophobes who sought to subvert the inextricable processes of change. However, it *was* a conscious decision on his part to suppress the other genres he had mastered. That decision was signposted by something he said on his return from Italy. Walking with Dick Farina in London, he asked a rhetorical question, ostensibly of Joan Baez: 'She's walking around on picket lines, she's got all kinds of feelings, so why ain't she steppin' out?' The real emergence of Dylan the protest singer, though, went back to the fall of 1962, and the first of a number of recordings he had made for *Broadside*.

Throughout 1962, Dylan had gradually become more active in his contributions to *Broadside*, 'Sis' Cunningham's mimeographed compendium of topical songs. In November 1962, he recorded eight songs at Cunningham's apartment, of which only the previously unrecorded 'I Shall Be Free' and Dylan's first Old Testament song, 'I'd Hate to Be You on That Dreadful Day' were not in the finger-pointing vein; and only 'I Shall Be Free' and 'Oxford Town' were earmarked for second-album duties. Reworking the hand-clappin', foot-stompin' brand of gospel music to embrace the needs of egalitarian emancipation, Dylan had already taken the traditional spiritual 'Ain't Gonna Grieve My Lord No More' and written a secular equivalent, 'Ain't Gonna Grieve.' He now gave *Broadside* more of the same. 'Walkin' Down the Line,' 'Train A-Travelin',' and 'Paths of Victory' were all rallying calls for the civil rights cause.

Returning to New York in mid-January, Dylan had a slew of new finger-pointing songs to introduce to his friends. He made a rare appearance at a Gerde's hootenanny the Monday after his return, to premiere 'Masters of War' to the by-now-usual plaudits from those recognizing a peer outstripping their own efforts. Within a couple of days he was recording the song for *Broadside*. In attendance at that session were 'Sis' Cunningham, Happy Traum, Suze Rotolo, and Phil Ochs. Ochs, the new kid on the block, was destined to be the first 'new' Dylan. When his mentor finally turned his back on the protest genre, Ochs obligingly took over as *Broadside* mascot.

The recordings continued at Cunningham's. A week or so later, Dylan was recording 'Only a Hobo' for the magazine, along with a stumbling 'John Brown.' By this point, though, there seems to have been a slightly grander purpose to these recordings. Both of these performances, fluffs and all, appeared on an album of *Broadside Ballads* put out by Folkways in the summer, along with the impromptu 'Talkin' Devil' and Happy Traum's rendition of 'Let Me Die in My Footsteps,' with vocal harmonies by Dylan. Ironically, despite the fact that the likes of 'John Brown' and 'Talkin' Devil' were hardly top-drawer Dylan, his songs still sound much smarter and more incisive than the other songs cluttering up Folkways 05301. Here was a niche for the taking.

Dylan also found himself temporarily relieved of the need for songs of hurt and loss. Released from the despair hinted at on 'Boots of Spanish Leather,' Bob found himself reconciled with Suze upon his return from England. Despite Suze's quickly rekindled expressions of doubt about the nature of their relationship, Dylan was happy to have her back in the fold. He even persuaded her to move back into his 4th Street apartment, negating her original intention of keeping the relationship on a more manageable basis. The flood of finger-pointing songs that spring and early summer seemed to provide both an alternative focus for his pen and a chance to share in Suze's sense of commitment to 'the Cause.'

Dylan's new direction that winter also seems to have led him to reconsider the songs he had already selected for his second album, *The Freewheelin' Bob Dylan*. There remains a common belief that he was forced by Columbia to pull 'Talkin' John Birch Society Blues' from the album *after* he walked out on *The Ed Sullivan Show* on May 12, 1963, when the head of program practices—i.e., the censor—considered the song potentially libelous. Indeed, Clive Davis, who was Columbia's general attorney at the time, and who broke the news to Dylan, states in his autobiography that 'the problem began with Ed Sullivan.'

However, when Dylan came to see Davis to have the decision explained to him, John Hammond was with him. Not that Davis recalls Hammond saying much, for Dylan was deeply angry, demanding to know, 'What *is* this? What do you *mean* I can't come out with this song?' It seems inconceivable that Hammond would have accompanied Dylan to Davis's office in May 1963, given that Grossman had finally succeeded in convincing Columbia to replace Hammond as Dylan's producer some time in April.

The animosity generated between Hammond and Grossman never abated, and Dylan and Hammond were estranged for some years after he was ousted. Hammond's replacement was a young black jazz producer, Tom Wilson. If Wilson had no knowledge of folk music, he quickly recognized someone who was not merely folk, and Dylan liked the idea of someone young, gifted (with an ear, that is), and black behind the console.

Tom Wilson: I was introduced to Dylan by David Kapralik at a time when I was not properly working for Columbia. I was being used by them, shall we say. He said, 'Why don't you guys stick around and do a coupla things?' I said, 'What do you mean? I don't even work for Columbia.' . . . I didn't even particularly like folk music. I'd been recording Sun Ra and Coltrane . . . I thought folk music was for the dumb guys. This guy played like the dumb guys, but then these words came out. I was flabbergasted.

Freewheelin' was released on May 27, 1963. If 'Talkin' John Birch' was pulled after the Sullivan debacle, this would have given Columbia two weeks to recut the album, reshoot the cover, and press up the new version. That hardly seems possible—even with replacement songs in the can. In fact, Dylan had gone back into the studio at the end of April (the 24th) and cut five of his newest songs, having already confessed serious reservations to an old friend about his original sequence for *Freewheelin'*.

Bob Dylan: There's too many old-fashioned songs in there, stuff I tried to write like Woody. I'm goin' through changes. Need some more finger-pointin' songs in it, 'cause that's where my head's at right now. [1963]

Possibly the April 24 session was originally scheduled to be for Dylan's next album. However, *Freewheelin'* was not even in the shops, and if this were the case, it would not really explain the self-conscious inclusion of a talking blues, a song format he had all but abandoned. The talking blues equivalent of 'Hard Rain,' 'Talkin' World War III Blues,' was apparently worked up spontaneously in the studio, Dylan working through four incomplete attempts before nailing his first complete take. Here was a very deliberate attempt to provide a substitute for 'Talkin' John Birch.'

All the evidence points to a decision by Columbia's lawyers to replace 'John Birch' being forced on Dylan some weeks prior to the Sullivan show. Rather than simply substitute one of the eighteen outtakes already left over from the 1962 sessions, Dylan decided to take the opportunity to reconfigure the album, using songs he had written in England to replace the likes of 'Let Me Die in My Footsteps,' 'Ramblin' Gamblin' Willie,' 'Rocks and Gravel,' and 'Talkin' John Birch Society Blues,' all songs he had composed in the winter of 1962 and all, save 'Talkin' John Birch,' songs he felt he had outgrown.

Such a chronology puts a whole different slant on Dylan's non-appearance on *The Ed Sullivan Show* on May 12. If Dylan had already been instructed by Columbia lawyers to pull 'Talkin' John Birch' before the April 24 session, then the fact that he attempted to perform it on a CBS TV show three weeks later suggests a very deliberate act of confrontation. If he had managed to get it past the head of program practices, as he might well have, Columbia Records and CBS-TV would have been made to look very stupid, and Dylan would have succeeded in publicly ridiculing the John Birch Society.

As it was, during the afternoon rehearsal Dylan was informed that his satirical blues about the John Birch Society might upset those he was seeking to satirize, and that he couldn't perform it. His response was remarkably calm and measured. He was asked if he wanted to do something else and he apparently replied, 'No, this is what I want to do. If I can't play my song, I'd rather not appear on the show.' It was almost as if it had all come down as he expected. Publicist Billy James, who had accompanied Dylan to the rehearsal, vividly recalls his stoical response.

Billy James: I recollect us leaving the studio, with him not too terribly disappointed. Because he was tough—he was used to rejection.

Ironically, the uproar about this blatant act of censorship probably did Dylan more good, by portraying him as a rebel and counterculture hero, than if he had appeared on the show and performed a single tune to an uncaring national TV audience. As it was, the *New York Times* and *Village Voice* both ran stories on the furore, while *Time* and *Playboy* referred to the incident in articles on the folk-music revival, emphasizing Dylan as the most promising up-and-coming folksinger. Nat Hentoff's profile in *Playboy* even included an account of Dylan's original audition for *The Ed Sullivan Show,* at the time his first album was released. His friends had told him that they would eventually call back and Dylan had replied, 'Well, they won't tell me what to sing.' Izzy Young, ever the radical, endeavored to picket Columbia. Dylan, though, felt he had made his point—as indeed he had.

Izzy Young: I had an idea to make a demonstration against CBS for cutting out 'Talkin' John Birch Society Blues' from the album, and Al Grossman encouraged me. I printed up a sheet with the song text and an explanation why it was wrong to censor the song: freedom of speech. I called everyone, I called the newspapers and went to the CBS office which was then located on 5th Avenue. There were eight policemen on horseback but there was no Bob Dylan, no Suze Rotolo, no Al Grossman, nobody from his office, just me and six or eight other people.

Though the Sullivan fiasco delayed Dylan's debut on national TV, he did appear on two local folk-music specials broadcast that summer, performing two and three songs for WBC-TV and WNEW-TV respectively. Grossman had encouraged him to refrain from New York club gigs, even though he was as yet an unknown commodity in larger venues. The result was a frustrating period without gigs, awaiting the slow-motion sound of Columbia's publicity machine whirring into action. The occasional radio appearance, such as he had made in 1962 on the shows of Cynthia Gooding, Billy Faier, and Henrietta Yurchenco, and now made on Bob Fass Skip Weshner and Oscar Brand's syndicated *World of Folk Music,* kept Dylan focused but were mere blips in Grossman's grand design.

If the Sullivan show was Dylan's most publicized non-appearance that spring, his debut at New York's Town Hall on April 12th garnered reviews of the actual event in *Billboard, Variety,* and the *New York Times* (courtesy of Bob Shelton, of course). Though he failed to sell out all nine hundred seats, even a three-quarters-full Town Hall was a remarkable achievement given that his groundbreaking second album had yet to be released, his first album had bombed, and less than eighteen months earlier he could hardly find fifty people to turn up at Carnegie Recital Hall to hear him perform.

Never one to give the audience what they expected, Dylan did not play a single song from his one and only released album. Nor did he include 'Blowin' in the Wind,' at this point his best-known composition. However, he did play a sixteen-song set wholly composed of original work, three of which would ultimately appear on his forthcoming album (though he had yet to record 'Bob Dylan's Dream' or 'Masters of War'); and two of which would make the following long-player. The remainder of the set largely comprised what can only be described as a wave of new songs from his finger-pointing pen, many destined to fall between the cracks created by his album-a-year contract, undemanding for the times.

Wisely mixing the lightweight and the topical, Dylan combined rag-time tunes like 'New Orleans Rag' and 'All Over You' with the type of social commentaries he was becoming known for. Along with earlier songs like 'John Brown,' 'The Ballad of Hollis Brown,' and 'A Hard Rain's A-Gonna Fall,' he debuted four brand-new finger-pointing songs: 'Masters of War,' 'Walls of Redwing,' 'Who Killed Davey Moore?' (boxer Davey Moore had died just eighteen days earlier, from wounds sustained in a title fight), and 'With God on Our Side.' Dylan even had the remarkable self-assurance to encore by reading an eight-minute poem, entitled 'Last Thoughts on Woody Guthrie.' Columbia recorded the show, ever mindful of the advantages of some live material in the vaults should they require product during a fallow period. That fallow period was a long time coming, and when it came Dylan was able to restrain Columbia (though not the bootleggers) from any archival trawls. The first Town Hall bootleg appeared in 1970, bearing the apposite title *While the Establishment Burns*.

Despite maintaining a fine balance between jocularity and social com-mentary for most of his ninety-minute set, by far the most moving moment came midway through, when Dylan performed an achingly lovely rendition of his most tender song, written for Suze during her absence in Italy, 'Tomorrow Is a Long Time.' Dylan and Suze had had a terrible row just before the show, which cannot have helped steady already taut nerves. 'Tomorrow Is a Long Time' sounds like the most beautiful of mea culpas.

In late April, though, Dylan found himself back in the clubs, one of which was a thousand miles from New York, being Chicago's latest alternative to the Gate of Horn, the Bear. Grossman had a part interest in the club, and while Dylan was in Chicago he managed to schedule an appearance on the *Studs Terkel's Wax Museum* radio show. Terkel was a renowned social commentator and his show attracted healthy listening figures in the Midwest. During his time in Chicago, Dylan was also to encounter two key figures in his forthcoming folk-rock reinvention. Victor Maymudes, already working for Grossman, became Dylan's road manager the following year. Dylan also jammed with a talented local guitarist called Michael Bloomfield, though Bloomfield's original intention had been somewhat different.

Michael Bloomfield: I had heard the first Bob Dylan album. I thought it was just terrible. I couldn't believe that this guy was so well touted. So I went down [to the Bear in Chicago] to see him y'know, to meet him, to get up there and blow him off the stage. But to my surprise he was enchanting. He couldn't really sing y'know, but he could get it over . . . better than any guy I've met.

Dylan returned to Cambridge that April, to renew acquaintances and to finally make his Boston concert debut, two nights at the Café Yana, having been hyped as 'the latest folk giant' by the *Boston Broadside*. Afterward, he stayed over to make an impromptu appearance at a Club 47 'hoot,' where he also had an opportunity to check out the Queen of Folk, Joan Baez. Baez had first met Dylan when he was playing at Gerde's Folk City in 1961, but had been unimpressed by the 'little vagabond.' At a later meeting, Dylan was too busy trying to impress her gorgeous younger sister Mimi, with whom Dylan seems to have remained permanently smitten, to take any undue notice of Joan. In the interim, though, Baez's manager Manny Greenhill had given Baez an acetate of his songs (probably a test pressing of the original *Freewheelin'*), at which point she apparently 'began to realize the power of the lyric content.'

After the Club 47 hoot everyone adjourned to Sally Schoenfeld's apartment, and Baez and Dylan got to spend some time together. Presumably she also got to hear 'With God on Our Side,' which Dylan had premiered nine days earlier. When they met again at the Monterey Folk Festival three weeks later, she would join Dylan on stage for 'With God on Our Side,' which qualified as an important endorsement, and they picked up where they had left off, Dylan ending up spending several days after the festival at Baez's home in Carmel. Their romance had made it to second gear.

It became semi-public the third weekend of July, at the second Newport Folk Festival. The festival had been in limbo since 1959, but the times demanded its revival. It was here that Dylan got to act out his role as princeling of the New Revival. With Peter, Paul and Mary's 'Blowin' in the Wind'—accorded singalong status as the second of Sunday evening's ensemble encores—now sitting at number two on the

Billboard pop charts, Dylan was attracting a lot of unwelcome attention, and it was already introducing some psychological worry lines.

Bob Fass: Bob . . . told me after the first time he had been to Newport, 'Suddenly I just can't walk around without a disguise. I used to walk around and go wherever I wanted. But now it's gotten very weird. People follow me into the men's room just so they can say that they saw me pee.'

Dylan had turned up at Newport with Suze, but he ended up singing with Baez twice, once on her set, once on his. Baez cannot have been in any doubt as to Suze's status. She was, after all, plastered across the front cover of Bob's latest album, arm in arm with him, walking down a snowy 4th Street. But Baez couldn't resist introducing her version of 'Don't Think Twice' as a 'Bob Dylan song . . . [but] the only thing he's protesting in this, is a love affair that lasted too long.' Suze, who already suspected Dylan of having an affair with Baez, was furious. Her demeanor cannot have improved when he informed her that he was going on a brief tour with Baez that August, playing half a dozen shows as Baez's guest, singing a couple of songs solo and then duetting with her on three or four more of his own tunes. The mini-tour, culminating at Forest Hills Stadium in front of twelve thousand fans, would give him some much-needed exposure.

Joan Baez: I was getting audiences of up to ten thousand at that point, and dragging my little vagabond out onto the stage was a grand experiment . . . The people who had not heard of Bob were often infuriated, and sometimes even booed him.

Suze, tired of living the dichotomies a possessive, polygamous boyfriend threw up, moved in with her sister Carla. This only resulted in Dylan becoming a virtual resident at Carla's apartment, where a series of rows ensued between him and Carla about Suze's needs and best interests. Because of the self-evident commercial gains Dylan stood to make through his relationship with Baez, and the cavalier way he has treated her over the years, some have doubted the sincerity of his feelings for her at this point. All the evidence suggests he felt little of the soaring heights and gaping depths of emotion his relationship with Suze clearly engendered. He was still unable to conceive of a life without Suze, even the Suze who had returned from Italy a little more worldly wise. It was Suze who accompanied Dylan to the Columbia sales convention that summer and, surprisingly, Carla was permitted to tag along, too, ending up the recipient of a particularly vicious Dylan 'truth-attack.'

The location for the 1963 convention was the Hotel Americana in San Juan, Puerto Rico, and Dylan was being actively championed by record division president Goddard Lieberson. However, he continued to be suspicious of his label and, when he got up to sing, took the opportunity to remind the reps that the man censored by the CBS-TV network was still singing a few home truths.

Tom Wilson: In the first Columbia convention, in '63, I had two acts, Dylan and Terry Thornton. I'd just joined the company . . . Dylan had just written that song about Emmett Till [sic] and another one called 'With God on Our Side' . . . he sang it and half the cats in the convention got up and split. All the Columbia guys just started to walk out: they didn't want to hear this. Those were his two strongest songs at the time and he didn't spare them.

The song that Dylan actually sang *at* the Southern reps was not the long-forgotten 'Emmett Till' but a brand-new song about another unjust murder of a black man. 'Only a Pawn in Their Game' had been premiered less than two weeks earlier at a registration rally in Greenwood, Mississippi, where he had flown to provide some moral support to those fighting the civil rights battle at the sharp end, and to sing a few of his new finger-pointing songs to the news cameras. Medgar Evers had been the Mississippi leader of the NAACP (National Association for the Advancement of Colored People). His murderer was portrayed by Dylan as just another poor dumb white bigot, denied a name in song as he had been denied a voice in life. If he did himself no favors by winding up the Southern reps this way, Dylan already knew he was succeeding, commercially and artistically, *despite* Columbia, not because of them.

Billy James: I was aware of the fact that Dylan was ignored for two years at the label. I went to that first Newport Folk Festival, where he closed it with 'Blowin' in the Wind.' There were two record dealers who had kiosks and there were less than twenty Columbia Records LPs of Dylan in all of Newport, Rhode Island. I came back and went ballistic . . . They did not have that sense until after Peter, Paul and Mary had a hit with 'Blowin' in the Wind' on Warner Brothers and then someone said to me, 'Why doesn't he save his best material for himself?' . . . I didn't go to San Juan, but . . . I can remember expressing my concern back in New York when I heard about the negative reaction that he received at that convention and I can remember being 'assuaged' with the comment, 'The Southern boys will get in line in due course.'

Columbia's idea of promotion was to issue a single of his less radio-friendly version of 'Blowin' in the Wind' a month after Peter, Paul and Mary scaled the charts with it. Ironically, Dylan's best support, record company-wise, was now coming from Warners and Vanguard, thanks to the gradual ransacking of his song catalog by the likes of Peter, Paul and Mary, Odetta, and Joan Baez. Despite Columbia, and at least one highly critical review from a previously supportive quarter, *Freewheelin'* finally cracked the *Billboard* album charts the first week in September, where it would remain for some thirty-two weeks, peaking at twenty-two.

If *The Freewheelin' Bob Dylan* had taken a few months to get up a head of steam, it had been mostly by word of mouth that sales accrued. Few in the mainstream press reviewed the album, and in the folk world, though he had *Sing Out*'s unequivocal endorsement, it had garnered one unexpectedly hostile review from Minneapolis's own *Little Sandy Review*. Back in 1962, when reviewing his first album (favorably), *Little Sandy Review* editors Paul Nelson and Jon Pankake exhorted Dylan to avoid the 'topical song' vein: 'We sincerely hope that Dylan will steer clear of the Protesty people, continu[ing] to write songs near the traditional manner, and continu[ing] to develop his mastery of his difficult, delicate, highly personal style.' When he failed to heed their advice, Pankake and Nelson felt it necessary to straighten the young cub out:

A fine local singer recently made a most perceptive remark about the urban folk scene in general, not particularly about Dylan. He said, 'Some singers are 98 percent personality and only two percent folk music, but that two percent is a whole lot better than most of the people in folk music today.' It seems a good summation of *The Freewheelin' Bob Dylan*, an album that, like Arthur Miller's salesman, is 'way out there in the blue, riding on a smile and a shoeshine,' and nothing else. Dylan bases everything here almost 100 percent on his own personality; there is hardly any traditional material, and most of the original material is not particularly folk-derived [sic]. It is pure Bob Dylan (Bob Dylan's dream, as it were), with its foundations in nothing that isn't constantly shifting, searching, and changing. What Dylan needs to do is to square the percentages between traditional and original back to 50–50 (as in his first album) to give some anchor of solidarity to his work; his absurd concoctions and blendings miss their mark here (whereas before they landed dead center), and the album floats away into never-never land, a failure.

Little Sandy Review was, by its own admission, a pissant lil' fanzine aimed at a few hundred subscribers whose bent was the purer strains of traditional American music. However, its comments stung a Dylan who had known and grown with this scene, and when he returned to Minneapolis in mid-July he sought out the editors for a showdown. Though Pankake bailed out of a head-to-head, feeling he had little to prove, Paul Nelson turned up at Tony Glover's apartment on July 17, where he and Dylan got into a friendly but heated discussion about the role of politics in folk music. Nelson once again attempted to convince Dylan to abandon the 'topical song,' which clearly subverted music to the Cause. Dylan insisted that 'politics'—in the widest sense—were the binding force in most of his lyrics, and that social issues 'were more important than music.'

Paul Nelson: After [*Freewheelin'*] we had this debate. I went, Jon didn't go. Tony [Glover] taped it but Tony was interested in getting the songs on tape. When it got interesting he turned on the tape . . . It went on and on. We were sort of the anti-topical-song people, not because we disagreed with it politically but just because we thought it was such shitty art, y'know. These songs were like fish in the barrel stuff. I didn't like the Phil Ochs songs much . . . It's like patting yourself on the back music, it just seemed so obvious and not particularly well done. And Dylan was arguing, 'No, no, this is really where it's at.' But he also made the point that the easiest way to get published if you wrote your own songs was to write topical songs 'cause *Broadside* wouldn't publish if you didn't, and you had a tough time getting in *Sing Out*. Jon just didn't want to go, he figured it right, 'If you go, you're gonna have twenty of Dylan's friends all aiming their guns at your head, and he's gonna be out to wipe you out.' [But] we did take this stand against topical songs, 'We oughta go and answer it,' and I think he respected me for coming . . . And he was kinda drunk and really brilliant that night and he was out to impress everybody, and I wasn't a very impressive talker and he wiped the floor with me—with the one exception. I kept saying, 'You're way too talented to be in this blind alley. You can only express A thru B by writing [like] this. Why would you want to stay there?' . . . 'And you won't,' I said. But it didn't take a genius to figure that. But we sorta made friends that night, because I showed up and because I did *argue* and I didn't cave in. But he out-argued me a hundred to one. He was really a brilliant talker then. He'd play 'Who Killed Davey Moore' and he'd say, 'Whaddya think about that?' 'I don't like it much.' And everybody would give me a hard time. And Dylan'd say, 'You've almost got it.' But it was a very uncomfortable night.

The respect Nelson perceived Dylan developing for him that night was not his imagination working overtime. Dylan didn't want Nelson to cave in because, in truth, he was arguing with his own soul, seeking to convince his Gemini self of the position he was taking. The following May, in a letter to Irwin Silber at *Sing Out,* Dylan asked after 'good critic Paul.' Nelson had taken up the offer to work at *Sing Out* in New York, where he would be when it came time to champion Dylan's inevitable change of heart.

Interestingly enough—though Dylan sought to prove his argument that night by playing Nelson his latest finger-pointing songs—'Only a Pawn in Their Game,' 'With God on Our Side,' and 'Who Killed Davey Moore?'—he also played his friends another new song, 'Eternal Circle,' that went beyond B. That night in Minneapolis Dylan won the argument with Nelson, but he lost it with himself. His last topical song was only a couple of months away, as the truths he felt the need to express began to assert themselves in opposition to the historical facts.

In September Dylan visited Baez again, at her home in Carmel, prior to sharing the stage with her at the Hollywood Bowl. His ostensible purpose was to find some necessary solitude, in order to write some more songs for his third album, even though he had fourteen already in the can—not that Suze greatly cared to listen to his lies anymore. And writing songs *was* one activity that occupied him in Carmel.

One song he wrote during his September idyll was another tale of the death of a black person, one Hattie Carroll, at the hands of a white man, William Zantzinger. A brilliant evocation of the kind of miscarriage of justice the color of a woman's skin could bring, 'Hattie Carroll' was Dylan's 'Vanity of Human Wishes,' a grand statement undercut by its tenuous grasp on the facts of the case. The man who, nine months earlier, had been walking 'in the pre-dawn London fog' with Richard Fariña, berating Baez because 'she's still singin' about "Mary Hamilton" . . . where's that at?,' was now sitting in her cabin, writing a ballad utilizing that very tune, and with as sound a relationship to circumstance as the largely apocryphal story of the 'Four Maries.'

Dylan's portrait of William Zantzinger in 'The Lonesome Death of Hattie Carroll' verges on the libelous, depicting him as a privileged son who killed a black maid, Hattie Carroll, by striking her with his cane at a Baltimore 'society gathering,' escaping with a nominal sentence because of his political connections. The reality of the case is that 24-year-old Zantzinger got drunk at a party and began tapping people with a wooden carnival cane. One of the people he tapped was a 51-year-old barmaid with an enlarged heart and severe hypertension. When she questioned his need for another drink, he became verbally abusive. Carroll became very upset, and on returning to the kitchen complained about Zantzinger to a co-worker. She then collapsed, and was taken to hospital, where she died the following morning.

The extent of Zantzinger's 'political connections' was a grandfather who had served on the state planning commission in the thirties. Though Carroll did not die as a result of any blow from Zantzinger, his conduct had played its part in 'a tremendous emotional upsurge' that ultimately killed her, and he was eventually charged with involuntary manslaughter and sentenced to six months in prison. He also paid $25,000 in damages to Carroll's family. Dylan's concern, though, was not the facts themselves but how they might fit his preconceived notions of injustice and corruption. That the song itself is a masterpiece of drama and wordplay does not excuse Dylan's distortions, and thirty-six years on he continues to misrepresent poor William Zantzinger in concert.

Indeed, the finger-pointing songs seemed to be pouring out of him that summer, on any pretext and with one purpose—to proclaim a new order where all are equal, and one can check into a hotel dressed how one wants. 'When the Ship Comes In' was a joyously vengeful lyric about the coming apocalypse written that August, in a fit of pique, in a hotel room, after his unkempt appearance had led an impertinent hotel clerk to refuse him admission until his companion, Joan Baez, had vouched for his good character. This song was debuted, appropriately enough, at the Washington Civil Rights march at the end of the month, to the bemused throng half a million strong. If Mary Hamilton's unjust death sparked Dylan's account of Hattie Carroll's demise, it was 'Jenny's Song' from Brecht and Weill's *Threepenny Opera* that inspired this particular retort. As Pirate Jenny dreams of the destruction of all her enemies by a mysterious ship, so Dylan envisages the neophobes being swept aside in 'the hour when the ship comes in.' If Suze and Bob were drifting apart emotionally, she was still managing to impart her tastes in his direction.

Suze Rotolo: My interest in Brecht was certainly an influence on him. I was working for the Circle in the Square Theater and he came to listen all the time. He was very affected by the song that Lotte Lenya's known for, 'Pirate Jenny.'

With Suze's encouragement, and the gentle prodding of the Van Ronks, both voracious readers, Dylan was starting to expand his intellectual frontiers. While in Britain at the beginning of the year he had begun to read Robert Graves's 'historical grammar of poetic myth,' *The White Goddess,* in which Graves categorically asserted that 'the function of poetry is religious invocation of the Muse.' He also began to immerse himself in the French symbolists—Rimbaud, Baudelaire, and Verlaine.

However, the most important literary resource for this lapsed Jew remained the Bible. 'When the Ship Comes In' betrays considerable knowledge of the good book. Allusions to the apocalyptic tracts of the Old Testament abound, as they do in the next song to flow from his typewriter ribbon. Taking as his starting point a line from the Gospel According to Matthew, in which Jesus says of the Last Judgment, 'But many that are first will be last, and the last first,' Dylan wrote a song which fused the anthemic nature of 'Blowin' in the Wind' with the apocalyptic conceit of 'A Hard Rain's A-Gonna Fall.'

'The Times They Are A-Changin',' though, had a self-consciousness these two earlier works lacked, as if it had been written to form. In September, Tony Glover came to visit Dylan at his apartment on 4th Street. He was in town to make an album for Elektra with Dylan's other Dinkytown pal, 'Spider' John Koerner. The night at Glover's place in July had not been forgotten. Indeed, Dylan had written an eloquent defense of his position in an open letter to Glover, and enclosed it in the program notes to the 1963 Newport Folk Festival.

When he got to the apartment that day, Glover recalls seeing some typed pages of song lyrics and poems lying on Dylan's table. Picking one up, he read a line from a new song: 'Come senators, congressmen, please heed the call.' Turning to Dylan he said, 'What is this shit, man?' Dylan simply shrugged his shoulders and said, 'Well, you know, it seems to be what the people like to hear.' It would take another thirty years for the song to find its true home—in a TV advertisement for a Canadian merchant bank.

'The Times They Are A-Changin'' was rapidly adopted by causes far wider than the civil rights activists. The rebellious young considered it a song as much about the generation gap as about liberal and conservative forces. Dylan would once again be forced to emphasize a wider meaning.

Bob Dylan: It happened that maybe those were the only words I could find to separate aliveness from deadness. It had nothing to do with age. [1964]

Bob Dylan: I can't really say that adults don't understand young people any more than you can say big fishes don't understand little fishes. I didn't mean it as a statement . . . It's a feeling. [1965]

If Dylan needed warning about the hard and fast image he was developing as a civil rights activist, an interview in the left-wing *National Guardian,* conducted by editor Jack Smith, should have provided it. Having talked for twenty minutes about his youth and twenty minutes about the civil rights struggle, the *National Guardian* inevitably chose to concentrate on the latter:

Bob Dylan: I don't think when I write. I just react and put it down on paper. I'm serious about everything I write. For instance, I get mad when I see friends of mine sitting in Southern jails, getting their heads beat in. What comes out in my music is a call to action. [1963]

Though he moaned to friends about the way he had been portrayed in the *National Guardian* piece, topical songs continued to dominate his art. 'The Lonesome Death of Hattie Carroll,' 'When the Ship Comes In,' and 'The Times They Are A-Changin'' were the first three songs he attempted to record when he resumed making his third album, the third week in October, at his familiar Columbia stamping ground, Studio A. If the recording of *Freewheelin'* spanned a whole year of Dylan's life, *Times* came almost as an afterthought. Ten of the songs recorded for *Times* had been written prior to the final *Freewheelin'* session—though only three of these would make the final sequence: 'Hollis Brown,' 'With God on Our Side,' and 'Boots of Spanish Leather'; and none of these matched the quartet of songs cut at the April session and placed on *Freewheelin'*.

Though fourteen songs had been recorded at three sessions in August, only six of these were under serious consideration for the album. When Dylan entered Studio A on October 23, he had with him another six songs to add to the August cache, more than enough for a strong successor. Unfortunately, perhaps the two best songs, 'Percy's Song' and 'Lay Down Your Weary Tune,' would not make the final album, failing to fit within the narrow bounds Dylan had decided to impose on himself. 'Percy's Song,' along with the August outtakes of 'Seven Curses' and 'Moonshine Blues,' showed that Dylan's command of traditional themes, housed in traditional melodies, remained undiminished by the topicality of other efforts.

'Lay Down Your Weary Tune' was something quite different. Along with 'Eternal Circle,' which he attempted at both August and October sessions, it marked a new phase in Dylan's songwriting. It is the all-important link between the clipped symbolism of 'A Hard Rain's A-Gonna Fall' and the more self-conscious efforts to come the following year. A celebration of song itself, 'Lay Down Your Weary Tune' was also an admission that there were certain songs 'no voice can hope to hum.' With this almost pantheistic expression of the power of nature, his muse sought to lead him down 'yon narrow road . . . thick beset wi' thorns and briers.' But the twenty-two-year-old had yet to learn to fully place his faith in the sweet lady.

As such, the album ended up being given over largely to recent finger-pointing songs, with just two 'invocations of the muse,' in both cases an errant muse who had broken the singer's heart ('Boots of Spanish Leather' and the exquisite 'One Too Many Mornings'), and a single act of introspection in a traditional style ('North Country Blues'). The one burning question that remained, as Dylan wrapped up the 'final' session with a Mexican piano rag and a cough, was how to close out such an unremitting catalog of hard times and moral outrages. After all, an album containing 'The Ballad of Hollis Brown,' 'North Country Blues,' 'Only a Pawn in Their Game,' 'With God on Our Side,' and 'The Lonesome Death of Hattie Carroll' could hardly be said to paint an unduly optimistic view of the world. The stark black-and-white cover, shot by Mary Travers's husband, Barry Feinstein, only served to reinforce its mono-chromatic feel.

It was a more rounded Dylan on show at Carnegie Hall two days after that final session. As with his Town Hall concert in April, he used his Carnegie Hall show—a sell-out—to present a new Dylan, though this time he *did* perform 'Blowin' in the Wind.' More importantly, he performed eight of the songs scheduled for his third album, and four further songs he'd recorded for *Times*. The fans who attended the show must have been very disappointed when the album appeared without 'Lay Down Your Weary Tune,' 'Percy's Song,' and 'Seven Curses,' all of which he performed superbly that night. He even had his parents fly in from Hibbing to see his triumph.

Beatty Zimmerman: We knew he was gifted when we went to Carnegie Hall . . . We stayed for a few days and we knew that he was really enjoying what he was doing, and that was important to us.

One wonders what the Zimmermans thought of one of their son's latest compositions, 'North Country Blues,' debuted that night at Carnegie Hall. Told in the third-person guise of a miner's mother, it is a blunt evocation of the North Country mines from the time 'when the red iron pits ran plenty' until 'the mining gates [were] locked and the red iron rotted.' Though almost no one in the audience that night knew of Dylan's Minnesotan roots, they were about to find out what he meant when he said, 'I am my words.'

From the Carnegie Hall stage he also chose to lay into part of a review of *Freewheelin'* by *Village Voice* journalist J. R. Goddard, an early champion of Dylan's work. A couple of days earlier, he had taken exception to another journalist's words, unaware that her response would be considerably less stoic than Goddard's. He had reluctantly agreed to be interviewed by *Newsweek* reporter Andrea Svedburg after she had dug up aspects of his Minnesotan past and threatened to use the material if he did not agree to the interview. Meeting up after a day in the studio, their conversation soon deteriorated into a slanging match, and Svedburg decided to proceed with publishing a vicious hatchet job:

Why Dylan . . . should bother to deny his past is a mystery. Perhaps he feels it would spoil the image he works so hard to cultivate . . . He says he hates the commercial side of folk music, but he has two agents who hover about him . . . He scorns the press, but wants to know how long a story about him will run. . .

The unveiling of his Hibbing past was only a minor (and inevitable) deconstruction of previous myth-making, long ago figured out by those who knew him well.

Eve MacKenzie: One time I asked him about his background. He said he was from New Mexico. I said, 'Do you have parents there?' He said, 'No. I had a lot of foster parents.' I said, 'What was the name of your last foster parents?' He said, 'Aw, there were so many of them I don't rightly remember.'

Svedburg, though, also brought up a story that had recently been circulating, of a high-school graduate named Lorre Wyatt writing 'Blowin' in the Wind' and selling it to Dylan for a thousand dollars. While Svedburg carefully avoided saying Wyatt *had* written the song, she sought to sow seeds of doubt by aspersion and implication. Because the interview had been brokered through Billy James, Dylan appeared to blame him for what he saw as a setup. When the article appeared a couple of days after his Carnegie Hall triumph, he was straight on the phone to James, brandishing threats.

Billy James: Dylan got angry with me. 'I don't want to meet any of your friends. You say you're my friend. Well, if you're my friend you'll know

I'm a writer and all I need is my pen . . . I oughta come up there and punch you.' . . . Later John Koerner told me that Albert had tried to get me fired for that . . . See, there was this snide, vengeful aspect to the story. It may have forever colored his relationship with reporters and editors.

Dylan was barely any calmer when he got through to Bob Shelton, persuading him to pen a letter to *Newsweek* questioning their journalistic standards. He told Shelton, 'I'm sticking to my friends from here on in.' And he remained true to his word. As James astutely observes, the *Newsweek* story 'forever colored his relationship' with the media. The new Dylan would turn on the press before they could turn on him. But he was still going to have to get used to the media painting portraits of him that he did not, or chose not to, recognize. As it was, his only available response lay in song. And it was to song that he turned to pierce Svedburg's 'dust of rumors' with his first truth-attack-in-song, and his first outline for an epitaph.

1963: Troubled and He Don't Know Why

7

The time can't be found t fit / all the things that I want t do.

—*Bob Dylan, 1963*

One immediate consequence of Svedburg's provocative open letter was that Dylan returned to Columbia's New York studios on the final day of October to record a direct response. The epitaph-in-song he'd written was based on a traditional Irish drinking song called 'The Parting Glass.' Originally called 'Bob Dylan's Restless Epitaph,' and with the above two-line introduction, it suggested that, at the age of twenty-two, Dylan already felt time was not on his side. 'Restless Farewell' gave fair warning that he was no longer content to remain the Woody Guthrie of his generation.

Dylan may even have envisaged a restless farewell to song. In the next three months, he would write a profusion of other 'epitaphs' (eleven of which would appear on the back cover, and as a special insert, to his third album) but none of them carried melodies, original or appropriated. The only new song that he appears to have recorded during this period was a publishers' demo (possibly written earlier) of the ironic 'Guess I'm Doing Fine,' in which he halfheartedly seeks to convince himself that he should count his blessings.

That 'Restless Farewell,' a first-person plea for understanding, was scheduled to close out an album of third-person topical songs was doubly ironic. It would be 1971 before Dylan would write another finger-pointer. Unfortunately, with his third album barely recorded, he had little choice but to present the persona he had seemed so determined to defend four months earlier as the current Bob Dylan. It was an identity he was increasingly uncomfortable with, especially after the chilling assassination of President John F. Kennedy in Dallas three weeks after he completed his album. Dylan later told Anthony Scaduto that he played a show in upstate New York the day after the assassination and he began, as always, with 'The Times They Are A-Changin',' 'That song was just too much for the day after the assassination . . . I couldn't understand . . . why I wrote that song, even.' With the song not even commercially released, it had already been superseded by events. Perhaps writing for the moment was consigning his art *to* the moment.

With his responsibilities to Columbia completed for another year, Dylan withdrew from public gaze for three weeks at the end of October. He stayed at Grossman's upstate retreat, hung out with Terri and Dave Van Ronk and Barry Kornfeld, and wrote a lot of poetry. He had come to feel he could best express the thoughts still knotting up his mind if he did not have to deal with the restrictions that song imposed. Already, he was looking for a way to step out of the traditional forms that had, so far, framed his songs. Already, he knew that his third album had been treading the same troubled waters as its predecessor. On the day he set about recording his next album, he discussed the constrictions the song form imposed with the trustworthy Nat Hentoff.

Bob Dylan: It's hard being free in a song—getting it all in. Songs are so confining. Woody Guthrie told me once that songs don't have to do anything like that. But it's not true. A song has to have some kind of form to fit into the music. You can bend the words and the meter, but it still has to fit somehow. I've been getting freer in the songs I write, but I still feel confined. That's why I write a lot of poetry, if that's the word. Poetry can make its own form. [1964]

Dylan enjoyed writing the occasional free-form piece and, like Woody, he used an innate rhythmic sense as a substitute for rhyme. The talking blues had in many ways been his first attempts at free poetry. Indeed he had penned a talking blues on the page for Izzy Young back in March 1962. 'Talkin' Folklore Center' and 'Go 'Way Bomb,' another piece for the page written for Young, seem to have been his two earliest attempts at the freestanding word. By the following April, when he presented two rambling poems to the audience at his Town Hall show, he had hit upon a style that suited him. The bio-poem 'My Life in a Stolen Moment' was included in the Town Hall concert program, while 'Last Thoughts on Woody Guthrie' was performed as an encore at the show, the only known example of Dylan actually reading his poetry aloud. He sounds mighty nervous, and it is interesting that the experiment was never attempted again.

'My Life in a Stolen Moment,' regularly reprinted in concert programs and bookleg productions prior to the *Writings & Drawings* collection, is a surprisingly straightforward account of his past. Though embroidered to include the myth of running away as a child, and taking the typically anti-intellectual stance of attending university 'on a phoney scholarship

that I never had,' most of the poem rings true, save most obviously for
an outrageous travelogue where young Bobby, between Minneapolis
and New York, manages to take in Texas, California, Oregon, Washington, New Mexico, and Louisiana. He refers to learning to play guitar, to
sing, and to write, 'but I never ever did take the time to find out why.'
'My Life in a Stolen Moment' was the start of a yearlong flirtation with
a form of rambling proetry. In that time he willingly contributed to
concert programs, album sleeves—his own and friends'—even to magazines published by friends.

Bob Dylan: I used to get scared that I wouldn't be around much longer,
so I'd write my poems down on anything I could find—the backs of my
albums, the backs of Joan's albums, anywhere I could find. [1965]

He also wrote and rewrote sections of some prototypical biography
along similar lines, a series of 'Incidents in a Stolen Moment.' In a
memorable statement to Studs Terkel on his Chicago radio show, a
couple of weeks after the Town Hall concert, Dylan suggested that he
had already begun to apply himself seriously to the task:

Bob Dylan: It's about my first week in New York . . . It's about somebody
who has come to the end of one road, knows there's another road there but
doesn't exactly know where it is, and knows he can't go back on this one
road . . . It's got all kinds of . . . thoughts in my head . . . I'd never been to
New York before, and I'm still carrying these memories with me. So I
decided to write it all down. [1963]

That the process was ongoing is seemingly confirmed by what appears
to be a two-page excerpt from the same 'autobiography' among the
so-called Margolis & Moss manuscripts, acquired by Graham Nash in
1989 but dating from the fall of 1963. The 120-line typescript takes the
form of college recollections, specifically about the 1959 Christmas
vacation, which he wanted to spend with Judy Rubin. It is a surprisingly
frank account of remembered feelings:

I love judy. judy says she loves me but she also says she's busy. I told her I
love her . . . I hate her cause I sence [sic] she don't love me . . . I wish I
didn't love her I wish she'd invite me for christmas for christ's sake.

The poem ends with Dylan phoning Judy, losing his cool, insulting
her, and having her hang up on him. He admits that 'girls have hung up

on me an have hung me up as far back as I remember . . . each one promises t be the last.' As a coda to his musings upon that Christmas, he unleashes one of many tirades directed at those willing to go through with the indignities attendant upon a college education:

what I saw connected with the fraternity house summed up the whole established world . . . underpants . . . cats standin in underpants being inspected by others with serious looks in their eyes . . . jive wide smiles in hairy sweaters . . . what the fuck thats got t do with learnin I never will know . . . never hope to either.

This particular rant coincides with Dylan's description to Terkel of the kind of 'thoughts' he wanted his autobiography to contain:

Bob Dylan: All about teachers and school and all about hitchhikers around the country . . . college kids going to college it's got and these are all people that I knew every one of them's sort of a symbol for all kinds of people. [1963]

The autobiographical 'excerpt' is part of a sheaf of papers that appear to date from the weeks following President Kennedy's assassination on November 22, 1963. As Dylan was struggling to find ways of expressing his many frustrations, he was working on the eleven poems that would later form the sleeve notes to his third album. These 'Eleven Outlined Epitaphs' would require an insert with the album, such was the stream of free-form proetry flowing from his pen at this point.

In Epitaph Two, Dylan again recalls his youth in Hibbing, clearly something he was coming to terms with in the wake of *Newsweek*'s public disrobing of his past, for the benefit of 'unknowin eyes.' In Epitaph Four he is questioning Jim (presumably Jim Forman of the Emergency Civil Liberties Committee) about the validity of party politics. In Epitaph Six he ponders how and why Woody Guthrie was his last idol. Epitaph Eight is the confession of a self-acknowledged plagiarist: 'Yes, I am a thief of thoughts / not, I pray, a stealer of souls.' Epitaph Nine is a further attack upon Svedburg and her ilk, debunking the journalistic exposé by pointing out that he exposes himself 'every time I step out on stage.'

The final two epitaphs seem more conciliatory variants on 'Bob Dylan's Restless Epitaph,' expositions indeed on that song. Here, as there, he seeks to recall the wrongs he may have committed, the causes fought, and the battles lost. Three albums into his career, Dylan was already trying to relive hard times. In the tenth epitaph he muses on whether the cockroaches 'still crawl' around Dave and Terri Van Ronk's apartment. Not that his autobiographical musings at this time were restricted to his outlined epitaphs or unpublished bio-poems. Sleeve notes that he wrote for Peter, Paul and Mary's second album recollected his first New York winter: 'Snow was piled up the stairs an onto the street that / first winter when I laid around New York City / it was a different street then.'

A couple of months earlier he had composed the most ambitious of his bio-poems for another album sleeve. Presumably written in September, when he was staying with Joan Baez in Carmel, the poem appeared in October on the rear of her *In Concert 2* album. It starts in Hibbing, with a young Zimmerman crouching on the grass, watching the trains roll by. Passing through a time when his adopted idols were role models—choosing his idols 't be my voice an tell my tale'—he finally transcends them ('I learned that they were only men / An had reasons for their deeds'). He begins to define his own terms, like beauty—'the only beauty's ugly, man'—before learning to recognize beauty in all forms, pure and impure. The coda, in which he realizes that the pure Baez caterwaul might somehow be 'beautiful,' reads like an ill-conceived tag to an otherwise powerful piece of poetry.

Dylan's 'Poem to Joannie' proved that his free-form poems could move to their own rhythm. It gave him new confidence in his free verse as he began to utilize even freer forms in prose-poem letters to friends. Baez has also suggested that much of the material he wrote for his book at her house, but never reclaimed, was equally biographical:

Joan Baez: He wrote some beautiful things about running up to his own house and trying to get in . . . Something about his mother behind the screen door, and he was jumping up—he had to pee . . . He never edited anything. He couldn't bear to take anything out of the sentence he'd written.

But Circumstance proved it still had the power to twist Dylan's visions. As John F. Kennedy got caught in the crossfire of someone else's cause, he was given the same crash course in Realpolitik as the rest of America. He later insisted, 'If I was more sensitive about [the J.F.K. assassination] . . . I would have written a song about it,' as if his post-assassination self couldn't admit to buying into Kennedy's dreamscape in the first place, but at least one eyewitness well remembers sitting with Dylan at Carla Rotolo's apartment the day of the shooting, and the impact it had on someone who had sung out loud at the March on Washington, less than three months earlier:

Bob Fass: We spent some time together the night Kennedy was shot . . . It
affected him very deeply . . . He said, 'What it means is that they are trying
to tell you "Don't even hope to change things." If you try to put yourself
up against the forces of death, the military, forget about it, you're done for.'

Dylan was being disingenuous when he told his first biographer that
Kennedy's death didn't directly inspire any songs. This was because he
had temporarily departed from his chosen path. On the other hand, the
Margolis & Moss manuscripts include several unfinished poems about
the assassination, clearly written as an immediate response to the events
in Dallas. In one he admits 'it is useless t' recall the day once more.' In
another, he uses one image repeatedly to rail against the bullets and
assassin/s: 'there is no right or left there is only up an down.'

Three weeks, to the day, after they shot J.F.K. down, Dylan was
stumbling to express the same feeling to a couple of hundred well-to-do
liberals, using the same idea to inform them, 'There's no black and white,
left and right to me anymore; there's only up and down.' This time he
admitted, 'And down is very close to the ground.' Rather than empathiz-
ing with Dylan's sense of dislocation, the suit-and-tie brigade that was
his audience that night began to boo.

The occasion was a dinner at the Hotel Americana in New York, at
which Dylan was due to receive the annual Tom Paine award for his
contribution to the civil rights struggle, given by the Emergency Civil
Liberties Committee. The dinner proved to be a total fiasco. Dylan was
a poor choice as recipient of such an award, unschooled as he was in the
art of public speaking, and a chronically nervous performer at the best of
times. Surrounded by middle-aged liberals beneficently donating money
for 'the cause', he was immediately uptight and began drinking heavily.
According to Edith Tiger, when it came his turn to speak, she found
him vomiting in the men's toilet. Led to the high table, he announced,
'I haven't got any guitar—I can talk though.' His subsequent speech
proved otherwise. Proclaiming that this was a 'young man's world,' he
then confessed that he saw something of himself in Lee Harvey Oswald,
Kennedy's alleged assassin. Since the dinner was primarily a fund-raiser
for the ECLC, his ill-considered speech cost the committee a considerable amount of money.

Afterwards he penned an open letter, 'A Message to the ECLC,' in
which he set out with the intention of apologizing for his actions, but
ended up doing anything but. Forced to speak publicly, he wrote the
ECLC, 'I tore everything loose from my mind / an said "just be honest,
dylan, just be honest."' He defended his comments concerning Oswald,

insistent that he was 'speaking of the times.' In conclusion, he stated that he was no speaker, and that, in future, he should confine himself to speaking out in song:

I am a writer an a singer of the words I write / I am no speaker nor any politician / an my songs speak for me because I write them / in the confinement of my own mind an have t cope / with no one except my own self.

In less than six months he had turned full circle from the protest singer who baited Paul Nelson into someone determined to write only songs that 'speak for me.' He had been guilty in the recent past of doing no such thing. The ECLC dinner taught Dylan to let the songs do the singing, and leave the talking to speakers and politicians. When, a couple of months later, he finally made his national TV debut on *The Steve Allen Show,* and was asked about 'The Lonesome Death of Hattie Carroll,' he both ducked the question and summarized his position for many years to come by informing Allen, 'If I talked about it, I could talk about it for a very long time; if I sing about it, it would only take as long as the song lasts.'

Dylan's ambitions as a writer for the page, rather than as 'a singer of the words I write,' may have been further fed at the end of December when he met renowned beat poet Allen Ginsberg, author of *Howl* and *Kaddish.* Dylan had first been introduced to Ginsberg's writings back in Minneapolis. Along with the French symbolists, the beats were a primary influence on his development as a songwriter, as he passed from immediate folk sources to a polychrome of literary styles.

Bob Dylan: I didn't start writing poetry until I was out of high school. I was eighteen or so when I discovered Ginsberg, Gary Snyder, Phillip Whalen, Frank O'Hara and those guys. Then I went back and started reading the French guys, Rimbaud and François Villon. [1985]

The meeting had been brokered by *New York Post* journalist Al Aronowitz, who made a habit of introducing leading lights to one another, enjoying the frisson of the moment. Aronowitz was an old friend of Kerouac and Ginsberg, and was more interested in hanging out with Dylan than writing about him, which suited Dylan. They would become friends, though largely on Dylan's terms, in the coming year.

Al Aronowitz: I courted his friendship until it got to a point where it was more important to me to be friends with him than to write about him . . .

You write about someone, and they don't like it when you start really telling the truth.

Ginsberg had only recently returned to New York, and was intrigued to meet the author of 'A Hard Rain's A-Gonna Fall' and 'Masters of War.' Though they discussed poetry, Ginsberg perhaps had other things on his mind.

Al Aronowitz: Allen was really a flaming queer. He came on to everyone I introduced him to—and he came on hard [to Dylan].

Despite his enduring desire to sleep with Bob, Ginsberg turned down Dylan's offer to fly with him to Chicago, where he was due to play the following night, because, in his own words, he was 'afraid I might become his slave or something, his mascot.' The Chicago date was another rung up the ladder, from the Bear Pit to the Orchestra Hall, as Dylan continued to play-act the man depicted on *The Times They Are A-Changin'*.

In private, though, it was the prospect of publishing a book, or maybe staging a play, that now preoccupied him. Dylan makes references to both a novel and a play in a letter to *Broadside* at the beginning of January. The novel was frustrating him: 'it dont even tell a story / it's about a million scenes long / an takes place on a billion scraps / of paper.' It would come to frustrate him a tad more. The play that Dylan was writing seemed to have taken him over, providing a new channel for his artistic energies:

an I'm up to my belly button in it. / quite involved yes / I've discovered the power of playwritin means / as opposed t song writing means / altho both are equal, I'm wrapped in playwritin / for the minute.

The play that occupied Dylan at this point was probably the untitled, unfinished fifteen-page typescript that later emerged as part of the Margolis & Moss papers. The play concerns a number of characters with names like John B. Pimp, Mrs. Agnas McBroad, and Eeny Weeny, who meet in a combination church/barroom/hotel because they have been told they must do so or they will die; it shows that whatever power the play exerted over him, he himself had little control over the play. Little more than a series of portentous conversations, it defied resolution and, at some point, he seems to have moved on to another idea for a play. In May 1964 he informed Max Jones he was working on two plays, and a fragment of another appears among the *Another Side* manuscript material (of which more later). The idea, more than the realization, continued to intrigue him through the first half of 1964.

By the end of January, he was in Canada filming a half-hour TV special for the Canadian Broadcasting Company. While there, he talked to two Canadian journalists, informing both that he was working on a novel and a play, telling the journalist from *Gargoyle* magazine that the play would be finished before the novel, and that he wanted to see it performed. The novel as a project, though, would endure considerably longer than either play, even if it passed from quasi-autobiography to a more nebulous form of wordplay as contractual demands began to formalize. Dylan himself has always liked to give the impression that he was cajoled into producing a book after the success of John Lennon's two collections of whimsical prose and verse (*In His Own Write* and *A Spaniard in the Works*):

Bob Dylan: I was doing interviews before and after concerts, and reporters would say things like 'What else do you write?' And I would say, 'Well I don't write much of anything else.' And they would say, 'Oh, come on. You must write other things. Tell us something else. Do you write books?' And I'd say, 'Sure, I write books.' After the publishers saw that I wrote books, they began to send me contracts . . . We took the biggest one, and then owed them a book. [1969]

In truth, it was Dylan who fancied himself to be an author of sorts, talking up the autobiographical novel to interviewers until he had not one but two contracts on which he was expected to deliver. If the book he had originally discussed with Studs Terkel in April 1963 had been no surreal voyage through language, but rather loosely historical, by the winter of 1964, the project had changed. In the fall of 1963, Dylan had met beat poet Lawrence Ferlinghetti and discussed the possibility of producing a book for City Lights, publishers of poets. A City Lights book carried a certain prestige. However, by April 1964 he still had not forwarded any manuscript. Writing to Ferlinghetti about the 'material' he had accumulated, he betrayed the seeds of confusion that would leave his literary ambitions unrealized:

I do got things of songs an stories for you. my hangup is tho that I know there will be more. I want t send the more more then I want t send the got. yes I guess that's it. [1964]

Meanwhile, he found himself contracted to produce a series of little vignettes to accompany a quite different book, a collection of photos of the 'old Hollywood' at its *fin de siècle*, taken by Barry Feinstein—husband of Mary Travers and the man responsible for the stark portrait of Dylan about to grace the *Times They Are A-Changin'* cover—between 1958 and 1962, when he worked first for Columbia Pictures and then as a freelancer in Hollywood. According to Feinstein, he had already secured a contract with Macmillan when he approached Dylan to provide brief 'commentaries.' Dylan, having agreed to the task, discussed the book with *Melody Maker*'s Max Jones in London in May.

Bob Dylan: It's just pictures and the words I'm going to write that [not so much] coincide with the photographer's, but somehow fall into the same direction or mood. All the pictures were shot in Hollywood: shots of everything, a whole picture of Hollywood from the beautiful sign on the hill to Marlon Brando speaking while someone holds up a sign saying Nigger-Lover. [1964]

Whatever problems Dylan had conceptualizing his own book, he had no such problem with Feinstein's, delivering his text with a minimum of fuss, only to find that the publishers were nervous about the controversial nature of some of its content: an image of the sign behind the bar at Barney's Beanery reading 'Fagots [sic] stay out'; of the exact bottle of pills that killed Marilyn Monroe, sitting empty on a table; and the photo Dylan described, of Brando on a CORE march, as a young punk walks alongside, carrying a banner saying, 'Brando is a Nigger-Lovin' Creep.' In the end, Macmillan passed on the book and reverted the rights to the two parties, leaving the original advance unrecouped.

Where Macmillan editor Bob Markel comes into the picture is not clear. Macmillan was not in a position to demand the return of any monies and, anyway, it was essentially Feinstein's book, not Dylan's. However, at some point, Grossman decided to use the 'in' created at Macmillan to broach the subject of a Bob Dylan book. However much Dylan may have been enticed by having his name in City Lights, Grossman was not about to sign his boy up to such a small operation. Grossman managed to convince senior editor Bob Markel to sign Dylan up for an unspecified project. It was little more than an option on a future work, should there be one.

Bob Markel: I met Albert Grossman before I met Bob Dylan . . . Bob was just beginning to make an impression as a singer and writer. Albert explained to me that he thought Dylan was a very hot property who might want to do a book one day, and that if I were interested, we might be able to work out a contract for a book . . . We gave him an advance for an untitled book of writings . . . The publisher was taking a risk on a young, untested potential phenomenon. In time we'd figure out a book, but it was worth having a contract. He was uncertain what the book would be.

When Markel first met Dylan, Dylan was no nearer defining what his own book might be than when he had written to Ferlinghetti:

Bob Markel: Our first meeting took place in the great big marvelous old downtown Macmillan offices . . . When I spoke to Bob on the telephone he asked that the meeting take place after dark, as he felt he couldn't travel in broad daylight. He was driving a motorcycle around New York in those days . . . There was no book at the time . . . The material at that point was hazy, sketchy. The poetry editor called it 'inaccessible.' The symbolism was not easily understood, but on the other hand it was earthy, filled with obscure but marvelous imagery . . . I felt it had a lot of value and was very different from Dylan's output till then. [But] it was not a book.

It was to remain 'not a book' for some time. If the material at that point was 'inaccessible,' it was as nothing to what Dylan would eventually deliver. But then Dylan's 'obscure but marvelous imagery' had not as yet become shot through with the stuff its author was ingesting. It remained like his other page-bound writings, little more than 'thoughts in my head.' Haphazard ideas from his free-form poetry, though, were beginning to feed back into his songs. At the beginning of February, for the first time on record, he had expressed disenchantment with the topical-song genre:

Bob Dylan: I used to write songs, like I'd say, 'Yeah, what's bad, pick out something bad, like segregation, okay here we go' and I'd pick one of the thousand million little points I can pick and explode it, some of them which I didn't know about. I wrote a song about Emmett Till, which in all honesty was a bullshit song . . . I realize now that my reasons and motives behind it were phoney. I didn't have to write it. [1964]

Though his politically conscious audience may have hoped that this was the statement of someone seeking to transform the genre, he was already looking to transcend it. Though most of his free poetry was bound to stay on the page, a few lines here and there began to sing to

Dylan. In particular, on one of the sheets in the Margolis & Moss papers, attached to a poem about his own response to the Kennedy assassination, was a six-line coda with a familiar ring to it:

the colors of friday were dull / as cathedral bells were gently burnin / strikin for the gentle / strikin for the kind / strikin for the crippled ones / an strikin for the blind.

This reads like a refrain. It is also the onset of a 'chain of flashing images' that, bound together, would form 'Chimes of Freedom,' and then lead on to 'Mr. Tambourine Man,' 'Gates of Eden,' and 'It's Alright Ma (I'm Only Bleeding).' There can be no real doubt which Friday's colors were dull—Friday, November 22. So much for Dylan's assertion that if he had been more sensitive to Kennedy's assassination, he'd have written a song about it! With this sad refrain, Dylan would pass from topical troubadour to poet of the road. After all, he had been away from song too long.

1964: On the Heels of Rimbaud

8

'64 was the year of the greatest Dylan concerts. It was just Bob and Victor Maymudes in a blue Ford station wagon with perpetual bottles of Beaujolais.

—*John Cooke*

Dylan's first trip through the Union, in February 1964, has become something of a cause célèbre. Scaduto, Shelton, and Spitz have each devoted a respectful chunk of pages to the man's own 'on the road' trek. In each instance, their primary source has been Pete Karman's notes and recollections of the trip. Karman seemed like a strange choice for a touring companion in the first place. He was a close friend of Suze and Carla Rotolo, a journalist, and hardly an uncritical fan of Dylan's work. The only plausible reason he was allowed to tag along was to serve as unofficial chronicler (much like Larry Sloman in 1975). Imbued perhaps with the notion that he could yet recreate a beat mythos, Dylan may have felt that the trip portended something important—as indeed it did.

Karman was a meticulous chronicler. When Dylan spent the night with a girl student after his Emory University concert, Karman was there to record it. As a result, when they reached San Francisco, and Dylan's presumably long-awaited liaison with Baez, Karman was sent packing. Dylan later told Shelton, 'We had to kick Pete out and send him home on a plane.' Karman insists he had to pay his own way back. The other two companions on Dylan's trek were more trustworthy, and, above all, 'cool.' Paul Clayton and Victor Maymudes knew how to play his moods.

In less than three years, Clayton had gone from being an important mentor to the very mascot Ginsberg had feared to become. Dylan started out in awe of Clayton, and ended up discarding him, an occasion apparently documented in one of his most poignant songs, 'It's All Over Now, Baby Blue.' Born in New Bedford, Massachusetts, in March 1933, Clayton heard Lead Belly at the age of eleven and immediately acquired a guitar, had his own radio series at fifteen, made his first record at nineteen and had, by the time Dylan recorded Clayton's 'Gotta Travel On' in Karen Moynihan's apartment in May 1960, already recorded some three hundred songs for the likes of Riverside and Folkways. He was a folklorist par excellence, and the acknowledged source of at least two tunes appropriated by Dylan—'Who's Gonna Buy Your Chickens?' and 'The Wind and the Rain,' which spawned 'Don't Think Twice, It's All Right' and 'Percy's Song' respectively.

Unfortunately, Clayton had a speed habit to dwarf those of even the unholiest of Village rounders, and while Dylan and Maymudes were at this point partial themselves to the odd popper, Clayton saw fit to work his way through a veritable medicine cabinet of amphetamines on their February jaunt. If Clayton was along on an expenses-only basis, Maymudes was road manager, his 'official' role being to insure that Dylan made it to the shows, and to use his common sense (and, if necessary, imposing height and stare) to make sure that it was a hassle-free trip Karman ended up documenting.

The twenty-day trek by station wagon, to California from the New York island, first weaved its way through Virginia and North Carolina, where they stopped off to find biographer, historian, poet, and folk collector Carl Sandburg in Hendersonville. Sandburg's *American Songbag* (1927), though more of a ragbag than a thorough overview of American folk song, had been an inspirational resource for nigh on forty years. However, he was apparently unimpressed by Dylan's hard sell of his credentials as a folk poet. In fact, Clayton had far more in common with Sandburg, and one suspects that, of the two albums Sandburg was given that day, it was Clayton's that got played first if either got played at all.

On to South Carolina, Georgia—where Dylan played at Emory University—Mississippi, and Louisiana, where they arrived on the afternoon of the 11th, intent on experiencing that night's New Orleans Mardi Gras. Setting out from New Orleans on the 12th, for the second leg of their journey, Dylan's trio of companions took it in turns to floor the pedal, roaring through Texas, Oklahoma, Kansas, Colorado—where Dylan premiered a new song at a concert at the Denver Civic Auditorium—and on through Utah and Nevada into the Golden State, where he had a few more dates scheduled.

Dylan's own version of this three-week journey through America was typically fanciful. In his version, 'We hit forty-six halls from Augusta, Ga. to Berkeley, Calif. We talked to people in bars, miners. Talking to people—that's where it's at, man.' In fact, he played just three shows, and on the one occasion he came into direct contact with the 'people'— when he stopped at a record shop in Charlottesville, Virginia, and was recognized by fans—he apparently said, 'Man, there's a lot of people in here. Let's split.' He was better able to deal with admirers when expecting public attention, as when he stopped by at the Denver Folklore Center on the day of his Denver concert. He had to accept that he was now a famous figure, and three-week trips spent 'talking to people in bars' were no longer possible.

The primary motivation for the trip was to find enough inspiration to step beyond the folk-song form, if not in the bars, or from the miners, then by peering deep into himself. Dylan regularly sat in the back of the station wagon tapping away at his typewriter, working on songs and, presumably, poems. The song he spent most time working on as they drove down to New Orleans was called 'Chimes of Freedom.' The refrain 'strikin for the gentle / strikin for the kind / strikin for the crippled ones / an strikin for the blind' had obviously been haunting him. As his three companions generally dissuaded Dylan from taking his turn at the wheel, knowing him to be a notoriously bad driver, he was free to complete the song in time to debut it at the Denver concert on the 15th.

In many ways the antecedents of 'Chimes of Freedom' can be found in the material discarded from his third album. Its sense of the power of nature—the song is set during a storm, as two friends or lovers huddle in a church doorway witnessing 'the chimes of freedom flashing'—closely mirrors 'Lay Down Your Weary Tune.' Unashamedly apocalyptic, it no longer advocates the chosen-few exclusivity of 'The Times They Are A-Changin'' or 'When the Ship Comes In.' The song is sung 'for every hung-up person in the whole wide universe.' The composition of 'Chimes of Freedom' represented a leap in form that permitted even more intensely poetic songs to burst forth.

He undoubtedly worked on other songs on the trip, though nothing that self-evidently made it into the canon, even if taking lines of poetry to spark a song was beginning to become a working methodology. While in New Orleans, Karman recalls Dylan speed-talking in elliptical, flashing images: 'No one's free, even the birds are chained to the sky.' The line would have to wait three months to find its place in a song.

According to Dylan, in the notes accompanying *Biograph,* he also began 'Mr. Tambourine Man' in New Orleans—two months before his first documented acid trip. The Pied Piper aspect of 'Mr. Tambourine Man' certainly ties in with Dylan's experience of the Mardi Gras, as he wandered the streets, frequenting bars, following the sounds. As the Mardi Gras stretched through the night and into the early hours of the morning, 'skippin' reels of rhyme' continued to haunt the streets, until the Dylan party collapsed into dreams. At such times visions would come with relative ease, Dylan later saying he got 'some amazing projections' from staying up all night. However, 'Tambourine Man' remained just another 'amazing projection' for the moment, one more thought hinted at in some other kinds of song, as when he wandered N'Awlins with 'joe b. stuart / white southern poet . . . arm in arm / stoned galore.'

Another kind of song was breaking out during Dylan's February trek, as America was shaken by a new wave of popular music from the other side of the pond. The record that most occupied the airwaves that month was the Beatles' first US number one, 'I Wanna Hold Your Hand.' If the Beatles' incursion into American culture was about to redefine rock & roll, Dylan had already been keeping tabs on them, probably since their American TV debut in November 1963, filmed in concert from the English coastal enclave of Bournemouth.

At the time, though, Dylan seems to have been put off by the hype that already surrounded the Fab Four. On the other hand, Suze Rotolo and Al Aronowitz got into them immediately, and began to champion their sound to Dylan, even as, in Aronowitz's words, Dylan 'tried to put them down as bubblegum.' Legend has it that Dylan first heard 'I Wanna Hold Your Hand' in Colorado, and that he stopped the car, running around it, banging his head on the bonnet and shouting, 'It's great!' A mite overenthusiastic for our Bob, but the song undoubtedly struck home.

Bob Dylan: We were driving through Colorado, we had the radio on, and eight of the Top 10 songs were Beatles songs . . . 'I Wanna Hold Your Hand,' all those early ones. They were doing things nobody was doing. Their chords were outrageous, just outrageous, and their harmonies made it all valid. You could only do that with other musicians . . . I knew they were pointing the direction of where music had to go. [1971]

If evidence of the sorry state of American pop music at this time should be required, the five number ones on the Hot One Hundred before the Beatles' onslaught were Jimmy Gilmer and the Fireballs, Nino Tempo and April Stevens, Dale and Gracie, the Singing Nun, and Bobby Vinton. No wonder the folkies held pop music in such contempt! Dylan would later claim that 'the English thing' not only returned rock & roll to its former status, but that folk music had only ever been 'a substitute.'

Bob Dylan: All you heard [back in the late fifties] was rock & roll and country & western and rhythm & blues music. Now, at a certain time the whole field got taken over into some milk(?), you know—into Frankie Avalon, Fabian and this kind of thing . . . So everybody got out of it. And I remember when everybody got out of it. And then folk music came in as some kind of substitute for a while, but it was only a substitute . . . Now it's different again, because of the English thing . . . What the English thing did was, they proved that you could make money at playing the same old kind of music that you used to play. [1966]

Though it is hard to believe that Dylan ever believed folk music to be a substitute for anything, on his return to New York in March he immediately rented himself an electric guitar. Meanwhile, across that lonesome ocean, the Beatles were spending part of January trying to woo a surprisingly resistant French market with a week of shows at the Paris Olympia. They, too, were on the lookout for something new when George Harrison returned to their hotel one day with a Bob Dylan album—*En Roue Libre*.

George Harrison: We got a copy of *Freewheelin'* and we just played it, just wore it [out]. The content of the song lyrics and just the attitude!

On February 22, as the Beatles returned home from their first American sortie, Dylan was playing a sell-out concert at the Berkeley Community Theater. Apart from a brief appearance at the Monterey Folk Festival the previous May and a badly received guest slot at Baez's Hollywood Bowl show in the fall, he had not played in California, and the level of anticipation for the concert was unseasonably high. As Richard Fariña recalled, in his essay 'A Generation Singing Out,' it was as if the students 'seemed, occasionally, to believe he might not actually come, that some malevolent force or organization would get in the way.' Only Clayton's or Maymudes's erratic driving threatened to 'get in the way.' In the end, though, they made San Francisco with a day to spare.

Dylan's performance that night may not have had the impact of the Beatles' US debut, but it was a stunning tour de force that even convinced respected *San Francisco Chronicle* jazz critic Ralph J. Gleason to recant a previous dismissal. Dylan gave his hip West Coast audience a foretaste of new directions by performing 'Chimes of Freedom' and 'Eternal Circle.' Inevitably, Baez donated her dulcet tones for a few duets, but Dylan no longer required her endorsement. Though he dedicated a song to her in Los Angeles, he did not join her on stage at any of her shows that winter. And yet, returning to her home in Carmel for a few days after the brief West Coast tour at the end of February, he was seemingly still prepared to continue—or perhaps disinclined to discontinue—their romance.

Suze, though, had had enough of Dylan's double values. Happy to gallivant around the States on a steady diet of sex, drugs, and topical folk, he remained fiercely possessive. The argument that finally ended their stormy relationship came almost immediately on his return from California, at Carla's Perry Street apartment, where Suze was now encamped. When they were interrupted by Carla's return, Dylan turned on Carla, accusing her of setting Suze against him. Suze finally just 'freaked out.'

Barry Kornfeld: [Paul Clayton and I] walked in and there was Carla practically foaming at the mouth, Dylan practically foaming at the mouth, and Suze sitting in bed, literally in shock. Suze had just sort of tuned out. Bob and Carla were still going at it—they were both totally incoherent.

Carla ordered Dylan out of the apartment and, though he later returned in a desperate attempt at reconciliation, Suze's mother Mary arrived just in time, to snatch her from his arms. With Mary's intervention, their romance was officially over. Looking back on their relationship now, Suze is remarkably forgiving of Dylan. She recognizes that the nature of his ever-increasing fame—and a certain inner hunger for that status— altered their relationship irrevocably, and made it impossible for them to work out their problems by themselves.

Suze Rotolo: We were young and vulnerable. A lot of crazy things happened. It is strange to think that so much is made of us together in those years. It could have run its course naturally, but it was shaded and formed by all these outside influences, because of his growing fame . . . He began snubbing his old friends. But it was all so understandable in an odd way. He could see these things happening to him and he wanted to make sure they would happen, so . . . he didn't have time to just hang out anymore . . . There was a period when I was part of his possessions. I don't think he wanted me to do anything separate from him. He wanted me to be completely one hundred percent a part of what he was.

Dylan was distraught. However badly he had behaved towards Suze, he still loved her, and found it hard to accept her loss. Neither the gradual emotional detachment indicated by her time in Italy, nor her moving in with Carla, had impinged on his consciousness enough to allow him to accept his fate with good grace. Nor did he turn to the more-than-welcoming arms of Baez in his grief, but looked for more chemical solutions to his emotional imbalance.

Al Aronowitz: For him, it was a long step farther into loneliness.

Bob Dylan: After Suze moved out of the house . . . I got very, very strung out for a while. I mean, really, very strung out. [1966]

The idea of a 'very strung out' Dylan as early as the spring of 1964 raises a number of questions, the two most pressing, in biographical terms, being: one, how bound up was his adoption of the Rimbaudian creed of the 'disordering of the senses' with a new level of drug experimentation, and two, what relationship, if any, was there between hallucinogenics and the breakthrough that came with 'Mr. Tambourine Man'?

Just as his life became more chaotic and his poetry more self-conscious, Dylan began to take upon himself the visionary mantle Rimbaud demanded of the true poet: 'The poet makes himself a seer by a long, prodigious and rational disordering of the senses . . . He reaches [for] the unknown and even if, crazed, he ends up by losing the understanding of his visions, at least he has seen them.' So had an adolescent Rimbaud written to his old teacher Georges Izambard in May 1871, when the options were limited to absinthe and opium. In February 1964, when Dylan was shuttling between Beaujolais, grass, and speed, he was telling his companions, 'Rimbaud's where it's at. That's the kind of stuff means something. That's the kind of writing I'm gonna do.' He seems to have been true to his word.

In 'Mr. Tambourine Man' the singer certainly seems to be searching for that 'dérèglement de tous les sens' of which Rimbaud wrote so eloquently. It is this that will open him up to the unknown, and through which he must follow the Rimbaudian seer onto his magic swirlin' ship (Dylan's version of Rimbaud's drunken boat). With 'Mr. Tambourine Man' Dylan leapt beyond the boundaries of folk song once and for all, with one of his most inventive and *original* melodies. Inevitably, many have seen 'Mr. Tambourine Man' as evidence that the 'long, prodigious and rational disordering of the senses' was being nudged along by copious amounts of drugs—specifically, LSD (lysergic acid diethylamide), first synthesized in 1938 and legal in the US until 1966.

The only source prepared to date Dylan's first hit of acid is producer Paul Rothchild, who told Bob Spitz that it was after a show at Amherst College, Mass., in April 1964, and that it was in the company of Maymudes and himself that Dylan learned to tune in to the eternal rhythms. Certainly Victor and Bob were no longer satisfied with 'perpetual bottles of Beaujolais,' though knowledge of Dylan's early drug experiments continues to be clouded by his penchant for exaggerating his own kingdom of experience.

Al Aronowitz: When I first met Dylan he told me he had been a junkie. I don't know. [But] we all used to smoke marijuana . . . He wrote ['Mr. Tambourine Man'] at my house. He stayed up all night listening to music and had it the next morning. He threw out all his reject slips in the garbage. I picked them up and put them in a file.

When not on the road in the blue Ford station wagon that spring, Dylan would, as often as not, stay at Aronowitz's apartment in the city. After finding out Suze didn't want to live with him no more, Dylan was finding it hard to live with himself. 'Mr. Tambourine Man' was finally penned some time between the middle of March and the end of April. The drugs-explain-inspiration brigade would doubtless prefer a composition date during the week and a half between his Amherst concert and a brief trip to Monterey in early May. Dylan himself later insisted that the drugs *never* prompted a song, they only kept him 'up' long enough to pump them out, a clear reference to the copious amounts of speed that force-fed his nocturnal writings. But there is an undeniable trippiness to 'Tambourine Man' that extends beyond mere lyrical references, even if Dylan insists, in his *Biograph* notes, that he began 'Tambourine Man' in New Orleans, two months before he encountered LSD, and that it was directly inspired by an instrument Bruce Langhorne was known to brandish:

Bob Dylan: On one session, Tom Wilson had asked [Bruce] to play tambourine. And he had this gigantic tambourine . . . It was as big as a wagonwheel. He was playing, and this vision of him playing this tambourine just stuck in my mind. [1985]

My initial response on reading this was to place the man's explanation alongside the one that 'Tangled Up in Blue' was inspired by Joni Mitchell's 1970 album *Blue*—one more for the 'Sure, Bob' file. Dylan hadn't worked with Langhorne in a year and a half, and certainly not when Tom Wilson was producing. However, the tambourine Dylan describes was quite real; it really was (and is) owned by Langhorne, who *did* make a habit of walking around the Village at odd hours, playing on it. Could it possibly be?

Bruce Langhorne: I used to play this giant Turkish tambourine. It was about [four inches] deep, and it was very light and it had a sheepskin head and it had jingle bells around the edge—just one layer of bells all the way around. You play it with fingers on your left hand. I bought it 'cause I liked the sound. Hanza El-Deen showed me how to play it . . . I used to play it all the time, I used to carry it around with me and pluck it out and play it anytime. It had a bass tone, and it had an edge tone and it had jingles.

The mundanity of Dylan's explanation may be unappealing to some, but there is something awfully convenient about Rothchild's dating of his first trip and the writing of his most famous (and least vulgar) 'drug song.' If his first trip was really that April, then he showed the same aptitude for drug experimentation as he had shown with the harmonica back in 1960.

By the second week of May, he was well on with his spring cruise on that magic swirling ship, making his first trip to that cradle of civilization, Manchester, England, where he found himself in a dressing room at a TV studio in West Didsbury one overcast Tuesday. A young fan, Neville Kellett, 'a kind of hospitality go-fer,' had been put in charge of the American folksinger and his manager, and as they waited to film an appearance on a Sunday TV program called *Halleluiah,* Albert leaned over and said to Neville:

'Do you think I could ask you a favor?'

'Of course, man,' replies Neville, only too eager to help out his two new friends.

'Bob and I need to be on our own for a few minutes. Do you think you could go outside and mind the door?' Grossman asks politely.

'Yeah, sure man,' Neville replies.

'And no one. Repeat, no one is to come in, Neville. Do you understand?' Grossman quizzes Neville.

Neville smiles at Dylan, who nods back at him as Neville closes the door. His last glimpse is of Dylan walking towards Grossman, who is reaching into his briefcase . . .

[When] Grossman opens the door and lets Neville in, Dylan is coming out of the toilet. Grossman smiles enigmatically as he ushers Neville through the door.

'Bob's ready now,' says Grossman.

Neville looks at Dylan and can't quite believe his eyes. Dylan is actually stumbling toward his guitar. After a brief struggle he manages to get the strap over his head, and then begins the monumental struggle to put on his harmonica holder.

The story, if it was related accurately by Neville Kellett to C. P. Lee more than two decades after the event, suggests that Grossman was 'carrying' for Dylan, and that Dylan was indulging in something a lot more intricate (and fast acting) than a sugarcube of acid or a reefer of grass. Though it seems inconceivable that Grossman would be carrying 'works' at this point—for shooting speed or junk—the fact is that Dylan was stoned to Betsy and back in a matter of minutes. Nor does Kellett make any reference to the telltale aroma of pot. Dylan's description, that he was 'very strung out' after Suze and him split up, begins to acquire a degree of credence. And, on the evidence of the only two clean sound-board recordings of performances at this time—Newport in July and New York in October—this was no one-off occurrence. Dylan was finding it increasingly difficult to perform in public without a little help from a 'friend.'

For the moment, he was lucky. Any habit he was acquiring had not impaired his songwriting skills. If anything, it was improving them. 'Mr. Tambourine Man' may have been the only Dylan composition of note he wrote in those couple of months in New York, but it changed everything. As William Lhamon has written, 'In both his own and his interpreters' hands the song was at once beautiful and commercial. It was his farewell and hello song . . . He said goodbye to overt protest and ballads and hello to the culture of his day.'

If Dylan was becoming unconscionably nervous about live perform-ances, he saved the live debut of 'Tambourine Man' for one of the landmark concerts of the sixties, attended by at least one influential reviewer who compared him to Segovia. During a two-hour marathon, one Sunday afternoon in mid-May at London's Royal Festival Hall, he debuted both 'Mr. Tambourine Man' and another, newer *meisterwerk*, 'It Ain't Me Babe,' which the same London *Times* reviewer perceptively observed had a chorus—'No, no, no, it ain't me babe'—that struck him as a quite deliberate parody of the Beatles' 'She Loves You.' It was Dylan's first tip of the hat to the Fab Four.

The audience that afternoon also heard 'Chimes of Freedom' and 'Eternal Circle,' which must have led anyone paying attention to believe that his fourth album would surpass all that had come before. Unfortu-nately, neither 'Tambourine Man' nor 'Eternal Circle' would appear on that album, and the remaining songs would follow the path laid down by 'It Ain't Me Babe.' Though Columbia had the extraordinary foresight to record the Festival Hall concert, the tapes have never been excavated and so we know not whether the 'It Ain't Me Babe' Dylan performed on May 17 has the extra verse that his handwritten manuscript, on Mayfair Hotel notepaper, contains.

Many have seen 'It Ain't Me Babe' as some kind of address to his audience and its ceaseless demands. In its original form, there is no mistaking the singular identity of the song's addressee, Suze, nor its relationship to a prototype he had written during her time in Italy, 'Hero Blues.' In this earlier song, 'She wants me to be a hero / So she can tell all her friends.' In its original form, the final verse of 'It Ain't Me Babe' accuses the former object of affection of looking for someone from her dreams, someone who would terrify her enemies, someone who would even up scores on her behalf, someone she could ultimately 'count on not t leave.' Inverting all that he professed to feel for Suze, he now insists that if she is 'looking for a heart t be so true,' then it ain't him. Making fidelity seem like an unreasonable demand, he succeeds in becoming the injured party in another 'make yourself feel better' song, again using an inventive reworking of the 'Boots/Girl' arrangement of 'Scarborough Fair' to tell his tale (at one show in September 1993, he even began singing 'Boots of Spanish Leather' and then, four lines in, remembered he'd already sung it, and reverted to the ubiquitous 'It Ain't Me Babe').

Not that Dylan's ever-expanding audience wasn't preying on his mind. The week of his arrival in London, *Freewheelin'* finally cracked the UK Top 20, and the Festival Hall show was a sell-out. It was a very different situation from sixteen months earlier, when the young Bob had scuffed around London anonymously. After his two-hour set, he also found out what it was like to be a pop idol in the land of the Beatles.

Anthea Joseph: We were walking out of the stage door—now this tells you that nobody realized what a star he was—we were going out to get a taxi to go to an Indian restaurant for supper. I mean, CBS hadn't laid on anything. I don't think there was anyone from CBS there even. And Bob was going out in front of me, and I was walking along with Albert, and Bob disappeared under this wave of humanity who were sort of grabbing at his clothes and his hair. He was terrified! And Albert and I dived in and hoisted him out, the two of us being the tallest and the largest people about, and got him back inside . . . It wasn't something you expected. I mean, that happened to pop stars . . . but not singer-songwriters.

Ken Pitt, who was Dylan's publicist on this and subsequent sixties visits, remembers Dylan's reaction somewhat differently. In his account, if this was what being a pop idol was about, Dylan, for one, wanted to savor it.

Ken Pitt: [The Festival Hall] was the very first time Bob experienced fan hysteria. We'd ordered a taxi after the show, but when we got there, there was an enormous crowd between us and the cab. Bob was chuckling with delight, going 'Wow, wow, wow!' and he was determined that we should push our way through the crowd to the taxi . . . [The taxi driver] put his foot down and tried to zoom off, but Bob was having a great time, thoroughly enjoying his new experience, shaking hands, kissing girls . . . The driver pushed on through a sea of waving arms and radiant faces, eventually getting clear of the hall, while Bob was now leaning out of the window, still protesting. As we reached the open road, Bob tried to lay his hands on the driver . . . and he slammed on his brakes and ordered us out of the cab. As we stood in the road . . . we suddenly saw the crowd coming chasing after us . . . Fortunately, another taxi, a welcoming beat-up old thing, came along.

Joan Baez also recalls a Dylan (back then) who almost delighted in stage-managing fan fever when leaving a concert, that he would plan 'these big getaways,' perhaps because, in his insecurities, 'he needed people pounding on the car.' He certainly can be seen in the 1965 and 1966 tour documentaries, *Don't Look Back* and *Eat the Document,* reveling in the moment as he makes it to the safe haven of his limo (in the nineties 'authorized' stage invasions during encores became a regular occurrence).

If Dylan was enjoying the attention of screaming girls, he remained less enamored with the popular press. However, since he was playing only one show in London, extracting maximum mileage out of his visit required he make himself accessible to the media. After all, it had taken a year to get *Freewheelin'* into the UK charts, and Grossman intended to keep it there. As it was, Dylan had to allow himself to be interviewed by several journalists, Max Jones from *Melody Maker* being the only one to whom he seemed to respond well. Other interviewers he treated cavalierly, in particular Maureen Cleave of London's *Evening Standard*. He did not take to the uninterested and ill-informed Cleave, and she was not used to such an uncooperative subject.

Anthea Joseph: He didn't like her but he flirted with her unmercifully. That's when he started [the games], having this posey young woman coming up and asking stupid questions, really beginning to get the hang of how to handle these idiots.

If the *Newsweek* story had taught him anything, it was to recognize someone who doesn't get it (as evidence: Cleave is the one asking about the Bible at the beginning of *Don't Look Back*). Cleave later suggested that Dylan was rocking backward and forward in a simulation of masturbation throughout the interview. She was obviously unaware of Dylan's lack of basic motor control when it came to his legs, which invariably acted like barometers of an inner impatience. His old school chum John Bucklen remembers more than once telling him to stop shaking his legs, that it was driving him nuts, 'like he was always looking for something to do but he couldn't find what he wanted.' What Dylan was really telling Cleave was that he wanted to get the hell outta there, outta the Mayfair, outta Piccadilly, outta London. On May 21 he tucked a drawerful of Mayfair notepaper in his bag, ducked into a hackney cab, directed it to London Airport, and hopped aboard a plane, destination Paris.

In Paris, Dylan looked up Hugues Aufray, who had translated some of his songs into French. Though he later complained to a friend that 'he failed to meet Brigitte Bardot as usual,' he was introduced by his traveling sidekick, Ben Carruthers, to a striking German model, Christa Paffgen, who now went by the name of Nico. Intrigued by her bit part in Fellini's *La Dolce Vita* and attracted to her carefully cultivated icy detachment, Dylan visited her studio flat for a meal and ended up inviting her to accompany him across Europe.

Dylan's eventual destination was a village in Greece, but he had decided to proceed via Berlin, where Aufray's cousin was living with Mason Hoffenburg, co-author, with Terry Southern, of the 1958 underground classic *Candy*. Availing himself of Hoffenburg's hospitality, Dylan spent a day looking for Nazis in West Berlin and, not finding any, concluded that they'd all moved to Arlington. He also ventured into East Berlin but it was apparently Liberty Day, and everything was closed. Unimpressed by Germany, he set out for Vernilya, a small village just outside Athens, where he stayed for just over a week, writing the bulk of the songs that appear on his fourth album, which he was due to record on his return to New York.

The material written on his May jaunt, and completed in Vernilya, comprised at least nine 'finished' songs: 'All I Really Wanna Do,' 'Spanish Harlem Incident,' 'To Ramona,' 'I Shall Be Free No. 10,' 'Ballad in Plain D,' 'It Ain't Me Babe,' 'Mama You Been on My Mind,' 'Denise Denise,' and 'Black Crow Blues,' all of which appear in a recently emerged set of manuscripts and typescripts, many on Mayfair Hotel notepaper. Along with the largely handwritten pages comprising these songs came a whole series of poems, almost all typewritten, from which he would cull the album's sleeve notes, the epigrammatic 'some other kinds of songs,' and dedicate to 'Bernard, Marylou, Jean Pierre, Gerard Philip an Monique for the use of their house.'

One song also written in Europe, but not contained in the various manuscripts, was 'I'll Keep It with Mine.' Offering to relieve Nico of some private sorrow she was carrying, Dylan donated one of his finest songs for her use, when he was perhaps in need of it himself.

Nico: He did not treat me very seriously, but at least he was interested in my story . . . As I was from Berlin, he asked me if I knew the playwright Brecht . . . For a man who was preaching about politics he did not know his history too well . . . We went . . . to Greece for a short time . . . and he wrote me a song about me and my little baby.

The other songs he was writing were considerably less gracious. On the basis of the manuscript, the song he seems to have worked on the most in Vernilya was 'Ballad in Plain D,' which took its tune (and the 'my friends say unto me' refrain) from a fine old British folk song, 'Once I Had a Sweetheart,' a.k.a. 'The False Bride.' The song graphically details the night of his breakup with Suze. It starts as a simple lyric of loss, then the singer admits to himself that 'in soft, selfish ways, many times I did lie.' In the original manuscript Suze's mother, Mary, comes off considerably worse than in the final song, being described as an overly possessive woman who, despite her constant creeping, overlooked her daughter's creative instincts completely. Carla is portrayed as her sister's shadow who, reflecting on her own failures, causes Suze's instincts to be 'constantly ridden upon.' Dylan's portrayal of Carla as the 'parasite sister' remains a cruel and inaccurate portrait of a woman who had started out as one of his biggest fans, and changed only as she came to see the degrees of emotional blackmail he subjected her younger sister to. Interestingly, when asked in 1985 whether there were any songs he regretted writing, Dylan singled out 'Ballad in Plain D.'

Bob Dylan: That one I look back at and say, 'I must have been a real schmuck to write that.' I look back at that particular one and say . . . maybe I could have left that alone. [1985]

Despite the numbers of drafts that the song seems to have passed through, beginning, it would appear, in London, 'Ballad in Plain D' was a long way from being fully realized when he recorded it. As David Horowitz wrote in December 1964, shortly after the release of *Another Side*, ' "Ballad in Plain D" . . . is not really a song at all, but only the raw material for a song. One has a feeling, in listening to it, of reading someone else's mail.'

Other songs that Dylan worked on in Greece were more sympathetic studies of a shattered relationship, though pain and sorrow still clouded his artistic vision. 'To Ramona,' the most realized song on *Another Side*, began life as a couple of scattered lines in 'I Shall Be Free No. 10,' and ended up as a particularly fine portrait of a woman whose friends betray her with their words of advice. Indeed, some of the more humorous songs seem to have been put together out of stray lines written as relief from the serious stuff. Verses of 'All I Really Wanna Do' and 'I Shall Be Free No. 10' interrupt 'Ballad in Plain D' and 'To Ramona' in the manuscript pages.

Perhaps the most poignant song written in Vernilya, 'Mama You Been on My Mind,' Baez would later claim for herself. However, there can be little doubt that this was Dylan's first attempt at 'If You See Her, Say Hello,' and that it was Suze to whom his professed nonchalance was directed. Rather than envisaging his messenger making love to her, he professes not to care who strokes her skin. In its original form, he does not ask her to say yes or no, but insists he is 'not putting any pressure on you to come back to me at all.' Methinks he doth protest too much. Here was a man who very much wanted another chance to get along with Suze.

Though 'Mama You Been on My Mind' failed to make the album, it is a song Dylan has remained attached to, even performing it regularly in concert in the nineties. Of the other songs he wrote on this trip, only 'To Ramona' and 'It Ain't Me Babe' would endure. The others merely provided some much-needed catharsis.

Suze Rotolo: People have asked how I felt about those songs that were bitter, like 'Ballad in Plain D,' since I inspired some of those, too, yet I never felt hurt by them. I understood what he was doing. It was the end of something and we both were hurt and bitter. His art was his outlet, his exorcism. It was healthy. That was the way he wrote out his life . . . the loving songs, the cynical songs, the political songs.

Now that his records were selling—*The Times They Are A-Changin'* had made the Top 20 Stateside—Columbia was pressing him to keep the albums coming. After all, this was an era when the Beatles and the Rolling Stones regularly issued two (or, once their respective American labels had bastardized their UK albums, three) albums a year. By the time Dylan returned to New York, the first week of June, it had been over eight months since he had been in a Columbia studio, and the powers-that-be wanted a new album in time for their fall sales convention. Studio time was hastily allocated.

When he arrived at the familiar Studio A on June 9, Dylan informed Nat Hentoff, who was writing a profile for *The New Yorker* magazine, that he would be recording the entire album in a single night. He also informed Hentoff that what he was about to record was very different from previous efforts.

Bob Dylan: There aren't any finger-pointin' songs in here. Those records I've made, I'll stand behind them, but some of that was jumping into the scene to be heard and a lot of it was because I didn't see anybody else doing that kind of thing . . . You know—pointing to all the things that are wrong. I don't want to write for people anymore. You know—be a spokesman . . . From now on, I want to write from inside me, and to do that I'm going to have to get back to writing like I used to when I was ten—having everything come out naturally. The way I like to write is for it to come out the way I walk or talk. [1964]

While polishing off a couple of bottles of Beaujolais, Dylan did indeed record some fourteen songs, eleven of which would constitute his fourth album, in a single night. By the time he recorded the official take of 'My Back Pages' at one-thirty in the morning, all that was needed were a couple of edits, and there would be a new Dylan album for the fall convention. The *Another Side of Bob Dylan* session was a prodigious effort, even for a man used to recording quickly and with a minimum of fuss, and over the years the session has taken on a certain mythical hue. As Paul Cable wrote in his *Bob Dylan: The Unreleased Recordings*:

It was a brilliant day. Around twenty tracks recorded [sic], many of them classics, and that is just the ones we know about. It illustrates that the use of the word 'genius' in referring to Dylan is not just something that has arisen out of the semantic excesses of pop journalism.

In reality, the *Another Side* session was another typical Dylan session—flashes of sheer brilliance, improvisational flair, songs coming together and falling apart (in fairly equal measures) in the studio. Though he had never recorded quite so many songs at a single session, he had already cut a dozen or more songs at two consecutive afternoon sessions on at least three occasions. Only with the first album, though, was it felt that these two sessions sufficed. This time, he decided to construct an album entirely from one session rather than going back and working on some of the songs again, or writing the couple of songs required to drop-kick 'I Shall Be Free No. 10' and 'Motorpsycho Nitemare'—two not-very-funny humorous songs—into the trash can. Presumably he included these efforts to provide some light relief among the songs of sorrow and pain. He certainly could have substituted a lovely version of 'Mama You Been on My Mind' recorded the same night, or even the version of 'Mr. Tambourine Man' he cut with Jack Elliott.

Ramblin' Jack Elliott: I knew he was going to try to record 'Tambourine Man' and he invited me to sing on it with him but I didn't know the words, 'cept for the chorus, so I just harmonized with him on the chorus.

The *Another Side* 'Tambourine Man' was cut in a single take. At six and a half minutes, with its harmonica intro (dropped before the January 1965 recording), and with Dylan stumbling over a couple of lines, it is not quite realized. Its slightly sluggish pace also suggests the Beaujolais is catching up with him. Indeed, it appears three-quarters of the way through the session, with mostly lighter songs to come. The three best performances on the album—'It Ain't Me Babe,' 'To Ramona,' and 'Spanish Harlem Incident'—had been recorded second, third and fourth at the session, after warming up with the as-yet-unreleased 'Denise Denise.' He wisely decided 'Mr. Tambourine Man' was too important a song to fix on vinyl in such a halfhearted form.

Unfortunately, the other songs were treated with more disdain. For the first time, Dylan permitted inserts to be recorded into live studio performances, on 'Ballad in Plain D' and 'I Shall Be Free No. 10' (Wilson can be heard pushing Dylan into doing an insert on the unedited 'I Shall Be Free,' Dylan says he'd rather start all over), while 'Chimes of Freedom,' the one song to have featured regularly in live performance, took seven takes before he rendered a complete take. Perhaps he already felt disconnected from this four month-old song. Certainly when he sang it at his next major performance, the Newport Folk Festival, he would sound like a man forcing his way through a song, and by his Halloween concert in New York it would have passed from the set.

As Columbia prepared *Another Side* for release, Dylan premiered his new songs at the end of July at the Newport Folk Festival, scene of his greatest triumph twelve months earlier and of his greatest controversy twelve months later. Between these two pillars of Dylan iconography, his 1964 appearance has been largely passed over. In fact, his two sets generated their fair share of controversy, and prefaced the mixed reception awaiting the album.

Dylan's first appearance that weekend, at a Friday topical-song workshop, was brief. In a perhaps ironic gesture, he opened with 'It Ain't Me

Babe' before performing 'Mr. Tambourine Man,' which met with instant acclaim from the large workshop crowd, who stood to acclaim another work of genius from their favourite troubadour. The response evidently encouraged Dylan to include it in his Sunday set, where he introduced it as 'a request from one of you,' along with three *Another Side* previews. Though Dylan dispatched 'All I Really Wanna Do' and 'To Ramona' with reasonable aplomb, by the time he got to 'Chimes of Freedom' he was bobbing and weaving, clearly out of control. The audience seemed unconcerned, and when he signaled that it was the end of his set, they were 'frantically calling for more.' He did return but only to perform a duet with Baez. The ubiquitous 'With God on Our Side' was an odd choice for the new Dylan, as they could presumably have reprised the almost solo 'It Ain't Me Babe' he had sung 'with Baez'—her burblings being largely off-mike—at the conclusion to her Friday set.

If Dylan was well received by the fans, the true hit of the 1964 festival was a man who had already been through all the changes he was seeking to excuse, Johnny Cash. To put Dylan's later apostasy in context, Cash was accompanied throughout his set by electric guitar and bass, courtesy of Luther Perkins and Marshall Grant, and his eight-song set was a delightful fusion of the rockabilly sides he had cut at Sun, the country-folk of A. P. Carter ('Keep on the Sunny Side') and Lead Belly ('Rock Island Line'), and a couple of covers from the topical-song canon: Peter La Farge's powerful 'Ira Hayes' and Dylan's 'Don't Think Twice, It's All Right.' The latter was introduced with a sincere testimony to the young songwriter, 'Got a special request from a friend of ours. I'm very honored, I've never been so honored . . . [off-mike] Hi, Bob—our good friend Bob Dylan. We'd like to do one of his songs and we've been doing it on our shows all over the country, trying to tell the folks about Bob, that we think he's the best songwriter of the age . . . Sure do.'

Cash and Dylan had spent the previous night jamming together in Baez's room at the Viking Motor Inn. It was their first meeting, but according to Cash, they were 'so happy to [finally] meet each other that we were jumping on the beds like kids.' Not that either was a new convert to the other's art. Dylan had been listening to Cash since his Sun singles in the fifties (he can be heard talking about Cash on one of John Bucklen's home tapes in 1958), and Cash had been playing *Freewheelin'* backstage before his concerts all year long. The mutual admiration society, started up by a letter from Cash the previous year, was to last well beyond both Dylan's *and* Cash's flirtations with the topical-song genre.

Cash seemed equally enthusiastic about Dylan's new songs. He would record his own 'It Ain't Me Babe,' and with a full 'rock' sound. However, the press reception for the new songs, at least those debuted at Newport, was less than celebratory, even among the previously reliable bastions of folkdom. Irwin Silber wrote a famous open letter to Dylan in the November issue of *Sing Out* in which he commented, 'your new songs seem to be all inner-directed now, inner-probing, self-conscious— maybe even a little maudlin or a little cruel on occasion.' Silber, though, did not confine his comments to Dylan's new songs:

I saw at Newport how you had somehow lost contact with people. It seemed to me that some of the paraphernalia of fame were getting in your way. You travel with an entourage now . . . buddies who are going to laugh when you need laughing, and drink wine with you . . . and never challenge you to face everyone else's reality again.

Silber was not the only one to believe that the pressures of fame were starting to tell on Dylan's art. David Horowitz's 'explanation for this sudden and unqualified failure of taste and self-critical awareness'—by this, he meant *Another Side of Bob Dylan*—was as telling as Silber's assessment of the Dylan he encountered at Newport:

In a culture in which the driving force of social existence, the pretext for art itself, is commercial, 'silence' is a luxury (and freedom) that few artists can afford. By sheer force of his public success, Dylan has ceased to be 'merely' an artist and has become a commodity, a 'hot property' in common parlance. The pressures . . . must have been terrific.

Another Side was another transitional album, as the original version of *Freewheelin'* would have been. For the first time, Dylan was simply too close to the experiences he was drawing upon to translate them into art. He was also still experimenting with the imagery found on 'Chimes of Freedom' and 'Mr. Tambourine Man.' 'My Back Pages,' the least success- ful example of the new style, was replete with bizarre compound images ('corpse evangelists,' 'confusion boats,' etc.). The fact that he was still fumbling his way toward a fully realized poetic language, encompassing 'chains of flashing images,' inevitably brought its own share of flak. The most cutting of critiques came in *Hi-Fidelity*, in which one O. B. Brummel shamelessly parodied Dylan's own sleeve-note scribblings:

some o bob's early ballads
are pretty good. . . .
but these new ones
ain't much
in fact most o them
sound like he wrote em fast
maybe three
*   or four*
*   per day*
includin bad days. . . .

n now
whenever you buy one o
bob's releases
columbia don't bother with
no album notes
they jus fill the sleeve
with bob's leftover verse
n man that's culture
*   with a capital*
*   cull*

but bob
he got two problems
small ones
the language he writes in
aint english
the measures he beats out
aint song

Inevitably, Dylan was forced to defend the album on its release in August. Writing to Ralph J. Gleason shortly afterwards, he insisted:

The songs are insanely honest, not meanin t twist any heads an written only for the reason that i myself me alone wanted and needed t write them. i've conceded the fact there is no understanding of anything. at best, just winks of the eye an that is all i'm lookin for now i guess.

Matters were not helped by the album's title, which was (quite reasonably) interpreted as a declaration of intent. The title seemed to invite resistance before the results could be heard. It seemed he did not wish to let his listeners down gently. Dylan later denied that the choice of title was his:

Bob Dylan: I didn't want them to call [my fourth album] *Another Side of Bob Dylan*. . . because I thought it was just too corny . . . I just felt trouble coming when they titled it that. I figured if they could have titled it something else, I wouldn't have had the resistance to it. [1978]

Shelton also followed the party line, insisting it was Tom Wilson's title, which Dylan had only reluctantly approved. However, the idea that Dylan by 1964 was not in a position to impose his own title on his albums is simply not credible, betrayed as it is by his own pen. In the *Another Side* manuscripts are two references to the album title. One is in an early draft of 'I Shall Be Free No. 10,' where a poor boy cries, 'You're on another side.' The other, more telling reference, the only line occupying the final page of the manuscript, insists that 'there is no other side of bob dylan.'

Another Side fared considerably worse than the previous two albums, failing to crack the all-important Top 40, indicating that sections of his existing audience were no longer listening. If he was understandably reluctant to admit that *Another Side* was a mistake at the time, within a year he would recognize some of its more evident faults. Meanwhile, certain voices from the underground managed to recognize the birth pangs of a new Dylan from the halfway house that was *Another Side*. In the issue of *Sing Out* after Silber's open letter, the letters page ran several defenses of Dylan, the most insightful of which came from one John Sinclair, in Detroit, Michigan:

Dylan was never the run-of-the-mill folksinger the hippies seem to want . . . Even his 'committed' songs had a deeper irony and a more profound intelligence to them than any other of the worker-war-bomb polemics everyone sings . . . Anyone with a simple awareness, an elementary grasp of what's going on in this world, can talk about the obvious evil around him (but this is just), superficial. Dylan has begun to go beneath the surface . . .

1964–65: The Ghost of Electricity

9

The songs I was writing [previously], songs like 'Ballad in Plain D,' they were what I call one-dimensional songs, but my new songs I'm trying to make more three-dimensional. There's more symbolism, they're written on more than one level.

—*Bob Dylan, 1965*

The hamlet of Woodstock, two hours upstate from the big city, had by now become a regular haven for Dylan. The previous summer he had enjoyed an idyllic month at Peter Yarrow's cabin with Suze. With Grossman giving him free rein at his house, from the summer of 1964 he began to spend more time there than he did in New York. Another incentive to visit was a dark-haired beauty named Sara Lowndes, a regular guest at Grossman's house. Sara was an old friend of Sally Buhler, the lady draped across the sofa on the *Bringing It All Back Home* album cover, and soon to become Mrs Grossman. If Joan Baez had formed the opinion that she was the only name in Bob's book, she was in for a shock, albeit someway down the road.

Joan Baez: When I finally met and became friends with Sara [in 1975], we talked for hours about those days when the Original Vagabond was two-timing us. I told Sara that I'd never found Bob to be much at giving gifts, but that he had once bought me a green corduroy coat, and had told me to keep a lovely blue nightgown from the Woodstock house. 'Oh!' said Sara, 'that's where it went!'

Sara has, over the years, proved even more mercurial than the man she was to marry. Information about her background seems permanently shrouded in Cornish mist. According to Aronowitz, she originally came from Delaware, 'where her father, a scrap metals dealer, had been shot to death in a hold-up.' Lowndes was not her real name, but rather her married name. Like Dylan, she seems to have abandoned her maiden name, Shirley Noznisky (or, according to her future in-laws, Novolet-sky), with relative ease. Having been briefly married to a photographer named Hans Lowndes when she first came to New York, she had reverted to that most New York of stereotypes, the waitress/actress. However, with her sultry looks and bewitching eyes, she soon evolved into a bunny, named Vicky, at the Playboy Club. Her roommate, Barbara, worked at the Gaslight, and since they lived on MacDougal Street, Sara too became part of the whole Village vortex. According to moviemaker Mel Howard, her acting ambitions weren't entirely fanciful.

Mel Howard: Back in the early sixties, my first wife and I introduced Sara, who was a friend of ours, to Bob. We ran a popular coffeeshop on MacDougal Street in the Village, where he occasionally sang. Ironically, at the same time, Sara was acting in the Broadway production of *Dylan,* a play about the great Welsh poet Dylan Thomas.

If Dylan and Sara first met when he had become more than just another folkie in the crowd, the name meant nothing to Sara. According to Sally Grossman, when they sat and watched Dylan's first network TV appearance together (presumably *The Steve Allen Show* in February 1964), Sara thought they were going to watch Bobby Darin. Whether the Howards were indeed the original intermediaries or not, the introduction came at a time when Sara was living in a one-room apartment with her baby daughter, Marie, and working part-time for Time-Life. Dylan had gone through his painful breakup with Suze, and was looking for calmer climes.

Al Aronowitz: From the first, Sara . . . ruled with regal radiance and with the power to calm troubled waters. She'd never lose her cheerful cool or pull a scene but, when she was really pushed to it, she knew how to do an icy slow burn.

If her 'regal radiance' and 'icy slow burn' set Sara apart from previous muses, she had one factor in common with Suze: she was a Scorpio, and, as Carla Rotolo acidly observed, 'Geminis are supposed to devour Scorpios.' Sara, though, was a rare breed of Scorpio, a triple Scorpio—sun, moon, and rising sign—untempered by other astrological aspects. Dylan was evidently struck not only by her cool charm but by her willingness to suppress her own ego, rendering herself part of the background.

Larry Keenan: [Sara] kept herself anonymous. She never stood near Dylan at all . . . Most girlfriends *hang* and she didn't . . . She was never where she could be photographed; she was so far removed from the scene.

Her ability to fade in and out of situations meant that many of Dylan's closer friends were wholly unaware of her role in his life, and the impact she had on him. According to Aronowitz, he'd been informed soon after they met that Bob intended to marry her. Dylan even went so far as to ask Aronowitz to make arrangements for the ceremony, though it would be another eighteen months before he was prompted to follow through on his expressed intention. Though photographer Daniel Kramer managed to capture Sara and Dylan together in Grossman's Woodstock cabin, the photo he took—for the cover of Dylan's 'book'—was rejected by Dylan, doubtless in part to preserve Sara's anonymity.

For the moment, though, Sara was required to make herself scarce, as Dylan turned up at Grossman's that August with Joan Baez in tow. If Baez was unaware of Sara's existence, her nemesis was not fitted with the same blinkers. According to Baez, her beau was concentrating more on the pen than his sword that summer.

Joan Baez: Most of the month or so we were there, Bob stood at the typewriter in the corner of his room, drinking red wine and smoking and tapping away relentlessly for hours. And in the dead of night, he would wake up, grunt, grab a cigarette, and stumble over to the typewriter again. He was turning out songs like ticker tape, and I was stealing them as fast as he wrote them.

Despite Baez's 'ticker tape' recollection, it is not clear what songs Dylan would have been working on that August. Of the two major works he wrote that summer—'Gates of Eden' and 'It's Alright Ma (I'm Only Bleeding)'—'Gates of Eden' is the closer to the 'chains of flashing images' conceived by 'Chimes of Freedom' and fully realized with 'Mr. Tambourine Man.' But it was almost certainly already written. It appears alongside the 'some other kind of songs' poems in the *Another Side* manuscripts, and was presumably contemporaneous with this material. If the manuscript is anything to go by, the song came to him almost whole, save for its resolution, originally at verse eight, with an ominous 'there's nowhere t hide inside the gates of eden.' 'Gates of Eden' proved that 'Tambourine Man' was no isolated, inspirational instance. Like its precursor, it was a song of vivid experience, constructed in the form of a dream, that came to him in 'a house that is not mine.'

Of the other two songs to definitely date from this lull, 'If You Gotta Go, Go Now' would hardly have taxed Dylan's pen for long, though its subtext—if you're not coming to bed with me, go home, so I can find someone who will—perhaps has the whiff of autobiography. 'It's Alright

Ma,' on the other hand, opened up a whole new genre of finger-pointing song, not just for Dylan but for the entire panoply of pop. When he had informed a journalist in February, 'I used to write songs, like I'd say, "Yeah, what's bad, pick out something bad, like segregation" . . . and I'd pick one of the thousand million little points I can pick and explode it,' he had come to realize that there was a better way. In 'It's Alright Ma' he took 'the thousand million little points' and exploded each one, producing a damning roster of America's societal malaises, and perhaps more memorable aphorisms than any other Dylan song: 'Money doesn't talk it swears'; 'He not busy being born is busy dying,' and so on. Before 'It's Alright Ma,' popular song was not a medium for critiquing society, only for isolating specific injustices. Dylan had irrevocably advanced beyond that position, aware that he had no choice but to live his life (and his life only) amongst pragmatic agnostics, stumbling blindly around the perimeters of Eden.

Dylan continued to be preoccupied by poetry and prose in Woodstock that summer. Working on the Macmillan book, he found himself somewhere between a walk down a crooked highway and a tarantella, taking relief in writing letters of prose-poetics to friends and other strangers. When he caught Baez writing to her mum he insisted on penning one of his finest parodies—this one of the letter home: 'i'm up in woodstock at uncle alby's . . . i'm with you-know-who . . . mummy you must believe me. i was gonna stay at the foremans as planned . . .'

The best evidence of Dylan's increasingly surreal approach to prose comes in four letters he wrote to Tami Dean, a student at Oklahoma State University, through 1964. The letters—not published until 1984, sixteen years after Dean's death in a car accident—vividly display his stylistic development. The first letter, from early March 1964, judging by a reference to a visit to Dallas three weeks earlier, is similar to free-verse letters to Tony Glover, Sis Cunningham, and the Emergency Civil Liberties Committee the previous year: 'I'll see you sometime. on a strange nite. when the leaves 're blowin. an it's close t shiverin. when the headlights pass above the bluff yes I'll meet you by the crossing. on the edge of town. in the brown dust.' The second letter, which probably dates from spring, continues in the same style, but with an oblique reference to 'Chimes of Freedom': 'I gaze out of cathedral windows when I can. at other times I gaze up at them from the rainy street.'

Letters three and four, though, are a world apart from such chains of thought. Apparently dating from the late summer or fall of 1964, both slip easily into a stream of consciousness, piling the incongruous upon the absurd. Neither directly addresses Tami Dean, reading more as expositions upon Dylan's state of mind. The third letter, the more coherent, is another parody of the 'dear ma, everyone's fine' letter. The character of doctor zen shares kith and kin with syd dangerous, Silly Eyes and herold the professor in *Tarantula;* or the family of lunatics portrayed in 'On the Road Again':

doctor zen says hello. i told him you were off in oklahoma. he says no she's not. i say ok i dig. there is no oklahoma. he says you asshole there is no she. i say ok ok he says say hi to her. doc gets weird sometimes. he stuffs lsd in his turban most everyday.

If the LSD was going in his turban, the amphetamine was not. The letter howls of speed and speed-writing. The fourth letter, a direct ancestor to *Tarantula* in its use of prose poems and free-verse 'epistles,' reads like a Dadaist chronicle. Opening with 'so there I was. riding on this umbrella,' it progresses through a travelogue which closely parallels the insane world found in songs like 'Bob Dylan's 115th Dream,' and winds up in a subterranean-style confessional:

watch for cave ins an dont be too good t nobody. they might get wrong idea. sneer at graveyard. make patty cake thank you mam good gawd son is that london bridge about t go? i mix up crazy phantoms. exchange their eyes bust into plate glass predictions. get in two timed position. try to make it with the manacans.

This advisory tone can also be found in the first of this new brand of prose poems to be published. In the program for his first New York concert in a year, the famous Halloween '64 show, he included a piece called 'Advice for Geraldine on Her Miscellaneous Birthday.' Dealing with conformity in his usual sardonic way, he advises the mysterious Geraldine never to create anything—'it will be misinterpreted.' His advice, when asked what one does for a living? 'say you laugh for a living.' At the show itself, he certainly made his audience laugh. In response to a request, he says, 'Hey, I'll do anything. Hope I never have to make a living.' On 'I Don't Believe You' he completely blanks out on the opening verse and has to ask the audience for assistance, but he manages to do it with enough good humor that they laugh along with him, not at him. For the second time in three months, at a high-profile performance, he was stoned and dangerously spinning. Again, though, he negotiated the tightrope successfully, introducing 'Gates of Eden'— as a 'sacrilegious lullaby'—and 'It's Alright Ma' to the appreciative crowd.

If getting stoned had been a favored pastime since his Dinkytown days, getting others stoned had only recently taken its place in the man's mantra. The occasion when Dylan descended from Woodstock to meet the Beatles, at their New York hotel, may have become overly imbued with Import, but on the night of August 28, 1964, two cultures fumbled for a common creed via a bag of weed. In the company of Victor Maymudes and Al Aronowitz, Dylan ascended the Delmonico elevator that evening to meet the current arbiters of change in pop culture. When he entered the Beatles' suite and went in search of 'what he usually drinks, cheap wine,' he was informed by Brian Epstein that they only had champagne. Apparently offered some pills, Bob suggested some pot, and proceeded to roll a joint. As the Fab Four partook for the first time, enlightenment apparently dawned, though in the cold light of the following morn, it proved illusory.

Paul McCartney: I was wandering around looking for a pencil because I discovered the meaning of life that evening and I wanted to get it down on a bit of paper . . . Mal [Evans] handed me the little bit of paper the next morning . . . and on it was written, in very scrawly handwriting: THERE ARE SEVEN LEVELS.

Aronowitz has written about how 'after they met, the Beatles' words got grittier and Bob invented folk-rock,' as if these logical developments were the by-product of their meeting. In truth, the example set by Dylan's lyrical preoccupations was there for anyone tuned in who wished to make a statement with pop. It didn't require a personal meeting or a shared spliff. Nor did Dylan's skirting the precipice of electricity truly spring from the Beatles' example. What the Beatles' success provided was an environment for experimentation such as occurs only rarely in any popular medium. That said, the evening established a personal dimension to the very real rivalry that would endure for the remainder of a momentous decade.

It would be a fine piece of synchronicity if, driving down to the city that August afternoon in his trusty station wagon, Dylan had turned on the radio and heard for the first time a new single by one of the bright young bands of Britpop. The Animals' version of 'House of the Rising Sun' had entered the American charts two weeks earlier, and was a week off the number one slot. It was the Animals' second single, and the second A-side they culled from Dylan's eponymous debut, having first tackled 'Baby Let Me Follow You Down.' Their version of 'House of the Rising Sun,' though, was a dramatic reinvention, an unconscious rerouting of the melody, a derivative of a sixteenth-century English ballad, along an almost entirely black avenue, by a quartet of decidedly white North Country blokes.

Whatever credit Dylan himself may wish to take for the folk-rock genre, the Animals' 'House of the Rising Sun' was unquestionably its first manifestation, and it shook him in a way no Beatles harmony, however outrageous, ever could. For the first time he heard a way to house 'the only, true valid death you can feel today' within a contemporary sound. Such was the song's impact that Dylan's producer, Tom Wilson, went into the studio with Dylan's acoustic version and dubbed on an electric backing track, clearly modeled on that of the Animals.

Tom Wilson: We tried by editing and by overdubbing to put like a Fats Domino early rock & roll thing on top of what Dylan had done, but it never quite worked to our satisfaction . . . That's where I first consciously . . . started to try to put these two different elements [folk and rock] together.

Dylan, though, was not interested in putting 'a Fats Domino early rock & roll thing' atop his impressionistic musings. The sound he heard in his head was far richer than the one Wilson placed astride his own 'Rising Sun Blues.' It was a sound much like the one he heard on a new album by his old friend John Hammond, Jr. Hammond had just signed to do an album for Vanguard Records, and though he wanted to record many of the blues songs that framed his acoustic sets in the Village, he decided to confront the electric R&B coming out of Britain head-on by making an electric album that would reflect urban R&B better than anything made by students from the London School of Economics.

Levon Helm: John, a scholar of the music we'd grown up on, realized the electric blues was the medium of the moment . . . [John] was one of the first to see the possibilities of having an electric band.

Hammond had a very specific electric combo in mind. The core components of his new sound were provided by three members of a Canadian bar band he had met back in 1963, guitarist Jamie Robertson, drummer Levon Helm, and organist Garth Hudson.

John Hammond, Jr.: I played a show up in Toronto at a place called the Purple Onion. This guy Stan Thomas, a folksinger, came backstage and said, 'Listen, I got to take you to this club after your show so you can hear these guys play.' . . . They were called Levon and the Hawks. They were playing

at the Concord Tavern . . . I flipped out when I heard them. Stan introduced
me to Robbie, Levon, and all the guys, almost instantly we hit it off . . . I
played often in Toronto and when they came to New York we'd hang out
. . . I was going to do a record for Vanguard and they were in New York
. . . so I said how about you guys back me up on an album, and they said
sure. We went into the studio, and . . . made [*So Many Roads*]. My friend
Michael Bloomfield was in from Chicago, and his friend Charlie Mussel-
white, who I had never met before. It was his first recording date ever, he
played harmonica . . . I invited Dylan down to the session, he heard Robbie
and it freaked him out.

So Many Roads is certainly the closest Robertson ever came in the
studio to those 'ghost of Buchanan' sounds he twisted out of his Fender
at the 1966 shows. However, Hammond remains the only one to claim
that Dylan attended the sessions for *So Many Roads*. Helm makes no
mention of it in his autobiography, though he dates the sessions to the
summer of 1964, when the Hawks were playing their first East Coast
residency since coming out from behind Ronnie Hawkins's considerable
shadow; and neither Robertson nor Bloomfield have ever referred to
Dylan's presence. Unlikely as it is that Dylan ventured down to the actual
sessions, there is little doubt that he heard the results *before* his own
electric excursions. Nor is it likely to be a coincidence that when he
recruited two Hawks for his first post-Newport band, it should be two
of those who contributed so much to *So Many Roads*. One Village
compatriot well remembers Dylan's enthusiasm for Hammond's
initiative.

Danny Kalb: Bob was really excited about what John Hammond was doing
with electric blues. I talked to him in the Figaro in 1964 and he was telling
me about John and his going to Chicago and playing with a band and so on,
and the next thing, Bob was making *Bringing It All Back Home*.

It may have taken Dylan several months, and much soul-searching,
but the path laid out by Hammond and the Animals proved irresistible,
even though when he turned up at Columbia Studio A for the first time
since the *Another Side* session, it was to record solo, with piano and guitar.
There has been some dispute about the purpose of this session on January
13, 1965. One Dylan scholar has sought to dismiss the session, at which
he managed to record ten complete songs and a couple of ideas-awaiting-
verses, as one 'at which Dylan laid down guide demos that he would use
at the two later sessions to introduce the studio musicians to the songs

he was going to record.' In fact, for his fifth album, Dylan clearly conceived of some kind of mix of acoustic and electric, as with the original *Freewheelin'*.

The songs recorded in both guises seem to have been made because he was genuinely unsure which format best suited them. According to Daniel Kramer, who was photographing the sessions, Dylan even attempted an electric 'Tambourine Man' at an evening session on the 14th (the tape of which appears to have been lost). It would end up acoustic on the album, but with embellishment from Bruce Langhorne. At that first session, Dylan tried acoustic versions of 'Subterranean Home-sick Blues,' 'If You Gotta Go, Go Now,' 'On the Road Again,' 'Bob Dylan's 115th Dream,' and the prototypical 'California' (a.k.a. 'Outlaw Blues'), all of which ended up electric. But he also cut acoustic versions of 'I'll Keep It with Mine' and 'Farewell Angelina' on the 13th that are hard to fault, and were not superseded (though 'I'll Keep It with Mine' was also attempted at the lost electric session).

Likewise, on the 13th, Dylan kept his options open with an exquisite acoustic rendition of one of his great love songs, the ethereal 'Love Minus Zero No Limit,' surely inspired by a lady of regal radiance. And yet, when he resumed recording the following afternoon, he and the musicians managed to craft an even more perfect performance from the song in a couple of takes at the outset of electric activities. The musicians given a pep talk at Studio A at 2:30 on the 14th were mostly producer Tom Wilson's choices—the beatmeister Bobby Gregg, bass player William E. Lee, pianist extraordinaire Paul Griffin—but when it came to lead guitarist, Wilson was required to defer to Dylan. Bruce Langhorne recalls being given some kind of advance warning as to the shape of things to come, presumably from Dylan:

Bruce Langhorne: Well, I showed up [for the sessions] with a pickup for my guitar and an amp, so there was that much 'prep' . . . I remember that we didn't do any rehearsal, we just did first takes and I remember that, for what it was, it was amazingly intuitive and successful. Everyone enjoyed playing with everyone else, and Dylan was sort of the thread that held everything together. His intent and his inertia—in physics terms—was very easy to hook onto.

If the session that afternoon was certainly 'amazingly intuitive and successful'—with 'Love Minus Zero,' 'Subterranean Homesick Blues,' 'Outlaw Blues,' 'She Belongs to Me,' and 'Bob Dylan's 115th Dream' all being wrapped up in a couple of takes—Dylan evidently wanted to explore every musical option. After a break for dinner, he continued recording in the evening, with John Sebastian and John Hammond, Jr., on bass and acoustic guitar, and Langhorne as the only retainee from the afternoon. This foursome ended up recording six songs, all subsequently scrapped, suggesting some successes still resembled failures.

When work resumed the following afternoon, Dylan reverted to Wilson's chosen few, and an easy camaraderie returned to the sessions, evidenced by the first take of the day, the only take they ever needed to do of 'Maggie's Farm':

Daniel Kramer: It was obvious from the very beginning that something exciting was happening, and much of it happened spontaneously. When the playback of 'Maggie's Farm' was heard over the studio speakers, we were all elated. There was no question about it—it swung, it was happy, it was good music, and, most of all, it was Dylan. The musicians were enthusiastic. They conferred with one another to work out the problems as they arose. Dylan bounced around from one man to another, explaining what he wanted, often showing them on the piano what was needed until, like a giant puzzle, the pieces would fit and the picture emerged whole. Dylan worked like a painter covering a huge canvas with the colors that the different musicians could supply him, adding depth and dimension to the total work. All in all, most of the songs went down easily and needed only three or four takes before they were accepted. In some cases, the first take sounded entirely different from the final one because the material was played at a different tempo, perhaps, or a different chord was chosen, or solos may have been rearranged . . . His method of working, the certainty of what he wanted, kept things moving. He would listen to the playbacks in the control booth, discuss what was happening with Tom Wilson, and move on to the next number. If he tried something that didn't go well, he would put it off . . . In this way, he never bogged down—he just kept on going.

Despite successfully rerecording many of the songs cut acoustically on the 13th with full electric backing, Dylan never intended to issue a wholly electric album. The three epic songs he had been performing at his acoustic shows—'Mr. Tambourine Man,' 'Gates of Eden,' and 'It's Alright Ma'—did not lend themselves to electric arrangements. Nor did 'It's All Over Now, Baby Blue,' another song attempted on the 13th that he now returned to, minus one of its melody lines. 'It's All Over Now, Baby Blue' was another of his 'go out in the real world' songs. À la 'To Ramona,' it was less conciliatory, the tone crueler, more demanding. If

Paul Clayton is indeed the Baby Blue he had in mind, as has been suggested, Dylan was digging away at the very foundations of Clayton's self-esteem (the 'seasick sailors' may be a little reference to the album of sailoring songs he recorded for Tradition).

According to legend, Dylan recorded the three songs he had already been performing live in a single stint, the tapes left rolling. In fact, though 'It's Alright Ma' and 'Gates of Eden' were both single takes (as was the 'It's All Over Now, Baby Blue' remake), he required six attempts to get 'Mr. Tambourine Man,' possibly because of an audacious decision to let Langhorne's electric lead play off Dylan's acoustic, on the song he had unwittingly inspired. The results more than justified Dylan's dedication, and illustrated the wisdom of his intuitive decision to leave it off his fourth album.

Five days later, and three thousand miles away, in another Columbia studio on the opposite side of the continent, another combo of producer's favorites, purporting to be the Byrds, were struggling with the selfsame song. Like Dylan, Jim 'Roger' McGuinn and his band of ex-folkies had made their first studio recording of 'Tambourine Man' back in '64, at World Pacific Studios in LA, having acquired a copy of the Dylan/Elliott *Another Side* outtake through their producer, Jim Dickson. McGuinn, Chris Hillman, David Crosby, and Michael Clarke's original recording was a very folkie version, with harmonies, tambourines, and maracas but no ringing twelve-string Rickenbacker refrain within audible range. According to Jim Dickson, Dylan visited the Jet-Set, as they were still calling themselves, during the World Pacific sessions, to give his blessing, but again it is hard to see when. Dickson, as a friend of Dylan's, probably just played him the demo when he was in town in late November/early December. It was still quite a gesture on Dylan's part to allow the Byrds to record such an important unreleased song, even if the Byrds themselves were initially unconvinced as to its suitability.

Whatever their feelings, the Byrds were signed to Columbia that month on the basis of Dickson's demos, and installed in a studio in January to record their version of the unreleased song. The band members themselves seem to have had little say in the matter, Jim Dickson and co-producer Terry Melcher taking matters into their own hands, even dispensing with all the Byrds save McGuinn at the recording session (though Crosby and Gene Clark were allowed in to sing harmony). That's Hal Blaine, Larry Knetchel, Jerry Cole, and an almost inaudible Leon Russell playing behind McGuinn. That chiming twelve-string intro, though, was all McGuinn, even if it took him eighteen takes to get it right. The single was scheduled for an April 12 1965 release, by which time the *Bringing It All Back Home* version would be in the shops, directed at album buyers, still leaving the AM airwaves to McGuinn and his newfound friends.

As Columbia set about releasing Dylan's first 'folk-rock' album and his second 'folk-rock' single ('Subterranean Homesick Blues'), he was making his American farewell to acoustic shows with a brief tour with Joan Baez. Now that Dylan's commercial stock was as great as Baez's, a joint tour seemed practicable. The difference was that Dylan's star was in the ascendant, Baez's assuredly was not, putting her manager in a lather about the whole affair.

Bobby Neuwirth: The feeling around that [Dylan/Baez] tour was pretty good. The only one who was in a sweat about it was Manny [Greenhill]. As far as Bob was concerned, Albert was the guy who took care of all that shit . . . Albert would ask him if he wanted to do something, and he'd say yes or no. There was never any of the evil shit that a lot of people imagined.

Despite the seeming camaraderie, the tour was Dylan's way of raising a parting glass to Baez, the underlying vibe being that this wasn't going to happen again. The final show coincided with the release of *Bringing It All Back Home,* and their joint return to the West Coast, in Dylan's case to play a few solo shows and share in the hype surrounding two new Columbia 45s, Baez to the refuge of her Carmel home to figure out where this relationship might be heading. With her powerful ego, she was never going to be able to live in the shadow of her increasingly influential beau. Yet when Dylan casually invited her to tag along on his forthcoming English tour, she had no idea playing tag was all he had in mind. The intensity of what was happening to Dylan only occurred to Baez with hindsight.

Joan Baez: It was not love that made me such a nuisance . . . it was desperation. For the first time in my short but monumentally successful career someone had stolen all my thunder from under my nose.

A presentiment of the pressures to come occurred during Dylan's brief visit to LA at the end of March. Columbia had thrown a press promotion party the afternoon before his sellout show at the Santa Monica Civic Auditorium, where he became taciturn and playful in turn. When an LA journalist asked for a word to the fans, Dylan responded, 'Astronauts.' Others noticed a new reticence from the original vagabond.

Kim Fowley: At that point it had gone from 'Notice me, Hollywood' to 'I hope nobody notices me.' It went from 'Here I am' to Garboesque. Billy James brought me to Ciro's in the afternoon and there was one of those in-crowd meet & greets where they have tiny sandwiches and everyone stands around acting gay-effete . . . hoping to come or hate or startle, and here comes Bob Dylan, who by then wasn't a lesbian-cowboy-rockabilly God . . . He was a scruffy guy who might have slept on somebody's sofa that day. It was certainly a more accessible person than the person [I saw] posing in front of [the] Bullwinkle [statue in 1963]. I was introduced to him and I asked him a question, What is your concept? He said, 'I ask questions and tell stories.'

That night, Dylan found himself at a party at Mickey and Ben Shapiro's, but quickly felt uncomfortable when required to schmooze and booze, and when Fowley and Love guitarist Bryan MacLean gate-crashed the party, Dylan welcolmed the opportunity to split with them, though not before reconciling with his ex-publicist Billy James, who was now based in LA and stage-managing the Byrds' rapid flight.

Billy James: He said that long rambling thing about the man threatening to commit suicide, there are people dying all over the planet, and you've got that [*Newsweek*] thing [still] running around [in] your head.

The Santa Monica show went well enough, Dylan reverting to acoustic versions of two songs—'She Belongs to Me' and 'Love Minus Zero'—found in electric guises on his new album. However, it was an impromptu appearance at a private gig the following day that generated real publicity for Dylan and his new sound. In the afternoon, he heard what the Byrds had done to his beloved 'Tambourine Man' and, though they had stripped every ounce of meaning from the lyric, he loved it.

Roger McGuinn: We showed him our arrangement of 'Tambourine.' Dylan said, 'Wow, man, you can dance to that.'

Dylan then witnessed the Byrds having to play the song themselves at Ciro's. After one photo op on the steps of the club, he could not resist another, joining the Byrds onstage, on another Dylan original they had already consigned to tape, 'All I Really Wanna Do.' Though he was clearly loving the attention these instantly accessible Byrds versions were garnering on his behalf, he was soon given an insight into how quickly fickle fans could turn when he refused to sing for his supper:

Kim Fowley: All of Hollywood appeared [at Ciro's]. He looked like the album covers. Sonny and Cher were there that night, and they later covered 'All I Really Wanna Do' . . . Everyone was going across the street to an apartment building. Some guy had a party. All of the apartments were connected and all of the doors were open. They had hundreds of people, maybe six hundred, eight hundred. We're all crammed in . . . and all of a sudden we found ourselves with hundreds of people in a room. They all started to yell and scream, it was like a lynch mob, and Bob Dylan had lost his handlers and was against the wall . . . all of a sudden alone, and all these lesser male guys saying, 'Sing for us, you bastard . . . Are you too good for us?' . . . I stood up and said, 'I'm better than Bob Dylan. I will sing for you and he will play for me.' 'Do you know any Bob Dylan chords?' I said to Bob Dylan. 'Play me one and give me a Bob Dylan title.' So he says, 'Walls.' Well, the room . . . got too confused to beat me up. Then the bodyguard types came back for Mr. Dylan. Before he left he said, 'You sing as good as I do.'

Ever since Irwin Silber had published his tirade against Dylan's 'entourage,' he had been taking a good deal of flak for the human barrier he was, out of necessity, forced to construct (and reinforce). One interviewer who had talked to Dylan back in December in Santa Barbara, Bob Blackamar, wrote to *Sing Out,* affirming Silber's view and berating Dylan for his newfound isolation:

He really has lost contact with his audiences and much of reality . . . I met part of Mr. Dylan's clique as well, and it is true that Bob is only interested in singing for their enjoyment.

If incidents like the Hollywood party gave Dylan cause for concern, his entourage of sidekicks like Bobby Neuwirth and Victor Maymudes were not merely silent heavies, protecting their boss from physical harm, they were verbal sparring partners, assistants to the game master as Dylan resorted to a form of verbal intimidation, running numbers on the neophobes for the mutual gratification and entertainment of the Unholy Hipsters. Baez, an old friend of Neuwirth's, was one of the butts for such jousting as was any journalist—even those given honorary membership in the inner circle. Robert Shelton, Nat Hentoff, Al Aronowitz, Ralph J. Gleason, and J. R. Goddard were never immune, save when they were assisting the game master in a grander design, as when Goddard ran a script of a wholly fictional press conference, composed by Dylan, in the *Village Voice* in March. A series of inside jokes, the 'conference' concluded with the question, 'Who do you think can save the world?' to which the reply was 'Al Aronowitz.'

Al Aronowitz: To be the constant targets of digs from Bob was the price each of us paid for hanging out with him. He was, after all, some kind of messiah to each of us and so each one of us in his inner circle willingly paid the price. Bob liked to feel big by making his hangers-on feel small.

If the insiders in Dylan's coterie were quite capable of fending for themselves, outsiders rarely were. In February 1965, he appeared on Les Crane's popular TV show and duly demolished Crane on air. Referring to his host throughout as 'Less,' he neatly sidestepped each and every question. When, predictably, he was asked for his main message, he replied, 'Eat.' Asked about a movie he was planning to make, he informed Crane it would be a horror cowboy movie. Asked if he played the horror cowboy, he asserted, 'No. I play my mother.'

Ramblin' Jack Elliott: Crane dressed up like Bob Dylan and wore some funny pegged pants and Spanish boots. He had a necktie on and Dylan teased him about the necktie. Les asked Bob a lot of stupid questions, which Dylan loved and answered them all in his usual irascible manner . . . Crane loved it but it made him look like a jerk. Afterwards, we went in a limo to some fancy nightclub uptown . . . Some girl fan appeared and wanted to get his autograph and talk to him. This girl was made to feel unwelcome but she hung in there . . . He was making fun of her, trying to make her feel miserable and kept saying, 'Through the hoop! Through the hoop!' and holding up this imaginary circus hoop.

The cruel tone creeping into his songs had begun to permeate everything Dylan said and did. An inevitable side effect of persistent amphetamine use, his cruel streak became bound up with a peculiarly sixties conceit, hip versus square. With an anti-intellectual streak as wide as the water, he had always rebelled against accepted wisdom. Now, with those around him convinced that his words had an almost prophetic quality, he too began to believe his ship was about to come in.

In many ways, it was. *Bringing It All Back Home*, released March 22, may well be the most influential album of its era. Almost everything to come in contemporary popular song can be found therein. With 'Subterranean Homesick Blues,' Dylan even presaged the advent of rap and the promo video, even if the riff was a shameless cop from Chuck Berry's 'Too Much Monkey Business.' That such an obvious homage kicked off the album was as deliberate and as provocative a statement as calling his previous album *Another Side*. Littered with drug references and street talk, Dylan's anti-establishment tirade was a tone down from its original self, when it was 'teachers, preachers' not 'cheaters, users' looking to trade blows. The folk references were there to be found, but to them had been added everything from the beats to the Beatles. Even if 'Subterranean Homesick Blues' gave the Byrds' 'Mr. Tambourine Man' no real contest up the charts, stalling at number thirty-nine, it said a lot more about where pop music was bound, and who was driving the plane.

1965: Over Your Shoulder

10

Don't Look Back was . . . somebody else's movie . . . I don't think it was accurate at all in terms of showing my formative years. It showed only one side. He made it seem like I wasn't doing anything but living in hotel rooms, playing the typewriter and holding press conferences for journalists. Throwing some bottles, there's something about [that] in the movie. Joan Baez is in it. All that is true, you know. But it's one-sided.

—*Bob Dylan, 1978*

I think, in *Don't Look Back*, that Dylan's enacting his life—as he wishes to enact it. Not necessarily as it *is*, and not necessarily as he wishes it *were*, but just as he wants to act it. *Don't Look Back* is a kind of fiction, but it's Dylan's fiction, not mine. He makes it up as he goes along.

—*D. A. Pennebaker*

The brief English tour Dylan undertook at the beginning of May 1965 remains well documented and fondly recalled. The main reason is Don Pennebaker's cinema-vérité study *Don't Look Back*, a ninety-minute black-and-white docudrama of life on the road with America's premier folk poet. And certainly the film is a remarkable study of the pressures of fame as they begin to affect a self-assured, talented young singer-songwriter. But, as Dylan suggests, the portrait composed for that movie has become forever fixed in people's minds as representing the Young Dylan, something with which Dylan has never been entirely comfortable. When Pennebaker completed the movie in April 1966 and showed it to him in Los Angeles, just before he embarked on that famous world tour, he insisted that there would have to be a lot of changes. However, at a second screening the following day, Dylan's Gemini self decided to let the film stand as is.

Dylan's original intentions in making the film have never been clear. Clearly the *idea* of making a movie appealed to him. He had told Les Crane in February he would be making a movie shortly, though *Don't*

Look Back was hardly a horror cowboy movie. Presumably, like his 'novel,' he felt it was one more medium to conquer—perhaps he just hoped they'd screen it at the Edelstein multiplex.

D. A. Pennebaker: I think that Dylan had a very parochial sense about his operation. He was going to do things totally differently from the way they'd been done; he was gonna revamp network schedules; he was gonna revamp movies; he was gonna make everything in a new way—without being quite sure how he'd do it.

Having abandoned the horror cowboy movie in favour of a documentary, Pennebaker's name came about because, in his words, 'Sara Lowndes was working for us, at the main Time-Life office. She had shown Bob a copy of [my short film] *Daybreak Express*, and he apparently had seen me somewhere by chance at some party.' Accompanied by Bobby Neuwirth, Dylan met up with Pennebaker at the Cedar Tavern in New York sometime in March, intending to test his suitability in the usual way—a few verbal games. Pennebaker wisely played along. The one idea Dylan brought to the tavern table that day was for a promotional video that would parody the out-of-sync, Ringo-rides-a-bicycle efforts that passed for the form in 1965.

D. A. Pennebaker: We were down in the Cedar Tavern . . . and he said, 'I was thinking of making up these cards and holding them up and running them like for a song,' where the words would be the words for the song . . . It would be a takeoff of what the Beatles had to do when they had to play the playback, which was demeaning. They accepted it because they were told you had to do this to sell records . . . Dylan wanted to put a little needle into that, by doing it as a gag.

Pennebaker, in deciding to go along with Dylan's ill-defined celluloid conceits, was taking something of a risk. The deal Grossman made with Pennebaker required Leacock-Pennebaker Inc. to put up the costs of making the film, and any profits would be divided equally. So Pennebaker was taking an awful lot on faith. He did not really know a lot about Dylan's work, nor what filming would be like, though his meeting with Dylan and Neuwirth gave him something of a foretaste. Yet, as soon as he arrived in London, on April 26, he could see that some fascinating process was about to unravel before the camera's Eye.

D. A. Pennebaker: Dylan . . . was under a number of pressures, including those from Joan Baez (personal) and the concerts (public). I had to take it on faith the film would not be a series of press conferences, and getting in and out of concert halls . . . It became clear that Dylan was going through some kind of change, and I knew that if I could stick with him I'd see something of it.

The first indication of the pressures Dylan now faced came the minute he landed at London Airport. How aware he was of his newfound popularity in England is not clear. His UK publicist, Ken Pitt, had been keeping Grossman fully informed, and he must have known his records were selling in England, but the commercial snowball that had been rolling since his appearance at the Festival Hall in May 1964 had achieved critical mass by April 15, 1965. At the beginning of the month his first UK single had entered the charts. It was, rather incongruously, 'The Times They Are A-Changin',' a song he had spent the last eighteen months trying to disown. Two weeks later, the steadily escalating sales of *Freewheelin'* finally took it to number one on the album charts, where it had been a regular feature for nigh on a year. This was quite an achievement. Since March 9, 1963, when *Please Please Me* first made it to number one, there had only been six chart-topping albums, four by the Beatles and two by the Rolling Stones. Such was the hegemony of English pop.

Not only did *Freewheelin'* create the first chink in the Beatles/Stones edifice, but Dylan's entire acoustic catalog had gone Top 20 in the previous six months, and *The Times They Are A-Changin'* and *Another Side* re-entered the Top 10 on his arrival. Evidently he was not some popular folksinger, but a star, and Britain had a well-established, tabloid-dominated national press who knew the importance of stars. An event that in America might have warranted a mention in the gossip column of the *New York Post* was national news in Britain.

If Dylan almost certainly did not appreciate how famous he now was, he knew the press would be awaiting his arrival, as he entered the VIP lounge at London Airport for his first genuine press conference carrying a large industrial lightbulb. Confident that he would be asked about his main message—after all, no American journalist had resisted asking the question in the last two years—he responded with, 'Keep a good head and always carry a lightbulb.' The press games had begun, even if on this occasion he seemed happy to talk.

A further press conference the following day at the Savoy Hotel found him less cooperative and, as the round of interviews filled up the three days before his first concert in Sheffield, the interminable questions—

always obvious, often patronizing his work and his fans; witness Maureen Cleave's question in *Don't Look Back:* Do your fans understand a word you sing?—rapidly burned out his short fuse. Subsequent interviews with the 'straight' press would be exercises in obfuscation, Dylan always mercilessly putting on his interviewers. Yet in the company of hipper members of the music press, like Ray Coleman of *Melody Maker* or the amateur student journalists he occasionally encountered along the way, he dropped the game board to give straight answers to honest questions. Interviewed in Sheffield for the university paper, he even gave a surprisingly frank explanation of his treatment of 'newspaper reporters.'

Bob Dylan: They ask the wrong questions, like, What did you have for breakfast, What's your favourite color, stuff like that. Newspaper reporters, man, they're just hung-up writers, frustrated novelists, they don't hurt me none by putting fancy labels on me. They got all these preconceived ideas about me, so I just play up to them. [1965]

The most famous of Dylan's verbal batterings was undoubtedly with *Time* reporter Horace Judson. In *Don't Look Back,* he is already working on Judson as the camera rolls, and it cuts away only after Dylan informs the shell-shocked Judson that not only can he sing as well as the great operatic tenor Caruso, but, 'I can hold my breath three times as long.' According to Anthea Joseph, who can be seen in the background, Judson did not just crawl away meekly after Dylan's onslaught.

Anthea Joseph: Bob was being absolutely appalling, but so brilliant. By this time I'd learnt that he could pull strips of skin off people, verbally . . . [But Judson] was quite abusive as well. He was extremely upset, he really was; and in a way I suppose it was not really his fault — not properly briefed, treating Bob as some sort of curiosity, not as a serious artist.

Not all victims fed to Dylan by uncomprehending editors took umbrage. Laurie Henshaw of *Disc and Music Echo* encountered a Dylan even ruder than the one who had launched into Judson. However, his stream of put-ons delighted Henshaw, who published the interview as it was, under the banner MR SEND UP, claiming it was 'the most fantastic interview that the amazing Bob Dylan has ever given!' having indeed secured Dylan's most outrageous interview to date.

BD: You don't ask me where I was born, where I lived. Don't ask me those questions.

LH: Why be so hostile?
BD: Because you're hostile to me. You're using me. I'm an object to you. I
went through this before in the United States, you know . . . Why should I
have to go along with something just so that somebody else can eat? Why don't
you just say that my name is Kissenovitch . . . and I come from Acapulco,
Mexico. That my father was an escaped thief from South Africa. Okay. You
can say anything you want to say.

Terry Ellis not only survived the verbal battering given him as a naive
science student, backstage at Newcastle City Hall, but went on to found
Chrysalis Records, manage Jethro Tull, and become a millionaire.

Terry Ellis: I remember he had a wicked glint in his eye—I couldn't tell
you if that was chemically induced.

That that glint in his eye *was* chemically induced, by this point, is not
really in doubt. And Dylan was not alone on his speed trip. For his
entourage to be able to withstand the verbal barrage, from Dylan and
Neuwirth in particular, speed was almost a necessity. As Dylan camped
out at the Savoy Hotel for the duration, almost commuting to his shows
around the country, the number of hangers-on began to grow.

Marianne Faithfull: We all sat on the floor of Bob's room talking, drinking,
and playing guitars while Bob pretended none of this was happening. He
would walk in and out of the room, sit down and type, talk on the phone,
he would even answer incredibly stupid questions, but only if he felt like
pulling that particular thing into focus. Otherwise we might as well have
been invisible . . . They were all so hip, so devastatingly hip. They were all
so fucking high. Every five minutes or so someone would go into the
bathroom and come out speaking in tongues.

It was clear that Dylan was becoming increasingly dependent on
drugs. Faithfull, who in her autobiography states that methedrine (i.e.,
methamphetamine) was the drug of choice at the Savoy in '65, seems to
have been the most reliable, and regular, witness to the goings-on. That
Dylan and the others were using the bathroom suggests shooting or
snorting, probably the latter—popping pills no longer did the trick. That
his drug habit was starting to wear Dylan down was noted by Nico, who
was now in London trying to replicate Marianne Faithfull's successful
launch as a pop diva with Stones manager Andrew Loog Oldham and
his Immediate label:

Nico: He looked terrible. Bob was completely drugged up and moody and arrogant as ever. I had not seen him so thin and white, like a matchstick. He was asking me all the time about the Stones and their clothes . . . He looked like a handyman.

Of course, it wasn't just the drugs that were working their charms on Dylan's physiology. The pressures that in America were already impinging on his personal freedom were on a whole other level in the pressure cooker of a pop-mad Britain. Inevitably, Dylan turned to his fellow sufferers for guidance.

D. A. Pennebaker: Watching Dylan go through the process of becoming more and more celebrated was really interesting because I don't think anybody can ever imagine that. For a normal person, you have no idea what the stresses are, what the downside is . . . If the only other people in the world that are as famous as you are the Beatles, they are your friends.

An article in *Melody Maker,* 'The Beatles Dig Dylan,' published that January, had given Dylan's commercial standing in the UK a major fillip. The Beatles were also in regular attendance at the Savoy, even if the awe they felt for Dylan erected a barrier that neither party seemed entirely able to breach. The Rolling Stones were equally intimidated by Dylan's presence, but felt the same compulsion to participate in acts of homage.

John Lennon: I just remember . . . that we were both in shades . . . and all these freaks around us . . . Ginsberg and all those people. I was anxious as shit.

Dana Gillespie: [Dylan] was the one person that both the Stones and the Beatles had great admiration for, so when he held court in one of the hotel rooms, everyone sat and listened.

Don't Look Back features a Dylan who is 'on' at all times, always onstage, meeting fans, entertaining friends and hangers-on, or putting the press on. Even the hotel jam with Baez is a performance, albeit for a chosen few: Neuwirth, Baez, Grossman, and Pennebaker. Indeed, the portrait Pennebaker paints is one of a private man required to react to the prying onslaught of others. As Dylan himself said, it's one-sided. And yet he could still revert to the shy, wry individual of yore, as those who shared time with him on his two previous visits have confirmed.

Anthea Joseph: I think he was being over-peopled . . . It was quite extraordinary the difference . . . When it was just us he was perfectly comfortable, perfectly relaxed, and perfectly easy. But once the place was full of people there was a little gear change and he became the public person. But every now and then he'd go and disappear and start bashing away at the typewriter, which was on the desk.

Ken Pitt: I quickly discovered that while you were on your own with him, he was an absolute delight to be with, but when his henchmen and his minders and his hangers-on came into view, he turned into 'Bob Dylan.'

Pitt's subtext suggests that the game master no longer controlled the game. An example of how Dylan was beginning to feel the pressure came the day before his Royal Albert Hall debut. Enjoying hanging out with assorted friends at a folk club in Soho, he heard that his whereabouts had become known, and that some fans were heading his way. Forced to return to the security of the Savoy, he then proved incapable of saying no to another party on room service.

Anthea Joseph: There was Donovan, the Pretty Things, assorted other odds and sods . . . We take over a table downstairs [at Les Cousins] . . . Baez wasn't there. She was still in the hotel in a sulk . . . And then . . . a friend of mine came into the pub—and said, 'Did you know they've heard that Dylan's in here and they're beginning to come up the road.' So I said to him, 'We [need to] leave.' So Dorothy [Carthy] and me hoiked him out and this taxi came round the corner into Wardour Street with his light on. I stopped him and got in and there was this blonde person in it, and we do not know where she came from. However, she paid the fare. We were halfway to the Savoy [before we] realized that none of us had enough money for the fare . . . [Having managed to reach the Savoy], the three of us [were] planning to just have a really nice chat [but] Bob invited this girl to come up—she didn't say no. And so we were sort of milling around talking about old times and that sort of nonsense and the phone rang. It was the porter saying, 'There's an awful lot of people downstairs saying you're having a party.' I said, 'Are you having a party?' He said, 'No.' I said, 'Well, they seem to think you're having a party.' He said, 'Well, I suppose we ought to have a party.' So I said, 'Okay, you get onto room service and order the booze. I'm not taking responsibility for this.' . . . All sorts of people turned up. Allen [Ginsberg] was there. I mean, everybody was there. And I was going around dishing out the drinks. And then this row broke out . . . These two bozos had locked themselves in the bathroom, where it had beautiful glass shelves—Those wonderful sort of thirties bathrooms! They were just chucking them out [the window].

Once again, Pennebaker was on hand to capture the denouement, as Dylan exploded, 'WHO THREW THAT FUCKING GLASS?!?' Joseph witnessed a side of Dylan she had not previously seen that night: 'Bob was sort of jumping [up and down]. I'd never seen him lose his temper before. It was really quite frightening. He went up like a little torch. And rightfully so.' That he allowed his out-of-context explosion to be part of Pennebaker's film suggests a degree of empathy for the cinema-vérité form, one-sided or not.

The evening here described by Joseph was no isolated example. The suite at the Savoy was constantly overrun with people. If it was not cocktail parties arranged by Grossman, it was journalists wanting one-to-one interviews; if not journalists, Allen Ginsberg and his beat friends; if not them, assorted members of England's thriving beat-group scene come to pay their respects.

In *Don't Look Back* an indication of the mayhem that usually filled the suite comes when Neuwirth, Dylan, and Baez are finally left alone (save for Pennebaker's Eye), and Neuwirth says, 'Welcome home. It's the first time that this room hasn't been full of a bunch of insane lunatics, man, that I can remember . . . It's the first time it's been *cool* around here.' Even then, Baez's presence makes relaxation all but impossible until, in classic 'who can rid me of this woman' fashion, Dylan looks on impassively as Neuwirth turns on Baez, telling her, 'Sister, you fagged out long ago,' articulating something to Baez that Dylan himself could not, or would not, admit to himself.

Joan Baez: One night I went to Neuwirth's room crying. He put his arms around me and mopped a pint of tears off my cheeks and chin, and begged me to pack up my bags and leave the tour. 'But Bob asked me to come. He asked me,' I protested. 'I know, but he don't know what's happening anymore, can't you see? He's just out there spinnin' and he wants to do it by himself.'

Whatever Baez's expectations may have been—and she was planning her own concerts in England that summer, where she remained considerably less well known than in America—Dylan clearly had no intention of introducing her at his concerts. If that rebuff hurt, it was only the beginning of his ruthless deflating of Baez's considerable ego. When, some years later, one of Dylan's girlfriends, on reading Baez's version of events in her autobiography, accused him of hurting her, he snapped back, 'She hurt herself.' Perhaps he had come to realize that a certain brutality was required to get the message through. One incident witnessed by Faithfull should certainly have provided the necessary message, writ large.

Marianne Faithfull: [Baez] insisted on singing her high vibrato version[s] of 'Here Comes the Night' and 'Go Now,' which Dylan complained about. He hates her voice and tells her so. At one point he held up a bottle as she sang a high note, and drawled, 'Break that!' She just laughed.

Baez was not the only lady friend on the receiving end of Dylan's sudden mood shifts. Marianne Faithfull was a witness to one such character swing one night at the Savoy. A nervous young Faithfull, in awe of Dylan, just didn't know how to deal with the situation when he finally came on to her. Stoned, and equally uncertain, Dylan's reaction to her gentle rebuff smacked of a man in permanent arrested adolescence, unused to hearing the word *no*—i.e., a rock star.

Marianne Faithfull: Without warning he turned into Rumpelstiltskin. He went over to the typewriter, took a sheaf of papers and began ripping them up into smaller and smaller pieces, which he let fall into the wastepaper basket. 'Are you satisfied now?' he asked. I was witnessing a little tantrum of genius. With that he stormed out in a rage. I sat there pinned to my chair. He returned a moment later with renewed fury and threw me out.

The women who responded to his minimal coaxing almost exclusively conformed to his preferred type. When he met up with the amply endowed Dana Gillespie at an official welcoming party on the first day of his visit, Baez discovered at first hand the sort of philandering that had tortured Suze before her.

Dana Gillespie: Dylan and I started talking almost as soon as I walked in . . . He was fairly blatant about it, and made some remark about my forty-four-inch bust.

Baez may have been able to dismiss Dylan's relationship with Gillespie as essentially physical, but she found it harder to deal with the presence of Sara Lowndes, the ravenlike American beauty who appeared for the first time in his company on his return from the Continent. Lowndes had joined him in Paris after the English tour, and they had traveled together to Portugal for a brief holiday before returning to London. Lowndes answered the door of Dylan's hotel suite when Baez called to see if he had recovered from a bout of food poisoning. Baez was stunned, but finally took the hint, even if she would continue to address Dylan in song, and continue to believe that he was addressing her in song.

D. A. Pennebaker: A peculiar situation [exists] around royal entourages, palaces, courts in general, politics, and that is that you can be number four or five, but if you're used to being number one or two it's a big jolt—and that's what that was about. There were other people in Dylan's life—there was Sara—and Baez kind of knew it.

Most viewers of *Don't Look Back* don't realize how brief is the time span covered in the film. Dylan spent longer in England (and Europe) at the end of his tour than on the road. The film covers barely two weeks in the life, and during that time he played just eight concerts, hardly the most rigorous schedule ever devised. The concerts themselves were well received, though his performances were beginning to sound a tad stale. Pennebaker has said that he didn't feel that playing live was the most important part of what was happening to Dylan in 1965, hence the lack of live footage in *Don't Look Back*. The tapes of these shows bear his assessment out. Though the performances are not exactly lackluster, they sound almost formulaic, something of which Dylan himself was acutely aware.

Bob Dylan: I was doing fine, you know, singing and playing my guitar. It was a sure thing . . . I was getting very bored with that . . . I knew what the audience was going to do, how they would react. It was very automatic. [1965]

Of course, part of the problem was that, in England, he was still seen as the man responsible for *Freewheelin'* and three other acoustic albums. Only at the end of the tour was *Bringing It All Back Home* released, and 'Subterranean Homesick Blues' began its steady climb up the charts. In fact, *Bringing It All Back Home* was already at number one on the UK album charts by the end of May, suggesting considerable commercial acceptance for his new sound. Irrespective of sales, though, Dylan was no longer comfortable in his acoustic guise. When a fan tells him in *Don't Look Back* that she does not like his new single, he tellingly mutters, 'Oh, you're one of those. I understand now.' In the film he can also be seen talking to a band who play electric versions of his songs, keen to hear how they sound.

Fascinated by the English R&B scene that had sprung up in the previous couple of years, Dylan decided that he wanted to record with one of these homegrown bands. One suspects that he was looking for something similar to the sound John Hammond, Jr., had harnessed with the Hawks, perhaps even hoping to record an album's worth of songs in a couple of sessions, like Hammond. A desire to achieve something usable seems borne out by Tom Wilson's presence at the session at Levy's Recording Studio on May 12, having flown over from New York to produce. Wilson told an attending journalist, 'We're going to try a little experimental stuff tonight.' Dylan's choice of combo was an intriguing one. Having only recently acquired a young guitarist named Eric Clapton from the Yardbirds, John Mayall's Bluesbreakers had released just one badly recorded live album and a 45, 'Crawling up a Hill,' at the time of the session. R&B was all they played, or cared to play.

Eric Clapton: John had recorded a song called 'Life Is Like a Slow Train Going up a Hill' [sic] and that interested Bob. Bob came in, looked for John Mayall. I was just the guitar player on the session. He had a friend called Bobby Neuwirth who was a fantastic player. Bobby Neuwirth was his kind of court jester at the time. [He] kept coming up to me and saying, 'You're playing too much blues, man. He needs to be more country!'

The first surprise of the session, drummer Hughie Flint recalls, was that 'when he came in, Dylan immediately sat down at the piano and started playing.' Though he had played piano on occasions in the studio prior to this, it had always been as a solo artist. After one less-than-together run-through of 'If You Gotta Go, Go Now,' with Dylan at the piano, it sounds on the session tape like Mayall observing, 'You haven't worked much with bands, have you?' Despite Neuwirth's input, the session was wholly unproductive, both Dylan and Wilson, upon realizing that they weren't about to record a British *So Many Roads,* giving themselves up to more Bacchanalian pursuits.

Hughie Flint: All through the session it was just messing around. I don't think we played a complete number. It was a real mess. There was a lot of booze there, crates and crates of wine—I'd never seen so much wine, and everybody got very pissed, very quickly, no one more so than Dylan.

Nico was one of the 'girlfriends' who sat around at the session 'like the chickens waiting for our rooster.' According to her, Dylan took this opportunity to cut a piano demo of 'I'll Keep It with Mine' for her use, and indeed just such a demo was registered with Witmark around this time. Nico, though, 'felt too old for this,' and left Dylan in the arms of another 'chick,' Nadia Catouse. That the session did not work out was no big deal in the scheme of things; but that Dylan had only two songs, both outtakes from his previous album to record, five months after he wrapped up *Bringing It All Back Home,* should have been a source of considerable concern to any Columbia executive hearing the results of Dylan's second London recording session.

The songwriter was focused on more literary pursuits. Through the fall of 1964 and the first few months of 1965 Dylan seemed to be working flat out on his book, despite not having found a title he was happy with. An excerpt in *Sing Out* in January 1965 gave the title as *Walk Down Crooked Highway*; in March 1965 he told Paul Jay Robbins in LA that it was 'tentatively [called] *Bob Dylan off the Record. . .* [but] the book can't really be titled, that's the kind of book it is.' At least the samples published in *Sing Out* and *Pageant* that winter, neither of which appears in the final book, showed that he had arrived at a stylistic form. Staying with Baez in Carmel, or at Grossman's in Woodstock, he wrote and wrote. According to Baez he left a huge wad of papers for the book at her house, never reclaiming them.

By the time he arrived in England at the end of April, he had nearly completed the book. He had also finally come up with a title, which he revealed to Michael Hellicar of the *Daily Sketch* prior to embarking on his English tour. The choice of *Tarantula* as the title has rarely been convincingly explained. Like the name Dylan, only its inventor knows the real reason for its choice. However, there can be little doubt that he had by now read a particular chapter from a classic philosophical work of the nineteenth century, entitled 'On Tarantulas':

Behold, this is the hole of the tarantula. Do you want to see the tarantula itself? Here hangs its web; touch it, that it tremble! There it comes willingly; welcome tarantula! Your triangle and symbol sits black on your back; and I know also what sits in your soul. Revenge sits in your soul: whenever you bite, black scabs grow. Your poison makes the soul whirl with revenge . . . therefore I tear at your webs that your rage may lure you out of your lie-holes and your revenge may leap out from behind your word justice. For that man be delivered from revenge, that is for me the bridge to the highest hope, and a rainbow after long storms.

Thus spake Nietzsche, via Zarathustra; the same Nietzsche who would get a name check in the sleeve notes to *Highway 61 Revisited*. Though

the style of *Thus Spoke Zarathustra* hardly conforms to that of *Tarantula,*
as a book of prose poems portraying the visions of a traveling seer it may
have provided some kind of inspiration. Another book of prose poems,
the visions of a seer whose memory served him well, Rimbaud's *A Season
in Hell,* provides equally little clue to *Tarantula*'s style, though the blurring
of poetry and prose Rimbaud achieved with his little 'Nigger book' was
evidently something Dylan aspired to. With no obvious literary role
models, Dylan suggested to Paul Jay Robbins in early April that cutups
had a large part to play in the way the book was being constructed.

Bob Dylan: I've written some songs which are kind of far out, a long
continuation of verses, stuff like that . . . I haven't really gotten into writing
a completely free song. You dig something like cutups? . . . I wrote the
book because there's a lot of stuff in there I can't possibly sing . . . Something
that has no rhyme, all cut up, no nothing except something happening
which is words. [1965]

In truth, *Tarantula* was nothing of the sort, much as the seemingly
random synchronicity of words appealed to Dylan. When he was required
to actually explain the relationship between the cutup technique and his
own work he was undone.

Marianne Faithfull: One afternoon he was trying to explain his novel, the
as-yet-unpublished *Tarantula,* to a journalist. He'd written it, he told her,
using William Burroughs's and Brion Gysin's cutup technique. The woman
was initially intrigued: 'Oh, what's that?' she asked. 'Is it a literary theory?'
She'd obviously never heard of it, so Dylan proceeded to explain it to her,
using a copy of the *Daily Telegraph* and a pair of scissors. But as soon as he
started trying to assemble the scraps of newspaper, you knew he'd never
actually done it.

Another of the phrases he had given to Robbins, 'a long continuation
of verses,' was a more accurate description of the book's eventual contents.
If the line between his songs and poems had become increasingly blurred
since the death of Kennedy, the original draft of 'Subterranean Homesick
Blues' could as easily have found its home in the pages of *Tarantula* as
between the grooves of *Bringing It All Back Home.* Indeed his sometime
sidekick Ben Carruthers had only recently taken one of his poems from
the back of *Another Side,* 'Jack o' Diamonds,' set it to music, and put it out
as a single (while Dylan was in the UK Carruthers played it to him).
Whatever *Tarantula*'s antecedents—and a healthy dose of the beats lies

therein—its symbolism was uniquely Dylan's, so uniquely his that he soon began to realize that his book was little more than a series of in-jokes that would be lost on those literary critics waiting for an excuse to denigrate the so-called bard of the airwaves. In his own words, he recognized that 'the folks back home just aren't going to understand this at all.' Later that fall, he confided in Nat Hentoff serious doubts concerning the book's merits. Though he delivered almost a parable to Hentoff, about a novel he was working on 'one time,' it is undoubtedly *Tarantula* he was alluding to:

Bob Dylan: One time I wanted to write a novel; and so I was putting a lot of time in. It must have been about six months, off and on . . . and finally I just came to the conclusion . . . Is this gonna be THE novel, THE statement? Is this my message? My thing? And no matter how many pages—I had about five hundred pages of it—I said, 'No, of course not.' That's bullshit. This is nothing. If I finish this novel, it's not gonna come out until at least a year and a half to two years from now. It's gonna be a completely different thing by the time it does come out . . . Meantime, I'm not even gonna be there any more . . . It won't even be me that wrote that novel. And from then on I have to live up to that novel . . . People are gonna ask me what I'm doing . . . I'm gonna HAVE to say I'm writing another novel! [1965]

His problem now was that everyone expected a book called *Tarantula*. Journalists wanted him to talk about the book. Dylan, accordingly, developed a potpourri of descriptions for it, vague, generic hints of some hidden theme. Thus 'it's about spiders . . . It's an insect book . . . My next book is a collection of epitaphs'; alternatively, it was 'a book of confusion, tiny little sayings. It's like a splash on the wall'; or in a fit of honesty, 'I can't really say what it's about. It's not a narrative or anything like that.' As the year grew on, he carried the galleys with him from show to show, from state to state, all the while reading it to friends and other strangers, seeking their honest opinion, but also hinting to others of a seismic shift in perspective.

Bob Dylan: I have a lot of words written for it but I can't use anything I've written . . . before a year ago . . . I can't really use the ideas. They're so deformed and just not really right ideas. Stuff which has been expressed a million times in the past . . . I don't write now unless it just happens. [1965]

That final telling remark, to the unctuous Allen Stone in October 1965, was a form of confession. *Tarantula* was the product of a time when he felt compelled to type and, in a speed-driven frenzy, would write (and write and write . . .). The blurb accompanying the hardback publication of *Tarantula* would allege that '1965–66, the most crowded and energetic period of his career, the years which produced . . . "Like a Rolling Stone," "Desolation Row" . . . "Visions of Johanna" and "Ballad of a Thin Man" . . . [was the] period Dylan also wrote *Tarantula*.' In fact, it was those songs, specifically 'Like a Rolling Stone', that led Dylan to abandon conventional literary ambitions.

Bob Dylan: I found myself writing this song, this story, this long piece of vomit about twenty pages long, and out of it I took 'Like a Rolling Stone' . . . After writing that, I wasn't interested in writing a novel, or a play. [1966]

'Like a Rolling Stone' had started out as one of those 'long continuation of verses . . . something that has no rhyme, all cut up,' but as Dylan extracted the elixir from its poisonous venom, he left his spider book for dead. Originally an ill-formed mass of words whose direction was uncertain, 'Like a Rolling Stone' may not have delivered Dylan from revenge, but it was a rainbow of sorts after a stormy season.

Bob Dylan: [When] it was ten pages long, it wasn't called anything, just a rhythm thing on paper, all about my steady hatred, directed at some point that was honest. [1966]

Dylan has, on occasion, been coy about what drove him to focus his 'steady hatred . . . at some point that was honest,' for 'Like a Rolling Stone' is a truly vengeful song—on a level of misogyny even the Stones had yet to scale. But he has not always sought the benefit of the doubt. At the famous San Francisco press conference in December 1965, one of the 'hipper' journalists asked Dylan whether he wrote such songs to help the people they were directed at. He shoots back, 'I just want to needle them.' The subject matter of 'Like a Rolling Stone' is a woman who has not really known hardship, but on whom hard times are about to descend. Written a matter of days after Baez finally took the hint, 'Like a Rolling Stone' may even be that rare beast, a song directed at Joanie. If so, Dylan was not entirely unconcerned about her feelings. On the page, at least, he wanted to know, 'How does it feel?'

After 'Like a Rolling Stone,' Dylan realized he could fit everything he felt compelled to say into song, even if he had to redefine the form in the process. His last prose poems (save for sleeve notes to *Planet Waves* and *Desire*) would be included on the rear sleeve of *Highway 61 Revisited* and in the program for the 1965 Newport Folk Festival. The events that fateful weekend suggested a new direction home, one in which no spiders would be tempted to tarantella after him.

1965: I Accept Chaos

11

Last spring, I guess I was going to quit singing. I was very drained. I was playing a lot of songs I didn't want to play. I was singing words I didn't really want to sing . . . It's very tiring having other people tell you how much they dig you, if you yourself don't dig you.

—Bob Dylan, 1965

The decision to quit singing was no frivolous whim. Dylan's final days in London had been troubled ones. A week in bed from food poisoning after a holiday in Portugal with Sara had given him a lot of time to think. He became convinced that he could go no further with his music. He would later talk to journalists about this fleeting decision, on his 1965–66 tour with the Hawks.

For most acts in pop music the imposition of fame happens so rapidly that there is little opportunity to step back and isolate oneself from the phenomenon. The process in Dylan's case, however, had been percolating for three years, ever since 'Blowin' in the Wind' had been a huge hit for Peter, Paul and Mary; his ambivalence a good deal longer—until no more good times would he crave. At the end of May he presented himself with a choice. He could commit himself to his boyhood dream and embrace rock & roll stardom, or he could walk away from it all. It would be unwise to underestimate how seriously he considered the latter option. He would tell Nat Hentoff in 1966, 'People have one great blessing—obscurity.' It's fair to say that, by then, he knew what he had given up.

On one level his dilemma was simply artistic restlessness. In the fall of 1963 he had come to realize the shallowness of the topical-song stream. In the spring of 1965 he was hard at work on his first book. Such diversions were part of a thirst for something more than the acoustic music he was making. If *Bringing It All Back Home* found him back on terra firma, it also seemed to represent, initially at least, the outer limits of where he could see himself going musically. His attempt to record with an authentic rhythm & blues band in England had been a disaster, and the five months since *BIABH* had resulted in no new chains of flashing images.

'Like a Rolling Stone' opened up that unseen levee, out of which poured many of his greatest songs. Though he had been impressed by the sound that the Beatles, the Animals, and the Byrds had succeeded in getting, he wanted something that truly brought it back home—a rhythm & blues sound with a folk sensibility. When 'Like a Rolling Stone' introduced it to the world, it would be called folk-rock, though Dylan always justifiably hated that expression.

Bob Dylan: What I'm doing now, it's a whole other thing. We're not playing rock music. It's not a hard sound. These people call it folk-rock— if they want to call it that, something that simple, it's good for selling the records. As far as it being what it is, I don't know what it is. I can't call it folk-rock. It's a whole way of doing things. [1965]

Dylan required a sound that lent meaning to the words, enabled them to cohabit without conflict. He had evidently decided to consolidate his success on the pop charts, and to signpost his chosen course, by recording 'Like a Rolling Stone' *as a single*. The first computation required in his new mathematical sound was to come, as always, from the guitarist. The problem solver on *Bringing It All Back Home* had been Bruce Langhorne. This time it was to be Michael Bloomfield, the young white blues guitarist Dylan had jammed with in Chicago back in April 1963. Why Langhorne was not recalled is unclear. Perhaps he was simply unavailable, perhaps Dylan wanted something imbued with the blues, but not the blues. Curiously, Bloomfield later informed Langhorne that he was constantly being told to play like him throughout the ensuing sessions.

Dylan had run into Bloomfield on a couple of occasions since the Bear, at an after-gig party when he played Chicago's Orchestra Hall in December 1963 and at the *So Many Roads* session, if he was truly in attendance. But what presumably prompted his renewed interest in the young colt were tapes Paul Rothchild had been making for Elektra of the Paul Butterfield Blues Band, for whom Bloomfield was now whipping up a storm. Rothchild probably played these to Dylan just after his return from Albion. The Butterfield Blues Band was as close to England's Bluesbreakers as America could provide in 1965. This time, though, Dylan sought to enjoin only the guitarist. He invited Bloomfield to Woodstock the weekend before the session now booked at Columbia.

Michael Bloomfield: I didn't even have a guitar case. I just had my Telecaster. And Bob picked me up at the bus station and took me to this house where he lived . . . Sara was there . . . and she made very strange food, tuna-fish salad with peanuts in it, toasted, and he taught me these songs, 'Like a Rolling Stone,' and all those songs from that album, and he said, 'I don't want you to play any of that B. B. King shit, none of that fucking blues, I want you to play something else.' So we fooled around and [I] finally played something he liked. It was very weird, he was playing in weird keys which he always does, all on the black keys of the piano.

Like Clapton, Bloomfield was essentially a blues guitarist. Dylan alone knows exactly what sound he did hear Bloomfield playing, if it wasn't 'any of that B. B. King shit.' Whatever it was, the 'Like a Rolling Stone' Bloomfield heard that weekend had been composed at the piano, and it was in waltz time (3/4), rather than the conventional 4/4 to which it would revert in the studio.

The session at Columbia Studios in New York on June 15, 1965 is one which has now passed into pop lore. The main source of the lore is Al Kooper's version of events in his autobiography, *Backstage Passes*. Kooper had secured an invitation to the session from Tom Wilson, the producer, harboring hopes of persuading Dylan to let him play guitar. When Dylan arrived, though, he was already accompanied by Bloomfield, whom Kooper soon realized was way out of his own league as a guitar player. When Dylan started recording his new song, though, he decided he needed both piano and organ, and Kooper volunteered his services at the organ. As Kooper tells it, he felt his 'way through the changes like a little kid fumbling in the dark for a light switch. After six minutes they'd gotten the first complete take of the day down, and all adjourned to the booth to hear it played back.' Dylan apparently liked the sound Kooper was making, and halfway through the playback asked Wilson to turn the organ up. Thus was born that organ-guitar mix that so identified Dylan's 1965–66 sound.

According to the Kooper gospel, that 'fumbling for the light switch' take was all they needed to create the immortal 'Like a Rolling Stone,' proving only that there are lies, damn lies and Al Kooper's recollections. Though Dylan may indeed have racked up more classic first takes than any jazz great, the June 15 session was his most labored to date, and Kooper may have been included on the final take of the day simply as a last resort. He is certainly not audible on the four false starts that preface the only complete 'Like a Rolling Stone' of the day, nor is he evident on the eight takes of a fast blues jam (what became 'It Takes a Lot to Laugh' in the fullness of tape) or the six takes of a medium-cool vamp ('Sitting on a Barbed Wire Fence') that occupied the remainder of the afternoon's slog. According to Bloomfield, a large part of the problem was producer Tom Wilson.

Michael Bloomfield: They had a great bass player named Russ Savakus, a terrific guy. It was his first date playing electric bass. He was scared about that. And they had the best studio drummer [Bobby Gregg]. But no one understood nothing. The producer was a non-producer . . . I think it was a black guy named Tom Wilson. He didn't know what was happening, man! . . . We did twenty alternate takes of every song, and it got ridiculous because they were long songs . . . It was never like: 'Here's one of the tunes, we're gonna learn it, work out the arrangement,' that just wasn't done. The thing just sort of fell together in this haphazard, half-assed way . . . It was just like a jam session, it really was.

Work on 'Like a Rolling Stone' resumed the following afternoon with Al Kooper on organ. Immediately Tom Wilson suggested a run-through: 'Okay, Bob, let's do one, and then I'll play it back to you and you can take it apart.' Even this run-through now had the right piano sound, fitful organ vamps, and Bloomfield's cascading fills, even though it broke down as they reached for the chorus, just as Dylan is blurting out, 'Nah, we gotta work that part out.' A couple more breakdowns and then suddenly, remake/retake four, everyone began playing on radar for perhaps the most important six minutes in modern rock.

And yet, as if reaching for something that he was not sure existed, Dylan continued to drive the musicians through another eleven attempts at a fully realized 'Like a Rolling Stone,' including some three complete takes. But by now everyone was trying too hard, playing too much. Finally they returned to the booth to hear the playbacks. Only then does Dylan seem to have realized that, back on take four, he had achieved what he had renounced on the back sleeve of his previous album— perfection. Returning to Grossman's apartment with music publisher Artie Mogull and a couple of friends, he put on the acetate to remind himself how it felt.

Bob Dylan: We took an acetate of it down to my manager's house on Gramercy Park and different people kept coming and going and we played it on the record player all night. My music publisher just kept listening to it, shaking his head saying, 'Wow, man, I just don't believe this.' [1987]

Not surprisingly, one of the 'different people' invited down to Grossman's to hear the new Dylan A side was the man who had been

producing Bloomfield's other current session work. Elektra producer
Paul Rothchild realized that the single was some way beyond the conventional pop-blues forms he had been dabbling in, not merely original but
radical:

Paul Rothchild: I knew the song was a smash, and yet I was consumed
with envy because it was the best thing I'd heard any of our crowd do and
knew it was going to turn the tables on our nice, comfortable lives.

Others shared Rothchild's suspicion that something had changed.
Indeed, it would be fair to say that the impact 'Like a Rolling Stone' had
on many second-generation rockers would never be replicated. Not that
it was just rockers who recognized its import. Paul Nelson was in another
New York studio with Dylan's old buddies John Koerner, Dave Ray,
and Tony Glover, making their second folk-blues album for Elektra,
when someone appeared with a copy of the song.

Paul Nelson: I thought, 'Oh boy, this just makes what we did obsolete . . .
this is where it's gonna go! And these guys know it too.' [But] they were all
for it. They knew a big change had come.

Across the ocean, Paul McCartney remembered going around to John
Lennon's house in Weybridge and hearing this six-minute single: 'It
seemed to go on and on forever. It was just beautiful . . . He showed all
of us that it was possible to go a little further.' Bruce Springsteen, a callow
Asbury juvenile with big dreams, later said that when he heard the song
for the first time, driving in the car with his mom, listening to WMCA,
'that snare shot that [kicked it off] sounded like somebody'd kicked open
the door to your mind.' Even the avant-garde outer echelons of pop
culture felt the shock waves, though some were less than convinced that
the song's intended audience really knew what was happening here.

Frank Zappa: When I heard 'Like a Rolling Stone', I wanted to quit the
music business, because I felt: 'If this wins and it does what it's supposed to
do, I don't need to do anything else.' . . . But it didn't do anything. It sold,
but nobody responded to it the way that they should have.

Though the other two and a half songs cut at the June sessions were
presumably an attempt at a B side that reinforced Dylan's new direction
in song, he was unhappy with the results, and perhaps with his producer.
In a hurry to get his new single on the airwaves and into the shops, Dylan

picked the surreal 'Gates of Eden' as the single's other side. Columbia would manage to get the 45 out in under a month.

Dylan knew that before he could start in earnest on his next album, he had some songs to write, even if his course was now charted. Thus began a month of intense writing upstate, near to Woodstock, where he had just bought a house of his own in Byrdcliffe. His relationship with Sara had been intensifying in the last couple of months, and this probably pushed him to purchase his own place.

Before resuming work on his third album in a year, though, he had another major commitment. Dylan's electric set at the 1965 Newport Festival may well be the most written-about performance in the history of rock & roll. Even at the time it was recognized as an important demarcation—the point where Dylan went his way and folk purists went theirs—even if there are as many opinions about the events that weekend as there are witnesses. Most of the major protagonists have axes to grind, looking through hindsight's rearview mirror—particularly those who feel a need to defend their initial resistance to change.

Dylan himself, talking about those events twenty years on, made a telling remark: 'I had a hit record out so I don't know how people expected me to do anything different.' Not only had he already released *Bringing It All Back Home* with an electric side, but he had had a hit single with 'Subterranean Homesick Blues.' More importantly, 'Like a Rolling Stone' was issued as a single the week before Newport, entering the charts within four days of its release, and seemingly blaring from every radio carried by the fifteen thousand fans who made it to Freebody Park that July weekend.

Joe Boyd: There was a tremendous anticipation at Newport about Dylan— 'Is he here yet? Has he arrived?'—and instead of this blue-jeaned, work-shirted guy who'd arrived in 1964 to be the Pied Piper, he arrived rather secretively; he was staying in a luxurious hotel just on the outside of town and he arrived with Bob Neuwirth and Al Kooper; that was the entourage, Neuwirth, Kooper, and Dylan. And they were all wearing puff-sleeved dueling shirts—one of them was polka dot—and they were not wearing blue jeans ... They wore sunglasses. The whole image was very, very different.

One question never adequately resolved is whether Dylan arrived at Newport with any specific intention of playing with a band. According to Kooper, they did not meet up until he arrived at the Festival and he was informed by Grossman that Dylan had been looking for him. This contradicts the usually reliable Boyd, who says that Kooper arrived *with* Dylan. If Dylan was trying to get hold of Kooper, it clearly suggests an intent to play with him at Newport. Joe Boyd also recalls already knowing 'that Dylan was going to do something with more than just himself'.

According to Eric Von Schmidt, Dylan 'heard [the Paul] Butterfield [Blues Band] in the blues workshop a couple of days earlier and realized they were a great blues band, and . . . said, 'Wanna do "Maggie's Farm"?' But, even if Bloomfield's membership in that combo was not what prompted Dylan's call in early June, he cannot have been unaware of the band given his friendship with their producer. Rothchild had already asked Grossman if he would be interested in managing the band. Grossman, a Chicago native, came and saw them play at the Café A Go-Go and apparently told Rothchild, 'I'll see them at Newport.'

It may simply be an instance of Dylan's unswerving belief in the powers of serendipity, that he would arrive at Newport minus a band and yet expect to play electric. Or perhaps he planned to play 'Maggie's Farm' and/or 'Like a Rolling Stone' solo! At least one acoustic Dylan set was scheduled that year. On Saturday afternoon he appeared at a songwriters' workshop (akin to the topical-song workshop the previous year) at which he played a cursory version of 'All I Really Wanna Do.' Making friends, though, was not on that year's curriculum. The workshop, which was on one of the side stages set up for such events, quickly grew to resemble Bedlam, and Dylan's set had to be cut short because of the chaos his presence created. The tension was mounting, and inevitably the resultant fury was directed not at Dylan but at his high-and-mighty manager, Albert Grossman. It now dawned on the festival commitee that Grossman's boy was bigger than the festival itself.

Joe Boyd: The crowd around the songwriters' workshop was so immense that it was swamping the other workshops. People were complaining: 'Turn up the Dylan one, because we're getting bleed from the banjo one on the other side!' This was very much against the spirit of what the festival was supposed to be about . . . Grossman became a focus of hostility for a lot of [the officials]. He'd never been popular among these people. He'd always been seen as one of the moneychangers at the gate of the temple. And Grossman was arrogant, particularly with Dylan now being so big. Grossman was being very cool, but Grossman's way of being cool got up people's noses.

The tide of resentment spilled over later that afternoon, during another workshop. Newport was always billed as the Newport Folk and Blues

Festival, and with the likes of Son House, Lightnin' Hopkins, Sonny Terry & Brownie McGhee, and Muddy Waters on the bill, there was no shortage of noteworthy bluesmen that year. The fact that Muddy Waters was known primarily for electric R&B recordings was evidently a trade secret, as he arrived with acoustic guitar in hand. The Paul Butterfield Blues Band, hardly exponents of acoustic blues, were also scheduled to play at the blues workshop, amps and all. The band's appearance on the bill had already been a source of some contention even before respected musicologist Alan Lomax stepped up to introduce them.

Joe Boyd: There had been a lot of pressure from Peter Yarrow on adding the Paul Butterfield Band to the lineup of the festival—he really put a lot of pressure on the other members of the board to get the invitation, and Lomax was really against it. Against Butterfield. Against white boys doing the blues, really . . . Lomax was forced to introduce the Butterfield Band at the blues workshop, and he gave them an introduction which was very condescending.

Paul Rothchild: After the traditionalists, and ahead of the Butterfield set, [Lomax] got up and said something like, 'Today you've been hearing music by the great blues players, guys who go out and find themselves an old cigar box, put a stick on it, attach some strings, sit under a tree, and play great blues for themselves. Now you're going to hear a group of young boys from Chicago with electric instruments. Let's see if they can play this hardware at all.'

Joe Boyd: As the group started to take the stage Lomax came offstage to be confronted by Grossman . . . Next thing you know, these two men, both rather oversized, were rolling around in the dirt throwing punches. They had to be pulled apart. Lomax then called an emergency meeting of the board of the festival that night . . . The board actually voted in favor of banning Grossman from the grounds of the festival. George Wein, who was a nonvoting advisor to the board, had to step in and say, 'Look, I don't have a vote, it's up to you, but I can tell you right now that if you do bar Grossman you have to prepare yourselves for the walk-out of Bob Dylan, Peter, Paul and Mary, and Buffy St. Marie!' . . . So the board reconsidered, and dropped the action against Grossman, but there was obviously a tremendous simmering of feeling.

It needs to be recalled that the Newport Festival was run by a nonprofit organization, and that the performers were paid only nominal fees, certainly not the sort of fees someone like Dylan now commanded. Grossman, apparently, told the Butterfield Band after their set that he wanted to manage them; and Bloomfield, presumably as a result of that decision, told Dylan that he could not go on the road with him. However, Grossman may also have convinced Dylan that the Butterfield Blues Band had the frame around which he could erect an impromptu electric backing for the coming Sunday's revivalist meeting.

Having already enlisted his keyboard components, Kooper on organ and Barry Goldberg on piano, and with Bloomfield as a given, Dylan just needed a rhythm section—and Butterfield's seemed as good as any. Unfortunately, as with Mayall's Bluesbreakers, what Butterfield's all-black rhythm section, comprising Jerome Arnold on bass and Sam Lay on drums, knew how to play was the blues, pure and simple.

Jonathan Taplin: The problem [with] the rhythm section [was that] they were great blues players, but Dylan didn't play twelve-bar music. He played very bizarre music in terms of its structure [and] they didn't really understand what was going on at all.

Michael Bloomfield: We were all at Newport, Kooper, me, Barry [Goldberg], and this schwartze Jerome [Arnold] from the Butterfield Band playing bass, and he's fucking up everything. We're practicing there in a room, and Odetta's staring at us, and Mary Travers is there, and we're playing and it's sounding horrible. Finally it's time for the gig, and Barry and me are throwing up in these outhouses.

They worked up only three songs, two of which were hardly radical departures from the Butterfield band's regular stock-in-trade—'Maggie's Farm' and the equally sweet home 'Phantom Engineer' (yet to evolve into 'It Takes a Lot to Laugh, It Takes a Train to Cry')—and by dawn Dylan was happy enough to proceed with the unveiling. Shelton and Spitz have both claimed that there was no sound check for Dylan and the band, evidently unaware of the footage in Murray Lerner's fine documentary of those Newport weekends, *Festival,* in which Peter Yarrow can be heard coaxing the musicians to 'get your instruments into your heads,' a difficult procedure at the best of times. Joe Boyd, perhaps the most reliable eyewitness to events both backstage and onstage that weekend, well recalls the sound check.

Joe Boyd: By the time the concert had finished that [Sunday] afternoon, and before the start of the Butterfield set that evening, we had two hours

. . . so the whole area was cleared and we got to do our sound checks. Now we had known that Dylan was going to do something, with more than just himself, and that he was going to need a sound check . . . Anyway, so on came Dylan with the Butterfield Band and Al Kooper on keyboards. We set up the stage the way they wanted it set up. It was set up anyway for Butterfield in the first set. They started playing. We all knew that this was significant.

The organizers had been given their first intimation of what Dylan had in mind for Sunday evening.

Pete Seeger: It wasn't a real sound check. They were tinkering around with it and all they knew was, 'Turn the sound up! Turn the sound up!' They wanted to get volume.

The basic sound was also previewed for the fans at the beginning of the Sunday evening concert, when the Paul Butterfield Blues Band found themselves on the main stage, opening the proceedings, because of a downpour that had washed out their scheduled afternoon set. The organizers rightly recognized the dangers that came with electricity. Throughout the early evening, Dylan stayed backstage. When he came onstage as the penultimate act in the first half he was dressed all in black.

Murray Lerner: I think I was more struck by the oddity of his clothing . . . the way Dylan was dressed, in the leather, it signified motorcycle, a tinge of Hell's Angel . . . I don't remember booing, but I remember consternation.

Liam Clancy: I was up a twelve-foot platform, filming with a telephoto lens, so I could zoom in close. And [when] Dylan came out . . . it was obvious that he was stoned, bobbing around the stage, very Chaplinesque actually.

There have been numerous accounts of the twenty-five minutes that Dylan occupied the stage that evening. Those who prefer their history infused with myth have Pete Seeger attempting to wrest the mixing board from Paul Rothchild throughout Dylan's set. One suggestion made is that the sound was so bad that fans began shouting because Dylan was inaudible. The punchy soundboard tape does not lend credence to this theory, though Tony Glover, who was watching from Chip Monck's lighting trailer out front, insists 'the PA sound basically sucked . . . vocal and guitar volumes surged and/or disappeared and the keyboards were

virtually inaudible.' Though he was not being distracted by an enraged
Seeger, Paul Rothchild was having a hard time hearing what was going
on 'because of the furor.'

Joe Boyd: So out comes Dylan and I'm out there onstage before he comes
out, setting up all the amps to exactly the right levels, and Rothchild's got
everything cranked up, and when that first note of 'Maggie's Farm' hit, I
mean, by today's standards it wasn't very loud, but by those standards of the
day it was the loudest thing anybody had ever heard. The volume. That was
the thing, the volume. It wasn't just the music, it wasn't just the fact that he
came out and played with an electric band . . . You didn't have some square
sound guy fumbling with the dials and having the thing creep up to where
it should have been. You would have had just badly mixed rock & roll. It
wasn't. It was powerfully, ballsy-mixed, expertly done rock & roll . . . As
soon as I had gotten the stage set, I ran around to the press enclosure which
was the front section, press and friends and people, and stood sort of at the
door of the gates, and watched at the side of the stage, and I thought, 'This
is great!' I was lapping it all up. Somebody pulled at my elbow and said,
'You'd better go backstage, they want to talk to you.' So I went backstage
and there I was confronted by Seeger and Lomax and, I think, Theodore
Bikel or somebody, saying, 'It's too loud! You've got to turn it down! It's
far too loud! We can't have it like this. It's just unbearably loud.' And they
were really upset. Very, very upset. I said, 'Well, I don't control the sound,
the sound is out there in the middle of the audience.' And so Lomax said,
'How do you get there? Tell me how to get there, I'll go out there.' I said,
'Well, Alan, you walk right to the back—it's only about half a mile—and
then you walk around to the center thing, show your badge, and just come
down the center aisle.' And he said, 'There must be a quicker way.' So I
said, 'Well, you can climb over the fence.' I was looking at his girth, you
know! And he said, 'Now look, you go out there. You can get there, I
know you know how to get there. Go out there and tell them that the board
orders them to turn the sound down.' I said okay. So I went out—there
was a place where anyone could climb on top of a box and get over the
fence from backstage. By this time, I think, it was the beginning of the
second number, and there was Grossman and Neuwirth and Yarrow and
Rothchild all sitting at the sound desk, grinning, very very pleased with
themselves . . . Meanwhile the audience was going nuts . . . There were
arguments between people sitting next to each other! . . . I relayed Lomax's
message and Peter Yarrow said, 'Tell Alan Lomax,' and extended his middle
finger; and I said, 'C'mon, Peter, gimme a break!' He said, 'Well, just tell
Alan that the board of the festival are adequately represented on the sound

console and that we have things fully under control and we think that the sound is at the correct level.' So I went back, climbed over the fence, and by this time all I could see was the back of Pete Seeger disappearing down the road past the car park . . . I was confronted by Lomax and Bikel again, frothing at the mouth, and I relayed Yarrow's message and they just cursed and gnashed their teeth. By this time the thing was almost over.

Seeger was furious with Dylan but only, he insists, because the sound was so distorted that nobody could understand the words. He insists he saw nothing fundamentally heretical about playing with electric instruments: 'It's all how you use it.' And yet, as he readily admits, 'I *was* ready to chop the microphone cord.' In truth, Seeger saw the carefully orchestrated theme he had announced at evening's outset—'songs babies would like to grow up with'—disappearing down the same whirlpool of irrelevance as the union songs he used to sing with the Weavers. If the organizers were incensed, they weren't alone. As Dylan wound to the end of 'Maggie's Farm,' paying fans began to boo. Consternation Dylan undoubtedly expected, but it had been a while since he'd been booed.

Paul Nelson: I was right in the photographers' pit so it was hard to hear what the crowd was doing. I could hear some boos. I don't know how loud the boos were, but they were there . . . Dylan was just caught in the circumstances of wanting to debut some rock & roll on the night we were all supposed to be babbling.

Jac Holzman: Paul Nelson . . . was standing alongside, and we just turned to each other and shit-grinned. This was electricity married to content. We were hearing music with lyrics that had meaning, with a rock beat . . . All the parallel strains of music over the years coalesced for me in that moment . . . Then suddenly we heard booing . . . It grew into an awesome barrage of catcalls and hisses. It was very strange.

Bob Dylan: I did this very crazy thing. I didn't know what was going to happen, but they certainly booed, I'll tell you that. You could hear it all over the place. [1965]

Initially oblivious to the boos, the musicians still knew had their own problems. Sam Lay had turned the beat around on 'Maggie's Farm,' so that he was playing on the upbeats (one and three), not the downbeats (two and four). Dylan quickly led them into 'Like a Rolling Stone', but the rhythm section was floundering—not that anyone out front was concentrating on the actual music. The idea of 'Rolling Stone' was enough for some. Finally, Dylan called out 'Phantom Engineer' and, having found solid ground, the blues boys took off. Before the initial shock could wear off, they riproared through the still jet-fueled 'Phantom Engineer', and then Dylan said, 'That's it,' and it was all over. Time onstage, just under sixteen minutes.

Kooper's version of events, which by now we might have learned was suspect, is that 'they were booing . . .'cause he only played three songs . . . but at the festival there definitely was a dispute about electric people playing, so I think they got meshed together in the booing legend.' He remains alone in this interpretation from stage right. Dylan knew better, and according to eyewitnesses galore, he was 'real shook up.'

Paul Nelson: I think he was pretty stunned by it. It looked to me like he was quite moved and upset by it, and I was only about ten feet away. I thought it was tremendous.

Jonathan Taplin: I saw Dylan backstage from a little bit of a distance, and he seemed to be crying. Johnny Cash came up and gave him a big Gibson guitar, a jumbo, much too big for Bob, and told him to go back out there . . . It was unbelievably dramatic.

Dylan seems to have had no plan beyond playing his three songs with the guys, and going down the road feeling bad. Taplin says it was Johnny Cash's idea to coax him into returning alone, but Peter Yarrow was also on hand, and as the crowd roared its (dis)approval, he came back out and announced that Bob was getting an *acoustic* guitar—a renewed roar. Again, the mythologizers have Dylan playing 'It's All Over Now, Baby Blue' as a grand gesture, and leaving the stage. In fact, he climaxed his set with 'Mr. Tambourine Man,' returning the controversy full circle to his previous year's performance and the fuss that song had caused then. It now sat atop the charts, courtesy of the Byrds. Point made.

After the intermission Seeger and Lomax got their wish, a set composed of all the things they held dear, but the drama of what had happened cast a shadow not only over the remaining proceedings, but over the whole folk revival.

Joe Boyd: After the interval for some reason the scheduling misfired and every washed-up, boring, old, folkie, left-wing fart you could imagine in a row, leading up to Peter, Paul and Mary in the final thing—Ronnie Gilbert,

Oscar Brand, Josh White, who was very much beyond his powers at that point, Theodore Bikel—they all went on, one after another. It was like an object lesson in what was going on here. Like, you guys are all washed-up. This is all finished. There's something else now that we're dealing with . . . You knew, as it was happening, that paths were parting.

Surprisingly, Dylan had not taken off after his set, entourage in tow, but stuck around for the traditional post-Newport party for performers, at which, ironically, the Chambers Brothers played their brand of electric blues. Dylan, though, remained largely by himself. John Cohen, from the New Lost City Ramblers, engaged him in earnest conversation, and the other performers were mostly supportive of him, but he clearly felt isolated from it all.

Maria Muldaur: Dylan was off in a corner buried, and [Richard] Farina told me to go over and ask Dylan to dance . . . So I went over to him and said, 'Do you want to dance?' and he looked up at me and said, 'I would, but my hands are on fire.'

Bloomfield, on the other hand, suggests that the after-effects of Newport wore off quickly enough. Twenty-four hours later, at another party, the old Bobby was back and, hopefully, his hands were no longer on fire:

Michael Bloomfield: When I saw him afterwards, he looked real shook up and I didn't know the nature of what made him all shook up. But the next night he was at this party and he's sitting next to this girl and her husband, and he's got his hand right up her pussy, right next to her husband, and she's letting him do this and her husband's going crazy.

Dylan had made an essentially selfish statement intended to create artistic elbow room, and cannot be held accountable for its more unfortunate consequences (i.e., self-absorbed singer-songwriters). And yet the fact is that Newport 1965 marked not only the death of the second folk revival and the assimilation of folk conceits (albeit Dylanized) into the new rock sounds, but the return of folk music—'the only true valid death you can feel today'—to the outer ring roads of popular song, barely in the peripheral vision of the mainstream Dylan now embraced.

He is quite correct when he reiterates that folk music can never die. Nevertheless his actions, and his alone, put it on a life-support machine. It was a renunciation for which he soon began to feel a need to atone.

Karl Dallas: When Northumbrian traditionalist Louis Killen did a small concert at Woodstock at the height of Dylan's withdrawal from the music business, Dylan turned up disguised in dark glasses and revealed afterwards to Killen that one of the reasons he had hidden himself away had been not so much the trauma of folkdom's refusal to accept his electric experiments, as their later overenthusiastic move from acoustic to electric music . . . He had been pursuing a personal vision, not charting a recommended course of action for his peers.

Bob Dylan: I was telling somebody . . . about when you go to see a folksinger now, you hear somebody singing his own songs. And the person says, 'Yeah, well, *you* started that.' And in a sense, it's true. But . . . there's no *dedication* to folk music now, no *appreciation* of the art form. [1984]

Bob Dylan: Folk music . . . got swept away by fashionable things . . . British invasions and pop art and medium-is-the-message type of things. But it didn't die. All modern music is based on those forms and structural verses. [1989]

There were enough old fans who came following him, and enough new fans, period, for him not to care about those he left behind. He had managed a trick rarely achieved in popular culture. He had replaced one popular audience with another, almost overnight, and actually increased his fan base in the process. His previous audience would largely accept the path he carved out in the fullness of time, but it would be a laborious process for some. Joan Baez would record her next album with bass and electric guitar, but not drums; Tom Rush would record an album with one side acoustic and one side that made *So Many Roads* sound halfhearted; even Pete Seeger would record an all-electric album by 1968—by which time, of course, Dylan had gone acoustic. Some responded more immediately. Phil Ochs wrote to the *Village Voice* championing Dylan's cause:

Dylan is being violently criticized for using amplified rock & roll as his medium on the Newport folk stage . . . I understand that even most of the festival directors were quite upset at his performance . . . I think the best way to judge for yourself who was making the most valid musical point is to listen to a couple of Newport records of previous years and then listen to Dylan's new single, 'Like a Rolling Stone.'

Paul Nelson, who had played an unwitting role in Dylan's previous renunciation of the topical-song genre, had only recently assumed the editorship of *Sing Out*. In a strong defense of Dylan, Nelson described Newport '65 as 'a sad parting of the ways for many, myself included. I choose Dylan, I choose art.' It was a powerful statement, even if Irwin Silber sought to counteract it with his own view of Dylan's set—'not very good "rock" . . . [and not] very good Dylan'—published at the front of the same November issue.

Paul Nelson: I quit *Sing Out* over Newport, I resigned, I wrote a piece in defense of Dylan and resigned. I didn't trust Irwin [Silber] to print the piece I wrote and I went in to Moe [Asch], [and said,] 'Will you make sure this gets printed right?' I got free tickets for [Dylan] concerts for years.

Nelson's resignation did not end the war, it just drew battle lines. The *Sing Out* letters pages would wring the debate to death over the coming year. By then, the scale of Dylan's achievement with his electric fusion, and the inability of the folk world to replace him, would render all contrary views moot. Dylan himself would continue to address his 'old fans' in song—one of the first songs he recorded after Newport had the provocative title 'Positively Fourth Street'—even as he ridiculed them in print.

Bob Dylan: There were a lot of people there who were very pleased that I got booed. I saw them afterwards. I do resent somewhat, though, that everybody that booed said they did it because they were old fans. [1965]

When he returned to the familiar Studio A four days after Newport, Dylan had dispensed with the producer of his last three and a half albums, Tom Wilson. Why Wilson was replaced has never been explained. Despite the assessments of Mike Bloomfield—'a non-producer'—and Paul Rothchild—who claims that Wilson was inclined to move sessions along at the expense of good takes—the fact is that Dylan and Wilson *both* liked to record quickly, with a minimum of fuss, relying on a percentage of simple twists of fate. Though Wilson had a reputation for telling his artists, 'Just go ahead and do it, don't mind me,' Dylan at this stage hardly needed the producer's creative input, and Wilson deserves a chunk of credit for pushing Dylan toward a full-fledged electric sound (though not as full-fledged as Wilson's greatest noisefest, the Velvet Underground's *White Light White Heat*).

Dylan and Wilson had also seemed the best of buddies, departing arm in arm from that London session in May. When asked by Jann Wenner in 1969 why Wilson was replaced, Dylan ducked the question. Wilson, now dead, also played dumb about the reasons for his removal, though he did make it clear to Chris Charlesworth of *Melody Maker* in 1975 that he and Dylan had had a major disagreement, and Dylan had said to him, 'Maybe we should try Phil Spector.' What Phil Spector would have made of *Highway 61 Revisited*, I fear to speculate. As it is, Dylan once again found himself with another in-house producer, Bob Johnston. If he was looking for someone with greater imagination and technical expertise, he had fallen short. If he was looking for someone happy to roll tape, Johnston was his man.

Al Kooper: I think Tom Wilson was more *something* than Bob Johnston . . . more soulful. Plus he was a real experimenter . . . Bob Johnston I would say is the kinda guy that just pats you on the back and says you're fantastic, and just keeps you going.

While Dylan's instinctual genius continued to work overtime, Johnston's lack of creative input was not a major issue. Dylan retained the input of other musicians, his manager, and his key sidekick.

Tony Glover: As far as I could tell, producer Bob Johnston was from the John Hammond school of production: call out take numbers, keep the logs, make phone calls, and stay out of the way. The only people I heard making comments about the takes were Albert and Neuwirth. The sessions seemed loose but businesslike. The session men would gather around Bob as he ran down a tune for them, singing a few verses as they noted down the changes, then sit down with their instruments and try out lines and rhythms.

Dylan was increasingly confident about his ability to harness his musical ideas. As Bloomfield later observed, it was Dylan who was responsible for selecting the mix on *Highway 61 Revisited* and 'it was astutely mixed . . . He knew he had a sound in mind.' He also knew he did not want to record sixteen takes of each song. He needed musicians who could respond to his energy and ideas. In Dylan's book, technical expertise was no substitute for a willingness to wing it. Russ Savakus, bass player on 'Like a Rolling Stone,' was finding the whole thing a bit fraught and apparently 'freaked out a bit' during one of the twelve takes of 'Tombstone Blues.'

Harvey Brooks: I got to know Russ . . . He was a very straight shooter and a real good bass player, but I think he did also have some difficulty with the style of music, because as I was [about] to learn, this was a case of just go for it—you were only going to get one or two shots, maybe, at each song.

At some point, probably on July 30, Savakus bailed out. Kooper assured Dylan that he knew a suitable replacement, and secured the gig for his friend Harvey Brooks. Dylan clearly loved Brooks's bass playing— he would ask him to play in his first live band—and though Kooper and Brooks were relative rookies, Dylan still had Bobby Gregg holding the sticks and Paul Griffin on the piano, both of whom had contributed so much on *Bringing It All Back Home*. Bloomfield also remained at the peak of his playing powers through the three days it took to wrap up *Highway 61 Revisited*, during which Dylan's focus was something to behold.

Harvey Brooks: Bob comes into the studio and . . . it goes quiet, and [everyone] starts listening to him, to what he's gonna say and what he wants to do. He ran the whole session. Bob Johnston was there just to keep it going. He was supposed to say if somebody was in tune or out of tune, but that was a useless concept, to try and get *anything* in tune . . . I was amazed that Bob could write his songs and perform them at the same time. He'd be writing the next song, changing his lyrics around . . . constantly . . . I really had no idea what was going on.

It wasn't just the lyrics that were getting changed around. On day one, they had warmed up with a couple of takes of his Newport sign-off, 'Phantom Engineer,' but something wasn't right and after a morning of working on 'Tombstone Blues,' Dylan spent the lunch break sitting at the piano, while Tony Glover watched and listened, 'and [he] worked over "Phantom Engineer" [into "It Takes a Lot to Laugh"] for an hour or more. When the crew was back in place, Bob ran down how he wanted it done differently—and in three takes they got the lovely version on the album.' The final song cut that day was 'Positively Fourth Street,' which made 'Like a Rolling Stone' sound like 'I Wanna Hold Your Hand.' Surely a response to the neophobes of Newport, it was issued as a single the first week in September, whence it followed 'Like a Rolling Stone' into the Top 10.

If the first July session produced 'Tombstone Blues,' 'It Takes a Lot to Laugh,' and 'Positively Fourth Street', the second session, on Friday, July 30, proved that Dylan's reliance on serendipity had its downside. Though the slight 'From a Buick Six,' a written-by-numbers paean to fast living and speed, was taped quickly enough, Dylan and the band got bogged down with his latest rewrite of 'Baby Blue' with added bile, 'Can

You Please Crawl Out Your Window?' Seventeen takes and a lot of breakdowns later, they finally got a take that was in time, but it still sounded like little more than, in Glover's choice phrase, 'a paler version of "Positively Fourth Street," with less interesting lyrics.'

Michael Bloomfield: There were chord charts for these songs but no one had any idea what the music was supposed to sound like . . . it all sort of went around Dylan. I mean he didn't direct the music, he just sang the songs and played piano and guitar and it just sort of went on around him . . . But the sound was a matter of pure chance . . . the producer did not tell people what to play or have a sound in mind . . . I was there, man, I'm telling you it was a result of chucklefucking, of people stepping on each other's dicks until it came out right.

After an afternoon and early evening of chucklefucking, they attempted to record a take of Dylan's most ambitious song to date, an eleven-minute voyage through a Kafkaesque world of gypsies, hoboes, thieves of fire, and historical characters beyond their rightful time. Though the full combo apparently got through the whole song, 'Desolation Row' did not suit its electric children.

Tony Glover: The last song attempted was . . . 'Desolation Row.' By the first verse into it, it was obvious that Bob's guitar was rather painfully out of tune. Both Neuwirth and I pointed it out, but Albert didn't want to stop the take. 'Let him go,' he said inscrutably. Some twelve minutes later, Bob called for a playback and as it began he scowled, 'It's way outta tune— why didn't you stop me? It's a long song.' Albert replied, 'You'll get it next time.'

After the Friday session, there was a two-day break, sessions resuming Monday evening. Dylan, Al Kooper, Tony Glover, and a lady friend drove up to Woodstock, where Dylan spent most of Saturday writing out chord charts with Kooper and polishing the half dozen songs he had yet to record.

August 2, 1965, was one of those extraordinary sessions where Dylan's focus was unfailing and the other musicians were servants of the sound. Preferring the tricks of the night, he began the session at eight in the evening. With Sam Lay guesting on drums, 'Highway 61 Revisited,' complete with a 'cigar-sized toy siren-whistle that Bob ended up sticking in his harp-holder,' was the first cut of the day, followed by the positively rippling 'Just Like Tom Thumb's Blues' and the insouciance of 'Queen

Jane Approximately.' As the session stretched into the early hours, Dylan
and the band managed to cut 'Ballad of a Thin Man' in a couple of takes.
Mystifyingly Dylan wound up mixing Kooper's ghost-train organ way
down, perhaps feeling that it was a distraction from the song's words,
which said more than any song to date about his current worldview.
If 'Desolation Row' was Dylan's *The Trial*, 'Ballad of a Thin Man' was
his *Freaks*. He would suggest in 1978 that he had written the song
from the viewpoint of a 'geek,' a man who made his living biting the
heads off chickens, for whom the only freak in the song was Mr.
Jones, but a rap he gave in concert in 1986 probably came nearer the
truth:

This is a song I wrote in response to people who ask questions all the time
. . . I figure a person's life speaks for itself, right? So every once in a while
you gotta do this kinda thing—put somebody in their place . . . This is my
response to something that happened over in England, I think it was '63 or
'64 . . .

By the time he recorded 'Thin Man' at two in the morning, Dylan
was looking forward to wrapping up his second album of 1965. The
final song of the session was again 'Desolation Row,' this time with
accompaniment confined to acoustic and electric guitar and electric bass,
and after four false starts he finally got a take he was happy with. Lyrically,
the song is wholly realized (save for a single snip: rather than trying to
get Casanova to feel more assured, they're feeding him 'the boiled guts
of birds'), it may even have the better vocal, but it would still be subject
to a final rerecording in wholly acoustic guise.

It would appear that Dylan was given a test pressing (presumably on
the third) of all the songs recorded over the three days (plus 'Like a
Rolling Stone'), with a view to honing the material down to a single
album from these fifty-nine minutes. It may well have been this test
pressing that convinced Dylan the only logical conclusion to such an
audacious work was an acoustic 'Desolation Row.' A session was hurriedly scheduled for the fourth, at which he was joined by Charlie
McCoy, a respected Nashville guitarist, who had been flown to New
York at Johnston's instigation. Unsure what was expected of him,
McCoy bluffed it.

Charlie McCoy: They just told me to go out and pick up a guitar and play
what I felt like playing. I finished and I went in and asked Dylan if it suited
him . . . He said, 'Yeah, that's fine.'

It was more like sublime. Thus was *Highway 61 Revisited* completed, an album that consolidated everything 'Like a Rolling Stone' (and *Bringing It All Back Home*) proffered. In a world before *Pet Sounds* and *Rubber Soul*, and a world away from *Bound for Glory,* Dylan conjured up an amalgamation of every strand in American popular music from 'Gypsy Davey' to the Philly Sound. The rich, textured sound was folk-rock realized. The competition were still tuning their Rickenbackers and wondering how to hide their love away. Dylan, though, was not about to stand still. That wild mercury sound beckoned.

1965–66: Seems Like a Freeze-Out

12

Bob was sort of oblivious to the whole fact that people were not turned on by his music . . . There was this cat, playing like they were clapping, when they were really booing.

—*Echo Helstrom, describing the Golden Chords*

Dylan has sold out to God. That is to say, his command was to spread his beauty as wide as possible. It was an artistic challenge to see if great art can be done on a jukebox. And he proved it can.

—*Allen Ginsberg, 1966*

Nat Hentoff: What made you decide to go the rock & roll route?
Bob Dylan: Carelessness.

—**Playboy** *interview, March 1966*

The brewing of a combustible concoction of previously popular forms like country blues, R&B and Appalachian folk into musical moonshine messed with the neat categories of sound carefully formulated by the RIAA (Recording Industry Association of America) and *Billboard* magazine, who between them had devised such wonderfully divisive notions as separate charts for country, R&B, and pop. By allying the hoary with the hip, the venerable with the vital, folk with rock, Dylan did not merely dispense with the neat tabulations of *Billboard,* he dissolved them irrevocably. That this act sent 'folk' back to its commercial cul-de-sac and made all guitar-toting hippies consider themselves Artists should not be held against the man. Even the embittered Nik Cohn, in his *Pop in the Beginning,* measuring Dylan's impact from within the cauldron of the late sixties, gave him the benefit of the doubt:

Almost everyone has been pushed by him . . . and almost everything new that happens now goes back to his source. Simply, he has grown pop up, he has given it brains . . . He hasn't so much changed rock as he's killed off one kind and substituted another. And if the kind he killed was also the kind I love, well, that wasn't hardly his fault.

Dylan may have been out front, but other willing cohorts were happily trailing through his dust. Riding the man's tailgate were a retinue of ex-folksingers anxious to reap their share of the commercial rewards. Folkie Jim McGuinn had become Roger, tuned his twelve-string Rickenbacker to the key of E and come up with the jingle-jangle required to turn Dylan's first surreal opus, 'Mr. Tambourine Man,' into a number one single. Jugband 'muso' John Sebastian, having sat through the sessions for Dylan's first 'folk-rock' album, decided to ask the public 'Do You Believe in Magic?' Others were more reluctantly co-opted into the new sound. Tom Wilson dubbed Dylan's studio crew over the acoustic duo Simon & Garfunkel, without Simon's (or Dylan's) knowledge, giving Paul and Art a number one 45—'The Sounds of Silence'—and a new sound that sustained them through 'I Am a Rock.'

When exactly this new sound became dubbed folk-rock (or, as Paul Nelson promptly satirized it, folk-rot), nobody seems sure, though credit is normally directed at *Billboard*'s Eliot Tiegel. It was at least six months after the Animals topped the charts both sides of the pond with Burdon's raw wail through the previously acoustic, stolidly traditional 'House of the Rising Sun,' another song reconfigured for public consumption from Dylan's prototype. That Dylan was the centrifugal force around which the new sound spun was not a source of debate.

Constantly required to define 'folk-rock' for a concussed media, Dylan simply changed the blueprint from session to session, show to show, before it could be sanitized by the folk-rock dilettantes. Whatever really had happened at the Newport Folk Festival, it was immediately written up as Dylan playing his new brand of folk-rock and the folkies roundly booing him for his arrogance. The controversy only heightened media interest in Dylan, who was rapidly turning into the pop-music phenomenon of 1965.

Though the Byrds managed, in less than a year, to get from 'Mr. Tambourine Man' to 'Eight Miles High,' they were still twanging their way through 'All I Really Wanna Do' on the charts that August, vying with the Turtles' lightweight 'It Ain't Me Babe,' Sonny and Cher's 'I Got You Babe' (proof that even the Dylan whine was up for grabs), and the man who put the *esque* in Dylan, Barry McGuire, decrying the 'Eve of Destruction.' While Sonny and Cher were keeping 'Like a Rolling Stone' from that number one slot, Dylan decided to take his new sound out on the road.

'Cept that the sound he was taking out on the road was even less beholden to the *Highway 61* template than his Newport combo, which had contained two of its prime ingredients, Al Kooper and Michael

Bloomfield. Though Kooper was willing to play a couple of prestigious open-air shows lined up for the end of August, and his buddy Harvey Brooks—who had played on half the album—was prepared to take bass duties, Dylan needed to replace both Bloomfield and the mighty Bobby Gregg, who was too busy with session work.

How Dylan hit upon the idea of using two members from Canadian bar band Levon and the Hawks has never been adequately resolved. According to Rick Danko and Levon Helm, Grossman's secretary, Mary Martin, a fan from the ol' homestead, would fly home at weekends to see the Toronto-based Hawks playing at Friar's. She may well have pushed their names forward. Robbie Robertson thinks it may have been Canadian folk duo Ian & Sylvia who recommended them. Dylan, though, was only looking for a guitarist and a drummer, and it undoubtedly clicked that Mary Martin was vouchsafing for the same good ol' boys on *So Many Roads*. Levon and the Hawks were pushing themselves through another residency in Nowheresville, New Jersey, when one of Dylan's sidekicks first checked them out.

Levon Helm: We heard from Mary Martin that Bob had sent some of his people down to see us at Tony Mart's [in New Jersey]. Then Robbie went up to New York to see Bob. They met in a studio somewhere, and Bob was looking at a bunch of electric guitars . . . They sat on a couch in a room with a couple of guitars. It was the first time Robbie had heard Bob, and he was playing a little rough, [but] Dylan seemed to want it that way.

Ronnie Hawkins, the Hawks' former bandleader; Robbie Robertson; and, to a lesser extent, Levon Helm have all been responsible for developing a cogent legend of this barely known band of white rabble-rousers whacking out a brand of R&B in the bars of Canada and Arkansas that would have put the entire roster of British R&B exponents—the Yardbirds, the Bluesbreakers, the Pretty Things, the Rolling Stones, etc.—to shame. Although not one of the many sides they cut with Ronnie Hawkins between 1961 and 1963, or the two singles Levon and the Hawks cut in their own name in 1964, backs any of this up, the legend lingers. As Greil Marcus said of the A side of one of the singles, it had 'all the ambition, a bit of the sound and none of the poetry of *Music from Big Pink*.' In truth, and with the ample evidence of good soundboard tapes from Texas and Arkansas in late '64, Levon and the Hawks were a bar band of unassuming ambition, playing standard fare without flash or fire. Robertson's lead-guitar work, copped largely from the mercurial Roy Buchanan (a brief resident of Hawkins's combo), rarely peeked above the parapet, and it was usually left to Richard Manuel's showstopping vocal tour de force, 'Georgia on My Mind,' to ratchet things up a gear.

That Robertson was prepared to forsake one and all for a shot with Dylan should not be a source of doubt, much as he would later insist that the hottest name in pop meant nothing to him. Nothing but deliverance. When Dylan told him they were playing Forest Hills and the Hollywood Bowl, Robertson knew he would be playing to as many people in just two forty-five minute sets as he would in a hundred shows with the Hawks. The first of these two major gigs—the fifteen-thousand-capacity Forest Hills Stadium in New York—was scheduled for August 28, and this time Dylan intended to be prepared. His new four-piece ensemble rehearsed with him at Carroll's Rehearsal Hall for two weeks, though not initially with Levon Helm on the drums.

Levon Helm: I met Bob for the first time in a New York rehearsal studio . . . Robbie hadn't been impressed with the drummer Bob was using and suggested he hire me instead, so I had to come to sit in on a rehearsal . . . So the boys strapped on their guitars, and I got behind the drums . . . and we began, ragged at first. Real ragged. We worked out parts for eight or nine songs . . . I couldn't believe how many words this guy had in his music.

On the day of the show, the sky was overcast and the wind blew cold, whipping through the open-air stadium, as Dylan ran through the full electric set one more time during a lengthy afternoon sound check. He knew that, sell-out or not, it was going to be a tense evening. In a pre-concert telephone interview with Robert Shelton, written up for the *New York Times*, he had told his old friend that if his so-called fans 'can't understand green clocks, wet chairs, purple lamps, or hostile statues, they're missing something.' For the first half of the performance, though, he had decided to 'placate everybody' by 'playing by myself,' and, sure enough, for forty-five minutes he mystified new fans and delighted the folk-loving section of his audience with a version of the old Dylan. In fact, it was no such thing. Only 'To Ramona' was drawn from his pre-electric canon, and for ten minutes he weaved a spell with the new, and on first hearing largely incomprehensible, 'Desolation Row.' The displaced images brought titters and even chuckles from the audience, the only time the mood shifted from deadly serious among the lightly chilled fans. Dylan, though, wasn't fooled, and at the interval he gave his first and last pep talk to a band.

Harvey Brooks: We talked about just remembering the music and having a good time with it. Bob said, '. . . If they don't like it, too bad. They'll have to learn to like it.'

Al Kooper: He knew something was gonna happen . . . He said, 'Now there's gonna be some kinda circus out there. Just ignore whatever happens and play the show.'

The more perceptive members of the audience had probably realized there was a reason for all those imposing speakers and amps enfolding the stage. However, when America's fastest-talking DJ, Murray the K, walked out to introduce Dylan, the folkies' worst fears were realized. As Jack Newfield wrote in the *Village Voice*, Murray was 'the leading symbol of commercialization and frenetic "Top 40" disc jockeying [and] was greeted with a cascade of boos.' Albert Grossman was apparently equally unhappy, screaming, 'Who the fuck let Murray the K out there? Get that asshole out of here!'

If it took three of Murray the K's introductions to coax Dylan on stage, once he was there he quickly led the band into 'Tombstone Blues,' one of five previews from his forthcoming album that conspired to make the experience as disorienting as possible for the fans. Not that even the well-known 'I Don't Believe You' and 'It Ain't Me Babe' were overly familiar in their new electric guises. By the third number, 'From a Buick Six,' the fans with faith had firmly set themselves apart from those suffering unbelief.

Paul Nelson: There were very few people applauding the electric set [at Forest Hills]. Some woman walked up to me and said, Joan Baez wouldn't sell out like this, and I thought, 'Joan Baez? What's she got to sell out?'

Newfield reported that 'the first wave of Rockers [now] erupted from the stands and sprinted for the stage. This ritual was repeated by co-ed guerrilla bands after each succeeding song. The Mods [!], meanwhile, responded to the ultimate desecration of their idol by throwing fruit.' Robertson, Brooks, Kooper, and Helm just followed Dylan's edict, keeping their heads down and concentrating on playing. Though the only circulating tape of the concert is a poor audience recording, a fine soundboard of the following show in LA proves that this was a remarkably musical combo. Dylan is still concentrating on singing his *Highway 61 Revisited* songs, and Robertson and Kooper complement each other well (as they would on *Blonde on Blonde*), with the lead breaks shared, not fought over. Though the rhythm section rarely extends beyond the basics, on a musical level it would take the Hawks a good six months to approach the same harmonious edge.

A story that has gained currency has Dylan instructing the band at Forest Hills to play the introduction to 'Ballad of a Thin Man' over and over again until the crowd quieted down. In fact, there is no evidence of this on the audience tape of the show, though he undoubtedly wanted his disenchanted fans to hear the immortal refrain: 'Something is happening and you don't know what it is.' 'Like a Rolling Stone' led to renewed boos, convincing Dylan to abandon two possible encores he had worked up with the band.

A couple of days later, before flying to LA, then-journalist Nora Ephron asked Dylan how it had felt to be booed by such a crowd. He told her, 'I thought it was great, I really did. If I said anything else I'd be a liar.' He was riding the crest of his particular wave, and in some perverse way he was feeding off all the negative energy his new music inspired. When, six days later, after performing an identical set to a considerably more appreciative audience at the Hollywood Bowl, Levon Helm told Dylan that he was glad the audience had been more friendly, Dylan replied, 'I wish they had booed. It's good publicity. Sells tickets.'

And he was right. The Forest Hills performance had made the front page of the *Village Voice,* beneath the immortal headline MODS, ROCKERS FIGHT OVER NEW THING CALLED 'DYLAN.' The relatively sedate Hollywood Bowl concert generated considerably less newsprint. Controversy was news. It didn't just sell tickets, it sold magazines and newspapers. Thus it was that the day after the Hollywood Bowl show, Dylan gave his first bona fide American press conference, at the Beverly Hills Hotel, where he was offered the opportunity to expound on teenage fans, the new folk music, Joan Baez, his monkey-wrench collection and the power grabbers, about whom he still had much to say:

Bob Dylan: They can't hurt me. Sure they can crush you and kill you. They can lay you out on 42nd and Broadway and put the hoses on you and flush you in the sewers and put you on the subway and carry you out to Coney Island and bury you on the Ferris wheel. But I refuse to sit here and worry about dying. [1965]

Whenever questions threatened to delve into the source of his success, Dylan would become flippant. Asked if his songs now had more urban imagery, Dylan replied, 'Well, I watch too much TV, I guess.' Press conferences gave him the best opportunity for such word games, because they did not allow journalists the opportunity to nail him down and say, 'I'm sorry, but what exactly do you *mean* by that?'

Throughout the fall of 1965, and into 1966, Dylan became the *enfant terrible* of interviews, partially because his moods had become wildly unpredictable. Two press conferences in San Francisco and Los Angeles in December, conducted a mere two weeks apart, were worlds apart in mood. In San Francisco his fifty-minute press conference—broadcast on local TV – showed him being witty, sharp, playful. In Los Angeles thirteen days later he looked tired, his answers seemed tinged with bile, and there was a cynical air to his words. When asked about honest emotions, he insisted he had none.

An underlying contempt for his antagonists in the press prompted him to 'rewrite' two major articles in the fall of 1965, providing two of his best comedy scripts. The first such piece was published in the *New York Herald Tribune* in December 1965, accompanying a portfolio of photos by Daniel Kramer. It was called 'A Night with Bob Dylan.' Jointly composed by Aronowitz and Dylan, it took the reader through a surreal journey of New York nightclubs and hotel rooms, peopled by characters like Soupy Sales and Mr. Egg:

The doorbell rang. It was Brian Jones of the Rolling Stones with a limousine waiting outside. Dylan wiped Soupy Sales's face off the TV tube, Robbie Robertson wiped the autoharp off his lap and everybody split. Dylan was the last to leave. He took the Temptations record off the turntable, hid it under his double-breasted corduroy jacket and winked at a light bulb. The tea, unsipped, was left to cool in its cup.

His second rewrite was the legendary *Playboy* interview, conducted by Nat Hentoff in the fall of 1965, which says more in its seven pages (reprinted in Craig McGregor's *A Retrospective*) than *Tarantula* managed in 137. For years, fans found it hard to believe that even Dylan could be as sustainedly, spontaneously funny as the March 1966 issue of *Playboy* implied. Anthony Scaduto then suggested that Dylan had recomposed the whole interview, but that Hentoff was reluctant to discuss it. In fact, Hentoff seemed perfectly happy to come clean when pressed by Brian Styble for *Zimmerman Blues* in 1976:

Nat Hentoff: There were two [*Playboy*] interviews. The first was really an almost unusually straight interview. As I recall, it was a quite sober, almost historical, biographical account, a lot of opinion, a certain amount of his—

you know he can't avoid being sardonically funny, but just a straight interview. The galleys were sent to him and I don't recall him making more than two changes of no significance. Then the final set came to him after they messed with it in Chicago. I don't know what they did but I think they put some words in his mouth. They fooled around with it. I got a call and he was furious. I said, 'Look, tell them to go to hell. Tell them you don't want it to run.' And he said, 'No, I got a better idea. I'm gonna make one up.' I said it probably will work if they very much want to have a Dylan interview. We were on the phone and I did not have a tape recorder then. This was all by hand. I'll never forget, I could hardly move the damn thing for a day. He made up an interview. I helped, I must say. Some of the good straight lines in there are mine, but all the really funny stuff . . . is his. It was run as was with absolutely no indication it was a put-on. I remember I saw him two or three times in the month or two after and he'd say, 'Hey, when's it coming out, when's it coming out?' He thought it was a very funny caper, which it was.

Both Aronowitz and Hentoff were in on the joke, playing from both sides of the fence. Other journalists found Dylan to be unconscionably judgmental. Self-appointed dispenser of badges to the hip, Dylan largely dismissed journalists outside his immediate circle as a bunch of C. W. Joneses. When Jules Siegel spent a few days in Dylan's company at the time, for a *Saturday Evening Post* cover story, he found him to be 'an unbelievable pain in the ass.'

Jules Siegel: This was when I was in my Brooks Brothers suit and wire-frame glasses phase. Dylan contemptuously dismisse[d] me as an academic, and ask[ed] me what my father did. 'He was a stick-up man. Eight years special solitary confinement . . . in Dannemora, the New York State maximum security prison.' . . . Silence . . . He [still] attacked me viciously for being an Establishment tool. 'You can't print the truth,' he shrieked. 'The truth is a tramp vomiting in the gutter. Can you print that?' I just kind of sat there and waited through this . . . A few weeks later, I went to the [preview] screening of *Don't Look Back* and there was Dylan running exactly the same routine, in exactly the same words, on another hapless reporter. It was just boilerplate.

The Dylan verbally lashing out was inwardly spinning out of control. The pressures were such that he seemed to need stronger and stronger stimulants to maintain his ability to perform, both on- and offstage. His 'official' position on drugs, as stated in the published *Playboy* interview in 1966, was that opium and hash and pot were fine:

Bob Dylan: I wouldn't advise anybody to use drugs—certainly not the hard drugs; drugs are medicine. But opium and hash and pot—now, those things aren't drugs; they just bend your mind a little. I think everybody's mind should be bent once in a while. [1966]

Dylan's real position was even less equivocal. His actual statement to Hentoff during the original interview for *Playboy* magazine, conducted back in the fall of 1965, was an endorsement of all forms of drug use:

Bob Dylan: It's fine if they use pot and LSD and heroin . . . everything. I mean, that's groovy . . . To know pot—or to know any drug—is fine; and it's not gonna fuck you up . . . I mean, LSD is a medicine. You take it and you know . . . [that] you don't really have to keep taking it all the time. [1965]

The rings forming around his eyes, and the ghostly look coming out of those blue and white orbs, suggested that they *were* 'gonna fuck you up.' Dylan would later dismiss the influence of drugs on his songs, saying that they just helped him keep pumping new ones out. He would also later dismiss the importance of the psychedelics that came into vogue in the mid-sixties:

Bob Dylan: When psychedelics happened, everything became irrelevant. Because that had nothing to do with making music, or writing poems . . . People were deluded into thinking they were something that they weren't: birds, fire hydrants, whatever. [1978]

As of the end of 1965, though, Dylan had yet to lose any close friends to the new drugs of choice, and his contemporary comments—though largely in code, referring to 'powerful medicine'—make it clear that he had yet to wake up to the way his own drug regime was transforming him into an irascible night owl. The drugs, especially methamphetamine, played a major role in sending his worldview spiraling down into an all-embracing paranoia. As Sterling Morrison once said, about the Velvets' contemporary methamphetamine abuse, 'We took them for old-fashioned reasons—it made you feel good, braced you for hostile audiences and criticism.' That Dylan was already taking the purest form of speed, and the one that accentuated all its nastiest aspects, is confirmed by a prescription, dated the day after a show in Hempstead in February 1966, from a Dr. Rothschild, for a quantity of methamphetamine, as well as Desbutal and Pentobarbital (Nembutal), both downers, designed to counteract some of the more unpleasant effects of coming down from pure meth.

Dylan seems to have reserved his less irascible side for the all-night girls. After the Hollywood Bowl show, he fulfilled a minor ambition when he got to meet Marlon Brando at the post-concert party. When Brando told his voluptuous actress-girlfriend Pat Quinn he was 'going home with the black bitch,' apparently a reference to Miles Davis's wife, Quinn drove over to the Chateau Marmont, knocked on Dylan's door and said, 'Well, here I am.'

Three months later he was back in LA at the infamous Castle, with Bobby Neuwirth and Edie Sedgwick. Sedgwick, who had become a starlet-in-the-ascendant in Andy Warhol's celluloid experiments, was looking for a new Svengali. She latched onto Dylan and Neuwirth, who were both patently attracted to her, and set about extricating herself from Warhol's influence. To Sedgwick has been attributed the inspiration for at least three songs from Dylan's pen that fall and winter: 'She's Your Lover Now,' which even refers to 'the Castle stairs;' 'Leopard-Skin Pill-Box Hat,' and 'Just Like a Woman,' the latter both expositions upon 'Vanity, thy name is woman.' Dylan, though, was never a serious suitor for Edie's affections, something Warhol delighted in revealing to Edie one night.

Paul Morrisey: The Dylan relationship came up one night when we saw Edie at the Ginger Man. She told us that she didn't want Andy to show her films anymore . . . She told us that she had signed a contract with Bob Dylan's manager Albert Grossman . . . Dylan was calling her up and inviting her out, telling her not to tell Andy or anyone that she was seeing him. He invited her up to Woodstock and told her that Grossman hoped to put her together with him. She could be his leading lady . . . She signed with Grossman at Dylan's urging . . . She said, 'They're going to make a film and I'm supposed to star in it with Bobby.' Suddenly it was Bobby this and Bobby that, and we realized that she had a crush on him . . . So Andy couldn't resist asking, 'Did you know, Edie, that Bob Dylan had gotten married?' She just went pale. 'What? I don't believe it.'

The Warhol circle, exemplified by photographer Gerard Malanga, would later insist that though 'the Dylan group were [not] responsible for Edie's demise . . . they probably helped it along.' Nico was probably closer to reality when she observed, 'Some things you are born to, and Edie was born to die from her pleasures,' though Dylan's flame was already starting to singe a few fellow candle burners. Nico herself had arrived in New York that fall hoping to attach her star to Dylan's, but he proved elusive, anonymously soaking up the *fin-de-siècle* feel of the Chelsea Hotel, on 23rd and 8th, with his heavily pregnant bride.

Edie and Nico were not the only ones amazed by the revelation that Dylan had married Sara Lowndes. Sara was largely unknown to the habitués of Dylan's nightly gatherings at the Kettle of Fish. Nor did some of his nocturnal activities suggest someone bound by marriage vows.

Part of Sara's appeal was that she was not like so many of the others, after a piece of the legend. Despite her Zen-like detachment from the paraphernalia of fame, though, the marriage seemed a surprising move, particularly when Dylan was due to spend most of the next six months on the road. When he was asked, after the marriage ended in acrimonious divorce, about his reasons for getting married, Dylan told one journalist, 'I'd rather not tell the world why I got married. Even though my ex-wife and I don't have a relationship now, she is still the mother of my children and I see fit to protect her.' The first of those children was already well on his way when, on November 22, 1965, the former Shirley Noznisky and Robert Allen Zimmerman got married in a civil ceremony, out on Long Island.

If Dylan really was sketching out 'Sad-Eyed Lady of the Lowlands' for his muse that winter, those nightly gatherings at the Kettle of Fish were providing him with a different kind of inspiration. Ever since 'Like a Rolling Stone,' he had begun penning a series of put-downs-in-song that betrayed a level of cruelty beyond anything found on previous platters. These songs were bound up with 'insights' arrived at in the course of those evenings, when even those who genuinely liked Dylan found him taking an unmistakable glee in the games played.

Michael Bloomfield: He changed . . . I would see him consciously be that cruel, man, I didn't understand the game they played, that constant insane sort of sadistic put-down game. Who's king of the hill? Who's on top? To me it seemed like much ado about nothing, but to David Blue and Phil Ochs it was real serious.

Tom Paxton: I strongly think that the stuff happening with Bob and Phil at the Kettle of Fish was about 80 percent schtick. Some of it was real. Phil was very envious of Bob. All of us were envious of Bob's success. What the hell! We all started out with the same equipment—guitars and voices—and one of us was suddenly a comet. It's unsettling, and nobody's going to handle it perfectly.

Ochs, in particular, was increasingly pierced by Dylan's verbal 'bay-onet,' to use Carla Rotolo's apposite phrase. Though Ochs himself would later describe those evenings as 'an endless series of great conversations . . . a huge speed trip,' Dylan knew Ochs was not so self-assured as to withstand all the barbs directed at him—he liked to call him a journalist, one of his favorite put-downs. And yet it was Dylan who proved incapable of taking the thrust of criticism when Ochs, for once, turned the bayonet back on him:

Phil Ochs: I had a fight with Dylan. He used to come around to the Kettle of Fish, and he was . . . super-arrogant then. He used to try to categorize all the other writers, in terms of how good he was. He used to say, well, Eric Andersen, you're not really a writer, or he'd say Phil, you're not really a writer, you're a journalist, you shouldn't try to write. And he went through this whole fantastic riff of how we shouldn't try to write, and that he was really the writer. Which, on straight aesthetics, I would admit was true. Y'know he was the best writer. Anyway, one day he was being photographed by Jerry Schatzberg and he was playing one of his new singles. And he was asking everybody what they thought. And he asked me what I thought, and I said I didn't like it. And he said, 'What do you mean, you don't like it?' I said, 'Well, it's not as good as your old stuff, and speaking commercially I don't think it'll sell.' We were all in a limousine, David Blue was there . . . and Dylan had gotten furious. He said, 'Get out of the car.'

The new single Dylan played Ochs was a rerecorded version of the song Tony Glover had considered 'a paler version of "Positively Fourth Street,"' 'Can You Please Crawl Out Your Window?' and Ochs was right on both counts. It was not as good as 'Like a Rolling Stone' and 'Positively Fourth Street,' the chorus being but a marginal rewrite of an idea more successfully explored on 'To Ramona' and 'It's All Over Now, Baby Blue.' He was also proved correct about its sales potential. After two Top 10 singles, 'Can You Please Crawl Out Your Window?' peaked at a mightily disappointing fifty-eight.

The sentiments, expressed as brilliantly as ever, may have become familiar enough to be tiresome, but the sound of 'Can You Please Crawl Out Your Window?' was something quite new: Dylan's first studio recording with his touring band, Levon and the Hawks. Recorded at the beginning of October, the single was one of two songs realized at their first joint session, the other being Dylan's cross-breed of 'I Wanna Be Your Man' and 'Sitting on a Barbed Wire Fence,' 'I Wanna Be Your Lover.' The Hawks' sound in the studio, wrapped around some manic

Manuel piano-work, Hudson's organ swirl, and Robertson's pinprick leads, had a whole set of dynamics that came from years attending the same brotherhood. And yet, Dylan and the Hawks had played just three concerts together when the session was booked.

Despite their successful performance at the Hollywood Bowl, Al Kooper had finally plucked up the courage to tell Dylan that, far from looking forward to the prospect of converting the heartland of America to Dylan's new music, he wanted out. The news of Kooper's decision prompted Levon Helm to confront Grossman with an ultimatum: 'Take us all, or don't take anybody.' Robertson might have been willing to go along with Dylan's own choice of compadres, but Helm wanted to be back with 'his' band of Hawks. Fortunately, Dylan agreed to a try out. Whether he had even heard Levon and the Hawks play live at this point is debatable.

Dylan traveled to Toronto a week before the shows in Texas to rehearse with the newly reconstituted Hawks, back playing a hometown residency at Friars. Though Robertson and Helm had already fully briefed the band, Dylan insisted on two all-night rehearsals. Of course, he would have been truly stuck if the Hawks had not worked out. Fortunately Dylan and the Hawks jelled, and there were two warm-up shows in Texas to iron out any problems before they made their New York debut on October 1. The shows in Austin and Dallas were surprisingly well received, and Dylan and the Hawks managed a few days' rehearsals in Woodstock prior to Carnegie Hall. Even the New York show was well received, though Paul Nelson recollects that 'most of the people from *Sing Out* made a point to leave at intermission—it was a very ostensible [sic] walkout.' The fans, though, were determined to show their enthusiasm for his new sound and his new band.

Levon Helm: At Carnegie Hall a couple of hundred people rushed the stage at the end, shouting for more. I could see Bob standing at the microphone. He was exhausted, spaced out, but really beaming. 'Thank you,' he mumbled. 'I didn't think you'd feel that way.'

But if Dylan felt that the tide had turned, he was in for a shock. The out-of-town shows he played most weekends in October continued to attract their share of hecklers, suggesting he 'Go back to England!' or 'Get rid of the band!' If he was upset by the renewed hostility, he took consolation in his new backing band. The Hawks were determined to make great music, leaving the waxing poetic to Dylan.

Levon Helm: We found a *way* of performing with Bob [that fall]. It was a hell of a challenge, because he was still learning about a band. He would suddenly stop and break the beat, and we'd get confused and not know where we were. We'd look at one another and try to figure out if we were playing great music or total bullshit.

Unfortunately, there are no audiotapes of Dylan backed by Levon and the Hawks to test Helm's belief that they 'found a *way* of performing.' Perhaps he was as deluded as to the merits of what they were now doing as he had been about the sound they made before Dylan recruited them. By late November Helm had resolved that, whether it was a way of performing or not, it was not great music, and it was not what he wanted to do. In truth, Helm had quickly tired of the barracking. He felt that perhaps there was a genuine fault with the sound, which they were unable to hear. He was also tired of the backseat role he was being forced to take with 'his' band.

Levon Helm: The audiences kept booing . . . The more Bob heard this stuff, the more he wanted to drill these songs into the audiences . . . We didn't mean to play that loud, but Bob told the sound people to turn it up full force . . . He'd bend and grind, stage front, miming Robbie's solos . . . I began to think it was a ridiculous way to make a living: flying to concerts in Bob's thirteen-seat Lodestar, jumping in and out of limousines, and then getting booed.

Robbie Robertson: [Levon] said, 'I don't want to do this anymore.' . . . To me it was like, 'Yeah, but the experience equals this music in the making. We will find the music. It will take some time but we will find it and eventually we'll make it something that we need to get out of it.' In the beginning, it was a little too much bashing.

Robertson's assessment is borne out by a tape from December 3, 1965, at the Berkeley Community Theater, made by Allen Ginsberg. Helm had quit just before their two-week tour of the West Coast, leaving Dylan little time to break in a new drummer. Thankfully, Bobby Gregg agreed to step in, though only for the West Coast leg. As the drummer on both of Dylan's two previous albums, Gregg knew the songs and was comfortable with Dylan's thirst for spontaneity.

Gregg acquits himself well on the Berkeley recording, but fans of the majestic '66 world tour tapes wouldn't necessarily welcome this particular devolution of sound. Though Robertson had begun to uncoil as a guitarist by December 1965, the three tiers of lead instruments—guitar, organ, harmonica—had yet to disentangle themselves from the mire. Dylan's attempt at a rocked-up 'Baby Let Me Follow You Down' comes closest to its Free Trade Hall '66 brethren, but the latest song from Dylan's pen, 'Long Distance Operator,' is a kitchen-sink bash with the usual dislocated lyrics; and the stop-start 'It Ain't Me Babe' simply lacks drama. To paraphrase Greil Marcus, Dylan and the Hawks still had the ambition, and bits of the sound, but some of the lyricism of the Holly-wood Bowl performance had gone.

The day after the Carnegie Hall deluge, *Highway 61 Revisited* entered the charts, residing there for the remainder of Dylan's 1965–66 touring schedule. However, he was already having to give serious thought to recording a follow-up. Having raised the stakes once with the isolated splendor of *Bringing It All Back Home*, *Highway 61 Revisited* had upped the ante again. In the fall of 1965, he was telling reporters that he thought *Highway 61 Revisited* represented the best he could do. As the single instance of 'Long Distance Operator' suggested, he was again having serious problems coming up with a successor that could replicate its impact.

Inspirational as the recorded performance was on his latest single, 'Can You Please Crawl Out Your Window?' was the solitary usable cut from two days of sessions in October, and a castoff from his previous incarnation. Dylan had arrived at the studio with three fragments of songs—'Medicine Sunday,' 'I Don't Want to Be Your Partner,' and 'Jet Pilot'—that he hoped to flesh out, but it was not to be.

Allen Ginsberg: Dylan always did improvise quite a bit. Round '65, he told me . . . he used to go into a studio and chat up the musicians and babble into the microphone, then rush into the control room and listen to what he said, and write it down, and then maybe arrange it a little bit, and then maybe rush back out in front and sing it!

The proto-takes of these three fragments certainly sound like a man grabbing a ragbag of images from the lexicon of *Highway 61* and 'bab-bl[ing] into the microphone.' Though 'I Don't Want to Be Your Partner' did manage to evolve into the fully fledged 'I Wanna Be Your Lover,' as a method of composition it was flawed, placing its reliance on inspiration arriving on demand, by clock-ticking studio time. Nevertheless, Dylan persevered with the method through the first set of Nashville sessions in February 1966.

If the October sessions were primarily for trying out ideas, a session booked for November 30, 1965, had a very specific purpose. Much like the June 15 session, Dylan set up the date—less than twenty-four hours before he and the band were booked on a transcontinental flight—with the specific purpose of cutting a new song. Much like 'Like a Rolling Stone,' 'Freeze Out' seems to have excited Dylan so much that he insisted on transferring it to tape pronto. Writing 'Freeze Out' opened another new door for Dylan the songwriter, and he wanted to see where it led in the studio. Slotting this session into such an unrelenting schedule suggests a resolve on Dylan's part to record while the initial vision remained. That he persevered through fourteen takes, six of them complete, of an eight-minute opus, affirms that resolve.

With 'Freeze Out' (a.k.a. 'Visions of Johanna'), Dylan once again leapt beyond the precepts of popular song, delivering what may well be his most perfect composition. The song's imagery is bone-chillingly precise, even as its subject matter, the omnipresent yet physically absent Johanna, hovers nebulously out of reach. The November 30 version, driven initially by some impromptu harmonica whoops, features a surprisingly defiant vocal, but the Hawks, though they play with energy to spare, seem lacking in any idea beyond getting to song's end. Dylan's exhilaration, though, is crying to be heard. The sheer joy of creation has yet to leave him and, even at the press conference three days later, he cannot resist mentioning his new 'ten-minute' song, nor can he resist playing it to Ginsberg, Ferlinghetti, Michael McClure, and their friends at his Berkeley concert, as if finally prepared to cop to being a poet, knowing it and hoping he don't blow it.

That Dylan had Bruce Langhorne, Paul Griffin, and Al Kooper all on standby throughout the 30 November session suggests a determination to get it right first time around. That he had them there at all suggests that, even at the time he recorded 'Freeze Out,' he was unsure whether recording with his touring band was a good idea. Nevertheless, he persevered with the Hawks and in January 1966—off the road awaiting the birth of his first son, Jesse—he took three days out at Columbia to record what he later admitted was an attempt at an album. What resulted, though, was a single usable song, and that required another call-up for the A team. Dylan recalled Bobby Gregg, William E. Lee, and Paul Griffin, the nuts and bolts of the *Bringing It All Back Home* sound, and Al Kooper, to metaphorically fumble for the light switch, simply to get 'One of Us Must Know' done and dusted after a record-breaking twenty-four takes, eight complete, had eaten up three consecutive three-hour stints of studio time. How many of the Hawks finally got to put their brand on the single has not been documented, but it is undoubtedly

Kooper's trademark organ, and probably Griffin's piano, burbling away beneath one of Dylan's finest exercises in tonal breath control.

Part of the blame for failing to turn a single into an album sat squarely with Dylan, who had simply not brought enough songs to the party. Allowing for mislabeled Columbia reels, a rerecorded 'Freeze Out,' the equally grand 'She's Your Lover Now,' a throwaway 'Leopard-Skin Pill-Box Hat', an impromptu 'I'll Keep It with Mine' and the new single, 'One of Us Must Know,' even realized in all their ragged glory, do not an album make. As it is, Dylan and the Hawks couldn't even make it through a complete 'She's Your Lover Now' in nine hours of session time. That Dylan ended up canceling three of the last four sessions suggests the level of despair this failure induced. And with the final, canceled session scheduled the day before he went back on the road, it meant that his next album would now have to be recorded between shows, somehow, somewhere. By the time Dylan spoke to Robert Shelton in Lincoln, Nebraska, in March, he had accepted the Hawks' inability, as yet, to translate their ideas to tape, having found the combination he needed in a studio down south:

Bob Dylan: I wouldn't be lucky if I couldn't produce. That's what I thought the last six months. Oh, I was really down. I mean, in ten recording sessions, man, we didn't get one song . . . It was the band. But you see, I didn't know that. I didn't want to think that. [1966]

Bob Johnston had been trying to convince Dylan to record in Nashville for some time. A session booked for November 1965, canceled at the last minute, represented months of cajoling. Now he renewed his arguments, and Dylan finally agreed to give it a go, though he still had very specific ideas about how he wanted to sound, insisting on sticking to the twin engines of organ and guitar that had worked on 'One of Us Must Know,' courtesy of Robbie Robertson and Al Kooper. The Robertson/Kooper combination—in tandem with musicians like Charlie McCoy, Kenneth Buttrey, and Joe South, who played with a mutual understanding acquired over innumerable sessions—represented the culmination of that 'wild, mercury sound' Dylan has been forever seeking.

Bob Dylan: The closest I ever got to the sound I hear in my mind was on individual bands in the *Blonde on Blonde* album. It's that thin, that wild mercury sound. It's metallic and bright gold, with whatever that conjures up. That's my particular sound. I haven't been able to succeed in getting it all the time. Mostly I've been driving at a combination of guitar, harmonica, and organ. [1978]

The musicians had no real idea who Bob Dylan was, illustrating just how focused on Music City USA these Tennessee ramblers were, but the beauty of the relationship lay in the fact that they had no preconceived notions of how they should play, nor were they intimidated by the *idea* of Dylan, or his potential importance to their future livelihoods.

Al Kooper: Everybody gets treated the same way down there, with a lot of respect and a lot of room. They knew he was *somebody*.

If the January sessions had cured Dylan of one misguided assumption, it had not seemingly persuaded him to arrive at a set of sessions with a bunch of songs, teach them to the musicians, and then attempt to record them. Using studio time to *write* songs was not something that the Nashville musicians expected. Studio time was expensive, particularly as these guys were mostly making double scale, and it was their ability to cut songs quickly and professionally that enabled them to command such fees. Dylan, though, had only finished a single song, 'Fourth Time Around,' since the January New York sessions, and that was a deeply surreal pastiche of a piece of John Lennon whimsy, 'Norwegian Wood.'

Charlie McCoy: When he first came in, he had his manager Al Grossman and his organ player Al Kooper. Everybody was introduced and he asked us if we'd mind waiting a while. They had stopped at an airport in Richmond and he didn't have a chance to finish his material. He asked us if we'd mind waiting a minute while he worked on a song. So we all went out and let him have the studio to himself. He ended up staying in there working on that song for six hours . . . He finally told us to come in and we cut it. It turned out to be fourteen minutes long . . . The whole session followed a pattern like that.

McCoy is mistaken in suggesting that the first session was an exercise in songwriting. In fact, that first day, February 14, Dylan and the guys managed to cut all three songs he'd held in reserve: 'Fourth Time Around,' 'Leopard-Skin Pill-Box Hat,' and a stunning 'Visions of Johanna' that was somehow cut in a single full take. Over the next three days, though, they would indeed wear the edges off a couple of decks of cards awaiting Dylan's presence, song in hand. Just two songs would occupy those extraordinary late-night—indeed, all-night—sessions, and both cuts required no more than three complete takes. That said, 'Stuck Inside of Mobile with the Memphis Blues Again' and 'Sad-Eyed Lady of the Lowlands' were hardly the sort of three-minute, major-key, verse-chorus-middle-eight-fade fare the Music Row musos were used to cutting. Whether any of 'Sad-Eyed Lady of the Lowlands' was written at the Chelsea Hotel in New York, as Dylan would later claim in song, must be open to doubt. The studio logs confirm that no actual songs were recorded at the two sessions booked for the 15th and the early-morning session on the 16th. Only at four in the morning did Dylan finally summon the musicians into the studio, and Bob Johnston duly set the tape machine rolling.

Ken Buttrey: He ran down a verse and a chorus and he just quit and said, 'We'll do a verse and a chorus then I'll play my harmonica thing. Then we'll do another verse and chorus and I'll play some more harmonica, and we'll see how it goes from there.' That was his explanation of what was getting ready to happen . . . Not knowing how long this thing was going to be, we were preparing ourselves dynamically for a basic two- to three-minute record. Because records just didn't go over three minutes . . . If you notice that record, that thing after like the second chorus starts building and building like crazy, and everybody's just peaking it up 'cause we thought, Man, this is it . . . This is gonna be the last chorus and we've gotta put everything into it we can. And he played another harmonica solo and went back down to another verse and the dynamics had to drop back down to a verse kind of feel . . . After about five, six minutes of this stuff we start looking at the clock, everyone starts looking at each other, we'd built to the peak of our limit and, bang, [there] goes another harmonica solo . . . After about ten minutes of this thing we're cracking up at each other, at what we were doing. I mean, we peaked five minutes ago. Where do we go from here?

Perhaps it is that very first take, which the studio sheets mark as complete, that now occupies the whole of side four of *Blonde on Blonde,* though Dylan and the band went at it two more times before the musicians were allowed to retire to their beds, to await another crazy all-night session, scheduled for six that evening. 'Stuck Inside of Mobile,' at a mere eight minutes, proved a breeze once they had got a handle on how to kick it off, and Dylan left his shell-shocked troops the evening of the 17th, heading for the plains of Ontario. After the successful recording of three such epic performances—'Mobile,' 'Sad-Eyed,' and 'Visions,' each groundbreaking in its own right, nudged close to half an hour's worth of record time—the idea of a double album now seems to have been allowed to form in his mind. Further sessions were booked for March, and this time he promised himself he'd write some songs in advance.

In fact, the four March session dates—from the 7th through the 10th—were something of a contrast to the extraordinary February happenings, with Dylan bringing some eight songs with him, all in the three- to four-minute range, containing some of his most inspired melodies—'I Want You,' 'Just Like a Woman,' and 'Absolutely Sweet Marie.' His writing methodology, though, remained abstract. A couple of typescripts surrounded by scribbles, written in this interim, suggest the songs retained their amorphic status until Dylan came up with a hook on which to hang his many extraordinary images. Thus the line 'i got five fevers & fourteen believers' would separate into two songs ('Absolutely Sweet Marie' and 'Obviously Five Believers').

On one typescript—to which he added the 'riverboat captain' verse in 'Absolutely Sweet Marie'—Dylan typed a list of themes and songs. Ideas for an 'if nothing comes outta this, you'll soon know' song ('Pledging My Time'), a 'guilty for just being there' song ('Temporary Like Achilles'), an 'i did it so you wouldn't have to (do it)' song ('Most Likely You Go Your Way and I'll Go Mine'), appear alongside the considerably more cryptic 'White Love & Song' and 'Yellow Monday Song.' Though he continued to write and rewrite his material in Nashville, this time he used downtime at the hotel to hone the songs he was looking to record. Kooper was present during these hotel writing sessions, learning the melodies well enough to be able to run them down for the Nashville musicians.

Al Kooper: He had a piano in his room at the hotel and during the day I would go up there and he would teach me the song. I would be like a cassette machine. I would play the song over and over on the piano for him. This served a double purpose. One, he could concentrate on writing lyrics and didn't have to mess with playing the piano; two, I could go to the studio early that night and teach it to the band before he even got there, so they could be playing the song before he even walked through the door.

The March sessions introduced some pop sensibility to the double album Dylan now seemed bent on recording, making *Blonde on Blonde* his most fully realized collection to date, even if it would not replicate the impact of his two previous albums on his fellow music-makers. Among the eight titles recorded at the March Nashville sessions were three songs—'Rainy Day Women 12 & 35,' 'I Want You,' and 'Just

Like a Woman'—which, between them, would return him to the status
of important singles artist, providing him with three Top 40 singles
before the end of 1966 after the surprising failure of 'One of Us Must
Know.' 'Rainy Day Women' would even duplicate the success of 'Like
a Rolling Stone,' reaching number two in the American charts and
generating some controversy among those unconversant with Proverbs
27:15.

Delighted with the way the album, and a double album at that, had
come together in Nashville, Dylan completed the mixing in Los Angeles
in April, proclaiming to Jules Siegel as he played him an acetate of
'Sad-Eyed Lady of the Lowlands,' 'Now that is religious music! That is
religious carnival music. I just got that real old-time religious carnival
sound there, didn't I?'

Though 'Rainy Day Women' would open the *Blonde on Blonde* album
with 'a Salvation Army sound,' and 'Sad-Eyed Lady' would close it with
'that real old-time religious carnival sound,' the search for salvation that
suffused the remaining songs was not about to be found among charitable
institutions or in dusty old fairgrounds. When he was asked, a month
later, on arriving in Australia, what his songs were now about, he would
reply in deadly earnest, 'The Second Coming.' Asked what he had to
look forward to in the *Playboy* interview, published that March, he
replied, 'Salvation. Just plain salvation.'

The Dylan who, having stayed an extra day in Los Angeles to complete
the task of supervising the final mix of *Blonde on Blonde,* on April 7
packed four one-sided acetates of his new album with a few belongings
and flew to Hawaii, was physically and psychologically exhausted. And
yet his trip to Honolulu was no holiday, it was gig number one on a
two-month world tour. It represented two more months away from Sara
and his newborn son (at least Sara and Dylan had spent a few days
together as he completed the final leg of another two-month tour of the
States less than two weeks earlier).

He was once again required to be a thief of fire, to play before
unknowing eyes in Hawaii, Australia, Sweden, Denmark, Ireland, England, Wales, Scotland, France, and then England again. As he boarded
the plane in LA, he perhaps recalled Rimbaud's sobering thoughts about
confronting the unknown: '[When] the poet makes himself a seer . . . he
reaches [into] the unknown and even if, crazed, he ends up by losing the
understanding of his visions, at least he has seen them!' It seemed the
crazier Dylan became, the more durable the visions that remained.

1966: A Curious Way to Make a Living

13

The two loudest things I've ever heard are a freight train going by, and Bob Dylan and the Band.

—*Marlon Brando*

Dylan is very disturbing. Dylan gets up there and sings great thoughts and great poetry to everybody, and when you say everybody you mean also to neurotics, to immature people, to the lumpen proletariat, to people not in control of themselves. Dylan is forcing everybody to listen to him, the quality of his work is so good and so communicative . . . I wonder what's going to happen. I don't know if Dylan can get on the stage a year from now. I don't think so. I mean, the phenomenon of Dylan will be so much that it will be dangerous . . . He's gotten inside so many people's heads—Dylan has become part of so many people's psyches—and there're so many screwed up people in America, and death is such a part of the American scene now.

—*Phil Ochs, October 1965*

The world tour of 1966 reads as a very small-scale affair these days, both in terms of the size of venues which Dylan chose to play (primarily theaters of two to four thousand capacity), and the breadth of the tour itself, which consisted of one show in Hawaii, seven in Australia, three in mainland Europe, and thirteen in Britain and Ireland—a mere twenty-four shows over fifty days. On the face of it, hardly a punishing schedule. However, his lifestyle and the nature of his newfound fame made these twenty-four dates seem more like 124.

Though the only audio documents from America in 1966 are three poor audience tapes from February, all incomplete, it is clear from the many excellent tapes that exist from the world tour that Dylan and his band were reaching ever deeper into Rimbaud's unknown. On a musical level, the replacement of Sandy Konikoff with Trini Lopez's drummer, Mickey Jones, changed the dynamics dramatically. Suddenly, the Hawks had a drummer who was as unwilling to take a backseat as their erstwhile leader, Levon Helm. Jones, though, simply asserted himself on a musical level, driving the other boys to match his intensity as he gave his kit a kicking night after night. The Hawks had also finally found Robertson's 'something that we need[ed] to get out of it.'

Robbie Robertson: By the time we did the Australia and Europe tours we had discovered whatever this thing was. It was not light, it was not folky. It was very dynamic, very explosive and very violent.

By this point, Dylan, Robertson, and Co. knew instinctively that what they were doing was right, in every sense of the word. If the Hawks had been a little hesitant in their playing back in the fall of 1965, the music they were producing now was stately, immense, compelling. The sound itself had a thousand precursors, but no precedent. It was, indeed, 'very explosive and very violent.' As Paul Cable once observed of the opening to the 1966 electric sets, 'you hear a few vague foot-stomps and a just audible "one-two-three" and then suddenly they are all in together. It is a pinpoint in time, yet they are all on it absolutely simultaneously. From then on every instrument except Dylan's guitar is a lead. But nobody is upstaging anyone—it is totally integrated, inspired rock music. In no way could Dylan or the Band be accused of specifically copying anybody.'

The only contemporary comparisons would have been the Who and the Velvet Underground, bands also seemingly comprising only lead instruments, all pushing their dynamic ranges to the limit. But the Who had yet to tour America, and therefore were known only by their relatively tame singles and album (though Dylan did lay some 'black beauties' on a temporarily bereft Keith Moon in London that May), while the Velvet Underground had already been checked out by Robbie Robertson, at Al Aronowitz's behest. Aronowitz had been quasi-manager of the Velvets during their first fitful forays into the real world and, having secured them a residency at the Café Bizarre, took Robertson down to check out the competition. Robertson hated them, presumably convinced that there was a distinction between noise and dissonance. And yet he may have taken something from the experience—the element of threat that had been missing from the Hawks' music at Berkeley, but was all too real in Manchester and Liverpool.

The electric set underwent its last structural change in February 1966, when 'Tell Me Mama' became the set opener and 'One Too Many Mornings' and 'Leopard-Skin Pill-Box Hat' replaced the novelty electric arrangement of 'It Ain't Me Babe.' The world-tour shows, save for dispensing with 'Positively Fourth Street' post-Sydney, followed the same course laid out by the North American dates, meaning that the band could concentrate on refining the familiar rather than arranging the unfamiliar.

However, the biggest change came from the man in charge. Dylan himself has admitted that the pace of the tour was relentless. If he was not playing concerts, then he was filming, or being interviewed, or giving press conferences (he gave a press conference for every single concert in Australia and mainland Europe, though only one in Britain).

Bob Dylan: We were going all the time, even when we weren't going. We were always doing something else, which is just as draining as performing. We were looking for Loch Ness monsters, staying up for four days running—and making all those 8 o'clock curtains, besides. [1974]

Required to be 'on' at all times, Dylan became ever more imperious and conspiratorial. In Melbourne, Australian writer Adrian Rawlins was temporarily admitted to the inner sanctum, showing Dylan, Robertson, and Victor Maymudes around Fitzroy, Melbourne's slum district, and hanging out with him after his first Melbourne show.

Adrian Rawlins: Bob Dylan came into the [hotel] room. His entrances at that time were very choreographed, athletic events. He danced everywhere and couldn't keep still—head moving, feet shuffling . . . He said he and Robbie Robertson had been driving around Melbourne looking for me. 'Where have you been . . . come up and talk.' Then he twirled around and said: 'You, you, you, and you can come too.' It was very much a power situation . . . We went upstairs and we talked and talked and talked. We were like the knight in the game of chess: we jumped from subject to subject and maybe two hours later we'd say, yeah, and this fixes up what we said before. We both knew intuitively what we were saying . . . He said things like, 'I don't like *Time* magazine, I prefer *Newsweek*, I don't like Hemingway.' . . . I could agree with everything he said . . . He took my poem [about him] out of his pocket and it was already tearing from being opened and closed so many times. And he said, 'Did you write this? Do you realize this is true? Do you realize this is the only thing in the world that's been written about me?' . . . At dawn he said, 'Come out on the balcony.' And we just looked at the light growing in the sky over the Fitzroy Gardens, because we were stoned, but also because we had, as it were, gone back into the essence of ourselves.

The all-night session Rawlins describes was typical of many on the world tour. Shelton details a similar session in Denver in March, as does another Australian temporarily befriended by Dylan, an actress called Rosemary Gerrette, whom he had met at his final Australian press conference in Perth. She hung out with him for the remaining three days in Australia. According to Mickey Jones, these extra days were an unscheduled result of the Australian government temporarily confiscating all commercial airplanes in order to send Australian troops to Vietnam. Gerrette was a witness to one of the 'composing' sessions that had become a routine for Dylan and Robertson when sleep would not come.

Rosemary Gerrette: I sat up with the group until dawn ... They were leaving for Stockholm for concerts. They were trying to get tired so they could sleep through the twenty-seven-hour flight and I was able to listen to a composing session. Countless cups of tea; none of the group drinks. Things happened, and six new songs were born. The poetry seemed already to have been written. Dylan says, 'Picture one of these cats with a horn, coming over the hill at daybreak. Very Elizabethan, you dig? Wearing garters.' And out of the imagery, he and the lead guitarist work on a tune and Dylan's leg beats time with the rhythm, continuously, even when the rhythm is in his own mind. Six A.M. and he asks me am I tired? Later he plays a melody to us, a very special one. 'I'll never have it published, recorded. I wrote it for this way-out moon chick. We just sat on the floor on these mattresses ... and like for two hours I spoke to her with my guitar. And she understood ... Of course, this isn't quite like I played it, because it meant something to me at the time, but now it doesn't.'

Dylan had alluded to such nightly occurrences at the San Francisco press conference the previous December, when he noted that 'sometimes [Robbie and I] play the guitars together—something might come up ... I'll be just sitting around playing so I can write some words.' The sessions, which remained a necessary by-product of the drug regime Dylan had now adopted, seem to have been highly productive, though since only a couple were taped, many songs were lost to the morning air.

He admitted to one journalist at the time that 'it takes a lot of medicine to keep up this pace.' What he didn't reveal was how much his prescription had been changed, and with it so had he. Old friends of his had begun to notice the first signs in the winter of 1965–66. Van Ronk told Spitz that 'Bobby tended to fall asleep a lot at the wrong times ... I knew he was playing with heroin.' Until now, Dylan had managed to steer clear of this most deleterious of drugs. Heroin was not hip, even among hippies. Not that everyone in the Village was immune to its undoubted charms—the somnambulent Fred Neil was often to be seen nodding at the back of the Wha, and Lou Reed was already performing 'Heroin,' his paean to junk, at the Café Bizarre and the Dom. Adrian Rawlins was convinced, even before meeting Bob, that he knew the needle, if not the damage done:

Adrian Rawlins: When I heard Dylan's version of 'House of the Rising Sun' in about 1964, my intuitive response was: This guy knows that experience from within. This is somebody who has sold his body for money . . . If you were in New York, you used junk and you hustled . . . [A female reporter] met Dylan in Melbourne at the same time [as me] and noticed stuff that she thought was heroin [but] I was able to say . . . it was something else. It was an earlier form of methadone called apomorphine.

Rawlins is mistaken to suggest that (i) Dylan was using apomorphine and (ii) that he had stopped using junk by the time he got to Australia in April. Apomorphine is not 'an earlier form of methadone,' it is a compound formed by boiling morphine with hydrochloric acid. It has, as William Burroughs notes in his introduction to *Naked Lunch,* 'no narcotic or pain-killing properties.' And it is quite clear to anyone with ears that the Dylan who sings, and sways, his way through that mesmerizing acoustic set at Melbourne is narcoticized up to the eyeballs. Witnesses speak of their amazement that the man did not literally slump from his stool. The self-absorption, the sense that this man was only focused on his internal world for the forty-five to fifty minutes his solo sets were lasting, points unmistakably to someone marooned on the selfsame Chinese rock Richard Hell came to occupy and describe as 'the archetypal drug, partly because, by inducing such an extreme form of self-absorption and by being so highly addictive . . . the country of heroin is the country of the self-referring self.'

Yet by the time Dylan took the stage for the second half, the droopy eyelids were no more, and it wasn't no dose of Zimdon that had cleared his head, it was something that made it all but impossible to sleep and 'braced you for hostile audiences and criticism.' That Dylan was still taking speed has been testified by at least two eyewitnesses.

Anthea Joseph: I was the only one that drank. They were all dropping pills and eating acid and generally misbehaving . . . Anything that was going to tear my mind to pieces I had no interest in whatsoever.

D. A. Pennebaker: Bob was taking a lot of amphetamines and who-knows-what-else, and he was scratching all the time. He was very edgy, very uptight, and he stayed up for days on end, without sleep.

However, Dylan's transformation into Rimbaud's bastard grandson, howling at the moon, after a half-hour intermission was simply too stark for a few pills to have snapped him out of his sustained solo nod. It was the 'who-knows-what-else' that gave Dylan that edge, and everyone save Dylan cause for concern. Pure speed playing piggyback to junk would have tipped Dylan off the edge and into psychosis. Logic and history suggest that Dylan was operating on a regime of junk, probably snorted, not shot, for that first swirling ship, followed by an interval 'speedball,' junk plus coke or speed, again probably snorted. The intent was to restore his equilibrium, though, measure for measure, Dylan could be smooth like a rhapsody or ready to smoke a few eyelids.

Of course, any man whose cure-all for smack was smack and speed was like-as-not gonna be wired to the national grid. If there had been a power failure at any of these shows, they could probably have plugged Dylan straight into the P.A. The side effects were obvious enough: Dylan had a long, long way to come down, often going for a couple of days without sleep, but with wild mood swings to come as the drugs began to wear off.

D. A. Pennebaker: I don't know what kind of chemicals he and Robbie were putting down, but I'm telling you it made him very irascible and very peculiar. He never slept—and I just couldn't take it after a while . . . Oh, there was a lot of weird behavior on that trip, [but] . . . the pressures were enormous.

Not only were the pressures enormous, so was the need for discretion. The quantities of drugs Dylan was 'putting down' were such that, at the end of the tour, Grossman booked the hotel for a further two days and instructed trusted chauffeur-bodyguard Tom Keylock, on loan from the Stones, to 'strip his gear, clean it out, pills, anything.' According to Keylock, it took him 'a day and a half to do those two trunks he had.' Dylan seems to have been very careful to keep the chemical cause of his nightly metamorphosis to himself. If it was apparent enough to all the musicians and crew, their interpretation of cause and effect could be a mite wayward.

Mickey Jones: At the intermission, he started to get pumped up. He was

walking around backstage . . . and could not wait to get out there and rock
& roll . . . As soon as he strapped on that black Telecaster, he was ready to
rock. He would jump around in the dressing room. He could not wait to
get on that stage . . . [but] sometimes Bob would hardly face the audience
in the electric set. He played to the band.

D. A. Pennebaker: In general, he was having so much a better time with
the band than he was by himself that you could see right away that the
difference was night and day in terms of his performance . . . Dylan was so
happy, he was jumping around like a cricket in the middle of the thing.

Both Gerrette and Rawlins played witness to Dylan's wildly oscillating
moods. When Rawlins turned up at his hotel room after the first Melbourne concert, Dylan turned and said, 'Where the fuck have you been?'
but then proceeded to be nice as pie. In Gerrette's case, he seems to have
flipped out, ordering her out of the hotel room and becoming verbally
abusive when she insisted on ordering a cab home. Like many who came
across Dylan on the tour, Gerrette was convinced that he was on some
kind of death trip. His dark moods, the apocalyptic conceit in his new
songs and utterances to the press, his copious consumption of chemicals,
his refusal to sleep, and the intensity of his performances on stage all
seemed to support the theory of a man awaiting public crucifixion and
sainthood. Dylan and some of his closer companions refused to call it a
death trip, attributing everything to the pressure cooker of expectation.

Bob Dylan: The pressures were unbelievable. They were just something
you can't imagine unless you go through them yourself. Man, they hurt so
much. [1971]

Anthea Joseph: I don't think he was on a death trip. I just think he was
working unbelievably hard. He was constantly working. I mean, if he wasn't
actually on the stage he was traveling, he was writing. He just never ever
stopped . . . You get so wired on adrenaline and you daren't stop 'cause you
know if you do you'll be in bed for a week.

Death, though, was most certainly on Dylan's mind, even if it was not
his own. On his arrival in London, he learnt of Richard Fariña's death
in a motorcycle accident on April 30, on the way home from the
book-launch party for his long-awaited novel, *Been Down So Long Seems
Like Up to Me*. However, it was the suicide of Paul Clayton that most
preyed on his mind. Night after night, as he sang 'It's All Over Now,

Baby Blue,' there seemed a new underlying sorrow to its performance. The Melbourne performance, just two weeks after Clayton was found dead from electrocution in his bathtub on April 6, 1966, would make even a rolling stone weep tears of rage. Dylan's estrangement from Clayton, once the closest of confidants, as his speed habit had taken him to the borders of psychosis, was undoubtedly a factor in Clayton's final break-down. When Dylan found out about Clayton's death is not clear, but Victor Maymudes, another old friend of Clayton's who had witnessed his irremediable collapse, was in Australia with Dylan. He would surely have conveyed the message to Dylan upon his arrival on tour.

Maymudes's stubbly visage also pops up in the background of several scenes in the final cut of *Eat the Document,* a one-hour 'documentary' of the European leg of the tour that would be broadcast just once, on a local New York TV station in 1979, having been commissioned by ABC for a series to be called *Stage 66.* Dylan insisted on complete control of the finished product. D. A. Pennebaker was again enlisted to shoot the footage along with Howard Alk, though he would not be the film's producer-director, as in 1965, but simply its cinematographer, on filming assignment, for which he would be paid a flat fee. Dylan wanted some-thing quite different from the as-yet-unreleased *Don't Look Back,* but he seems to have had very few specific ideas about what kind of film it should be. Cinema vérité it was not going to be, coming closest to Welles's later *F for Fake* in its inter-cutting of pseudo-documentary episodes, live footage, and scenes Dylan would orchestrate.

D. A. Pennebaker: After *Don't Look Back* was finished, Dylan came to me and said, 'You've got your film'—which he called 'Pennebaker by Dylan'—'now I want you to help me make my film, but this time there's gonna be none of this artsy fartsy documentary cinema vérité shit. This is going to be a *real* movie.' He had some kind of vision of it, but no idea in the world how to get it. He'd occasionally say, 'Shoot that, shoot some of this over here.' That kind of direction. He would occasionally get people to say things or set up situations. For instance, he would get rooms filled with strangers who appeared out of nowhere and get them all into the scene. I don't know what he was smoking, but he was pretty far up in the air a lot of the time! . . . It wasn't bereft of ideas. It's just that the ideas in his head . . . what we were going to get on film wouldn't be that . . . I was never quite sure what I was meant to be doing.

Dylan saved most of his interest for scenes like the one where he and Richard Manuel attempted to buy a Swedish boy's girlfriend from him.

When the boy finally names a price—as the girlfriend edges ever farther away from him—Manuel shoots back, 'Will you take Australian money?' A beshaded Dylan looks on impassively.

D. A. Pennebaker: Making home movies . . . simply doesn't interest me very much . . . I'm not sure how to . . . make other people's home movies for them . . . And in a way, we were doing that. Howard [Alk] was doing some of that himself.

One of the 'little scenes' involved Dylan and John Lennon in the back of a limo being driven around London by Tom Keylock. Though the actual film contains only thirty seconds of Lennon and Dylan over London, the full ten-minute sequence that Pennebaker shot most certainly qualified as cinema vérité, with the pair of them clearly 'fucked up on junk,' as Lennon concisely put it in his 1971 *Rolling Stone* interview. Dylan at one point asks rhetorically, with a degree of self-loathing and disgust, 'What if I vomit into the camera? I've done just about everything else into that camera, man, I might just vomit into it.'

Pennebaker came to feel that Dylan was missing a remarkable opportunity, failing to exploit the real-life drama taking place every time he stepped on stage. One night in Glasgow, Pennebaker actually filmed Dylan with the Hawks, right under his nose, 'film[ing] the whole thing by just walking around on stage with him.' Unfortunately Pennebaker did not have his camera in hand when the most dramatic confrontation between disenchanted fan and ex-icon took place, that afternoon, in the Glasgow hotel room.

Tom Keylock: [There was a] knock on the door and it was the waiter, with some buttered toast for Dylan, and some tea and honey . . . The waiter come[s] in, puts it down there, I sign for it, and he [suddenly] says, 'Fuck him! I want to talk to him! [To Dylan:] You're a fucking traitor to folk music!' . . . Albert looked at me, 'Get him out of here!' I shoved open the door and shoved him out. He pulls a knife on me—I've still got the scar on me to prove it—so I give him a good kicking . . . [Then] Mickey [Jones] comes up the stairs. I said, 'Stay away!' . . . [Afterwards] Albert said, 'I don't believe it.' So Mickey said, 'Yeah.' . . . [But] Bob wasn't quite there, like, he was somewhere else—he was a bundle of nerves.

Glasgow, in keeping with most of the northern shows, had fans shouting 'Rubbish!' and 'Shut up!' When Dylan was slow-handclapped before 'Leopard-Skin Pill-Box Hat,' something he had begun semi-

orchestrating with an extended tune-up, he began burbling into the
mike until curiosity got the better of the hecklers.

Mickey Jones: In fact, the little thing that Bob did when the crowds would
get unruly, and he'd go [mutter, mutter], well, he did that on a lot of
occasions. He didn't end with the same thing, he'd say something different,
but . . . that really got their attention and they'd stop.

Dylan also pulled the same stunt prior to 'One Too Many Mornings'
at both Liverpool and Manchester. Electric instances from these two
shows, just three days apart in the merry month of May, were released
by Columbia thirty-two years apart. Though it is Manchester that was
immortalized on bootleg and was finally released in 1998 in its entirety,
the crowd response at Liverpool was perhaps even more vehement, one
heckler shouting, 'Woody Guthrie would turn in his grave,' to which
Dylan retorted, 'There's someone up there looking for the savior,' before
standing at the piano and declaiming 'Ballad of a Thin Man.' The Hawks
also played with perhaps more bite than they had ever done, and certainly
ever would again, the guitar playing on 'Leopard-Skin Pill-Box Hat'
being the apotheosis of dynamic, explosive violence. Unfortunately the
only audio document made of the Liverpool show was a mono line feed
recorded on the film crew's Nagra reel-to-reel at 7 ½ inches per second.

Robbie Robertson: The only reason tapes of those [1966] shows exist
today is because we wanted to know, 'Are we crazy?' We'd go back to the
hotel room, listen to a tape of the show and think, 'Shit, that's not bad. Why
is everybody so upset?'

They already knew they weren't crazy. Crazed, maybe, but not crazy.
Robertson's explanation for the decision to record shows fails to take
account of the needs of the film, for which Pennebaker was shooting
live footage most nights. Initially shows were recorded to provide a
musical soundtrack for that documentary. A nightly ritual, which
involved Dylan in another set of late-night sessions, was the process of
making preliminary selections for the soundtrack, a ritual witnessed by a
French reporter the night of the Sheffield show (May 16):

The entire group meets in a suite. Five musicians, four film-makers and
sound-technicians, one sound-man, Tom—the driver of the Rolls who is
also acting as Dylan's bodyguard, Henri—who looks after the guitars, Al
Grossman, Bob Neuwirth, Fred Perry [the tour manager], Bob Dylan and

myself, plus a few girls picked up at the end of the show . . . They have to listen and choose the recordings made of the concert. It's a daily routine. Sitting on the floor, on cushions, everyone listens in silence . . . The music is played very loudly, and apprehensive waiters come and go with trays full of cups of tea and beer. The night will go on for a long time yet. Bob is having a film made of the tour for American television and these recordings have to be synchronized later with the pictures. Gradually people begin to leave; one by one they go to bed. At 6 A.M. there are only three or four people left: Bob, myself and a couple of musicians.

In fact, Sheffield was the first show where there were two recordings made of the performance, one on the Nagra for the film, the other on a three-track, 15 i.p.s. stereo machine, arranged at Columbia's behest. The acoustic set that night featured a particularly stoned Dylan, and perhaps the sublimest example of that 'extreme form of self-absorption,' his two harmonica breaks on the acoustic finale, 'Mr. Tambourine Man,' the second of which, beautifully shot by Alk, appears in the final *Eat the Document*, in close-up, lest it need to catch a falling star.

The following night's show in Manchester, erroneously immortalized as the '*Royal Albert Hall*' bootleg album, featured a considerably more controlled Dylan, even though it constitutes the most notorious battle-ground on the tour. The May 17 acoustic set may actually be the most unrepresentative solo set of the entire world tour. Gone are those gently gliding syllables, almost as if the previous night's cocktail had left him little in reserve. The electric set, though, was particularly loud, and the reaction particularly explosive.

C. P. Lee: I felt like I was being forced back into my seat . . . like being in a jet when it takes off.

Rick Saunders: The level of sound was something that I'd never heard before, especially being so close up to it. I was just blasted out of my skin. It was physical rather than just listening to music. It took a long time before I could recognize what the tunes were.

The slow-handclapping from sections of the audience started after 'I Don't Believe You,' though Dylan refrained from introducing 'Baby Let Me Follow You Down,' as he had in Birmingham, as 'a folk song my granddaddy used to sing to me.' Nevertheless, it was cultivated from a particularly savage garden that night; and after 'Just Like Tom Thumb's Blues,' which, as Paul Cable says, 'just lags slightly behind the

Liverpool version,' one ex-fan had had enough, as eyewitness C. P. Lee recalled:

A young, longhaired woman walked up the central aisle to the front of the stage. Dylan stopped tuning up and bent down towards her. She reached up and passed him a note. Dylan bowed and blew her a kiss to thunderous applause from the crowd. Then he glanced at the note, put it in his pocket and turned back to the Band . . . The tuning and slow hand-clapping resumed. On the tape of the gig you can make out fragments of onstage conversation. Robertson asks Dylan, 'What's it say?' . . . [Dylan replies,] 'I dunno—pick it up, man.'

In fact the note said, 'Tell the band to go home.' Not that the audience participation ended there. After the almost ubiquitous slow-handclap and burble before 'One Too Many Mornings,' Dylan took his usual place at the piano, standing to pound out the rudimentary chords of 'Ballad of a Thin Man.' The message, though, was not getting through, and tuning up for the 'Like a Rolling Stone' finale, Dylan was stung by a single-word taunt: 'Judas!' Though others took up the challenge after a smattering of applause—one barely audible shout sounding like 'You took your name from Dylan Thomas'—it was to the man with a penchant for biblical analogies that Dylan responded, 'I don't believe you . . . you're a liar . . . [turns to Mickey Jones] Play Fucking Loud!' Again, though, the message didn't get through, as our heckler, Keith Butler, a twenty-year-old student from Keele University, near Stoke, had had enough, and split from the theater before the song was through. It would take another thirty-two years before Mr. Butler, now resident in Canada, found out about the historical kerfuffle that arose out of his ill-considered allusion. Nor did he get off entirely scot-free on the night, being caught by Bobby Neuwirth, microphone in hand, as he left the theater, and captured on film being asked what he thought of the show. What did he think of the show? What did he think of the show??!?

Pennebaker had had business at the Cannes Festival that year and missed two or three shows during the British leg, giving his assistant Howard Alk the ideal opportunity to film *his* type of footage, which more closely accorded with Dylan's own concept. One of those shows was Manchester (not that any footage from the actual show appears in *Eat the Document*). It was presumably Alk's idea to capture some immediate post-concert interviews with disgruntled fans coming out of the show. Their angry responses are cleverly cut up in *Eat the Document* with parts of a particularly fierce version of 'Ballad of a Thin Man,' the centerpiece of which is the earnest young Butler telling us what he thought of the show: 'Any pop group could produce better rubbish than that. It was a bloody disgrace, it was. He wants shooting. He's a traitor.'

If, in the final end, Dylan won the war, he was losing a few battles to the hecklers. The hype surrounding his Paris concert was considerable. L'Olympia had been sold out for weeks, even though the tickets were priced at an unprecedented forty and sixty francs. On the plane, Dylan interrogated a journalist from *Salut les Copains* as to what might be the response of the French fans and media (unaware that *France-Soir* had already announced Dylan's arrival with typical Gallic sourness, calling him Champion of the Singing Beatniks):

[Dylan said,] 'Can you tell me what I'm doing in a country where nobody understands a word I say? Do you think they'll boo at the Olympia?' As we assured him that this wouldn't happen he went on: 'What questions are they going to ask at the press conference?' Nothing important, don't worry— what you think about the war in Vietnam, why you changed your style, what you think of long hair, that kind of stuff. 'Good. In that case I'll say the first thing that comes to mind.'

He proceeded to give the French his most unambiguous statement to date about his 'politics' at a press conference conducted at the deluxe Hotel George, V the day after his arrival. Carrying an old puppet, which he introduced as Finian, he informed the attendant media, 'I don't belong to any movement. I've only got some ideas in my head and I tell them. I don't support anybody's cause. No revolution ever came about because of songs.' But nerves seem to have gotten the better of him the night of the show and, when his acoustic guitar refused to stay in tune, he began to visibly unravel.

Tom Keylock: I went to Paris with him. He was in a bit of a state with his pills and that—[he was] well gone—and he wouldn't come out of the dressing room. Albert and Tito couldn't get him out . . . It took me about fifteen minutes to get him onstage, [and then it] took him twenty minutes to tune his guitar . . . He got it together after twenty minutes, and he was having [a] conversation [with the audience] as he was going along, 'I can't get this thing together, like, what's happened?'

Having genuine difficulty tuning an unfamiliar acoustic guitar, after he had been forced to dump his favorite Martin when it 'got broke' in Australia, his usual forty-five-minute acoustic set was drawn out to over an hour. When fans expressed dissatisfaction, he told them to read their newspapers or go down to a bowling alley.

Tom Keylock: After [a couple of] numbers, I'm on the side of the stage, he said, 'How long have I got to go?' I said, 'Keep going. You got a long way to go.'

Having already failed to endear himself to the bemused Parisians, Dylan then appeared for the electric half with a large American flag draped across the rear of the stage—a highly provocative act in the light of America's much-criticized involvement in Vietnam—prompting shouts of 'Get rid of the flag!' and 'US go home!' The French headlines were suitably brusque. *Paris-Jour* suggested 'Bob Dylan Go Home!,' *24 Heures* considered 'Mr. Dylan's Reputation Too Flattering,' while for *France-Soir*, 'Bob Dylan Disappointed the Most Loyal Audience of the Season.'

After the controlled aggression of the Manchester show, Dylan seemed to be finally losing his cool with his recalcitrant fans. The two final shows of the world tour, back in London at the Royal Albert Hall, were no less traumatic. At the penultimate show, Dylan suggested to one fan, 'Come up here and say that!'

D. A. Pennebaker: Albert Hall was the wildest . . . people were really shouting at him and he was screaming back. He was very wild at Albert Hall.

The same night he told the London audience, before 'Visions of Johanna,' in the most stoned voice imaginable, that this was what the English press would call a 'drurrg song.' He informed the Londoners that he didn't write 'drurrg songs . . . it's just vulgar to think so,' and then proceeded to jam out on 'Like a Rolling Stone' Grateful Dead style. In taking the song to nine minutes he proved that the Hawks were ill-equipped improvisers, and that his instincts were beginning to fail him. As the *Daily Telegraph* reviewer of the second London show observed, 'He is beginning to show the signs of a man who does not care whether he communicates or not.' At a party after the final show, to which he was conveyed by poet Spike Hawkins, he confirmed the reviewer's insight.

Johnny Byrne: Dylan was visibly vibrating. I should imagine it was the exhaustion and a good deal of substances. He was totally away, there was a yawning chasm between him and any kind of human activity.

Perhaps Dylan felt that he had done it all. Two days earlier he had made it to twenty-five. In just five years he had transformed popular music beyond recognition, and it was hard to see where he might now go. The three songs he was filmed working on with Robbie Robertson in Glasgow on a rainy afternoon featured a couple of his most insidious melodies, but they suggested no great advance on the insights of the about-to-be-released *Blonde on Blonde*—not that he sensed a great deal of competition from his peers. His most famous contemporaries, on the other hand, still felt a clear need for his approval.

In Alf Bicknell's diary of his times as the Fab Four's chauffeur, he refers to two nights Dylan spent in the boys' company after the Royal Albert Hall shows, 'watching some of his home-movies that he is turning into a film.' Bicknell suggests that 'John treats Bob almost like a God,' whereas 'George [just] want[s] to sit down and play with Bob, [which] the others do as well in their own way.' If so, there is no evidence that they actually jammed with Dylan, though McCartney had already swung by his room at the Mayfair with an acetate of the Beatles' latest musical experiment. McCartney's recollection of the incident is refreshingly self-deprecating.

Paul McCartney: It was a little bit *An Audience with Dylan* in those days: you went round to the Mayfair Hotel and waited in the outer room while Bob was in the other room, in the bedroom, and we were ushered in one by one . . . I was quite happy to pay homage. The only trouble really was that occasionally people would come out and say, you know, Bob's taking a nap or make terrible excuses, and I'd say, 'It's okay, man, I understand, he's out of it,' you know . . . I'm pretty sure it was *Pepper* [I played him] 'cause I remember him saying, 'Oh I get it, you don't really want to be cute anymore.' And I was saying, 'Yeah, that's it.'

Needless to say, it was not *Sgt. Pepper* that McCartney played to him, though it was the track from *Revolver* that most evidently led down to that particular abyss. Marianne Faithfull was back in Dylan's good books, and got to hear the song, too.

Marianne Faithfull: Paul got a very cool reception. I saw him come in . . . with an acetate of a track he'd been working on which was very far out for its time, with all kinds of distorted, electronic things on it. Paul was obviously terribly proud of it, he put it on the record player and stood back in anticipation, but Dylan just walked out of the room.

The track 'with all kinds of distorted, electronic things' that the Beatles had recorded in April, for their forthcoming *Revolver* album, had a working title of 'Mark 1' but was released as 'Tomorrow Never Knows.' Though the single-chord drone was in fact one of Lennon's, and therefore an unusual choice for McCartney to play, the tape loops and sound effects, designed to disguise the lack of a tune from rock's favorite tunesmiths, were almost exclusively McCartney's.

If Lennon might have been dissuaded from his chosen path by Dylan's a(nti)pathy, McCartney was not about to abandon the opportunity to use the studio as a tool. Dylan had just raised the stakes with *Blonde on Blonde*, whose acetates he played to the chosen, giving the Beatles a signpost, off in the distance, to emulate. Dylan was just relieved to find the end of this particular road in his sights, unaware that there was one last hairpin curve to negotiate.

Part Two

Learning to Do Consciously

1966–67: Evening Things Up

14

[When] I had that motorcycle accident . . . I woke up and caught my senses, I realized I was just workin' for all these leeches. And I didn't want to do that. Plus, I had a family.

—Bob Dylan, 1984

Given the extraordinary pace at which he had been moving for the previous eighteen months, the fact that the two months that separate Dylan's final show at the Albert Hall from the legendary motorcycle accident were punctuated by little activity suggests that psychic exhaustion had already set in. Some confirmation for this comes from suggestion that he was apparently treated for exhaustion by an English nurse in Paris after the tour. By this point, Sara had flown to Europe to join him. After the rigors of the world tour, he must have mused upon the unrelenting pressure of the cauldron he had allowed himself to be deposited in.

His trusty sidekick, Victor Maymudes, had also endeavored to reveal to him, during the British leg of that brutal world tour, just how much Grossman had engineered his own fortune out of Dylan's. Dylan, though, did not take heed, and the revelation drove a wedge between Maymudes and him that would take a long time to heal—far longer than it would take Dylan to realize the truth of Victor's charge. In the here and now, Grossman was already arranging a daunting fall schedule of concerts in America, to publicize the imminent release of *Blonde on Blonde* (according to Columbia records the album was released on May 16, but since an overdub on 'Fourth Time Around' was not recorded until June, and the album did not enter the US charts until the day after his motorcycle accident, on July 30, a release-date of mid-July is far more likely).

Meanwhile, *Tarantula* was just about ready for publication, and an hourlong TV special on the European tour was also expected for the fall, composed from the footage Pennebaker and Alk had shot throughout May. Thus Dylan's two immediate concerns were to approve the galleys of *Tarantula* and to compose a rough cut of the documentary to present to ABC. His heart was no longer in either project. When Macmillan's editor Bob Markel sought final approval of the galleys for *Tarantula,* he had to travel up to Woodstock, where he found Dylan attempting to disentangle the usable from the footage Pennebaker had shot in Europe. Even then Dylan was still threatening to make 'a few changes,' in the face of dust jackets already printed, and promotional badges sent out to stores.

Bob Markel: We brought a set of galleys to him so he could take one last good look at it before we printed it and bound it, and started to fill all the orders that had come in. Bob took a break from some film editing he was doing. We talked a little about the book, and about Rameau and Rimbaud, and Bob promised to finish 'making a few changes' in two weeks. A few days after that, Bob stopped working [altogether].

The 1966 *Tarantula* galleys were to remain untouched. Dylan simply could no longer relate to the man who had written those words. Nor was he any happier at the prospect of making a film of the events of May, and he soon sought to return that task to the film crew, contrary to a previous agreement:

D. A. Pennebaker: He came sometime in July. He drove down and looked at stuff—we spent two or three days looking at stuff in the studio and then he said, 'Well, I want you guys to go ahead and make some sort of a rough edit to get an idea of what you did because ABC is coming after it.' . . . So Neuwirth and I started to edit something together . . . a twenty- or thirty-minute thing . . . Then . . . Albert got pissed at me 'cause he said I wasn't helping him edit enough and I explained to him that I was never supposed to be editing it [in the first place].

Pennebaker was understandably unhappy to be placed in the position he now found himself in. A cut of that film still exists in Pennebaker's private collection. It is, needless to say, a very different film than the one Dylan and Alk would produce. David Dalton, writing of the film recently, in a profile of Pennebaker in *Gadfly,* described it thus:

You Know Something Is Happening, in its unfinished, sketchy state, is more intimate and at the same time more artificial than *Don't Look Back* . . . Dylan, drawing a filigree mustache and beard on his face with a pen. Dylan, outside a London shop, reading a notice that offers to COLLECT, CLIP, BATHE, AND RETURN YOUR DOG and then, like some inspired monkey grammarian, spinning this unpromising material into epic permutations, the combinations becoming more and more surreal until the words are no more than notes that he can rearrange in any order . . . The performance footage of Dylan singing . . . is wildly chromatic and strange.

So in the period before the accident Dylan was pretending to make 'final' changes to *Tarantula,* getting Neuwirth and Pennebaker to produce a film on his behalf, and precious little else that we know of. He was seen down in the city at the end of June, when he attended another John Hammond, Jr., session in the company of Robbie Robertson, but he studiously avoided 699 7th Avenue. He also attended a party for the visiting Rolling Stones at the Chelsea Hotel in early July, prior to their playing Forest Hills. Otherwise he remained in Woodstock with his bride of seven months and his baby son, Jesse. But whatever regime he had reverted to on his return does not suggest someone who 'had taken the cure.' A set of photos taken shortly before the accident, up in Woodstock, show Dylan carrying a walking cane, standing and kneeling in the woods, still with the sunken cheeks and ghostly stare of the death-ridden.

On July 29, 1966, the whole wheel on which Dylan was bound came crashing down, bringing him with it, when he crashed his Triumph 650 Bonneville motorcycle. The English bike had been one of his few ostentations, and he used to love riding it around the woods, but he had always been a notoriously uncoordinated, not to say reckless, biker. His old school buddy John Bucklen recollects his first motorcycle spill at the age of seventeen:

John Bucklen: I was never confident when I was riding on the back seat of his motorcycle . . . I remember one time he almost got creamed. It was near Brooklyn, which is a little suburb of Hibbing. I was riding with Leroy Hoikkala and Bob was on his own bike. We were waiting anxiously at a train stop, gunning our motorcycles. The train goes by, he guns it—only he didn't see the train coming in the opposite direction. He almost slipped down under the wheels. That was one of the few times that I saw old Bobby ever shaken up badly.

Al Aronowitz recalls Dylan in Woodstock retaining that reckless streak.

Al Aronowitz: I always felt a strange twinge of guilt about the spill because I was the one who had driven him to pick up his new Triumph bike in the first place. I remember an ominous foreboding as I followed him while he rode the motorcycle home. But I never told him about this feeling—he wouldn't have heeded my warning anyway.

Dylan himself has been asked about the motorcycle accident on many occasions, part of an ongoing attempt to unravel the great change that occurred after the accident as if there were some cathartic point as he sailed over the handlebars when he realized All Is Phoney. Ray Lowry, the respected cartoonist, would deliciously parody such notions in a drawing where Dylan is flying over the bike as a lightbulb labeled 'Country Rock' comes on over his head. According to Aronowitz, the truth was more mundane:

Al Aronowitz: He told me that, as he hurtled through the air, when he was thrown from the motorcycle to the side of the road, he thought sure he was going to be killed. 'I saw my whole life pass in front of me,' he said.

Dylan later told Robert Shelton, 'It happened one morning after I'd been up for three days,' clearly confirming that he had not abandoned his punishing lifestyle during this break from the road. However, his most extensive answer was given to Sam Shepard, in an interview published as a one-act play in *Esquire* some twenty-one years later.

Bob Dylan: It was real early in the morning on top of a hill, near Woodstock. I can't even remember how it happened. I was blinded by the sun . . . I was drivin' right straight into the sun, and I looked up into it even though I remember someone telling me a long time ago when I was a kid never to look straight at the sun . . . I went blind for a second and I kind of panicked or something. I stomped down on the brake and the rear wheel locked up on me and I went flyin' . . . [Sara] was followin' me in a car. She picked me up. Spent a week in the hospital, then they moved me to this doctor's house in town. In his attic. Had a bed up there in the attic with a window lookin' out. Sara stayed there with me. [1987]

If a shade metaphorical, Dylan's account here rings reasonably true. The extent of the physical damage seems to have been cracked vertebrae and mild concussion. Though conspiracists love the idea that the accident might never have happened, it does not seem to have immediately occurred to Dylan that this was a way out of his ongoing commitments. When he lost his back wheel down a country road, the only thing he seemed bent on was 'keeping on.'

Bob Dylan: I . . . didn't sense the importance of that accident till at least a year after that. I realized [then] that it was a real accident. I mean I thought that I was just gonna get up, and go back to doing what I was doing before . . . but I couldn't do it anymore. [1969]

Only as 1966 wore on did Dylan realize that he was no longer interested in honoring contractual obligations at the expense of his health and sanity. Though he was taken to the hospital—from where he apparently personally phoned the band members to tell them the August shows at Shea Stadium and the Hollywood Bowl were not going ahead—in little more than a week he was back in Woodstock, where he seems to have temporarily recuperated at a local doctor's house. Pennebaker found Dylan in a neck brace when he arrived in Woodstock a few days after the accident, but he was fully functioning.

D. A. Pennebaker: I heard about the accident when I was in California and then I came and I saw him a couple of days later, walking around with a brace. He didn't appear very knocked out by the accident, so I never quite knew what happened . . . But he was very pissed [off] at everybody and I don't know whether it was because they were putting pressure on him to get the film ready for TV.

Aronowitz also recalls him being in 'pretty good shape,' considering. His stay at the doctor's house seems to have been for something quite distinct from his physical injuries. Another visitor who came to call on Dylan was Allen Ginsberg. On August 19, exactly three weeks after the accident, Ginsberg brought him some reading matter. Dylan told Ginsberg he did not expect to be up and about for another two weeks.

Allen Ginsberg: I brought him a box full of books of all kinds. All the modern poets I knew. Some ancient poets like Sir Thomas Wyatt, Campion, Dickinson, Rimbaud, Lorca, Apollinaire, Blake, Whitman.

A quarter of a century on, Dylan's motorcycle accident is still viewed as the pivot of his career. As a sudden, abrupt moment when his wheel really did explode, it has become a convenient demarcation, allowing one to shut out what comes after—as if beyond this point the shuddering of his genius becomes too erratic, too hard to put one's finger on. The great irony of this is that 1967—the year after the accident—remains his most prolific year as a songwriter.

His full recuperation from the crash was undoubtedly hindered by the poor physical shape he was in. The physical punishment his body had undergone in the previous six months was more than enough to tax a healthy man, but the 'powerful medicine' he had been liberally taking cannot have improved his constitution. Thankfully, the press at the time seemed determined to portray the accident as a near-death trauma. *Time* magazine claimed, in its August 12 edition, that Dylan was not wearing a crash helmet and had sustained 'severe face and back cuts.' The *New York Daily News* hinted that Dylan might never perform again, so disfigured was he from the accident. The suits from Macmillan, ABC, and Columbia (to whom he owed one more album under his existing contract) were hardly likely to trek up to Woodstock to remind a badly injured man of his contractual obligations.

Even though, pre-accident, Dylan seems to have been waiting for the next wave of ideas to hit, after the accident he seems to have quite self-consciously turned off the tap. Initially a somewhat dazed Dylan seems to have elected to sit down and view the footage shot on the 1966 tour. The man center stage on celluloid, even in the offstage scenes, must have seemed truly crazed to one who had lost the understanding of that man's visions—if that is, indeed, what had happened. The post-accident Dylan was certainly less than impressed by the quality of the footage shot.

Bob Dylan: They had made another *Don't Look Back,* only this time it was for television. I had nothing better to do than to see the film. All of it, including unused footage. And it was obvious from looking at the film that it was garbage. It was miles and miles of garbage. That was my introduction to film. [1978]

He decided to set about re-editing an entirely new movie from the footage Pennebaker had discarded (hence *Eat the Document*). Pennebaker believes their methodology had a whole other conceit: 'They took these pieces of footage and jammed them together. They were trying to make a point by doing that. It was a sort of putdown of documentaries.' Two friends attuned to Dylan's concept, Howard Alk—an old friend of Grossman and Dylan, who had shot much of the footage in the first place—and Robbie Robertson, were now encouraged to come up to Woodstock to help him in his weakness.

Robbie Robertson: I went up and lived at his house and worked on the film for a while, and Bobby Neuwirth was kind of in and out . . . It seemed like a nice scene.

Robertson, christened the Barnacle Man on the world tour by some of the crew, had been angling for Neuwirth's role—right-hand man— for some time, and now that Maymudes was out of the picture and Neuwirth's touring role was obsolete, the position was pending, going on vacant. Pennebaker happily bowed out of the project. He had never considered Alk's conceptual ideas to be compatible with his own, and was clearly annoyed that Dylan was going to produce a movie that did not represent what he thought had really happened on the tour.

D. A. Pennebaker: I've always felt that he made [*Eat the Document*] out of our cuts . . . he set out to make his own film. How much of it is his film, and how much was Howard Alk's film I don't know . . . I think he was very influenced by Howard's film ideas, which didn't interest me much . . . They tend to be sort of intellectual ideas . . . not visual ideas.

Indeed, while Dylan and Alk were hard at work editing *Eat the Document*, Pennebaker finally arranged for the release of *Don't Look Back*. With Dylan's sudden disappearance from the public gaze, Pennebaker's 1965 documentary, premiered in San Francisco on May 17, 1967, seemed to allow fans a rare glimpse of the 'real' Dylan—in turn warm, funny, abusive, gentle, sarcastic, Up, Down, onstage, backstage—all in ninety grainy minutes. The film reinforced a general perception of Dylan that was already outmoded. Alk and Dylan, on the other hand, were using a lot of fast cuts to reflect a sense of the amphetamine pace of the 1966 tour. Unfortunately they found that 'the Eye,' a.k.a. Pennebaker, had limited the scope of their more ambitious ideas, ideas not fully realized until nine years later, when they began work on *Renaldo and Clara*.

Bob Dylan: What we had to work with was not what you would conceive of if you were going shooting a film. What we were trying to do was to make a logical story out of this newsreel-type footage . . . to make a story which consisted of stars and starlets who were taking the roles of other people, just like a normal movie would do . . . That's not what anyone else had in mind, but that is what myself and Mr Alk had in mind. And we were very limited because the film was not shot by us, but by 'the Eye,' and we had come upon this decision to do this only after everything else had failed . . . What we tried to do was to construct a stage and an environment, taking it out and putting it together like a puzzle. And we did, that's the strange part about it. Now if we had the opportunity to re-shoot the camera under this procedure, we could really make a wonderful film. [1968]

Among the 'intellectual ideas' Dylan and Alk discussed was one that the film should present a pretense of reality, reflective of an inner truth, much as a song like 'Ballad of a Thin Man' did. Indeed, the 'Thin Man' sequence constitutes one of the cornerstones of the released *Eat the Document*.

Murray Lerner: From what Howard described, [*Eat the Document*] had a very unusual idea behind it—I don't know whether it was Howard's or Dylan's or both—but it was to fracture reality, to deliberately take a scene and strip it apart and deconstruct it. In a way that's his strength and some people might think it's his weakness. [But] I think [*Eat the Document*] started out being a literal project.

Mel Howard: The point of [*Eat the Document*] was that you could take the footage and make it say anything. He made a surrealistic film from what had been a very good, but more conventional, film.

Eat the Document appears to open with Dylan snorting substances unknown from a dining-room table in the Georges V Hotel in Paris, serving to emphasize the disorienting nature of the handheld speed trip on which the viewer is about to embark. Whether it was an illicit substance inhaled on film, only Dylan knew. Perhaps it was meant as an admission of past weaknesses. In the latter months of 1966 Dylan was certainly re-evaluating where he had come to at the age of twenty-five, and reviewing the raw film footage was only part of that process.

It was not the accident, but the breathing space it gave Dylan, which afforded him the opportunity to reinvent himself in a calmer guise. He came to realize that he no longer had the will to play live. Yet the accident had only compounded Dylan iconography. With his decision to retire came an awareness of his responsibilities. The last people he wanted to consider were the agents and managers who wanted him back out in the marketplace. Talking about the period after the accident, as he returned to the road, he recalled a particular night in Woodstock.

Bob Dylan: The turning point was back in Woodstock. A little after the accident. Sitting around one night under a full moon, I looked out into the bleak woods and I said, 'Something's gotta change.' There was some business that had to be taken care of. [1974]

He made a similar reference to outstanding business—his chosen phrase was 'even[ing] things up'—when interviewed by Michael Iachetta in May 1967. Iachetta, who had interviewed him back in 1963, pre-*Newsweek*, tracked him down to his house in Woodstock, obtaining his first public pronouncements in a year. Dylan spoke forthrightly to Iachetta of the kind of self-analysis that his rest had afforded.

Bob Dylan: What I've been doin' mostly is seein' only a few close friends, readin' little 'bout the outside world, porin' over books by people you never heard of, thinkin' about where I'm goin', and why am I runnin', and am I mixed up too much, and what am I knowin', and what am I givin' and what am I takin' . . . Songs are in my head like they always are. And they're not goin' to get written down until some things are evened up. Not until some people come forth and make up for some of the things that happened. [1967]

By the time Iachetta got to Dylan the songs in his head were not necessarily being written down, but they *were* starting to be put down on tape, along with a number of covers spanning the full gamut of Anglo-American popular song. That the someone expected to atone 'for some of the things that happened' was none other than Albert Grossman, he made demonstrably clear in a song recorded within weeks of the Iachetta interview. The song in question was not a Dylan original (even if it was impertinently copyrighted by Dylan's music publishing company in 1973), but a song recorded by Bobby Bare back in 1959. The song was called 'All-American Boy' and, in its original guise, it was a thinly veiled series of digs at Elvis and the Colonel, with verses like:

> *Up stepped a man with a big cigar,*
> *He said, 'Come here, son, I'm gonna make you a star.*
> *I'll put you on Bandstand,*
> *Buy you a Cadillac,*
> *Sign here, kid.'*

Dylan, though, substituted disturbingly autobiographical rewrites in lieu of some of the song's original sentiments. The verse just quoted became particularly outlandish:

> *Well, sooner or later a boss gonna come*
> *He gonna take a look at ya, look at your drum,*
> *Drink this sonny, it comes in a cup,*
> *Yeah, he'll take you out to his farm,*
> *Where he's fixing it up.*

Well, sooner or later you're bound to meet his wife
You'll come and have the time of your life.

Just two of the implications in this rewrite are that the manager of the 'new' All-American Boy offered him the sexual favors of his wife *and* a choice of drugs—even helping him to apply the needle. Dylan had evidently taken to heart the comments of Maymudes about Grossman, even though they had resulted in Maymudes's excommunication. Having said he realized he was 'just workin' for all these leeches,' 'All-American Boy' offered no prizes for guessing the identity of Boss Leech.

Though it would be twenty-five years before aficionados would get to hear Dylan's take on 'All-American Boy,' the first hint that he was preparing to emerge from his self-imposed hiatus in music-making came in an article by old friend Al Aronowitz, published in *Cheetah* in the summer of 1967. Aronowitz had visited Dylan in Woodstock that spring and sat listening to him jam on new songs with the drummerless Hawks (Levon Helm had yet to return to the ranks, Mickey Jones having returned to LA the previous summer):

'Dylan has been doing nothing, absolutely nothing,' said Jamie Robertson, Dylan's guitarist, to an inquiring reporter . . . But that was just a contribution to the Dylan mystery. Actually, Dylan was writing ten new songs a week, rehearsing them in his living room with Robertson's group, the Hawks, and trying to complete a one-hour film TV special for ABC, which said it couldn't use the program because it was seven months late.

There seems some doubt about when the sessions that would result in the legendary basement tapes commenced. Rick Danko said that the residual Hawks did not join Robbie in Woodstock until February 1967, and that the sessions began in March. Evidently, at some point, Dylan was reminded that all these guys were still on retainer, and they might as well be made to play for their supper. The usual starting point is given as April, though the official album's sleeve notes say it was June, and it may well be then that the songs on the official album began to be recorded. The first couple of months of sessions seem to have been 'killing time,' to use Robertson's phrase. Not that there wasn't a process going on, just that it had yet to flower into perhaps Dylan's greatest collection of songs.

What these early tapes display, aside from the sheer wealth of American music these guys seemed to know, was an unfolding, not merely of Dylan's muse but of a sensibility that Robbie and the guys could really latch onto. For the Band, Dylan's rediscovery of his music set an example that would finally transform their music into something genuinely unique. Robertson is in no doubt that this was Dylan's intent all along:

Robbie Robertson: With the covers Bob was educating us a little. The whole folkie thing was still very questionable to us—it wasn't the train we came in on. He'd be doing this Pete Seeger stuff and I'd be saying, 'Oh God . . .' And then, it might be music you knew you didn't like, he'd come up with something like '[The Banks of the] Royal Canal,' and you'd say, 'This is so beautiful! The expression!' He wasn't so obvious about it. But he remembered too much, remembered too many songs too well. He'd come over to Big Pink, or wherever we were, and pull out some old song—and he'd prepped for this. He'd practiced this, and then come out here, to show us.

The diversity of popular songs they recorded is quite remarkable: everything from Johnny Cash to the Stanley Brothers, from Ian Tyson to Eric Von Schmidt, from sea shanties to country tearjerkers, from pure gospel to morality tales, culling their material from the English and Irish dales, the Appalachian Mountains, the Mississippi Delta, Nashville's Music Row, and even Tin Pan Alley. It was almost as if Dylan were attempting to tap into some common constituency in American popular music in order to remind himself not only of his roots, but of his audience. Though the Americana aspect of the basement tape recordings has been overstated—after all, there are forty-three known covers on the basement tapes, of which barely a quarter are traditional songs—the covers are an integral part of the 'basement' experience, and their absence from the official set makes for a vacuum the Band songs hardly begin to fill.

So in the spring of 1967 Dylan began hanging out every day with the Hawks, who had found themselves a rented house in West Saugerties. With its distinctive bright pink exterior, it was known locally as Big Pink. Initially these musical gatherings convened at Dylan's house, in the equally color-conscious Red Room. However, the daily distractions of family life were such that the boys soon decided a relocation was in order. The routine was established early on.

Robbie Robertson: We used to get together every day at one o'clock in the basement of Big Pink. And it was just a routine. We would get there and to keep [every] one of us from going crazy, we would play music every day . . . There was no particular reason for it. We weren't making a record. We were just fooling around. The purpose was whatever comes into anybody's mind, we'll put it down on this little tape recorder. Shitty little tape recorder.

In fact, Robertson is being slightly disingenuous when he talks about this 'shitty little tape recorder.' The sessions appear to have been recorded on the trusty old Uher that had served them well on the world tour, using a couple of Altech PA tube mixers, allowing up to three microphones to be input per channel, and four or five studio-quality Neumann microphones. Not your average 1967 home setup! Though Garth Hudson, the overseer of the recording equipment and the one who leaned over and pressed stop at song's end, may have just enjoyed the challenge of getting the best sound he could, after a couple of initial bass-heavy, overamplified recordings, the results have a warmth and intimacy that Dylan has found hard to rediscover on subsequent studio sessions. That Dylan has often wanted to get back to such informality is not in doubt. He has continually sought the self-same feel on post-basement recordings, and he would tell Jann Wenner in 1969:

Bob Dylan: You know, that's really the way to do a recording—in a peaceful, relaxed setting, in somebody's basement, with the windows open and a dog lying on the floor. [1969]

When Dylan resumed his music-making that spring it had been over a year since his last recorded work, and there is no evidence that he had been writing songs since his return from Europe. If there had been an air of deliberation to this drought, Dylan was now taking a series of whiffs from the very wellspring of his art—Anglo-American traditional song—to ease himself back into songwriting. In years to come (specifically, in 1970, 1987, and the early nineties) this would become almost a methodology, but in 1967 it was uncharted territory. The first batch of basement originals were almost invariably semi-improvised, usually taking as their springboard some image from the lexicon of American song: 'One man's loss is another man's gain,' 'One for my baby, one more for the road,' 'I can't make it alone.'

Garth Hudson: We were doing seven, eight, ten, sometimes fifteen songs a day. Some were old ballads and traditional songs . . . but others Bob would make up as he went along . . . We'd play the melody, he'd sing a few words he'd written, and then make up some more, or else just mouth sounds or even syllables as he went along. It's a pretty good way to write songs.

The reel on which Dylan's exposition of Bobby Bare's 'All-American Boy' was recorded, also contained two John Lee Hooker covers, 'I'm in the Mood' and 'Tupelo'; Ian Tyson's 'Four Strong Winds' and 'The French Girl'; Eric Von Schmidt's 'Joshua Gone Barbados'; Gid Tanner's 'You Gotta Quit Kickin' My Dog Aroun'; and a couple of pastiches, seemingly improvised: 'Next Time on the Highway' (with lines grab-bagged from 'any number of old chain-gang songs,' to quote Dr. Marcus), and the hilarious teen-prom doo-wop of 'I'm Your Teenage Prayer.' Crucially, it also contains perhaps the first two sightings of Dylan's returning muse, 'Tiny Montgomery' and 'Sign on the Cross.'

With 'Tiny Montgomery,' Dylan rediscovered his flair for characters out of left field. Skinny Moo, Half-Track Frank, and Tiny Montgomery himself presaged a whole steel-driving crew of basement eccentrics, from the Mighty Quinn to Turtle and Silly Nelly, Mouse, Molly, and Moby Dick. He also rediscovered a love of choruses. With 'Sign on the Cross' he found something else, something long lodged in his id. Over seven and a half minutes of searching for 'that old key to the kingdom,' Dylan first confronts, then disavows, fears that the sign on the cross may hold the key, that one day he 'might want to enter [the kingdom] but, of course, the door it might be closed.'

The way that the Band's music ebbs and flows with Dylan's extemporizing is proof positive that telepathy exists. Dylan seems particularly attuned to the astral plane as he launches into preacher mode in mid-song, though the original source of the persona here adopted can be found on one of the many country covers recorded that summer: '(Be Careful of the) Stones That You Throw,' a song about gossip written by Hank Williams in his adopted guise of Luke the Drifter, a character who specialized in this type of moralistic monologue. The culmination of this style would come on the *John Wesley Harding* album with 'The Ballad of Frankie Lee and Judas Priest.'

Of course, taking into account Dylan's probable state of mind by this point in the afternoon, his wild exhortations on 'Sign on the Cross' might best be taken with a truckload of salt. Though it is unclear how much of this particular reel of tape was recorded in a single day, on the earlier songs the musicians sound like they'd been whacked out of the trees and landed on their heads. On 'Next Time on the Highway,' Dylan lights into Richard Manuel for 'playing that piano shit-faced,' before exhorting him to 'piss on that piano.' 'The Spanish Song,' in the words of Marcus, 'seem[s] to be what the maddest of the basement adventures were pointing to all along: complete dementia.' 'All-American Boy,' the song before 'Sign on the Cross,' is full of Manuel's interjections and asides, ever goading Dylan on. The audio evidence makes it clear that Dylan had no more abandoned all drugs of choice post-accident than he had abandoned folk music post-Newport.

The daily regime invariably commenced with a communal joint, or three, Woodstock being apparently redolent with the aroma of the finest pot money could buy that summer. Not that they confined themselves to some mighty weed. As the tape rolls, on take one of 'Yea Heavy and a Bottle of Bread,' Dylan can be heard clearing his throat, not of catarrh but in that telltale way that bespeaks a quick snort of speed or coke that has gone a little too far down the nasal passage. These boys were evidently flying low over the Rockies by the time music-making commenced.

The informal sessions served to unlock Dylan's muse. Once he was writing again, the flood of new songs was even greater than during his days in New York City. In a matter of months, Dylan and the Hawks recorded at least thirty new Dylan compositions, including some of his finest (and most-loved) songs: 'I Shall Be Released,' 'This Wheel's on Fire,' 'Quinn the Eskimo (The Mighty Quinn),' 'Million Dollar Bash,' 'Tears of Rage,' and 'You Ain't Going Nowhere.' Less familiar fare, like 'I'm Not There (1956),' 'Sign on the Cross,' 'Going to Acapulco,' and 'All You Have to Do Is Dream,' were equally shot through with the insights of a man returned from the precipice. Amazingly, some of the more inspired songs were semi-improvised on the spot, notably 'Apple Suckling Tree,' 'I'm Not There (1956),' and 'Sign on the Cross.' If Dylan had always improvised in the studio, it was never to this extent and with this level of results. Spontaneously experimenting with country and blues forms, he was mouthing line upon line of oblique images from the id.

On 'I'm Not There (1956),' the most inspired example of Dylan's ability to capture a moment on tape as a vision begins to fragment, he seems to be free-forming words around the rudest of rudimentary outlines. A typescript purporting to be Dylan's original was published in *The Telegraph* and, on the face of it, seems genuine. If so, almost all the great lines in the Big Pink performance—'she's my Christ-forsaken angel, but she don't hear me cry'; 'she knows that the kingdom weighs [or is that *waits*?] so high above her'—were spontaneous. The slightly bitchy tone of the typescript, in which our heroine is 'a drag queen . . . a drag-a-muffin . . . a drag,' is replaced by an exquisite remorse for the singer's inability to save her from herself. The words become props to a mood that only the music can dissolve, given up to 'a dyslexia that is music itself,' as Marcus put it in *Invisible Republic*.

Unfortunately, not everything they ran through was even recorded.

(At one point Dylan tells Hudson, 'You don't need to record this. You're just wasting tape.' Aargh.) There are no recordings of Dylan, Robertson, Danko, Manuel, and Hudson fumbling through the genesis of songs. The basement tapes we have, and those we do not, are snapshots from the end of the day. The procedure was to work up an arrangement of a song, either an original or a cover, and, if they liked it, record it.

Robbie Robertson: When we were inspired, we'd go down to the basement and put something down on tape. Eventually it became quite a collection of songs that we had there.

Dylan's process of 'educating us a little' was not confined to showing the Band the roots of American popular song. He also pushed them into writing their own songs. Indeed, two of the best songs from the sessions were co-written with members of the Hawks: 'Tears of Rage' and 'This Wheel's on Fire.' In both cases he presented the typewritten lyrics, to Manuel and Danko respectively, to see if they had some music 'that fit.' The words were now coming thick and fast, even if they remained as bemusing to the musicians as to their eventual audience.

Richard Manuel: He came down to the basement with a piece of typewritten paper . . . it was typed out—in line form—and he just said, 'Have you got any music for this?' I had a couple of musical movements that fit . . . so I just elaborated a bit, because I wasn't sure what the lyrics meant. I couldn't run upstairs and say, 'What's this mean, Bob: "Now the heart is filled with gold as if it was a purse"?'

Though over the summer they had mined more than an album's worth of rough diamonds—and despite the fact that Dylan still owed Columbia an album before he could consider his options—he seemed to have no real idea what to do with all this homemade produce. At the end of August, ten of the songs penned in the preceding months were dubbed down from their original stereo to mono and deposited with his music publishers, Dwarf Music, jointly formed by Dylan and Grossman at the end of 1965, as demos for other artists to cover. Dylan has even given the impression that the songs were 'sort of' written with others in mind.

Bob Dylan: They were written vaguely for other people . . . I don't remember anybody specifically those songs were ever written for. They must have been written at that time for the publishing company . . . We must have recorded fifty songs at that place. At that time psychedelic rock was overtaking the universe and we were singing these homespun ballads. [1978]

Peter, Paul and Mary were the first to chart with a basement tapes song, releasing their version of 'Too Much of Nothing' as a single in November 1967. They were soon followed by Manfred Mann, who topped the charts with 'The Mighty Quinn,' and, in the UK, by Julie Driscoll and the Brian Auger Trinity, who made it into the Top 5 with 'This Wheel's on Fire.' The Band also cherry-picked their share for their debut album, *Music from Big Pink*, while the Byrds signposted another change in direction with countrified versions of 'You Ain't Goin' Nowhere' (also a hit single) and 'Nothing Was Delivered,' on their groundbreaking foray into country-rock, *Sweetheart of the Rodeo*.

And yet Dylan and the Hawks continued their music-making, even as the songs became darker and deeper, even as Levon Helm was preparing to rejoin the fold. 'Tears of Rage,' 'Quinn the Eskimo,' 'Nothing Was Delivered,' and 'Open the Door Homer' were all copyrighted as part of a second batch of publisher's demos in January 1968, though they were almost certainly the product of sessions in September or early October (drum duties continuing to be filled by Manuel).

If Dylan was already preparing to move on, the Band's music remained permanently imbued with the spirit they found collectively in the basement of Big Pink. Helm was stunned by the music his old buddies were making when he flew back from Memphis in early November. As he concisely put it, 'The boys had discovered how to write songs. Bob Dylan had opened it up for 'em.'

By the time the Band came to release *Music from Big Pink* (conceived in West Saugerties, though not recorded there), some fans were already aware that the three Dylan songs contained within were part of a far larger store of hidden goodies. The same month, June 1968, the recently founded fortnightly rockzine, *Rolling Stone*, ran a cover story on 'The Missing Bob Dylan Album,' under the headline DYLAN'S BASE-MENT TAPE SHOULD BE RELEASED, where they concluded that:

There is enough material—most all of it very good—to make an entirely new Bob Dylan record, a record with a distinct style of its own . . . These tapes could easily be remastered and made into a record. The concept of a cohesive record is already present.

The fourteen-song acetate of publishers' demos was now written up as the missing link between *Blonde on Blonde* and *John Wesley Harding*, and given that all fourteen songs had been widely circulated on tape and acetate, it was inevitable that the huge demand for Dylan's own renditions of the likes of 'I Shall Be Released,' 'Tears of Rage,' 'This Wheel's on Fire,' and 'Quinn the Eskimo' would be fulfilled, if not by Columbia then by some other able-bodied brigands. Sure enough, in July 1969 came the first and most famous of albums from the 'other' recording industry, *Great White Wonder*, assembled by the legendary 'Dub' Taylor, primarily from the Dwarf Music acetate and Glover's 1961 'hotel tape.' It was rapidly followed by the ten-track *Troubled Troubadour,* the fourteen-track *Waters of Oblivion* and the thirteen-track *Little White Wonder,* which were wholly subterranean.

Over the next six years, the basement tapes would become the most bootlegged recordings of all time. As Paul Cable once pointedly asked, 'What else . . . did Dylan expect?' The official double album, released in 1975, temporarily stilled the golden calf, but when another twenty or so recordings from Big Pink (and the Red Room) passed into trading circles in 1986, and a further fifty in 1990, more bouts of bootlegging were inevitable. With the likes of 'I'm Not There (1956),' 'Sign on the Cross,' 'All You Have to Do Is Dream,' and 'All-American Boy' continuing to reside among Dylan's unofficial canon—and some forty-plus covers that between them make Dylan's five official albums of other people's songs (count 'em) sound like the bootlegs—the basement tapes remain Dylan's greatest secret. Since the contents remained unknown for some time outside of Woodstock, the evidence they provided of Dylan's continuing fecundity at the end of the summer of love was unavailable to those fans eagerly awaiting his response to the 'psychedelic rock . . . overtaking the universe.'

1968: Drifters, Immigrants, Messengers and Saints

15

Woodstock is a very womblike place. It's very special there . . . It's filled with personal spiritual growth opportunity there . . . and people who go to Woodstock are transformed, people who live there that is. And [Dylan] was going through a transformation, I feel . . . He was learning love and learning to feel love and express it and experience it in the family way . . . [making] very introspective, very countrylike, very havenlike music.

—*Elliott Landy*

He became weirder yet after the motorcycle accident.

—*Al Aronowitz*

The backdrop to the basement tapes, commercially and culturally, hardly lent itself to 'very havenlike music.' Grossman had waited five years to extract Dylan from his imminently expiring Columbia contract, and had seemingly negotiated a seven-figure advance—a quarter of which would go into the Grossman account—and a 12 percent royalty with the struggling record division of movie moguls MGM. If the fans knew nothing of Dylan's summer songwriting spree, Grossman gave Mort Nasatir at MGM some of the acetate songs, 'to give me a feel for what he was doing and what he had in mind.' Convinced of Dylan's creative well-being, Nasatir voted to proceed. The one immovable object in the way was a fellow member of the MGM board, the resolute Allen Klein, who felt that the deal set a bad precedent.

Klein had an ally, equally determined to keep Dylan from MGM: the operating head of Columbia, Clive Davis. Davis, who recognized that Dylan was not simply a financial asset to the label but gave Columbia kudos, had an important weapon at his disposal—Dylan's original contract with Columbia, which had yet to be fulfilled. According to the terms of that contract, Dylan still owed them 'a minimum of fourteen 78 rpm record sides . . . embodying fourteen different musical compositions not previously recorded by [him]' and these 'said master recordings shall be recorded pursuant to all of the terms and conditions of the Term

Contract including, without limitation, the basic royalty rate of 4%.'
Accordingly, Dylan was notified on February 9, 1967, that Columbia
had 'put into effect the suspension provisions of sub-paragraph 14 c) of
the Term Contract.' On March 27, 1967, Dylan etched a surprisingly
childlike signature to an agreement to 'render [his] services at recording
sessions at our studios . . . for the purpose of making [fourteen] satisfactory
master recordings.' To be free of Columbia, he would have to deliver
another album, and at a royalty rate a third of what he stood to gain from
the MGM deal.

Davis also had other weapons in his armory. He began a two-pronged
campaign to retain Dylan by furnishing Klein with the real sales figures
for Dylan's albums, which were less than spectacular simply because
Dylan's fans tended to buy his albums immediately, sending them up the
charts, but their shelf life was limited. He then reminded Grossman that
Dylan was due substantial back royalties from Columbia that, if paid in
their entirety in a single year, would be all but swallowed whole by the
taxman. And it wasn't only back royalties that Columbia had a surfeit of.
They had hours of studio outtakes, at least four albums' worth—some
very, very good—and at least nine complete concerts lying in their
vaults, wholly owned by Columbia, to do with as they saw fit.

Grossman's counter-proposal to Columbia was an unheard-of 10
percent royalty (twice their previous ceiling) but no advance, and a
five-year term, with no stipulated minimum number of albums. Davis
grabbed this no-risk deal, and Dylan's lawyer sent a telegram to MGM
rescinding Dylan's signature on their contract. It had apparently not
occurred to Klein that Dylan's low profile since July 1966 might have
actually increased his saleability. His next two albums would generate
higher initial sales than any of his pre-accident albums. And the new
contract he signed with Columbia on July 1, 1967 countermanded the
agreement signed in March, so Dylan stood to make his 10 percent on
every copy of his next album, as and when he felt like recording one.

By the time he began work on his eighth album, in the fall of 1967,
eighteen months had passed since the completion of *Blonde on Blonde*:
months that had seen the Beatles record their two most perfect singles
and their most unsatisfactory album; the Beach Boys record two even
more perfect singles while failing to realize their most ambitious album;
and the Velvet Underground presage a whole new form of rock music
based on dissonance, noise, and confrontation. As so often, the greatest
immediate impact was made by the most retrograde of these long-players,
the Beatles' *Sgt. Pepper's Lonely Hearts Club Band*—a cornucopia of studio
gimmicks designed to obscure lightweight tunes, and two steps back

from the inspired *Revolver*. Its surface sensibilities caused a lemminglike rush of hippies intent on recording psychedelic versions of their most recent acid trip.

Dylan, though, now knew that one didn't need to tune in and turn on to drop out. Indeed, only by turning off and tuning out had he found a degree of inner peace. If there was much speculation at the time as to how he would attempt to top *Sgt. Pepper*, Dylan himself had no interest in such an exercise. He had been even less impressed by what he had heard from Abbey Road studios that summer than he had been by McCartney's loopy experiment 'Tomorrow Never Knows.'

Bob Dylan: I didn't know how to record the way other people were recording, and didn't want to. The Beatles had just released *Sgt. Pepper*, which I didn't like at all . . . I thought that was a very indulgent album, though the songs on it were real good. I didn't think all that production was necessary, 'cause the Beatles had never done that before. [1978]

Though, at the time, Dylan kept his disdain for the new Beatles album to himself, he did insist on hiding pictures of the Fab Four in the trees on the cover of the *John Wesley Harding* album. Perhaps Vera's comment to Frank, in the album's sleeve notes, was another way of summing up his intentions: 'Why didn't you just tell them you were a moderate man and leave it at that?'

The passage from the basement tapes to *John Wesley Harding*—a transition no more fathomable than from, say, *The Winter's Tale* to *The Tempest*—marked an even deeper immersion in the well of traditional balladry. Though the most powerful covers recorded at Big Pink were the handful of ballads attempted—'Young but Daily Growin',' 'The Hills of Mexico,' 'Bonnie Ship the Diamond,' 'The Banks of the Royal Canal,' 'Joshua Gone Barbados,' and 'Spanish Is the Loving Tongue'—Dylan continued omitting the form from his own craft. Until, that is, a peculiar ballad by a young country singer, Bobbie Gentry, began to storm the charts in August. 'Ode to Billie Joe'—a cleverly constructed yarn about the undertows sometimes tugging beneath inane dinner conversations—prompted Dylan's first parody since 'Fourth Time Around,' and his first ballad since 'Bob Dylan's 115th Dream.' 'Clothesline Saga,' or 'Answer to Ode,' as it was originally identified on the basement reels, revolves around a far more surreal event than the suicide of Billie Joe McAllister—'The Vice President's gone mad!' The way that this extraordinary event barely impinges on the mundane lives of the song's characters—and is dismissed with a pragmatic recognition of this fact, 'Well, there's nothin' we can do about it'—provides for a richly detailed depiction of life in Normal, USA.

Whether 'Clothesline Saga' was written before October 3, 1967, has not been documented, but it certainly suggested a man returning to 'the only true, valid death.' The death, that day, of the author of 'This Land Is Your Land,' from the degenerative disease that had long rendered the 'very great man' mute, passed the wider world by. Woody Guthrie's demise, though, clearly impacted on Dylan. Within two weeks, he would be in a studio in Nashville, recording three brand-new ballads that reiterated some of Guthrie's favorite motifs. 'I Dreamed I Saw St. Augustine,' based on the familiar 'Joe Hill,' portrays a man whose resemblance to St. Augustine is moot, since it was union organizer Hill who was 'put . . . out to death'; while 'Drifter's Escape' exercises the deus ex machina of a 'bolt of lightning' to save Guthrie's favored drifter from a 'cursed jury'; and 'The Ballad of Frankie Lee and Judas Priest' adopts the style of the western ballad, much as Guthrie had with some of his most cutting critiques, for a disquisition on morality housed in the familiar message-song format.

The October 17, 1967, session, at which he managed to cut all three of these morality-play ballads, was an impressive start to the eighth Dylan long-player. As extraordinary as the new songs' pared-down lyrics was the austere sound. With just Kenny Buttrey on drums and Charlie McCoy on bass augmenting his guitar and harmonica, Dylan recorded the songs in a single three-hour session—just like the old days. McCoy and Buttrey were stunned at the transformation from manic ragamuffin into this calm, clean-cut professional in a mere year and a half.

The songs were also suffused with a new religiosity that perhaps suggested the sign on the cross continued to bother Bob. Their language was the language of the King James Bible, their characters, adrift in some postlapsarian American frontier town, were bound by an Old Testament morality. Beatty Zimmerman, talking to Toby Thompson in 1968, spoke of how her son had recently rediscovered the Bible.

Beatty Zimmerman: In his house in Woodstock today, there's a huge Bible open on a stand in the middle of his study. Of all the books that crowd his house, overflow from his house, that Bible gets the most attention. He's continuously getting up and going over to refer to something.

The *John Wesley Harding* album is certainly replete with allusions to both Old and New Testaments. In his study *The Bible in the Lyrics of Bob Dylan*, Bert Cartwright cited some sixty-one biblical allusions on the album, the breakdown for each song being 'As I Went out One Morning' (1); 'All Along the Watchtower' (5); 'I Dreamed I Saw St. Augustine' (3); 'The Ballad of Frankie Lee and Judas Priest' (15); 'Drifter's Escape' (4); 'Dear Landlord' (6); 'I Am a Lonesome Hobo' (5); 'I Pity the Poor Immigrant' (16); and 'The Wicked Messenger' (6).

'All Along the Watchtower' features perhaps the most overt biblical allusions, drawing its setting from the section of Isaiah that deals with the fall of Babylon. Yet the thief that cries 'the hour is getting late' is surely the thief in the night foretold in Revelation, Jesus Christ come again. It is He who says, in St. John the Divine's tract: 'I will come on thee as a thief, and Thou shalt not know what hour I will come upon thee.' Dylan remained unsure of the hour at which he might come, later saying of *John Wesley Harding* that he had been 'dealing with the devil in a fearful way.'

The album's morality, though, was not wholly Judeo-Christian in outlook. Dylan had also taken on board some ideas from a band of traveling minstrels, the Bengali Bauls, who had come to the United States at the request of Albert Grossman. While staying on Grossman's estate in Woodstock, they were introduced to Dylan. The Bauls sang songs based on traditional forms dating back to the ninth or tenth century. Containing elements of Buddhism and Sufi Islam, their songs had some similarities to Western popular song, using a repetitive refrain after each verse, but it was the primary theme of all their poems and songs—the right of the individual to develop freely—that most imbued the songs Dylan wrote that fall.

Levon Helm: The Bauls of Bengal were a family of itinerant street trouba-dours that Albert Grossman had met on a visit to India . . . They were real gypsies and real players, happy to get high and sing all night about rivers and goddesses and play their tablas, harmonium, and fiddles.

Two of the Bauls, Purna and Lakhsman Das, flank Dylan on the cover of *John Wesley Harding*, an album full of outlaws, drifters, immigrants, messengers, and saints. What the album was not laden down by were those wild kaleidoscopic images that had flowed from Dylan's pen before the accident. The surrealism of *Blonde on Blonde* had been pensioned off, even if the sleeve notes suggested it remained at his command. According to Dylan, he was looking to strip his language bare, something he discussed with Allen Ginsberg at the time.

Bob Dylan: What I'm trying to do now is not use too many words. There's no line that you can stick your finger through, there's no hole in any of the stanzas. There's no blank filler. Each line has something. [1968]

Allen Ginsberg: In '68 he was talking poetics with me, telling me how he was writing shorter lines, with every line meaning something. He wasn't just making up a line to go with a rhyme anymore; each line had to advance the story, bring the song forward. And from that time came some of the stuff he did with the Band—like 'I Shall Be Released', and some of his strong laconic ballads like 'The Ballad of Frankie Lee and Judas Priest'. There was to be no wasted language, no wasted breath. All the imagery was to be functional rather than ornamental.

Part of the new functional imagery was a result of Dylan writing the words to the songs before devising an appropriate tune. Over the next month, he continued to write songs in the style of the three songs already recorded for *John Wesley Harding*. After recording 'All Along the Watchtower', the title track, 'As I Went Out One Morning', 'I Pity the Poor Immigrant', and 'I Am a Lonesome Hobo' in another single session in Nashville, the first week in November, the album was wrapped up three weeks later, also in Nashville. Only now did Dylan partially abandon his modus operandi, writing the words and music together for two of the songs.

Bob Dylan: There's only two songs on the album which came at the same time as the music. The rest of the songs were written out on paper, and I found the tunes for them later. I didn't do it before, and I haven't done it since. That might account for the specialness of that album. [1978]

The two exceptions—'I'll Be Your Baby Tonight' and 'Down Along the Cove'—had none of that 'sense of fear' found in 'Dear Landlord' or 'The Wicked Messenger'. They were also bereft of all biblical allusion. If *John Wesley Harding* was the album made the morning after a dark night of the soul, these two songs suggested a newly cleansed singer returning from the edge. The light, breezy pedal steel of Pete Drake also seemed to presage a more country-directed sound, not just for Dylan but for a whole enclave of sixties survivors, from the Band to the Byrds. If the sound of the album was initially startling in its austerity, Dylan may have originally intended a quite different sound. After the first two sessions for the album, he considered adding further embellishments, suggesting to Robbie Robertson and Garth Hudson that they overdub some guitar and organ onto the basic tracks.

Bob Dylan: I didn't intentionally come out with some kind of mellow sound. I would have liked . . . more steel guitar, more piano. More music . . . I didn't sit down and plan that sound. [1971]

Robertson, though, felt that the album worked as it was, and pushed Dylan to release it as is. The addition of Pete Drake, and the two upbeat closers to the album, were perhaps a concession to a more varied musicality, but the sound on the other cuts was destined to remain as pared down as the new imagery.

Robbie Robertson: As I recall it was just on a kind of whim that Bob went down to Nashville. And there, with just a couple of guys, he put those songs down on tape. Then we did talk about doing some overdubbing on it, but I really liked it when I heard it and I couldn't really think right about overdubbing on it. So it ended up coming out the way he brought it back.

The final session for *John Wesley Harding* was on November 29, 1967. In under four weeks it was in the racks. The album was issued in the States with only minimal publicity, at Dylan's request—'I asked Columbia to release it with no publicity and no hype, because this was the season of hype'—but the wait alone ensured that it shot to number two in the charts, the real meat sandwiched between the latest platters of the Beatles and the Rolling Stones. Though the rock press was barely out of diapers, *Rolling Stone* gave the album two reviews, one as part of Ralph Gleason's regular column, predictably laudatory:

These are myths and legends perhaps, and maybe even parables on the edge of time. Whatever they are, Dylan has returned, cleansed, as a whole man with a new kind of serenity to illuminate his visions and a deeper artistic impulse from within himself.

The other, two weeks later, by Gordon Mills, in the record-review section, was more measured, recognizing 'another major musical step for Bob Dylan,' and emphasizing 'the predominance of country blues— white and black—from Hank Williams to Leadbelly . . . [something] unprecedented in the new electric music.' Though Dylan's 'new kind of serenity' was not henceforth to 'illuminate his visions,' *John Wesley Harding* remains one of Dylan's most enduring albums. Never had Dylan constructed an album-as-an-album so self-consciously. Not tempted to incorporate even later basement visions like 'Going to Acapulco' and

'Clothesline Saga,' Dylan managed in less than six weeks to construct his most perfectly executed official collection.

Though the album was met with a certain disappointment by those for whom the roar of electric instruments and the rush of drugs continued to drown out the real world, this did not dissuade Dylan from his chosen path. When *Nashville Skyline* came out eighteen months later, many fans re-examined the earlier album and recognized its quality. Critics would also note the way he had previewed his movement towards a fuller country sound with the final two songs on *John Wesley Harding*.

A further clue that Dylan had already marked out his next sound, if not his next persona, by the beginning of 1968 resides on what appears to be the final shared session at Big Pink between Dylan and the Hawks. On this session, with Helm back in the fold, they confined themselves exclusively to covers, two of which were culled from Harry Smith's six-album *Anthology of American Folk Music*, the Carter Family's 'Wildwood Flower' and Blind Lemon Jefferson's 'See That My Grave Is Kept Clean.' The latter of these is here sung by Dylan in an extraordinary country twang that might have surprised even Bonnie Beecher, if she had had the foresight to call on Dylan that day.

Bonnie Beecher: I was startled when I heard him again on *Nashville Skyline*. [In 1960] he got this bronchial cough that lasted almost a year, and he wouldn't take care of it because he thought the rougher his voice sounded, the more [it was] like Woody Guthrie. I thought he had lost . . . that sweet voice altogether.

It certainly must have stunned the Band, who had traveled the world with a nasal folksinger who now sounded like a cross between Jimmie Rodgers and Hank Williams. Elements of that voice were even road-tested on Dylan's return to live performance a few weeks after the final Big Pink jam, snugly integrated into the more raucous style worked up on summer demos of 'Down in the Flood' and 'Odds and Ends.' That return to live performance comprised just two fifteen-minute sets. In October 1967, when he had heard about Guthrie's death, Dylan had phoned Harold Leventhal, Guthrie's longtime friend and manager, and said that if there was going to be a memorial show he wanted to be there. Thus, on 20 January 1968, he shared a bill at Carnegie Hall with the likes of Judy Collins, Tom Paxton, and Guthrie's son Arlo for the first Woody Guthrie Memorial Concert (a second was held on the West Coast in 1970). Dylan asked the Band, billed as the Crackers, to back him.

Despite the fact that all the acts played sets composed of Guthrie songs, Dylan's first concert appearance in twenty months was more of an event than Guthrie's death as far as the media were concerned. The three songs he did perform—'Grand Coulee Dam,' 'Dear Mrs. Roosevelt,' and 'I Ain't Got No Home'—were hardly in the folk style Guthrie had espoused, and which all the other performers adopted for the occasion. The sound the Crackers whacked out was a darn sight closer to rockabilly, while Dylan's singing was part twang, part *John Wesley Harding*, but precious little folk.

Robbie Robertson: Everybody else was taking a different plane musically, you know, it was a very folk-orientated show. But we just played what we were doing at the time. I can't help but think Woody Guthrie would have approved. I mean, if a song is going to live, it must live in its contemporary surrounding.

If the fans hoped that Dylan's appearance might whet his appetite for live performance, they were to be sorely disappointed. In his June 1968 interview for *Sing Out*, Dylan made it clear that his touring days had been put on hold: 'I did it enough to know that there must be something else to do.' Now bearded, he looked like a country squire who had accidentally wandered through the door marked *Stage*. His newfound serenity, however, was not extended to all and sundry. He was still capable of treating some with icy indifference.

Levon Helm: [At the Guthrie benefit,] we noticed that Bob and Albert weren't speaking to each other.

Speculation had been rife that one song on *John Wesley Harding*, 'Dear Landlord'—Dylan's plea to some individual not to put a price on his soul—was directed at Grossman. Though Dylan himself would later deny it, it certainly seems an appropriate address to a man who had pushed him so hard during that grueling world tour, and whose contracts continued to give him a huge cut of Dylan's earnings. Though the deal with Witmark Music had come to an end in 1965, Grossman retained a share in Dylan's current music publishing company, Dwarf Music, and his management contract was scheduled to run until August 1971. Though Grossman continued to protect his client's interests, Clive Davis at Columbia was concerned that, without his manager's input, Dylan might lose contact with his record label and public.

Clive Davis: [Dylan and Grossman had] stopped working together. He did not have another manager; I had the feeling that he needed someone to bring him ideas, goad him a bit, make suggestions, offer help if he needed it . . . I had to tread very softly. I began calling him. I could never reach him directly, for he guards his privacy very carefully. The technique was to call his secretary Naomi, who would call him; then, if he chose to, he would call back.

Though Dylan seems to have valued Davis's input, he was not about to embrace the mores of a product-driven world. When Davis urged him to pull a single from *John Wesley Harding,* he preferred to maintain its low-key integrity (it would be left to Jimi Hendrix to take 'All Along the Watchtower' into the Top 20 at the end of '68). At the end of 1967 Dylan must have been pleased with life in Woodstock, both personally and artistically. Sara had given him a daughter that summer, named Anna. He had signed a lucrative new contract with Columbia, and recorded and released his first album in two years, which had proved both a major addition to the canon and a popular success. He had even been reconciled with his estranged parents, who had visited him in September to see for themselves their first granddaughter.

To his parents, it must have seemed that their son had been transformed by his new responsibilities, and on some level that was certainly true. Indeed, his love of children has never left him. But the man now wrapped up in Woodstock domesticity just could not be reconciled with the man looking to slam like a drake on 'Please Mrs. Henry' or blow his plums on 'Going to Acapulco,' let alone the wild child in *Eat the Document*. It wasn't just that the man had mellowed out, he had thoroughly reinvented himself as, in the words of John Hammond, Jr., 'a human being who was also a huge star . . . [who] was recuperating and having babies.' Everybody who had contact with him in the 'Woodstock period' commented on his new self. Bob Markel traveled to Woodstock in February 1968 to see if Dylan could be pushed into allowing publication of *Tarantula*.

Bob Markel: He was far more friendly, far less distracted. He was more grown up and professional, easier to be with. He said he didn't know if he wanted the book published at all. It wasn't something he wanted to improve; it [just] didn't interest him anymore. He'd gone past it. He [still] wasn't sure if he wanted it published as a 'relic,' or an unfinished work.

Because galleys had been made, and discreetly circulated, back in 1966, *Tarantula* had created almost as large a demand as the basement tapes and, sure enough, *Tarantula* booklegs appeared in tandem with the *Great White Wonder* bootleg album. However, Dylan informed Macmillan that he preferred to work on a new book. In June, talking to Happy Traum and John Cohen, he dismissed *Tarantula* as 'nonsense.' It would take some time for him to revise that opinion.

Bob Dylan: I just put down all these words and sent them off to my publishers and they'd send back the galleys, and I'd be so embarrassed at the nonsense I'd written I'd change the whole thing. And all the time they had 100,000 orders . . . The trouble with it, it had no story. I'd been reading all these trash books, works suffering from sex and excitement and foolish things. [1968]

Perhaps the most surprising consequence of his Woodstock retreat was that he fell in love with his wife again. Not that Dylan hadn't always been smitten by Sara, simply that her charms had previously failed to subjugate more polygamous instincts. Having reinvented himself as a family man, he now embraced the role, just as his own father had, making babies taking precedence over making records. According to Shelton, a third child was due in June:

Al Aronowitz: After Sara and Bob moved into Byrdcliffe, situated where the mountaintop sticks its head into the clouds, my wife and I and our children continued visiting them, often spending the night. I would bring film cans full of the latest Hollywood hits, obtained from a friendly New York movie mogul. During this period, Bob and Sara grew to be one of the tightest twosomes I've ever known . . . In the years following his motorcycle accident, Bob acted like a romantic cornball when he was with her. More and more, he depended on her advice as if she were his astrologer, his oracle, his seer, his psychic guide. He would rely on her to tell him the best hour and best day to travel . . . They flirted with each other constantly . . . [and] she was always just as hip as he was.

Shortly before Sara gave birth to their third child, though, came the devastating news that Dylan's father had died of a heart attack, aged just fifty-six. Dylan flew to Hibbing-Chisholm airport alone. After the funeral, he got his younger brother, David, to drive him around Hibbing in the rain. Sleeping in his father's old bedroom, Dylan immersed himself in the faded photographs, tapes, and records of his youth, but the sense of things left unsaid would not leave him. Rather than have to return to Hibbing again, he sought to persuade his mother to sell up and move. He then caught the plane home, seemingly to witness the birth of another son. A photo by Elliott Landy taken in Woodstock in the fall of 1968 appears to include this son, held firmly in Sara's arms, Marie, Jesse, and Anna at her feet. However, no such son was cited in the 1977 divorce proceedings, nor is there any record of him being bar mitzvahed.

In June 1968, Dylan honored another commitment from a past life. He had told Happy Traum, when he had moved to Woodstock the previous year, that he might be prepared to do an interview for *Sing Out*. *Sing Out* was experiencing considerable financial difficulties, and a Dylan interview might yet dig them out of this particular hole. It would, after all, be his first major interview since the accident. Traum suggested that John Cohen, of the New Lost City Ramblers—who had also photographed Dylan in the early sixties—conduct the interview. Dylan agreed. However, his mellow new persona was in full noncommittal mode the day of the first interview, and he seemed reluctant to express *any* opinions about the pressing political issues of the day. A second interview went the same way, despite Traum's intervention. The interview appeared to indicate that Dylan had not merely reinvented himself, but had awoken one morning to find he had become the papa in his own clothesline saga.

Happy Traum: He was totally not giving interviews. In fact he was so changed by his accident that he had become religious; he had become a family man; he'd stopped smoking. You know, there'd been a total change in his personality . . . So I called John [Cohen] and he came up, stayed with me at my house, and we went out and saw Dylan. Through most of the interview I just sat and listened, I didn't say anything. I was letting John do it, because John is a very smart fellow, he has a very specific point of view. He's an artist, he's a photographer, as well as being a musician. Then about three-quarters of the way through the interview—I believe it was two separate sittings—I began to feel that John was being too careful with Bob, he wasn't pushing him on anything . . . He was intimidated by the fact that he was doing an interview with this man . . . And I felt that in order to be a good interview it needed some life, it needed somebody to stick something in there . . . Now at this time—you've got to remember it was 1968—there was still a lot of talk about him leaving politics, about him not singing political songs anymore. He was writing only love songs and he had made some statements about how he had finished with politics and he wasn't interested, and all that kind of stuff. So I thought it was important to try to get some answers out of him, something of his ideas about politics, because

people wanted to know that . . . At the time the Vietnam War was on and
we were upset about that, and I really wanted him to say something about
that. I was trying to get Bob to make some definitive statement about
where he stood. But he didn't say anything, he was just talking about this
stonemason he knew.

Dylan had already told reporter Hubert Saal that winter that he didn't
consider 'living in the country is a retreat from anything. It's not as if I
were getting ready to go out in a bouncing wave or anything like that.
You have to be let alone to really accomplish anything.' And yet,
starved of the musical interaction he had enjoyed with the Band, as they
completed work on their own communiqué from Big Pink, and with a
newfound interest in painting beginning to supplant that of song, it
seemed like he had bought long on the backwoods vibe of this rural
artistic community of yesteryear. Though a sense of retreat and other-
worldliness was exactly what he had required when he sporadically
retired to Woodstock during his New York days, and even more so as
he recovered from his accident and discovered the joys of family life, by
1968 it was stifling his creative spirit.

Elliott Landy: Everybody had rented beautiful, big, old wooden houses
that are typical of Woodstock, or they lived on farms. Dylan's house in
Woodstock, for example, had a huge living room with a high wood-paneled
ceiling, all a little gloomy and spooky. Upstairs it looked like an old-fashioned
hotel—long walkways with wooden floors and a red carpet, numberless
children's and guest rooms. It was a so-called Byrdcliffe house, named after
the man who built it. Byrdcliffe was a wealthy man who at the turn of the
century had tried to found an artists' colony at Woodstock, and with his
money had splendid and solid houses built.

Landy befriended several musicians living in this artists' colony, including the Band, Dylan, and Van Morrison, who would move to Woodstock
because of the Dylan association. He was taking photos of all of them,
communicating that vibe over a number of album covers. Landy visited
Dylan on several occasions throughout 1968 and 1969, and he noticed
that Dylan was increasingly committing his energies to his palette. The
first public evidence of Dylan the painter graced the cover of the Band's
debut album, *Music from Big Pink,* that summer.

Elliott Landy: I've seen the original Big Pink painting and it's incredible.
It doesn't look so good on the album cover . . . He started painting when

he was in Byrdcliffe. His neighbor was a painter and taught him how to use the tools of painting. That's what you do in Woodstock . . . It's in the air.

At the time Dylan was happy to celebrate having 'air to breathe and water to wash in,' though he would later coin a phrase for what happened to the songwriter in him in the period after the release of *John Wesley Harding*—'the amnesia.' Though a certain wayward journalist has suggested that Dylan consciously turned off the tap in 1968, to deny Grossman his share of the music publishing, Grossman would continue to collect from Dylan's songwriting skills until July 1970, when he was certainly writing again, albeit not very well. Dylan's own explanation was more simple and poetic:

Bob Dylan: One day I was half-stepping, and the lights went out. And since that point, I more or less had amnesia . . . It took me a long time to get to do consciously what I used to be able to do unconsciously. [1978]

Though Dylan had no more prosaic explanation for 'the amnesia,' he did write in 1974 in an early draft of 'Idiot Wind' that it was like strangers telling him where he'd been. In other words, he forgot not only how to write, but who he was. Unrelated to the motorcycle accident, the amnesia was considerably more unexpected.

Bob Dylan: What I survived after that was even harder to survive than the motorcycle crash. That was just a physical crash, but sometimes there are things in life that you cannot see, that are harder to survive than something which you can pin down. [1978]

When George Harrison visited him around Thanksgiving, he found him uncommunicative and out of touch. Even in the quartet of lines he gave to Harrison, nothing was revealed: 'All I have is yours. All you see is yours. All you see is mine . . . I'd have you anytime.' The only other songs he is known to have written at this time were 'I Threw It All Away' and 'Lay Lady Lay'—the latter written for the *Midnight Cowboy* movie but submitted too late. They hardly suggested the voice of a generation, unless it was Lefty Frizell's.

George Harrison: He'd gone through his broken neck period and was being very quiet, and he didn't have much confidence—that's the feeling I got with him in Woodstock. He hardly said a word for a couple of days.

Ane yet Dylan was already looking to escape from his self-imposed retreat—or perhaps, more accurately, locate a suitable alternative retreat. Earlier in the summer, he took his family out to Fire Island for a few days. Fire Island, with its no-car policy and plentiful beaches, was equally otherworldly, but with a quite different vibe from the artists' colony upstate. Al Aronowitz arranged with composer David Amram to rent a place, anonymously, for the weekend.

David Amram: I was out at the beach at a place called Davis Park, he came off of a boat [with] Al Aronowitz [who'd] called up and said, 'David, I'm coming out to the beach with Bob Dylan. I know he hasn't seen you in a while, and we need a place to stay. Can you meet me at the ferry, he'd like to hang out with you.' . . . I went to the ferry and Bob got off with all these kids and his wife Sara, whom I had known before Bob met her, [through] her husband Hans Lowndes . . . it was so great to see her because [the last] time [I'd seen her] she and her husband had split up, she was with a little baby and struggling, and [now] she looked terrific, she looked happy and beautiful and she had these beautiful children with her . . . It was in September, after Labor Day. [They] all stayed for the weekend and they had a wonderful time. I talked to him a little about Jack Kerouac . . . He had an abiding interest in Kerouac . . . and [the film] *Pull My Daisy,* which he was interested in. I recalled [for him] the whole thing of how Jack sat down with me playing the music, and improvised the whole narration of the film and didn't want to do it a second time. And . . . we stayed in touch.

In the winter of 1969, Dylan moved his family to the southern part of Woodstock, purchasing a larger house, previously owned by economist Walter Weyl. The Weyl place was considerably more secluded, and far fewer people knew about it than the house at Byrdcliffe, which remained on the market while a young musician named Steven Soles was asked to house-sit. He remembered Dylan would occasionally 'come over with his son and just look around, take a lamp or get a book!' In reality, he was probably looking for something less concrete that the new house didn't have and the old house hadn't kept: some clue as to who he had been and how he might get back there. His time in Woodstock was coming to an end, just as the rest of the world was beating a path to its door.

1969: What's the Matter with Me?

16

On *Nashville Skyline* you had to read between the lines. I was trying
to grasp [for] something that would lead me on to where I thought I
should be, and it didn't go nowhere—it just went down, down,
down.

—Bob Dylan, 1978

In February 1969, Dylan flew to Nashville to record—or begin to record,
depending on who you believe—the follow-up to *John Wesley Harding*.
It had been fifteen months since those sessions, and he had not ventured
into a recording studio, or involved himself in his songwriting craft, in
the interim. However, he *had* previously managed to construct something
as masterful as *John Wesley Harding* in six weeks, from blank page to metal
master. According to Dylan, he only went to Nashville to lay the
groundwork for an album, much as he had on October 17, 1967.

Bob Dylan: The first time I went into the studio I had, I think, four songs.
I pulled that instrumental one out . . . then Johnny [Cash] came in and did
a song with me. Then I wrote one in the motel . . . pretty soon the whole
album started fillin' in together, and we had an album. I mean, we didn't go
down with that in mind. [1969]

Dylan was being quite upfront about his work here. He did indeed
record four songs at the session on the 14th, including the two definitely
penned in 1968—'Lay, Lady, Lay' and 'I Threw It All Away.' He also
wrote perhaps the best song of the sessions, 'Tonight I'll Be Staying Here
with You,' in the Ramada Inn, on motel notepaper; and recorded 'a
song,' or seventeen, with Johnny Cash. But no matter how Dylan
tinkered with the songs he had, made fragments and half-ideas whole,
exhumed instrumentals, or covered previous work with Johnny Cash,
an album's worth he could not make.

Much like *Another Side*, the kernel of a fine album, and another
significant change in direction, resides among the padding that fills out
Dylan's ninth collection. 'Tonight I'll Be Staying Here with You' is a

fine cousin to *John Wesley Harding*'s 'I'll Be Your Baby Tonight.' 'I Threw It All Away' remains one of Dylan's most convincing songs of loss, despite the platitudes that clutter up verses 1, 3, and 4 (making that flash of the old Dylan in verse two—'Once I had mountains . . .'—all the more unexpected). 'Lay, Lady, Lay' proved that, if good pop was now the extent of his artistic ambitions, good pop he could make, even if the lovely percussive feel of the album take was largely fortuitous:

Ken Buttrey: Sometimes . . . I go to the artist and say, 'What do you hear on the drums?' Because sometimes when people write songs they can hear it completed, they hear everything they think's gonna be on it . . . I went over to Dylan and said, 'I'm having a little trouble thinking of something to play. Do you have any ideas on this song?' He just kind of looked back . . . and he said, 'Bongos' . . . I went, 'Okay.' I immediately disregarded that, I couldn't hear bongos in this thing at all, so [I thought] I'll go and ask Bob Johnston. So I walked into the control room and said, 'Bob, what do you hear as regards drums on this thing?' And he just sort of rolled his eyes back . . . and said, 'Cowbells.' . . . Kris Kristofferson was working at Columbia Studios at the time as a janitor and he had just emptied my ashtray at the drums and I said, 'Kris, do me a favor, here, hold these two things . . . hold these bongos in one hand and the cowbells in the other,' and I swung this mike over to the cowbells and the bongos . . . I had no pattern or anything worked out. I just told Kris, 'This is one of those spite deals. I'm gonna show 'em how bad their ideas're gonna sound.' . . . We started playing the tune and I was just doodling around on these bongos and the cowbells and it was kinda working out pretty cool . . . Come chorus time I'd go to the set of drums. Next time you hear that [cut], listen how far off-mike the drums sound. There were no mikes on the drums, it was just leakage . . . But it worked out pretty good . . . To this day it's one of the best drum patterns I ever came up with.

'Lay, Lady, Lay' also illustrated Dylan's 'new' voice to optimum effect. The media was initially taken aback by his mysteriously acquired country twang. Even though he put it down to giving up smoking, family and friends soon pointed out that his new voice bore a remarkable similarity to the voice he used to sing with when he played the Ten O'Clock Scholar and the Purple Onion in the winter and spring of 1960.

There was nothing instrinsically heretical about Dylan advancing from a country-tinged sound to a full-out country collection, clichés and all. In the fifteen months since *John Wesley Harding,* country-rock had acquired its own currency. In May 1968, Jann Wenner had written in

Rolling Stone, 'Country and western music . . . is an idiom that is at the historical core of rock & roll and has returned, with Bob Dylan's *John Wesley Harding,* to the spiritual core of contemporary rock & roll. Soon it will become a rock style with the forthcoming release of a new Byrds album now being recorded in Nashville.'

Though the Byrds' *Sweetheart of the Rodeo* would suffer a number of delays, as McGuinn's ego got in the way of its original conceit, its November release, on the back of the Band's country-folk debut, *Music from Big Pink,* made for another trend which Dylan was credited with instigating (as well as enjoying the royalties from five basement tape songs featured on these two albums). Whereas *Sweetheart* was the Byrds' folkiest album to date, though, *Nashville Skyline* was the Music Row version of country, absent of all the roots so inspiringly explored back at Big Pink. The songs came quickly, but only because simplistic lyrics and downright obvious arrangements had replaced that legendary chemistry between Dylan and the musicians he worked with.

Bob Dylan: We just take a song; I play it and everyone else just sort of fills in behind it . . . At the same time you're doing that, there's someone in the control booth who's turning all those dials to where the proper sound is coming in. [1969]

After three days of sessions, Dylan had recorded just seven songs, less than twenty minutes of music, much of it trite. Plans were made to resume recording after a two-day break. He evidently now intended to complete some kind of album. Awaiting an old friend to lend a hand, Dylan resumed recording on the 17th, cutting one of his finest album closers, 'Tonight I'll Be Staying Here with You,' while it remained fresh off the pen. He then ran through the Nashville equivalent of a Mexican rag he'd recorded six years earlier, a clear sign that his pen was all writ out. When the Man in Black, Johnny Cash, stumbled in from next door, where he had been recording with his own band, it was a spontaneously prearranged attempt to record a couple of 'historic' Bob Dylan–Johnny Cash duets.

The three songs they chose to record were the familiar 'Don't Think Twice' and 'One Too Many Mornings,' and a song they had last sung together, pilled to the gills, backstage at Cardiff, on that infamous world tour. This time 'I Still Miss Someone' sounded like a valedictory to Dylan's absent muse. Though none of the trio was deemed worthy of release, the Cash TV documentary *A Man and His Music* captured Dylan squirming his way through a playback of 'One Too Many Mornings.'

Despite the Dylan–Cash idea having almost nothing to recommend it, save as a competition to see who could sing on one note the longest, they decided to reconvene the following day to record an entire album of standards for a possible joint release.

The results were painful enough to be consigned to the back shelf, though 'Girl from the North Country' was eventually tagged onto Dylan's new album, an afterthought. A ten-track acetate exists, with *Nashville Skyline* written in Dylan's hand (presumably the idea of calling the album *John Wesley Harding Vol. 2,* referred to in a later interview, was only a whim). The acetate retains the same songs as the released album, minus its eventual opener, the strictly-for-chuckles duet on 'Girl from the North Country.' It would appear that Dylan at one point was considering releasing a twenty-three minute album, since the acetate was cut *after* three overdub sessions in late February. If so, commercial pressure pushed him to give Cash another outlet to add to a TV series, a live album from San Quentin, and a hit single about a boy named Sue.

Though *Nashville Skyline* proved to be one of Dylan's bestselling albums, thanks to the success of its three singles—notably 'Lay, Lady, Lay,' which gave him his first Top 10 single since 'Rainy Day Women'—and the national TV coverage his appearance on *The Johnny Cash Show* garnered, the distance between Dylan and his 'real' audience was growing greater with each commercial concession.

Clive Davis: Our area of greatest difficulty was singles. Bob always said that he would leave the choice up to me—yet he was invariably surprised by my choices, and sometimes balked at them. He didn't think about singles, he said, and he didn't think AM radio was that important. None of his friends listened to it.

It was not just that none of Dylan's friends listened to AM radio: the rock audience itself was splintering at the end of a momentous decade. If Dylan was concerned about retaining a hold on the rock constituency, making albums with Johnny Cash in Nashville was tantamount to abdication in many eyes. The Dylan who appeared on Cash's new TV series in June was clearly not the man who had hung 'Less' Crane out to dry on his last national TV appearance four years earlier. What was immediately apparent to most of his longstanding friends was that this was a man terrified out of his wits. Given that this was the public unveiling of his *Nashville Skyline* persona, he was perhaps entitled to be so. Not for the first time, the new Dylan envisaged a stormy reception.

Johnny Cash: When he went out to rehearse they had an old shack hanging from wires behind him to try to give it a backwoods look. He came offstage upset. He said, 'I'm gonna be the laughing stock of the business! My fans are gonna laugh in my face over that thing!' I said, 'What would you like?' He said, 'Have 'em get that out of the way. Just put me out there by myself.'

Nashville Skyline was already descending from its number three peak when *The Johnny Cash Show* was broadcast on June 7. Even with 'Girl from the North Country' as its opener, the twenty-eight minute album wasn't so much thin as transparent—though not to the new cabal of rock critics, all of whom had grown up listening to Dylan lay out the shape of things to come, time after time. The new emperor of country-rock might sometimes have had to stand naked, but no one at *Rolling Stone, Crawdaddy,* or *Fusion* was going to render him so. When Jann Wenner, the editor of *Rolling Stone,* actually got to speak to the man himself, he made no attempt to question Dylan seriously about his apparent change of direction, even when he sought to justify the banality of songs like 'Country Pie' and 'Peggy Day.'

Bob Dylan: These are the type of songs that I always felt like writing when I've been alone to do so. The songs reflect more of the inner me than the songs of the past. They're more to my base than, say, *John Wesley Harding.* There I felt everyone expected me to be a poet so that's what I tried to be . . . [My old] songs were all written in the New York atmosphere. I'd never have written any of them—or sung them the way I did—if I hadn't been sitting around listening to performers in New York cafés and the talk in all the dingy parlors. [1969]

If the songs on *Nashville Skyline* really reflected the 'inner me', then Dylan-the-artist was now hollow to the core. And yet the reviews for the album were largely positive, with the 'Daren't Dis Dylan' factor certainly playing its part. The usually astute Paul Nelson wrote in *Rolling Stone*:

Perhaps . . . it is more difficult to convey meaningfully a total fulfillment of marriage and family than it is to create a nightmare world of complex hallucination, even though the latter seems more painfully our own. In many ways, *Nashville Skyline* achieves the artistically impossible: a deep, humane, and interesting statement about being happy. It could well be what Dylan thinks it is, his best album.

Even *Newsweek*, to whom Dylan gave his second and last promotional interview for the album, seemed to buy into the party line, the reviewer enthusing about 'the great charm of the album ... and the ways Dylan, both as composer and performer, has found to exploit subtle differences on a deliberately limited emotional and verbal scale.' Dylan's cultural import was clearly getting in the way of honest, undiluted criticism, something even the Beatles were denied (lest we forget, *Sgt. Pepper* was slammed in both the London *Times* and *New York Times* on the day of its release). Geoffrey Cannon addressed the problem in his level-headed review in *The Guardian*:

The magnetism of Dylan is so much to do with his experience being knit into our shared consciousness, that listening to *Nashville Skyline* privately, before it is broadcast, gives me the sensation of being inside a time-warp, and makes the task of commentary, prickly and arduous.

Fully dissenting voices were few, though Ed Ochs, at *Billboard*, stripped the album bare as he laid into Dylan's creative soul: 'the satisfied man speaks in clichés, and blushes as if every day were Valentine's Day.' The idea of a Dylan who was not being ironic was a scary one to those who invested Dylan's music with the power to institute cultural change. In Britain, where the album went straight to number one, only Tim Souster, in the BBC's *Listener* magazine, had the courage to suggest, 'One can't help feeling something is missing. Isn't this idyllic country landscape [simply] too good to be true?'

Though this landscape was as much of a dreamscape for Dylan as his audience, it was one to which a man seemingly bereft of ideas now returned. On his trip to Nashville at the end of April, to tape his appearance for the Cash show, he took the opportunity to record an album's worth of country covers, having apparently already sounded out Clive Davis about the idea.

Clive Davis: Bob asked my opinion of the album's concept early on. My objections wouldn't necessarily have stopped the album, but I knew he'd been having some difficulty coming up with his own material ... so I encouraged him.

Some eleven songs were recorded over the three sessions. The one original—'Living the Blues'—was scheduled as a single, before Davis got his way, and 'Lay, Lady, Lay' showed what it could do with the requisite airplay instead. If there was a concept to the exercise at this stage, it was less than evident, save perhaps that they were mostly songs

Dylan would have heard growing up: a couple of Everlys songs, a couple by Cash, a latter-day Elvis. The idea of Dylan recording songs like 'Blue Moon,' 'Take Me As I Am,' and 'Take a Message to Mary' was enough to make even *Rolling Stone* rethink its 'Question Not Dylan' stance. When *Rolling Stone* reviewer Bill Reed got to hear these tapes the following winter, he would write:

If you've a predisposition against country and western, but the hybrid sound of *Nashville Skyline* didn't offend your anti-roots sensibilities, be warned. There are still-unreleased Dylan sides that, quite likely, would drive you up the wall—some of them songs with lyrics out of the 'bliss-kiss-fingertips-lips' school of prosody.

Reed unwittingly prophesied a world where Dylan crooning through 'Blue Moon' would come on the radio. For now, though, the April/May sessions were simply Dylan's second attempt of 1969 to record an album of standards in country mode. They were also the second such attempt to be put aside, awaiting a day when it really poured. He wasn't quite ready to further alienate his remaining fans.

Dylan spent the remainder of his time in Nashville checking out potential properties. Another Woodstock summer was not an option he was willing to consider. When he drew a blank in Nashville, he decided to reconsider Fire Island as an option. Thus it was that Dylan was able to disappear from view at the height of the Woodstock madness, and find a degree of peace for himself and his family.

David Amram: He decided . . . he'd liked it so much he rented a place down the beach, a place called Bay Berry Dunes, and as soon as he came out he got in touch with me. I used to go down almost every day and hang out with him and Sara and the kids, and it was so nice to see him with his family. At that point he hadn't really retired, he'd just stopped for a while.

The picture Dylan later painted of these times (in the song 'Sara') certainly suggests a momentary idyll. He even found time for music-making with Amram, with whom he almost recreated the Big Pink vibe on Fire Island, though this time minus Hudson's tape recorder.

David Amram: We used to sit and play music, I'd bring my little penny-whistle and my French horn over. He was just playing, I would just accompany him. Then he used to come down to my little part of the beach, he would leave Sara and the kids, and he'd just come down, different people would just come by to play music and just jam and, whatever they would play, I would play with them. One time we had an electrician named Jack Lovinger and a very good drummer and he was playing on pots and pans, and they were really having fun and we played for about three hours and Bob was having a ball. So I walked him back home up the beach, and we were walking in silence and he turned to me and said, 'Boy, you really *enjoy* doing this, don't you?' And he said it . . . in a way that [suggested] he was surprised. I said, 'Man, I love it.' And he kinda chuckled. Obviously, he loves to play too, but in the highly competitive world of rock & roll that he was thrust into . . . that wasn't considered to be part of the picture . . . Bob used to talk about that, how he just wanted to play music and, even though he wanted to be appreciated, how hard it was sometimes to be stared at, or be treated like some kind of a person from outer space, when all he wanted to do was tell his stories through songs. And I told him what it was like for Jack [Kerouac] when he suddenly became a worldwide celebrity overnight [with *On the Road*], and how devastating it was for him—he just wanted people to read his books.

These jam sessions catered to two of Dylan's deepest desires, the quest for anonymity and an environment where he could just play, making music stripped of any expectations, simply for the moment. Indeed, such was the incongruity of the situation he found himself playing music in, and the sheer mystique that surrounded his semi-mythical persona, that when two young outsiders intruded on the music-making, they refused to believe the evidence of their own eyes:

David Amram: [One] time I said let's go over to Jack Lovinger's place [at] somewhere called Skunk Hollow, and we went there for a jam session, and Bob was sitting there playing for about two hours and suddenly these kids, who were 'clammers,' walked in, and they were staring at Bob and looked completely freaked out. We played two tunes, then in the middle of the third tune they got up and staggered out. So we stopped a while [later] and we walked back, and Bob turned to me and said, 'Did you see that? Those two kids walked out on us!' The next day I found out these two kids had been taking LSD before they came to our place and they thought that they saw Bob Dylan. They thought they were having some kind of weird acid trip. They were so freaked out that they walked out to go swimming in the bay, to get their heads together!

And yet, ever the Gemini, Dylan still wanted to be a contender, just an anonymous one. Perhaps those Fire Island jam sessions only served to

scratch the itch to perform. When two English promoters suggested to
Bert Block—who had taken over the day-to-day management of Dylan's
affairs from his boss, Albert Grossman—that perhaps he might like to
play a festival on a small island just off the south coast of England, and
that he and his family could travel first class on the QE2 and have a
two-week holiday on the Isle of Wight into the bargain, he expressed
interest in the offer.

Ray Foulk: One thing I had discussed with Block was the way we could
entice Dylan to do it. So we came up with the idea of making it a holiday
for him and his family. We obtained a farmhouse in Bembridge which was
suitable. It had a swimming pool and a barn that had recently been converted,
which was suitable for rehearsing in . . . We were offering Dylan a fortnight
stay there, no expense spared, car with driver. Also we would have him
come over on the QE2, [and] the fee offered to Block was $50,000.

Before he signed on the dotted line, Dylan decided to remind himself
what playing to a large crowd was like. Thus, on July 14, the familiar-
looking 'Elmer Johnson' joined the Band on stage during their set at the
Mississippi River Festival in Edwardsville, Illinois. As if trying to recreate
Big Pink in the Midwest, Dylan gave one of his three-song précis of
American song, performing Guthrie's 'Ain't Got No Home,' Lead Belly's
'In the Pines,' and Little Richard's 'Slippin' and Slidin'.' That he had
been missed was not left in doubt by the fans, and Dylan returned to Fire
Island assured that he still had an audience.

David Amram: I remember one day he went off mysteriously to a place
in the Midwest and just showed up at a surprise concert down by a river,
and [then] came back. I said, 'How was it?' He said, 'Man, there was
something like thirty thousand people and they didn't forget me . . . It was
a good feeling, [but] it's good to be back here, at the beach, in silence.'

Another incentive for making the trip to England was provided, gratis,
by a couple of hippie promoters bent on staging the biggest rock festival
to date right in Dylan's backyard. Through July, plans moved ahead for
a huge pop festival on a mid-August weekend in Woodstock. There was
no way Dylan wanted to be around when a few hundred thousand baby
boomers started wandering through the brush, trying to locate the home
of their guru. He knew that the choice of Woodstock as a site was no
accident.

Al Aronowitz: In essence, the Woodstock Festival was nothing but a call to Bob to come out and play.

Bob Dylan: It was like a wave of insanity breakin' loose around the house day and night. You'd come in the house and find people there, people comin' through the woods, at all hours of the day and night, knockin' at your door. It was really dark and depressing. And there was no way to respond to all this . . . They kept comin'. We had to get out of there. This was just about the time of that Woodstock Festival, which was the sum total of all this bullshit . . . I couldn't get any space for myself and my family, and there was no help, nowhere. I got very resentful about the whole thing, and we got outta there. [1984]

Thanks to the Foulk brothers, the Isle of Wight festival promoters, the Dylans were planning to set out from New York Harbor on August 13— two days before half a million people descended on Max Yasgur's farm on the outskirts of Woodstock—and head due east on the *QE2*. The Band would join them by plane after the Woodstock weekend jamboree, at which they were scheduled to act as surrogate Dylans. Unfortunately, a slight mishap scuppered this best-laid plan. Boarding the *QE2*, Dylan's eldest son, Jesse, temporarily lost consciousness after banging his head against a cabin door, and the ship's doctor refused to accept responsibility for the boy should they make the voyage. They disembarked and took Jesse to a doctor in New York. So much for a sailing trip to England!

A nervous twelve days followed for the Foulks, as they awaited confirmation that Dylan would be flying to England instead. When he and a very pregnant Sara finally flew into Heathrow Airport, minus the children, it became apparent that Dylan had again seriously under-estimated the interest in his return to the stage. Though there would be no airport press conference this time around, the British media ran stories every day about 'the British Woodstock' until it became clear that Dylan would have to make some concession to the UK press. On the Wednesday before the festival, he held his first press conference since May 1966. The results were suitably farcical, as his affected *Nashville Skyline* twang only served to bemuse the natives. When asked about drugs, he responded, 'I think everyone should lead their own lives, you know.' Asked about his previous British tour, he insisted, 'That stuff was all for publicity. I don't do that kind of thing anymore.' There was little doubt that this was a different Dylan, even if the graphic on the fluttering posters advertising the festival was a stark black-on-white shot of a beshaded Dylan in classic '66 pose.

With press duties attended to, Dylan and the Band got down to some proper rehearsals in the barn at Forelands Farm. Though they had briefly rehearsed in Woodstock, at the end of July, they were relying on three or four days playing together on the Isle of Wight to whip their set into shape. Unfortunately, when three of the Beatles arrived by helicopter on Friday, with necessary supplies and a few tennis rackets, hoping for a game of tennis and a jam session, Dylan and the Band were still tinkering with the set. By Sunday, when a van came to convey Dylan to the festival site, they still had not arrived at any kind of running order.

The scale of the event clearly took Dylan by surprise, though he presumably realized that the fifty grand he was being paid—ten times what the previous night's headliners, the Who, had received—implied a large crowd. But by the time the Band took to the stage to play their own set there were at least two hundred thousand fans milling around the festival site. If Dylan was unnerved, his mood was not improved by a two-hour delay between Ritchie Havens's set and the Band's, as the press enclosure spilled over from a surfeit of hangers-on. As the huge crowd became impatient, an edgy Dylan tipped over.

Al Aronowitz: The audience was getting tired . . . Both Bob and I knew that the crowd must be feeling drained and worn out. Bob started pacing again. 'I wanted to catch the crowd when it was still at the peak of its psychic energy,' Bob said grimly. 'Now I'm really getting into a bad mood! This is spoiling everything that I came here to do. Everything I'd wanted to accomplish!'

Dylan's one-hour set at the Isle of Wight on August 31, 1969, has been a source of contention ever since. Though few who were there remember it as anything other than anticlimactic, his choice of songs was intelligently ambitious, and after he got a family of frogs out of his throat on 'She Belongs To Me,' 'I Threw It All Away,' and 'Maggie's Farm,' his four-song acoustic set was a delight, capped as it was by an incomparable rendition of the traditional Scottish air 'Wild Mountain Thyme.' However, it quickly became clear that fans fed on tall stories in the press, of a three-hour performance climaxing with an all-star jam, were in for a lean time.

Dylan was sticking doggedly to his *Nashville Skyline* persona, even down to his showbizzy spoken intro, 'Great to be here. Sure is.' Indeed his whole appearance drew unfavorable comments, his beard and white suit making him look like a Hasidic scholar on an exchange program. Only once, on a raucous 'Highway 61 Revisited,' did some of the old fire return to his singing. After a unique live romp through 'Quinn the Eskimo'—his last number one in England, albeit via Manfred Mann— he left the stage, barely fifty minutes after he had taken to it. The crowd was not about to let him leave it at that, and he was required to summon up a two-song encore. But not even a sing-along 'Rainy Day Women' could revive fans' flagging energy.

Levon Helm: I would've liked to have gotten carried away . . . Bob had an extra list of songs with eight or ten different titles with question marks by them, that we would've went ahead and done, had it seemed like the thing to do. But it seemed like everybody was a little bit tired and the festival was three days old by then; and so, if everybody else is ready to go home, let's all go.

If the English hippies were anxious to return to the mainland, Dylan wasn't far behind, departing for London the following day, where he briefly jammed with Lennon on 'Cold Turkey' before flying back to New York on Tuesday morning, where he informed waiting pressmen that he would not be returning to England in the foreseeable future: 'They make too much of singers over there. Singers are front page news.' His attempt to 'get away from it all, and give myself a chance to break back in,' as he put it to the candy-chewing newspapermen, had not been a great success.

His personal dissatisfaction with the performance manifested itself most obviously with the scrapping of an official live album of the event (the bootleggers showed no such aesthetic concern). Having enlisted Elliot Mazur to engineer the recording, Dylan gave the tapes the once-over before they were sent to Nashville, where Bob Johnston couldn't resist a remix. The disappointing performance also seems to have scuppered any plans to resume touring, even though Dylan had informed Jann Wenner in late June that he would be going back on the road in the fall. Having tested the water at the Isle of Wight, he had clearly decided to stay on the beach.

Even out on Fire Island, though, his competitive urges could still be stoked by one of his peers. Sometime that summer Paul Simon came out to spend the day with his old nemesis. According to Dave Amram, Simon had never actually 'gotten together' with Dylan—though Dylan had checked out Simon and Garfunkel at Gerde's back in 1964—and they ended up 'playing together . . . kinda getting to know each other, and swopping tunes.' No matter how many sales he has racked up, Simon's sense of living in Dylan's shadow has always remained acute. Now he found himself in the Top 10 with a song widely interpreted to be *about* Dylan. 'The Boxer,' using the boxer/singer motif established by Elvis in *King Creole*, seemed to be a particularly bitter account of a young colt seduced by 'the whores on Seventh Avenue' (i.e. Columbia). Ever competitive, even when there was no contest, Simon apparently took the opportunity of a day out on Fire Island to play 'The Boxer' to Dylan, who seems to have been quite taken with the song.

If Simon sensed someone who felt he was being left behind, he was not alone. Eric Andersen recollects meeting Dylan at this time and him 'saying nice things about my records . . . but you could tell that behind it [all] a lot of things were going on.' Aronowitz also recalls George Harrison bringing an acetate of the just-completed *Abbey Road* to the farm on the Isle of Wight, and playing it through one of the amps in the rehearsal shed. This time, Dylan had to admit, the Beatles had truly extended themselves, even as they were imploding.

With the imminent prospect of arranging his children's education, and with Woodstock having long ceased to purvey any magical quality, Dylan's thoughts turned to returning to the maelstrom known as Manhattan. Rekindling 'the New York atmosphere' now seemed like a necessity if he was ever going to be anything more than an anachronism, at the age of twenty-nine. As the swinging sixties turned—in the instant a Hell's Angel's switchblade entered Meredith Hunter—into the cynical seventies, Dylan decided to return to his old stamping ground, 'Bleecker and MacDougal'—the vortex 'of the so-called Urban Folk Revolution,' Skip Weshner wrote on Fred Neil's 1965 album of the same name. Whether or not, five years on, it retained 'an improbably high percentage of talent perform[ing] their songs, about their own world, and the way they see it,' it was certainly no longer the Village a so-much-younger Bob had arrived in when 'snow was piled up the stairs an onto the street . . . it was a different street then—it was a different village—nobody had nothin—There was nothin t get.'

1970: A Restless, Hungry Feeling

17

Lookin' back, it really was a stupid thing to do. But there was a house available on MacDougal Street, and I always remembered that as a nice place. So I just bought this house, sight unseen. But it wasn't the same when we got back. The Woodstock Nation had overtaken Mac-Dougal Street also. There'd be crowds outside my house.

—*Bob Dylan, 1984*

The worst times of my life were when I tried to find something in the past. Like when I went back to New York for the second time. I didn't know what to do. Everything had changed.

—*Bob Dylan, 1989*

By January 1970, Dylan had just about renounced his previous view that 'you have to be let alone to really accomplish anything.' Perhaps, he reasoned, he needed 'the New York atmosphere' to write songs—even if there was little prospect of him anonymously enjoying 'performers in New York cafés and the talk in all the dingy parlors.' As the new decade kicked in, he had decided to purchase a town house on MacDougal. Its communal square at the back of the house could only be accessed by fellow residents, allowing the children a large playing area to cavort in without the usual urban dangers. The local schooling also garnered its share of plaudits. However, if Dylan held a notion that he might be able to blend into the hubbub of the Village, it was rapidly dispelled.

Inevitably, his return to New York became common knowledge. Even those who did not know Dylan's exact address would wander the Village in the hope of a sighting. The most famous of these devotees was A. J. Weberman, who had also devoted a series of articles in underground magazines like *East Village Other* to interpreting Dylan's work, in particular his 'Currant Bag,' i.e., his current state of mind. Except that Weberman was not really a fan of the current Dylan. A.J. had convinced himself that Dylan had consciously abandoned the counterculture in order to produce capitalist shucks like *Nashville Skyline*.

As in 1965, Dylan felt the need for some artistic elbow room, so that he

could continue his career free of preconceptions. Should later pronouncements be believed, he now hit upon a plan to drive his fan base away—
not that *Nashville Skyline* hadn't already got some reaching for the door.
According to this Dylan, the sense of a man parodying himself on his first
album of 1970, *Self Portrait*, was a deliberate, concerted attempt to dispel
much of the iconography surrounding him, once and for all.

Bob Dylan: That album was put out . . . [because] at that time . . . I didn't
like the attention I was getting. I [had] never been a person that wanted
attention. And at that time I was getting the wrong kind of attention, for
doing things I'd never done. So we released that album to get people off my
back. They would not like me anymore. That's . . . the reason that album
was put out, so people would just at that time stop buying my records, and
they did. [1981]

Bob Dylan: I said, 'Well, fuck it. I wish these people would just forget
about me. I wanna do something they can't possibly like, they can't relate
to' . . . And then I did this portrait for the cover. I mean, there was no title
for that album . . . And I said, 'Well, I'm gonna call this album *Self Portrait*'
. . . And to me it was a joke. [1984]

The album as released certainly seems to provide substantial aural
evidence that 'it was [all] a joke.' However, the decision to integrate the
results from three days in the studio in New York in March 1970 into
an extended parody of fans' expectations was surely made *after* the sessions
themselves, at which Dylan recorded a couple of dozen folk songs—
mostly traditional, some contemporary fare—in what might be termed
his classic nasal style, in tandem with two of his favorite musicians, Al
Kooper and Dave Bromberg. At the same time he laid down resolutely
restrained renditions of a couple of new songs, 'If Not for You' and
'Went to See the Gypsy.'

Many of the covers recorded were not the kind that Dylan would
have been inclined to parody. Songs like 'Pretty Saro,' 'Belle Isle,'
'Copper Kettle,' 'Railroad Bill,' 'The House Carpenter,' 'Little Moses,'
and 'Come All Ye Fair and Tender Ladies' directly reflected Dylan's
roots. They were truly his 'lexicon and . . . prayer-book.' If it is possible
to glean intent from a set of tape logs, then Dylan's 'original' intent was
the same as the one that inspired his attempt at a joint Dylan–Cash
project, and the album of country covers he recorded in Nashville in the
spring of 1969—to put together a set of covers that reflected something
of who he was, and how he came to be.

Any suggestion that a fine album could be constructed from the March 1970 sessions has to remain largely a matter of speculation, given that fourteen of the covers remain in the vaults, though he has performed 'House Carpenter,' 'Railroad Bill,' and 'Little Moses' magnificently on other occasions. The released versions of 'Copper Kettle,' and 'Belle Isle' also strike all the right chords—'Copper Kettle,' in particular, being one of the most affecting performances in Dylan's entire official canon. The other 18-carat nugget from the March sessions, buried amid the mountain of fool's gold that is *Self Portrait*, is a suitably croaky version of 'It Hurts Me Too.' The two 'Albertas' and the version of Gordon Lightfoot's 'Early Mornin' Rain,' clearly a personal favorite, also have something to commend them. Such performances were bound to confuse listeners when sandwiched between country tearjerkers.

There were clearly problems, though, with the tapes from the sessions, which ran March 3–5. The rhythm section—Alvin Rogers and Stu Woods—would eventually be mixed out, though they would still receive a name check on *Self Portrait*, and almost all of the songs were cut in single takes, as if Dylan was suggesting to the musicians, we either get this in one or we forget it. There were five exceptions to this approach: the three originals—'Come a Little Bit Closer' which remains unidentified, 'If Not for You' and 'Went to See the Gypsy'—already earmarked for some entirely separate project; and two covers omitted from *Self Portrait*—Eric Andersen's 'Thirsty Boots' and the traditional 'Pretty Saro.'

'Thirsty Boots' was mixed down (which many of the outtakes were not), and would crop up as a 'possible' for Dylan's next album, *New Morning*, perhaps suggesting it was too good for the project Dylan now had in mind. If the March sessions had started out as a serious attempt to produce a folk album of covers, then he evidently abandoned the idea upon hearing the tapes, deciding on an entirely different concept. As Greil Marcus recognized, in his famous review of the album in *Rolling Stone*:

Self Portrait most closely resembles the Dylan album that preceded it: *Great White Wonder* . . . [and] though it's a good imitation bootleg, [it] isn't nearly the music that *Great White Wonder* is.

Dylan admitted as much to Shelton the following year, calling *Self Portrait* 'my own bootleg record.' Just as *Great White Wonder* comprised a seemingly random selection of cuts from a 1961 hotel tape, a 1962 radio show, 'a bunch of basement noise,' and 'Living the Blues' from *The Johnny Cash Show*, so *Self Portrait* attempted to blend half a dozen cuts from the country covers sessions in April/May 1969 with a dozen of the March 1970 tracks, throwing in a couple of alternative takes for good measure and even a couple of instrumental jams, topping the whole she-bang off with four tracks from the Isle of White farrago. The result: an album of outtakes and live oddities from one of the least interesting periods of Dylan's career.

It was as much the way *Self Portrait* was constructed as the songs themselves—seguing from Dylanesque folk covers into syrupy Nashville croon-tunes via almost insulting Isle of Wight renditions of Dylan favorites—that left the bitter aftertaste of pastiche. Thus the opening song, a Dylan original, features no Dylan vocal. Instead a chorus of girl singers repeatedly sings, 'How'm I s'ppose to get any ridin' [shouldn't that be "writing"?] done.' Dylan's version of Paul Simon's 'The Boxer' features two versions of himself—one is the 'old' Dylan, considered by some to be the subject of the song; the other, the 'new,' smoother, richer *Nashville Skyline*, Dylan singing a painfully out-of-sync harmony vocal. The album also features two versions of 'Alberta' and 'Little Sadie,' the latter per-formed in a ludicrously fast rag version, and then as a more sympathetic, not to say sedate, folk ballad. Even the one original Dylan lyric, 'Living the Blues,' is a pastiche of Guy Mitchell's 'Singing the Blues.'

The choice of songs from the Isle of Wight concert also smacked of the deliberately perverse. Of the four songs selected, only 'Minstrel Boy'sounds remotely palatable, and perhaps that is only because we have no other version with which to compare it (according to the usually reliable *Writings & Drawings*, the first edition of Dylan's published lyrics, it dates from the Big Pink era). The Isle of Wight version of 'Like a Rolling Stone,' his most famous song, is definitely a joke, and in very bad taste at that. He not only forgets the words, but strips the song of any feeling. Even the Band fails to inject any enthusiasm into the proceedings. 'Quinn the Eskimo' is equally disappointing, despite being the first official Dylan version of the most successful of all basement tape spin-off singles, while 'She Belongs to Me' sounds like a very nervous Hasidic scholar playing in front of two hundred thousand people.

Certainly, if Dylan's ambition, with the material recorded at the March sessions, ever extended beyond simply parodying himself and insulting his audience, such thoughts soon evaporated. Within six days of the sessions, the tapes had been sent down to Nashville to be over-dubbed with new rhythm tracks, backing vocals, strings, dobro, trom-bone, kitchen sink. That he left the final act in this passionless play to his producer, Bob Johnston, suggests an extraordinary level of detachment from the exercise. To then enlist the musical chops of McCoy and

Buttrey, who had given such focus to *Blonde on Blonde* and *John Wesley Harding*, for the overdubs was perhaps the final in-joke on a project where artifice seems to have replaced an honest recognition of the need for product during an unprecedented creative drought.

Charlie McCoy: Dylan sent the tape down with instructions that we were to just play over what he'd already recorded on it . . . The tape was mostly other people's songs and it sounded like he was experimenting with them. The tempos didn't really hold together real well and he wasn't real steady with his guitar, either . . . I assumed . . . it was just stuff he'd thrown together for the heck of it.

Ken Buttrey: Charlie McCoy did his overdubs and I came in the studio as he was leaving . . . and he said, 'You're not gonna believe this.'

Having effectively disowned the idea of a simple album of covers for 'a concept record,' Dylan reserved his last creative input for the album cover, which was to be graced with one of his paintings, of a man's face. With no title emblazoned across the front, just this curiously expressionless visage, it was inevitable that people would assume it was a portrait of himself, even if that was not his intent.

Bob Dylan: The way it turned out, the album became a concept record with a title that could be taken a ton of ways. Staring at the blank canvas for a while encouraged me to blindfoldedly make a picture that would paste all the songs together between the sleeves . . . It wasn't my purpose to paint my own picture. [1991]

Not surprisingly, *Self Portrait* was panned on its release. The reviews were almost universally scathing. A lengthy review in *Rolling Stone* by Greil Marcus began with the question on most people's minds when first hearing the album: 'What is this shit?' In his deliberately sprawling review, Marcus recognized the conceptual nature of the finished artifact but called it 'a concept album from the cutting room floor. It has been constructed artfully, but as a cover-up, not a revelation.' Perhaps the most incisive remark of the whole review, and the one that probably prompted Dylan to label the article 'a piece of shit,' came halfway through the four-page spread, when he warned Dylan that 'unless he returns to the market-place, with a sense of vocation and the ambition to keep up with his own gifts, the music of [the mid-sixties] will continue to dominate his records, whether he releases them or not.' The irony is that

Dylan did eventually return 'with a sense of vocation and the ambition,' and still his audience would continue to 'take over his past.'

Marcus's review generated its own debate within fan circles, and the rock culture in general. Once again, though, Dylan's cultural import was such that *Rolling Stone* felt the need to print its own version of a retraction—another review, this one by Bill Damon, that gave Dylan the benefit of the doubt:

Though he has taken plenty of chances in the past, never before has he left himself so vulnerable. For one thing, *Self Portrait* is the most daring title Dylan has ever chosen, and he has used it for an album with little of his own writing . . . What counts, though, is that *Self Portrait* is alive musically. It is beautiful to listen to, an evolution in attitude and sound that works as well as anything Dylan has ever done . . . He has brought to *Self Portrait* his myth, his images and his past. These add force and interest to his work, we can't deny it.

Dylan's own apparent response was to issue another album, this one composed entirely of new originals, within four months of *Self Portrait*'s release. It was a brilliant coup on Dylan's part, and would have completely cut the ground away from the critics snapping at his heels—if only *New Morning* had been more substantial than a halfway decent collection from the man responsible for *Bringing It All Back Home*, *Highway 61 Revisited* and *Blonde on Blonde*. Fans and critics alike inevitably concluded that the vituperative response to the double album had prompted him to scurry into the studio, recording a 'proper' album to appease them, and to convince the world that he still had 'a sense of vocation.' As so often with Dylan, this was one more conjurer's trick.

Bob Dylan: I didn't say, 'Oh my God, they don't like this, let me do another one.' It wasn't like that. It just happened coincidentally that one came out and then the other one did as soon as it did. The *Self Portrait* LP laid around for I think a year. We were working on *New Morning* when the *Self Portrait* album got put together. [1975]

In fact, Dylan had all but completed *New Morning* at a series of sessions in New York the week prior to the release of *Self Portrait*. Only 'Day of the Locusts'—and rerecordings of 'If Not for You' and 'Time Passes Slowly'—postdate *Self Portrait*'s rocky reception. That said, the hostile response to the 'concept album' clearly had a bearing on the *type* of album he eventually elected to release. Only at the last minute, and after at least two alternate, sequenced versions had been provisionally approved, did Dylan decide to release an album entirely composed of originals—good, bad and indifferent—rather than his original concept, another album that contained both covers and originals, even if the balance, this time around, favored Dylan originals.

Though *New Morning* would, in its released form, contain no covers, the 1973 release of *Dylan,* an album of covers from the *New Morning* sessions (save for two stray *Self Portrait* outtakes), confirmed a continuing penchant and prompted Dylan to insist that 'they were just not to be used—I thought it was well understood—they were just to warm up for a tune.' In fact, the track sheets for the June sessions belie his version of events, as do the recollections of the musicians. Russ Kunkel, the drummer at the sessions, recalls it being the original songs that were the afterthought, and that the bulk of the sessions were occupied with recording traditional songs like 'Rock a Bye My Saro Jane,' 'Lily of the West,' and 'Mary Ann,' as if, having failed to realize an album of folk covers in March, he wanted to try again with a finer pedigree of accompanists.

The first of the five June sessions was devoted exclusively to covers, of which Peter La Farge's 'Ballad of Ira Hayes' was the only one earmarked as a 'possible' for the final album (though one of the seven takes of 'Saro Jane' later appeared on *Dylan*). The second session began with a magnificent solo piano take of 'Spanish Is the Loving Tongue.' It would eventually see light of day on the 'Watching the River Flow' 45. Jerry Jeff Walker's 'Mr. Bojangles' and the traditional 'Mary Ann' occupied most of the session. The only originals recorded that day—'If Not for You' and 'Time Passes Slowly'—had already been laid down twice in Columbia studios, at the March *Self Portrait* sessions and at a May Day session with George Harrison.

Indeed, three of the songs on *New Morning* had been attempted at the March sessions, but none of these versions would make the album, even though 'If Not for You' and the electric-piano version of 'Went to See the Gypsy' were both sent down to Nashville in July for some subtle overdubs, favored by Dylan's co-producer, Al Kooper, over their official brethren. It was the session with Harrison that represented the true starting point for Dylan's second album of 1970, and his fourth post-accident artifact, the same three originals being rerecorded at this May Day session, along with 'Sign on the Window' and the curious 'Working on the Guru.' Only 'Went to See the Gypsy' from the Harrison session, though, would make the final album, albeit uncredited. Evidently Dylan was determined to keep reworking these originals until he had either more originals or some usable covers with which to construct an album. Also recorded with Harrison were twenty covers, though only his own 'It Ain't Me Babe' was pulled from the reels. Of the others, Dylan's particularly brutal deconstruction of 'Yesterday' is probably the best reason to date for wishing the song had never been written.

That the two months since the final *Self Portrait* sessions had produced only the admittedly sublime 'Sign on the Window' and the eminently disposable 'Working on the Guru,' and that the previous nine months had only generated a sincere love song, an insincere memorial to country life, and an account of his long awaited meeting with Elvis in 'a big hotel' in Las Vegas, suggested that the amnesia had hardly abated. Dylan was simply not coming up with new songs, good or otherwise.

In the spring of 1970, he had become involved with the production of a new play by poet Archibald MacLeish. The play, which was intended to be a musical version of *The Devil and Daniel Webster,* was called *Scratch.* According to Dylan, in the *Biograph* notes, he eventually wrote three songs for the play—'New Morning,' 'Time Passes Slowly,' and 'Father of Night'—but he 'didn't see eye to eye' with the producer on 'Father of Night,' 'so I backed out of the production.' In fact, MacLeish wrote a letter to his publisher in October 1970 stating that Dylan 'proved simply incapable of producing new songs, and things looked desperate until [we] decided . . . to use old songs of Dylan's.' Al Kooper calls the songs he wrote for MacLeish's play 'pretty much the fulcrum for that album. [It was like,] "Well, I have these songs. Let's go in and cut these." That got him writing a little more.'

As it is, the early June sessions seem to have prompted Dylan to get down to some serious songwriting. At the last two June sessions, as *Self Portrait* began to be shipped, Dylan pulled from his pockets the likes of 'Three Angels,' 'If Dogs Run Free,' 'Winterlude,' and 'The Man in Me,' along with the MacLeish-inspired 'Father of Night' and 'New Morning.' The impulse to bookend his new songs with a couple of covers abided, though, and at those final sessions, Dylan continued to expend his energies on songs like Lead Belly's 'Bring Me a Little Water, Sylvie,' Joni Mitchell's 'Big Yellow Taxi,' and the traditional 'Lily of the West' and 'I Forgot to Remember to Forget.'

Though Bob Johnston continued to be credited with production duties, he was apparently absent from the last couple of sessions and it was Dylan and his old stalwart, Al Kooper, who began, at the end of the week, to put an album together. The sessions may have had their low spots—few comparable to the one instance of Dylan Does Joni—but they were offset by his decision to remind fans he was no slouch at the piano. Though he remained self-conscious about his self-taught style, he had recently received reassurance from the classically trained Amram.

David Amram: He said [one time], 'Y'know, I wanna work on my piano playing.' I said, 'Frankly, for your songs, I don't think anyone could do any better. It would be like telling Picasso not to use so much yellow. If you're trying to play a Beethoven sonata then you'd be in trouble, but for what you do, it's perfect.'

Dylan also decided to revive the voice that hit notes as well as Caruso, and could hold its breath three times as long, notably on 'Spanish Is the Loving Tongue' and 'Sign on the Window.' The Nashville twang was permanently pensioned off, though the *New Morning* version of Dylan was a particularly nasal one, thanks to a mild attack of influenza.

Ron Cornelius: Dylan had a pretty bad cold that week. You can hear it on one song, y'know, that bit about 'Brighton girls are like the moon,' where his voice really cracks up. But it sure suits the song. His piano playing's really weird; you fall over laughing the first time you see it, because his hands start at opposite ends of the keyboard and then sorta collide in the middle—he does that all the time—but the way he plays just knocks me out.

Dylan remained genuinely unsure of the worth of much that he had recorded. Nor was he sure how best to present the songs. With the reviewers not sharing the joke with *Self Portrait*, song selection and mixing became a tortuous affair. Al Kooper, co-producer in all but name, was driven to distraction by his constant vacillating. The first sequenced version of *New Morning* incorporated elements of both *New Morning* and *Dylan*, as well as a lovely reworking of his unreleased 1962 song 'Tomorrow Is a Long Time.' Kooper also pushed Dylan into sending 'Spanish Is the Loving Tongue' and the March versions of 'If Not for You' and 'Went to See the Gypsy' down to Nashville for some smoothing out of the edges. He also convinced him to add strings to 'Sign on the Window,' evidently having a far lusher album in mind. And initially, it seemed as if Dylan was in full accord. However, the man's previous sureness in the studio had seemingly absconded with his muse.

Al Kooper: When I finished that album I never wanted to speak to him again . . . I was cheesed off at how difficult [the whole thing was] . . . He just changed his mind every three seconds so I just ended up doing the work

of three albums . . . We'd get a side order and we'd go in and master it and
he'd say, 'No, no, no. I want to do this.' And then, 'No, let's go in and cut
this.' . . . There was another version of 'Went to See the Gypsy' that was
really good . . . It was the first time I went in and had an arrangement idea
for it and I said, 'Let me go in and cut this track and then you can sing over
it.' So I cut this track and it was really good . . . and he came in and pretended
like he didn't understand where to sing on it.

Unable to choose between versions of 'If Not for You' and 'Time
Passes Slowly,' Dylan finally just recut them, along with a song he had
written in the ensuing weeks, after he had accepted an honorary doctorate
in music from Princeton University, the week after the June sessions.
Dr. Dylan had not enjoyed the experience, from which he culled the
unconvincing, semi-surreal 'Day of the Locusts.'

David Crosby: I think we were staying at John Hammond's house. Sara
was trying to get Bob to go to Princeton University, where he was being
presented with an honorary doctorate. Bob didn't want to go. I said, 'C'mon,
Bob it's an honor!' Sara and I both worked on him for a long time. Finally,
he agreed. I had a car outside—a big limousine. That was the first thing he
didn't like. We smoked another joint on the way and I noticed Dylan
getting really quite paranoid behind it. When we arrived at Princeton, they
took us to a little room and Bob was asked to wear a cap and gown. He
refused outright. They said, 'We won't give you the degree if you don't
wear this.' Dylan said, 'Fine. I didn't ask for it in the first place.' . . . Finally
we convinced him to wear the cap and gown.

'Day of the Locusts,' along with the two rerecordings from an August
12 session, was tagged to the front of the album, at the expense of
'Ballad of Ira Hayes' and 'Mr. Bojangles.' Dylan had completed his first
collection of original songs since his return to New York, and when *New
Morning* was released in October, it was met with a certain euphoria. In
Rolling Stone, Ralph Gleason even proclaimed the album's release with a
rave review headlined 'WE'VE GOT DYLAN BACK AGAIN':

It came on the radio in the late afternoon and from the first note it was right.
Bob Dylan bringing it all back home again . . . This is a message from home
to all of us . . . There will be more. He will be back. He will sing for us
again . . . Come back, Bob, we need you. And thank you for that letter
from home.

Although the all-original *New Morning* was probably forced on Dylan by both critical and commercial considerations—from which no artist in the public arena, even one as contrary as Dylan, can entirely immunize himself—it provided only a fleeting form of solace for his fans. Though I'd trade 'Sign on the Window' for all thirty-five cuts on the two previous albums, nothing else on *New Morning* approaches such heights, and 'Three Angels,' 'Father of Night,' and 'If Dogs Run Free' inhabit depths even 'Peggy Day' feared to tread.

One key problem, as articulated by Richard Williams in his London *Times* review of the album, was that, though Dylan continued to hold the attention of those who remembered the impact of his earlier work, 'a newer generation finds it hard to understand what [all] the fuss is about.' This newer generation had found a new set of heroes, and those heroes were to be found on increasingly spacious stages in customized arenas, regularly peddling their wares. The Who, Cream, the Grateful Dead, the Jeff Beck Group, and Led Zeppelin all proved that they could simply bypass a certain critical distaste for their extended workouts, tapping into a new youth culture that favored the direct connection of live performance. Even the previously high and mighty Rolling Stones had responded to the dislocation by reinventing themselves as 'the greatest live rock & roll band in the world,' touring America in the fall of 1969.

In the fall of 1970, Dylan actually considered consolidating the commercial success of *New Morning* by going back out on the road himself. The notion even got as far as the rehearsal stage, trying a simple four-piece setup, featuring Al Kooper and Harvey Brooks, à la Forest Hills.

Harvey Brooks: [After *New Morning*] we talked a little bit about playing shows, but it didn't get very far down the line. We did have a few rehearsals at a place, a studio on Houston Street where he did a lot of painting . . . and we tried out a few different combinations of musicians, but it just didn't click.

In the end, Dylan decided he was not yet ready to embrace another disruptive period out on the road, especially as Sara was expecting another child (to be a son, Jakob), in the spring. Though New York had not turned the key or provided the requisite impetus, his family remained central to all his considerations. Nor could he any longer rely on the management skills of Albert Grossman to arrange and coordinate a tour on a grand scale. They had arrived at the formal dissolution of their business relationship on July 17, 1970.

Early in 1969 Dylan had sought to change the publishing arrangement he had previously agreed with Grossman through the jointly controlled Dwarf Music. Grossman consented to Dylan forming another publishing company, under his direct control, into which he would place future compositions. Grossman retained his right to half the net proceeds from the exploitation of such compositions and Big Sky Music was duly formed. Shortly afterward, Dylan retained Grossman's former secretary, Naomi Saltzman, on a full-time basis. Saltzman was to be a powerful weapon in the subsequent settlement. Dylan also took lawyer David Braun with him, leaving Grossman to find new counsel. He was prepared to argue the toss over how their agreement should be construed, if necessary in court. But what he most wanted was control of his work.

Grossman, through his lawyers, sought to clarify the terms of their previous agreement, from March 1969; and on July 17, 1970 Dylan and Grossman agreed to:

(A) terminate the Management Agreement, reserving to Grossman his right to royalties on works created during the management period;
(B) confirm Grossman's rights under the Witmark, Partnership (i.e., Dwarf Music), and Joint Venture (i.e., Big Sky) Agreements;
(C) shift the control and administration of the Partnership and Joint Venture catalogues from Grossman to Dylan, who became obligated to account to Grossman for his share of profits owed under the Partnership and Joint Venture Agreements.

Big Sky Music would be replaced by Ram's Horn Music before the close of 1971, effectively ending any joint ownership of publishing. As Dylan told Shelton in May 1971, Grossman 'had me signed up for ten years, for part of my records, for part of my everything. But I'll be out of that next month.' The impetus for a settlement in 1970 may have been forced on Grossman by financial irregularities. Though Grossman's cut, to which he would always be entitled on the work to date, continued to rankle with Dylan, he did gain complete control of all his music publishing, and personal management, as a result of the July settlement. The five-year CBS contract was also up for grabs in 1972 and—unbeknownst to Davis—Dylan had no plans to deliver any further albums under the conditions Grossman had secured for him back in July 1967. It was going to be a quiet couple of years.

1971–72: Smooth Like a Rhapsody

18

It may have been some five years after the scheduled date that my phone rang one morning, and my secretary came in to my office, and she whispers: 'It's Bob Dylan on the telephone!' . . . I picked up the phone. I said, 'Hi, how are you?' He said, 'Fine.' He said, 'Why don't we publish the book?' I said, 'Sure.' . . . [And then], 'You don't really feel that you wanna do . . . ?' He said, 'No. That's what I wrote. That's the way it is. We did what we did. That's it.'

—*Bob Markel*

Into every artist's life come periods of retrenchment. If 1970 began with Dylan's sprawling vinyl retort to the bootleggers, it ended with his response to the bookleggers. *Tarantula,* Dylan's 'lost' speed ramblings, had been enjoying an underground existence akin to Joyce's *Ulysses* or Lawrence's *Lady Chatterley's Lover,* being 'booklegged' from the original galleys sometime in 1969. The most overt pirate of Dylan's printed words was A. J. Weberman, who openly sold an unauthorized edition of *Tarantula* even as he was railing against Dylan's Currant Bag in print. Official publication was the only logical recourse.

At the same time, Dylan attempted to establish a dialogue with Weberman, presumably to find out something of A.J.'s motives. After talking to Weberman outside his house at the beginning of January, he phoned him the following day, and invited him to his Village studio to talk some more. He was disconcerted to discover that A.J. intended to write an article for the *East Village Other* about their informal meeting, and insisted on the opportunity to see a draft of the article.

In a final telephone conversation, on January 9, hoping to persuade him not to publish his article, Dylan informed Weberman, 'You don't have my permission to do any of this shit.' It was to be their last verbal contact, though sometime in 1972—after Weberman promised to stop rummaging through Dylan's garbage, searching for evidence of an abiding drug habit—he returned to the MacDougal Street town house with a reporter in tow, to hunt once more through Dylan's garbage, as part of a feature on his new 'science,' Garbology. Sara came out of the house and freaked out at Weberman's reappearance. Dylan, having returned home to a presumably distraught Sara, later went looking for Weberman.

A. J. Weberman: I was walking around with my head bowed down to my shoes, y'know. I was down on Elizabeth Street to get some Coca-Cola from the neighborhood store, when all of a sudden I felt this arm around my neck. I thought I was being mugged, y'know . . . I wrenched loose and I turned around and it was Bob Dylan. I said, 'Hey man, let's talk, man, what are you doing?' He started punching me, and I said, 'Come on, stop! Stop!' I thought, is this really happening to me? Could Bob Dylan be punching me out? My idol, the guy that wrote all that great poetry? And a punch to my head convinced me it was . . . I thought maybe I'd wrestle him down, calm him down a little. But that didn't work out 'cause he had spirit on his side. He got me down on the sidewalk and started banging my head against the pavement. And then some hippies came along and broke it up.

By the time he tried banging some sense into Weberman, Dylan had had enough of people imposing their own hang-ups on him and his family. Though 1971 was marked by a number of attempts to establish a dialogue with his audience, both through the forum of Scaduto's biography—which belatedly benefited from his direct input—and on AM airwaves, only his two live appearances of the year could be deemed entirely successful, and they simply reaffirmed a demand for a return to a stage he would prefer did not exist.

The dialogue ended in 1972, both with his audience and the voice in his head, as he occupied himself with an anthology of past words. As Dylan's silence grew, so did the clamor for his return to the pop vortex. Articles constructed out of rumors, spoofs, and supposition filled the papers, while bootlegs filled the racks, feeding off the absence of official wares, rewriting the pages and the text. The *Royal Albert Hall* bootleg finally gave fans a sound borne of Dylan's *dérèglement de tous les sens*, while the likes of *Seems Like a Freeze Out, Stealin'*, and *Talkin' John Birch Society Blues* charted the route to the precipice. Michael Gray, writing at the time, even suggested 'the release of so much bootleg material . . . once again poses the overexposure problem and . . . the best way to counter-act it is for [Dylan] to hold back for a substantial period before issuing anything else.' In fact, Dylan had already alluded to the true cause of the absence of product in line two of his first single of 1971: 'I don't have much to say.'

In one sense, 1971 and 1972 might both be considered 'lost' years. Neither produced albums, or even sessions for a Columbia album, though

Dylan would issue two singles of new material in 1971. The difference is that Dylan spent 1971 testing the water, and 1972 watching the river flow. Perhaps he had already decided to wait out the end of contractual obligations to Grossman and Columbia. The first suggestion of a movement away from his record company's welcoming confines came in March, when he booked three days of sessions at a small studio in the Village. The Blue Rock recordings were his first-ever official sessions held away from the shelter of Columbia. The sessions were to be produced by Leon Russell of *Mad Dogs & Englishmen* fame. Only two originals were recorded—'Watching the River Flow' and 'When I Paint My Masterpiece'—but both confronted the same subject matter, a continuing dearth of inspiration, in a refreshingly honest fashion.

The only song to date overtly concerned with Dylan's 'amnesia' had been 'Went to See the Gypsy,' in which he allegorically seeks out a gypsy who can drive him from his fear, and bring him through the mirror (a metaphor seemingly co-opted from Hermann Hesse's *Steppenwolf*), much as Elvis had broken through a second time with his '68 comeback TV special. 'Watching the River Flow,' a honky-tonkin' roller coaster of a single, opens with a classic Dylan couplet: 'What's the matter with me / I don't have much to say.' The implication of the song is that only in the city—'with the one I love so close at hand'—can the singer rediscover his muse, but he knows that the evidence is against him.

In 'When I Paint My Masterpiece,' the artist travels further afield, in time *and* space, searching for his muse. The song ostensibly opens in Rome, a city where two millennia of culture overawe the singer. He wanders the streets, looking for inspiration. Though he longs to return to 'the land of Coca-Cola' (lines omitted from the released version, though preserved on the Band's contemporaneous recording), the singer heads for Brussels, where he is once again caught up with his own notoriety. The irony implicit in the title—a suspicion that he will *never* paint his masterpiece—was to make the song such a perfect opener on the 1975 tour, when he could once again envisage being hung as a thief. 'When I Paint My Masterpiece' would be first released by the Band, on their *Cahoots* album, and later included as a 'bonus' track on Dylan's second collection of greatest hits. 'Watching the River Flow' was released as a single in June 1971, backed by the powerful solo 'Spanish is the Loving Tongue,' but failed to reach the Top 40, despite being his first non-album single since 'One of Us Must Know.'

In many ways, 'Watching the River Flow' and 'When I Paint My Masterpiece' conclude the second phase of Dylan's career—as he himself slyly admitted in his *Writings & Drawings* collection, which concludes with these two songs—even though he would make one more attempt at chart success in 1971. Having searched high and low for his muse, he now concluded that he must simply sit by that bank of sand and await her return.

By the time 'Watching the River Flow' was stuttering up the charts, Dylan was enjoying a holiday in Israel with Sara, though enjoy might be an overstatement. Planned as a second honeymoon, they made the trip without the children. Unfortunately, within days of their arrival, Dylan was snapped by a UPI photographer at the Wailing Wall in Jerusalem. When the photographer realized he had captured Bob Dylan, né Robert Zimmerman, in the homeland of his forefathers, on the very day he turned thirty, in front of one of the most powerful symbols of the religion he had been born into, he realized he had a photo he could syndicate around the world. Dylan thus found himself hounded by members of the local press, asking for an interview. Having been all around this world, it must have seemed that no refuge remained.

Dylan's desire to escape his self-imposed identity reached such a height on this trip that he even considered entering a kibbutz with his family, though not under the usual restraints. At some point in June, Dylan and Sara approached the Kibbutz Givat Haim, with a view to joining up for a year.

Eve Brandstein: The only thing was he wanted to get a guest house, have the kids go each day to the kibbutz for the experience, but that he and his wife would not have to work on the kibbutz. Rather, they'd stay in a guest house and pay for the stay and the keep of the children. He wanted to put some time in . . . He was turned down . . . He wanted special privileges, and they were afraid that if word got out the kibbutz would be overrun.

Dylan was still looking for a home away from home. His visit to the kibbutz coincided with a series of rumors that he was embracing the religion of his father. It seems the death of his father, in June 1968, had prompted him to begin exploring the Jewish heritage he had spent his younger days trying to disavow.

Harold Leventhal: After his father died, Bob became quite conscious of his Jewishness. He was very excited about Israel when he got back [in 1971], and it was around that time he started talking with Rabbi Meir Kahane, who formed the Jewish Defense League.

Dylan himself would later attempt to play down the importance of his May 1971 visit, and subsequent exploration of his heritage, but the fascination would endure, periodically stoked by devout lifelong friends like Louis Kemp.

Bob Dylan: There was no great significance to that visit. But I'm interested in what and who a Jew is, I'm interested in the fact that Jews are Semites, like Babylonians, Hittites, Arabs, Syrians, Ethiopians. But a Jew is different because a lot of people hate Jews. [1976]

If one half of Dylan was looking for a place to hide, another side was curious enough about his ongoing status to consider another return to the stage, albeit cushioned by a superstar bill he hoped might dissipate any unnaturally high expectations. Two benefit concerts at Madison Square Garden, organized by George Harrison to raise funds for Bangla-desh, threatened by both civil war and drought, gave Dylan a cause to champion, and a platform to play. George Harrison and Ringo Starr were sharing the scheduled bill with such luminaries as Eric Clapton and Ravi Shankar, and rumors even began to circulate that at least one more Beatle might also turn up. Though Dylan gave Harrison the impression that he was willing to appear, nothing was set in stone, particularly after the sound check, the day before the show, reminded him of the scale of proceedings.

George Harrison: Right up to the moment he stepped onstage I wasn't sure if he was going to come on. So it was kind of nerve-racking. I had a little list on my guitar and I had a point after 'Here Comes the Sun'—it just said 'Bob,' with a question mark. So it got to that point, I turned around to see if Bob was there, to see if he was going to come on. Because the night before when we went to Madison Square Garden [to sound-check] he freaked out, he saw all these cameras and microphones and this huge place. He was saying, 'Hey man, this isn't my scene, I can't make this.' . . . I was just tired of trying to organize the whole thing, and he was saying, 'Got to get back to Long Island, got a lot of business.' . . . [But] he was all ready, he was so nervous, he had his harmonica on and his guitar in his hand and he was walking right onstage, like it was now or never.

Though he was only on stage for twenty minutes, Dylan's presence again overshadowed an event with a higher purpose. The real surprise was not his appearance but the songs he chose to perform, all of which were from pre-accident albums. Particularly surprising was the inclusion of 'Blowin' in the Wind,' a song he had not performed in eight years, and one he initially took umbrage at Harrison requesting.

Phil Spector: [At the first meeting with Harrison,] George said to Bob, 'Do you think you could sing . . . "Blowin' in the Wind"'—the audience would just love it' . . . and Bob looked at him: 'You interested in "Blowin' in the Wind"? . . . Are you gonna sing "I Wanna Hold Your Hand"?'

Given that he sang in a particularly nasal style, even for Bob, and that the band accompaniment to his acoustic strums verged on the perfunctory, the response to his set was extraordinarily positive. Perhaps it was simply the visual evidence of his continued well-being, bedenimed and lean, that provided all the reassurance his fans needed. That he found an almost throwaway set, in which his singing sounds thin and pinched, taking up an entire side of a three-album boxed set, as well as forming the centerpiece of a general-release film, suggested a level of expectation still burning bright. A side of his personality continued to enjoy the immediacy of a crowd's response, if not the burden of expectation.

The other live appearance of 1971 was equally last-minute and was also recorded for posterity, part of a grander scheme. On the evidence of the one song to pass into collectors' hands, it also marked a return to some approximation of peak performing powers. His appearance at the Band's New Year's Eve show at the Academy of Music may technically have been after midnight, but it certainly featured a Dylan roaring against the dying light. The 'Down in the Flood' he sang that night has all the tonal breath control so evidently lacking at Harrison's million-dollar bash. It also reminded Dylan of the one Band capable of bringing the joys of the stage out in him. And yet when Levon Helm asked him, after the show—the last of four nights they were recording for the Band's live *Rock of Ages* album—'When are we gonna go on the road together again?' he looked perplexed, replying, 'I'm thinking of touring with the Dead.' He may even have been serious. The following July he caught the Dead at Roosevelt Stadium, headlining a bill with the Allman Brothers, and the association continued to fuel the rumor mill up until January 1974, when Dylan finally took Helm's recommendation to heart.

He still preferred the unexpected. When the Band made the decision to record a double album that captured their live sound, it made sense to make Dylan a component of that. But then, having delivered a five-song set blessed with power and commitment, he elected to apply his veto when it came to a release. It seemed equally curious for him to make a political statement of some cultural import, only to have it dismissed as nonsense by those who had spent the past five years getting on his case for abandoning the Cause. On November 3, 1971—having read a newspaper account of the death of George Jackson, the incarcerated black activist—Dylan wrote a straightforward elegy for the dead man. The following day he hurriedly assembled a small band in Blue Rock Studios to record his new song as a single. He recorded two versions, a simple acoustic version and a 'Big Band' version. Despite taking the opportunity to also record a country-flavored original called 'Wallflower,' he decided to put 'George Jackson' on both sides of his new single, presumably to ensure that radio stations could not get away with playing an innocuous B side as the new Dylan single.

The speculation aroused by this seemingly sincere expression of grief was something to behold. Even his recent biographer, Anthony Scaduto, questioned Dylan's motives for releasing the single, suggesting it was an attempt to get certain sections of his audience off his back (effectively ending any contact he was to have with the man). Despite the controversy, the single did not sell any better than 'Watching the River Flow,' suggesting that Dylan was not the only one for whom such political statements were passé.

Though the 'George Jackson' 45 would be his last contact with Columbia for over a year, Dylan entered New York's Record Plant five days later to begin recording his first album since *New Morning*. However, this time his role would be purely musical, deferring to his co-worker on the project when it came to speaking in tongues. The album, which would never be released—despite overtures from Apple at John Lennon's behest—was a collaboration between Allen Ginsberg and Bob Dylan. The idea originated at a poetry reading given by Ginsberg and Gregory Corso at the end of October.

Allen Ginsberg: That fall in NY [Corso] and I gave a poetry reading at NYU in Greenwich Village, and improvised for an hour on the theme 'Why write poetry down on paper when you have to cut down trees to make poetry books?' . . . Unbeknownst to us, Bob Dylan was in the audience, in the rear, with old musician fellow-actor companion David Amram . . . He called us up at our apartment in Lower East Side and said he liked the reading—so he came over the same evening and picked up a guitar that was around and began improvising. He started playing the blues and I started making up lyrics, just weird things that made him start giggling at first. Then Dylan said, 'Why don't we go over to the studio and do this?'

Of course, the idea of improvising poetry was nothing new to Dylan, several of whose songs from the peak years of 1965–67 were largely improvised. Though Ginsberg recollects Dylan being excited by the approach, Dylan's companion that night, Amram, believes that it was

Ginsberg who pushed Dylan into 'sponsoring' the project with his name, and who cajoled a reluctant Dylan into returning to Chez Ginsberg.

David Amram: Bob called me up at my apartment on 6th Ave. He said, 'Allen and Gregory [Corso] are giving a reading at Loeb Student Center at NYU, do ya wanna come?' I said, 'Sure.' Bob came over and played the piano a little bit . . . Then we got up and went over to Loeb Student Center. And Gregory was in top form! . . . During intermission, we went up to say hi to them. Gregory was just glad to see us, but Allen was thrilled. He said in a surreptitious whisper, 'D'ya think you could get Bob to come over to my place afterwards? I'm working on some music and stuff.' [So] we walked over there, banged on the door, Allen opened the door, said 'Awww, Great to see you. Okay, Bob, the key of G,' and handed Bob a guitar before Bob could even get in the door. He had this little harmonium, he pushed down one note, G, and started chanting something about the CIA and Cambodia and Laos and I could see in Bob's eyes, 'Oh my God, what's happening here?' So I took up my French horn and just as Bob was trying to get the guitar more or less in tune with Allen's harmonium, Allen pushed down a button on a tape recorder, which he had sitting up, plugged in, ready to start taping us. Bob looked over and said, 'Turn that goddamn thing off.' . . . I thought Dylan was gonna walk out, but he stayed there. So we began to plunk away and we played for about two hours and Allen had all these poems and speeches, dispatches from the *New York Times* about the CIA, and it was so outrageous. We mostly used one chord, maybe two chords, and then Allen would call out the chord changes—which weren't the right ones . . . It was fun, and Bob had a good time, and he wasn't used to doing this. And he said [on the way back], 'What did you think about all that?' . . . Frankly I never thought anything more would happen.

Despite Dylan's initial dismay, Ginsberg *did* record the evening's jam session, which involved a number of William Blake poems set to 'music,' as well as Dylan coaching Ginsberg as to the correct name for various chords. The evening prompted Ginsberg, who had been invited to read some of his poetry on New York's public TV station, channel 13, to attempt an improvised performance along the same lines, live on local TV. Persuading Dylan to tag along in the background, Ginsberg wheeled out his Blake poems and a new work entitled 'September on Jessore Road,' which was not so much improvised as memorized.

David Amram: Bob got all dressed up in a greenish suit. They did everything in one take live . . . [When] we watched it afterwards, we both

laughed because we were all the silent partners, with Allen doing his show
. . . As a result of that, we made a recording.

Ginsberg booked three days of sessions—November 9, 17, and 20—
at the Record Plant, paying for the studio time out of his own pocket,
and invited Amram, Happy and Artie Traum, and poet Anne Waldman
down to the sessions in the hope of putting Dylan at ease. The sessions
were predictably chaotic, the methodology being, in Ginsberg's words,
'he'd just start strumming—da da da dum, chang chang, and I'd start
babbling words.' When Ginsberg attempted to coax Dylan into improvising some lines of his own, he all but clammed up, asking leading questions
of Allen: 'What are we doing? What exactly is this?' The results proved
that relying on serendipity alone, without covering one's bases musically,
was not about to lead to the palace of visions.

Happy Traum: It was a very loose happening—as usual when Allen
organizes something—we were laughing and falling all over the floor. Corso
was running across the studio like a neurotic, accompanied by a Tibetan
female singer. The others were in a 'state of transition' and walked around
deliriously. Soon, only Allen, Bob, and I were left. [It was] then we recorded
the music.

Sadly for his own pocket, Ginsberg found few interested parties when
he attempted to get the album released. An entire album of improvised
poetry, however distinguished the musical accompanists, was not likely
to be a big money spinner. Another major problem was some of the
language on the record, which lay somewhere between the pornographic
and the scatological, particularly 'Jimmy Berman Rag,' Ginsberg's homo-
sexual paean to a newsboy. Though he did not push Columbia into
releasing the album themselves, Dylan continued to encourage Ginsberg
to develop such musical and lyrical experiments, visiting him in January
1972 to hear several new compositions, and volunteering to appear on
any further sessions that Ginsberg might want to arrange.

However, Dylan refrained from attempting his own album, improvised or otherwise, and continued to keep Columbia at arm's length,
though he did agree to a second greatest-hits collection at the end of the
year, as long as he was allowed to compile it himself, could make it a
double album, and could include a handful of songs that had not previously appeared in an official guise, but had been commercially covered
by other artists. Thus it was that his heartfelt 1963 Town Hall performance
of 'Tomorrow Is a Long Time,' his Blue Rock 'When I Paint My

Masterpiece,' and three new recordings of basement tape songs, cut that October with Happy Traum, were added to the official canon in November 1971.

Happy Traum: He knew that they had songs chosen out for this double album and there were some songs that he didn't agree with their choice. He felt there were some songs that he had written that had become hits of sorts for other people, that he didn't actually perform himself, and he wanted to fit those on the record as well . . . So we just went in one afternoon and did it, it was just the two of us and the engineer, and it was very simple. We cut about five songs and chose three on the spot and mixed them . . . in the space of an afternoon . . . Sometimes I wasn't even sure if it was a final take until we would just finish and Bob would say, 'Okay, let's go and mix it.'

The intent behind a largely rewritten 'You Ain't Going Nowhere' was not so obvious. A Mr. McGuinn was told to 'pack up your tent,' presumably a dig at the Byrds' own version of the song, issued as a single in its own right, but perhaps a reminder to all those who might have forgotten that nobody sang Dylan like Dylan. At the end of the session, Traum recalls, 'he told me that he felt stimulated to prove himself again.' If so, the feeling passed quickly enough. A year of sporadic activity had enabled Dylan to continue to be news, without adding any significant product to the brand name. When another year passed without any discernible activity on the recording front or the concert front, the suspicion began to form in the media that the man would prefer his public image to simply fade to black.

Between January and June 1972 the only evidence he was in New York at all was a reading he attended by Russian poet Andrei Voznesensky at the Town Hall. By this point, though, nobody was on the lookout for Dylan, and he had developed, as poet Jim Carroll noted, 'a slumping, camouflaged way of moving, like an aged and wise chameleon, perfected by years of ducking out of joints inconspicuously.' After the reading, a motley crew headed for the Kettle of Fish, with Voznesensky and his Russian 'companions' in tow, but the evening was hijacked by Ginsberg on one of his conspiracy kicks.

David Amram: Allen went into this whole big rap about America being a repressive right-wing country with no liberty, no freedom, and these two KGB agents were just sitting there staring at him in disbelief. Finally, after Allen has finished his rant, the KGB agent says, 'My dear boy, let me tell you one thing, the enemy is not capitalism or communism. It's television!'

Dylan had spent most of the first half of 1972 holed up near Tucson, Arizona, at a ranch he had recently acquired, possibly not the ideal location 'to cool out for a while.' Retreating ever more into himself and his family, he began to write one of his most enduring songs, 'Forever Young,' for his youngest son, Jakob, born the previous year. He had been prompted to take up his pen again by the persistent airplay of a particular single that assailed the airwaves that spring. The single in question was not one of his, though it might as well have been. Rather, it was Neil Young's breakthrough 45, 'Heart of Gold.'

Bob Dylan: I used to hate it when it came on the radio. I always liked Neil Young, but it bothered me every time I listened to 'Heart of Gold' . . . I'd say, 'Shit, that's me. If it sounds like me, it should as well be me.' There I was, stuck on the desert someplace, having to cool out for a while. New York was a heavy place. Woodstock was worse, people living in trees outside my house, fans trying to batter down my door, cars following me up dark mountain roads. I needed to lay back for a while, forget about things, myself included, and I'd get so far away and turn on the radio and there I am, but it's not me. [1985]

Though Neil Young had been around almost as long as Dylan himself, and had developed a style that was, if anything, even more nasal, harnessed to the quintessence of ramshackle, it is hard not to recognize the Dylanisms on the self-consciously referential 'Heart of Gold.' But then, Young was hardly alone in alluding to Dylan in his absence. Don McLean was portraying Dylan as 'the jester [who] stole [the King's] thorny crown' in his chart-topping 'American Pie,' while English singer-songwriter David Bowie's 'Song to Bob Dylan' pleaded for someone to tell Dylan that 'they've lost his poems / so they're writing on the wall,' before asking the man to 'give us back our sanity / you're every nation's refugee.' Though he insisted that 'this is how some see B.D.,' there was no mistaking Bowie's intent, to establish himself as the English Bob Dylan.

As Dylan became increasingly invisible, the search for a 'New Dylan' became an ongoing activity for both the media and those in A&R. Dylan even gave one of the candidates, ex-Chicago postman John Prine, an endorsement of sorts by making a brief guest appearance at the beginning of September, at the Bitter End in New York, when Prine was playing his first New York residency, on the back of a fine debut album.

John Prine: I gave Dylan one of the first pressings of the record. Two weeks later I played my first gig ever outside of Chicago. I was playing with

David Bromberg and Steve Burgh and [Steve] Goodman, but I needed a harmonica player. I asked if there was anyone around. Now, this is only my second night, and Dylan comes up. He had brought a harmonica and learned the words to all the choruses of my songs. I introduced Dylan, and about two people were clapping. No one believed it. They thought Dylan was either dead or on Mount Fuji.

Around the same time, Dylan's old producer John Hammond was signing to Columbia a kid from New Jersey who had an album of subterranean homesick blues he wanted to record. It would take Bruce Springsteen three years or so to live down the New Dylan tag, a period in which it also clearly stuck in Dylan's throat. If in September 1974, when recording the original version of 'Idiot Wind,' he referred non-specifically to 'imitators [who] steal me blind', at his first meeting with Bruce Springsteen, backstage at the Rolling Thunder Revue in November 1975, he apparently extended his hand and said, 'Hi, I hear you're the new me.'

If the bevy of New Dylans weren't enough to prompt Dylan to resume the good fight, a summer of performances by contenders and pretenders convinced him that, if he was ever going to be a contender again, a change was gonna have to come. Even Elvis was retreading the boards, and at the beginning of July, Dylan caught the King at Madison Square Garden. If Elvis was by now all pizzazz, at the end of July he also caught the post-*Exile* Rolling Stones at the Garden, perhaps the grandest rock & roll bonanza to date.

Arthur Rosato: I think the Stones' [1972] tour had a big influence on him. That was the biggest thing going and Bob's a major rock & roll fan. It was right after that he came out of retirement.

The itch almost got scratched three days earlier, at a festival in Toronto that he'd attended with Dave Bromberg, but this time it was the organizers who were reluctant to accede, and Dylan who was anxious to get up and play. The clamor that had greeted his simple presence was such that an actual set was clearly out of the question.

John Cohen: The New Lost City Ramblers were singing at the Mariposa Folk Festival, held on an island near Toronto. We had just finished getting off the stage. Suddenly there was this tremendous buzz around. Someone had discovered Bob in the middle of the crowd in the audience. He was disguised as a hippie and had on a red bandanna . . . Someone suddenly recognized him and everybody was making a big circle around him—several thousand people. He walked two foot to the left and they all moved that way. It was very strange. Slowly, slowly he moved over to the performers' area and then walked in there . . . I happened to be the first one he recognized when he came inside. It was a scary situation. Nobody knew what to do, but they wanted to take him apart. It's a very inhuman relationship to do that to somebody, you know, to gang around him like he was a queen bee.

What he would have played at the festival one can only guess. New songs had been a long time coming (he was still tinkering with 'Forever Young'). Not that he needed a further reminder of how to write lyrics. He had spent most of 1972 overseeing the completion of his second book, another cast through the past, a collection of all his lyrics and poems, to be entitled *Words*. At some stage he decided to illustrate a few of the songs with his own line drawings, changing the title to *Writings & Drawings*. Though the book did not appear until June 1973, the last songs to be included were the two-year-old 'Watching the River Flow' and 'When I Paint My Masterpiece.' This was clearly deliberate, part of Dylan's ongoing role in the book's production, as publisher Robert Gottlieb recognized:

Robert Gottlieb: At the time that this came to me as a publishing project the manuscript was complete. Bob demanded, and had every right to have, complete artistic control over his book. No editorial changes were made in the text . . . Bob was involved in all its aspects and phases . . . I know it wasn't a rushed, overnight piece of hysteria because too many books happen that way and I can recognize the signs. There was nothing sloppy or careless or rushed or hysterical about this. It seemed to me very carefully worked, and I imagine over quite a period of time.

One disconcerting aspect of this lavish book was the air of finality that hung over it. At the time, it really seemed as if Dylan was saying, 'Well here it is. Don't expect any more,' even if, with hindsight's kinder gaze, he was really saying, 'This is my past. I have dispensed with it, and cleared the decks.' After all, it had been nearly three years since he had issued his last official studio album, and the imminent release of a largely instrumental movie soundtrack hardly suggested a major creative renaissance.

Further evidence of the dearth of current inspiration could seemingly be found on opening the book. On the inside of both front and back covers were endpapers with drafts of songs, presumably contemporary with the final stages of the book's composition. If songs like 'Bowling

Alley Blues' and 'Field Mouse from Nebraska' were indeed representative of his current output, it was clear why there had been no Dylan album since *New Morning*. But then, perhaps there was something to one particular question Dylan chose to ask on the very last line of the inside front cover: 'Is it right to think about what [one] can do, or . . . what one has done?'

1972–73: Alias What?

19

Sam's really . . . the last of a dying breed. They don't hire people like
that to make movies anymore.

—*Bob Dylan, 1973*

Pat Garrett and Billy the Kid, the Sam Peckinpah-directed film that landed
Dylan in Durango, Mexico, for two and a half hellish months in the
winter of 1972–73, is generally considered to be a minor episode in the
Dylan story. In fact, the filming proved to be the necessary jolt to get
him writing again, pushing him to finally abandon New York for sunnier
climes, and providing him with a most unexpected return to the charts.

It has always been something of a mystery how Dylan ended up in a
western by the notoriously eccentric Peckinpah. He had been out of
circulation for some time—in terms of popular perception he had never
really returned from the accident—and talk about acting in movies,
prevalent in 1965–66, had long since subsided. As it is, the writer of the
original screenplay for *Pat Garrett and Billy the Kid*, Rudy Wurlitzer, was
an old friend of Dylan's. It was Wurlitzer who initially approached him,
hoping to persuade him to provide something for the film's musical
soundtrack.

Bob Dylan: Rudy needed a song for the script. I wasn't doing anything.
Rudy sent the script, and I read it and liked it and we got together. And then I
saw *The Wild Bunch* and *Straw Dogs* and *Cable Hogue* and liked them. The best
one is *Ride the High Country*. . . So I wrote ['Billy'] real quick. [1973]

'Billy' was a perfect précis of the film, and a fine return to the ballad
form he had forsaken after *John Wesley Harding*. It also showed that the
young Zimmerman's days of study at the Edelstein cinemas had not been
in vain. Dylan even began to hanker for a small role in the movie, an
idea first mooted by Wurlitzer. He was keen to escape New York, and
several weeks in Durango would allow him to savor at first hand the
Mexican culture he had always professed to love.

Around Thanksgiving, Dylan traveled down to Durango with his wife, to meet the fabled Peckinpah and play him the two songs—'Billy' and 'Goodbye Holly'—he had written for the movie. Peckinpah was genuinely unaware of Dylan's status, and required some coaxing from Kris Kristofferson and James Coburn—who were scheduled to play the two title roles—even to approach Dylan.

James Coburn: Rudy was a friend of Bob's, and he'd written this song about Billy . . . Sam says, 'Who's Bob Dylan? Oh yeah, the kids used to listen to his stuff. I was kinda thinkin' of that guy Roger whatsisname, King of the Road guy, to do it.' And we all said, 'What!! You gotta see Dylan.' . . . He said, 'Okay, bring Dylan down.' And Dylan had been in hiding—meditating or something—since his motorcycle accident and he came down with his tall Indian hat and his little mustache. Very strange cat . . . wonderful guy. He was like quicksilver. You could never put your finger on Bobby . . . So the night we were over at Sam's house and we were all drinking tequila and carrying on and halfway through dinner, Sam says, 'Okay, kid, let's see what you got. You bring your guitar with you?' They went in this little alcove. Sam had a rocking chair. Bobby sat down on a stool in front of this rocking chair. There was just the two of them in there . . . And Bobby played three or four tunes. And Sam came out with his handkerchief in his eye: 'Goddamn kid! Who the hell is he? Who is that kid? Sign him up!'

Peckinpah, delighted with Dylan's songs, offered him a role in the film without really being sure who he was—a legend—and what he was not—an actor. Wurlitzer was delighted, recognizing that 'Dylan . . . brings a different point of view, especially to a western. The part is small, but it's important in a funny sort of way. Do the two of them have any common ground to meet on?' It was left to Wurlitzer to suggest the actual role Dylan should play, one which he volunteered to expand to create something worthy of Dylan's stature. The character he had in mind was as enigmatic and elusive as Dylan himself. His name: Alias. Alias anything you please. Dylan, in the ensuing years, has given the impression that Alias was an invented character, introduced into this celluloid border ballad simply to provide him with a role in the film.

Bob Dylan: I don't know who I played. I tried to play whoever it was in the story, but I guess it's a known fact that there was nobody in that story that was the character I played. [1974]

In fact, not only did Alias appear in Wurlitzer's original version of the script but he was a real historical character, mentioned by Garrett himself in his own *Authentic Life of Billy the Kid*. More than merely a member of Billy's gang, he was Billy's right-hand man, something suggested by the two of them riding side by side during the Turkey Chase sequence, the first scene filmed with Dylan—hence the mustache (so much for continuity!). If anything, Alias's role in the film was gradually reduced. Wurlitzer implying it was at Dylan's request. According to Kristofferson, it was simply one of the many by-products of Peckinpah's ongoing problems with MGM, the film studio whose folding bills he was spending.

Kris Kristofferson: Sam . . . was never able to sit down and figure out what Dylan was in the movie . . . Bob kept sayin' to me, 'Well, at least you're in the script.'

The stuttering character Wurlitzer created in the original script was soon gone, presumably because it required a degree of acting technique quite beyond Dylan. He also only joined Billy's gang after witnessing his escape from the Lincoln jail. In one of the most powerful scenes in the film, he unties his butcher's apron, casts it to the ground, and rides out to join the gang. Footage of a stuttering Dylan was doubtless shot, but was junked, along with much of the early footage, as a major disaster wiped out two weeks of filming.

James Coburn: Somebody dropped the main camera and for a while we had focusing problems—the left and right of the screen were fine, but the bottom wasn't in focus. We needed to reshoot when we finally got the camera fixed.

Unfortunately the studio did not share perfectionist Peckinpah's assessment as to the usability of the footage. They refused to finance any reshooting. The underlying tension this dispute generated affected everyone. The film's producer, Gordon Carroll, soon became Peckinpah's adversary as the director fought to retain artistic control of the film. Disregarding MGM's wishes, Peckinpah endeavored to reshoot scenes without the producer noticing. The conflict took its toll on Peckinpah—an eccentric character at the best of times—and his behavior became progressively more unstable.

Gordon Dawson: Sam would tell me to set up a scene. Carroll would veto it because it wasn't authorized. Then there'd be a race to see if I could get a wrap before they could rip it out.

Bob Dylan: That was Peckinpah's kingdom—and he was sort of a madman. He kept saying, 'It's my movie, my movie.' [1986]

Dylan, like his fellow actors, naturally sided with the auteur in his struggle with the powers-that-be. Peckinpah's problems confirmed in Dylan a long-held suspicion that artistic concerns were anathema to big-business interests, helping to shape his own jaundiced view of the film studios, which later manifested itself in the way he set about releasing and distributing his own grandiose celluloid experiment, *Renaldo and Clara*.

Bob Dylan: I learned by working in *Pat Garrett* that there is no way you can make a really creative movie in Hollywood . . . You have to have your own crew and your own people to make a movie your own way. [1978]

Cast adrift by Peckinpah's problems, Dylan became ever more diffident. However, he occasionally permitted his delight in the kind of games played in his medicine days to come to the fore.

Kris Kristofferson: This one scene, Sam wanted him to come riding up to me, and as usual, it wasn't in the script. So they put Bobby on a horse and told him what they wanted. Now it's hard for Bobby to hit his marks in a scene with his own feet 'cause he doesn't think like that. But he's supposed to come through these sheep to where I'm standin' and old Sam says, 'Okay, Bobby, you just come straight by the camera here.' Well, Bobby went into a gallop, man, scaring sheep, horses, cameramen, and everybody. And I was laughin' so hard I was in tears. So was Sam. And old Sam says, 'No, Bobby, I really didn't mean that.' . . . I don't know whether Bobby did that on purpose or not.

Members of the press, who were at least as interested in Dylan's acting debut as in a crazed Peckinpah, found him uncommunicative. But it wasn't only to journalists that he remained subdued, and eventually his wife began to question the point of the exercise.

Kris Kristofferson: I never know where his head's at. There are times when it can really be upsetting when somebody doesn't talk. Hell, he doesn't even talk to his old lady sometimes for weeks . . . according to her . . . [But] I admire him for sticking it out.

Bob Dylan: My wife got fed up almost immediately. She'd say to me, 'What the hell are we doing here?' [1985]

During a two-week Christmas break, Sara managed to persuade Dylan to fly over to England to spend some time with George and Patti Harrison. Though this break temporarily restored their flagging spirits, a further four weeks of filming awaited the pair of them on their return— along with the recording of a soundtrack album, Dylan's first studio work in over a year. As Super Bowl weekend approached, Dylan arranged to fly to Mexico City, where Columbia owned its own studios, to record the title song, 'Billy,' and some incidental music. By this point, it was not only he who needed a respite from Durango. On the last plane out of town were both of the film's stars, its scriptwriter, and assorted wives and girlfriends.

Rudy Wurlitzer: Sam knows he's losing to Dylan. He's giving a screening of *The Getaway* in town tonight, but everybody wants to go to Mexico City with Dylan. [Sam] also just called a 6:30 rehearsal for Monday morning because he knows we won't be back till after eight. But I don't care, man. I've got to get away.

It had been a while since Dylan had conducted a studio session with a band, and the January 20 session did not start auspiciously. Dylan and the in-house engineer failed to hit it off, and after the first take the engineer complained about him hitting the mike a couple of times. He just snorted and muttered, 'Too bad.' He also found an unnecessarily large number of musicians trying to get in on the act, some from Kristofferson's band, some local Mexicans. Dylan, though, refused to abandon his traditional method of cutting songs live, with a minimum of preparation, even if his seemingly undisciplined approach to recording infuriated some of the other musicians.

Kris Kristofferson: I flew my band down figuring they would love to pick with Bob Dylan. Because of the Mexican musicians' union they had to have one Mexican musician for every American musician on the session. Bob doesn't speak Spanish, so I asked him if he wanted me to talk to the trumpet players. I figured he wanted border trumpets. So I went over to talk to them and he said something real curt like, 'You can do that on your own song!' . . . so I left him alone . . . I didn't understand what he was goin' through. I didn't really understand how he records. My band would come up to me and say he was barely showing them something, they would almost learn it, and he'd move on to the next one. And they were trying to be so perfect for Dylan! But he wanted their first impressions. He's like a certain kind of painter. But . . . I thought he was just fuckin' with my band.

None of the repeated takes of 'Billy' satisfied Dylan, and he began to pare the sound down, though not before recording an instrumental with the Mexican trumpeters, 'Peco's Blues,' which bore more than a passing resemblance to the traditional 'What Does the Deep Sea Say?' However, the main task was to record a satisfactory 'Billy.' Having dispensed with trumpets, then drums, then organ and electric guitar, he finally cut a take of the Billy ballad accompanied by just Terry Paul on bass—an approach he would later adopt on *Blood on the Tracks*. Apart from the final take of 'Billy' (later issued as 'Billy 4') and a brief instrumental called 'Billy Surrenders,' thirty seconds of which found its way into the released cut of the movie, there would be no takes used from this session in the film. Even the other vocal track, 'Goodbye Holly,' ended up on the cutting-room floor. The session ended at four in the morning, Dylan crawling off to his hotel bed to catch four winks before flying back to Durango.

Dylan knew that it would take more sessions to round out the soundtrack. Additional pressure had been brought to bear by Peckinpah, who had brought in Jerry Fielding, an experienced hand at scoring movies, to 'supervise' Dylan's musical soundtrack. The long-forgotten Fielding considered Dylan an amateur who had written 'a lot of nonsense which is strictly for teenyboppers,' an attitude which did not endear him to Dylan, who knew that Fielding was not going to approve of the results from Mexico City, as one off-mike comment he made during the session made clear: 'This guy Jerry Fielding's gonna go nuts when he hears this.'

Nevertheless, Dylan did his best to comply with Fielding's recommendations. Fielding's first idea was to have 'Dylan sing a relevant verse' of the 'Billy' ballad 'as it fit the story at roughly nine separate points throughout the picture' (the idea was modified to 'Billy' appearing at four appropriate points). Fielding recommended Dylan's other lyrical contribution to the soundtrack, 'Goodbye Holly,' be dropped and another song substituted, this time representing the death, not of Holly, but of Sheriff Baker. When Fielding heard the song Dylan had written to replace Holly's lament, he was not impressed.

Jerry Fielding: I set up two dubbing sessions. Dylan had this song ['Billy'] he'd written for which he had a limitless number of verses that he would sing in random order . . . So I had to tape Dylan's song, because he had nothing written down, and have it transcribed. Dylan never understood what I wanted. At the same time I asked that he write at least one other piece of music because you cannot possibly hope to deal with an entire picture on the basis of that one ballad. So finally he brought to the dubbing session another piece of music—'Knock-Knock-Knockin' on Heaven's Door.' Everybody loved it. It was shit. That was the end for me.

The egregious Fielding was destined to remain in a minority of one for not responding to the transcendental grace of 'Knockin' on Heaven's Door,' one of Dylan's most evocative songs. With its plaintive gospel feel, the song made no attempt to glamorize the bloody tapestry of death that was Peckinpah's trademark. Aside from providing the film with a signature tune, it would also give Dylan a much-needed hit single. The effect on the musicians who played on the studio recording, at the rescheduled soundtrack sessions in LA, was as profound as on all those, save Fielding, who heard it first in Durango.

Jim Keltner: It was very early in the morning on the Warners soundstage. I think the session was 10 A.M. and again it all fell into place . . . There weren't even any overdubs on that, the singers were singing live, little pump organ, Roger McGuinn I think played [guitar]. This was for a particular scene in the movie when Slim Pickens is dying and that's the first time I ever cried while I played. It was the combination of the words, Bob's voice, the actual music itself, the changes, and seeing the screen . . . In those days you were on a big soundstage, and you had this massive screen that you can see on the wall, [with] the scene . . . running when you're playing. I cried through that whole take.

With shooting finally completed, and editing of this complex, at times confused, narrative due to commence, Dylan and his family headed for California, ostensibly to complete recording of the soundtrack at Burbank Studios. Dylan's main concern, though, was to ensure that one of his children, who had become ill during filming, received the sort of treatment unavailable in Durango. Los Angeles was as good a place as any to obtain the necessary medical supervision.

The sessions at Burbank Studios, which lasted just a couple of days, were considerably more upbeat than the Mexico City session. Dylan was working with some of his favorite musicians, including Bruce Langhorne, who had moved to Los Angeles to work on movies after the death of Farina; the ultimate session drummer, Jim Keltner; Terry Paul from Kristofferson's band; and Roger McGuinn. They even found time to jam out on 'Sweet Amarillo' and a seemingly spontaneous 'Rock Me Mama,' though Dylan continued to be exasperated by some aspects of the process, informing producer Gordon Carroll prior to an instrumental

'Knockin' on Heaven's Door,' 'This is the last time I work for anyone in a movie on the music. I'll stick to acting.'

His resolve must have further hardened when he saw the released cut of the movie (thankfully discarded, after Peckinpah's death, in favor of one of those fabled 'director's cuts'), in which much of the music Dylan recorded was used inappropriately and ineffectively. Though Wurlitzer thought the shooting script had 'reduced [the story] to its most simplistic components,' Peckinpah's own cut remains a poignant commentary on the way two old friends confront the demands of the New West. The film as it was initially released, though, cut several important scenes, including the opening sequence where Garrett is gunned down by Poe (the film was intended to be a flashback by Garrett, as he faces his own death). Indeed, Poe's crucial role was all but cut from the finished film.

In the shooting script, Garrett's reluctance to track down his old friend is made explicit by his wandering in a convoluted way around Fort Sumner, aware all along that Billy is hiding there. Eventually Poe is required to inform him of Billy's location, thus galvanizing Garrett into providing the inevitable sacrifice. Other scenes cut by the studio included Poe's brutal beating of two old codgers, to establish Billy's location; a vignette in which Garrett's wife informs him that she will leave him if he guns down the Kid; and an extended sequence where Peckinpah himself plays an undertaker, building a child's coffin at Fort Sumner, as Garrett rides in to kill the Kid. With the final edit by MGM these pivotal scenes vanished, the tempo of the film was irrevocably altered, and the careful synchronizing of musical soundtrack to appropriate scenes was all but forgotten. All the leading players involved in the drama of making *Pat Garrett and Billy the Kid* were bitterly disappointed with the released version.

Bob Dylan: Sam himself just didn't have final control and that was the problem. I saw it in a movie house one cut away from his and I could tell that it had been chopped to pieces. Someone other than Sam had taken a knife to some valuable scenes that were in it. The music seemed to be scattered and used in every other place but the scenes in which we did it for. Except for 'Heaven's Door,' I can't say as though I recognized anything I'd done [as] . . . being in the place I'd done it for. [1985]

In this re-edited form, the film was not initially well received, though posterity has again proved more generous. The soundtrack album was also subject to a particularly ill-judged review in *Rolling Stone*, by Jon Landau. Lacking the insights of a Marcus, or the feel for authenticity of a Nelson, Landau dismissed the album as 'Merely Awful,' accusing Dylan of stage-managing a decline into cultural irrelevance. The review incensed Dylan.

Bob Dylan: Landau's . . . got his head up his ass. He wrote that article from a very inexperienced and immature position . . . He wasn't connecting it to the film. He's into rock & roll, man, the way it was in the fifties . . . [but] Landau I had already crossed off as someone who just didn't understand. [1975]

Landau was one of many guilty of unreasonable expectations. Landau's frustration seemed to stem from the fact that it was 'merely' a soundtrack album. In truth, though, he simply resented an artist who fitted into none of his preconceived roles for the rock & roll star. Disenchanted with the real McCoy, he would champion New Jersey's New Dylan over the originator in the ensuing decades.

If Landau didn't recognize a stirring in Dylan's soul, the public was more perceptive. The obvious single, 'Knockin' on Heaven's Door,' gave him his first Top 30 single since 'Lay, Lady, Lay,' as well as providing an unexpected boost to the film's flagging receipts. Yet, despite the single's innate commerciality, it almost ended up not being released. After three years waiting for a new album, Columbia almost hijacked Dylan's mini-renaissance. Through his lawyer, David Braun, he had been negotiating the terms of a new contract with Clive Davis. Davis knew that he had also been having discussions with Warner Brothers and Atlantic Records.

Atlantic, in particular, had been carefully courting Dylan, who had made guest appearances on two albums recorded in the fall of 1972 at Atlantic's New York recording studios. He had sat in on two weeks of Doug Sahm sessions, playing keyboards and guitar, and even providing backing vocals on his own 'Wallflower,' which he had donated to Sahm. He recorded with Steve Goodman, too, and popped in on sessions for Bette Midler's debut album, both Atlantic acts. He also managed to secure a one-album deal with Atlantic for Barry Goldberg, on condition that he co-produce the album in question. Clive Davis, though, was determined to return Dylan to Columbia, unaware that it would be in his absence.

Clive Davis: Early in 1973 I finally did conclude negotiations for a new contract with Bob. Basically, it was limited to a commitment for two more albums, plus the *Billy the Kid* soundtrack album—there was no time period involved . . . the guarantee was about four hundred thousand dollars per album . . . Columbia [then] backed out of the deal after I left. Since the *Billy the Kid* movie had just been released, Braun screamed that the soundtrack album commitment had to be honored; they couldn't go elsewhere in so short a time. So Columbia released it at the royalty rate agreed upon during my negotiations with Braun . . . When the single broke out of the album, and clearly showed Dylan's continued fertility, [Columbia head Goddard] Lieberson tried to resume negotiations.

Davis had been about to finalize details for the new contract when he was fired by CBS president Arthur Taylor on May 29. Met at the door of Taylor's office by two CBS security men, he was then served with a civil complaint, alleging ninety-four thousand dollars' worth of expense-account violations over six years, this from a man whose income in 1973 alone totaled over three hundred thousand dollars. The whole thing stank of a corporate coup, which mortified Dylan almost as much as Davis himself. Dylan eventually testified on Davis's behalf in the civil case, when it came to court in July 1975. Though it did not take long for Columbia to realize the error of its ways, Dylan had clearly decided to teach the company a lesson. A year after his less-than-ceremonious departure, Davis would write in his autobiography:

It is now very apparent that Columbia will spare nothing to bring Dylan back into the fold. They finally understand that they need Dylan, and have no choice but to lure him with an outstanding royalty, not only on new albums but also on his extensive catalog.

By this point Dylan, having explored his options, had signed to the West Coast-based Asylum Records, and secured the first number one album of his career. The change to Asylum reflected a significant shift in outlook for the previously East Coast-bound Dylan. After a couple of pleasant months in California, he was seriously considering settling there. In April 1973, he leased a property in Malibu. Back in December 1971 he had bought a modest property on the Pacific coastline from an LA sportswriter, part of his ongoing portfolio of property investments. But the original house, to which he was now able to add some adjoining land, needed to be extended if it was going to accommodate the entire Dylan clan. As such, leasing 21336 Pacific Coast Highway was a temporary measure, even though he intended to remain in Malibu. He was enjoying four seasons rolled into one, hanging out with old friends, writing songs, and making music again.

Roger McGuinn: [I'd] been hanging out a lot with Bob in Malibu, playing basketball and . . . one day, he was sitting on my couch and we were trying to write a song together and I asked him if he had anything and he said he had one that he'd started but he was probably gonna use it himself, and he started playing 'Never Say Goodbye.'

He had also completed 'Forever Young,' and reaffirmed the central role his wife continued to play in his life with 'Nobody 'Cept You.' These three songs were demoed in June for his new music publishing setup, Ram's Horn Music, marking the beginning of a new phase of the man's varied career. It was time to haul himself back to the marketplace.

1973–74: Into the Flood

20

The risk was not that Dylan would destroy his myth, which was
exactly what he intended to do, but that in the process he would lose
his old audience without gaining a new one.

—*Ellen Willis, 1974*

When I got back [on the road], I was looked upon as a songwriter of
a generation, or mouthpiece of a generation . . . I had to meet that
head on.

—*Bob Dylan, 1997*

Dylan's insistence that there was nobody 'cept Sara for him provided
some much-needed reassurance in the summer of 1973. However synonymous Sara had once been with his muse, their comfortable domesticity had transformed their relationship irrevocably. As long as he
remained content to live in the shadow of former glories, they were the
same cozy couple, and she remained 'his astrologer, his oracle, his
seer, his psychic guide.' But Sara had known Dylan through all the
amphetamine years. She knew *that* Dylan just as well and, on the evidence
of the songs her husband was now writing, greatly feared his return.

For the moment, though, Dylan confined himself to playing with old
friends and considering options. Robbie Robertson relocated to Malibu
that summer. Robertson was suffering an even greater creative drought
than his former master. After four albums in as many years—the second
of which, 1969's *The Band*, was a work of such stature that Dylan himself
must have wondered whether his pupil might yet outstrip his own
efforts—there had been two and a half years of silence from Robertson
and Co., punctuated by a stopgap live double album and a collection of
rock & roll covers.

Robertson's presence in Malibu was clearly no coincidence—he was
as keen to push Dylan to the brink as Sara was to keep him tethered at
home. He, too, was being pushed in a particular direction, and that
direction was west. Starting in the spring, David Geffen, presiding
potentate at the fledgling Asylum label, very obviously began courting

Robertson. Robbie was quite aware that, when Geffen phoned him out of the blue, 'it was a business move.' Any move by Geffen was a business move. Flying Robbie to Paris with Joni Mitchell and himself was a business move. Suggesting the Band sign to Asylum was a business move. But the underlying strategy was a grand one—to rejoin Dylan with the Band, put them on the road, and record and release the results.

As Robertson recalls the chronology, he spoke to Dylan shortly after the Band's own return to live performance on July 28, playing to 300,000-plus Woodstock refugees in upstate Watkins Glen. Dylan was very interested in the Band's instant rapport with this huge crowd: 'He went for it all the way. He asked me more questions. And then . . . when I went out there [Dylan and I] picked up on our talks . . . and we were coming out with a more positive attitude.' These 'talks' revolved around the possibility of Dylan and the Band returning to that endless highway. Robertson may have taken longer to tire of life in upstate New York, but he sensed the same restless, hungry feeling in them both. He sounded out the other members of the Band.

Robbie Robertson: All of a sudden it seemed to really make sense. It was a good idea, a kind of step into the past . . . The other guys in the Band came out [to Malibu] and we went right to work.

Thus it was that, sometime in September 1973, Dylan, Helm, Manuel, Danko, Hudson, and Robertson convened at what passed for Robbie's rehearsal studio in Malibu, to run through a few songs and decide if that old black magic could yet be recreated by such an unabashed 'step into the past.'

Robbie Robertson: We sat down and played for four hours and ran over an incredible number of tunes, just instantly. We would request tunes. Bob would ask us to play certain tunes of ours, and then we would do the same, then we'd think of some that we would particularly like to do.

If Dylan was really going on the road again, corporate 'wisdom' considered such an idea unthinkable without new product to promote. The days of playing shows, releasing records, and playing more shows were over. Tours on this scale were organized on the back of albums. And, anyway, he needed to prove to himself that there was something more to this than a wish to bask in (and cash in on) an already burgeoning sixties nostalgia. Surprisingly, given Dylan's previous determination to leave town, and his failure to reignite the old spark in the early seventies, it was to the Big Apple he flew in October to compose some new songs for album sessions, scheduled for the beginning of November. Equally surprisingly, he returned to California twenty days later with half a dozen new songs to add to those he had demoed in June. It was almost like the old days: an album session was imminent, so dash off a few songs. And as usual, he would continue to hone them in the studio between takes.

Not as yet committed to Asylum, Dylan joined the Band in Village Recorder Studio A in Los Angeles on November 2 to begin recording his first album in three and a half years, and their first joint sessions since the aborted attempt to record a sequel to *Highway 61 Revisited* in the winter of 1965–66. Helm was still returning from the East Coast when, in time-honored fashion, Dylan attempted to get the three oldest songs he planned to record out of the way, even though engineer Rob Fraboni recalls that first Friday session being scheduled simply 'to get set up and to get a feel for the studio.' As well as jamming out on an instrumental called 'Crosswind Jamboree' and a reconfigured 'House of the Rising Sun,' Dylan and the same four-piece that had shared the Big Pink basement, in another lifetime, managed to cut the album version of 'Never Say Goodbye' and good takes of 'Forever Young' and 'Nobody 'Cept You.'

However, the meat of the matter would have to await Helm's presence the following Monday, at which point the sessions began in earnest. Though Dylan never returned to 'Never Say Goodbye,' the other two June demos would eat up more than their fair share of tape, without ever being realized quite the way Dylan had in mind. 'Nobody 'Cept You' occupied most of the second Monday session—by which point Robertson had thankfully put away the wah-wah pedal he'd applied in dollops over the Friday recording (released on *The Bootleg Series*)—but never lent itself to an electric arrangement and ended up being cast aside (though, in an acoustic guise, it would be a highlight of the 1974 tour).

'Forever Young' was something else. It was an important statement for Dylan, an attempt to write something hymnal and heartfelt that spoke of the father in him. It would occupy large chunks of studio time over four of the five remaining sessions. But the more he recorded the song, the less sure he was that he and the Band were bringing it into focus. On the second weekend—after cutting some seven tracks with the five-piece Band, during four days of sessions—Dylan recorded the song acoustically, at what was planned as the final session for the album. He told Fraboni that afternoon, 'I been carrying this song around in my head for five years and I never wrote it down and now I come to record it I just can't decide how to do it.' In fact, Dylan had recorded a beautiful slow waltz of a performance the previous night, with the Band slipping unobtrusively into the groove after a couple of false starts, but his new-found inner insecurity in the studio was fed by one particularly dumb broad his childhood chum, Louis Kemp, had brought along to the session.

Rob Fraboni: We only did one take of the slow version of 'Forever Young.' This take was so riveting, it was so powerful, so immediate, I couldn't get over it. When everyone came in nobody really said anything. I rewound the tape and played it back and everybody listened to it from beginning to end and then when it was over everybody sort of just wandered out of the room. There was no outward discussion. Everybody just left. There was just [a friend] and I sitting there. I was so overwhelmed I said, 'Let's go for a walk.' We went for a walk and came back and I said, 'Let's go listen to that again.' We were like one minute or two into it, I was so mesmerized by it again I didn't even notice that Bob had come into the room and I felt somebody standing behind me. I turned and I said, 'Where were you?' He said, 'I went to a movie across the street.' So when we were assembling the master reel I was getting ready to put that [take] on the master reel. I didn't even ask. And Bob said, 'What're you doing with that? We're not gonna use that.' And I jumped up and said, 'What do you mean you're not gonna use that? You're crazy! Why?' Well, [it turns out] during the recording . . . Lou Kemp and this girl came by and she had made a crack [about 'Forever Young'] to him, 'C'mon, Bob, what! Are you getting mushy in your old age?' It was based on her comment that he wanted to leave [that version] off the record.

Only when Fraboni refused to back down did Dylan decide to give preference to his engineer's ears over those of Kemp's lady friend. If 'Forever Young' was already old, the half a dozen songs written leading up to the sessions clearly suggested a man psychologically preparing to confront his public for the first time since he blew a gasket on a country back road. 'Tough Mama,' which features one of his raunchiest vocals, found him cavorting with his muse for the first time in quite a while. However, the song which came in for the most intense speculation from those seeking to connect Dylan's art with his life was recorded solo, the Saturday he attempted an acoustic 'Forever Young.' It was called simply 'Wedding Song.'

Rob Fraboni: We were assembling . . . around noon. Bob said, 'I've got a song I want to record later,' and I said, 'Fine.' He said, 'I'm not ready right now. I'll tell you when.' We were doing what we were doing, and all of a sudden he came up and said, 'Let's record.' So he went out in the studio, and that was 'Wedding Song' . . . Usually he wouldn't sing unless we were recording. That's the way he was. You couldn't get him to go out and just sing, unless he was running something down with the Band . . . [This time] he asked, 'Is the tape rolling? Why don't you just roll it?' So I did, and he started singing, and there was no way in the world I could have stopped him to say, 'Go back to the top.' It was such an intense performance. If you listen to the record, you can hear noises from the buttons on his jacket. But he didn't seem to care . . . I mentioned recutting it to eliminate the button sounds, at one point, and Bob said, 'Well, maybe.'

Though it was not in fact the culmination of the sessions, 'Wedding Song' was clearly written as the album closer. It begins with the narrator attempting to convince his lady love that he loves her 'more than life itself'—'pledg[ing] his love by outbidding every other love song claim ever,' to quote Simon Frith—in what was a clear return to 'Nobody 'Cept You' territory. The references to babies and saving his life suggested a very direct connection to Dylan's own life and wife. However, the focus begins to turn when he informs her, 'we can't regain what went down in the flood,' suggesting that their search for a new Eden was always doomed to failure. By the sixth verse we have come to the crux of the song—the singer's protestation that he does not wish 'to remake the world at large,' because he loves her 'more than all of that'. Clearly this was a plea for his wife to accept his decision to go out on the road again.

If 'Wedding Song' was the first parting address to his wife, 'Dirge'— the last song to be recorded for the album—was a pre-tour address to his audience. Both songs seem to have been penned over the course of the sessions. Though Fraboni believes that 'we had recorded a version [of "Dirge"] with only acoustic guitar and vocal a few days earlier,' the studio sheets list no such take, and Dylan went to the trouble of recalling the Band—six days after their part in the sessions had 'formally' ended— to attempt yet another rearrangement of 'Forever Young,' with Robertson playing mandolin and Danko on fiddle, and to record the song listed on the tape box as 'Dirge for Martha.' Even though Dylan had decided to place two alternative 'Forever Youngs' back to back, and omit the now abandoned 'Nobody 'Cept You,' the album needed at least one more song—not that 'Dirge' reads as one of Dylan's written-to-order efforts. He reserved the most possessed vocal of the album for this, his most twisted song since the accident. He also decided that a sparse arrangement would keep the emphasis roundly on the words.

Rob Fraboni: Bob went out and played the piano while we were mixing [the album]. All of a sudden, he came in and said, 'I'd like to try "Dirge" on the piano.' . . . We put up a tape and he said to Robbie, 'Maybe you could play guitar on this.' They did it once, Bob playing piano and singing, and Robbie playing acoustic guitar. The second time was the take.

Whether or not Martha was ever a real muse, her 'Dirge' represents a quite astonishing catharsis on Dylan's part. As the narrator expresses an underlying hatred for 'the need that was expressed' by her presence, he encapsulates all the ambivalence this popular artist felt for both muse and audience. Though the imagery was not as finely honed as he would manage on his next album, 'Dirge' came in for much praise at the time of the album's release. It also provided further proof that nobody played piano like Dylan. Sadly, few took either 'Dirge' or *Planet Waves* at face value, though *The New Yorker*'s Ellen Willis managed to tell it like it is:

Planet Waves is unlike all other Dylan albums: it is openly personal . . . I think the subject of *Planet Waves* is what it appears to be—Dylan's aesthetic and practical dilemma, and his immense emotional debt to Sara.

Later, as the subsequent tour faded from memory, some critics even began to question the worth of *Planet Waves*. A predictably disparaging Dave Marsh expressed the hope that 'he writes an album about the tour that illuminates something beyond his joyous domesticity . . . it just isn't interesting.' Surprisingly, several thought the album a disappointment after the 'promise' of *New Morning*, few seeing it as 'the bridge building effort' that *Let It Rock*'s Mick Gold recognized it for. The sheer quality of the musical interplay, and Dylan's return to a strongly melodic vocal style for the first time since *John Wesley Harding*, generated almost no comment. Nor did many critics praise the directness of his lyrics, as Willis had chosen to do.

Robbie Robertson: *Planet Waves* was as good as we could make it in the situation . . . he really didn't have a bag of songs there so it was just a last-minute thing . . . Under those circumstances, I thought it was extraordinary . . . But it wasn't an appropriate Bob Dylan album, that's what the problem was, and it wasn't superunusual, so it got a different kind of credit. People put so much weight on the words that it really limited that album. All those songs . . . [were] as simple as he's ever done, and people just thought it wasn't a real effort.

Planet Waves itself not only passed most critics by, but seemed almost incidental to many so-called fans, wrapped up in the euphoria surrounding the 1974 tour. Despite 'Shipping Gold,' shooting to number one—his first in the US—on the basis of advance orders, it only sold a disappointing six hundred thousand copies. Dylan found this very hard to equate with the $92 million of ticket orders from around ten million applicants for the tour, even though part of this was down to his last-minute decisions to change the album title (from *Ceremonies of the Horsemen*) and to substitute some as-yet-uncomposed sleeve notes, his first since *John Wesley Harding*, which pushed the album's release back from the opening night of the tour to two weeks in.

The delay could have cost David Geffen, whose Asylum label was stamped across all these *Planet Waves*, a pretty penny in pulped plastic. If the word on the early shows had been less than laudatory, he stood to catch a serious financial cold. As it was, he was operating almost at a loss on the venture. Though Geffen went around proclaiming that he'd given Dylan no advance for the album, he had apparently offered him, in Richard Goldstein's choice phrase, 'a higher profits percentage than I got on my bar mitzvah gifts,' an unprecedented eighty cents an album. Unfortunately for Dylan, having forsaken a four-hundred-thousand-dollar advance per album from CBS, he found that the inexplicably high returns insured he was no better off. The one advantage for Dylan from the deal cut, which was not finalized until December 6, was that he retained all rights to the master, Geffen effectively leasing the album for seven years.

Part of Dylan's bemusement undoubtedly stemmed from the surprising success of CBS's own churlish response to his departure from the label, *Dylan*, an album of outtakes from *Self Portrait* and *New Morning*, comprising only covers, which sailed surprisingly high in the *Billboard* charts (peaking at number seventeen). But then, Columbia had managed to get their album out a week before the December 1 announcement that Dylan and the Band would be venturing out on a forty-date, twenty-one-city tour, starting January 3, 1974, when the stakes had yet to be confirmed by press and pundits. It is difficult now to conceive of the risk Dylan was taking by touring with the Band in 1974. This was testing the water by jumping in head first. A syndicated article by Lynn Van Matre, voicing the fears of many, appeared the week he opened in Chicago:

Dylan will always sell no matter what he does—or doesn't—have to say, or how he says it. The memories are there, and it is the memories and the mystique that spurred millions of ticket requests on this long-awaited tour.

What sort of musical [sic] Dylan takes to the stage remains to be seen and heard . . . There is always something fascinating about watching a performer try to live up to his legend and emerge stronger than his mystique. There is generally something depressing about it as well . . . Whether or not the clock of Dylan's creativity has ticked out all this time is the question.

The statistics for the 1974 tour remain remarkable—even in an era when the most banal country-rock combo can command $150 a ticket to replicate their greatest-hits CD in the flesh, so to speak. An unprecedented top-dollar ticket price of $9.50 led to 5.5 million pieces of mail, applying for up to four tickets each, some $92 million in check and money orders, sent by close to 4 percent of the American population.

Bob Dylan: It wasn't a tour where a bunch of guys get together and say, let's go out and play. There was a great demand for that tour and it had been building up, so we went out and did it. You know, we were playin' at that point three, four nights at Madison Square Garden and three, four nights at the Boston Garden but what justified that? We hadn't made any records. When we were playin' out there earlier in the era we weren't drawing crowds like that. [1989]

The last thing he had wanted was this level of media interest, and the crushing burden of expectation it carried in its wake. The painfully shy, diffident side of Dylan felt nothing but embarrassment. The confidence of youth had been replaced by a self-consciousness that he now needed to overcome.

Arthur Rosato: When we did a rehearsal pre-tour, at the Coliseum (*sic*) in LA, Bob is on the court with the basketball, and he's trying to look like a basketball player, and he's not that tall and not that good. In his socks, he's trying to look like he knows what he's doing, but he doesn't. [And it suddenly struck me,] this guy is *so* self-conscious.

Though Dylan and the Band had rehearsed for two whole days between Christmas and New Year at the cavernous Inglewood Forum in LA, ideal preparation for touring around such chambers of acoustical horrors, Levon Helm admits, in his autobiography, that '[we] felt very unready when we hit Chicago.' Dylan's own frame of mind was conveyed by a piece of writing he decided to place in at least six hundred thousand pairs of hands, the poem scrawled across the back of his latest album (and then omitted from both *Lyrics* and the CD reissue): 'I lit out for parts unknown, found Jacob's ladder up against an adobe wall & bought a serpent from a passing angel.'

The notes, finished 'for the last time' on New Year's Eve, were Dylan's first thoughts in a sketchbook he had bought with the express intent of keeping a diary, in words and images, of the road ahead. He would dub the exercise book *A Book of Dreams,* perhaps a knowing nod at Peter Reich's autobiography. Though Dylan would only sparingly record his feelings out on the road, the day of the opening show he observed that he had outlived both Billy the Kid and Jesus, two of his favorite outlaws, but that it had taken its toll. He also wondered whether he still had the will to succeed, before deciding he was better off not allowing such self-doubts to bother him.

On January 3, 1974, Dylan and the Band opened their first tour in seven long years and two hundred days at Chicago Stadium, in front of 18,500 fans. Deliberately opening away from the coasts, Dylan did not succeed in dissuading a single major daily or weekly publication in America from sending a representative. Nor did his typically perverse decision to open with a rollicking rendition of the unreleased, and ultra-obscure, 1962 composition 'Hero Blues'—its new lyrics, announcing a singer 'walking down the highway just as fast as I can go,' largely trapped in the stadium's tin rafters—succeed in fazing the fans.

The two-hour opening show attempted to interleave the Band's songs with Dylan's own. Indeed, for the only time on the tour, Dylan became briefly just another Band member, playing harmonica on Manuel's tour de force, 'Share Your Love.' However, the general consensus, at show's end, was that it didn't work, and the set reverted to a format favored for the remainder of the tour—six-song Dylan/Band set, five-song Band set, three more Dylan/Band songs, five-song Dylan acoustic set, three/four-song Band set, joint finale. The choice of songs, after that surprising opening salvo, was predictable, and became more so as the tour wore on.

Though Dylan was asked by *Rolling Stone*'s Ben Fong-Torres, a week into the tour, about the lack of songs from *Self Portrait* and *New Morning,* and was reassured that 'we'll do some from *New Morning,*' the only post-accident, pre-*Planet Waves* material played on all forty dates were nightly excursions for a whorehouse-holler of a 'Lay, Lady, Lay,' a heavily Hendrixized 'All Along the Watchtower,' and a three-verse 'Knockin' on Heaven's Door.' The shows were almost entirely a leisurely stroll through nostalgiaville. As Nat Hentoff noted, 'Dylan's sound and beat are of the past . . . the gestalt is anachronistic.' Even the *Planet Waves* songs that cropped up at the early shows—'Tough Mama', 'Something

There Is About You,' 'Wedding Song,' and a riveting 'Nobody 'Cept You'—were dropped, leaving 'Forever Young' a lonely orphan at the later shows, something that cannot have helped ship all those boxes of the new album out of the warehouse and into the shops. But then, in the seven and a half years that Dylan had been out of the loop, his audience had also elected to buy into the American Dream:

Lucian K. Truscott IV: The crowds came dressed shabbily, elegantly, all the ways that people who can afford the choice turn themselves out. They lit up $40-an-ounce grass, snorted $75-a-gram coke, flashed gold rings and fancy platform boots, wore prefaded jeans and enough Indian jewelry to have bought Wounded Knee, snapped pictures with the most expensive photographic equipment money can buy, and shelled out upwards of $100 to scalpers for tickets. *This* was not a crowd without a home.

Dylan recognized the sea change. In his diary, he wrote about the encore for the third show, in Philadelphia. He had had the house lights turned up and put his glasses on to see the crowd—something he rarely did, preferring the batlike blur his chronic nearsightedness normally induced—and he did not like what he saw! Not that the fans weren't enjoying the shows, which were being extraordinarily well received. The acoustic set in particular was invariably met with a scattershot of whoops and a volley of cheers at every stop, especially when he sang the prophetic line from 'It's Alright Ma,' 'Even the president of the United States sometimes must have to stand naked.' As the Watergate scandal reached critical mass, it seemed that songs composed a decade ago had retained their political resonance.

But still some had harbored hopes that Dylan's ascension to the arenas of America might somehow psychically reignite the flames of social change. It was now clear that the moment Greil Marcus defined, when 'Bob Dylan seemed less to occupy a turning point in cultural space and time than to be that turning point,' had passed. This was just a rock & roll show.

If Dylan proved surprisingly willing to cater to a nascent nostalgia for a decade barely four years past, the one aspect of the shows that worked against a series of benign flashbacks was his voice, which generated its own degree of controversy. Though Fong-Torres's initial posting for *Rolling Stone* from Chicago suggested 'the voice was reminiscent of *Highway 61*, the transitional rock voice, with less of the harshness, more of the confidence,' critics at later shows were less kind. Lucian K. Truscott IV, when he caught Dylan working his way through 'Just Like Tom

Thumb's Blues' at the first New York show, recognized a man who 'refused to allow the song to carry him as much as he carried the song. He would not plumb the lyrics for the experiences, feelings, and ideas that gave it birth, allowing them to bring the song back to life.' Mimi Farina, who attended the Oakland show with her sister, heard 'a branch of that old nastiness coming through, by the intonation of his voice.'

Perhaps Mimi really did hear some nastiness in the way Dylan spat out 'The past is gone' during the afternoon performance of 'Wedding Song.' Perhaps something had caused him to re-evaluate the song's mawkish sentiments. Or maybe Mimi simply caught a particularly jaded Dylan. After all, the Oakland shows were the last shows before the LA finale, by which point he was so drained that, when his old sidekick Bobby Neuwirth introduced him to a truck driver named Bob Gardner after the final show, Gardner told his companion, 'He had the same look on his face as I remember seeing on Bobby Kennedy's face in 1968 when he came through Kentucky.' Dylan himself wrote in his diary that, though he felt the last three shows were all good, he had done them on little sleep. What he chose not to record in his *Book of Dreams* was the reason for the sleepless night he'd spent before the Oakland show.

Ellen Bernstein: I was working for Columbia. I was running the A&R office in San Francisco . . . I was living at Sausalito in a really great place, beautiful view, and Bill Graham had a party at the Trident for Bob—I had lived with Bill for, like, a year and a half—the Trident was the quintessential flower-child restaurant, all these beautiful waitresses, everybody was beautiful. There were more beautiful women there than I've ever seen at any party, every gorgeous woman in Marin County was there. I remember getting a little bit drunk, not like plastered, and he kinda appeared, sitting next to me. And I was a little out of it—I started talking with someone who was talking to me—[but] I wasn't so out of it that it didn't dawn on me that this was Dylan. The next thing that happened we were walking up to my house, which was up the hill, and we stayed up all night playing back-gammon. He was much funnier than I thought he would be, a really good backgammon player. I was a single twenty-four-year-old girl. The attention was very flattering. The next day was the concert at Oakland, and we['d] literally stayed up all night, so I couldn't figure out how he was going to play a concert, but he said, 'You should come. Be with me at the show tonight.' It was fantastic, and I can't remember the hotel, but I went back there. They left the next day.

Save for a solitary reference to a banker's niece in St. Louis in his diary, there is no evidence that Dylan hadn't previously been a good boy on the tour, even if Richard Manuel's insistence on members of the crew taking Polaroids of the groupies before they were allowed backstage ensured an appropriately high standard of starfucker, to cop a phrase. Sara had even surprised Dylan one afternoon in Houston, flying in from LA to remind him of the benefits of connubial bliss, as well as taking the opportunity to share some thoughts and feelings. But Ellen represented Sara's worst fear. She was no groupie, just a young, vital, beautiful, intelligent girl. And though Ellen figured she would not hear from Dylan again, in this she was assuredly mistaken.

Flying down from Oakland to Los Angeles on February 12th, Dylan must have been pleased with the way the tour had gone. He had caught up with many an old friend, from the Gleasons and Mike Porco in New York to Ronnie Hawkins in Toronto, even Victor Maymudes, who had appeared in a snowstorm in Denver in a large white coat. And he was returning now to the starting point, the LA Forum, for three shows, to be recorded for the inevitable live album.

The decision to release a live album seems to have been made before the tour. This was Dylan's first tour since the advent of bootlegging, and, as the reluctant father of the other record industry, he could be assured that the bootleggers would be out in force. Sure enough, fourteen bootleg albums, culled from eleven gigs, sought to document the shows. Though it would satiate most fans' desire for a memento, an official album was not about to quell the demands of obsessives. Not that the serious collector wasn't entitled to seek out recordings of the earlier shows, which featured a more balanced set and less theatrical vocals. Unfortunately the LA shows, from which all but one of the songs on *Before the Flood* were to come, featured a Dylan singing with 'just full-out power,' something hindsight alone brought home to him.

Bob Dylan: When [Elvis] did 'That's All Right, Mama' in 1955, it was sensitivity and power. In 1969, it was just full-out power. There was nothing other than just force behind that. I've fallen into that trap, too. Take the 1974 tour. It's a very fine line you have to walk to stay in touch with something once you've created it . . . Either it holds up for you or it doesn't. [1980]

The one exception at the final show—from which the bulk of the live album came—was an audacious electric arrangement of 'Mr. Tambourine Man' with Garth Hudson on accordion, presumably played for Sara's benefit, since it was her favorite song. Sara must have been mightily relieved when she was reunited with her husband in Los Angeles for those final shows, taking his arm for a final post-tour party at the Forum Club on the evening of the 14th before accompanying him to the Beverly Wilshire Hotel for a more intimate gathering early the next morning. Having hauled himself to the marketplace one more time, Dylan had seemingly returned to the fold.

Dylan seems to have been as relieved as his wife to have got through the tour. As he later recalled, 'From the first moment I walked onstage at the opening concert, I knew that going through with the tour would be the hardest thing I had ever done . . . The problem was that everyone had his own idea of what the tour was about. Everybody had a piece of the action . . . I had no control over what was going on.' Well, perhaps it was all gonna work out fine, for Dylan, if not for an exhausted and dispirited Geffen, whom he visited the morning after the final show. At least he had proved to himself that he could still do it and, if he was going to get up and do it again, he no longer felt like he needed to call on his disciples, the Band.

Arthur Rosato: It was the most magical tour, but it was personalities. 'Stage Fright' was a little poke at Bob . . . All those years he played with Robbie, he never showed [Dylan] anything. He always turned his back [onstage], so you could never see what Robbie was playing . . . By the end of that tour there was a little separation. By that time Bob was kinda figuring out what he wanted to do.

For the Band, too, it made no sense to repeat the exercise. As Helm observed in his autobiography, 'the tour was damn good for our pocket-books, but it just wasn't a very passionate trip for any of us.' Even if this time 'they were more than a backing band,' it was time for the Band to forge their own path back to former glories, following them northern lights.

As he looked through the photos his old friend Barry Feinstein had taken on the tour, up in his home studio in Malibu, winding down from the nightly adrenaline charge, Dylan began to ask himself whether he was really back where he started, or whether perhaps it was still his duty to remake the world in some small way. Coming to the end of his book of dreams, he concluded that perhaps he *was* the Messenger, after all.

1974–75: Spring Turns Slowly to Autumn

21

A lot of people thought . . . that album, *Blood on the Tracks*, pertained to me . . . [but] I don't write confessional songs.

—*Bob Dylan, 1985*

Despite the naysayers, *Planet Waves* and the 1974 tour were certainly greeted as some kind of Grand Return. It required a shift in the matrix by Dylan himself to make hindsight a crueler instrument. Only when he truly painted his masterpiece were many able to assign the previous five albums their proper place in the canon. To those closest to him, the conclusion of the 1974 tour must have seemed like the end of a period of frenetic activity. In truth, it was the beginning of the end of something— Dylan's marriage. Whatever air had been cleared between Sara and Bob in the stuffy Houston hotel, the presence of a new woman in Dylan's life suggested a man still looking for room to breathe. By the time he reconnected with Ellen, Sara had seemingly already moved out of their house.

Ellen Bernstein: I heard from him fairly quickly, about a week or so later. He would come up and visit me. I would come down and visit him. He had a house in Malibu Canyon that didn't have much in it, some mattresses. This big house, but it was like a crash pad.

Meanwhile, as Rob Fraboni and Phil Ramone edited down the multitracks accumulated from New York, Seattle, Oakland, and Los Angeles into a double-album souvenir of the tour, Geffen attempted to take the moral high ground, seeking to remind Dylan of an obligation to release the album of the tour on the label that had supported him throughout. Though Dylan had attended a very showbizzy thirty-first birthday party for Geffen at the Beverly Wilshire Hotel a week after tour's end, even serenading him with a solo 'Mr. Tambourine Man,' he remained a man capable of separating business from his personal life.

Dylan had hit upon the idea of selling the album by mail order, using a TV campaign. Given that he stood to make three to four times more

Bob riffles through another record collection, January 1962.

Opposite: 'I heard ya—ya booed!' Newport Festival, July 25, 1965.

Above: 'Man, I'm not even twenty-five!' Paris airport, May 23, 1966.

Bob goes for a stroll backstage at the Isle of Wight, August 1969.

Top: 'And I can't even read a note!' Bob with
Dave Amram at the Songwriters' Hall of Fame, March 1982.
Bottom: A portrait, 1983.

Above: Bob ponders his future, August 1985.

Opposite: Tom Petty and Bobby D. on the verge of True Confessions, April 1986.

Bob meets the Pope barely four months after nearly meeting his Maker.

per disk than he could make through Geffen's operation, the idea had obvious attractions. Eventually he realized that such a scheme would require a whole marketing apparatus for it to succeed. But Geffen again ended up paying over the odds for what was, after all, the sort of album record companies usually *excluded* from their contractual tally, and Dylan had found an extra way to shake the moneymaker. The contract for *Before the Flood* was not signed until May 6, just six weeks before the album appeared in the racks, to mixed reviews, peaking at number seven on the Hot Hundred, a very high placing for a live double album, but some way short of *Planet Waves*, let alone *Frampton Comes Alive*. The side and a half of cold cuts from the Band probably helped consign it to life among the cutouts.

The day Dylan signed on the dotted line, he was in New York, having flown there at the end of April. He had already been seen scouting around the Village, trying to get a sense of the scene. Even through the 'amnesia,' he had maintained a rapacious interest in what was happening in the live music scene, particularly those singer-songwriters who had emerged from his own shadow (the first act he caught that spring was Buffy Sainte-Marie, performing at the Bottom Line). Returning from his lawyer's office, he ran into Phil Ochs, who was desperately trying to arrange a benefit for the recently ousted socialist government in Chile at the Felt Forum, part of the Madison Square Garden complex.

With fifty-five hundred seats to fill, and the same ol' stable of folk revivalists stuck in a time loop on the bill, Ochs was having a serious problem selling out such a large venue. Dylan was the answer to his prayers. After plying the troubled troubadour with some Beaujolais, Ochs gave him a hard sell about the plight of the Chileans, and in a typical shake-on-it kinda way, Dylan agreed to appear at the benefit three days hence. Ochs immediately went on WBAI and announced that Dylan was appearing, selling the show out in hours.

Fortunately for Ochs, Dylan honored his promise, arriving anonymously enough, acoustic guitar in hand, well ahead of time, to pass the hours drinking wine and chatting with old friends like Dave Van Ronk, Pete Seeger, and Arlo Guthrie. Remembering the old days, he proceeded to get in the kind of state he used to have to, just to get up on stage. By the time it was his turn, he could barely stand, let alone sing. Declaiming a set he could easily have sung at Gerde's—one Guthrie song ('Deportees'), one traditional tune ('Spanish Is the Loving Tongue'), and one of his early efforts ('North Country Blues')—he finally excused himself after a communal 'Blowin' in the Wind.' Ochs, though, had pulled off his last great coup, even if it affected the situation in Chile not a jot.

Though nobody seems quite sure why Dylan was in town that spring, it would appear that he had come to New York to look somebody up, an art teacher named Norman Raeben, on the recommendation of some friends in California. He had continued to work on his painting and, at this point, was more concerned with refining that aspect of his art than dealing with any inner calling. Ironically, Raeben would prove to be the man who would teach him to 'do consciously what I used to do unconsciously' when it came to a form he genuinely excelled in—the power of words.

Bob Dylan: [Some friends] were talking about truth and love and beauty, and all these words I had heard for years, and they had 'em all defined . . . I asked them, 'Where do you come up with all those definitions?' and they told me about this teacher. I made a point to look him up the next time I was in New York, which was in the spring of 1974. I just dropped [in] to see him one day and I wound up staying there for two months . . . Five days a week I used to go up there, and I'd just think about it the other two days of the week. I used to be up there from eight o'clock to four. That's all I did for two months. He was a painter . . . He came to this country in 1930 and he made his living boxing. He's a big guy. And then he started making his living painting portraits, but in the thirties in France he roomed with Soutine, the painter. He knew people like Modigliani inti-mately . . . Anyway he didn't teach you how to paint so much. He didn't teach you how to draw. He didn't teach you any of these things. He taught you [about] putting your head and your mind and your eye together—to make you get down visually something which is actual . . . He looked into you and told you what you were . . . My mind and my hand and my eye were not connected up. I had a lot of fantasy dreams. He doesn't respect fantasy. He respects only imagination . . . In this class there would be people like old ladies—rich old ladies from Florida—standing next to an off-duty policeman, standing next to a bus driver, a lawyer, just all kinds. Some art student who had been kicked out of every art university. Young girls who worshiped him . . . Needless to say it changed me. I went home after that and my wife never did understand me ever since that day. That's when our marriage started breaking up. She never knew what I was talking about, what I was thinking about, and I couldn't possibly explain it. [1978]

Dylan paints a very idealized portrait of Raeben, who never roomed with Soutinen nor was intimate with Modigliani. Raeben, on the other hand, never held him in particularly high esteem. To him, he was just another pupil, and a particularly idiotic one at that, as one of Raeben's ex-students recalled during a WBAI special on Dylan in 1986:

Norman Raeben . . . used to call everybody an idiot because they couldn't see the nose on their face. They couldn't understand that it was a shadow and a light put together . . . He called Dylan an idiot all the time, and Dylan stayed for about six months [sic], and [then] took off . . . Never said a word to any of us and just left. But he took a lot from Norman.

Dylan would be the first to agree that he took 'a lot from Norman.' In 1978, he would talk at great length about his time with Raeben, having finally decided that Sara 'never knew . . . what I was thinking about,' and having taken some of Raeben's ideas and placed them in a film of his own making, the much-maligned *Renaldo and Clara*. Both that film and the two albums that precede it share a fascination with identities that stems as much from Raeben as Dylan.

Bob Dylan: [My time with Raeben] locked me into the present time more than anything else I ever did . . . I was constantly being intermingled with myself, and all the different selves that were in there, until this one left, then that one left, and I finally got down to the one that I was familiar with. [1978]

The one he was familiar with was a more self-conscious version of the old Dylan. As the amnesia passed, he found himself writing a flurry of songs that had 'no sense of time.' Throughout the summer he applied techniques he had learned from Raeben, techniques primarily intended for use on canvas, in a little red notebook. The results were unlike anything he had attempted before—revealing portraits of the artist as a mature man.

Bob Dylan: [Norman Raeben] taught me how to see . . . in a way that allowed me to do consciously what I unconsciously felt. And I didn't know how to pull it off. I wasn't sure it could be done in songs because I'd never written a song like that. But when I started doing it, the first album I made was *Blood on the Tracks*. Everybody agrees that that was pretty different, and what's different about it is there's a code in the lyrics, and also there's no sense of time. [1978]

Though Dylan has not always wanted to make it clear what prompts him to reinvent himself, the songs have always spoken for him. Because his albums, with only a couple of exceptions, have always been intended to stand as a totality (the main reason why compilations fail to replicate their impact), there is usually one song that sits astride, rattling the keys to the kingdom. Though it need not be the most realized composition on the album, the other songs take their points of reference from it. On *Bringing It All Back Home*, 'Mr. Tambourine Man' gave depth to Dylan's chains of flashing images; 'Like a Rolling Stone' took the man down *Highway 61;* and 'Visions of Johanna' applied blonde to blonde. As it happens, we know that these songs were starting points for each of those albums, chronologically *and* conceptually.

For *Blood on the Tracks* there are clues, but no hard facts, to confirm my confidence that 'Tangled Up in Blue' was the song that opened up his new album all the way. Dylan himself has said it was a song that took him ten years to live and two years to write. It is also the second of seventeen songs he wrote into the notebook that summer, prefaced only by a not-quite-realized 'Lily, Rosemary and the Jack of Hearts.' Though 'Lily, Rosemary and the Jack of Hearts' shares with 'Tangled Up in Blue' a delight in playing with identities, it exists unto itself, the one vision on *Blood on the Tracks* its narrator painted whole (at one point Dylan even had discussions with Jonathan Taplin about realizing this ballad visually on the big screen). On the other hand, 'Tangled Up in Blue' could have been given a full-length movie to be disentangled, and even then the images themselves would not have added up to more than the sum of the parts, as 'Tangled Up in Blue' so clearly does.

Bob Dylan: 'Tangled Up in Blue' . . . was another one of those things where I was trying to do something that I didn't think had ever been done before. In terms of trying to tell a story and be a present character in it without it being some kind of fake, sappy attempted tearjerker. I was trying to be somebody in the present time, while conjuring up a lot of past images. I was trying to do it in a conscious way. I used to be able to do it in an unconscious way, but I just wasn't into it that way anymore . . . See, what I was trying to do had nothing to do with the characters or what was going on. I was trying to do something that I don't know if I was prepared to do. I wanted to defy time, so that the story took place in the present and the past at the same time. When you look at a painting, you can see any part of it, or see all of it together. I wanted that song to be like a painting. [1985]

Once again Dylan was utilizing images in a completely original way, whether it was Rimbaud or something as lodged in his subconscious as Fred Astaire ripping gay divorcée Ginger Rogers's dress when trying to 'help her out of a jam.' On a set of songs that, at points, embraces Verlaine and Rimbaud, Woody Guthrie, Jesus Christ, Bonnie and Clyde, Tom Paxton, the Magician, Robert Johnson, and Astaire and Rogers, he created so much more than an album of songs about Suze Rotolo ('Simple Twist of Fate'), Ellen Bernstein ('You're Gonna Make Me Lonesome When You Go'), Sara Lowndes, and himself.

After two and a half months in New York, Dylan had flown to Minnesota, to once again be in the company of Ellen. This time, though, they were sharing their downtime with his own children, a significant step forward in the relationship, even if Ellen wisely continued to take the whole affair as it came. Jesse, aged eight, and Anna, aged seven, must have been disconcerted by the absence of their mother, something alluded to in one of the 'lost' songs from this period, 'Call Letter Blues,' where the narrator has to tell his children, 'Mother took a trip.'

Ellen Bernstein: He wanted me to come to Minnesota . . . this was when all the kids were little, running around like little children. [Marie] wasn't there. I would cook and we would run around. He was at his best there, at his most comfortable, with his brother's house down the road. He had a painting studio out in the field, and the house was far from fancy, out in the middle of nowhere. He was very relaxed, and that's where and when he was writing *Blood on the Tracks*.

Despite the very obvious pain that comes through in the songs—the pain of separation from a wife for whom he clearly still carried a torch—Ellen remembers this man on his farm as someone trying to remind himself what it felt like to be a normal human being, someone who liked to know whether his woman could 'cook or sow, make flowers grow.'

Ellen Bernstein: He was treating me very well and a very caring, loving person and lots of fun to be with so I didn't tend to sit around and analyze what his state of mind was, or why he was doing this stuff. I was much more involved in an appreciation of knowing someone who had that kind of ability to express himself, and how interesting it was to see it in process, and be a part of that process. I think that he's always in some measure of pain, being that creative. That kind of artistic genius goes hand-in-hand with demons . . . [But then] I think he is generally uncomfortable in his own skin. [And yet,] when he was on the farm, nobody [was] around . . . [who] was looking at him, or wanting from him, it was just me and the kids and his brother, in a state where he felt comfortable, with his paints and his guitar and some food. He would get so excited by my homemade granola.

I think I sewed him a black vest while I was there, and he just thought that was fantastic.

Of course, this 'ordinary man' also happened to be writing perhaps the finest collection of love songs of the twentieth century, songs filled with the full spectrum of emotions a marriage on the rocks can engender. But these songs were written when he was alone in his study, raking over the past. Only when he had a fully formed prototype for the song would he show it to Ellen, and invariably, by then, it had been copied into the little red notebook from the scraps of paper on which his initial thoughts had been sketched (the lyrics in the notebook, though still subject to change, were something more than first drafts).

Ellen Bernstein: He would do his writing early in the morning and then kinda materialize around midday, come downstairs and eventually, during the day, share what he had written. It was in the notebook, but he would play it, and ask me what I thought, and it was always different, every time, he would just change it and change it and change it. You definitely had this sense of a mind that never stopped.

The songs he was now writing certainly came from somewhere deep down in his soul. They also contained a whole other set of layers from the songs he had been writing. The symbolism was no longer merely evocative, it had a precision and internal consistency that even the songs from his amphetamine years lacked. And yet, ever determined to play dumb, he insisted on disconnecting himself from the songs' conception. When he finally completed 'Lily, Rosemary and the Jack of Hearts,' he told Ellen, 'Everyone's gonna wonder who the Jack of Hearts is. I have no idea who it is.' Presumably, Dylan would insist it was mere coincidence that the Jack of Hearts tallies so well with the attributes attached to the magician, the Magus, in A. E. Waite's tarot pack, and that this particular tarot pack—featured on the inner sleeve of Dylan's next album—paints the Magus surrounded by two flowers, the lily and the rose.

If Dylan has professed disdain for prosaic analysis, he has also delighted in leaving clues for literary sleuths. The one song on *Blood on the Tracks* addressed directly to Ellen, 'You're Gonna Make Me Lonesome When You Go,' even managed to mention the town where she was born, Ashtabula, along with a host of other references that were hers, and hers alone.

Ellen Bernstein: I remember . . . when we were walking out in the fields somewhere and I found a Queen Anne's lace, and he didn't know that that's what it was called . . . this was in Minnesota. I would come up there for long weekends and then I would leave. I did say I was planning a trip to Hawaii. And I lived in San Francisco. Honolulu, San Francisco, Ashtabula— to put it in a song is so ridiculous. But it was very touching.

One other song on the final album left a series of literary clues that its subject matter was not Sara, but a muse from another lifetime. 'Simple Twist of Fate', which took the singer back to the last time he had been struck down by such romantic anguish, when his affair with Suze had gone sour, may well be up his most beautiful remembrance of things past. In the notebook, he even gave the song a subtitle, 'Fourth Street Affair,' perhaps to reinforce a connection for those who couldn't recognize his reference to hunting 'for her by the waterfront docks.' But then the song lost its subtitle in the studio. For the fortunate few who saw him forget himself, one night in London in the summer of 1981, and sing about 'Suze, and the way that she talks,' it only made explicit what the sense of the song had always demanded.

But the songs to Ellen and Suze were mere refractions from the primary focus of his mind, the loss of his wife of nine years. Making such a public declaration of the pain the separation from his wife was causing him—particularly after placing half a dozen tributes to her on his last album—took a certain amount of inner strength. And yet, when the album was released and he did an interview for Mary Travers's radio show, he told her that he found it hard to understand how people could enjoy hearing that type of pain. But still he felt compelled to write about the breakup—allegorically on many of the songs on *Blood on the Tracks,* literally on several of the songs he discarded prior to any sessions—even if it became a subject *verboten* on the farm.

Ellen Bernstein: It felt sorta like, 'Don't ask, don't tell.' I was a very young twenty-four. I was not terribly sophisticated. This was brand-new stuff to me, so I never thought to ask, 'So what's going on with your wife?' . . . I didn't want to get married, and I wasn't being asked to leave.

As he bared his soul, Dylan knew that, when *Blood on the Tracks* was finally released, he would be allowing himself to be, for the first time, the subject of intense speculation about his personal relationships, most especially with his wife. Not that his problems entirely escaped the media, even as he prepared to document the breakup in song. On August 1,

Rolling Stone reported that 'Dylan is [apparently] furious over two gossip items—in two syndicated columns and on CBS-TV—about the breakup of his eight-year marriage.' The gossipmongers had managed to light on the wrong lady, Lorey Sebastian, former wife of John Sebastian, prompting Lorey to make a series of disclaimers, and prompting Dylan to write one of his most memorable opening couplets: 'Someone's got it in for me / They're planting stories in the press . . .'

If the songs Dylan was writing were filled with regret, kindled by remorse and tinged with sadness, there was one that showed the darker side of his marriage, a dirge on family, fame, and fortune. He may have moved from 4th Street, but this was positively the same man. 'Idiot Wind' began as Dylan's 'Ballad in Plain D' for the seventies, but unlike its predecessor, it was subjected to a number of wholesale changes, over a five-month period, turning it from being 'right on target, so direct' into an allegory on contemporary America seen through the eyes of two star-crossed lovers caught up in forces beyond their control, forces as imponderable as gravity and destiny.

Ellen Bernstein: ['Idiot Wind'] was one in particular that I remember changing a lot, whole verses would come and go . . . it was a real organic process for him.

In its original form it once again had that 'feeling . . . of reading someone else's mail,' Dylan even punning on his lack of sexual prowess, writing that he waited for his lover forever, and then she said that he came too fast. The insights into their relationship come thick and fast, but there is none of the epic sweep of the final song. It remains an exclusive song, for and about one woman, one relationship. In this room full of memories, there is no room for the listener, except as a voyeur, peeping through a lyrical keyhole. In this airless room, the narrator insists, it would be nice to work things out, but only if it's for love, rather than money. By the time he came to record the song in New York, he was telling her that if she wanted 'the best there is,' it was gonna cost her all her love—'You won't get it for money.' Seemingly already preoccupied by how much this separation was going to cost him, in the original draft he'd pulled up stakes and gone for broke. On the first recording, he simply shrugs and says, 'Why go on, what's the use?'

That original draft of 'Idiot Wind' was more of an outpouring than a lyric. If it is possible to build up a psychological profile from the order of the songs in the notebook, 'Idiot Wind' comes after the promise to change ('I swear') in 'You're a Big Girl Now' and the recognition of loss

('If you're makin' love to her / kiss her for the kid') in 'If You See Her, Say Hello,' but before the devil-may-care insouciance of 'Up to Me.' Of all the songs in the fabled notebook, 'Idiot Wind' alone was wholly rewritten *after* its inclusion in the notebook.

At the end of the notebook, after the seventeenth song of the summer, 'Little Bit of Rain' (a title copped from Fred Neil), Dylan starts again, and this time 'Idiot Wind' is suffused with some of his most poetic turns of phrase. The prophet, who had told him too much pride was a disease, is now lovesick. The blue strangers in the back room tell him where he's been (a reference to his 'amnesia'). The man packing up his uniform this time is silhouetted by a moon in Capricorn. The lyrics, though, in the words of Betsy Bowden, continue to 'express consistent resentment toward the sweet lady, the only hint of reconciliation or shared blame coming in the switch to first-person-plural pronouns for the last refrain.' This was a recognizable prototype for the song he would record in New York that September, though it would be but a second cousin to the song as released.

Though the notebook would join Dylan in New York, neither of the songs penned there, to complete the album, would find their way into its remaining pages. Before that trip, though, he wanted to try out these songs on some songwriters and musicians. On July 22, he played Stephen Stills and Tim Drummond at least half a dozen of the new songs. This solo session, in a room at the St. Paul Hilton Hotel, after a Crosby, Stills and Nash gig, was the first evidence that he had enough songs to record a new album. According to Tim Drummond, the new songs were of a very high quality.

Tim Drummond: Dylan's got an album. It's great . . . it's gutsy, bluesy, so authentic. I heard eight or nine new songs, and it's the first time I've sat in a room and liked everything I heard.

Of the seventeen songs written in the notebook, only ten would be recorded at the sessions proper. For the first time, Dylan was editing down his songs prior to starting work on an album, presumably basing his choices on those that felt right when he played them, or received the most positive response. Lyrically, the songs he discarded from the process were mostly light on insight and heavy on the reiterated wisdom of others.

Ellen Bernstein: I think, as he wrote the songs, and as he played them for people, the sequencing decided itself . . . He was really definite when he went in, he knew what he was going to do and he knew how he was going to do it.

Some of the lyrics in the notebook read more like alternative versions of the same template. Thus 'Belltower Blues' and 'Call Letter Blues' were kith and kin, based around the same twelve bars (and, eventually, would be superseded by another frequenter from the same bars, 'Meet Me in the Morning'). Indeed, the songs he was playing on his acoustic guitar already had a unity of sound, primarily because they had mostly been written in open E tuning. Most commonly found in Elmore James–style urban blues, this tuning suggested a very bluesy album. Thus when Dylan found himself staying at Ellen's Oakland home in August, he decided to take the opportunity to track down his old partner in classic recordings, Mike Bloomfield, with a view to asking him to accompany him into the studio. Unfortunately, rather than putting Bloomfield at ease and teaching him the songs, he preferred to compound the confusion his surprise appearance engendered by playing all these ballads in open E with nary a pause.

Michael Bloomfield: He came over and there was a whole lot of secrecy involved, there couldn't be anybody in the house. I wanted to tape the songs so I could learn them so I wouldn't fuck 'em up at the sessions . . . and he had this look on his face like I was trying to put out a bootleg album or something . . . He started playing the goddamn songs from *Blood on the Tracks* and I couldn't play, I couldn't follow them . . . There was this frozen guy there. It was very disconcerting . . . He took out his guitar, he tuned to open D [sic] tuning, and he started playing the songs nonstop! And he just played them all and I just sort of picked along with it . . . He was singing the whole thing and I was saying, 'No, man, don't sing the whole thing, just sing one chorus and if it's not gonna change, let me write it down so I can play with you.' And he didn't. He just kept on playing. He just did one after another, and I got lost. They all began to sound the same to me, they were all in the same key, they were all long. It was one of the strangest experiences of my life . . . He was sort of pissed off that I didn't pick it up . . . I just felt this big wall, this enormous barrier that was so tangible that there was no way you could say, 'Hey man, how are you? You getting much pussy? Drinking a lot still? How are your kids?'

On the trip to the Bay Area he seemed particularly anxious to play his songs, and Bloomfield was not alone in finding 'this enormous barrier' to the normal parameters of communication. Bluegrass picker Pete

Rowan, who had been fortunate enough to witness one of the *Blonde on Blonde* sessions, was another one treated to an impromptu private concert.

Pete Rowan: We went down to a private room and we took out my guitar and we traded songs, in this sort of music meditation room we had set up. He was playing all the songs from *Blood on the Tracks*. . . It was about three in the afternoon, we were sitting there, we both had dark glasses on. Neither one of us was going to take our dark glasses off. And we played there until finally the sun went down.

Ellen also took the opportunity to introduce Dylan to Shel Silverstein, one of his favourite country songwriters. Their visit to Silverstein's fairly luxurious houseboat culminated in Bob sitting down and playing him 'every song on *Blood on the Tracks*, every single one—and Shel loved it.' The fact that Dylan insisted on playing these word-rich love songs to Silverstein and Rowan, and initially wanted Eric Weissberg to embellish them, perhaps suggests that he originally conceived of an album with a country-blues feel. If so, Buddy Cage's pedal steel on a couple of the New York recordings is all that remains of that conceit.

The final dry run for the album came a couple of weeks after the Silverstein session, in Crown Heights, New York. By now, the songs Dylan had in mind to record were in place. He had flown to New York the second week in September to commence work on his second studio album in a year. Ellen was along, too, and not simply for the ride.

Ellen Bernstein: He was very interested in people's reaction to [the material]. When Bob and I went to New York to do *Blood on the Tracks* he wanted to go and visit this friend of his in some Hasidic neighborhood, I think it was Crown Heights . . . and we had to drive there, and he was driving and it was really scary. But he wanted to go and see this friend of his. We get lost, but finally we find this guy's house. We pull up into the driveway and there are several people sitting in the front yard, and this friend of his and his sister and his sister's husband, who happens to be my cousin! We go in and have a meal with this family of Hasidic Jews, this is when he was becoming fascinated with all of that. He found it really interesting. And after the meal we went out in the backyard and he played the songs for these friends of his—this group of Hasidic Jews. It was wonderful . . . But it was a real unusual experience to have before the recording of the album.

Ellen now found her Columbia employment brief being extended to helping her paramour complete his first album back in the fold. On

August 2, 1974, Columbia president Irwin Segelstein announced that Dylan had signed a 'long term contract' with Columbia at the CBS Annual Convention at the Century Plaza Hotel in LA. (The contract, which actually only required the delivery of three studio albums, would be fulfilled in less than a year.) Negotiations had been going on since early spring. At one point it even seemed that Columbia might secure the live album of the 1974 tour. Though Geffen was given that album as a sop, Dylan had clearly decided that—after reaffirming the demand for new product—he could now benefit from the sort of commercial muscle only a company the size of Columbia could offer.

He was also doubtless keen to insure that Columbia issued no more product like *Dylan,* their November 1973 'revenge' album. A cursory trawl through the vaults had in fact already been undertaken, early in 1974, with a view to further archival releases should the label's wayward son prefer to remain gone. But Columbia now pulled out all the stops to entice him to return, even reverting rights to previous album masters on the delivery of new product, another move on Dylan's part to gain control of his own work.

Though Ellen insists that she played no part in Dylan's decision, she now found herself playing liaison officer between Dylan and her employer. The sense that Dylan was taking one step back in order to make his latest quantum leap was reinforced by his choice of studio— A&R Studios in New York, better known as the old Studio A, where he had made six albums' worth of historic recordings a decade earlier. Its lack of cutting-edge technology was more than compensated for by its sense of space and incomparable acoustics.

Ellen Bernstein: The theme of returning ran through the sessions. The sound of the album was such a return that it made a lot of sense to do it [at A&R].

The first visitor at the sessions must have felt equally at home with his surroundings. John Hammond, Sr., popped in on the first day of the sessions to welcome Dylan back, and found a surprisingly relaxed Bob recording acoustically. He told Hammond, 'I want to lay down a whole bunch of tracks. I don't want to overdub. I want it easy and natural,' and, sure enough, the first day generated at least nine songs, of which six, according to the studio sheets, were recorded with Eric Weissberg and his band.

Larry Sloman, in his *Rolling Stone* report on the sessions, wrote that when Dylan entered the studio the first afternoon, September 16, he began recording solo, while his office attempted to track down Eric Weissberg, the renowned guitarist and banjo player whom Dylan had first met in Madison, Wisconsin, back in December 1960. When Weissberg finally answered his phone, the intermediary knew not which of the many instruments he played should be brought to the studio. When Weissberg arrived at A&R at six in the evening, he was no wiser as to what Dylan had in mind. When he asked Dylan whether he wanted his band, Deliverance, to come to the studio, he said, 'Sure, bring the whole band over.'

But then, once the five-piece arrived, Dylan again seemed determined to make things difficult. Just as Bloomfield had struggled to learn the new songs, so Weissberg, equally respected in his field, found Dylan's reluctance to explain the open tuning a major hindrance to the recording process. Perhaps, as at the Mexico City session in January 1973, 'he [just] wanted their first impressions.'

Eric Weissberg: It was weird. You couldn't really watch his fingers 'cause he was playing in a tuning arrangement I had never seen before. If it was anybody else I would have walked out. He put us at a real disadvantage. If it hadn't been that we liked the songs, and it was Bob, it would have been a drag. His talent overcomes a lot of stuff.

Weissberg remembers not only Dylan drinking a lot of wine, but that he seemed uninterested in 'correcting obvious mistakes.' Certainly, he refused to be fazed by something like the buttons on his jacket rattling against his guitar, as they do most audibly on both New York recordings of 'Tangled Up in Blue.'

Ellen Bernstein: There were certain ones where you can hear the sound of his fingernails on the guitar. That didn't matter to him. None of that stuff was important to him. What was important was the overall weight of the song.

Though he apparently attempted a number of songs with the full sound of Deliverance, they are only heard on a single cut on the album ('Meet Me in the Morning'). Dylan also attempted to record a couple of the songs he had been playing solo with a battery of acoustic guitars— even himself, Weissberg, and Charlie Brown attempted to pick their way through the original, open E tuning of 'Tangled Up in Blue' at the end of that first evening. If Weissberg was less than bowled over by the experiment, Brown seemed to recognize the reasoning behind Dylan's seat-of-the-pants approach.

Charlie Brown: He seemed to be having a good time. His whole concept of making an album seemed to be go ahead and play it and whichever way it comes out, well, that's the way it is. It's what happens at the moment. He didn't want to do a lot of takes, and I don't blame him 'cause some of the songs are so long. We'd just watch his hands and pray we had the right changes.

Dylan evidently felt that the session was not a great success, and given that he had already played this batch of songs more than anything he'd recorded since *The Times They Are A-Changin'*, he was keen to get them down on tape as effortlessly as possible. As Ellen says, 'He worked so instinctively, more so than anyone I've ever worked with.' And, in his heart of broken hearts, he knew that the songs needed paring down again. Accordingly, he requested that Deliverance bassist Tony Brown alone return for the subsequent sessions.

Using a sound similar to the one he had gotten down in Mexico with 'Billy 4,' Dylan locked into the songs, and in just two sessions— intersected by a night on the town, checking out Little Feat at the Bottom Line—he got the songs off of his chest and onto the tracks (just solo recordings of 'Lily, Rosemary and the Jack of Hearts' and 'Idiot Wind' from the 16th made the test pressing, overdubbed with bass and, on 'Idiot Wind,' organ). The sessions on the 17th and 19th—the first also attended by his old sidekick, Paul Griffin, whose glissando through 'You're a Big Girl Now' alone should have made its omission from the finished album a felony—featured an inspired Dylan. If 'Shelter from the Storm' lost a verse in the process, he had plenty more in store.

Dylan arrived on the 17th with a musical upbeat closer to the album. 'Buckets of Rain' superseded 'Little Bit of Rain,' with the melody line from Tom Paxton's 'Bottle of Wine' lending a hand, too. On the 19th, he asked to do perhaps the most un-Dylanesque of activities: to overdub a new lyric over the electric blues he had recorded with Weissberg's Deliverance three days earlier. The man who had, an album earlier, balked at a single vocal overdub on 'Going, Going, Gone,' complaining, 'I don't even know if it's the right thing to do,' overdubbed the 'Meet Me in the Morning' vocal onto the 'Call Letter Blues' backing track.

Dylan, engineer Phil Ramone, and the ever-constant Ellen returned the following Tuesday to assemble the album, already earmarked as *Blood on the Tracks*. With eleven completed tracks and alternates of 'Idiot Wind,' 'Tangled Up in Blue,' and 'Up to Me' that Dylan wished to consider, the sequencing was no simple matter. Apart from anything else, he had a fifty-eight-minute album he needed to trim. The loser was 'Up to Me,' presumably because it would have ended the album on a slightly sour note—'If we never meet again, baby remember me'—and it shared its few chords with 'Shelter from the Storm,' which probably also sealed its fate. 'Buckets of Rain,' though equally fatalistic, seemed to say *que sera sera*, as the singer was going bust. Having sung for fifty minutes about the inevitability of loss, 'Buckets of Rain' left an 'and yet' in parentheses at album's end.

Dylan had completed the album in less than a week, and Columbia was anxious to issue *Blood on the Tracks* before Christmas 1974, even though it would have been Dylan's third album of 1974. Dylan himself seemed very pleased with the results, playing the test pressing to Robbie Robertson and others on his return to Malibu. However, it also appeared that, whatever demons he had exorcised with the album, Ellen was attached to a couple of them. Without ever formally breaking up, Dylan began to make their emotional distance as great as their physical distance, until Ellen finally began to take the hint.

Ellen Bernstein: We became less involved [after the sessions]. He was down here, I was up there, and he wasn't terribly communicative, and I was left to do a lot of guessing. But it was definitely on a downswing . . . When I did [go to Malibu] it didn't have the same flavor as it had before . . . The press had written about the musicians [on the record] and I remember him calling me, and not coming directly out and saying, Did you give this information out? But he was trying to find out, without asking me, and I remember thinking, This is really weird . . . It was just too hard, the distance, and I didn't know what was going on.

It is possible that Sara was hinting at a reconciliation, and Dylan was now ready to grasp the olive branch. The last person Ellen could ask was Dylan, who had even written her a song, and perhaps a verse in 'Buckets of Rain,' about the inevitable parting of their ways. But she was particularly mortified when she heard through the Columbia grapevine that he was seriously considering rerecording some or all of the album.

Unfortunately, one of the people Dylan had played his test pressing to, his younger brother David, told him that it would never sell, presumably based on the sheer starkness of the sound, rather than the nakedness of his brother's soul, and convinced him to rerecord half a dozen of the songs in Minneapolis, with a set of local musicians that he would assemble at a studio he knew well, Sound 80, making himself producer for a day (or two). Inevitably, three months on from the New York recordings, and a further two months on from the songs' composition, Dylan took the opportunity to do more than simply reconfigure the sound.

The songs he decided to recut included the three most ambitious songs of the sessions—'Idiot Wind,' 'Lily, Rosemary and the Jack of Hearts,' and 'Tangled Up in Blue'—and the two songs most obviously sung for Sara—'You're a Big Girl Now' and 'If You See Her, Say Hello.' An argument could even be made—though not by me—for all three epics being improved by the emotional distance that now lay between the songs and their composition. No such argument could, or should, be made for what Dylan proceeded to do to 'You're a Big Girl Now,' which was a mere reflection of the ghost of a pale shadow of its New York self, or 'If You See Her, Say Hello,' which was another casualty of his desire to clothe his previously shorn soul.

'You're a Big Girl Now' may have retained the same lyrics, if little of the necessary blood, but 'If You See Her, Say Hello' was subjected to a number of minor changes and one line—'If you're making love to her' became 'If you get close to her'—that stepped back from the intimacy and real hurt in the original. But, inevitably, it was 'Idiot Wind' that was subjected to whole new verses, in keeping with its endless evolution, and though the rewrites made for a more poetic lyric, they worked at the expense of the song's sense, which, when aligned to its Minneapolis performance, is overwrought, and belies all the underlying sorrow rippling through the original vocal. As Betsy Bowden equivocates, in her Ph.D. thesis on Dylan, *Performed Literature:*

Until one begins analyzing the printed lyrics, one does not notice that the [released] 'Idiot Wind' narrator is cruel at the beginning, has a heroic vision, gradually admits his own confusion, and becomes gentle and sorrowful at the end. A listener instead simultaneously experiences all these emotional states . . . The development of emotional mood during the course of [the released] 'Idiot Wind' makes it work better in print than does the outtake. But . . . these are songs, not poems.

Though the versions of 'Lily, Rosemary and the Jack of Hearts' and 'Tangled Up in Blue' from Minneapolis may have the edge on the New York takes, it is difficult not to conclude that Dylan copped out by issuing the Minneapolis version of the album, compromising his art to tone down his audible pain. Three months on from the original sessions, he decided he had laid a little too much of himself on the line with the original New York recordings. He also perhaps believed his brother when he said it wouldn't sell. Though it is hard to agree with David's assessment, the album as released did shift veritable units, remaining perhaps his most consistent seller.

Having said which, the one aspect of the album that convinced writers to wield their critical scalpels was the playing on it. *Crawdaddy*'s reviewer, Jim Cusimano, referred to 'the lp's instrumental incompetence,' calling the Minneapolis cut of 'Lily, Rosemary and the Jack of Hearts' 'the most significant casualty.' *NME*'s Nick Kent described 'the accompaniments [as] often so trashy they sound like mere practise takes,' and singles out the organ on the Minneapolis 'Idiot Wind' as something that 'could only have been vamped spontaneously on a single playback.' It was Jon Landau, in *Rolling Stone*, though, who used a few bum notes to definitively dismiss Dylan 'as a record maker,' suggesting that, much as he loves some of the new songs, 'the record itself has been made with typical shoddiness. The accompanying musicians have never sounded more indifferent.'

Landau spent most of his three-page review berating Dylan the record maker, but his final assessment of the album suggested someone who genuinely could no longer tell why a song like 'Tangled Up in Blue' exists on a somewhat higher artistic plane than the Ronettes' 'Be My Baby' (a record he actually suggests, in his review, has no equal in the Dylan canon):

To compare the new album to *Blonde on Blonde* at all is to imply that people will treasure it as deeply and for as long. They won't . . . *Blood on the Tracks* will only sound like a great album for a while. Like most of Dylan, it is impermanent.

Landau was not alone in requiring a new set of critical bifocals. Michael Watts's *Melody Maker* review was almost dismissive, suggesting that the album, which could apparently 'have marked a transition between *Harding* and *Nashville Skyline*,' was evidence of Dylan 'moving laterally.' Other, dare one say more perceptive, reviewers recognized that, whatever *Blood on the Tracks* was, a move sideways from *Planet Waves* it was not. Cusimano, in *Crawdaddy*, insightfully wrote, '*Tracks* takes the logical step after *Planet Waves*. Where that album investigated the contradictions of domestic love and life, this resolves them—through separation.' Jonathan Cott, in an alternative *Rolling Stone* review, also recognized that 'there was an uneasy, diseased buttress lodged within the generally rhapsodic framework' on *Planet Waves,* and that 'the wage of this attitude is the title of Dylan's magnificent new album, *Blood on the Tracks*.'

Rolling Stone's decision to let the pro- and anti-Dylan camps fight it out over four pages of the magazine was indicative not merely of their cautious regard for Dylan's uncanny ability to outguess them, but of a general caution that greeted an album of such lyrical insight, devastatingly vocalized. After the false dawns of *New Morning* and *Planet Waves,* NME's Kent confessed, 'I don't honestly know what *good* Dylan is anymore.' But at least he admitted he was 'enthralled with this album to a point where I can't even remember a time before when I've been *this* drawn to a recorded work.' Paul Williams also called it 'the best album of the last five years *by anybody,*' though, like Dylan, he was a survivor of the sixties. Only Michael Gray, author of *Song and Dance Man*, attempted to come to terms with the historic importance of the album in his review in the English monthly *Let It Rock:*

I don't know how, but some adjustment in our consciousness must now follow from the fact that it is Bob Dylan who has produced, in *Blood on the Tracks*, the most strikingly intelligent album of the seventies. That seems to me to change everything. It transforms our perception of Dylan—no longer the major artist of the sixties whose decline from the end of that decade froze seminal work like *Blonde on Blonde* into a historic religious object . . . Instead Dylan has legitimized his claim to a creative prowess as vital now as then—a power not, after all, bounded by the one decade he so much affected.

No other artist in white rock & roll can be said to have done this. The issue Gray raised in his review would become a central one in succeeding years—whether *Blood on the Tracks* did indeed legitimize 'his claim to a creative prowess as vital now as then.' *Blood on the Tracks* remains not only the central pivot of Dylan's career but of the rock aesthetic itself. With this album, the man shifted axis. Ten years after he turned the rock & roll brand of pop into rock, a self-conscious, albeit populist, art form, he renewed its legitimacy as a form capable of containing the work of a mature artist. He also gave it a new self-consciousness, just as the linchpins of first-generation rock were coming to the end of their respective streaks of inspiration. The Rolling Stones would never top their four albums from *Beggars Banquet* through *Exile on Main Street,* 1968 through 1972; neither Lennon nor McCartney would come close to the quality of *Revolver, The White Album,* or *Abbey Road;* Pete Townshend was rock-operaed out after 1973's *Quadrophenia;* even David Bowie had concluded his early seventies trilogy of consecutive rock classics.

Only Dylan, whose mid-sixties canon was more daunting than all of the above, succeeded in producing an album that stoked up his genius quotient nearly ten years after he was thought to have left it by the roadside. And he had done it by reinventing his whole approach to language. Gone were the surrealistic turns of phrase on *Blonde on Blonde,* gone was the 'wild mercury sound' surrounding those mystical words. In their place was a uniformity of mood, a coherence of sound, and an unmistakable maturity to the voice—as if he had had to make *Nashville Skyline, Self Portrait,* and *New Morning* to assimilate those aspects of his voice into a stronger whole. He had never sung better.

Blood on the Tracks was not only markedly superior to the juvenile angst of *Another Side,* Dylan's last 'confessional' album, but the album of a man in his mid-thirties, coming to terms with all the water that has passed under the old bridge. For the first time he was confronting the previous decade as a survivor, willing to reminisce about a time when 'revolution was in the air,' while insisting that his primary concerns lay elsewhere. And the fans seemed to share his need to confront the past. *Blood on the Tracks* became Dylan's second consecutive number one album in the US, and his sixth in the UK (*Pat Garrett* excepted).

And yet an air of self-delusion blows through many of the songs. On 'Idiot Wind' and 'If You See Her, Say Hello,' the male narrator paints himself as the wronged party while the central male figures in 'Tangled Up in Blue' and 'Lily, Rosemary and the Jack of Hearts' take on quite heroic proportions. The Jack of Hearts, in particular, is a figure who wins hearts readily, and whose outlaw lifestyle embodies freedom from responsibility. After Rosemary kills Big Jim to save the Jack of Hearts, he leaves behind all consequences of his incursion into their lives. The narrator in 'Tangled Up in Blue,' though less cavalier, is no less idealized, devoting his life to a romantic quest, perpetually 'heading for another joint.'

In real life, though, it was Dylan who had been unfaithful and, far from behaving heroically, he had simply kept running from responsibility until he was too tired to carry on, at which point he sought to sing himself back home. The reconciliation, though, would take more than a simple 'I'm back, honey.' Though Sara was very visibly in his company in San Francisco in March, when they permitted themselves to be photographed backstage at the SNACK (Students Need Athletic and Cultural Kicks) benefit in Golden Gate Park, a sense of separation was destined to endure for some time yet, bridge-building not being one of Dylan's stronger suits.

Sara was in fact supposed to accompany Dylan to France the following month, but in the end chose not to—though she threatened on occasions to join him, she never did. While he was in France, they stayed in daily contact, though he experienced a loneliness perhaps even more terrible than the previous summer's. His companion this time was less obliging than Ellen, being the painter David Oppenheim, whose painted mural graces the rear cover of *Blood on the Tracks* (after the first pressing contained sleeve notes by the writer Pete Hammill that addressed the original test pressing. Oops!). Predictably, Dylan continued to disguise his loneliness with the occasional lusty liaison.

David Oppenheim: At that time I had just built myself a house in Savoie . . . He arrived at two in the morning. We stayed together for two months [sic] . . . Two of us together here alone. To see this bloke completely despairing, isolated, lost—I didn't want to be like him—He was having problems with his wife. She was supposed to have come with him but she hadn't arrived. He phoned her every day . . . We lived an adventurous life. No complications. We screwed women, we drank, we ate . . . Pathetic and superb at the same time, Dylan is a bloke who invents everything. He's the most egotistical person I know. That's what makes him an incredible person, his amazing self-confidence . . . When I got him to understand that he was completely mad, he would grow pale in the face, and that made me feel good because I identified with the person that I thought he was in those moments of inner understanding . . . This bloke who talked of nothing but love was very, very much on his own.

The portrait Oppenheim paints is a harrowing one. And yet Dylan had recently delivered one of his great artistic triumphs, confirming his return to a creative peak. He was not about to abandon his muse again, whatever the cost.

The one song definitely inspired by his six-week stay in France was 'One More Cup of Coffee,' a result of attending a large Gypsy festival on his thirty-fourth birthday. Though 'One More Cup of Coffee' is written from the viewpoint of someone seduced by a daughter of the king of the Gypsies, it was the king of the Gypsies himself who truly fascinated Dylan.

Bob Dylan: I . . . went to see the king of the Gypsies in southern France. This guy had twelve wives and a hundred children. He was in the antique business and had a junkyard, but he'd had a heart attack before I'd come to see him. All his wives and children had left . . . After he dies, they'll all come back. They smell death and they leave. [1977]

One other song seems to date from the period just before Dylan finished mining the rich vein of language struck on *Blood on the Tracks*. Written from the viewpoint of someone 'despairing, isolated, lost,' 'Abandoned Love' suggested someone whose 'amazing self-confidence' as an artist had returned, but for whom the problems in his marriage were no nearer a happy solution. It was also the first song in a while where he heard his muse whispering to him, 'It's time to make a change.'

1975: From the Bottom Line to the Bitter End

22

I was just sitting in a field [in France] overlooking some vineyards, the sky was pink, the sun was going down, and the moon was sapphire, and I recall getting a ride into town with a man with a donkey cart and I was sitting on this donkey cart, bouncing around on the road there, and that's when it flashed on me that I was gonna go back to America and get serious and do what it is that I do. Because by that time people didn't know what it was that I did . . . Only the people that see our show know what it is that I do. The rest of the people just have to imagine it.

—*Bob Dylan, 1975*

On June 26, 1975, a double-album of *The Basement Tapes* was released, some eight years after the sessions themselves. Dylan could now afford such a reminder of his heyday. Hard on the heels of the critical and commercial acceptance of *Blood on the Tracks*, it was an ideal time to confront those songs from happier times. After *Blood on the Tracks, The Basement Tapes* no longer had the status of 'final reminder of Dylan's lost genius.'

It was Robbie Robertson, rather than Dylan, who was the prime mover in the project. Once again, a Dylan album was being released to shore up the Band's depleted funds. Likewise, it was Robertson who compiled the songs for the album, which included eight songs by the Band, of which only four originated at Big Pink. If the Band songs detailed the search for an independent voice, they were subsequently replaced by superior material on *Music from Big Pink*, which may explain why, in subsequent conversation, Robertson has seemed slightly defensive about his own motives for releasing this set.

Robbie Robertson: It wasn't put out to combat anything. All of a sudden it seemed like a good idea . . . It just popped up one day. We thought we'd see what we had. I started going through the stuff and sorting it out, trying to make it stand up [as] a record that wasn't recorded professionally. I also tried to include some things that people haven't heard before, if possible . . .

[I] just wanted to document a period, rather than let them rot away on the shelves somewhere. It was an unusual time which caused all those songs to be written, and it was better it be put on disc in some way than be lost in an attic.

Robertson's attempts 'to make it stand up [as] a record' did not involve the inclusion of 'I Shall Be Released,' 'Quinn the Eskimo,' 'Sign on the Cross' or 'I'm Not There,' while 'Goin' to Acapulco' and a tuneless first take of 'Too Much of Nothing' were the only recordings new to collectors. Robbie also insisted on dubbing piano, guitar, and/or drums over four of the Dylan–Band performances. Given that he even managed to exclude four of the fourteen original oft-bootlegged demo recordings, he had done Dylan fans a major disservice. Dylan had been asked about the release by Mary Travers in March, but continued to dismiss the work as unfinished therapy:

Bob Dylan: We were all up there sorta drying out . . . making music and watching time go by. So, in the meantime, we made this record. Actually, it wasn't a record, it was just songs which we'd come to this basement and recorded. Out in the woods . . . The record's been exposed throughout the years, [and] somebody mentioned it might be a good idea to put it out as a record, so people could hear it in its entirety, and know exactly what we were doing up there in those years. [1975]

The album as released hardly gave a real idea of what they had been doing in Woodstock. Not even the two traditional songs pulled to the master reels—'Young but Daily Growin'' and 'The Banks of the Royal Canal'—made the final twenty-four cuts. Dylan, though, was hardly interested in archival releases. The day *The Basement Tapes* was released coincided with his popping up in the Village, once again the center of a happening scene, though the focal point was not the folk clubs but a seedy little dive on the Bowery known as CBGB's. It was there that bands like the Ramones, Blondie, and Television had been playing for almost a year, slowly acquiring reputations and reviews. In their wake would follow bands like Talking Heads, the Heartbreakers, Pere Ubu, Richard Hell and the Voidoids, and so on.

If the Village clubs were not at the epicenter of New York's new musical explosion, first-generation New York punk outfits like Television and the Patti Smith Group still aspired to graduate to more esteemed establishments like Max's Kansas City and the Bottom Line. The Bottom Line, in particular, remained a showcase venue for promising new acts, as well as for established artists still seeking a little contact with their audience. In August, it would be the venue for some of the most famous performances of the seventies, when Bruce Springsteen became 'the main contender' over five nights of consecutive two-hour sets.

But it was at the (previously Bitter) Other End, on June 26, that Dylan caught New York's latest and most androgynous new Dylan—Patti Lee Smith. On the verge of signing to Arista and recording the most remarkable debut long-player of the seventies, *Horses*, Smith's uninhibited performances combined frenetic rock & roll with long between-song raps and smatterings of poetry. Smith's shows at the Other End were landmark performances—her first shows with drummer Jay Dee Daugherty, the culmination of four years spent compiling a unique rock & roll sound. Dylan was totally fascinated by Patti, and loved the easy informality of her band. Having been dissuaded from devising his own standing band after the 1965 Hollywood Bowl concert, he had never known the joys of touring with a band of his own making.

Patti Smith: He started getting really turned on by the idea of the band— my guys following me or pushing me and not faltering or wondering about what musical changes to go into because I've just spread the song out like a hand. He saw somebody doing something that he didn't think was possible, and he said, 'I wish I would have stayed with just one group.'

Patti's looseness seemed to rub off on Dylan, who happily hugged her backstage as photographers snapped away, while asking if she read Rimbaud in the original French. Though Patti would pass up a position on Dylan's forthcoming tour, remaining faithful to her band, she provided some much-needed proof that his influence was still strong enough to jump a generation. She duly became a part-time member of nightly after-hours gatherings around the man at the Other End.

Patti Smith: He started hanging out more—he liked the fact that he could be in a club and people didn't maul him to death, because there were a lot of things happening at that time. And we were all hanging out there, and it was really great 'cause we'd all get drunk and stuff, and be falling around. People just started turning up in the Village. It happened very fast. Jack Elliott was around—everybody was around. Then one night, Bob started going up onstage, jamming with these people. I saw him start getting attracted to certain people—Rob Stoner, Bobby Neuwirth—it was great to see [Neuwirth] and Bob back together, because he really brings out the worst in Dylan, which is what we usually love the best. And he was working out this Rolling Thunder thing—he was thinking about improvisation, about extending himself language-wise. In the talks that we had, there was something that he admired about me that was difficult to comprehend then.

The week after Dylan caught Patti's act, he finished off 'Abandoned Love.' He had also begun work on a symbolic travelogue called 'Isis.' At this point, according to Jacques Levy, it was 'almost a dirge, slow, unlike anything I'd ever heard before, obviously setting you up for a long story.' It was in this form that Dylan's next accompanist believes the song was first played to her. In late June 1975, Dylan seemed to be on a scouting mission, looking for a new sound. Driving around the Village, he ran across an exotic-looking violinist by the name of Scarlet Rivera, and invited her to his rehearsal studio to run through some songs. Perhaps he wanted to explore a guitar–violin blend, perhaps he just wanted to get to know this particular gypsy soul. Rivera spent the afternoon playing along to some new songs from Dylan's pen. There was a mantralike quality to Rivera's violin playing, and though she was always fractionally sharp in tone, there was an obvious chemistry between her and Dylan.

Scarlet Rivera: [I] played all afternoon with him on songs that I could never have possibly heard before, at his studio in the Village. And he played them on guitar. I'm sure [he] consciously didn't play anything that he had recorded before, so that I couldn't have a head start on knowing how it sounded, or how to play it. There was a little half smile after playing a few songs . . . 'One More Cup of Coffee' was one of the first songs we did that afternoon . . . [We did] 'Mozambique,' 'Isis.' Then he moved to piano and tried some of the same songs in different keys. And so it progressed.

Only one recording exists of Dylan and Rivera attempting to blend acoustic guitar and violin, but it is an extraordinarily powerful one—a recording for an aborted TV special in Florida in April 1976. The song they are attempting to perform is one of the songs played that afternoon in late June 1975, 'One More Cup of Coffee.' Allen Ginsberg would write, at the time, of Dylan's voice on the studio recording of this song 'lift[ing] in Hebraic cantillation never heard before in US song,' and the tremulous way he wavers through the final word of each line certainly bears a stronger resemblance to Middle Eastern song than 'Be My Baby.' Sadly, the ten-minute duet at Clearwater, from a so-so audience tape, provides the only known example of Dylan's original guitar–violin concept. His wish for Scarlet to sign on for the duration became apparent as the June evening wore on.

Scarlet Rivera: By late, late afternoon we left [the rehearsal studio] and he said he wanted to take me to a club to see a friend, and that turned into his sitting in with Muddy Waters . . . After that show was my moment of acceptance . . . We went to Victoria Spivey's house that very night. I think it was [in] Queens or Brooklyn. The entire Muddy Waters band went, and Bob and I spent many more hours jamming, talking to her, listening to old records. He was really excited by the whole evening.

Dylan's surprise appearance at the Bottom Line with Scarlet was the start of a hectic two-week period when he would be seen in the Village clubs and bars almost every night, sometimes sitting in with old friends, often just enjoying the show. It was the highest profile he'd maintained in years. Two days later, he was back at the Other End, sitting in a booth at the back, checking out the latest guise of Ramblin' Jack. The following night, he was unable to resist joining Jack on 'Pretty Boy Floyd' and then, as Elliott graciously turned over the stage, debuting 'Abandoned Love,' which in its original guise contained a couplet that may well suggest the state of mind he was in at the end of these evenings out on the town: 'Send out for St. John the Evangelist / All my friends are drunk, they can be dismissed.' Dylan's intrusion into Elliott's set that night was only the beginning. As the week wore on, the intrusions gradually became longer than the set.

David Amram: At the time, Ramblin' Jack Elliott was playing, and Bobby Neuwirth came along, and we all sat in with Jack. Suddenly, everybody started singing and carousing and it wasn't Jack Elliott's set any more.

Sitting in on several of these late-night jam sessions was Elliott's sometime bass player, Rob Stoner. Stoner had his own band, Rockin' Robin and the Rebels, but backed Elliott on occasion, and was in the Village most nights Bob was hanging out. They had first met back in 1971 in San Francisco, when Stoner was playing with the Greenbriar Boys, and had briefly hung out together in Los Angeles in 1973. Dylan knew Stoner's sound, and respected his knowledge of rockabilly. Like Rivera, Stoner would get the call when the time came to recruit the musicians necessary to promulgate Dylan's latest soundscape.

The remaining components for the standing band Dylan hankered after came from a week of jam sessions that passed for a residency at the Other End by Bobby Neuwirth. Neuwirth had stayed in touch with Dylan since their 1974 reunion, and it was presumably he who had told Dylan about Patti Smith, whom Neuwirth had first coaxed into being a performing poet three years earlier. Once again, Neuwirth was the conduit through whom all who sought the inner sanctum needed to pass. Steven Soles, who had last seen Dylan when he was house-sitting Byrdcliffe back in '68, bumped into Neuwirth at a Village hangout called the Locale, and was promptly invited down to the Other End to meet up with the twin Dylans—Bob and Patti.

Steven Soles: We all wound up at Larry Coombs's loft. We stayed up all night and Bob played us all his new songs from what was gonna be *Desire,* which he hadn't recorded at that point, and we all just played songs.

Inevitably Soles, who was now based on the West Coast, found himself recruited into Neuwirth's little band, little knowing he was undertaking some kind of audition for a notion that Dylan and Neuwirth had been ruminating over for a couple of weeks.

Steven Soles: Neuwirth had a gig at the Other End . . . for a week, so he said, Well, Steven, what are you doing? Come and play with me? . . . Every night someone new came—Ronson and Ian Hunter came down, suddenly Ronson became lead guitar player, John Belushi and Dan Ackroyd came down, they sat in, Gordon Lightfoot came down, he sat in. It became a jam every night. Then 'the Bobs' got together and said, 'This is such a cool thing, what if we took this on the road but we went around in a station wagon, we just showed up and played, no advertising.'

Not that the idea of a touring revue had started at the Other End. It was an old Bob Dylan dream. He had told Phil Ochs the previous May that he would love to tour small clubs 'and give the money away.' And back in 1972, he had said to Maria Muldaur, 'Wouldn't it be great if we got a train, and put a revue together that would travel across the country?' He had even discussed the idea with Robbie Robertson during 'the amnesia.'

Robbie Robertson: This thing has been a thing that Bob's been talking about for years. I'm sure he would have liked to have taken it all the way and done it by train. He's always wanted to have that kind of gypsy caravan situation happening where it was loose, and different people could get up and do different things at different times, and nothing would be out of place.

If Soles had some inkling of what 'the Bobs' were cooking up that July, others who stumbled into Neuwirth's web remained unaware of a higher purpose. A seventeen-year-old David Mansfield was another multi-instrumentalist Neuwirth roped into this scene, inviting him up onstage one night, and keeping him there for the remainder of the week.

David Mansfield: [Neuwirth] didn't really have a band as such, he had a gig and for this gig he sort of put together this group of people that kept growing and growing and growing . . . A lot of people joined up along the way and I was one of them . . . [My girlfriend] was my biggest promoter and she brought me into the back room, introduced me to Neuwirth, said, 'This is my boyfriend, he's an incredible violin player,' and Neuwirth in a tequila haze said, 'Well, take it out and let's hear you play!' That week of gigs coalesced into what later became the Rolling Thunder Revue . . . all the boundaries completely blurred within days [of rehearsals] and most of the people who'd played with Bobby [Neuwirth] ended up playing with Bob Dylan. The stage at the Bitter End was so crowded you could barely find a place to stand . . . This crazy, swirling thing that was the RTR was what Neuwirth was at the time, and what he did when he went onstage at the Bitter End. He was getting paid something by Paul Colby, [but] he immediately starts sending friends plane tickets . . . [all] to create this scene. And that was very much the spirit of the tour.

The LA-based Steven Soles, the New York-based David Mansfield, and a tall Texan, T-Bone Burnett—recipient of a Neuwirth plane ticket—had never played together previously, but complemented each other well enough to eventually form the Alpha Band. Along with the bass and violin components Dylan had already found, this trio would form the basis of the first touring band he'd ever composed from scratch. Though he had assembled such motley crews for studio duties, when it came to the stages of the world, he had previously stuck with the Band. But the Band, for all their musicality, were no great improvisers. Dylan was now looking for a band who could respond when, to quote Patti, he sought to 'spread the song out like a hand.'

If the musicians were somewhat in the dark as to the real purpose of these onstage auditions, Dylan was actively talking to those who might help it happen. As early as mid-July, a rep from Columbia was indicating to *Rolling Stone* just how seriously Dylan was considering taking 'this cool thing' on the road:

You get the feeling he really digs being back in New York. He's looking into doing a show on Broadway . . . But most of all, after these nights down here at the Other End, he'd like to tour small clubs like this. There has been some talk of getting a van and driving around the country, dropping in, unannounced like tonight, playing a couple of nights and moving on. Nobody would know he was there until he showed up, so there wouldn't be a crowd scene. And nobody would know where he would strike next.

The rep in question was presumably Don Devito, a company man about to be entrusted with production duties on a Dylan session scheduled for July 14. If so, he caught some of the songs he was expecting to record, sung for the chosen few in the Other End bar after Neuwirth and co. had wound down for the night. As well as 'Abandoned Love,' Dylan sang an almost entirely rewritten 'Isis' and a brand-new twelve-verse ballad about the gangster Joey Gallo, both co-written with lyricist and stage director Jacques Levy, one of those with whom Dylan had discussed the practicalities of a low-key tour. After running into each other the previous spring and promising to get together, the two of them had again hooked up in early July. Dylan ended up spending more time with Levy that month than with all his old friends combined.

Jacques Levy: Bob didn't have any specific idea about what he wanted to do. He knew one thing he didn't want to do. He did not want to jet from here to there like he had done before on tour with the Band. He hated that . . . The two of us spent a lot of time talking about what kind of a tour would be possible. Bob started to call a few people about musicians . . . [and] Bob and I started to conceive of this traveling circus notion.

For the moment, though, the traveling circus notion was incidental to the primary purpose of their alliance: writing some songs. As a songwriter Levy was probably best known for his collaboration with Roger McGuinn on 'Chestnut Mare,' though he had also stage-directed the risqué *Oh! Calcutta!* when it had first come to New York. The subject of a possible songwriting collaboration had come up one night during a typically informal discussion at the Other End. Dylan, on the spur of the moment, suggested going up to Levy's loft and playing him some 'bits and pieces of some songs I was working on . . . on the piano.' Almost the first thing Levy got to hear was the original version of 'Isis.' Levy made some suggestions, and suddenly Dylan started finding a thread tying the song together.

Jacques Levy: We were just sitting, just talking . . . and then he went to the piano, sat down, and he started to play 'Isis.' But it was a very different style of 'Isis' than you hear now . . . So the two of us started working on that together. I started writing words, then he would say, 'Well, no, how about this, what about that?'—a totally cooperative venture.

Bob Dylan: I . . . asked him if [the words] meant anything to him, and he took it someplace else, and then I took it someplace else, then he went further, then I went further, and it wound up that we had this song ['Isis'] which was out there. [1975]

Jacques Levy: We were having a hell of a time, a terrific time, just the two of us. It got to be three in the morning . . . I typed [the song] up and we went over all of it. Then the two of us went out. We wanted to catch the Other End before it closed. He took the paper with him. We had a beer. There were a few people in there hanging out. Then he did something that was very surprising to me. He announces to these people sitting there that we had just written a new song, did [they] want to hear it? Everybody, of course, says, 'Sure, sure.' He doesn't sing the song. He opens up the piece of paper and he reads it to them like you read a poem to somebody . . . They all responded unbelievably to it. It was a really great atmosphere, which made us both feel good . . . The next day we got together and he told me he had been trying to write a song about Rubin Carter.

Dylan had discovered a companion for his passage back to a more storytelling mode of songwriting, a realignment of the ballad tradition, that incorporated some tricks he'd picked up from the likes of Joseph Conrad, Franz Kafka, and Sam Peckinpah. After 'learning to do consciously what he used to do unconsciously,' Dylan now stood to benefit from Jacques Levy's more deliberate, conscientious approach, which naturally complemented his inspirational, less disciplined way of working. Waiting for lightning to strike hadn't produced more than two finished songs in the six months since he'd completed *Blood on the Tracks*. Levy soon introduced him to an invaluable aid.

Roger McGuinn: Bob had never seen a thesaurus before, nor a rhyming dictionary. Imagine all the songs that Bob has written without a rhyming dictionary. When he saw one it blew him out . . . He's going, 'What! Think of all the time I could have saved.' He didn't even know they existed.

Dylan was looking to write some story songs again. Though no less cinematic than 'Lily, Rosemary and the Jack of Hearts,' they would advance the tale more directly, and with fewer dramatic lurches. Levy was an ideal collaborator. Inspired by Levy's directorial skills, Dylan even rewrote 'Simple Twist of Fate,' performing this new version on the John Hammond TV tribute in September. He had never really collaborated before. Composed the odd bridges, put lyrics to others' tunes many times. But not collaborated. It was a new and exhilarating experience.

The song Dylan had been trying to write about imprisoned ex-boxer Rubin 'Hurricane' Carter had been inspired by reading Carter's auto-biography, *The Sixteenth Round*, which Carter had sent him 'because of his prior commitment to the [civil rights] struggle,' and which he had taken with him to France. The book detailed the specious case that had been brought against Carter for a multiple murder 'that happened in a bar' back in 1967. Carter and his 'accomplice,' John Artes, were both found guilty of what was widely reported as a 'race killing' and sentenced to four consecutive life sentences each. Dylan visited the incarcerated Carter in Rahway Prison in Trenton, New Jersey, shortly after returning from France. According to Carter, 'We sat and talked for many, many hours. And I recognized the fact that here was a brother.'

Bob Dylan: I realized that the man's philosophy and my philosophy were running on the same road, and you don't meet too many people like that . . . I took notes because I wasn't aware of all the facts, and I thought that maybe sometime I could condense it all down and put it into a song. [1975]

The same penman who had detailed the fates of Hattie Carroll, Emmett Till, Medgar Evers, and George Jackson decided to bring Carter's case to public attention. Unfortunately, he was not really sure how to put across the story. After all, it had been twelve years since he had written a topical ballad. Levy suggested something unashamedly cinematic.

Jacques Levy: Bob wasn't sure that he could write a song . . . he was just filled with all these feelings about Hurricane. He couldn't make the first step. I think the first step was putting the song in a total storytelling mode. I don't remember whose idea it was to do that. But really, the beginning of the song is like stage directions, like what you would read in a script: 'Pistol shots ring out in a bar-room night . . . Here comes the story of the Hurricane.' Boom! Titles. You know, Bob loves movies, and he can write these movies that take place in eight to ten minutes, yet seem as full or fuller than regular movies.

Suffused with a sense of mission, and once again reinventing himself as a broadside balladeer, Dylan felt inspired enough to tackle another controversial murder 'that happened in a bar,' the gunning down of local hoodlum Joey Gallo in Umberto's Clam Bar, in Little Italy, on April 7, 1972. The inspiration for 'The Ballad of Joey Gallo' was twofold. One was the paperback publication of Donald Goddard's biography of Gallo that month, from which came the graphic depiction of Joey's death, and the song's eventual title, 'Joey.' The remainder of the song was composed after a dinner Dylan and Levy attended, given by two friends of the infamous Gallos.

Bob Dylan: Jacques . . . was going up to some place to have supper, and I was invited to come if I felt like it . . . I was hungry so I went with him. And it was up to Mary and Jerry Orbach's place, and as soon as I walked in the door, Mary was talking about Joey. She was a good friend of Joey's. They were real tight. I just listened for a few hours, they were talking about this guy, and I remembered Joey. At that time, I wasn't involved in anything that he was involved in, but he left a certain impression on me. I never considered him a gangster. I always thought of him as some kind of hero in some kind of a way. An underdog fighting against the elements. He retained a certain amount of his freedom and he went out the way he had to. But she laid all these facts out, and it was like listening to a story about Billy the Kid. So we went ahead and wrote that up in one night. [1975]

If Goddard's warts-and-all biography of Gallo had once again made him news, the eventual release of 'Joey' on *Desire* led to some pointed criticism in the press about a song that only appeared to glorify a vicious hoodlum if one disregarded the unanswered choral refrain: 'What made them want to come and blow you away?' Godfather to punk journos everywhere, Lester Bangs wrote a lengthy and unbalanced attack upon the historical veracity of the song in *Creem*, under the title 'Dylan's Dalliance with Mafia Chic.' Dylan defended the song as a valid re-creation of the traditional ballad form, which had eulogized outlaws for six hundred years, indeed evolved out of 'rymes of robyn hode.' Ironically, it remains the one song from Dylan's bestselling album to have regularly featured in concert in the nineties.

Bob Dylan: I always grew up admiring those heroes . . . Robin Hood, Jesse James . . . those guys who kicked against oppression and had high moral standards . . . It amazes me I would write a song about Joey Gallo . . . [but] I feel that if I didn't, who would? But that's an old tradition. I think I picked that up from the folk tradition . . . I used to sing a lot of those songs and it just kinda carried over. [1981]

'Joey' was also the first song from *Desire* to be recorded in the studio, along with one of Dylan's and Levy's more throwaway efforts, about lesbian writer Rita Mae Brown. However, the session on July 14 did not use any of the musicians, save for Scarlet Rivera, that Dylan had been checking out over the previous two weeks. Instead, Dave Mason's five-piece band, and three female singers, were augmented by violin, mandolin, accordion, and harmonica. Evidently, the new album was going to be a considerably grander affair than its predecessor. Though Dylan would persevere with a 'big band' sound, only the violin/girl-singer combination would survive until the finished artifact. Neither of the Dave Mason Band tracks would be short-listed for the album. Surprisingly, given the antiseptic sound of these cuts, Dylan would also persevere with Don Devito as producer. But before the process could resume, what was needed was a little quietude and an album's worth of songs.

Jacques Levy: What was happening was that we were going out and hanging out late at night and we were getting together the next afternoon and there were lots and lots of distractions. So we said, 'Let's get out of here,' and suddenly it became serious, that we were really going to do some serious work together. So we went out to a place out in the Hamptons. Nobody was around, and the two of us were just there for like three weeks together . . . We had already written a couple of songs so there was a feeling of confidence that . . . we could really do it.

In the seclusion of the Hamptons, Levy claims they wrote fourteen songs together in three weeks. In fact, it was less than two weeks and, on the evidence of the *Desire* sessions, they wrote half that number of songs. Two of these were complex travelogues, 'Black Diamond Bay' and 'Romance in Durango,' evidence that their collaborations were growing in sophistication. 'Durango' is the more conventional tale: an outlaw and his lover, on the run in an exotic Mexican landscape, the climax to an unmade Peckinpah movie in song. 'Black Diamond Bay' relates the destruction of a tiny island, observed from a hotel on the island itself, before pulling back at song's end to reveal a man watching a TV news report about an earthquake, which has left behind just a Panama hat and a pair of shoes.

Of the Hamptons songs, only the two travelogues and 'Oh Sister' suggested a real vein of inspiration, but they gave Dylan that album's worth of songs in less than four weeks of collaborative songwriting. He wasted no time recording the results. The man seemingly recognized a

roll. Unfortunately, he was determined to repeat the big-band experiment, despite failing to get a sound that worked in mid-July, lacking any
obvious aptitude as an arranger, and given the equally unsuccessful
attempt to record a more band-oriented version of *Blood on the Tracks*
with Weissberg's band the previous September. Two weeks after the
Mason experiment, Dylan was back in Studio E with around twenty-one
musicians waiting on him.

The July 28 session was a typically Dylanesque example of walking a
wire without a safety net. Determined to continue cutting songs live in
the studio—contrary to post-*Pepper* practice—he required a technically
adept producer who could keep the musicians in check and provide a
proper mix of instruments. Instead, Devito ended up 'stacking' organ,
violin, and percussion on the multitrack tape, precluding the possibility of
remixing or overdubbing Scarlet's occasionally off-key accompaniment,
while recording more guitar tracks than Steve Jones on the Sex Pistols'
Never Mind the Bollocks, rather than asking a couple of the musicians to
sit some songs out.

Neil Hubbard: There were far too many musicians there—five guitarists,
including me and Eric Clapton, played on the 'Hurricane' set. And there
was no one in overall control. No producer or anything.

Quite why Dylan needed any other lead guitarists when he had
someone of the stature of Eric Clapton begs for an explanation. Clapton
himself must have been somewhat surprised that the man's working
methods had not changed markedly since the May 1965 session with the
Bluesbreakers. Failing to figure out what exactly Dylan had in mind,
Clapton soon departed, though not before doing Devito's job for him,
venturing the opinion that some slimming down of the musicians was in
order.

Eric Clapton: He was trying to find a situation, you see, where he could
make music with new people. He was just driving around picking musicians
up and bringing them back to the sessions. It ended up with like twenty-four
musicians in the studio, all playing these incredibly incongruous instruments,
accordion, violin—and it didn't really work. He was after a large sound, but
the songs were so personal that he wasn't comfortable with all the people
around . . . We did take[s] on about twelve songs. He even wrote one on
the spot, all in one night. It was very hard to keep up with him . . . I had to
get out in the fresh air, 'cause it was madness in there.

The first session reached a crescendo of madness on a particularly outrageous 'nearly disco' version of 'Hurricane,' on which three electric guitars were stacked on top of each other, as were mandolin and accordion, as well as horns, trumpets, and saxophones. That Dylan had a core sound in mind was evidenced by the presence of Rob Stoner, Scarlet Rivera, and Emmylou Harris, the songbird from Gram Parsons's Fallen Angels who was now striking out on her own. But all three were unnerved by Dylan's studio methodology. Rivera, in particular, lacking studio experience, was having a hard time of it, particularly 'after having [previously] worked so intimately.' Emmylou Harris was considerably more experienced, and had sung harmony with the equally mercurial Parsons—presumably the credentials that impressed Dylan—but was left praying for the hard times to end after the first couple of sessions. Reading off lyric sheets, and with no opportunity for rehearsal, Emmylou found the whole experience of recording with Dylan quite bewildering.

Emmylou Harris: I'd never heard the songs before and we did most of them in one or two takes. There were no tapes, we sang live. His phrasing changes a lot, but Gram did that a lot, too. Gram and I had the same feel for phrasing, but I watched him all the time, so I did just the same thing with Dylan. I just watched his mouth and watched what he was saying. That's where all that humming comes from. You can hear me humming on some of those tracks . . . It does take me a while to work out harmony parts and Dylan works very fast. I'm more of a perfectionist. I would have liked more time. There were times when I didn't even know I was supposed to come in and had to jump fast. But I later realized that you just don't overdub on a Dylan album. He's not that kind of artist. I asked to come and fix my parts and he said, Sure. But I didn't have the time, and I really didn't think he'd use any of it.

Rob Stoner, almost a bystander at that first session, was in no doubt as to what was wrong with the setup.

Rob Stoner: They were trying to do a superstar session thing: they had Dave Mason, they had this band Kokomo, Clapton was up there. A lot of people. But it was just too much of a hanging-out scene. In fact, they had to empty out an adjacent studio to put [on] a . . . buffet for all these overflow people—everybody was bringing their friends, 'Hey, you wanna see me record with Bob Dylan?' . . . These guys from Kokomo, I think they were the main culprits, 'cause they were really into this very slick, professional [sound] . . . It became their record because they kept doing takes so they would get their parts together, and by that time Bob's bored.

Dylan also realized something was wrong with the whole setup. Though frontman Neil Hubbard subsequently insisted that six-piece English pub-rockers Kokomo had only ever been booked for the one session, Dylan proceeded to do A Deliverance, asking just two members of the sextet to return the following day, saxophonist Mel Collins and conga player Jody Linscott, promoted to drums this time around. The Clapton contingent was also lighting out for territories unknown. With half the number of musicians, and experienced session men Hugh McCracken and Vinnie Bell taking turns at lead guitar, Dylan set about rerecording much of the previous day's fare, as well as attempting the quirky 'Black Diamond Bay' with harmonica, horns, piano, and conga— as brave as such experimentation gets. However, by now Dylan was beginning to sense too much instrumental embroidery.

Bob Dylan: We tried it with a lot of different people in the studio, a lot of different types of sound . . . I even had backup singers on that album for two or three days, a lot of percussion, a lot going on. But as it got down, I got more irritated with all this sound going on. [1978]

Toward the end of the session, Dylan attempted a stripped-down 'Oh Sister.' Using just bass, drums, guitar, violin, and harmony vocals, he cut a version good enough to warrant overdubbing a new Emmylou Harris harmony vocal the following day. If Dylan was following one particular stream of thought, at least one musician wanted to row along. With precious little in the way of suggestions coming from the producer's chair, and having assumed the bedrock role sonically, Stoner was quite prepared to give it to Devito and Dylan straight, with rock salt and nails.

Rob Stoner: Devito came to me at the end of the night, when all these musicians had gone home, and asked me what I thought of it and I told him that I thought it was not a likely way to get a productive project out of Bob Dylan, that it was too crowded, it was too confusing, it was inefficient. Bob's music really is dependent on catching a moment—they're like snapshots, Polaroids . . . The first take is gonna be better—even if it's got some wrong notes or something . . . So Devito asked me what I would suggest. I said, 'Why don't you come in with a tiny band and like nobody, no girlfriends, no wives, no nothing! Just the smallest possible band you can get—bass player, drummer, and anybody else you wanna keep around.'

With the two remnants from the Kokomo contingent also about to fade out of the picture, Dylan was in dire need of a drummer if he wanted to keep cutting these long ballads. He had to date been blessed with an extraordinary array of four-star drummers in the studio—Bobby Gregg, Ken Buttrey, Russ Kunkel, Jim Keltner, and Levon Helm. He again sought out Buttrey, unsuccessfully, as well as Jim Gordon, of Derek and the Dominoes fame, before Stoner suggested a sidekick of his own, the positively metronomic Howie Wyeth. Howie found himself immediately immersed in the deep end when the musicians reconvened at Columbia Studio E for a third night of sessions.

Howie Wyeth: Emmylou and Bob had their own little table. It was like they were in a little French restaurant or something . . . the rest of us were all over here. It was like a separate scene. Bob would start a tune. He wouldn't tell us the names of the tunes. This is the gospel truth, man, I don't think people believe me—the first song we started to do—I had just barely met him—I think they were recording it, we played the song and we sort of fumbled the ending . . . He said, 'Okay we're gonna do that again.' And I said, 'Bob, are we gonna end this or is it gonna be a fade?' And he went into such a lengthy explanation, he went on and on, that everybody got so confused, it ended up we didn't even do the song [again]. He said, 'Let's not even do it.' And Stoner said, 'Don't ask him anything. Just play.'

Perhaps Dylan was beginning to despair of the recording process itself, which, for the first time in a remarkably serendipitous career, had been threatening to slide away from him. He had called Sheena Seidenberg, a percussionist at the sessions, that afternoon to tell her that he couldn't sleep, that 'the energy was so high, so intense.' And yet, despite a foul-up on 'Golden Loom,' and for perhaps the last time in his career, on July 30, 1975, Dylan was able to rely entirely on the fortuitous chemistry of a live studio setup to get an album's worth of songs in a single night. The remainder of the session was a revelation. Next up, they attempted 'Isis' and, straight away, Dylan and the band struck gold. Not since the days of *Bringing It All Back Home* had he hit such a creative groove and managed to maintain it throughout an entire session.

Rob Stoner: Right away that [first] version of 'Isis' was a take. Because it was a small group, there was no confusion . . . Right after we finished 'Isis,'

Bob came over to me and said, 'Your drummer's great, it sounds great,' and we all felt great because it was [so] intimate. It had the sound that you can hear on *Desire*, just a bunch of people playing in a room with no overdubs, all live, happening right before your ears. We could get that first-take spontaneity because we didn't have to keep going over and over things to show them to all these musicians who were faking it . . . We just listened to that take of 'Isis,' we just went back into the studio and started running through tunes, bam, bam, bam, just getting every complete take, every complete tune was a take . . . just like that. We were so hot we did 'Rita Mae,' which wasn't on the record, 'One More Cup of Coffee,' 'Joey,' 'Mozambique,' 'Hurricane,' 'Oh Sister,' 'Black Diamond Bay,' we did them all that night . . . I think we were still doing takes as late as five and six A.M., and we hung out listening to the playbacks until we had to go out to the street to move our cars, at eight, so they wouldn't get towed away.

Howie Wyeth: We had a lot of ESP that night. Even in 'Joey,' there was a place where I thought the song was ending, and I drop out for a second, and it wasn't the end. But it worked great.

Five of the nine *Desire* songs were cut on that night of 'commotion and magic,' as were a slow version of 'Isis,' Dylan's preferred take of 'Hurricane,' the 'Rita Mae' 45, and the *Bootleg Series* take of 'Golden Loom.' Neither the eleven-minute 'Joey' nor 'Black Diamond Bay' in swing time managed to throw Stoner, Wyeth, and Rivera. The spirit of the 30th pervades the finished album. Though Harris, even after a two-session baptism, fades in and out as Dylan's vocal idiosyncrasies wax and wane, the session on the 30th had given him a strong successor to the incomparable *Blood on the Tracks*. The relief was enormous. Dylan and Devito, in particular, had seen a great weight lifting from their shoulders as the evening progressed.

Howie Wyeth: I remember they drove me down [town] afterwards, and Bob and Devito each had cars, and they were like bumping each other, playing bumper cars. I mean, I thought we were gonna die. They dropped me off about eight blocks from here. I walked back in the middle of the street 'cause I thought something was gonna fall on me. I thought those guys were gonna kill each other, 'cause as they dropped me off they were stopped at a light, and Bob was pushing Devito on through the light.

The one dissenting voice was the person who had found it so hard to share singing duties. Stoner remembers Harris being 'really bummed out at the end of that night,' even confiding to him that she hoped that 'they don't put it out.' It was her final session. She had commitments with her own Hot Band that made further work impractical.

Though all concerned felt that the album had been all but completed on the 30th, the most convincing Dylan vocals on the finished album were to come at the following night's session, on which he at last sang alone. Perhaps he was unconsciously holding back when singing with Emmylou, but the Dylan on 'Isis' is bending notes with the best of 'em, while with 'Sara,' he returned to his Hebraic cantillations, wringing tiers of meaning from one of his least convincing lyrics. Wyeth recalls a slightly emotionally drained Dylan arriving at the session, after a day in court testifying as a character witness on Clive Davis's behalf.

Howie Wyeth: He was so bummed out . . . the night we played 'Sara' . . . We thought everything sucked at that point.

Only three songs were seriously attempted on the 31st, but all three were dispositions on the marital battleground, two of them composed in isolation: 'Abandoned Love,' shortly before Levy appeared on the scene, and 'Sara,' a solo effort from the Hamptons. These were the only songs from this period to cross the same border as the previous album. And who should have accompanied Dylan to this final *Desire* session but the lady he still loved more than blood, Sara Lowndes Dylan. But if 'Sara' was a hymn to Dylan's 'Scorpio Sphinx in a calico dress,' the portrait of the woman/women in the other two songs recorded that night—'Isis' and 'Abandoned Love'—was far more capricious.

To sing 'Don't ever leave me, don't ever go' and 'Won't you descend from the throne from where you sit?' in consecutive songs—at a session at which your wife and subject matter sits on the other side of the mirror—hardly suggests an unquestioning re-entry into the marriage arena. Unfortunately, 'Abandoned Love' sounds like the performance of an emotionally drained man, lacking the passion it contained the night of 'the flaming moon,' July 3. According to Rolling Thunder Revue chronicler Larry Sloman, Dylan then turned to his wife and said, 'This is for you,' before breaking into 'Sara,' the day's torpor having been drained from his vocal cords by 'Abandoned Love.'

The following day Dylan, Devito, and the band listened to playbacks of all the songs recorded with the stripped-down ensemble, as well as those from the big-band sessions. Dylan suggested recutting 'Romance in Durango,' but the others decided it should be the one and only example of the big band to make it to vinyl. The remainder of the album would be compiled from the previous two nights. *Desire* was now a reality, and Dylan had recorded a strong follow-up to *Blood on the Tracks* just seven months after concluding the sessions for that album. With the album completed, Dylan and Sara took a trip to their farm in Minnesota for a summer holiday with the children, which concluded with a family occasion, the marriage of his cousin, Linda Goldfine, at the Temple Israel Camp in Minneapolis.

An impromptu 'Forever Young' at his cousin's wedding suggested that the itch to perform remained, and a couple of weeks later Dylan was reassembling his new three-piece combo. He wanted them to accompany him to Chicago to perform three songs for a tribute to John Hammond, being filmed by PBS for screening in the New Year.

Scarlet Rivera: We had less than twenty-four hours' notice . . . Our rehearsal basically took place in the dressing room, talking over the songs, and what key they would be in, and just mental refreshers . . . We [also] ran over [the new] 'Simple Twist of Fate' in the dressing room.

Though Dylan didn't fly back to New York with Stoner, Wyeth, and Scarlet, but to Malibu for some further bridge work, he was back in New York by the middle of October. Enjoying the torn and frayed vibe of the Gramercy Park Hotel, he booked a couple of weeks' rehearsal time at the midtown Studio Instrument Rentals space. Suddenly the disparate elements of those balmy summer nights began to come together. The musicians who had lost out in the studio—Soles, Mansfield, and Burnett—found themselves being bolted onto the bare bones of the *Desire* trio.

Rob Stoner: [We] start rehearsing up at SIR in midtown there, 54th Street. We're rehearsing for like a day or two—it's not really so much a rehearsal as like a jam, tryin' to sort it out. Meanwhile all these people who eventually became the Revue started dropping in. Baez was showing up. McGuinn was there. They were all there. We had no idea what the purpose for these jams was, except we were being invited to jam. I think the only people who were being paid were the group that was already working for Bob—namely Scarlet, myself, and Howie. So we're up there jamming and it turns out what we're really doing is rehearsing.

Though the whisper was that they were rehearsing for a tour, tapes were left rolling. But for what? Wasn't the album done and dusted? Perhaps because the rehearsals themselves were part of a process, and only when the destination hove into view did the process crystallize into rehearsing for live shows.

David Mansfield: That was the nature of rehearsals—it wasn't like, here's the songs, we're gonna learn them, it was like he'd start playing a song and it might be a song that you were gonna be rehearsing for the tour, and it might be something like ['People Get Ready'], where you're playing it just to play.

That Dylan's new standing band ended up being an amalgam of the amorphous Neuwirth Other End Revue and the trio that had saved him from the madness of a big-band *Desire* was, in part, simply another act of faith. As with the big-band sessions, the SIR rehearsals began, and indeed ended, with Dylan just inviting a whole series of friends and other strangers to share the experience.

Arthur Rosato: [At SIR] I was the only [technical] guy. It was me and the film crew. Bob would come up with these weird set lists and we'd talk about [them, and I'd be thinking,] 'Why's he talking to me about set lists? He's got all these musicians.' But it's the weirdest group of people . . . Bob is infamous for asking people to come along. 'Yeah, come on down, I'm doing this.' Well, they were all friends of each other and it all kinda worked out. It did make sense. But they happened to be at the right place at the right time.

Lou Kemp: We'd go out at night and run into people, and we'd just invite them to come with us. We started out with a relatively small group of musicians and support people, and we ended up with a caravan.

Even as the sound of rolling thunder came crashing in, Dylan was looking to add to his 'traveling circus.' On October 22, he turned up at the Other End to watch David Blue perform (possibly intending to invite him along). Instead he met the ravishing Ronee Blakely, the actress-cum-singer who had just made an abiding impression as the frail country legend Norma Jean in Robert Altman's three-hour cult classic, *Nashville*. Blakely joined Dylan onstage for a few duets at the end of Blue's show and, with his mind already dovetailing plans for a tour *and* a film, Dylan asked her to join his medicine show.

Ronee Blakely: I don't know what possessed me but I got up and started playing the piano with him! He was playing all the new stuff from the *Desire* record . . . I was playing the same piano, singing along, just doing my best, and he said, 'Hey Ronee, you gotta come on tour with us!'

Though she had other commitments that initially made her turn down Dylan's offer, she rethought her position soon enough to find herself in the studio with him two days later. Another lady with other options, but little to lose, was one Joan Baez. In what was seen as a repayment of some old debts, Dylan had already signed up Roger McGuinn, Ramblin' Jack Elliott, and Bobby Neuwirth when he decided to give the bill true nostalgia appeal by asking Baez to tag along, too. Though Baez, predictably, played hard to get, there was never any question that she wouldn't finally play ball.

She didn't, however, get to add her dulcet tones to a rerecording of 'Hurricane,' required of Dylan because of the abiding nervousness of corporate lawyers. It was felt that a reference in the lyrics to Bello and Bradley 'robbing the bodies'—an unprovable assertion—could lead to litigation. Rather than punching in a new verse over the July tape, Dylan elected to rerecord the entire song (quite possibly because there was such leakage on the original tapes that a vocal 'punch-in' was out of the question).

Rob Stoner: The first or second day [of rehearsals] all these suits from CBS come in and they're all talking about this 'Hurricane' controversy, saying, 'Look, the band is here. You got these guys sitting here right now. Let's go across town and do another version of it now, so at least we got an alternate one.' So that's what it was. They interrupted this rehearsal/jam thing to go across town and just do this quickie thing that they put on the *Desire* album—they just slapped it on to appease the legal problems.

Ronee Blakley substituted for Emmylou Harris on harmony vocals and some congas were added by Luther Rix, but the rerecording lacked that summer spark. Warming up at the piano with 'Sitting on Top of the World' and 'That's All right Mama,' Dylan wanted to get the song down quickly. However, something was not right.

Howie Wyeth: We ended up doing it after we'd been rehearsing for about fourteen hours and they said, 'Okay, now we're gonna go and record.' Everybody was burnt. It was not the right night to record. Everybody was drinking. Ronee was starting to ad-lib more and more. At first, I think she hit an ad-lib that worked. Then, of course, everyone went, Yeah. Which we shouldn't have, 'cause then she started [really] ad-libbing. I think she was juiced.

If so, she wasn't the only one. Dylan kept stumbling over the rewritten words, and by five in the morning he'd simply had enough. According to Sloman, a witness to the session, after ten takes of the eight-minute song, Dylan just put his coat on and said to Devito, 'Man, I don't know. You mix it. You let me know which one you pick out.' In the end, Devito spliced the ending from take six onto the incomplete take two. The recording process was to try Dylan's patience a tad more in the ensuing quarter of a century, but at this point, he just wanted the song out. His mind had not been on recording. The album was a thing of the past. What mattered now was the tour.

Two nights later, Dylan and the band started out a whole lot looser as the Revue assembled at Gerde's for one last blowout, planned to coincide with a birthday party for owner Mike Porco, the man who first booked Dylan back in 1961.

Some of the losers in the lottery of singer-songwriters for the Revue were at Gerde's that night. Eric Andersen, passed over when he needed it most, proceeded to remind his old friend what he would be missing. Phil Ochs also showed up, ostensibly to play for Porco but, in truth, to confront Dylan. Ochs was by now dangerously psychotic. He had been showing signs of schizophrenia for months when, a matter of days before the Gerde's bash, he had been recorded by fellow oddball Harry Smith doing a long, rambling monologue in which he envisaged himself, as his alter ego Luke Train, killing Phil Ochs, then finding himself in the presence of his true nemesis. All his deep self-loathing, suffused with an abiding hatred of Dylan, comes out in this monologue, which appeared in slightly sanitized form in Marc Elliott's thin biography of Ochs:

Luke Train kills Ochs in the Chelsea Hotel, walks out the hotel and coincidentally there stands Bob Dylan, Ochs's friend, enemy, jealousy figure, rival in poetry and, in Ochs's opinion, sell-out—the greatest writer of all time, number one, and the greatest sell-out of all time, number two . . . Train grabs Dylan by the collar and says, 'Listen asshole . . . you were Shakespeare at twenty-five, and now you're dogshit.' . . . Dylan is really a cheap little Jew who happens to be a genius but only for five years [Harry Smith interjects]—okay two years—based on speed and other drugs, and a lot of help from Neuwirth and Grossman.

Among the people in Gerde's that night aiming to send off the Revue in style, was the one singer-songwriter who had turned down Dylan's invitation to tour, Patti Smith. Her choice of image to describe the standoff that evening was worryingly prescient.

Patti Smith: There was a lot of tension. Phil Ochs was there, and Phil Ochs could always bring out that *Don't Look Back* side of Dylan. Bob wouldn't talk to Phil Ochs . . . It was like there was a noose in the middle of the room, and they were circling around, trying to get each other to hang themselves.

Larry Sloman's account of the evening has Ochs finally mounting the stage, but when he sees a drunk in the second row with a knife, he glares at him and says, 'You better use it or I will.' A genuinely concerned Neuwirth then shouts out, 'C'mon, Phil, we're not making a snuff film.' In fact, 'the drunk in the second row' was a perfectly sober half-Indian musician named Roland Moussa, an old friend of Dave Amram's, and the knife that Ochs was glaring at was one Ochs himself had concealed between two cushions in his dressing room. Moussa had found it there and taken it upon himself to remove it. When Ochs was, in Moussa's words, 'looking at me . . . [with] this crooked stare, he knew I had it.' What Ochs intended to do with the knife can only be pure speculation, but despite clearly being in no fit state to tour, he felt torn between great bitterness towards Dylan for not making the offer and an equally deep need for his benediction—such that, when Dylan started for the bar, Ochs cried out, 'Where you going, Bobby? C'mon onstage and sing this with me.' Dylan reassured him that he was just going to the bar, but Ochs knew that he was going a lot further than that, and that Luke would not be invited along for the ride.

Dylan was going on the road with a package tour he had put together himself, to be billed as the Rolling Thunder Revue. First stop: Plymouth, Massachusetts, where those riding on the *Mayflower* had first spied some land. It was an appropriate first docking for a bicentennial tour. The night before the first show, after a further two days of rehearsals at the exotic Seacrest Motel in Falmouth, Massachusetts, Dylan found himself at a far more relaxed pre-tour party, in the company of Allen Ginsberg. Continuing to recognize the man's importance, Dylan planned to make Ginsberg the tour's bard. He engaged with Ginsberg in a brief conversation about God, in which he suggested that his time 'on the mountain' was finally up:

AG: *Well, is [the party] giving you pleasure?*
BD: *Pleasure? Pleasure? No, not at all. I wouldn't want that, would you? That's too dangerous . . . I do what I do without thinking of pleasure.*
AG: *When did you come to that state?*
BD: *Couple years back . . . I mean, at one time I went out [looking] for a lot of*

pleasure, all I could get, because see there was a lot of pain before that—but I found that the more pleasure I got, subtly there was as much pain, and I began to notice a correspondence, the same frame—I began to experiment and saw it was a balance— so now I do what I do without wanting pleasure—or pain—everything in moderation . . .

AG: Do you believe in God?

BD: God? You mean God? Yes I do . . . I mean, I know, because where I am I get contact with . . . It's a certain vibration . . . Yes, I've been up on the mountain and I had a choice—should I come down? So I came down—God said, 'Okay, you've been up on the mountain, now you go down—you're on your own, free— check in later.'

1975: You Come On to Me Like Rolling Thunder

23

It started out a revue, it became an indoor festival.

—*David Mansfield*

As we started sitting down . . . and doing some of the production aspects [of the tour], the film crew started making its presence known. And like the camel that sticks its head in the tent, it soon became the engine that was driving the [whole caravan].

—*Mike Evans*

The Rolling Thunder Revue was in part conceived as an antidote to the hullabaloo that had surrounded Dylan's return to the stage the previous year. By doing the exact opposite, playing with an assembled band of self-styled experimenters, singing largely new material and covers, sharing the stage with co-headliners, and playing mostly theaters, he hoped to remind 'the people that see our show . . . what it is that I do.' The veil of secrecy that surrounded the location of the Revue at any given point; the advocacy of Hurricane Carter; the new material that he was premiering; the fact that it was his first tour since *Blood on the Tracks;* his stated intention to play smaller venues; and the inclusion of Joan Baez on the same bill as Dylan for the first time in ten years—all contributed to a heady brew, albeit one that would be available only on the northeastern seaboard and in Canada's two largest cities.

The show that had been put together at SIR, and honed at the Seacrest, was intended to be a new kind of rock & roll drama. Jacques Levy, with his theatrical experience, was asked to put together a format for a very choreographed show. Though Dylan wanted to be able to push the show in new directions as the fancy took him, he wanted a framework that could house myriad options and yet retain its basic shape.

Jacques Levy: Bob said, 'Can you figure out a way of doing it—a presentation?' . . . I knew we were talking about a big show—four hours or more. So I wrote up a thing like that and I left open spots so there could be guests and shifts. It wasn't really a rigid thing at all, the key point [was] how exactly we'd get to the point where Bob came on, and when to play the new material. We rehearsed the show in New York for almost two weeks . . . And the idea was that it should not look staged. We didn't want it to be a flash show, because that didn't fit anybody's style. The thing was to make it appear like it was a spontaneous evening . . . like a traveling vaudeville show or a traveling circus . . . There was almost a hootenanny feel . . . [But] there was no tuning up between songs, there were no pauses. Big chunks of the show were the same every night.

As Levy also tagged along, his position once the show hit the road was akin to a playwright who, having written a stage play, insists on an ongoing right to tinker with the finished product. Thus, he made himself a little unpopular by taking it upon himself to call rehearsals 'when things were not going as well as I thought they should, or when I felt that things had gotten a little loose, or things were beginning to drift in a direction I didn't like.' When it came to Dylan's set, though, there was little point in rehearsing an arrangement, because he would, like as not, want to change the way a song was performed the following night, keeping the experience fresh for the audience and the musicians but, more especially, for himself.

Mick Ronson: He used to come on one night and play real fast. Then next night he'd play the same songs real slow. Either he was doing it on purpose or . . . he had a bad memory . . . 'Cause he was all over the place some nights. He'd just wander off somewhere, expecting us to follow him. Come to think of it, he had problems knowing what key he was playing in. We'd just have to look at him all the time, 'cause otherwise he'd have finished one song and be into another . . . He really forced you to look at him, what with him being a bit shaky on his timings, key changes and all, he didn't know what he was doing half the time . . . Plus he never played anything the same way twice.

Mick Ronson was one of the more incongruous ingredients in the Revue brew, coming fresh from a three-year stint in Bowie's backing band, the Spiders from Mars, where one always played the songs the same way, where every change was pre-agreed, every solo pre-planned. Though born by the Humber, Ronson had no grounding in English folk music, and was wholly unaware of the source of Dylan's musical eccentricities.

David Mansfield: I don't ever remember him starting a song in one key and lurching into another . . . but working with Dylan gave me a lot of training as an accompanist . . . What I recall that was challenging to learn was his phrase lengths, [which] were totally unpredictable—they were [clearly] based on American ethnic stuff, where it wasn't a neat eight bars, there might be a bar of 2/4, or it might just vamp on something for ten beats—a complete folk thing. I guess it all came from Appalachian music, where it really was a function of the text . . . and sometimes guessing harmonically, from voice-leading, what the next chord change would be, which [might] be necessary from either not knowing the songs, or the other typical thing that Bob would do: completely changing the arrangement . . . He might just one day decide to play something that had been a shuffle as a waltz the next day, and change the chord progression entirely.

Rob Stoner also recalls Dylan developing quite a penchant for rearranging songs during the actual performance. The new songs, in particular, not only excited Dylan but had yet to solidify into a fixed form. Stoner specifically recalls that, with 'Isis,' 'we did a reggae version, we did funk versions, we did the waltzy one, we did the fast metal version . . . Bob was really into that,' but his explanation was not quite as musicological as Mansfield's: 'He's not doing that to be a prick. He's doing that to keep himself from getting bored . . . Anybody who's gonna complain about that shit shouldn't be on his bus! That's the gig!' The most extreme example of this was an arrangement of 'It Takes a Lot to Laugh' that was interchangeable with an epic version of 'A Hard Rain's A-Gonna Fall.'

As rehearsals progressed, Stoner had become the de facto bandleader, the one who relayed Dylan's idiosyncratic jumps between chords, bars, and tempo. Dylan was lucky to find such a man among his assembled music makers, because without someone willing to play Hawkeye it would have been very easy for him and the band to end up playing entirely different songs (as later happened)—and he knew it, retaining Stoner as 'unofficial MD' until Stoner tired of the role in the spring of 1978.

David Mansfield: [Stoner] wasn't handing out parts or anything like that, but he was keeping order . . . I suspect with any of his bands the way that someone became the bandleader [was] by default, by a vacuum . . . Rob had one of those personalities . . . That's something [Dylan] never really knew how to do, basic rock & roll conducting, with your guitar neck you cut off the band.

The Rolling Thunder Revue shows remain some of the finest music Dylan ever made with a live band. Gone was the traditionalism of the Band. Instead he found a whole set of textures rarely found in rock. The idea of blending the pedal-steel syncopation of Mansfield, Ronson's glam-rock lead breaks, and Rivera's electric violin made for something as musically layered as Dylan's lyrics. He had lucked out in the rhythm-section department, finding two guys, Wyeth and Stoner, with inbuilt radar. He also displayed a vocal precision rare even for him, snapping and stretching words to cajole nuances of meaning from each and every line.

Not surprisingly, the new songs seemed to bring out an extra degree of vocal commitment. And every night a third of the Dylan set was devoted to performing two-thirds of the *Desire* album, 'Romance in Durango' and 'Isis' closing out his first set, 'Oh Sister,' 'Hurricane,' 'One More Cup of Coffee,' and 'Sara' setting up the grand finale of 'Just Like a Woman,' 'Knockin' on Heaven's Door,' and 'This Land Is Your Land.' But he was also trawling through his musical roots and, during the Dylan–Baez sets, would resurrect Merle Travis's 'Dark as a Dungeon,' Johnny Ace's 'Never Let Me Go,' or something as unashamedly traditional as 'The Water Is Wide' or 'Wild Mountain Thyme,' songs that allowed him to have a little fun tiptoeing around Baez's piercing soprano.

The other duet of the evening was shared with Bobby Neuwirth, who helped Dylan to announce his presence with 'When I Paint My Masterpiece.' Surprisingly, having truly painted a masterpiece the previous year, Dylan now brusquely disregarded *Blood on the Tracks,* save for interchangeable acoustic renditions of 'Tangled Up in Blue' and 'Simple Twist of Fate.' However much people might have enjoyed hearing that kind of pain, Dylan was evidently in a better place.

The circuslike atmosphere at all thirty fall performances was also reflected in a surprisingly theatrical gesture on Dylan's part: the donning of whiteface makeup. At a couple of the shows he even came onstage wearing a plastic mask, which he tossed aside when required to play harmonica on the second song, a reggae-inflected 'It Ain't Me Babe.' No one seemed too sure what the white mask was meant to symbolize, and only one hardy soul, at a show in Lowell, seemed prepared to ask.

Scarlet Rivera: There was a point where a heckler in the audience . . . said, like, 'Why are you wearing the mask? What is it all about?' And I think his response was, 'The meaning is in the words.' . . . I guess because he wanted to be understood.

Though he did not adopt the whiteface at all shows, all the footage in the film he was shooting drew from shows where he did, and in talking about *Renaldo and Clara,* he would cite the search for identity as the film's main thematic preoccupation. Clearly his whiteface was as connected with the making of the film as the overtly theatrical performances. Talking about the shows to tour chronicler Larry Sloman, Dylan let slip the likely source of his whitefaced self.

Bob Dylan: Ever see those Italian troupes that go around in Italy? Those Italian street theaters? *Commedia dell'arte.* Well, this is just an extension of that, only musically. [1975]

In the *commedia dell'arte* the majority of the players wore masks. The nature of the *commedia dell'arte,* as described by novelist Anne Rice, ran thus: 'Each actor had his role for life, and . . . they did not use memorized words, but improvised everything on the stage. You knew your name, your character, and you understood him and made him speak and act as you thought he should. That was the genius of it.' In this sense, then, the mask was the essential link between Revue and movie. The players, both onstage and in the film, were living out their roles to their logical conclusions. The musicians stuck to the same core material, yet every night it was different, spontaneous, and of the moment. The movie tried to capture that sense as well, though less successfully than the music. Every musician who played on the 1975 tour describes a unique atmosphere, a belief that they were redefining themselves in the process.

Scarlet Rivera: I felt this incredible freedom to express whatever feeling, whatever thought, whatever symbolism, and actually carry it out.

The tour operated as backdrop to a whole series of psychodramas, some of which were acted out for the camera crews that were an intrinsic element of the experience, some of which were acted out onstage, and a few of which managed to be contained behind closed doors. That Dylan somehow managed to occupy the center point of all these psychodramas, no matter how far removed he may have been from their genesis, just seemed part of the Revue's unique internal logic system.

Larry Johnson: [My wife] came to Niagara Falls to tell me it was over. I was totally useless, but I went to Bob: 'This is it. Have you got any advice for me? My wife's leaving me.' He said, 'Ah, ask Sara.' . . . I remember feeling at that point that there was a lot of personal stuff going on which I didn't know the undercurrent of.

Mel Howard: The great love of my life ended up having an affair with Dylan. Things like that were going on all the time.

The sense that, if one blinked, one might miss some significant shift in the vibe, meant that, as Steven Soles has said, 'We never slept . . . because it was so exciting—you're existing on so much adrenaline.' There were precious few on the tour existing only on adrenaline. As Wyeth vividly recalled, 'There was a guy carrying duffel bags full of coke on the tour and you could buy grams for twenty-five dollars, and just get 'em written off to your per diem.' Though speed was still part of many a cocktail, it was cocaine that had supplanted it as the musician's drug of choice. As in 1966, the large-scale drug abuse existed in tandem with a slightly surreal pretense of normality.

David Mansfield: There weren't any horrifying scenes, like someone overdosing, but the level of drug-taking was a good primer [for future tours] . . . like Mick Ronson was young but not a kid, but I don't think he had really tried cocaine before . . . I saw [very quickly] how much he learned to love that leisure activity . . . I remember Beatty Zimmerman back there with the grandkids in the wings of the stage. It was so wholesome. While people were getting wasted out of their minds, doing all kinds of crazy stuff, there were also kids and grandparents around, and this all sort of existed at the same time. While there might be somebody who would run off with you down the hallway to shoot up, or something, there would also be someone to wash your clothes and watch out for you, too.

As in 1966, the need to be 'on' at all times was compounded by the ever-present film crews—two of 'em—seeking to make *Son of Eat the Document*. Back in 1968 Dylan had told John Cohen that if he and Howard Alk had the opportunity to reshoot the sort of footage from which they had composed *Eat the Document*, 'we could really make a wonderful film.' Well, he had not given up on the idea. In October 1975, Alk picked up the phone at his home in Montreal to hear a distant voice saying a single cryptic sentence, 'Bob wants to know if you're ready.'

The two crews had begun filming scenes in New York just as the tour rehearsals whirred into life: David Blue telling stories about the early sixties in Greenwich Village while playing pinball; Dylan's surprise appearance for Mike Porco's birthday party at Gerde's; a meeting between Dylan and Walter Yetnikoff, Columbia Records division president, to discuss the release of the 'Hurricane' single. But it was in Falmouth that filming started in earnest.

Larry Johnson: We had no idea what to expect . . . we knew that the qualities we bring to [a project] are spontaneity and the ability to capture things in a cinematic way, in a theatrical style, in a documentary format. And we knew that he was looking to shoot a lot of material under cinema vérité [styles] . . . [But Dylan] definitely understood cinema vérité [as] an area where truth and fiction collide.

Johnson's partner in film, Mel Howard, was equally in the dark, but less than impressed by the early footage, little of which survived to the final film. Indeed, he voiced the same criticism that Pennebaker had made of the footage Alk filmed back in 1966.

Mel Howard: A lot of the stuff that we were shooting in New York and at the beginning was stuff that was conversational, and worse than that . . . To take that opportunity [to film Dylan] and just parade him around as though he were some lame dick, and everybody's gonna freak out over him, and we can take funny movies of girls giggling, that to me was lame and a drag . . . I thought the stuff was home movies.

If the younger Dylan 'was gonna make everything in a new way—without being quite sure how he'd do it'—the thirtysomething man continued to hanker after something grander than his sixties docudramas. Initially, he decided to bring in a writer to help him write scenes for the movie. At the time Sam Shepard got Dylan's call he was a promising New York playwright on his way to a reputation. As one of Patti Smith's more infamous ex-lovers, it may even have been Patti who had suggested him. They had, after all, spontaneously co-composed a play called *Cowboy Mouth* back in 1972. Neuwirth, whose role in the film's realization has gone all but unrecognized, was equally au fait with Shepard's credentials.

Whatever the initial connection, Shepard was summoned from California to New York, arriving during final rehearsals. His first meeting with Dylan was not auspicious, Dylan's first words to Sam being, 'We don't have to make any connections. None of this has to connect.' He asked him whether he had seen Marcel Carné's *Les Enfants du Paradis* or Truffaut's *Shoot the Piano Player*—ever ambitious, he told Shepard those were the types of films he wanted to re-create. *Shoot the Piano Player* was a rather intriguing choice, being a film about an ambitious girlfriend's attempts to get the anti-hero to resume his once-prominent concert career—seemingly the reverse of Dylan's own circumstances.

Shepard soon found his supposed role to be all but redundant. Even before they left Plymouth, it became apparent that the film would be almost entirely improvised and, as such, there was little need for a scriptwriter. On the road, Shepard traveled with Larry Johnson's film crew. Johnson recalled that 'Sam drove in our van, writing pages, also trying to figure out what was going on.' As Shepard himself later wrote in his fragmented chronicle of the tour, the *Rolling Thunder Logbook*, Dylan quickly 'abandoned the idea of developing a polished screenplay or even a scenario-type shooting script, since it's obvious that these musicians are not going to be knocking themselves out memorizing lines in their spare time . . . So we've veered onto the idea of improvised scenes around loose situations.' Shepard found himself transformed from scriptwriter to bit actor. Dylan, though, continued to insist that the film retained its *raison d'être*, even convincing others that the footage they were filming complied with it.

Bob Dylan: People were told this, this, this—the rest of it is up to you, what you say in this scene is your business, but at the same time beyond that, the only directions you have are: you're going to die in a year, or see your mother for the first time in twenty years. So far as instructions to actors go, less is more. [1977]

Larry Johnson: I got the feeling it was gonna be this traveling circus. As filmmakers it was great, because Bob had Howard [Alk], who was with Bob all the time . . . They knew there was a direct purpose through the whole thing, you always felt there was a journey that had a mission, but the mission statement never appeared . . . There were many scenes that have never seen the light of day that were phenomenal: Kerouac's grave, the old whorehouse with Arlo Guthrie, and the Thanksgiving dinner with the Indians, and somehow, without any written organization, they all became major events. They all became these things when spontaneity would just take off.

If Dylan was reluctant to reveal the 'mission statement' to the film crew or musicians (and the fact that Mansfield says, 'I didn't realize, until I saw [the film], that people were listed as characters, and Allen was the Father and I was the Son,' confirms it) he evidently shared some of his ideas with the tour bard. In Ginsberg's own diary, he noted that the film 'requires discrete scenes . . . with thematic relation but no need story

line plot.' This was fortunate, as the film was clearly evolving, or devolv-
ing, on a day-to-day basis, according to the whims of Dylan, Alk, and
Neuwirth.

David Mansfield: There was a certain level of unreality, hyper-reality,
around the whole thing anyway . . . One of the Bobs would say, 'Hey, let's
go do this. Let's call up the film crew.' I think that was the methodology,
pretty much.

Getting musicians to participate in the movie did not usually present
a problem. Indeed, when the crew arrived to begin filming, it simply
contributed to the Felliniesque atmosphere of most post-gig parties.

Mel Howard: Dylan and the musicians would come offstage and party in
the green room, where there would be lots of booze and drugs . . . We
knew that was the best time to show up with the cameras . . . Since
people rarely did anything without consulting Dylan, he quickly became
the 'director.'

Not that Dylan necessarily saw his role as directorial in any conventional sense.

Ronee Blakely: Everybody was constantly creating scenes for the movie,
and it was somebody's idea for Neuwirth to break a bottle of whiskey on
my door, and for Mick Ronson to carry me out down the hall. Of course,
I don't know about this plot, 'cause I was asleep! I can't remember whether
I had on my bunny pajamas or what, but I was incensed at having my room
crashed into, and Ronson carrying me over his shoulders, and so I said to
Dylan and Neuwirth, 'Who's directing this goddamn movie?' They [just]
pointed at one another.

Like the man standing at Richard Manuel's side as he tries to buy the
girlfriend in *Eat the Document,* Dylan saw himself as an observer after the
fact. Having orchestrated many of the situations, he clearly wanted the
scenes to resolve themselves in as internally consistent a way as possible,
his own role fulfilled, at least until the editing process, when a new level
of responsibility would pass to him (and Alk).

Larry Johnson: Bob really wanted to be the jester-mixer by throwing all
these people together [in order that] he could stand back . . . It didn't take
much for these people to get on . . . [But] I found him to be very sympathetic

to people . . . When you're filming people in a situation like that, there's a cruelty factor. When you invade people's lives, and they're that open, there's always that possibility, and I guess that's why he's sensitive about his own personal life, because he reflects it in the people around him.

Much as Dylan might like to suggest a consistent conceit, maintained from genesis to revelation, it was only as the Revue weaved its way through Massachusetts, Rhode Island, Vermont, New Hampshire, Connecticut, upstate New York, Massachusetts again, Maine, Quebec, and Ontario, that the film became something more than an expensive home movie, and began to attempt to 'wrap up all [the] questions—Ecology, Capitalism, Communism, God, Poetry, Meditation, America,' as Ginsberg noted in his journal at the midpoint of the tour in Niagara Falls.

By this point, certain figures on the fringe of the musical Revue began providing some real input into the film. Larry Sloman was scouting for potential scenes after nearly every show; Sam Shepard had devised several scenes, including one between an alchemist and an emperor, featuring Dylan and Ginsberg; and Ginsberg began to push the whole bicentennial idea, seeing the Revue as a reclaiming of America's heritage, viewing 'Dylan [as] rightly connected to the whole tradition of the beat generation and, through that, to the earlier poets, Poe, the whole sense of the American vagabond,' to quote Mel Howard.

The film, though, had yet to straddle its two preoccupations—a modern *commedia dell'arte* that sought a mythopoeic dimension—when they filmed a scene at Niagara Falls, the day after two concerts there. Straight off the frozen lake, Ginsberg noted, 'Dylan took us back to Duluth—A Mormon Household, everyone in Beards & polish-russian with furniture & big big church family in a church-like house—Big Dinner Coming—Sara said No she grew up in a convent.' It was the first of a number of scenes to involve Sara, Dylan's wife of ten years. And yet it doesn't appear as if it was Dylan's idea to bring Sara on tour. Indeed, according to Bob Spitz, Sara's appearance involved moving a pretty young 'publicist' out of Dylan's room.

Mel Howard: At some point, Howard Alk showed Dylan [my 1972 film] *Snapshots*, which was sort of a 'false documentary.' The film purported to be real, but was actually fictionalized . . . [and] Dylan was attracted to the form. He has always been reluctant to talk about himself and his own life, but he has always flirted with it . . . Howard Alk and I decided to invite Sara on the tour and see how much of this [tension] he would permit to be on film. Sara, who had given up acting after marrying Bob, was excited to be involved in the tour . . . [And, for Dylan,] things he couldn't confront in banal, conventional psychological terms in his own life, he would play out in mythology.

Suddenly, a whole new dynamic was added to the film. The scenes involving Dylan and Sara at times seemed to dissect his marriage for public consumption.

Larry Johnson: He was a brave man, [everything] was fair ground to shoot and film, and there's a subtext of content in [there] that's deeply personal. There'd be moments when I'd look away, knowing that we were getting into some pretty deep shit here, [wondering,] Where is this gonna go?

Not surprisingly, the intensely private Sara was not entirely happy about her newfound role. Her only comment about the filming—'After all that talk about goddesses, we wound up being whores,' a reference to the bordello scene where Sara and Baez reminisced about past loves— suggests that she was unconvinced they were acting out something entirely mythological. But then perhaps her view of cinema vérité was closer to Pennebaker's—watching someone 'going through some kind of change, [hoping to capture] something of it'—than Alk's—'an area where truth and fiction collide.' Though she presumably trusted her husband's artistic instincts, and had known filmmaker Mel Howard for many years, she revealed a little of her sense of isolation to Larry Sloman, admitting in conversation, 'I really can't take the traveling. And I have no real function here. Back home, I have the kids, and other things, but there's really nothing for me to do here.'

Whatever her reservations, Sara's presence pushed the film in a whole new direction, as a central story began to emerge, one involving Dylan, Sara, and Baez in some kind of *ménage à trois*. A preoccupation previously addressed on perhaps Dylan's two most perfect songs—'Visions of Johanna' and 'Tangled Up in Blue'—the notion had taken over the filming when Howard talked to Sloman on the flight from Montreal to New York at the end of the tour. However, the movie that Howard talked to Sloman about was only partially mirrored by *Renaldo and Clara* in its final form.

Mel Howard: The thing that started to evolve as a general theme was Dylan, Sara, and Joan. And Sara and Joan as opposing forces, in different mythological guises, Joan as a certain kind of energy, Sara as a different kind of energy, and Dylan in between, being attracted to both . . . I guess in the last two weeks [of] . . . the tour . . . Dylan was sufficiently secure, and the film just possessed him, and it took him over . . . But I'm afraid how the film is gonna turn out . . . I think it's important to push Dylan in some way to make the film that's there.

If Sara was ambivalent about the experience, Baez was actively hostile. She had told Nat Hentoff, who was preparing a cover story for *Rolling Stone*, 'The movie needs a director. The sense I get of it so far is that the movie is a giant mess of a home movie.' And though this contemporary assessment, made mid-tour, has been borne out by others, she would later offer a far more damning appraisal of the way the movie was shot in her autobiography, *And a Voice to Sing With:*

Joan Baez: One day I was trudging around in the snow on a farm in Canada with Dylan, doing a 'scene' . . . Naturally, I was playing a Mexican whore— the Rolling Thunder women all played whores. The scene opened with Bob shoving me through the snow toward a shack. In fact, there was neither a plot nor a script so the characters 'developed' as we went along . . . It was a cold day, and I wondered what I was doing in this monumentally silly project, and if Dylan was taking it seriously. Sam Shepard was there, supposedly directing it, or writing it, but it was never written, and barely directed. Bob would stand in back of the camera and chuckle to himself, and get everyone to run around and act out his mind movies. The filming happened in gleeful little happenings, enacting whatever dream Dylan had had in the night.

Baez had none of Sara's acting background, and was chronically self-conscious, ever concerned about how others would perceive her, making it difficult for her to adopt her 'mythological guise'—The Woman in White—convincingly. Nor was she willing to involve herself in the kind of 'spontaneity/pseudo-acting' others willingly embraced. Dylan presumably had Baez in mind when he later alluded to some of the problems that stopped him fully realizing some of the film's stronger thematic ideas:

Bob Dylan: A lot of good scenes didn't happen because we had already finished improvising them by the time the cameras were ready to film. You can't recapture stuff like that. There was a lot of conflict during filming. We had people who didn't understand what we were doing, because we didn't have a script. Some who didn't understand were willing to go along with us anyway. Others weren't and that hurt us, and hurt the film. [1978]

Not that Baez was alone in her refusal to go along with Dylan's filmic conceit. Joni Mitchell refused to allow any footage of her to be included in the finished film because of how she felt she looked, a decision that, after seeing the film, she said she would have reconsidered had she realized how jaded everyone else looked. But then Mitchell had not been an integral part of either tour or movie, joining it in the middle, apparently at her own expense, simply to share in the experience. Baez, on the other hand, was most assuredly an important part of tour *and* movie, Dylan delighting in nightly opportunities to puncture her sense of self-importance, even as he sought to convince her to assume her 'mythological guise' in his film. He would mercilessly lean into her face or microphone when she least expected it, stretching the notes, then snapping the lines in half, holding a measure, then forsaking the next, even agreeing on 'The Times They Are A-Changin,' and then singing 'I Dreamed I Saw St. Augustine.' But if Baez was a most unwilling captive offstage, onstage she was determined to ride roughshod through his vocal idiosyncrasies.

David Mansfield: He would do that Appalachian phrasing thing to the nth degree and give you no cues, and [Baez] would stick to him like glue. I seem to recall once or twice he would do that to her, and she would, like, kick him in the pants . . . It got playful and it was charming to watch.

Occasionally, she even managed to get into the actual spirit of this traveling circus, as when one night she appeared in whiteface to duet with Dylan or dressed up as Bob for the final benefit show, to be introduced as Bob Dylan. According to one Rolling Thunder musician, Baez even managed to put one over on Dylan at one of the shows:

Joan and Bob are doing a duet . . . She's really moving. I mean dancing. She starts doing the Charleston and the audience is digging it and we're digging it. Dylan, though, he's plunking his guitar, moving his eyes around quick, like he does, looking at Joanie, looking at us, looking at the audience. Like, 'What the hell is she doing that's going over so damn big?' It's over, and Joan walks offstage, grinning, sees a friend in the wings, and says to him, 'You won't be hearing that number again from this little old duo on this tour.'

The story must be apocryphal—Baez's dance routine was a nightly feature of her own set, never with Dylan—and it almost certainly originated with Baez herself. Here was a woman whose own insecurities appeared to feed on the insecurities of others, imaginary or real. And while the Revue was never a place for the fainthearted, when it came to ego bruising it was the women performers who proved most willing to go the distance. Larry Johnson called it the Battle of the Berets, because 'Joni and Ronee and Baez all showed up wearing berets, and 'cause there was a lot of competition going on with those women.' Baez, in particular, made little attempt to hide her distaste for Mitchell or Blakely.

Larry Sloman: Joan Baez . . . was not encouraging to anybody on that tour. I mean she was like a huge prima donna and felt incredibly threatened: one, that Ronee Blakely was on that tour, and two, that Joni Mitchell came in. There was all this horrible behind-the-scenes shit going on.

The endearingly naive Blakely was no match for giant ego bubbles like Baez and Mitchell. Joni had already turned her own pen on Blakely, dissecting her Norma Jean-like persona in her disarmingly beautiful 'Shades of Scarlett Conquering,' in which she mocked her 'mimicking tenderness [that] she sees / in sentimental movies.' If Joni remained secure in her judgments of others, Baez clearly viewed Blakely as competition of sorts, despite her minimal profile onstage. Even Sara seemed prepared to enter the arena when it came to Blakely, perhaps recognizing a 'type' that assuredly appealed to her husband. Their all-too-obvious mutual admiration only served to bring out a green-eyed Scorpio rarely seen since her husband careered off that country road.

Ronee Blakely: We were finishing up the movie, and Joan Baez dressed up in Bob's outfit, with a hat on, filled with flowers, and his white shirt and a black vest, and his jeans. I was supposed to be a hitchhiker who picked him up, he was just dressed in regular clothes, and we were supposed to go together into a rehearsal, where I was supposed to introduce the real Bob Dylan to the Joan Baez Bob Dylan . . . wherein he was going to audition to go on the road with us and play 'Like a Rolling Stone.' So there we were, along with his wife, Sara Dylan. And somewhere during the shooting of this scene I put my hand on Joan Baez Bob Dylan's shoulder. Sara put her hand on top of mine. So then I put my hand on top of hers, and she put her hand on top of mine. And it was funny. And after the director—whoever that might have been at that moment—yelled cut, I said to Sara, 'What was that . . . Why did you do that?' And she said, 'Nobody can put their hand on Bob while I'm around.'

The scene, needless to say, never made the movie, and Ronee's position on the Revue became such that she would not be invited back when it resumed its travels in the spring of 1976. Nor would Joni volunteer to join up the second time around. In that sense, Baez triumphed in the Battle of the Berets, though it was to prove a pyrrhic victory. She would find herself out on a limb when the Revue was wheeled out again, neither fellow musicians nor Dylan prepared to cater to her apparent sense of self-importance. Not that all the interactions between the women in this caravan were quite so fueled by petty jealousies. Poet Anne Waldman, who had become part of the cast at Ginsberg's behest, recalls discussing with Sara a shaman renowned for mushroom ceremonies, perhaps after filming the bordello scene Waldman was responsible for instigating.

As the tour crossed the border into Canada at the end of November, Dylan began to re-evaluate the financial status of tour and film. Clearly, the film had always been an important part of the motivation for him to go back on the road. Equally transparent was the fact that the type of film he had spent part of October and all of November 1975 making, whatever its final structure, was never going to be the sort of mainstream movie that lent itself to outside financing. Inevitably, the tour wound up funding the filming process.

Bob Dylan: My lawyer used to tell me there was a future in movies. So I said, 'What kind of future?' He said, 'Well, if you can come up with a script, an outline and get money from a big distributor.' But I knew I couldn't work that way. I can't betray my vision on a little piece of paper in hopes of getting some money from somebody. In the final analysis, it turned out that I had to make the movie all by myself, with people who would work with me, who trusted me. I went on the road . . . to make money for this movie. [1978]

The Revue had slotted in a couple of lucrative double-headers at the Civic Center in Providence and the Veterans Memorial Coliseum in New Haven earlier in the month, and as Advent beckoned, the musicians found they were scheduled to play out the tour in the same steel-and-glass canyons that Dylan had frequented last time out. Two shows at Toronto's Maple Leaf Gardens and a single show at the Forum in Montreal were considered to be against the original spirit of the Revue, or so the media implied. Dylan was forced to defend a position he insisted he had never advocated in the first place: 'It's not a nightclub show . . . We have played theaters and we're going to continue to play theaters.'

In fact, the Revue's musical chops were now such that their sound effortlessly slotted into arenas, and Dylan's singing, which had acquired a fine raspy quality in its nether regions, remained as expressive as at the earlier shows. The Montreal Forum show proved to be the best of the tour. It is from this set that the bulk of the live footage in the film comes, including a powerfully theatrical 'Isis,' 'a song about marriage' he dedicated to Leonard Cohen, but directed at the lady sitting in front of the stage, with whom its co-author now seemed reconciled.

The passage from bars to barns was completed on December 8 when the 1975 Rolling Thunder Revue ran its course with a benefit show for Hurricane Carter at Madison Square Garden in New York. They had played to a largely uninterested black audience at the Clinton Correctional Institute for Women the previous day, at which Baez couldn't resist playing to the crowd, expressing the hope that they make it as easy for the inmates to get out as they had made it for her to get in. But it had been a much abbreviated set that only caught fire, predictably, when Dylan sang 'Hurricane.' At the Garden, 'the next night, the revue went back to doing what it knows best,' as Les Ledbetter noted in *Rolling Stone*, Dylan and the Revue delivering a steaming four-hour show that ran on 'full-out power,' without forsaking the subtleties. The reviews were universally positive, even the usually truculent Nik Cohn delivering a rave. It was a triumphant end to a tour that returned Dylan to center stage. How long he wished to stay there, he had yet to decide. He knew that the decision involved not just how to use his newly restored performing powers, but which songs about marriage he might desire to play.

1976: A Hard Reign

24

The folly [in 1976 was] trying to recreate this wonderful thing that had spontaneously combusted months before. That first Rolling Thunder tour just worked because it worked, you couldn't have planned it.

—*David Mansfield*

The best thing I learned from that [1976] tour was that it's a small step from the limo to the gutter.

—*Kinky Friedman*

On January 16, 1976, *Desire* was released worldwide. Prefaced by the 'Hurricane' 45, a *People* magazine cover, and general recognition for *Blood on the Tracks* as the album of the year; coinciding with Nat Hentoff's cover story on the Revue in *Rolling Stone*, Jim Jerome's cover story in *Creem*, and twenty minutes of prime Dylan broadcast on the PBS special 'The World of John Hammond,' it seemed like Dylan was again on the verge of 'occupy[ing] a turning point in cultural space and time.' It was not to be. The seismic impact of new punks on the block, Patti Lee Smith included, was about to reconfigure the rock aesthetic irrevocably.

Not that *Desire* wasn't well received. Only Dave Marsh seemed prepared to admit, in his *Rolling Stone* review of an album apparently kept 'from greatness' by 'Dylan's adamantly antimusical approach,' that 'there are those of us who will always believe that Dylan is copping out until he returns to the fiery rock & roll that drove his middle Sixties work.' Marsh, resolutely mired in the past, represented the minority view, as *Desire* became the third and last album of Dylan's career to top the charts on both sides of the pond, and his bestselling album ever. More intuitive souls, like William Lhamon, an English professor at Florida State University and part-time album reviewer, recognized that this was an album about 'the moments of one more cup of coffee before we leave love for the valley below, the moments of wondering why Joey Gallo got blown away and Hurricane Carter framed, or the moments when we learn that our lovers forgave us not our trespasses.'

If Dylan had seemingly convinced his wife to forgive him his previous trespasses, the events of 1976 were finally to drive a wooden stake into the cadaver of their marriage. Specializing in burning down barely constructed bridges, he sought to reassemble the Revue with Twelfth Night barely passed. This time, though, they were rehearsing a swift swing down Highway 1 from Malibu, at Studio Instrument Rentals in Santa Monica. Not that his proximity to home made him any more inclined to return to his 'angel of the hearth.' An up-and-coming actress, Sally Kirkland, soon became, in Stoner's descriptive phrase, his 'motion of the moment,' as Dylan allowed his mind, and body, to wander from the rehearsals, which already showed signs of diffusion as the Revue worked on, but failed to work up, half a set of 'surprises' for a second Night of the Hurricane, originally scheduled to be held at the Louisiana Superdome but moved to the equally cavernous Houston Astrodome.

Night of the Hurricane II proved to be a fiasco par excellence, by being everything that the 1975 Revue had not been—one overblown ego junket for would-be superstars. Flying the entire Revue out to Los Angeles to rehearse for just one show would have been an expensive exercise in itself. The new venue, the Astrodome, another acoustical nightmare, was, with its seventy-thousand capacity, always unlikely to be filled by Texas bottoms. Dylan's solution was reasonable enough— to add some ticket-selling names. Stevie Wonder and Stephen Stills both volunteered to appear at the show, but they also insisted on bringing their own bands with them.

Howie Wyeth: It was just too much. That show went on forever. And the air—you couldn't breathe . . . The show was like twenty-four hours long, everybody did too much, everybody did too many songs, and there were too many stars there . . . All these guys brought their own bands. They weren't doing it the way we'd been doing it . . . We lost the whole togetherness thing.

As Hollywood starlets got in on the act, further swelling the size of the traveling circus, Dylan found himself again singing 'Sara' and 'Hurricane,' though not with the passion he had found in the fall. Instead, extra vocal commitment was worryingly reserved for some old songs addressed to those disinclined to forgive trespasses, 'One Too Many Mornings' and 'I Threw It All Away,' a licentious rewrite of 'Lay, Lady, Lay' ('let's go upstairs / who really cares?'), and a surprisingly barbed

'Positively Fourth Street.' The Night of the Hurricane II, which grossed some half a million dollars but netted a mere fifty thousand dollars for the Carter defense coffers, was 'the top of the end' of that 'wonderful thing that had spontaneously combusted months before.'

In March, Rubin 'Hurricane' Carter was finally released on bail, pending a retrial (at which he would, again, be found guilty), and Dylan had performed his last live version of 'Hurricane.' He had also performed his last-ever 'Sara,' a song he had quickly grown to regret writing. With arrangements for a spring tour of the Gulf Coast in the formative stages, and with no plans to record himself, he started turning up at sessions for Eric Clapton's new album, which was being recorded down the road at the Band's Shangri-La Studios.

It would appear that he just didn't want to go back to his house on Duma Point, whatever awaited him there, so hanging out with fellow musicians presented an ideal excuse to hide away—particularly when it came to musicians like Eric Clapton and Ron Wood, who were always good for a jam and a jar, as a particularly painful impromptu bootleg recording of Dylan working up 'Idiot Wind' and 'The Water Is Wide' on Clapton's birthday only serves to illustrate. Disinclined to record any new songs, he donated Clapton and Wood a song apiece. 'Sign Language,' a song about the problems two lovers have communicating, appeared on Clapton's *No Reason to Cry*, with Dylan in the unfamiliar role of harmony vocalist. 'Seven Days,' a song about waiting for one's true love to return, he gave to Ron Wood. The narrator insists he's been good while he's been waiting, suggesting it was not one of his more literal songs.

Ron Wood: This [one] session went on for a couple of days solid. There was a point where we stopped the master tape, and just ran a two-track. That's where I got 'Seven Days' from . . . He made this tent up from the clothes on my bed. He made off with my sheets and pillows and everything. At the sessions we very rarely got the chance to have a break, and crash . . . One night I went to creep off to my room and there were no bedclothes at all, and the window was wide open, and I looked out and I could see this tent in the distance, right in the middle of this big field. And Bob had made off with this girl, but she was in a plaster cast—her leg and her arms in plaster! . . . It was like *Invasion of the Zombies*.

Restlessness must have been an important factor for Dylan when he sought to reassemble the Revue at a large resort hotel in Florida at the beginning of April. Whether that restlessness was something he specifically wanted to feed into his music, night after night, was less clear. Reassembling the Revue may have been one way of avoiding going home, but it was almost immediately evident that he was not in the mood to revive the magical spirit created throughout the New England tour.

Arthur Rosato: When the next one came out, that was a strange one . . . I don't think I said two words to him on the whole tour . . . As soon as we got to Florida we knew that this wasn't it. It was way uptight. He was petulant. He didn't wanna be there, and he let everybody know about it.

Rob Stoner: The first time . . . we all holed up in a hotel and rehearsed in the ballroom, and it worked that time. But here everybody was too far from home.

The rehearsals did not start auspiciously, with the ballroom in which they planned to recreate the Seacrest Motel vibe being unavailable. If the first three days of rehearsals thus took place in the cramped confines of the Pool Studio, at least the Revue's frontman was in attendance. On the evening of the 10th, with the Starlight Room finally available, Dylan was having dinner with the band when he was shown the news that Phil Ochs had hanged himself the previous morning, in the New York apartment of his long-suffering sister.

Scarlet Rivera: I was sitting at the table when he got the word about that. And he was really upset and angry that he had done that to himself . . . It was a combination of real sadness and anger. A couple of days went by when he was missing. I think he took the news very, very hard . . . Before he came back to the rehearsals he wanted to clear his mind.

Despite his minimal contact with Ochs in the previous ten years, and the strange state of mind he had found Ochs in that night at Gerde's the previous October, Dylan was very shook up by the news. It doubtless brought back memories of the way Paul Clayton, another member of the same young band of folksinging companions, had taken his own life back in April 1966; and that he had heard about that death—almost ten years ago, to the day—at the start of another maniacal tour, reminding the world 'what it is I do.' If Dylan's rejection of Clayton had undoubtedly stirred that particular spiral, Ochs equally desperately wanted to be a part of Dylan's happy band. Though Dylan was all too aware how unstable Ochs had become, he doubtless blamed himself, as others did, for writing Phil's last rejection slip. Once again he had been reminded just how some got singed when his flame burned bright.

Dylan's efforts 'to clear his mind' evidently didn't work, as his mood did not substantially improve after two days of solitude, and though he returned to rehearsals, they became tortured affairs. Some of the rehearsal tapes that exist from Clearwater come close to the fabled Twickenham jams from January 1969, when the Beatles' torpor had reached such a state that they could barely finish their own songs before calling out old rock & roll standards, hoping to ignite some spark of yesteryear. In Dylan's case, the covers he chose were symptomatic of a troubled soul.

David Mansfield: The most fun was Joan and Bob sitting around with a couple of acoustic guitars and saying, D'you remember . . . ? It is sort of amazing that there were some moments like that . . . Speaking as a musician, whether he was doing it consciously, I am sure that he was [doing such things] to snap out of it . . . I do remember him not attending rehearsals for a while, and I do remember how black his mood was, [but] he didn't do the kind of haranguing that I've heard that he's done with other bands at other times.

The Dylan songs they were rehearsing were equally indicative of a change in the weather. Gone were many songs from *Desire,* replaced with some particularly gritty examples of *Blood on the Tracks.* 'Idiot Wind,' in particular, occupied Dylan's time and energies, and as Stoner observes, 'it definitely reflects what must have been going on with him.' In its new bitter, vengeful guise, it was a reminder of the one-dimensional version of *Blood on the Tracks* Lester Bangs heard in his head:

I discovered that I only really wanted to play this record whenever I had a fight with someone I was falling in love with—we would reach some painful impasse of words or wills, she would go home, and I would sit up all night with my misery and this album, playing it over and over, wallowing in Dylan's wretched reflection of my own confusion.

The Clearwater rehearsals at times resembled a more active version of Bangs's nighttime wallow. Needless to say, Dylan's melancholia affected the whole homesick Revue: 'A month and a half of this, and the boss won't talk to anyone,' to quote Rob Stoner, who did his best to keep the band in a groove.

Joel Bernstein: The rehearsals were in the Starlight Room of the Bellevue

Biltmore Hotel in Clearwater and they went on for some time before the tour. It was somewhat strange. Bob would show up late for rehearsals, he wouldn't talk to the band, he'd just start a song. I never liked Rob Stoner's playing very much but I have to give him credit. He really understood, could follow Bob by looking at his foot, following his heel, listening for the first note, and then he'd get a feel for the key, and the rest of the band took their cue from him. Bob spoke very little—he wasn't talking to me for a while—and it seemed a very strange way to proceed with rehearsals . . . He would just give them these *looks* . . . And the rehearsals went on for quite some time . . . Usually rehearsals began around noon, and Bob wouldn't show up until two or so . . . [then he'd] just pick up a guitar and play a song.

And yet, however bad his mood was at rehearsals, the act of singing these songs clearly helped fill some kind of void. Dylan is really trying, working on focusing the songs, refusing to abandon arrangements that aren't yet working. Three days before the Gulf Coast tour was due to kick off, in Lakeland, he even summoned the core trio of components— Stoner, Wyeth, and Rivera—for an impromptu after-hours rehearsal, just the four of them. The old Elmore James standard, 'The Sun Is Shining,' suggested it was raining in this man's heart, and—playing more electric guitar than he ever had—he roared his way through 'Just Like Tom Thumb's Blues,' 'Ballad of Hollis Brown' (never featured on the tour), 'Isis,' and 'Shelter from the Storm' with renewed power. When the Revue staged a full 'dress rehearsal' performance for the 150 employees of the hotel, on the 17th, Dylan proceeded to deliver one of his most potent performances. Playing a white National guitar—all fuzz, no tone— through much of the show, a newly energized Dylan insisted on continuing the 'rehearsal' even after the employees had returned to their chores. As in 1966, it seems he had found a way to externalize much of that negative energy and channel it into his music.

If he continued to communicate to members of the Revue only through the songs, he did not allow himself to suffer entirely in splendid isolation. If there had been something of a gypsy caravan attendant on the fall tour, it was as nothing to the one that traveled the Gulf Coast Highway with Dylan—an entire retinue of striking, idiosyncratic women able to operate as mirrors to his various moods.

Howie Wyeth: [There was] the tightrope walker—the girl from *The Dating Game* . . . she was a circus performer, she walked tightropes and stuff, [who] sort of seemed like a mystic, but then we found out she also wrote a book about *The Dating Game* . . . There was a real tall chick that was also a magician that was with Bob . . . off and on. They were on the tour, they had their own room. They didn't do anything else. There was a faith healer too, though she was real innocent. She was really a nice lady from Vermont, into all sorts of weird foods . . . My old lady at the time was an astrologer, and she was on the tour . . . and there was a guy on the tour that was into pyramid power, a cat from England, and he looked like a pyramid.

Rob Stoner: It was a big void in his life. The marriage was falling apart, and this thing which had seemed so exciting and promising—Rolling Thunder—that wasn't [working], and he couldn't figure out why, I don't think . . . It was like a midlife crisis. He was confused and he was searching. He tried a lot of chicks . . . he tried [every] kind of chick.

Though some of these 'witchy women' found themselves ensnared by Dylan's libido, it seems that he was more concerned with finding a healer for his state of mind than immersing himself in purely physical activities. As such, the herbalist from Vermont and the tightrope walker from LA found a far from uncommunicative man, albeit someone for whom the oppressions of being Bob Dylan were beginning to weigh heavily again. Susan Green, the 'nice lady from Vermont,' had first met Dylan back in 1962, when she had attempted to book him to play at the college she was then attending. When they met up again on the 1975 Revue, she had cooked him up a herbal brew when he was running low in Burlington and, remembering the benefits, he invited her to join him on the second leg of the Revue.

Susan Green: In April 1976, I was vacationing on the Gulf Coast of Florida at the same time that Rolling Thunder just happened to be there, gearing up for a spring swing through the South. Dylan invited me to become the tour herbalist, adding prophetically that 'people are going to be getting sick.' . . . At Disney World's Contemporary Resort Motel [in Orlando], the singer had a raw throat. So that I could have access to a stove for boiling water, Dylan's bodyguards parked his private camper near the artificial lake with a euphemistic name, the Seven Seas Lagoon. With the herbs steeping, we sat at the edge of the manicured forest in the Magic Kingdom, talking mushrooms. 'When I was in Mexico making *Pat Garrett and Billy the Kid*, everybody was eating mushrooms this big,' Dylan recalled, indicating something the size of a grapefruit. 'They would all be tripping, but I'd barely get a buzz. Drugs don't do it for me anymore. But herbs, man, they get me high. You know how people on acid see a tree come alive? . . . That's how I see things all the time.'

Dylan was prepared to open the door for Ms. Green—showing the same man who had told Jules Siegel, ten years earlier, 'I see things that other people don't see . . . It's terrible. They laugh.' However, it was the 'tightrope walker from *The Dating Game*' who proved willing to step inside. Stephanie Buffington had indeed spent a happy couple of years on *The Dating Game*, even writing a book about her experiences. Dylan was, in Buffington's own words, 'more curious about my own spiritual practice and experience. I think that was the focus between us. I'm a vegetarian, I don't drink, I don't smoke. The Rolling Thunder [was all] omelettes and drugs.' Dylan was equally fascinated by her tightrope walking, rigging up a basic setup at Clearwater so that he might practice daily. While watching Bob wobble across the wire, Buffington witnessed a good deal more of the inner Dylan than the other members of the troupe.

Stephanie Buffington: Big things were happening in his life: the dissolution of his marriage . . . friends dying. That changes you on a deep level. It makes you think of your own mortality . . . Everything's all screwed up in a personal way, it's part of the quest, [and] I think he was doing a lot of soul-searching at that time.

If all parties witnessed a dark side to Dylan at Clearwater, his mood was not improved by a whole series of problems that dogged the tour from the start. These problems had simply not occurred the previous year. Part of it was just the general vibe, part was the inexperience of the road management, and a large chunk was the decision to make this a Gulf Coast tour in the first place. At the first show in Lakeland, Dylan took to the stage after the acquired taste that was Kinky Friedman—he'd taken Blakely's place in the Revue—and immediately opened with his most complex vision, acoustic guitar in hand.

Kinky Friedman: I remember closing in Lakeland with 'Asshole from El Paso' and it went over extremely well, the crowd were laughing, and at that moment Bob chose to weave his way out onto the stage, wearing this weird turban, singing 'Visions of Johanna,' or some other eighteen-minute song, and it was a spectacle, seeing people actually laughing during Bob's song, because they were not really finished with my act. It almost got me pitched off the tour.

The question that had preoccupied Jacques Levy back in October, 'how exactly we'd get to the point where Bob came on,' seemingly no longer concerned the members of the Revue. Down south, a bill that featured Bob Dylan, Joan Baez, and Roger McGuinn was a Bob Dylan show with a couple of support slots by faded sixties bestsellers. The 1976 shows were also far less democratic on a musical level. If Stoner was still doing his best to keep in step with his key-changing, chord-switching frontman, Dylan's electric guitar was now assigned a whole new slot, way up in the mix.

David Mansfield: All of a sudden Bob became a lead guitarist on that tour, which he still hasn't grown out of . . . He now knows how to play a lead solo in the key that the band is playing in, but . . . in those days he really couldn't play [lead] at all.

Rob Stoner: [Dylan] had leaditis then. I don't know what the fuck came over him.

Dylan's electric-guitar playing has always been something of an acquired taste, but a sense of modesty had previously kept him burbling away in the lower registers of mixdom while Bloomfield, Robertson, or Ronson got on with embellishing musical motifs actually present in the songs. In 1976, he was either looking to communicate with his audience on an atonal level, or he wanted 'that scrub-board style that grates through everything,' to quote Arthur Rosato, as an integral part of the '76 sound. He certainly wasn't about to take on board any suggestions about how to introduce a few more textures to the distorted dissonance of that blasted white National he was playing.

Arthur Rosato: McGuinn is this total gadgets freak, but he knows that Bob isn't. But he wanted to show Bob these MXR effects pedals so he ganged like three of them together, stuck 'em right into Bob's guitar. So Roger's frantically trying to get everything together—and Bob's looking down at him—and finally he says to McGuinn, 'Will this make me play like Buddy Guy?' Roger looks at him, yanks the whole thing out.

If the sound of Rolling Thunder, this time around, was suitably abrasive, it was reflected not only in the choice of songs, but the way in which they came out. At the first couple of shows 'Mozambique' was the solitary inclusion from an album that had just spent five weeks at the number one slot. Dylan replaced 'Sara' with 'Idiot Wind,' a brutal substitution, as *Blood on the Tracks* became the featured album for the tour—eight of the ten songs making at least one appearance at these shows—but it was the arrangements that gave these songs a starker meaning than their multilayered lyricism originally suggested. 'Tangled Up in Blue' was given its own bump and grind arrangement halfway through the tour. 'Shelter from the Storm' and 'Idiot Wind' became savage electric denunciations. 'You're Gonna Make Me Lonesome When You Go,' in contrast, was given an easy, fatalistic vocal, in partnership with a wistful country arrangement.

But the most startling inclusion from *Blood on the Tracks* was an acoustic version of 'If You See Her, Say Hello,' performed as song number two at the opening show. In this new version, the singer is haunted by the lady but hates her power over him. Making it almost a 'Dirge for Sara,' his tone starts as dismissive ('She left here in a hurry / I don't know what she was on'); veers between threats toward a new lover ('If you make love to her / Watch it from the rear') and bouts of remorse; before the abject servitude she can still instill in him is allowed to return at the song's end: 'I know that she'll be back some day / Of that there is no doubt / And when that moment comes, dear Lord / Give me the strength to keep her out.' When it came to twisting the blade, Dylan knew the words he needed to summon, and the turns of phrase he could command. As he nightly vomited up 'Idiot Wind' in all its raging glory, he also took time out to hone his barbs in a contest with the game Stephanie Buffington.

Stephanie Buffington: Bob one time told me that he didn't think women could be poets. Because we had a lot of long, long, long conversations in these rides across the country in this motor home, about many things. I took it . . . personally. So then he'd say, 'You write the nastiest thing you can write, and then I'll write the nastiest thing I can write.' And then we'd just have these little games writing things back and forth . . . [It was like], 'Okay, [Bob], what is this thing that women can't experience, or write about, or verbalize, or put on paper? What is this place? You own this place, mister?'

If much of the effortless musicality of the previous tour had been forsaken, placing a far greater onus on Dylan to drive each performance, he had not sounded as close to the edge in ten years or more. The 'Just Like a Woman' at Pensacola reinvented whole melody lines afresh; the 'You're a Big Girl Now' at Hattiesburg uncoiled to reveal a newly independent Eve; 'Stuck Inside of Mobile,' debuted the night before Mobile, was an airtight cauldron of paranoia; 'Isis' and 'Like a Rolling Stone,' filmed for an aborted TV special back at Clearwater, three dates into the tour, traded the celebratory quality of the previous year for passion aplenty. Indeed, some within the band felt that the return to Clearwater was the moment when the '76 band started to click.

Howie Wyeth: The rehearsals sucked in that place . . . it just wasn't happening . . . Then we did the [Clearwater] concerts, and they were filming it, and it happened. That was the first day that the music started feeling right again. Bob did a really hip version of 'Like a Rolling Stone.' He did some tunes that he hadn't done at all.

Certainly the sets filmed for the TV special provided evidence of a man determined to rip up the set list. Brand-new electric arrangements of 'It Ain't Me Babe,' 'Leopard-Skin Pill-Box Hat,' 'Like a Rolling Stone,' 'Most Likely You Go Your Way,' 'A Hard Rain's A-Gonna Fall,' and 'One More Cup of Coffee' were added to the repertoire. Once he abandoned set lists, Dylan didn't look back, and every show would be introduced by an example of familiar fare, 'Mr. Tambourine Man,' and an unfamiliar acoustic surprise. The duets with Baez also dug deep— 'Dink's Blues,' 'Wild Mountain Thyme,' 'Railroad Boy,' and 'Deportees' operating a round-robin policy—before Dylan's highly personalized rendition of 'I Pity the Poor Immigrant' led the band back to that foreign country exposed to idiot winds.

The Clearwater film, shot by Bert Sugarman's *Midnight Special* crew, was never used. According to Wyeth, Dylan 'got into a big argument with [Sugarman] over the dinner table one night, after we'd already done half of it. And then he said, No! We're not doing it. Fuck it!' Though the second half of the show featured some terrific performances by all concerned, Dylan preferred to film one of the later shows at his own expense rather than permit the hokey NBC film to represent the Revue. As it is, the edges just kept getting sharper, the final TV film being almost voyeuristic in its close-up, in-your-face look.

Dylan's prediction to his herbalist, Susan Green, that 'people are going to be getting sick,' also proved more than a little prescient, even if those content to exist almost entirely on man-made medicine were having a better time of it than our man and his herbalist. A week after Clearwater, the Revue snuck into Mobile.

Susan Green: When we reached Alabama, I looked in the Mobile Yellow Pages and found a listing under herbs: Harold's Healing Arts Shoppe. A friend named Claudia and I walked miles until we found the place, in a run-down section of town. Stepping inside, we realized that Harold specialized in voodoo . . . Yet, next to a variety of love potions, I spotted familiar herbs . . . Maybe it doesn't matter where the herbs come from, I thought . . . as another Biblical quote popped into my head: 'It's not what comes into a man that defiles him but what comes out of him.' I didn't have the opportunity to test the voodoo herbs until the tour reached Hattiesburg. Dylan was sick again. Even after drinking my tea, however, his condition hadn't improved by showtime. Unfortunately, members of the tour began slipping him various other remedies as well. Before going onstage, he spent several minutes involuntarily purging all the Mobile balms, and then some. I've poisoned America's most charismatic musical poet, I thought despondently . . . Nonetheless, Dylan gave a terrific performance.

The May Day Hattiesburg show gave a particularly generous airing to *Blood on the Tracks*, with a bittersweet 'Simple Twist of Fate' in the surprise slot, and 'You're a Big Girl Now' and 'You're Gonna Make Me Lonesome When You Go' now redefined by the same ragman as 'Shelter from the Storm' and 'Idiot Wind.' Sara was due to catch up with the Revue in New Orleans, a couple of days later, perhaps prompting such fearless retrospection. If so, Dylan was not quite so fearless in real life, begging his tightrope walker to stay, even after Sara had made her presence known.

Stephanie Buffington: As far as I knew they were separated and she was living at a ranch that they had out in Southern California . . . [But] I did not go into my relationship with Bob with romance in mind—not really even being physically attracted to him. But it obviously turned into that kinda thing . . . [It was] very hormonal . . . For me it was a little difficult because this was like a traveling Peyton Place, and I'm not used to that, I'm repelled by that kind of situation. But I had a certain loyalty, and by that time I had really fallen in love with Bob, and then I was almost asked to stay. All Bob's girlfriends were jumping ship and I was asked not to leave. I wanted to leave because it was a very uncomfortable feeling there, especially after Sara came, I mean, 'Excuse me, you've got business to attend to. Get me out of here!' But I did stay, because I just had a commitment on another level . . . He just said, 'Oh, my wife is coming,' and at that moment I remembered that I had met her before . . . He just said, 'Oh.' . . . Sara had come to my house . . . to buy some Tibetan artifacts a couple of years before I ever met Bob. I [had] even forgot[ten] that I met her . . . I had traveled all over India, and read tarot, and was very involved in that sort of thing at that time, and did a lot of Eastern practices. We had a big conversation. She was a collector.

Confrontation was not Stephanie's trip. As Baez records in her autobiography, she 'vanished quietly when Sara was around,' unlike a local 'curly-headed Mopsy,' whom Baez perpetually paints as 'a lawless intruder.' Despite the ephemeral nature of their one previous meeting, Sara clearly remembered Stephanie and, when they finally met up again, the paranoia that life with Dylan was bound to induce flared up again.

Stephanie Buffington: She said, 'I thought it would be you!' Then I wanted to go, 'Listen, I'm not a homewrecker, this is supposed to be fun. I'm out of here.' I didn't see the whole picture. As far as I knew, he [had been] separated from her for four months and free to do whatever he wanted to. He certainly did [do] whatever he wanted to.

Having found Dylan's version of events wanting, Stephanie took off at this point, leaving him to his perfumed Mopsy and fuming wife. He wanted none of this either, and, when the man from NBC came around wanting to get his approval for the TV special, he realized it was once again time to opt out of a potential confrontation.

Mike Evans: Bert Sugarman showed up in New Orleans and wanted to show Bob the tapes of the Clearwater video thing, and Bob . . . [was] nowhere to be found . . . When I found [his bodyguard] Andy, he says, 'Hey, he got away from me!' . . . It turned out he'd climbed a tree out behind the hotel and was just sitting in the tree.

Not that hiding in trees was going to resolve another sticky situation with Sara. Only time spent together was likely to do that. Fortunately, after an afternoon and evening show in New Orleans—where Dylan sang of a familiar muse in 'Love Minus Zero,' and reconfigured 'Tangled Up in Blue' for the first time—and a show in Baton Rouge the following day, a three-day break opened up in the schedule, thanks to a canceled show at Lake Charles in western Louisiana, on May 6, the first of a number of shows about to be scrapped because of poor ticket sales. Immediately after Baton Rouge, in the words of guitarist Steven Soles, 'we commandeered a bus and we went to visit Bobby Charles in the bayou, somewhere outside New Orleans. We said, "Whoever's coming with us is coming with us," and Bob followed us in a little white van.' Sara, though, was not so keen a passenger.

Mike Evans: We pulled out of New Orleans late—it must have been after the [Baton Rouge] show. Bob and Sara were in one van and McGuinn was with me, but it seems that there was a disagreement between Bob and Sara.

Sara wanted to go back to New Orleans and Roger McGuinn . . . wanted to go on with Bob . . . [Finally,] Sara did continue with us and we finished up out at Bobby Charles's place out in the bayou, very deep, deep in the woods . . . [and] everybody got their guitars out, and it was just a wonderful, wonderful night.

All the musicians remember the time at Bobby Charles's place as the highlight of the 1976 tour. David Mansfield called those days 'a highlight to me of both tours . . . [and] an incredibly powerful experience . . . [just] the food, the music, the alcohol, the physical location.' For the first time, some of that 1975 vibe was allowed to infect their space, so much so that, according to Soles, when Barry Imhoff arrived to remind them that they had to be in Houston in a day's time for a show with Willie Nelson, the musicians said, 'Forget it, cancel the show, no one wants to come to the show anyway.' Even Dylan—though he kept himself (and, presumably, Sara) to himself—seemed to find Charles's place quite unlike anything he had experienced to date.

Arthur Rosato: When we went down further south, one place he came back raving, he was off in the swamp, saying he saw all these lights. I thought, 'Okay, he's getting into this.'

Though the stay at Charles's place seems to have recharged everyone's batteries, the tour was about to undergo further travails, necessitating a further crank of the dynamo. The date in Houston, on May 8, that 'no one want[ed] to come to' was the beginning of a disastrous sortie through the second largest state of the union. Less than five months after the Night of the Hurricane II, the Rolling Thunder Revue failed to sell out Houston's 11,000-seat Hofheinz Pavilion. Despite the late addition of Willie Nelson to the bill, the gig was barely three-quarters full, and the following day's show was canceled altogether.

Ever since September 1965, when he had played Dallas and Austin with his new rhythm & blues band, the Hawks, and had been enthusiastically welcomed by the locals, Dylan had been convinced that Texas was a good place to play. Now, the Revue ended up canceling shows in Dallas and Houston, and the Revue's San Antonio show was moved from the Hemisfair Arena to the somewhat smaller Municipal Auditorium. The two shows at Austin's Municipal Auditorium were also combined into one, again because of poor ticket sales, and reserved seating became general admission. Here was someone who two years ago had generated ten million applications for his American tour, had consolidated his commerciality with three consecutive number one albums, who was failing to sell out medium-sized arenas in Texas. Essentially, the problem was that Dylan had relied on Barry Imhoff at Bill Graham Productions to organize the tour. Unfortunately, Imhoff had no experience of the Lone Star State promoters.

Howie Wyeth: There was a whole bunch of hassles. The promoter didn't get along with the people out west. He was Jewish. I heard there was a whole bunch of stuff he just didn't know. He said the wrong things to the wrong people, and they were prejudiced . . . In Austin they booked us the same night as four other concerts, and then they made all the kids stay out in the rain all night to get the good tickets, and then they decided to make it general admission, after these guys had waited to get tickets so they could be in the front row. Oh boy, were they pissed [off]. They were ready to kill us.

Thus the Revue found themselves with large chunks of time on hand, to get into trouble, to drink themselves dry, or simply to bounce off walls. Sara had again abandoned Dylan to his adulteries in Houston. A general frustration only fueled a backs-against-the-wall mentality. Their best performance was reserved for a free concert at a boys' school in Gainesville, the day of the aborted Dallas gig, though their real intention may have been to steal the dean's daughter. The following day's concert at Fort Worth's Tarrant County Convention Center, recorded for a live album, documented a bunch of guys holding forth for all it was worth.

Relieved to leave Texas behind, shows in Oklahoma City and Wichita, Kansas, were beneficiaries of Dylan's continuing attempts to throw himself into the performances, perhaps to keep the ol' demons at bay, perhaps just to keep from being bored. Wichita witnessed the first documented live performance of 'One of Us Must Know,' a particularly twisted look at a relationship gone bad. After Wichita, the Revue headed into Colorado, where they again found themselves with a couple of days off in a well-appointed resort up in the mountains, where they could hang out and prepare for the Fort Collins open-air stadium show, which was being filmed for the long-scheduled TV special, as well as being recorded for a live album. But the two-day break stretched out to four as the skies continued to pour hard rain down upon their bandanna-covered heads.

Howie Wyeth: They said, You're gonna love this. We got you in this dude ranch up in the mountains. [But] it was raining so you couldn't go riding, and it was up in the mountains so you couldn't breathe. There was nothing to do. And we were all stuck up there. So, after all this adrenaline, it was like detoxing or withdrawal.

Rob Stoner: Bob was really hitting the bottle that weekend. That was a terrible fuckin' weekend. There was a lot of stuff that makes *Hard Rain* an extraordinary snapshot—like a punk record or something. It's got such energy and such anger . . . It was an outdoor stadium and it had rained for days before the gig. We had done this aborted Bert Sugarman special for NBC in Clearwater. I think the deal was that Bob had the right of refusal if he didn't like the videotape, but the terms were that he had to make good on it, at his expense, by doing his own thing to deliver to NBC. Therefore Bob had to hire video, sound crew, twenty-four-track remote truck, all this extra stuff . . . and they've all driven this shit from LA . . . We were supposed to do the gig [on] two or three consecutive days—each time the rain date was supposed to be the next day—but it was pouring for days and days and, meanwhile, it's costing Bob a lot of bread. Everybody's holed up in this little hotel up in the mountains in the middle of nowhere, with nothing to do except get drunk . . . Here's the last gig [sic] and it's taking forever to do it. The boss is getting in a progressively shittier mood . . . Eventually they just decided to go and do it in the rain . . . [and] the rain cleared up on the last fuckin' song—it was the first time that the sun had shone in a week.

The reluctant rehearser even cajoled the musicians into working up revamped electric arrangements of 'Tangled Up in Blue' and 'Just Like a Woman' for the largest show of the tour. If Dylan was hurting for a lost love, it was not Sara who was on his mind. He missed Stephanie. Having tracked her down, he again left it to one of his minions to ask her to come back. This time, though, Stephanie wasn't impressed: 'I wasn't gonna go unless he called in his own voice.' His bluff called, Dylan made the call himself, begging her to join him in Estos Park. Eventually, he prevailed, even if the time remained out of joint. As Stephanie says, 'I think I was there five hours and Sara arrived back too. It was like, What am I doing here? . . . I was a fish out of water. I don't get mixed up in people's tragedies or ego battles.' Stephanie was not about to face off against the missus again. Even as Dylan was pleading for her to stay, Sara was waiting outside, metaphorical rolling pin in hand.

Joan Baez: Sara showed up late in the tour, wafting in from a plane looking like a madwoman, carrying baskets of wrinkled clothes, her hair wild and dark rings around her eyes . . . Sara appeared airily at the front door dressed in deerskin, wearing her emerald necklace and some oppressively strong and sweet oils. She greeted me with a reserved hello and talked distantly about nothing in particular, all the while eyeing the closed door to the ballroom.

Presumably Sara had arrived all along with the purpose of confronting Dylan, though her ostensible intent was to help him celebrate his thirty-fifth birthday among family. With his children and mother in tow, Sara seemed determined to remind the man of his obligations. Dylan, though, was in no mood to listen as, according to Stoner *and* Wyeth, Sara lit into him in the parking lot. If anything, Sara had only deepened a slowly forming resolve.

Such personal retribution may not have been the best of preparations for Dylan's most important gig of the year, but it forms a fitting bookend to the whole tour. Finally, on the 23rd, the Revue performed their penultimate show to a wet, but surprisingly appreciative, Fort Collins audience. Perhaps predictably, Dylan and the band responded with one of the best shows of the tour. The sense of sheer desperation is there on both film and album (*Hard Rain*). It may be ragged, but it was all right—there was real fire in that firewater they'd all been imbibing.

Scarlet Rivera: There was a lot of pressure on that day to get that filmed [and recorded] . . . This was the last possible moment for this recording to be made, and it was under the worst circumstances.

Rob Stoner: Everybody's soaked, the canopy's leaking, the musicians are getting shocks from the water on the stage. The instruments are going out of tune because of the humidity. It was awful. So everybody is playing and singing for their lives, and that is the spirit that you hear on that record.

It was almost as if the whole tour had been building up to this confrontation in the rain. It cannot be coincidence that Dylan sang his most rancorous performance of 'Idiot Wind' the day Sara sat, one imagines stone-faced, in his sightline. Visions of her chestnut mare had turned into 'visions of your smoking tongue.' Every time he now came into her room, 'you leave me standing in the middle of the air.' Alk's film crew played war correspondent as Dylan relived each battle in a single performance until, on the final verse, the scales fall from his eyes and he roars, 'I *think* I finally see!' (a welcome equivocation). Whereas the narrator seems to accept his own idiocy at song's end, the man at Fort Collins rocks his head from side to side on the word *sorry* (or *sarreee*). Here was a man who felt no such remorse. If the message required reinforcement, he even added a new coda to 'One Too Many Mornings': 'I've no right to be here / And you've no right to stay / Until we're both one too many mornings / and a thousand miles away.'

The Dylan singing on *Hard Rain* had never been more attuned to his performance art. The results may be harsh (though not as harsh as many of the reviews), but as an example of audio-vérité it has few peers. For sheer, undiluted vitriol there can be few songs able to stand alongside 'Idiot Wind' at Fort Collins. 'Shelter from the Storm' brought an equally demonic performance from a man about to face the consequences of his own actions. This time, though, the line the man was bound to cross pointed away from shelter, and back into the storm. The final Rolling Thunder show was in Salt Lake City two days later. Playing in a half-empty seventeen-thousand-seat Salt Palace, the Revue gave another great performance.

Joel Bernstein: It was a very spirited show, perhaps because it was the last show. People knew that it wouldn't happen again.

It was a dispirited set of musicians who boarded the plane out of Salt Lake City, bound for LA. Though the tour had pushed Dylan in ways only the tapes can reveal, it had also been one of the most ramshackle, half-assed débâcles in modern touring times. The cherished traveling-circus conceit had been left with the excess baggage, and Dylan found few allies had stayed the course. Arthur Rosato's abiding image of that flight remains Joan Baez attempting a communal version of 'Happy birthday, dear shithead.'

It would be another twenty-one months before the not-so-young Dylan would emerge from another self-imposed retreat, and another two years before he would record any more of the visions that continued to come from his pen. In September, NBC screened the one-hour *Hard Rain* TV special, and managed to get Dylan on the cover of *TV Guide*, but to disappointing ratings and generally unfavorable reviews. In contrast to NBC's own sugared version, Alk and Dylan had seemed determined to make people uncomfortable, the visual intensity for once matching a live concert's audio track.

But Dylan and his old friend Howard Alk had more ambitious editing tasks to undertake. It was time to assemble their grand vision: *Renaldo and Clara*. Time in the editing suite was also time spent away from home. Rosato recalls that they got a first edit fairly quickly—unfortunately, it was eight hours long. Unwilling to allow any outside distractions, Dylan almost didn't go up to San Francisco in November for the farewell bash of the Band at the Winterland Ballroom.

Arthur Rosato: Bob asked me, Think I should go up for that? . . . [He was] in the middle of this and it [was] hard to drop it and run off and do this and come back and get back to editing again. [But] he ended up going up.

Levon Helm: Bob didn't really want to be in the movie because he was working on his own movie, *Renaldo and Clara* . . . We explained about Warners wanting to finance only if Bob appeared in the film, and . . . Bob said he would think about it . . . About fifteen minutes before we were due back onstage with Bob, he decided he didn't want to be in the film. I wasn't that surprised. Howard Alk had been saying all week . . . Bob didn't want to compete with himself by having *The Last Waltz* and *Renaldo and Clara* go head to head.

Though he finally obliged with a gutsy six-song set, for which the cameras were allowed to roll on three, he was a reluctant partner in *The Last Waltz*, and was going to make damn sure that his own film came out first. As Helm writes in his autobiography, 'Bob Dylan's lawyer [went] into the truck immediately after the show and seized the tapes Bob was on. So there would [still] have to be negotiations.'

That Dylan, ten years down the road, was again recuperating from an emotionally draining tour—where he had pushed his performance art to the limit, in complete disregard of all public perceptions—by staring into a Moviola with Howard Alk, trying to piece the whole thing together, was one of the scarier flashes of déjà vu from 1976. That he continued to exert bittersweet mental revenge for some unspoken sins his 'sweet virgin angel' had unwittingly fashioned made for an altogether more painful, not to say costly, period of retrenchment this time around.

1977: Everything Went from Bad to Worse

25

I can't go home without fear for my safety. I was in such fear of him that I locked doors in the home to protect myself from his violent outbursts and temper tantrums . . . He has struck me in the face injuring my jaw . . . My five children are greatly disturbed by my husband's behavior, and his bizarre lifestyle.

—*Sara Dylan, press report of divorce proceedings, March 1977*

The amount of 'blow' suctioned up by various parties during the filming of *The Last Waltz* may, line for line, make the quantity consumed by Alk and Dylan when piecing *Renaldo and Clara* together mere diaspora, but cocaine was a bad habit to (re)acquire. An anti-social, intolerant form of recreational self-abuse, it allows for no one save its participants. That on his return to LA Dylan also resumed his liaison with Sally Kirkland suggests that all thoughts of reconciliation with Sara had passed from his mind.

And yet the pretense that had become their marriage was maintained for some nine months after his return. With no access to the minds of the participants, one can only speculate on the degree of psychological torture inflicted on Dylan's long-suffering wife, based on his well-known reluctance to personally confront, to bring a closure to any relationship. Though it is hard to lend credence to the allegations of physical violence made by Sara in the subsequent divorce proceedings, and there is no independent evidence for it, there is little doubt that Dylan exacted a heavy psychological price for the return of her dowry, putting Sara in a psychiatrist's chair after the divorce, and driving her to the only proven act of violence in the whole sorry saga.

The final act of their marriage was played out according to Dylan's script. He spent several days in February 1977 at Gold Star Studios in the company of Phil Spector, Leonard Cohen, and Allen Ginsberg. The ostensible purpose was to help Cohen record a new album, *Death of a Ladies Man*, but, as with the previous year's superstar jam, it became largely an excuse for chaotic carousing. After one particularly drink-driven session, Dylan returned to his house in Malibu with an old friend of Leonard's in tow. According to a declaration by Sara Dylan's legal representative, released to the press in March 1977, 'On February 22nd of this year, [Sara] came down to breakfast and found Dylan, the children, and a woman named Malka at the breakfast table. She said that it was then that Dylan struck her on the face and ordered her to leave.'

Malka is not likely to have been the new lady in Dylan's life, though he doubtless bathed in the powerful Eastern European vibe of the very woman Joni Mitchell once described as having 'a mouth like yours / She knew your life / She knew your devils and your deeds' ('A Case of You'). Malka was one of those poetesses Dylan had his doubts about. Though Sara's press release made Malka seem a key player in the drama, she was one of a number of ancillary characters, albeit the one that finally triggered Sara's departure and divorce.

It was classic Dylan behavior: rather than simply ask his wife to leave (or leave himself), he preferred to allow an intolerable situation to develop, forcing the other party to show their hand first. In Sara's case, she had a strong suit, made stronger by her immediate retention of Marvin Mitchelson, the 'Palimony King,' as her attorney. If the prospect of a very public and acrimonious divorce had tabloid hacks sharpening their pencils, on the day proceedings commenced in her divorce suit, a plea was immediately made for the documents relating to the court case to be sealed. As the *Los Angeles Times* reported: 'Mrs. Dylan's attorney, Marvin Mitchelson, concurred in the request of Dylan's attorney, Marvin Burns, to prevent disclosure of the marriage dissolution, filed by Mrs. Dylan March 1st. Judge Raffedie additionally sealed other documents stipulating the assets of the Dylans, and ordered sealing of a response by Dylan yet to be filed.'

The divorce thus proceeded in a surprisingly sedate manner without, it would appear, any concerted effort by Dylan to be reconciled with Sara. The divorce became final in June, though the commissioner announced he was 'retaining jurisdiction of their communal property for future determination.' Sara reportedly received a $6 million settlement, as well as a half share of Dylan's ongoing royalties from those songs copyrighted in the period they were married. Resident in a state with community property laws, Dylan had very little room to maneuver. The most pressing question, though, remained the custody of the children, something that would not be settled for some time.

Not surprisingly, Sara initially retained legal custody of the children. The situation only became highly charged when she decided to go to Hawaii, apparently to look for a new home for herself and the children. She left a woman called Faridi McFree in charge of her home. McFree had originally been employed by Sara to help the children during the legal wrangles, using a technique called 'art healing,' which involved encouraging children to express themselves through painting. Unfortunately, years of living with her chameleon-poet husband had clearly taken its toll, and a destabilized Sara turned on the lady brought in by a friend to lend a helping hand.

Faridi McFree: Rosanna [Taplin] came to me and she said, 'Faridi, Sara is in such a bad way. Would you please help her with the children? You're doing art healing and the children [can] really benefit by it.' . . . So that's how I got involved with the children . . . We'd work together on the same piece [of art] . . . I started off with her, and then she really treated me very badly. I just said, 'I'm here to help you, I'm not here to be abused. I don't think you need my services anymore.' And [then] she went to Hawaii. But she said, 'Do me a favor. Just stay in the house, please. Do me this one favor, because I really want someone in the house, and I trust you.' I said Okay.

Though she had lived in Woodstock in the late sixties, McFree did not know Sara's ex-husband, though they had met at the wedding of Rosanna and Jonathan Taplin in 1975. However, as she tells it, McFree suddenly found herself awakening from an intense dream involving Dylan a couple of days after Sara had set out for Hawaii.

Faridi McFree: I fell out of bed. I mean it was so intense, this loneliness, and I didn't understand it. Then that morning the next door neighbor, [who] was a filmmaker, a very big one, called me and said, 'Did you hear, Faridi? Bob got a divorce last night from Sara in Santa Monica.' And I said, 'No, Sara's getting the divorce.' And he said, 'Uh-uh, he beat her to it.' And then I had this pain again in my heart all day. I [thought], I can't stand it, [and] I picked up the phone and I said, 'Bob, this is Faridi. I work with Sara and the children. I'm the children's art teacher. Are you okay?' And he said, 'No, I'm not okay.' So I said, 'I had this strong feeling that I should call you.' . . . And then he [asked me], 'What are you doing right now?' I said, 'Nothing.' He said, 'Why don't you come over? I really, really need to talk to someone.' I said, 'It's late. I don't really want to.' 'Cause he was thirteen miles from the house that she had rented at the colony . . . [and] I was a little afraid of him, so I said, 'I don't think so.' He said, 'I really do.' So I said, 'Oh, okay.' . . . I go there, and I was scared, because there are all these bodyguards, and it just seemed very scary, all these guys. [But] they let me in . . . And then Bob came toward the light and, as I was driving slowly, he looked like he was crazed. And I got so scared. I said, 'Oh, my God.

What am I doing here?' But he came to the car, and he drove with me to the house, and we just never stopped talking . . . We just talked into the night. I don't think we stopped talking until four or five o'clock in the morning. He just poured and poured and poured out his heart. All these grievances that he was feeling, grief and everything else . . . We talked right around the clock. And that's how [our affair] started.

Dylan's involvement with McFree was bound to make an already complex situation doubly problematic. Sara had spent her married life dealing with, and deflecting, the many women who sought to befriend her solely to get close to her husband. Though Faridi had none of Sara's radiant sensuality, there was clearly some deep, intuitive connection that she and Dylan divined on first meeting.

Faridi McFree: When she came back I was already with him. I had moved into his house. It was fast with us. She . . . totally freaked out. And I said, 'Bob, I don't know what's happening with us, but I feel it's the wrong move. I don't think I should move.' . . . But he insisted that I move in with him. And I said, 'She is going to misunderstand all this.' So he said, 'Well, is she your mother?' I said, 'No, she's not my mother but I don't want to start any problems.' 'Cause she had told me all these stories about all these women that would use her to get to him.

As another summer beckoned, he decided to take a temporary rest from editing the film, and head for his farm in Loretto, Minnesota. He planned to take the children along, as well as Faridi, with whom they had already established a rapport through her art healing. It really did seem as if it was 1974 all over again. That sense was reinforced when the calm of the farm again inspired him to begin writing a whole new set of songs.

Not that he hadn't penned a few lyrical directives during the divorce process. Steven Soles recalls Bob coming over 'unannounced' to his apartment one day in the spring, when T-Bone Burnett was in attendance, 'and played us, I don't know, ten, twelve songs . . . to get our take on [them]. And of course it just completely floored us, but it was very dark, very intense—none of those songs were ever recorded.' This seems to have been Dylan's intent all along. He alludes to the same set of songs in an interview with Robert Hilburn a year later, insisting, 'I cut that whole experience right off. I had some songs . . . They dealt with that period as I was going through it. For relief, I wrote the tunes. I thought they were great. Some people around town heard them . . . But I had no interest in recording them. I wanted to start off new on the album.'

It had been two years since the starburst of songs out of which he had produced *Desire*. If he had been writing songs in the interim, as he suggested, he always intended to exclude them from the authorized canon. The new songs he began writing were perhaps his most technically sophisticated lyrics to date. Songs like 'Changing of the Guards' are among Dylan's strongest lyrics, read off the page, and he evidently wrote them first, later putting them to music, something he had not attempted since *John Wesley Harding*.

Faridi McFree: He started to write *Street Legal* when we were together. He would show me some of the songs that he was writing. [It was] practically the entire album . . . It started when we were on the farm . . . He was very down. Don't forget, he was suffering when I met him. He was in a bad way. I brought him back to life. He was practically dead . . . this guy was shot emotionally and he had to get away from all the pressures in Malibu. The farm was really where he got back up on his feet again. But then that custody case was so vile and so treacherous. I mean, I kept running away 'cause I couldn't handle it. The kids were on the farm.

As Faridi says, 'practically the entire album' seems to have been written on the farm, six of the nine *Street Legal* songs certainly dating from 1977, including 'No Time to Think,' 'Where Are You Tonight?' and 'Changing of the Guards,' three of his most ambitious, not to say wordy works. Like *Blood on the Tracks,* he would spend some time honing the words, and trying out tunes (the original melody for 'Where Are You Tonight?' bears almost no resemblance to its studio guise), before letting outside musicians try them on for size. But, unlike *Blood,* indeed any previous collection, Dylan actually put off recording the songs for almost nine months—a most uncharacteristic decision, suggesting perhaps that he did not yet feel comfortable with the songs as they stood.

If his time on the farm allowed Dylan to get 'back up on his feet again,' one real moment of sadness came to him, and millions like him, during his time in Loretto. On August 16, 1977, at 3:30 P.M., Elvis Presley was pronounced dead at the Baptist Memorial Hospital in Memphis, Tennessee. He had been taking enough pills to poleax a herd of mules, but—despite his ex-bodyguards asking *What Happened?* in a book published shortly before his death—the world at large was unaware just how bent on oblivion Elvis had become. Like the death of Phil Ochs in April 1976, Elvis Presley's permanent siesta made Dylan, who had met him only once, temporarily morose and uncommunicative.

Faridi McFree: I was with him the night Presley died. It was in August. He really took it very bad. He didn't speak for a couple of days. He was really grieving. He said that if it wasn't for [Elvis] he would never have gotten started. That he opened the door.

Bob Dylan: I went over my whole life. I went over my whole childhood. I didn't talk to anyone for a week. [1978]

The time he spent with Faridi and the children down on the farm helped Dylan to make a quite extraordinary decision. He was going to fight Sara for the custody of the children. The odds were set against him. Leaving aside the courts' understandable bias toward the nurturing mother, and even allowing for Dylan's undoubted devotion to his children, his lifestyle alone, and the uncontested allegations Sara had made in her initial court statement, left him electing to fight a battle he couldn't win. Possibly he felt that he could set up a home with Faridi. If so, it would have to be in cloud cuckoo land. Inevitably Marvin Mitchelson, Sara's lawyer, set about exploiting the way that the relationship with McFree had come about.

Faridi McFree: Right after the divorce . . . he felt that he wanted [the children] and the children wanted to be with him, and that's when he decided to go to court and fight for them. And Marvin Mitchelson . . . used everything he could to win the case and Bob's lawyers knew that, and warned Bob to get rid of me. They said, 'Let her go. She shouldn't be around you 'cause you'll lose the case.' And he just wouldn't. So I used to go into hiding when they came over. This was both on the farm and in Malibu.

Matters came to a head in September. Mitchelson asked the court to give Sara permission to move to Hawaii, to live there with the children. Hearing of Sara's September 2 petition, and realizing that she intended to remove the children from his immediate influence, Dylan asked that the court grant him sole custody of the children. The original settlement required a court order, or the other parent's written consent, for the children to be taken out of California. Within four days Dylan's new attorney, Robert Kaufman, filed papers alleging Sara Dylan had violated that original court order by taking the children with her to Hawaii at the beginning of the summer. Mitchelson insisted that the legal action Dylan had taken was 'precipitous, hysterical and without foundation.'

In fact, the only participant who proceeded to act in a way that might be deemed precipitous and hysterical was his client. Sara had returned to Hawaii to make further arrangements to set up a home there, leaving the children in California. Dylan took the opportunity provided by Sara's absence to enjoy temporary physical custody of the children—according to a later declaration to the court, part of an attempt by Dylan and Faridi 'to brainwash the minor children and to deprive them and [Mrs. Dylan] of the natural love and companionship of each other.' Sara proceeded to obtain physical custody of the children in a surprisingly violent manner.

A further hearing had been set for December 1. Meanwhile, an interim court order had specifically ordered Dylan to return Jesse, the one kid old enough to abscond, to his mother. Within days of the hearing that resulted in this court order, though, Sara was being charged with assaulting a teacher at the children's school in Malibu. According to a syndicated report of the incident, Sara invaded a classroom 'flanked by three private detectives, chased the Dylan children through the school, frightening other students' and attacked teacher Rex Burke 'when he asked to see the court order.' The children 'apparently resisted going with Mrs. Dylan.' If the custody battle was wearing on Dylan, Sara was clearly becoming unglued. She was later fined for her assault on the teacher. Quite why she acted in this way is unknown, as she had a court order giving her custody of all five children (including Maria, Dylan's stepdaughter). Faridi McFree believes that the state of mind Sara found herself in was probably something originally intended for her.

Faridi McFree: I was always with the children and that was the first day that I wasn't, and she went into the school system and they took the children by force . . . It was really a traumatic experience for them.

Reaching a reasonable settlement with Sara had clearly become a major problem. Her perception of the relationship with Faridi was always going to color her thoughts, one of which, the thought of sharing her children with her ex-husband and this art teacher, was clearly too much to bear. When the settlement was finally made late in December—ensuring that the children remained in California, and that Dylan would have access to them—Sara Dylan and Mitchelson insisted on the complete exclusion of Faridi McFree from the children's circle of influence. Inevitably, Faridi became the sacrifice necessary to resolve a bitter custody battle.

Faridi McFree: When I came to New York, Mitchelson made him sign a piece of paper that he would never see me again, and then the case was settled. It was either me or the children . . . there was a lot of money involved too, and he didn't want that case to go on any longer. It was really painful. I don't know what all the details were, but he told me that, and I just knew it was the end for us . . . If your children are at stake and your life is upside down, you're gonna sign that piece of paper.

Though Dylan and Sara would ultimately come to terms with each other's way of giving, even genuinely considering getting remarried in 1983, it would be some time before the wounds of the custody battle faded away. When he was giving a number of interviews in January 1978, Dylan seemed to consider relations with Sara irrevocably breached.

Bob Dylan: No one in my family gets divorced. It's just unheard of, nobody does that. And so when I did get married, I never conceived of getting divorced. I figured it would last forever. But it didn't, and now there's a marriage and there's a divorce. And the circumstances in my life have led to the divorce really being a divorce . . . most people don't really get divorced. They keep some contact, which is great for the kids. But in my case, I first got really married, and then got really divorced. [1978]

That the custody battle operated as a backdrop to Dylan assembling his massive, sprawling cinematic opus, *Renaldo and Clara*, with Howard Alk, gave gossipmongers a field day. Though he could hardly omit the scenes with Sara from the film, it inevitably led to speculation that he was washing his dirty laundry in public. In fact, Mel Howard insists that 'Dylan obscured a lot of the personal revelations in the editing process. I know that he left out some of the most revealing material with Sara and Joan.' Not that the scenes with Sara that were edited out were left lonely. An enormous amount of footage had been shot on the tour itself and, though Dylan's co-editor Howard Alk would insist that the end product maintained 'the standard documentary ratio,' many of the most vividly recalled scenes ended up on the cutting-room floor.

Howard Alk: We knew from the beginning that the film was going to be too long [for some] . . . [though] our final ratio of what was shot to what's in the final film is the standard documentary ratio of 20 to 1 . . . Actual cutting took about six months. We began work on the film [in 1976] . . . but we were interrupted by the second leg of the tour and by the television show, so we were actually in the editing room for six months [in 1977].

Bob Dylan: I knew it was not going to be a short hour movie because we couldn't tell that story in an hour. Originally, I couldn't see how we could do it under seven or eight hours. But we just subtracted songs and scenes and dialogue until we couldn't subtract any more. [1978]

Renaldo and Clara, as released, clocks in at three hours 52 minutes. Dylan soon realized that the length of film would scare off any major studio. Though he approached at least one major studio before editing began, and another when it was finished, it was self-evident that there could be no rapprochement between Dylan's conceptual ideas and a Hollywood studio's understandable desire for something a tad more linear, and certainly 'something more definite than an improvisational film with just an outline based on death and rebirth.'

Bob Dylan: We took the movie to one of the major studios. They treated us like dogs. As far as I can remember they didn't want to see more than fifteen minutes of the film before they bought the picture. We felt it only proper they should see it all . . . They thought it should run for one and a half hours, and that it had to be all music. [1978]

Though the film would be attacked for its lack of cohesion, it was in fact structured very carefully. Dylan even gave out a set of production notes to accompany the film's release, detailing the types of scene shot for the movie (all quotes are Dylan's own):

(i) Dylan would set up a scene for improvisation, and let the actors work around a given concept. Various people such as Ronee Blakley, Ronnie Hawkins, and Mick Ronson had great talent in expanding on a Dylan idea, and they took off from this starting point and embellished with their own contributions. Dylan emphasizes that 'all the dramatic scenes are filled with reason, but not with logic.'

(ii) Dylan would give the cameramen an assignment to get a certain type of image, then he would let them go about their work, not being physically present during the shooting. These scenes add another texture to the film, outside of the Rolling Thunder Revue and the acted scenes.

(iii) After shooting proceeded and cast and crew had picked up on Dylan's modus operandi, the director opened the film up for people to create their own types of drama. Characters had taken on lives of their own, and actors were given free rein to extend these lives out to their logical conclusions. 'I'll tell you what my film is about: it's mostly about identity—about everybody's identity. It's about naked alienation of the inner self against the outer self—alienation taken to the extreme. And it's about integrity. The film is about the fact that you have to be faithful to your subconscious, unconscious, superconscious—as well as to your conscious. Integrity is a facet of honesty. It has to do with knowing yourself.'

(iv) Documentary coverage had its place in *Renaldo and Clara* when Dylan visited Jack Kerouac's grave in Lowell, Massachusetts, with Allen Ginsberg, or when he traveled to a New York CBS Records executive meeting, the camera was present to record the activities. 'You must be vulnerable to be sensitive to reality. And to me being vulnerable is just another way of saying that one has nothing more to lose . . .'

Having accrued these various types of footage, the film was constructed according to certain rigorous criteria. Unfortunately, few reporters were interested in how (or why) he had spent a year of his life putting the film together. All they wanted to know was why Bob Dylan ended up being played by someone else (Ronnie Hawkins); who exactly Bob Dylan played in the movie; and whether the *ménage à trois* of Renaldo, Clara, and the Woman in White reflected some aspect of the relationships of Dylan, Sara, and/or Baez in real life. Allen Ginsberg took it upon himself to interview Dylan extensively about the way the film had been made. Becoming an unpaid publicist, Ginsberg then went on radio shows and behind lecterns to talk at length about the film's composition.

Allen Ginsberg: It's built in a very interesting way. You'd have to study it like *Finnegans Wake,* or Cézanne, to discern the texture, the composition of the tapestry. He shot about 110 hours of film, or more, and he looked at all the scenes. Then he put all the scenes on index cards, according to some preconceptions he had when he was directing the shooting. Namely, themes: God, rock & roll, art, poetry, marriage, women, sex, Bob Dylan, poets, death—maybe eighteen or twenty thematic preoccupations. Then he also put on index cards all the different characters, as well as scenes. He also marked on index cards the dominant color—blue or red . . . and certain other images that go through the movie, like the rose and the hat, and Indians—American Indians—so that he finally had a cross-file of all that. And then he went through it all again and began composing it, thematically, weaving these specific compositional references in and out. So it's compositional, and the idea was not to have a 'plot,' but to have a composition of those themes. So you notice the movie begins with a rose and a hat—masculine and feminine. The rose is like a 'traveling vagina'—those are his words. The hat is masculine—crowns. The rose . . . travels from hand to hand . . . It's a painter's film, and was composed like that. I've seen it about four times, and each time I see it, it becomes more logical—not rational, but logical.

Bob Dylan: The film is no puzzle, it's A-B-C-D, but the composition's like a game . . . The interest is not in the literal plot, but in the associated texture—colors, images, sounds. [1977]

Ginsberg's allusion to it being 'a painter's film' came directly from Dylan, who assured one journalist that the purpose of the film was 'to put forth a certain vision which I carry around, and can't express on any other canvas.' Though he remained a devotee of the great Hollywood directors—deliberately tipping a hat to the grandest of auteur statements, Welles's *Citizen Kane*, by billing *Renaldo and Clara* not as directed by, but as 'a film by Bob Dylan'—the points of reference he made when talking about the movie came mostly from painters' palettes. To one reporter, he asserted, 'I've learned as much from Cézanne as I have from Woody Guthrie.' To his mind, only one previous movie 'stopped time'—*Les Enfants du Paradis*.

Dylan had already written a song that, in his own words, attempted 'to defy time, so that the story took place in the present and the past at the same time.' That song was 'Tangled Up in Blue.' And, in many ways, his conception of the film was an extension of that sensibility, one he acquired from Raeben. In 'Tangled Up in Blue,' Dylan uses a daydream as the basis for the song—'I was layin' in bed / wonderin' . . .'—and the song develops as a series of flashbacks, linked not chronologically but as a series of refracted images that set each other off, 'challeng[ing] our expectations of unitary narrative.'

In *Renaldo and Clara*, as in 'Tangled Up in Blue,' there is the strong journeying element—a constant procession of people coming and going, the rose and hat becoming linking symbols. As Aidan Day asserts about 'Tangled Up in Blue,' 'The order of events . . . is irrelevant to the archetypal figure of the lost love.' The film and song share many common elements: a deliberate confusion of identities, the use of flashbacks, the importance of the primary colors, a *ménage à trois* of sorts ('I lived with them on Montague Street . . .'). Even the end of the song and film suggest a central figure 'heading for another joint.' Dylan made it clear, to those who listened when he spoke about the film, that its dreamlike quality was deliberate, that the film was indeed Renaldo's dream.

Bob Dylan: The man on the floor [at the end], who's obviously dreaming, no one asks him anything—but the whole movie was his dream . . . Renaldo has faith in himself and his ability to dream, but the dream is sometimes so powerful it has the ability to wipe him out. Renaldo has no ordinary mind— he might not even have a soul. He may in actuality be Time itself, in his wildest moments. [1977]

The dream nature of the film allowed for all sorts of distortions of identity, not all of which Dylan felt the need to explain. Even when talking to Allen Ginsberg about the movie, he never resolved the question of whom Bob Dylan plays: 'Renaldo is everybody . . . He's Everyman in the movie, and he survives.' On the other hand, according to Dylan the whitefaced figure has no name, he is 'the Chorus of the movie,' the figure that Renaldo aspires to become, in his dreams.

Bob Dylan: The man in whiteface is what Renaldo cannot become at the moment. At the Indian party that isn't Renaldo, that is the man in whiteface. He represents the compelling figure of authority . . . Bob Dylan is being used here as a famous name, so we don't have to hire Marlon Brando! . . . Let's say that in real life Bob Dylan fixes his name on the public. He can retrieve that name at will. Anything else the public makes of it is its business. [1977]

But however much Dylan may have come to believe 'I is another,' the distinction was bound to be lost on many. The implication that beneath the whiteface of Bob Dylan-as-Chorus lies Renaldo, the real self behind the mask, was always going to be too oblique for a general filmgoing public and, unlike his record-buying public, these customers felt that they should understand the art form they chose to subsidize.

Nor did Dylan ever take the opportunity to explain the relationship between Clara, the Woman in White, and the White Goddess—Robert Graves's all-encompassing conception of the muse as Virgin-Lover-Hag—without which the film makes little sense. He did admit to Jonathan Cott that the Death Mother was represented in the movie, and Mel Howard observed, during filming, that 'Sara is very much into Robert Graves and his notion of the muse . . . that's probably a big part of their relationship.' Hence, presumably, the self-conscious use of white, red, and black in the movie—representing the three aspects of the Goddess. According to Ginsberg, one of the scenes cut from the final film was 'Sara on the Mother Goddess,' along with another scene that would have made the connection explicit.

Mel Howard: There was this scene in Niagara Falls where Sara played this kind of witch goddess creature and she set tasks for [Dylan] to fulfill, and nothing was ever good enough and that was the constant prod to keep him going. So we had a whole subplot, all of the women in the film, black magic and white magic, and the different powers of women and men, and the focus of all of this was Dylan himself.

Renaldo and Clara remains Dylan's most deliberate exposition of himself as a conscious artist, and the only public insight (*Drawn Blank*, his 1994 collection of drawings, excepted) into Dylan as a visual artist. In the many interviews he gave at the time, of which his conversations with Ginsberg are the most important, he seemed for the first time prepared to talk about his art in a self-conscious, expository kind of way. The source of this persona was unmistakable.

Bob Dylan: I am a conscious artist . . . I had a teacher who was a conscious artist and he drilled it into me to be a conscious artist, so I became a conscious artist.

Renaldo and Clara took up all of Dylan's creative energies through the last six months of 1976 and 1977. It was the most sustained, disciplined work he had ever done, or would ever do. If, in the recording studio, he could put his faith in serendipity, no such option existed in an editing suite, where progress was necessarily slow and painstaking. With such willpower applied, and given that the film had taken ten years to live, three months to film, and a year and a half to edit, the question still remained: Was he placing too much faith in the filmgoing public?

Having finished the film in September 1977, Dylan took time out to undertake some market research. In October, Allen Ginsberg spent a week with him, watching and discussing the movie. Ginsberg, not your average filmgoer, gave the film a thumbs-up. He also recorded at least three interviews with Dylan about *Renaldo and Clara*, intending to publish a brief study of the film. Two further major interviews were arranged in the fall, one with Ron Rosenbaum for *Playboy* magazine, the other with Jonathan Cott for *Rolling Stone*. Both were shown the movie, Dylan going to great lengths to explain queries these perceptive writers raised. Cott, in particular, seemed enthusiastic about the movie, though he did observe 'how easy it is to mistake people in the film for one another' and sought to warn Dylan about how 'some people will obviously think that this film either broke up your marriage, or is a kind of incantation to make your marriage come back together.'

Such erudite souls, though, were no substitute for a real preview audience, the kind who forever consigned *The Magnificent Ambersons*,

Welles's immaculately conceived follow-up to *Citizen Kane*, to the junkyard angels. In early December, Dylan stopped at a restaurant near Goldwyn Studios, where he had been completing the film, and invited some of the customers to a screening of the picture. The mixed response provided a clearer gauge as to the likely reception awaiting the film on its release. Though someone considered it 'an avant-garde piece of work,' and a handful of the random audience were just happy to watch the incomparable concert footage, it was the disgruntled attendee who moaned, 'I'm a little upset. I missed Carl Perkins on the Johnny Cash Christmas TV special for this,' who came closest to the critical consensus to come.

By the time the film critics got to stand in judgment on 'A film by Bob Dylan,' though, he had already sidelined his cinematic ambitions for another eight years, in favor of a return to the road for some necessary shoring up of funds. He had even taken on a rehearsal space, signing a five-year lease on an old three-story building on the corner of Ocean and Main that would come to be known as Rundown, suggesting he had a lot of rehearsing in mind. Perhaps surprisingly, given his plans, he had decided to reassemble the frame around which he had hung his previous revue:

Rob Stoner: I was really surprised when I got the call to do the '78 gig. Man, I thought the *Hard Rain* thing was the last I'd ever hear from Bob . . . Then suddenly I get this call—I think Bob [actually] called me up personally . . . and asked me to bring Howie, and a couple of other people, to LA to 'just try some things out.'

1978: Someone's Got It In for Me

26

I don't have anything but darkness to lose. I'm way beyond that.

—*Bob Dylan, 1978*

The Rundown era, which would extend from September 1977 through 1982, was to represent the last great era of Dylan songwriting—not that he wouldn't subsequently write great songs, simply that they would come in small clusters, divided by months, even years. These four and a half years, though, would see something of a flood from Dylan's quill, as he worked up songs on the spot with one of two standing bands, the first of which he had called Rob Stoner to LA to assemble.

For Dylan as a songwriter, the Rundown era would begin, effectively, with him running down the songs for *Street-Legal* to Rob Stoner, Steven Soles, and road-crew veteran Joel Bernstein, on December 26, 1977, and end with him working out a number of musical ideas that would coalesce into *Infidels,* with drummer Bruce Gary, at the beginning of June 1982. However, the primary purpose of Rundown rehearsals would remain performance-based, and in December 1977, Dylan was planning his first world tour in twelve years.

As of September, Dylan became a part-time resident at Rundown. What with the final editing of the film, the need to organize interviews, set up a proper rehearsal space, and the occasional court appearance, it was easier to convert one of the building's offices into a bedroom than return to Malibu nightly. Joel Bernstein and Arthur Rosato, from the 1976 road crew, were among the first full-timers to assemble at Rundown. Bernstein also ended up pretty much living there 'from about September 1977 until we left for the Japanese tour early the following year.' He recalls a nonstop procession of musicians: 'There were auditions and rehearsals all the time,' based around a familiar nucleus of players, 'members of the band that he knew that he wanted, like Steven Soles and Rob Stoner.'

The first of that 'nonstop procession of musicians' arrived in late November/early December. Along with the essential Howie Wyeth, Stoner recalls bringing 'a guy who used to play with Charlie "Bird"

Parker, Walter Davis, Jr., on piano . . . and Otis Smith, a great percussionist and singer, friend of Howie's and mine.' Dylan also brought
in the likes of Soles and Mansfield almost immediately, but what he did
not have in mind was a slightly reconfigured Rolling Thunder Revue.
Even the musicians were made to feel that certain elements of that sound
had been pensioned off for good.

David Mansfield: It wasn't at all like picking up where the Rolling Thunder
Revue left off. I remember that I brought my steel guitar and I had it in
rehearsal and every time I'd go to start unpacking it, Bob would go, 'We
don't need that.' All of a sudden the instrument that I played all over the
place in the previous band, he didn't wanna see it, let alone hear it.

Though Dylan had gone to the expense of bringing out these New
York musicians in the weeks leading up to Christmas, his new band
initially took a backseat, as he was required to deal with other distractions,
of which the custody battle was doubtless the most stressful. *Renaldo and
Clara* was also due to première in late January. Often absent from the
initial rehearsals, when Dylan did make it to rehearsals, his mind was not
on playing, and the musicians again found him difficult to communicate
with. The thought crossed a mind or three that a rerun of the 1976 tour
beckoned.

Rob Stoner: I brought this weird band out with me, and Bob kept us
sitting around for a week or two. He just never showed up . . . Meanwhile,
to pass the time and keep everybody together I was doing the surrogate
singing—I was just singing the tunes that I thought everybody should know,
in case Bob does show up. And we keep waiting. And [when] he drops in,
he's distracted. Maybe he didn't like the band. He was really fucked up
[mentally]. He was always bummed out. He was chain-smoking and he was
really in a bad mood. He was short with people. It just wasn't working out.

Perhaps Dylan genuinely 'didn't like the band.' He can certainly be
heard bemoaning the fact that 'I can't spring anything new on this band'
at the December 26 '*Street-Legal* piano preview.' Presumably he had run
down at least a couple of these songs with the band, as Stoner requests
'Señor.' Even by this point, though, the components that Stoner had
brought out from New York were being disassembled—in one key
component's case, at his own request.

Howie Wyeth: I went to LA [around] Christmas Eve. I showed up out there, and they weren't ready yet, and I tried to rehearse with them, and then I heard that Bob had a new manager and that the guy said, 'We're not gonna even have any grass on this tour.' I think they were serious. They were going to Japan. I was thinkin', 'Man, if they're not even gonna have grass, I'm really gonna be in trouble' . . . So I went out there and we tried to play, and it didn't feel right, and I was tryin' to kick [heroin] too, 'cause I knew I couldn't get high once we'd left . . . I realized I was either gonna get busted or I'd end up being tortured to death. So I literally had to just tell Bob one night, 'I can't do it.' That was terrible. He had his own problems. He felt bad that I wasn't gonna do it, and he called me up when I got back to New York and said, 'Are you sure?'

The phone call to New York was born as much from desperation as concern on Dylan's part. He knew that the Stoner-Wyeth combination was a tough one to replace, an impossible one to replicate. Stoner's familiarity with Wyeth also made for a happy couple. A whole new backbeat would require Stoner to make the kind of allowances bound to affect his own bass playing. The other problem was that Dylan himself was overly enamored of drummers who kept the beat, period. With the kind of band he envisaged this was never going to be a sustainable option.

Arthur Rosato: Bob's a big fan of the backbeat . . . On the '78 tour we went through so many drummers. I mean, Keltner came down and he was perfect, but he didn't want to come out. But there was one drummer, he was black, really strong backbeat but he played it through all the songs. Bob loved that. I said, 'Bob, he's playing the same thing for everything. He's not playing the song. That's not where you want to be.'

Joel Bernstein: He needed a drummer and he auditioned a number of drummers, maybe ten or a dozen. It was an interesting experience for me, watching all these different musicians trying to play Bob's songs . . . Bob [finally] settled on Denny Siewell.

Selecting Siewell, whose credentials included a stint with Paul McCartney's Wings, occupied the few days left before Christmas. He was a member of the new combo by December 30, 1977, when he joined Stoner, Mansfield, Soles, guitarist Jesse Ed Davis, and singers Katey Sagal, Debbie Dye Gibson, and Frannie Eisenberg in running through an odd set of rearranged Dylan classics, most of which bear almost no resemblance to their guises two months hence (the 'Like a Rolling Stone' arrangement on the tape of the 30th bears an uncanny resemblance to the yet-to-be-written 'In the Summertime'). Rehearsals were clearly still at the song-selection stage, with many cuts rehearsed at this point not making it to the tour set. *Blonde on Blonde*, well represented at the turn-of-year rehearsals, with 'Most Likely You Go Your Way,' 'Leopard-Skin Pill-Box Hat,' 'Fourth Time Around,' and—believe it or not—'Sad-Eyed Lady of the Lowlands' all tried out, would have to settle for the three hit singles it spawned. Dylan's input in these rearrangements varied, though at the beginning of the rehearsal tape from the 30th (they taped most rehearsals) he can be heard trying to guide the band through an idea for 'It's All Over Now, Baby Blue' at the piano.

The piano had only recently returned to favor as a sounding board for Dylan's music. Aside from using it for arrangement ideas, he had played it four days earlier when previewing two-thirds of *Street-Legal* and a 'lost' original named 'First to Say Goodbye' after the day's rehearsals. Seeking to gauge the reaction around him to his new songs, Dylan never completed any of the performances, though it is evident that songs like 'Señor,' 'No Time to Think,' 'True Love Tends to Forget,' 'We'd Better Talk This Over,' and 'Where Are You Tonight?' are already as formed as any of those in the *Blood on the Tracks* notebook. He had also previewed a similar selection of songs to Jerry Wexler at an Etta James session earlier in the month.

Jerry Wexler: That afternoon in Cherokee, Bob told me he'd been writing on the piano. Since Dylan famously composed on guitar, I was intrigued. He walked over to the piano and played a series of chord progressions with the enthusiasm of a child. I thought it was great.

By the time he was playing Stoner and Soles his new songs, Dylan seems to have begun to reapply himself to music-making. He almost immediately began to impose a grander vision on whatever sound the Revue veterans had initially conceived. With his love of fatback R&B, it should have come as no surprise that he hankered after a band with a saxophone player and some female singers, even if he had just told *Playboy* readers, via Ron Rosenbaum, that 'mostly I've been driving at a combination of guitar, harmonica and organ.' From the start of rehearsals, he seems to have planned taking a big band on the road. Indeed, the band he assembled in the two months before the 1978 world tour shares many similarities with the big band he had attempted to impose on *Desire*. The girls/sax/keyboards combination also reflected elements of the extravagantly presented shows Presley had been playing in the 1970s.

Dylan's method of recruiting female singers at times reflected his new proximity to Hollywood and its mores—preferring the casting couch to the microphone.

Rob Stoner: He starts inviting all these chicks to come down and sing and I felt it was like: Is he doing these things to impress these girlfriends of his? 'Cause they weren't professional singers . . . The first time he shows up to do anything serious it's 'cause he's got these chicks around. Oh God, and we tried rehearsing with them. It was a revolving door. Eventually we settled on the three or four that ended up doing the tour—but they were pros . . . When the chicks start showing up to rehearsals, then Bob starts to get interested in it. Suddenly he's in contact with me every day. He says, 'Well, call Jesse Ed Davis. Have him come down and play.' He tried to get Al Kooper, he couldn't make it, he had Barry Goldberg down there—Barry couldn't do it for another reason. We had Mickey Jones, the actor . . . He was calling up people from like twenty years ago. It was like he was gonna have a reunion party and check everybody in LA out. I was having a good time doing this! Every day we were having a jam with people who Bob had called to show up . . . [but] nothing was getting done, and there were gigs booked.

Among those who came and went during this process was Sally Kirkland, who continued to figure in Dylan's scheme of things, even if he was becoming increasingly attracted to Kirkland's roommate, Mary Alice Artes, an African-American actress also scuffling for parts on the perimeters of moviedom. Though Artes would not audition for the role of backing singer, she would be listed as 'Queen Bee' on the *Street-Legal* sleeve. Another of the actress-cum-singers who was put through the mill was Katey Sagal, who actually temporarily secured the gig, before going on to her own fame and fortune in the long-running sitcom *Married . . . With Children*. Sagal remembers a Dylan who seems to have taken a certain glee in showing up the girl singers:

Katey Sagal: I remember . . . he'd have three girls all sing a part that was not in our range, and we were too terrified to say anything.

Using rehearsals as an excuse to jam with musicians and gel with singers didn't delay the dates already booked in Japan for February. That the band, by mid-January, was not taking to its role with any greater coordination, drive, and discipline than its frontman convinced him that he needed to make a whole series of last-minute reconfigurations. Katey

Sagal and Frannie Eisenberg were considered surplus to requirements, and a whole new texture was added with the recruitment of novice singer Helena Springs and the eminently professional Jo Ann Harris.

David Mansfield: At that time Bob would make changes or do things in ways that were both enigmatic and inconsiderate. He might have someone rehearse with the band for a month or two and then one day an assistant would tell them don't come back on Wednesday. And Bob wouldn't ever deal with that himself, so you'd never know what caused the decision . . . There were some people you'd become friendly with, and it became painful to see them let go so inconsiderately.

Rob Stoner: The band that ended up being that band was something that I had to do hastily because we had blown our time having all these jam reunion things. But Bob had no relationship with that band. He wasn't hanging out . . . I had tried out a lot of people but [with] this casual attitude until the last week. Then everyone got scared. We had to get Steve Douglas, who costs a fuckin' fortune. He's one of the top sax men in Hollywood.

Stoner's increasing exasperation resulted in him inviting an old friend, Billy Cross, a lead guitarist from Sweden, to fly over for an audition. Though Cross played well within himself at the audition, he became increasingly carried away by his status in the band, firing off heavy-metal riffs at the most inappropriate junctures. Siewell had fit surprisingly well into what was an unfamiliar setup for him, but shortly before the band was finalized it became apparent that he wouldn't be allowed into Japan because of the Wings drug bust in Sweden. They were required to commence a whole new set of auditions.

Rob Stoner: I can't remember half the people that showed up to that . . . We had the guy from Derek and the Dominoes, Jim Gordon, great drummer. Man, we had all kinds of drummers. But y'see, because we waited so long to make the final cuts in the band, the deadline was pressing and eventually we had to settle on somebody. And [Ian] Wallace happened to be it . . . Wallace was just convenient—he was Mr. Right for the night. It's just that the night was too fuckin' long.

Ian Wallace, the man who put the work in workmanlike, had played with King Crimson, and so had a pedigree of sorts—though Bill Bruford he was not. But the main problem was that he played fractionally behind the beat, or, as Stoner colorfully put it, 'the man had a beat like a cop.'

In a band the size of this one, Dylan could not afford a drummer who was not *absolutely* on the beat, especially as he was accustomed to taking his cues from the man with the sticks. He had unwittingly set in motion the impetus for Stoner's premature departure, at the end of the first leg of the world tour.

With an eight-piece backing band, plus three singers, to play with, Dylan was suddenly required to do a little more than decide a key and expect the musicians to ride his tail. Though the *idea* of a big band had always appealed to Dylan, the reality was a whole series of new arrangements, to make each song different and to highlight the band's demonstrable versatility. This was presumably how they ended up with a number of Douglas/Mansfield pennywhistle/violin arrangements, and even a quasi-baroque version of 'If You See Her, Say Hello' (which actually worked surprisingly well). Often these arrangement ideas came from the band. As Stoner observes, when they put these arrangements to Dylan, 'Sometimes he'd like it and he'd use it, and other times he'd say, Forget it.' In the final two weeks of rehearsals, all ideas of what to do with the band were fashioned by tapes of each day's session.

Joel Bernstein: The [rehearsal] recordings were specifically for [Dylan] to listen back to, not for him to ever use, but to let the band hear how things were progressing, and for him to hear how arrangements were coming together. He was much more disciplined than . . . [on] the 1976 tour. Not only was everything taped, but he would have the band stay over after rehearsals finished and he would have me play back particular performances of the best versions of each song that day . . . and spend an hour, hour and a half, listening back to things . . . Rehearsals would usually begin about one o'clock . . . People would show up and have lunch and then we'd start around one and play until six . . . The band got bigger as time went on, and once it was reasonably together he got them to play certain songs in different ways, in one key and then another key and then half-time, then country, then reggae, then rocked up. It was really an experimental thing. And then listening to those songs he would just pick one, say, Yeah! That's the one! And I would inwardly groan and go, Oh no! Not the reggae one! But he had his own idea about what was the best one to do.

The main problem with the big band was that it was essentially anathema to his usual working methods. Not that the excitement of working out a whole new way of doing an old chestnut doesn't come through on a couple of the later rehearsal tapes—say, Alan Pasqua's vamped-up organ sound dueling with a pumped-up Dylan on 'It's

Alright Ma,' or the interplay with the girls on a lovely rewrite of 'The Man in Me' ('as for compensation / whatever you wanna bring')—but it perhaps had not occurred to Dylan that his own room for melodic maneuver might be savagely curtailed by the band's size, save on a couple of songs when he allowed himself to be backed by just keyboards, sax, and electric guitar.

David Mansfield: By the time we were doing anything in public the arrangements were much more straightforward and straitlaced than anything we'd done on the Rolling Thunder Revue and also, once he'd decided he was going to do an arrangement a certain way, he didn't vary it a whole lot.

The other uncharacteristic aspect of the tour—especially at its outset, when there was no new product to shift—was the return to the anachronistic gestalt of 1974, with four additional years' interest. Dylan was being forced into a musical straitjacket that his dire financial straits required him to wear for a full year, making for a strangely muted series of performances. For the first time in seven long years he also had a new manager, Jerry Weintraub, whose view of entertainment was almost vaudevillian. The incongruous connection led Dylan to take ideas from another Weintraub act, Neil Diamond, peremptorily dismissed at the Last Waltz, but whose show, caught one hot August night in 1977, had a strong influence on his impending direction. Weintraub, and his fellow promoters, foolishly imagined that Diamond plus repertoire equaled Dylan.

Rob Stoner: I'll never forget one day [at rehearsals] a telegram arrived from the Japanese promoter, and in it he had a manifest of the songs he expected Bob to do on this tour. In other words he was a jukebox, he was playing requests. We don't want you coming here and doing like your new experimental material, or getting up there and jamming.

Dylan's need for a commercial success, or just suitcases chock-full of hundred-dollar bills, was further necessitated by a media assault on his new film that at times resembled D-day, without the return fire. On January 25, *Renaldo and Clara* had premiered simultaneously in Los Angeles and New York. The reviews were not merely universally hostile, they were extraordinarily spiteful. Having accepted that Dylan had put the art in one art form, the critics found it inconceivable that another art form might have reconnected the man to his art. *The New Yorker* sent along the lady about whom Woody Allen once observed, 'She has everything a great critic needs except judgment.' Pauline Kael's view of Dylan suggested just how judgmental she could nevertheless be:

The Bob Dylan [his fans] responded to [in the sixties] was a put-on artist. He was derisive, and even sneering, but . . . *Renaldo and Clara*. . . is what Louis [XIV] and Marie Antoinette might have done at Versailles if only they'd had the cameras.

In fact, Kael's sour review was one of the least personalized assaults upon Dylan's movie. In most of the reviews, one could sense some personal grievance, as if the critics now believed that everything Dylan had pro-duced to date was somehow a 'put-on.' The fiercest attempt to assassinate the film's credibility came in New York's *Village Voice*, which sent no less than four reviewers to savage it. Faridi McFree, who was staying at Dylan's town house in New York, recovering from the custody battle and the end of their relationship, read the reviews to him over the phone.

Faridi McFree: It was horrible, absolutely horrible what they said about him, especially in the *Village Voice*. One guy said they hated him and they wished he'd die. And I said, 'Bob, they actually really wish you were dead.' And he said, 'It doesn't bother me . . . they say all kinds of things about me. I've just learned to live with it.'

In truth, the reviews certainly did bother him, in a way that nothing typeset had since the infamous *Newsweek* piece. He had just spent eighteen months of his life making his most overt statement as a conscious artist—now he was being reminded why he had previously insisted on being just 'a song-and-dance man.' Not surprisingly, he felt a need to justify himself and the movie.

Bob Dylan: Reading the reviews of the movie, I sensed a feeling of them wanting to crush things. Those reviews weren't about the movie. They were just an excuse to get at me for one reason or another . . . I was disappointed that the critics couldn't get beyond the superficial elements. They thought the movie was all about Bob Dylan, Joan Baez, and Sara Dylan. [1978]

In a sustained attempt to defend the movie to parts of the press—and to salvage part of what was a substantial financial commitment, even for Dylan—he committed himself to a further flurry of interviews on the film's release. *Renaldo and Clara* though, sank without trace. It opened in only one more city, Minneapolis, and disappeared from American cinemas within weeks, never to reappear. A consortium later persuaded him to edit the movie down to two hours—their two-million-dollar offer for the two-hour version helping to reduce the film's financial deficit—before rereleasing it to American cinemas. Dylan, though, chose to mock those who had savaged the film so mercilessly, giving the consortium the film all the critics had claimed the real version to be, an inchoate jumble of improvised scenes, edited in a random sequence without rhyme or reason. Including virtually all the concert footage in the original movie—though not 'Sara'—it was his final revenge on those responsible for the brutal reception given his film (save, perhaps, for his later decision to withdraw the film altogether, and refraining from a video release, making bootleg copies a collector's only option).

Ironically, when the film received its European debut at Cannes in May—in full four-hour form—it was enthusiastically received. And when it made its London debut in July it ran for a three-month season at the Camden Plaza cinema, becoming a regular favorite at repertory cinemas through the mid-eighties, when Dylan himself chose to remove it from distribution. Though reviews were still mixed, many considered it an audacious experiment, and even those less enamored showed a degree of restraint lacking in their American counterparts.

Having been subjected to the most intense critical barrage of his career, he finally flew to Japan on February 16, 1978, glad to have the opportunity to leave the American press behind. The audacious new arrangements of a cross-section of his finest songs drew nothing but praise in Japan and Australia. The two-hour-plus shows were considered well thought out, and Dylan seemed genuinely interested in being there. Though some of the Japanese shows lacked punch, as some of the more incongruous elements in Dylan's big band sound, such as flute and congas, gained a temporary ascendance, the more familiar guitar, harmonica, and organ gradually assumed a dominance as the tour progressed, and Dylan's voice became harder, more insistent. Whether the new professionalism suited Dylan was another question. Stoner believes that he was never entirely convinced about the wisdom of his decision.

Rob Stoner: He had in mind to do something like Elvis Presley, I think. That size band and the uniforms. [But] he wasn't very sure about it, which is why he opened way out of town. I mean, we didn't go any place close to Europe or England or America [for] forever, man . . . and I don't blame him. I think he knew, subconsciously, he was making a big mistake.

If Stoner represented a voice from one side of the divide, Weintraub was still whispering in Dylan's ear, I can get another million yen for ya. The Japanese tour, though it spanned a mere eleven shows, eight at the Budokan in Tokyo and three in Osaka, was Dylan's most lucrative set of shows to date. Keeping his contrary twin temporarily in check, Dylan largely conformed to the greatest-hits mentality of his manager and audience.

Rob Stoner: That guy [Weintraub] accompanied us to Japan and he was, like, always around. Suddenly we were The Entertainer, and it was a little too stodgy ... They want[ed] to see Bob Dylan doing 'Blowin' in the Wind,' like, on and on—the most predictable greatest-hits ten songs you could name ... By then I might as well have been working in Wayne Newton's band, or something.

The only major set variation on the Far East leg of the tour was the nightly opener, which could be one of a number of blues standards. Over the course of the Far East tour fans heard Dylan's versions of Billy Lee Riley's 'Repossession Blues'—presumably a dig at those who sought to dub this the Alimony Tour—Ernest Lewis's 'Lonesome Bedroom Blues,' Tampa Red's 'Love Her with a Feeling,' and at one show Robert Johnson's 'Steady Rollin' Man.' In Europe and America, Tampa Red's 'Love Crazy' and Willie Dixon's 'I'm Ready' would vie for inclusion with 'Love Her with a Feeling.' Otherwise, the sets were entirely drawn from Dylan's repertoire of familiar originals. The only new song introduced was 'Is Your Love in Vain?,' which Dylan performed at the two shows his Japanese record company, Sony, was recording for a live album.

The live album was all part of that lucrative deal Weintraub had cut for Dylan to tour Japan. By 1978, it was standard Japanese marketing practice to convince artists to record live souvenirs of their shows in Nippon, to be released subsequently in the Far East. Cheap Trick, Deep Purple, and the Runaways had all complied with the ruse before Dylan. Dylan had also been badgered into providing his own suggestions for a three-album anthology, entitled *Masterpieces*, to be released in Japan to coincide with the shows. The three-album set, a superb overview, lavishly packaged, even included a side's worth of rarities like the 'Mixed Up Confusion' 45 (a real rarity, because they accidentally used an outtake version), the Liverpool 1966 'Just Like Tom Thumb's Blues,' and a stereo 'Can You Please Crawl Out Your Window?,' providing a model for the later *Biograph,* and healthy sales in Japan and on export. The live album

Dylan gave them, creatively named *At Budokan,* though intended only as a souvenir for the Japanese, became the one and only testament to a 115-date world tour when it was subsequently released worldwide—in response to 'popular demand' (Dylan was able to insist that, if it *was* released worldwide, it became one of the five albums he was contracted to deliver under his February 1, 1978, recording contract).

Bob Dylan: They twisted my arm to do a live album for Japan. It was the same band I used on *Street-Legal,* and we had just started findin' our way into things on that tour when they recorded it. I never meant for it to be any type of representation of my stuff, or my band or my live show. [1984]

Dylan's earlier suspicion, that he couldn't 'spring anything new on this band,' was confirmed one night in Osaka, when he decided to respond to a request for 'One Too Many Mornings,' a song no one recalls them rehearsing. The ramshackle rendition convinced him not to try that one again! If the shows provided little more than a nightly ritual, Dylan was again enjoying other nightly rituals. He had quickly become smitten by the vivacious Helena Springs, a brown-skinned girl fresh out of school, and the youngest recruit to his gaggle of girl singers. Springs had been recruited at the end of the impressing-chicks phase of the rehearsals. She had never toured with any band, let alone one on this scale. If some frowned on her lack of experience, Dylan tried to encourage her to fully express herself. While in Brisbane in March, they even worked up a few songs together.

Helena Springs: We were together in Brisbane one evening and he was playing on the guitar and we were just goofing around, laughing, and I said, 'I can't really write' . . . He said, 'Well, come on, I'll write something with you. We'll write something together.' And I said, 'Okay.' He said, 'You start singing some stuff and I'll start playing.' So he started strumming his guitar and I started to sing, just making up lyrics. And he'd make up stuff, and that was when we got 'If I Don't Be There by Morning' and 'Walk Out in the Rain.'

Dylan's and Springs' 'goofing around' was not confined to writing songs, as the photo of the two of them in a Tokyo restaurant on the inner sleeve of *Street-Legal* suggests. In what was going to be a long year on the road, the Dylan–Springs relationship made for another dynamic—though not the only romantic dynamic. At the end of the Far East tour, Dylan enjoyed a three-day holiday in New Zealand with a native princess he had met in Auckland earlier on the tour, named Ra Aranga. And, when he returned to Rundown to begin work on his new album, he rekindled a few sparks with his old flame, Ellen Bernstein. For a few moments each evening the burden of being Bob Dylan was temporarily lifted by the obliging Ellen.

Ellen Bernstein: I wouldn't say [I] became reinvolved with him, but we did spend time together when he was rehearsing one of his tours, and he was rehearsing in this building on Main Street in Santa Monica. He had his own room set up upstairs, so I would go and visit him at the rehearsals and then stay afterwards.

If certain members of the crew remained unhappy with the new intimacy between Springs and Dylan, they wisely refrained from comment in his earshot. Stoner, on the other hand, because of his position as bandleader, was getting all the complaints musicians invariably liked to make, but not to their paymaster. Stoner himself was very unhappy, though the Dylan–Springs relationship was not the source of his dissatisfaction. He did not feel that the 1978 band suited the man, was bored by the lack of spontaneity, and was generally antsy about the direction in which the whole tour was heading.

Rob Stoner: The drummer sounds like fuckin' sludge . . . when he was playing with Bob he couldn't swing from a rope . . . I was not happy, and Bob knew this, and my not being happy meant that I was fucking every chick on the bus, and I was getting a little wild myself. Fortunately, you can't get drugs in Australia and Japan as easily as you can places that you know, [but] . . . I was drinking a lot.

When the Far East tour wound to an end on April 1, at the Sydney Fairgrounds, Stoner informed Dylan that he wanted out. And so Dylan found himself, on his return to Los Angeles, required to rehearse a new bass player and bandleader before setting about recording his first album in thirty months. Reinforcing the sense that he was carrying a baton passed on from Elvis, the new bass player was Jerry Scheff, who, like Steve Douglas, had made his reputation as part of Presley's touring band in the early seventies. But working with Dylan was most certainly not like playing with Elvis. The 'audition' rehearsal at which Scheff found himself being blooded saw Dylan running through one of his newest works, 'We'd Better Talk This Over,' aware that however much homework Scheff might have done, this would be a hard one to bluff. Within a fortnight of that fraught introduction, Scheff found himself back at Rundown, cutting the song for real, part of four days of sessions that would result in *Street-Legal.*

If recording an album as rich in potential textures as *Street-Legal,* and with as grand a band as this, in just four days, seems to suggest that Dylan's search for that 'wild mercury sound' had survived the seventies intact, nothing could be further from the truth. *Street-Legal* would be the first in a long line of song collections—lest we call them albums—whose failure to be realized in the studio would lay a 'dust of rumors' over Dylan as an abidingly creative artist that he has never been able to fully shake, no matter how steadfastly he has refused to look back.

Conceptually, it would appear that the album was fully realized. Dylan had nine songs that he wanted to record. Though they would record three of the songs written with Helena Springs at a fifth session, three days later, it was surely an excuse to use the mobile truck while they still had it booked. There is no evidence that any of these songs—'Coming from the Heart,' 'Walk Out in the Rain,' and 'Stop Now'—were ever under consideration for the album proper.

David Mansfield's recollection is that 'we [had already] rehearsed [the songs] enough that we had things well in hand by the time the mobile truck came.' The songs had also probably undergone all the major lyrical changes they were likely to (though, even at the Scheff audition, Dylan comes out with a great couplet—'Even when we're making love / it winds up in a fight'—that would not make the finished 'We'd Better Talk This Over'), and the songs themselves were melodically strong, save perhaps for 'No Time to Think,' which one critic appositely described as 'a long litany of verses in which musical variation is sacrificed to [a] difficult lyric meter.'

Dylan knew that he had very little time to record his new album. A European tour was scheduled to begin in June, and the members of the band were expecting a brief respite in the interim. There had never been any question that he would record these songs with the touring band, who were by now conversant with a fair number of his many idiosyncrasies. Initially, Arthur Rosato, who would be listed on the album sleeve as second-in-command, recalls that 'they had booked it at Record Plant, and the studio they had booked was [living-room size]. The [studio people] were so used to one guy coming in and doing his parts . . . and I said, "No, we do it all at once," and they were looking at us, like, "Totally live?"' By 1978, the idea of recording an album live in the studio had become all but unheard of. It was an idea, though, that Dylan cherished dearly, and was not going to be easily convinced to forsake.

He decided to use his own rehearsal space, Rundown, as the venue for the recording sessions, and to bring in a mobile truck with full twenty-four-track capability.

Bob Dylan: I didn't want to do it there; [I] couldn't find the right producer. But it was necessary to do it. So we just brought in the remote truck and cut it, [and] went for a live sound. [1978]

If writing the *Street-Legal* songs in many ways mirrored the *Blood on the Tracks* experience, the recording sessions resembled his previous attempt to record with a big band, at the early *Desire* sessions. Quite why he elected to use Don Devito as producer again, when recording with a big band had proved wholly beyond him three years earlier, is a mystery still residing in the man's cranium. *Street Legal,* an album only marginally flawed in conception, would be dramatically impaired in its execution. Neither Devito nor Rosato would be able to salvage these songs from their twenty-four-track morass.

David Mansfield: The biggest problem with *Street-Legal* was how it was recorded, with Bob getting impatient with the engineering assistants . . . baffling and checking levels and getting sounds in sync, [and saying,] 'Get rid of this crap, pull your stuff around in a circle and let's just play these songs,' and the recording crew just having to scramble to get mikes into place, and get something on tape, while we were playing the thing the few times we were gonna play it. Consequently, the music is very poorly recorded. But that stuff sounded marvelous in the room, tons better than *Budokan*. It really was sort of like Bob Dylan meets Phil Spector in the best way . . . as if it had [just] been recorded so the instruments sounded full and well-blended.

Dylan's Luddite tendencies when dealing with studio technology had not previously hindered the transition from vision to tape, odd exceptions notwithstanding. But he now needed someone to sit him down and patiently explain why 'stuff [that] sounded marvelous in the room' would not necessarily sound marvelous on tape. Part of the problem was that he had heard all these great-sounding tapes that Rosato and Bernstein had made of the rehearsals in January and presumably felt that, if they could make tapes like that on a shitty eight-track, recording with one of ·Wally Heider's mobile trucks would be a sea breeze.

David Mansfield: They had some old Atari eight-track [at the rehearsals] and Arthur was sort of tending it mostly, so there was no sophistication, like having outboard equipment, and compressing and EQing . . . But there was also no antagonism between the recording crew, namely Arthur Rosato, and Dylan. If there were mikes placed, they were pretty much where they were supposed to be, and . . . I do remember the thing of, 'We're going in now to make a record,' and of course that puts the kibosh on a number of things . . . I remember being struck with how Dylan would be hammering at something, and I'd never experienced him hammering at something before.

What Dylan evidently had in mind was a naturalistic approach to recording that maintained the interplay between each musician. Uninterested in redoing vocals, and with distinct limits placed on any musician's ability to overdub, he did achieve his first imperative—recording the songs quickly. But even overdubbing his own vocals proved impractical (something borne out by the way on the album he fluffs the key line in the final verse of 'Changing of the Guards'—'with tranquillity and splendor on the wheels of fire').

The use of floor-mounted monitors rather than headphones to achieve that naturalism in the studio was a no-no, purely on technical grounds. As Joel Bernstein, whose recordings on the Atari had convinced Dylan that he could record this way, notes, 'When you're recording, the last thing you want to have is a wedge with anything in it—including your voice . . . first of all, you've got to equalize it terribly just to make sure it's not gonna feedback. [And] no matter how you equalize it . . . you've got a lot of stuff going on there which is gonna really thin [the sound] out.' It is perhaps amazing, given his fixed view of recording, that it took Dylan seventeen years to make an album as poorly recorded as *Street-Legal*. Perhaps equally surprising is the fact that he would return to Rundown three years hence to record another album of strong songs unrealized.

(Twenty-one years after the fact, the radical 1999 remix/remaster of *Street-Legal* in fact suggests that much of the damage was done at the mixing stage. Rescuing the vocals from the mire, and resuscitating the drums, may not have made *Street-Legal* fully realized, but it has certainly restored some of the songs' strengths, suggesting a more than worthy successor to *Blood on the Tracks* and *Desire*.)

Though the album's sound would come in for a little stick on its release—Jon Pareles in *Crawdaddy* recognizing that 'Dylan still needs a producer'—the sonic flaws passed most reviewers by. Greil Marcus, in a *Rolling Stone* review that made his famous 'What is this shit?' piece read like a rave, attacked the singing on the album as 'simply impossible to pay attention to for more than a couple of minutes at a time,' failing to recognize the technical source of this lack of vocal gravitas. Marcus's disillusionment was born more of a creeping political correctness that made a shared worldview a prerequisite of any great work. Not that 'Is Your Love in Vain?,' in which Marcus accuses Dylan of 'speak[ing] to the woman like a sultan checking out a promising servant girl for VD,' was great work. But it was certainly Dylan being brutally frank—unlike 'Sara,' the one song Marcus felt had redeemed *Desire*.

If the American reviews took their lead from someone Dylan later characterized as 'one of our leading rock critics, whatever that is,' reviews across the pond, in contrast, coincided with a season of hype that threatened to put the summer of love to shame. As Michael Watts, still trying to live down his lukewarm review of *Blood on the Tracks*, wrote in *Melody Maker*, 'in the euphoria surrounding his British concerts, this is not quite the time to make heady pleas for this album.' He still proceeded to call it Dylan's 'best album since *John Wesley Harding*.' *NME*'s Angus MacKinnon also professed reservations, before buckling under: 'Hell, I'll state my case—*Street-Legal* is Dylan's second major album of the seventies.'

Of course, the fact that *Street Legal* was released as Dylan was embarking on his first European tour in twelve years did have a bearing. Arriving in London on June 13, two days before the album's appearance, he found the mayhem that had surrounded his visit to the Isle of Wight nine years earlier had now spread to the mainland. The English press had so hyped six sellout dates at London's acoustical death trap, the infamous seventeen-thousand-seat Earls Court, that people had begun lining up for tickets forty-eight hours before they went on sale. Even in the powerful English music press, which had self-consciously championed a punk revolution that had transformed the music scene beyond all recognition in the past eighteen months, each weekly devoted page-previews to the seven warm-up shows in LA, at which Dylan had unveiled a heavy-metal version of 'Masters of War' and a quite breath-taking organ/guitar arrangement of 'Tangled Up in Blue' that hinted of a greatness renewed and said everything necessary about Marcus's assessment that his 'new vocal style . . . [had] destroyed Dylan's timing and his ability to bring emotional precision to a lyric.'

The hype even extended to the national TV news, which for the first time devoted a two-minute segment to a mere rock concert the night of his London debut. The following day one tabloid review bore the headline 'The Greatest Concert I Have Ever Seen,' setting the tone for most UK press reviews. *Melody Maker* included an eight-page pull-out, which celebrated the residency with four enthusiastic reviews of the London shows. The slightly hysterical tone that now accompanied Dylan was not confined to England. From London, he headed for Rotterdam, where fifty-five thousands fans awaited him; then Dortmund, Berlin, and Nuremberg, where he played 'Masters of War' to eighty thousand fans (and a couple of dozen neo-Nazis, who threw things at him for his affrontery) in the stadium where Hitler had held his rallies.

Six shows at the Pavillon de Paris proved just as triumphant as the London residency, as were two shows in Gothenburg. He finally returned to England a month to the day after opening his European tour at Earls Court, concluding it with the largest open-air show ever held in Europe, at a disused aerodrome in the Surrey countryside, attended by an estimated 200,000-plus fans. The Blackbushe show represented the high point of the 1978 world tour. Dylan performed for two and a half hours, singing ten songs not performed at the Earls Court shows a month earlier, including six from the newly released *Street Legal*. The fans loved it, and accorded him a rousing reception.

And yet, try as he might, Dylan simply could not turn the critical tide in America. Even his ultra-catchy rewrite of Robert Johnson's 'Stop Breaking Down,' 'Baby Please Stop Crying,' which had gone Top 10 all over Europe that summer, failed to dent the *Billboard* Hot 100, while *Street-Legal* stalled at ten, decisively ending his run of American number one albums. After a quiet summer down on the farm, he returned to the North American stage in Augusta, Maine, on September 15, the first of sixty-five scheduled shows that fall, bringing his 1978 sound to every town that imagined itself to be a city.

This was his first nationwide tour since that legendary 1974 tour, when ten million people had scrambled for tickets to a mere forty shows, and save for parts of the East Coast and apathetic Gulf Coast enclaves, this was many fans' first opportunity to catch the post-*Blood* Dylan. This time, though, he was not even selling every show out, as the Alimony Tour was redubbed the Vegas Tour by the US press, content to paint a picture of the man belting out replications of those classic tunes from his sixties heyday. Dylan reacted to these new attacks in the press with understandable anger, sharpened by an underlying frustration.

Bob Dylan: The writers complain the show's disco or Las Vegas. I don't know how they came up with those theories. We never heard them when we played Australia or Japan or Europe. It's like someone made it up in one town and the writer in the next town read it . . . I don't know how radically different it is from things in the past, considering the elements that I have in this band I've . . . used before. I made an album called *New Morning,* and we used singers on just about every track, so I've done that. As far as using the horn sound, I used the horn sound in Nashville on 'Rainy Day Women' . . . there isn't really anything new, [it's] just a bunch of pieces put together. [1978]

In fact, the sound Dylan was presenting to the Americans was considerably harsher than the one so well received in the Far East and Europe, perhaps a response to early criticisms, perhaps just because he was beginning to tire of the formality of the band's sound. As it is, he was giving most songs a raucous, whiny delivery that sometimes stripped them of their sensitivity, notably 'Tangled Up in Blue,' whose torch-ballad arrangement had come in for such praise in Europe. But some songs really benefited from the treatment, notably the *Street-Legal* songs, which now came into their own. New arrangements of 'I Threw It All Away,' 'The Times They Are A-Changin',' and 'Mr. Tambourine Man' were also more inventive than on previous legs, the audacious mix of instruments and vocals providing a bedspring symphony off which Dylan's voice could bounce. Not for the first time, fans refused to follow the critics' lead, responding to the shows enthusiastically, and whatever his nagging dissatisfactions, Dylan visibly began to put himself into the songs.

David Mansfield: He generally fraternized with the help quite a bit. He was part of the band—he'd hang out, he'd drink, he'd talk his head off, he'd play, total reverse of '76. I recall when that year of touring ended, he didn't want to stop. He was having a ball. He had all kinds of stuff booked. He just wanted to get on an airplane or bus, and keep playing forever, [and] he started talking to the audience all of a sudden. He was just having a good time and he started playing around with the audience . . . He was reading reviews in America, but seemed to be able to do that and not be fazed [by the bad press]. They said Steve Douglas was impersonating Clarence Clemons—I mean, you couldn't take that stuff seriously.

The notion of Presley's saxophonist copying Springsteen's was not the only half-assed comparison hacks were prepared to draw between Dylan's 115-date world tour and Springsteen's 110-date *Darkness* tour. Dylan's two sets with an intermission format had also been adopted by the man from Asbury Park, determined to cram most of his four albums to date into his nudging-three-hours shows. If Dylan derived a single reciprocal debt from the Boss that fall, it was the notion of prefacing certain songs with little rap-stories. This way of prefacing songs—part autobiography, part tall tale—had been a trademark of Springsteen ever since he'd left the New Jersey shore behind. And, like Springsteen's raps, Dylan's generally came before the same songs each night, even though the raps themselves changed. The rap before 'Señor' originally evolved out of Dylan's subtitle to the song, 'Tales of Yankee Power':

I was riding on a train one time through Mexico, traveling up north to San Diego; and I must have fell asleep on this train and I woke up and it was about midnight . . . and the train had stopped at a place called Monterey . . . This bunch of children were getting off the train, this family—there must have been about seventeen children and a mother and father and they were getting off the train. And at the time I was watching it all through the glass; it was dark outside so the whole side of the train was like a mirror. So I was watching it all happen and I saw this old man stumble up onto the train and he gets onto the car; and he was walking down and he took a seat right across the car from me. I felt a vibration in the air. I turned to look at him and I could see he wasn't dressed in anything but a blanket; he was just wearing a blanket. He must have been 150 years old. I turned around to look at him and I could see both his eyes were burning out—they were on fire, and there was smoke coming out of his nostrils. I said, 'Well, this is the man I want to talk to.'

It is tempting to impose some underlying religious meaning on this rap, in the light of subsequent events. Indeed, it appeared in the shows alongside a rewritten 'Tangled Up in Blue' to which the words that 'glowed like burning coal' came not from Dante but from the Gospel According to Matthew—the very gospel written to convince Jews that Jesus fulfilled Old Testament prophecies regarding the Messiah. At the same time, Dylan began sound-checking a new song he was working on, entitled 'Slow Train.' He had first written about 'the holy slow train' on the back of *Highway 61 Revisited*. It now appeared that 'she . . . [who] prays for rain and for time to interfere' had begun praying for his soul, too.

Part Three

Busy Being Born Again

1978–79: On the Holy Slow Train

27

His conversion wasn't one of those things that happens when an alcoholic goes to AA. . . The simplest explanation is that he had a very profound experience which answered certain lifelong issues for him.

—*David Mansfield*

Jesus did appear to me as King of Kings, and Lord of Lords . . . I believe every knee shall bow one day, and He did die on the cross for all mankind . . . they call it reborn . . . it changes everything. I mean it's like waking one day and can you imagine being reborn, can you imagine turning into another person? It's pretty scary if you think about it . . . It happens spiritually, it don't happen mentally.

—*Bob Dylan, 1981*

Just writing a song like ['Slow Train'] probably emancipated me from other kind of illusions . . . On its own level, it was some kind of turning point.

—*Bob Dylan, 1995*

To all outward appearances, Dylan was reveling in his performance art, savoring the versatility of his band, and enjoying getting loose after hours with the musicians and girl singers as he found himself, in mid-November 1978, back on the West Coast, dedicating 'Girl from the North Country' to Bonnie Beecher in Oakland, dedicating himself to making it through the last third of a tortuous sixty-five-date American tour—his first nationwide tour in four years, and his most stamina-sapping in twelve. In this version of events, he would later insist, 'I was doing fine. I had come a long way in just the year we were on the road [in 1978] . . . but a very close friend of mine mentioned a couple of things to me and one of them was Jesus.'

The songs he wrote in the winter and spring of 1979 suggest some amendment bound by unbelief. In these lyrics, he refers to an inability to break repeated patterns, being truly emancipated, not from 'other kind of illusions' but from illusion itself. When revelation came, it came alone. Dylan only turned to 'a very close friend' *after* Jesus had appeared to him. The significance of that manifestation would be ineluctably shaped by contact between Dylan, his close friend, and her counsellors.

The cumulative effect of the negative receptions for *Renaldo and Clara, Street Legal*, and now the American tour—contrasting starkly with the response to both album and tour in Europe—cannot be discounted when considering Dylan's state of mind at this point. After an impressive show in his hometown, Los Angeles, on November 15, he had a month left on the road. In San Diego, two days later, something remarkable happened. He was no longer feeling quite so good. The show itself was proving to be very physically demanding, but then, he perhaps reasoned, he'd played a gig in Montreal a month earlier with a temperature of 105.

Bob Dylan: Towards the end of the show someone out in the crowd . . . knew I wasn't feeling too well. I think they could see that. And they threw a silver cross on the stage. Now usually I don't pick things up in front of the stage. Once in a while I do. Sometimes I don't. But I looked down at that cross. I said, 'I gotta pick that up.' So I picked up the cross and I put it in my pocket . . . And I brought it backstage and I brought it with me to the next town, which was out in Arizona . . . I was feeling even worse than I'd felt when I was in San Diego. I said, 'Well, I need something tonight.' I didn't know what it was. I was used to all kinds of things. I said, 'I need something tonight that I didn't have before.' And I looked in my pocket and I had this cross. [1979]

Stuck in a Tucson hotel room, after a lifetime of visions that caused divisions, Dylan experienced a vision of Christ, Lord of Lords, King of Kings. His state of mind may well have made him susceptible to such an experience. Lacking a sense of purpose in his personal life since the collapse of his marriage, he came to believe that, when Jesus revealed Himself, He quite literally rescued him from an early grave.

Bob Dylan: There was a presence in the room that couldn't have been anybody but Jesus . . . Jesus put his hand on me. It was a physical thing. I felt it. I felt it all over me. I felt my whole body tremble. The glory of the Lord knocked me down and picked me up. [1980]

On the road, 'heading towards the sun,' Dylan started to question his whole value system. The import of his experience, though, temporarily eluded him. Meanwhile, few clues were given to the thousands of fans he was playing to every night, in the final four weeks of his yearlong world tour. That small silver cross, though, clearly represented a new starting point. Six days on from Tucson, Dylan was in Fort Worth, playing the Convention Center. On stage, he was seen to be wearing a metal cross around his neck. For a man raised as a Jew, this could not have been a casual gesture.

He also began to improvise a new line for the stripped-bare arrangement of 'Tangled Up in Blue' he was performing at the time. Rather than having the mysterious lady in the topless bar quoting an Italian poet from the fourteenth century [sic], she was quoting from the Bible, initially from the Gospel According to Matthew. Gradually, though, the lines changed, until he settled upon a verse from Jeremiah—the one he would quote on the inner sleeve of the *Saved* album: 'Behold, the days come, sayeth the Lord, that I will make a new covenant with the house of Israel, and with the house of Judah' (Jeremiah 31.31), the same 'contract with the Lord' his 'covenant woman' was about to undertake.

His pen had not been quiescent since *Street Legal*. The new songs, though, seemed to continue his descent into a sexual battleground where victories were transitory, final defeat inevitable. The songs debuted on the American tour to date bore titles like '(You Treat Me Like a) Stepchild,' 'Coming from the Heart,' and 'I Must Love You Too Much.' But his best performances he gave up to the empty arenas, when he was sound-checking, as he worked on ideas for new songs, or ran through old favorites like Lowell Fulson's 'Reconsider Baby,' Shel Silverstein's 'Daddy's Little Girl,' or Tampa Red's 'But I Forgive You' that plowed the same terrain.

As he entered the final two weeks of the 115-date world tour, Dylan began to attack the shows with renewed vigor. He also began writing songs that addressed some of the more pressing issues whirling around in his head. At sound-checks he worked on a new song called 'Slow Train.' For the final show of the tour, in Miami, he introduced another new song. 'Do Right to Me Baby (Do unto Others)' was the first song he had ever written around a dictum from the Bible, indeed a saying directly attributed to Jesus himself: 'All things, therefore, that you want men to do to you, you also must likewise do to them; this, in fact, is what the Law and the Prophets mean' (Matthew 7:12).

For the first time in a long while, the questions running around his head only prompted larger questions, more ineffable answers. Not surprisingly, the first person he turned to for more definite answers was his traveling paramour, Helena Springs, the lady with whom he had been writing songs of betrayal and loneliness like 'If I Don't Be There by

Morning' and 'I Must Love You Too Much.' Of all his traveling band, she remained perhaps his only real confidante. She had also been brought up a Christian.

Helena Springs: I think he was having some problems . . . He called me and he asked me, and they were questions that no one could possibly help with. And I just said, 'Don't you ever pray?' . . . And he said, *'Pray?'* Like that, you know. And he said, 'Really?' And he asked me more questions . . . He started inquiring . . . He's a very inquisitive person, which is one good thing about searching for truth.

Not that others in his ensemble couldn't have suggested something more tangible than prayer. If Jesus appeared to Dylan that night in Tucson, He was presumably passing through on His way to the Alpha Band contingent in Dylan's band. Steven Soles and David Mansfield had both become members of a particularly Californian creed of Christianity, the Vineyard Fellowship, in recent months, their old compadre T–Bone Burnett having led the way.

David Mansfield: T–Bone was the first one to go through this experience, and Steven sort of followed him, and I eventually did, too. And T–Bone has more than a bit of preacher in him and was probably hammering at all of his friends in the ways that he could be most effective—arguing Christian apologetics. But there was this revival going on—there was a certain time when we were all going to the same church, and Bob would be way in the back incognito, but T–Bone, Steven and I were all playing in the church band.

An adamant Burnett insists he was not approached by an inquisitive Dylan at this juncture. Nor, says Mansfield, was he. Soles, though, recalls being subjected to Dylan's inquiries about the nature of his faith. One thing he said, in particular, struck a chord: 'I kept telling him that I was so glad that I didn't have to place my faith in man any longer.' As in 1976, though, Dylan seems to have largely reserved his inner philosophical struggles for the 'witchy women' who shared his battleground. Ever the pluralist, he continued to balance his affection for Helena with an infatuation for Sally Kirkland's ex-roommate, black actress Mary Alice Artes. Artes had also been brought up as a Christian; but, unlike Springs, her faith had faded—until, that is, she encountered the Vineyard Fellowship.

David Mansfield: Mary Alice Artes was one of these dynamic personalities that Bob's probably attracted to in general, and if they're black so much the better—she was really powerful. She could look really sexy, dress really sexy, without ever exuding sex, but meanwhile being one of those really competent mothers who would shower you with all this love and attention, and . . . tell you what you should do, and slap your bottom to get you off doing it. She would have been like the perfect Jewish wife . . . At the point I became a Christian she was so sweet and intense, and 'praise the Lord,' this and that.

Independently of the Alpha boys, Artes had attended a Vineyard Fellowship meeting in Tarzana, California. According to a press report at the time, she actually moved out on Dylan upon 'rededicat[ing] her life to the Lord,' a move guaranteed to impress a genuinely smitten Dylan. According to pastor Ken Gulliksen, she requested pastoral guidance for her boyfriend.

Ken Gulliksen: At the end of the meeting she came up to me and said that she wanted to rededicate her life to the Lord . . . That morning she did rededicate her life to the Lord. Then she revealed that she was Bob Dylan's girlfriend and asked if a couple of the pastors would come, there and then, and talk to Bob. And so Larry Myers and Paul Esmond went over to Bob's house and ministered to him. He responded by saying, Yes, he did in fact want Christ in his life. And he prayed that day and received the Lord.

If he was on the run from the Triple Goddess, Dylan was bound to need the protection of a strong, patriarchal religion, and the 'born-again' songs he wrote that year are littered with references to redemption *from* the power of women. In 'Trouble in Mind,' notably, Satan whispers to the singer that, when he grows bored of Miss So-and-So, 'I got another woman for ya.' On the verge of collapse from a five-year struggle with his various muses, he now found himself renewed by a God-given strength, and a new message.

Bob Dylan: Beauty can be very, very deceiving and it's not always of God. Beauty appeals to our eyes . . . The beauty of the sunset . . . that's God-given. [But] I spent a lot of time dealing with man-made Beauty, so that sometimes the beauty of God's world has evaded me. [1981]

By embracing the New Age brand of Christianity advocated by the Vineyard Fellowship, Dylan was about to become, in popular perception, just another Bible-bashing fundamentalist. In fact, though the Fellowship certainly shared the 'born again' precepts of more right-wing credos— believing such a change was an awakening from original sin ('Adam given the Devil reign / Because he sinned I got no choice')—it represented a more joyous baptism of faith.

David Mansfield: A big part of the fellowship of that church was music. I remember all those courses they offered—Dylan took the whole Discipleship thing! It was as intense as what was going on in fundamentalist circles, but it was culturally from an entirely opposite place.

Dylan had always been thorough in his reinventions of self. Never one for half measures, the man who after Newport became Rimbaud's spitting son, after *Nashville Skyline* became the cud-chewing country farmer, after *Blood on the Tracks* became the wronged party, after *Desire* became the dutiful husband, was bound to be attracted to the idea of another dramatic rebirth. Certainly the Born-Again Bob now preparing to preach out in the world was as thorough a reinvention as any since Elston Gunn had decided he'd rather be Bob Dylan.

Bob Dylan: Being born again is a hard thing . . . We don't like to lose those old attitudes and hang-ups. Conversion takes time because you have to learn to crawl before you can walk. You have to learn to drink milk before you can eat meat. You're reborn, but like a baby. A baby doesn't know anything about this world, and that's what it's like when you're reborn. You're a stranger. You have to learn all over again. [1980]

The first stage of this process was carefully supervised by the Vineyard Fellowship, who were bound to recognize the benefits of having the spokesman for a generation speaking out on their behalf. In having 'to learn all over again,' Dylan was required to return to school. An auto-didact of twenty years' standing, and never the best of students, he was his usual recalcitrant self when it was suggested he undertake an intensive course in learning to walk in the spirit of the Lord.

Bob Dylan: At first I said, 'There's no way I can devote three months to this. I've got to be back on the road soon.' But I was sleeping one day and I just sat up in bed at seven in the morning and I was compelled to get dressed and drive over to the Bible school . . . I didn't know myself if I could go for three months. But I did begin telling a few people after a couple of months, and a lot of them got angry at me. [1980]

One suspects that it was Dylan's way of 'telling a few people' that got them angry, not necessarily the message that Christ is Lord. References to 'so-called friends' and 'companions' who'll 'someday account for all the deeds [they] done' abound on the songs he was writing contemporaneously, songs of praise and damnation like 'Slow Train,' 'I Believe in You,' 'Precious Angel,' and 'No Man Righteous (No Not One).' If the simple acceptance of Christ did not imbue him with righteous fervor, the adoption of the Vineyard brand of Christianity most certainly did. And, when it came to righteousness, the author of 'The Times They Are A-Changin'' was still up there with the best of them.

The three-month course at the Vineyard School of Discipleship demanded regular attendance—four days a week. The regime itself perhaps reminded Dylan of the breakthrough he'd achieved with Norman Raeben back in 1974. The classes were held in a back room, above a Realtor's office in Reseda, California, and lasted from 8:30 A.M. till noon. An anecdote recounted in *Stairway to Heaven*, a thorough survey of Christian rock music by Gavin Seay and Mary Neely, reveals a Dylan surprisingly eager to participate in the process:

During class breaks, Dylan would often walk into the parking lot in back of the prefab building, dressed against the brisk morning air in a leather jacket and stocking cap, to smoke Marlboro cigarettes and talk with his girlfriend . . . One morning a student stood to report a dream he had the night before. In the dream, the members of the class were gathered in an upper room, a beautiful cedar-paneled loft lit golden by sun pouring through a skylight. One corner of the room, the student said, had been left unfinished, exposing insulation padding, ducts, and a tangle of dangerously frayed electric wiring. The hazardous wiring, it seemed, had to be pulled down before the room could be made safe for habitation. It was a difficult, dangerous job, and the dreamer was frightened, until an unidentified man assured him that only boldness was required. Encouraged, the dreamer thrust his hands into the wiring and pulled. It fell away, and through the hole in the roof, fresh, clean water began to flow. From his seat in the corner of the room, Dylan's eyes were bright. He was nodding and smiling as a moment of unmistakable recognition passed between the student and the star . . . Bob Dylan's interpretation of his classmate's dream of the upper room was the simple one: 'Old things are passed away, and all things are made new.' Old circuits must be stripped for the cleansing water to flow.

The course pounded into Dylan a responsibility that devolved to all fellowship members—to evangelize. Pastor Gulliksen insists, 'It was an intensive course studying about the life of Jesus; principles of discipleship; the Sermon on the Mount; what it is to be a believer; how to grow; how to share . . . but at the same time a good solid Bible-study overview type of ministry.' The important phrases here are 'principles of discipleship' and 'how to share.' The later controversy surrounding Dylan's conversion might have been considerably more muted if it had not been for this evangelical codex. Even fans who could tolerate a Dylan for whom Jesus was the savior foretold in the Old Testament found out there was 'no neutral ground' when it came to the 'principles of discipleship.'

Bob Dylan: That [born-again period] was all part of my experience. It had to happen. When I get involved in something, I get totally involved. I don't just play around on the fringes. [1983]

The Chambers Dictionary defines *evangelical* as 'Of the school that insists especially on the total depravity of unregenerate human nature, the justification of the sinner by faith alone, the free offer of the Gospel to all, and the plenary inspiration and exclusive authority of the Bible.' Taught to conceive of man as born into a state of sin; that the gospels represented not figurative, but literal truth; and that the Devil was at work every minute of every day, insidiously undermining man's morals, Dylan now denied himself all evidence to the contrary. A well-read man, for whom the Bible had previously been little more than a literary resource, he now made its allegories come out in black and white.

Bob Dylan: You would think the enemy is someone you can strike at and that would solve the problem, but the real enemy is the Devil. That's the real enemy, but he tends to shade himself and hide himself, and put it into people's minds that he's really not there and he's really not so bad, and that he's got a lot of good things to offer, too . . . What Jesus does for an ignorant man like myself is to make the qualities and characteristics of God more believable to me, 'cause I can't beat the Devil. Only God can . . . Satan's working everywhere. You're faced with him constantly. If you can't see him, he's inside you making you feel a certain way. He's feeding you envy and jealousy. [1981]

The message conveyed by the Vineyard Fellowship was not simply concerned with spreading the Gospel. It elevated the final book of New Testament allegories, St. John the Divine's Revelation, into a literal account of the end times. All one needed was the code. The end of the world was not merely nigh, it was NIGH, with a capital double-underlined N!

Bob Dylan: What I learned in Bible school was just . . . an extension of the same thing I believed in all along, but just couldn't verbalize or articulate. Whether you want to believe Jesus Christ is the Messiah is irrelevant, but whether you're aware of the messianic complex, that's . . . important . . . People who believe in the coming of the Messiah live their lives right now, as if He was here. That's my idea of it, anyway. I know people are going to say to themselves, 'What the fuck is this guy talking about?' but it's all there in black and white, the written and unwritten word. I don't have to defend this. The scriptures back me up. [1985]

Aside from the scriptures, the classes sought to provide a grounding in the works of one Hal Lindsey, the man to whom God in his infinite wisdom had revealed the true code of Revelation. Though no saint himself, Lindsey was closely associated with the Vineyard Church. His book *The Late Great Planet Earth* (1970), became Dylan's second Bible and added an apocalyptic edge to his worldview, allowing Christ Come Again precedence over Jesus the Teacher.

If Dylan's doomsday poems had always displayed a keen sense of the apocalyptic, he had rarely drawn from a wholly black, or cataclysmic, apocalyptic tradition. The only examples that spring to mind are 'I'd Hate to Be You on That Dreadful Day,' 'All Along the Watchtower,' and, maybe, 'Changing of the Guards.' He had previously preferred the red, or revolutionary, tradition (as in 'Ain't Gonna Grieve,' 'The Times They Are A-Changin','); or, commoner still, the green or pastoral, tradition (as in 'Chimes of Freedom,' 'When the Ship Comes In,' 'Gates of Eden'). The black tradition, which finds expression in the Old Testament prophets—Isaiah, Jeremiah, Ezekiel—and, in the New Testament, in the Revelation of St. John, carried a very exclusivist message, one Dylan had seemingly rejected back in 1963. Little versed in the Bible's historical happenstance, though, he became an ideal disciple for Lindsey's rhetoric.

According to Lindsey, current world events had been foretold in the apocalyptic tracts of the Bible. His basic premise, in *The Late Great Planet Earth,* was that the events revealed to St. John in Revelation corresponded with twentieth-century history, starting with the re-establishment of the Jews' homeland, Israel. By identifying Russia as Magog and Iran as Gog—the confederation responsible for instigating the final conflict, the Battle of Armageddon—Lindsey prophesied an imminent End. This scriptural snake oil was drunk whole by Dylan. There can be no question that in 1979—and for some time to come—he believed that the finishing end was truly at hand. A lengthy rap from one of his fall 1979 shows illustrates the unequivocal nature of this belief:

Bob Dylan: You know we're living in the end times. I don't think there's anybody . . . who doesn't feel that in their heart. The scriptures say, 'In the last days, perilous times shall be at hand. Men shall become lovers of their own selves. Blasphemous, heavy and highminded.' Now I don't know who you're gonna vote for, but none of those people is gonna straighten out what's happening in the world today . . . Take a look at the Middle East. We're heading for a war. That's right. They're heading for a war. There's gonna be a war over there. I'd say maybe five years, maybe ten years, could be fifteen years . . . I told you 'The Times They Are A-Changin'' and they did. I said the answer was 'Blowin' in the Wind' and it was. I'm telling you now Jesus is coming back, and He is! And there is no other way of salvation . . . There's only one way to believe, there's only one way—the Truth and the Life. It took me a long time to figure that out before it did come to me, and I hope it doesn't take you that long. But Jesus is coming back to set up His kingdom in Jerusalem for a thousand years. [1979]

His belief in the imminence of the End was reflected in almost all of the songs he now found himself writing. Indeed, the songs disturbed him on a very deep level, even as he felt compelled to get the news, good or not, out into the world. As a contemporary bumper sticker proclaimed, Jesus is coming back, and boy, is He pissed!

Bob Dylan: The songs that I wrote for the *Slow Train* album [frightened me] . . . I didn't plan to write them . . . I didn't like writing them. I didn't want to write them. [1984]

Powerful evocations of dread like 'Precious Angel,' 'Gonna Change My Way of Thinking,' 'When You Gonna Wake Up?,' and 'When He Returns'—all subsequently included on *Slow Train Coming*—drew heavily and directly upon the Book of Revelation. If *John Wesley Harding* had dealt with 'the devil in a fearful way,' the new songs dealt with Jesus in an equally fearful way. The scariest example of Lindsey's oddball eschatology, though, bought wholesale by Dylan, occurs in the song, 'Ye Shall Be Changed,' wisely omitted from the 1979 album but later included on *The Bootleg Series*. It was based upon Chapter 11 of *The Late Great Planet Earth,* in which Lindsey fantastically interprets I Corinthians 15:52—'In

the twinkling of an eye, at the last trumpet . . . we shall be changed'—
to signify that 'when God has the last trumpet blow, it means He will
move out all Christians—and at this point we shall be changed' into
Essence. Only at this point would the battle of Armageddon be fought.

Lindsey takes a classic pre-millennialist position—that Christ will
return before the thousand-year rule and defeat Evil—subjecting the
alternative, post-millennial view—Christ returns only after Christians
have established a thousand-year rule by 'their own efforts'—to considerable scorn. The gradual transformation into a truly Christian kingdom
on Earth was never likely to appeal to the author of "The Times They
Are A-Changin'" and 'When the Ship Comes In,' songs as steeped in the
language of Apocalypse as those on *Slow Train Coming*. In the early
months of 1979 Dylan was writing his most message-driven album in
sixteen years. This time, though, the pursuit of the millennium had
overtaken more sociopolitical concerns.

A positive aspect of Dylan's spiritual quest was that he was once again
writing songs for and about himself, and a wealth of them at that. Just as
his classes with Raeben resulted in the *Blood on the Tracks* songs, the
intense tutorship from the Vineyard Fellowship provided the necessary
inspiration for a number of memorable new songs. For the first time
since Suze 'approved' his early topical songs, his new songs were also
being vetted, by one of the pastors, lest he stray from the narrow path of
orthodoxy carved out for him.

Ken Gulliksen: He shared his music with Larry Myers, one of the pastors
who had originally ministered to him. I freed Larry to go with Bob as much
as possible. Bob asked him to come with the band on the road, so that Larry
would be there to lead them in prayer and Bible study, and to minister to
him personally. He and Bob became very close, and trusted each other.
Larry was often the backboard for Bob to share the lyrics.

Initially, Dylan was more than a little reluctant to put his name to
these songs of fear and loathing. He would later insist that he originally
wanted Carolyn Dennis to record the songs, intending merely to produce
the results, 'and not even put my name on them. I wanted the songs out
but I didn't want to do it [myself], because I knew that it wouldn't be
perceived in *that* way. It would just mean more pressure. I just did not
want that at that time.' In all likelihood, pressure was brought to bear for
him to confront these demons himself and, more importantly, to send
the Vineyard's message out into the world attached to a Bob Dylan
album.

The process of Dylan's conversion, his indoctrination at the school of discipleship, the songs that documented this process, and his coming to terms with his evangelical responsibilities as a recording artist of some import, all seemed to happen in a twinkling of the proverbial eye. Barely three months after he had wished his band of '78 travelers a merry Christmas—see ya in the New Year!—he was turning his back on his grand ensemble, feeling that he needed a more gospel-tinged sound for the album he felt compelled to record. The album he was planning was bound to be controversial, not to say aberrant to a large section of his audience, who had not always discerned the difference between personal restlessness and a willingness to instigate social change.

The essential ingredient in previously successful studio formulas had usually been the guitarist. This time, Dylan's choice was more ingenious than inspired. Arthur Rosato had played him a single, 'Sultans of Swing,' written by a young English guitarist who had the kind of tone that might slip real easy between the cracks his new songs opened up. As such, on March 29, 1979, a curious Dylan attended the final show of a successful residency at the Roxy, in LA, by Britain's most commercial recent rock export, Dire Straits.

In their homeland, the Straits were considered too twee to pass the New Wave entrance exam. But in America circa '79, when the average journalist's conception of 'punk rock' was Elvis Costello, the Straits were easily assimilated into that uniquely West Coast concept, AOR (Adult Oriented Rock). Songwriter Mark Knopfler's guitar tone, a homogenization of J. J. Cale, Richard Thompson, John Martyn, and a soupçon of Lou Reed, defined mellifluous. If Dylan had a bitter pill for his audience to swallow, a spoonful of Knopfler's sugar would sure help the medicine go down. After the Roxy show, Dylan approached Knopfler about playing on his next album. Knopfler, unaware of its contents, just wanted to know when.

Dylan, though, still needed a producer, preferably one with ideas of his own. Though he had succeeded in recording albums like *Highway 61 Revisited, Blonde on Blonde, John Wesley Harding,* and *Desire* with the producer serving as little more than a well-paid engineer, by 1979 he most assuredly needed technical help to get his vision onto vinyl. The multitrack era had raised the stakes—the complexities of arranging and recording a big sound onto sixteen-track almost destroying *Desire* before fully eluding him on *Street-Legal.*

The someone Dylan already had in mind was his co-producer on Barry Goldberg's solitary collection, Jerry Wexler. He remained a great admirer of Wexler's soulful amalgam of horns and a tight rhythm.

Synonymous with a small studio in Sheffield, Alabama, the sixties Atlantic recordings of Wexler defined the Muscle Shoals Sound. Though known primarily for recording a who's who of black soul artists, Wexler had also wrestled with the one great white soul singer of the sixties, Dusty Springfield. If Springfield found singing to a rhythm track strange, Dylan was never going to countenance such an idea. Yet Wexler was confident he could make the man embrace his methods:

Jerry Wexler: [Dylan] came to me because he wanted the sonority he'd heard in Aretha and Otis as opposed to those . . . out-of-tune, see-you-down-the-line, thirteen-and-a-half-measure, out-of-time phrases.

Wexler's confidence was to prove misplaced, though out of the conflict he would craft perhaps the finest-sounding album in the man's canon. He was also initially unaware of Dylan's real motive for enlisting that aural trademark: to make the most unequivocal Christian rock album since repentant rock & rollers came out of the First Era, bottle and Bible in hand. Wexler was caught hopping by a proselytizing Dylan, preaching redemption if he would turn from hell.

Jerry Wexler: Naturally, I wanted to do the album in Muscle Shoals—as Bob did—but we decided to prep it in LA, where Bob lived. That's when I learned what the songs were about: born-again Christians in the old corral . . . I liked the irony of Bob coming to me, the Wandering Jew, to get the Jesus feel . . . [But] I had no idea he was on this born-again Christian trip until he started to evangelize me. I said, 'Bob, you're dealing with a sixty-two-year-old confirmed Jewish atheist. I'm hopeless. Let's just make an album.'

For Knopfler, too, the experience of hearing such unequivocal songs played by his idol proved a tad disorienting. At some point he even voiced his concerns—'all these songs are about God'—to his manager, Ed Bicknell. On the other hand, Dylan's professionalism clearly impressed him as they sketched out arrangements, in much the way Dylan had done with Bloomfield prior to the *Highway 61 Revisited* sessions.

Mark Knopfler: Bob and I ran down a lot of those songs beforehand. And they might be in a very different form when he's just hittin' the piano, and maybe I'd make suggestions about the tempo or whatever. Or I'd say, 'What about a twelve-string?'

When work began in earnest, down in Alabama, on his last album of the seventies, Dylan knew which songs he wanted to record, and had agreed with Wexler who should play and sing on them. If two of the girl singers, Helena Springs and Carolyn Dennis, were the sole survivors from his 1978 touring band (and then, only on a couple of songs), veteran bassist Tim Drummond seems to have been a longtime preference, awaiting a slot. Straits drummer Pick Withers was Knopfler's suggestion. Keyboardist Barry Beckett had been an integral part of the Muscle Shoals Sound since 'Papa Don' Schroeder brought him down to Sheffield to record 'I'm Your Puppet' in 1966. The famous Muscle Shoals Horns seem to have been Wexler's idea, something he could overdub onto the basic tracks. All in all, Dylan had a most intriguing musical melting pot from which to pour a little ol' time religion onto the face of the world.

The first session, on April 30, though, proved to be a most Dylanesque disaster. For non-believers like Pick Withers, Mark Knopfler, and Tim Drummond, a day spent recording 'Trouble in Mind'—'easily the most naked of Dylan's recent songs,' as Paul Williams notes in *What Happened?*—must have been beyond strange. Withers admits, 'Things were a little strained the first day.' The first salvos in the battle for the album's sound were also fired off, with Wexler reining in Dylan's desire to vocalize unnecessarily, and Dylan refusing to don the dreaded headphones, determined to persevere with a 'live' sound, no matter how many of the twenty-four tracks required overdubs.

Jerry Wexler: Bob began playing and singing along with the musicians. We were in the first stages of building rhythm arrangements; it was too soon for him to sing, but he sang on every take anyway. I finally persuaded him to hold off on the vocals until later, when the arrangements were in shape and the players could place their licks around—not against—Bob . . . Bob was uncomfortable wearing headphones, and I could see that the thing still hadn't come together.

If the following day's proceedings were only marginally more successful, Wexler began to figure out the advantage of getting a good Dylan vocal and rhythm track, and worrying about overdubbing the melodic niceties at a later date. The seductively sly 'Precious Angel' was a May Day product, even if bass, guitar, organ, and horns would all be overdubbed at the following week's sessions. Ditto 'No Man Righteous (No Not One),' though even in its overdubbed state it wouldn't make the final cut. Thus was a pattern set, the basic tracks, lead vocals intact, laid down before Dylan's boredom threshold was reached. Adding and redoing bass parts, acoustic and electric guitars, background vocals, horns, organ, electric piano, and percussion would require their own set of sessions, but by then Dylan could be an interested observer.

Having reached a suitable rapprochement with Wexler, and with a tight musical setup now attuned to the Dylan methodology, the basic tracks for the remaining ten songs came in just six three-hour sessions over the next three days. 'I Believe in You' and 'Gonna Change My Way of Thinking' were first takes, though the former was one of two vocal overdubs Wexler convinced Dylan to redo at the overdub sessions the following week (the other being 'When You Gonna Wake Up?').

The songs recorded that first week in May fell neatly into two distinct categories: those that attested to Dylan's personal sense of redemption, such as 'I Believe in You,' 'Precious Angel,' 'Gonna Change My Way of Thinking,' and 'Trouble in Mind'; and those that admonished the unrepentant and foretold the imminent damnation of anyone who refused to embrace the Message to end all messages. The latter spanned the full gamut of browbeating, from the gentle cajoling of 'Do Right to Me Baby' to the fire and brimstone that suffuse 'When You Gonna Wake Up?' and 'Slow Train.'

As the musicians relaxed into their roles, arrangement ideas were often worked out on tape. 'Gotta Serve Somebody' was tried at the piano; 'Do Right to Me, Baby' was attempted à la 'Dirge'; 'When He Returns' began life as a full-band version. Dylan had, at least temporarily, abandoned his usual practice of recording songs without running them down for the musicians, and even Wexler seems to have been surprised by Dylan's ability to ride each and every happenstance.

Jerry Wexler: Whatever we did was live. Bob might run it down on piano or guitar, just singing and playing the background until we had a rough shape in our minds, then the Muscle Shoals band would start to play it. As soon as it sounded right, Bob and the girls would start to sing.

'When He Returns,' the penultimate song recorded, was the one that continued to unnerve Dylan. Though there was never any question but that it would conclude the album, with all-encompassing finality, he apparently originally planned for it to be sung by (one of) the female singers. However, when recording a demo vocal for the song, accompanied by Barry Beckett at the piano, Beckett's strident accompaniment made him think again. After practicing overnight, he pushed himself through seven vocal takes, over Beckett's original piano track, before the eighth endowed the album with perhaps Dylan's strongest studio vocal since 'Visions of Johanna.' Concluding the album, though, with this stark, intensely foreboding song was bound to bring its own fair share of righteous anger down upon his head, dealing, as Bert Cartwright put it, with 'the need . . . to dethrone self, surrendering your crown as the 24 elders did, before the throne in Revelation [4:10], on the "blood-stained ground" of Cain.'

With the album barely completed, the news of Dylan's conversion to Christianity began to filter through to the media. On May 22, he was required to give a pre-trial deposition in Beverly Hills to a defamation-of-character suit by Patty Valentine, regarding the song 'Hurricane.' Asked about his wealth, he replied, 'You mean my treasure on earth?' Asked about the identity of the song's 'fool,' he described that person as being 'whoever Satan gave power to . . . whoever was blind to the truth and was living by his own truth.' Five days later, the *Washington Post* reported this pre-trial statement, and quoted Ken Gulliksen revealing that Dylan had accepted Christ into his life, and had joined the Vineyard Christian Fellowship.

In June, Dylan provided London's Capital Radio station with an acetate of 'Precious Angel,' to premiere the song on Roger Scott's afternoon show. By July, pre-release tapes of *Slow Train Coming* were free-falling through media circles, prompting one of the last great *NME* captions, for their gossipy report on the conversion: 'Dylan & God—It's Official.' But when it came to reviewing the album, Charles Shaar Murray, while prepared to admit that *Slow Train Coming* was presented in a most beguiling musical shrink wrap, was deeply disturbed by the Message Writ Large: 'Bob Dylan has never seemed more perfect and more impressive than on this album. He has also never seemed more unpleasant and hate-filled.' Greil Marcus, in *New West,* shared Murray's concerns, asserting that 'Dylan's received truths never threaten the unbeliever, they only chill the soul.' Accusing him of trying 'to sell a prepackaged doctrine he's received from someone else,' Marcus isolated *Slow Train Coming*'s greatest flaw, an inevitable by-product of his determination to capture the immediacy of newfound faith in song.

The sense of betrayal in certain reviews did not, however, carry over to the all-important *Rolling Stone* review. *Rolling Stone* had not always been supportive of Dylan's artistic statements in the seventies and, as the only major US music journal, its opinion carried unwarranted weight with American consumers. That editor Jann Wenner assigned himself two pages to review the album, which he insisted was the man's finest work since *The Basement Tapes,* was as nothing to his closing statement,

seemingly borne on the unreliable wings of hyperbole, but in fact a
recognition of the extra dimension a new integrity had brought to the
vocal cords of 'the greatest singer of our times':

Musically, this is probably Dylan's finest record, a rare coming together of
inspiration, desire and talent that completely fuses strength, vision and art.
Bob Dylan is the greatest singer of our times. No one is better. No one, in
objective fact, is even very close. His versatility and vocal skills are
unmatched. His resonance and feeling are beyond those of any of his
contemporaries. More than his ability with words, and more than his insight,
his voice is God's greatest gift to him.

The care taken with the album's sound was reaping surprising rewards.
Despite preferring 'Gotta Serve Somebody' to the more instantly palatable 'Precious Angel' as a first single release, Dylan was again venturing
into the singles chart. 'Gotta Serve Somebody' provided him with his
first US Top 30 single in six years, and *Slow Train Coming* managed to
outsell both *Blood on the Tracks* and *Blonde on Blonde* in its first year of
release, even though it failed to make number one. Its twenty-six weeks
on the chart again suggested the man's extraordinary commercial dura-
bility. However, for many fans, *Slow Train Coming* was the only shot of
salvation they were ever gonna invest in. Christian rock buyers, though,
were finding a whole legion of lapsed agnostics in the racks that year.
Both Van Morrison's *Into the Music* and Patti Smith's *Wave* were less
preachy gusts from the same full-force gale.

Those who hoped that Dylan had made his statement, and could now
move on, were about to be bitterly disappointed. The man was not so
much moving on as pressing on. By the time *Slow Train Coming* entered
the charts in early September, he had already begun rehearsals for a fall
tour that would take his message into the theaters of North America. He
was also hard at work on more songs of faith and salvation. Wrapping
his words in palatable sounds was not about to obscure the message. Just
as in 1965–66, he needed a band that believed in the validity of what he
was doing. If none of those in the Fellowship made the short list, he at
last convinced the finest bedrocker in LA to forsake lucrative session
work for the vagaries of life on the road to Calvary.

Jim Keltner: Bob would say, 'You wanna come down and play?' and it
was actually for auditions. I would go down and I would hang around and
play, knowing that I wasn't going to do the tour, but I would go down just
to have the opportunity to be around him. And then at the end of the day

he would say, 'Well, whaddya think?' And I'd say, 'I can't really go on the road,' and they'd move on and find a drummer. That happened at least a couple of times. [But] in '79, when the same thing occurred, I went down again and I listened to the music and I heard the whole [of *Slow Train Coming*]. I went upstairs to Bob's room and knocked on the door. He answered and I said, 'Listen! I'm aware of [where] you're going. Whatever you want to do, I'm with you.' And that affected my life hugely. I stayed with him for two and a half years.

The band Dylan now assembled was almost entirely composed of fellow believers, save for Tim Drummond, whose contribution to the album prompted a personal invite, and Fred Tackett, who recalls that he got the gig 'by going down [to Rundown] and playing with him for three weeks—until he had to hire *somebody*.' Keyboard duties resided with one-half of the Penn–Oldham writing team ('I'm Your Puppet,' 'A Woman Left Lonely,' 'Cry Like a Baby,' etc.), the self-effacing Spooner Oldham; and a familiar gaggle of girl singers—Helena, Mona Lisa Young, and Regina Havis—added some gospel flavor to the soul food Dylan intended to force-feed his audiences nightly. Initially, the tour rehearsals were even more grandiose than the previous year's. Despite the more stringent practicalities of a theater tour, it took Dylan a while to face up to the impracticality of his original conceit—girls *and* horns.

Dave Kelly: They started [rehearsals] with a five- or four-piece horn section as well. Jim Horn, a well-known horn player, and some of the more famous LA session men. They were supposed to go with the horns on one side, and the girls on the other. He had percussionists. Russ Baboo, the Jamaican guy . . . [David] Lindley made two solo albums with Baboo, having brought him from Jamaica to America . . . He did all sorts of weird things. Playing saucepan lids and things. He's a real percussionist . . . About a week before we went on the road . . . he said, 'What do you think, the horns or the girls?' I was totally flabbergasted! He said, 'We can't really have both, financially. It's just ridiculous.' . . . I didn't know what to say . . . the horns were not doing a lot. The next day I came in, and there were no horn players.

Arthur Rosato: He was cutting it back. He had a different thought on what he wanted to do. He didn't feel like he [wanted to be] responsible for this big organization . . . You could see he was listening to things differently.

Dylan had assembled the nucleus of a band that would stand by him for the next two years, perhaps his most prolific period as a songwriter since 1967. Indeed, rehearsals were not so much occupied with working up arrangements of the *Slow Train* material as the songs he was now writing. His personal assistant, Dave Kelly, remembers him, 'writ[ing] an awful lot ... It was like nearly every day he'd come up with two or three new songs.' Less self-evidently apocalyptic, these new songs concentrated on affirming a personal sense of gratitude for his redemption. 'What Can I Do for You?,' 'Covenant Woman,' 'Saving Grace That's over Me,' 'Saved by the Blood of the Lamb,' and 'Pressing on to a Higher Calling' were more about the joys of salvation than the Lindsey-fueled Slow Train of Armageddon. He was already advancing on the position precipitately carved out on his newly charted album.

It seems a galvanized Dylan was already thinking about his next record. According to Kelly, Jerry Wexler even attended a couple of rehearsals, suggesting arrangement ideas for some of the new songs, in case he should be called upon to replicate the previous album's surprising success. Evidently, the imminence of the End was not dissuading Dylan from making plans, and he was aware that his next Christian album was likely to be more of a hit-and-run affair, slotted in during a respite from touring, much like *Street Legal*. This time, though, he had faith in the musicians, who would be fully conversant with the material from playing the songs night after night to some uncomprehending crowds.

As a final warm-up for what promised to be the 1966 tour plus God, Dylan and his slimmed-down touring band flew to New York on October 18 to perform three songs from *Slow Train Coming* on the popular late-night comedy show *Saturday Night Live*. Seemingly at pains not to crack anything that might pass for a smile, all three performances stood out from the body satirical. His last national TV appearance, the John Hammond tribute, by comparison had been positively loose. An uncharacteristically clear-eyed Dylan now harped on about those trying to drive him from town, having recommitted himself to singing uncomfortable 'truths.' The performance gave fair warning, to a huge audience, that the Vegas Dylan was a long time gone.

1979–80: Middle of the Road—
East Coast Bondage

28

Nat Hentoff: What do you have to look forward to?
Bob Dylan: Salvation. Just plain salvation

—**Playboy** *interview, 1996*

I was saying stuff I figured people needed to know. I thought I was
giving people an idea of what was behind the songs.

—*Bob Dylan, 1980*

The *Saturday Night Live* appearance did not resolve the most pressing
question: Did Dylan intend to perform both old and new songs on his
forthcoming tour? Larry Myers, 'the backboard for Bob to share the
[new] lyrics,' assured him that his old songs were not anti-God. But still,
he continued to refuse to 'sing any song which hasn't been given to me
by the Lord to sing,' even after one wag held up a sign at a concert that
said, 'Jesus loves your old songs too!' In part, it was simply a feeling that
he had just played a greatest-hits show, in arenas of the nation, barely a
year earlier. The decision to play an entirely new show in 1979, and to
play theaters, reflected a belief that it was time to make a change as much
as a recognition that 'all old things are passed away.'

Bob Dylan: In 1979 . . . we started out with a different show. We didn't
play any song you'd ever heard before . . . I thought that was interesting,
you know . . . I had never heard of . . . anybody who'd recorded songs for
twenty years and then one day just didn't play any of 'em again, just played
nothing but new songs . . . I got a kick out of that. [1981]

Arthur Rosato: He doesn't want to be a performer on command. He
wants to play the stuff he wants to play . . . So when we were doing the
gospel stuff he didn't want to be distracted by performing 'a show.' He
really wanted the audience to listen. Some city theater, the audience kept
yelling for 'Lay, Lady, Lay,' so he just started playing it, got halfway through

the opening and said, 'I thought you were gonna sing it.' . . . It was a tough battle. He was hanging himself every night.

On November 1, 1979, Dylan played his first show since his conversion, in the relatively intimate confines of a two-thousand-seat theater in one of the seedier parts of downtown San Francisco. Originally booked into the Warfield for seven dates, exceptional prior demand had led to a further seven shows being added. It was the beginning of a six-month onslaught on North America, at which he was indeed 'hanging himself every night,' even as his music was reborn. Having abandoned all the songs exhumed the previous year, the message he delivered that first, and every subsequent, night was unequivocal and uncompromising.

The evening would open with his three backing singers performing six gospel songs, concluding with the traditional 'This Train (Is Bound for Glory).' The tone would not change perceptibly when Dylan took to the stage. He would invariably launch straight into 'Gotta Serve Somebody,' following it with six more songs from his new album, initially without a single spoken comment. Finally a song would be introduced that shared a more joyous aspect of the man's newfound faith. 'Covenant Woman' was a captivating tribute to the one who had led him to the Lord. That opening night, it was the first song to be fully convincing.

After another spiritual interlude from one of the backup singers, Dylan ran through the two remaining songs from *Slow Train Coming*. By now it was dawning on the first-night crowd that there would be no concessions made to the paying customer, no memorable anthems of yesteryear. The remaining five songs of the set, all new, came with titles like 'Hanging on to a Solid Rock Made Before the Foundation of the World,' 'Saving Grace That's over Me,' 'Saved by the Blood of the Lamb,' 'What Can I Do for You?,' and 'When They Came for Him in the Garden.' There could be no doubting the message reiterated in each and every one of these songs, or the strength of the man's convictions.

Even with sections of the audience walking out, they returned for an encore, the traditional 'Blessed Is the Name,' before Dylan walked to the piano and, unaccompanied by the band, began singing of his resolve to press on 'to the higher calling of my Lord.' One verse in, he arose from the piano, walked to the front of the stage and, with no guitar separating him from the remaining fans, picked up the mike and sang straight from the heart: 'Shake the dust off your feet/Don't look back.' Despite the sheer artistic nerve displayed, and the svelte musicality of Dylan's new combo, the two most influential local reviewers, Philip

Elwood of the *Examiner* (Headline: 'Born-Again Dylan Bombs!') and Joel Selvin of the *Chronicle* (Headline: 'Bob Dylan's GodAwful Gospel!'), were obdurately unimpressed by this touchingly sincere display of faith. Though Elwood considered the show 'a pretty grueling experience,' it was Selvin's review that was more widely syndicated, and caused the greater damage. The conclusion of Selvin's review ran: 'Dylan is no longer asking hard questions and raising an angry fist. Instead, he has opted for the soothing soporific which the simple truths of his brand of Christianity provide.' Perhaps the most damaging part of Selvin's review was the reference to the 'cat-calls and boos [that] echoed throughout the ornate hall.' In fact, though the revivalist aspect of each night's affair prompted some to depart and not look back, there were few boos at this, or any subsequent, Warfield show.

Dave Kelly: Next morning we would go to this little restaurant next to the gig and he'd buy all the papers and we'd read the reviews, and you would not believe that these people were at the show . . . I mean yeah, there were some people that walked out, but they were small by comparison with people that were there.

The reviews clearly got under Dylan's skin, prompting an unprece-dented personal call to Selvin's house, in which he informed Selvin's then-wife that he was revoking her husband's right to review his shows. Later in the tour, he half jokingly asked one audience, 'I know you're gonna read in the newspapers tomorrow that everybody walked out, but will you tell them the truth?' He continued to resent the inaccuracies and untruths in the reviews for some time to come. Talking at the conclusion of his evangelical tour, he was prepared to admit that 'all my stuff at that time was influenced or written right off the Gospel . . . [but] that was no reason to say it wasn't a musical show.' As late as 1984 he would bemoan (to MTV's Martha Quinn) the media perception of his recent performances:

Bob Dylan: The reception's always good . . . The problem is media prob-lems. For some reason the media reportage of the shows I've done has never been entirely accurate since 1978 . . . They say it was all gospel or the crowd booed and walked out. This wasn't true. Maybe three or four people walked out. [1984]

Dylan had other problems at these shows, primarily from those seeking to insure that he remained an isolated, enthusiastic advocate of the

Vineyard Fellowship's particular brand of evangelism. His publicist, Paul Wasserman, was banned from backstage because he was an infidel. When he offered to resign, Dylan said he couldn't, he was the best in the business. The twin pressures of being Bob Dylan and the mouthpiece of someone else's constructed creed were already beginning to pull him apart.

Helena Springs: I remember a lot of people [backstage at the Warfield Theater] were from the Vineyard in Los Angeles . . . I remember a lot of them pressuring him about a lot of things . . . like if he'd drink some wine . . . They were not allowing him to live. They were just being too much of a headache. And I remember one time he said to me, 'God, it's awfully tight, it's so tight, you know.' And I thought and said, 'Yeah, it seems like you gotta get out from under it a bit.' And I felt a lot of pressure from those people . . . Also he found a lot of hypocrisy from those people.

Perhaps it was the hypocrisy he found among the fellows of the fellowship that prompted a particular rap at one of the later shows on the gospel tour:

Bob Dylan: I know a lot of country and western people do that. They sing, very often, 'You can put your shoes under my bed anytime.' And then they turn around and sing, 'Oh Lord, just a Closer Walk with Thee.' Well, I can't do that. That's right, you cannot serve two masters. You gotta hate one and love the other one. You can't drink out of two cups. [1980]

Given that this man would end up fathering children by two of his backing singers on his eighties tours, the reader might suspect that the master of Mammon still had a handle on this man's cup of salvation. Nightly tests of his resolve on stage, though, he continued to pass with flying colors. The fourteen dates at the Warfield gave him plenty of opportunity to work on the new songs, and to grow comfortable with playing live again, even if the sets remained as rigid as another medicine show, thirteen years earlier. Much like those performances, his demeanor was shaped night after night as much by the level of resistance as by his personal frame of mind. As 'straight' as he'd ever been onstage, he was having to fight his chronic stage fright using only the willpower given to him by God. Still, some nights he'd be playful with the singers, interjecting lines in 'Man Gave Name to All The Animals' ('wasn't too small, wasn't too big / think I'll call it a giraffe'), and talking with the crowd, not at them. Other nights, though, made the Free Trade Hall 1966 sound like a veritable jamboree.

Jim Keltner: The audiences didn't know what to make of it. A lot of them were thinking it was going to be a typical Dylan show, and so they were all out there with their pot and ready to party, ready to rock & roll, and so they would yell and scream. They'd holler at him, they'd curse. Right next to them would be a family: 'Bob, we love you, we love your new music.' It was the weirdest thing I've ever seen in my life. Up onstage I'm crying my eyes out, playing every song . . . There were moments on that tour when he played his harp like Coltrane. Bob [also] had complete mastery of . . . his vocals and the songs he was singing. You can't get any more poignant than that.

Starting in the second week of the Warfield residency, Dylan began to grow positively verbose as his between-song raps became an extension of his *raison d'être* for touring in the first place. If the dictionary definition of 'evangelize' is 'to make acquainted with the Gospel . . . to preach the Gospel from place to place,' that is exactly what he was aiming to do. Talking to the crowd allowed him to gauge the mood more accurately than just belting through his seventeen-song set. One night he informed the audience:

Bob Dylan: Satan is called the god of this world. Anyone here who knows that? That's right – he's called the god of this world, and Prince of the Power of the Air. [*someone shouts: 'he sucks!'*] That's right! He does! But anyhow, we know he's been defeated at the cross. I'm curious to know how many of you all know that? [1979]

In 1985, when talking about the element of righteousness in these shows, Dylan made it clear that his evangelizing energized the entire tour:

Bob Dylan: Self-righteousness would be just to repeat what you know has been written down in scripture someplace else. It's not like you're trying to convince anybody of anything. You're just saying what the original rule is, and it's just coming through you. But if someone else can get past you saying it and just hear what the message is, well then, it's not coming from you but through you. And I don't see anything wrong in that. [1985]

No matter how much ridicule Dylan was subjected to, it was something he felt he had to do, almost as if the tour itself answered the question raised in the penultimate song of the main set, 'What Can I Do for You?' He was certainly willing to give some fairly preachy sermons. Of the Warfield shows, the final one, on the 16th—one of the two or three finest performances the singer in him ever gave—also featured his most talkative self to date. As usual, it was before 'Slow Train' and 'Hanging on to a Solid Rock' that the sermonizing came. Before 'Slow Train' he gave the bare bones of a rap that would expand to epic proportions as the tour progressed:

Bob Dylan: You know we read in the newspaper every day what a horrible situation this world is in. Now God chooses to do these things in this world to confound the wise. Anyway, we know this world's gonna be destroyed; we know that. Christ will set up His Kingdom in Jerusalem for a thousand years, where the lion will lie down with the lamb. Have you heard that before? I'm just curious to know, how many people believe that? [*mixed response*] All right. This is called 'Slow Train Coming.' It's been coming a long time and it's picking up speed. [1979]

If Dylan gradually won over most of those San Franciscans who stayed to the end, those in attendance at his next four shows needed no such convincing. Two days on from the Warfield, he returned to Los Angeles for shows at the Santa Monica Civic Auditorium, his first concerts there in nearly fifteen years. As benefits for World Vision, a nondenominational Christian charity, and this being home territory for the Vineyard Fellowship, the shows were bound to be a quite different experience for Dylan and the band. On the first night, when he asked the audience how many knew that Satan had been defeated at the cross, the response suggested an ecumenical revival meeting. He was clearly delighted, affirming, 'Awright! At least we're not alone.' The following three shows found Dylan singing with a passion that only comes with burning conviction. His apocalyptic sermons were also becoming imbued with the same fiery fervor. The second night his pre 'Solid Rock' rap was his most lengthy pronouncement to date:

Bob Dylan: You wanna know something, we're not worried at all, even though it *is* the last of the End times; because we see all these hostages being taken here and drugs being outlawed there. All these sad stories that are floating around. We're not worried about any of that. We don't care about the atom bomb, any of that, 'cause we know this world is going to be destroyed and Christ will set up His kingdom in Jerusalem for a thousand years, where the lion will lie down with the lamb. Y'know the lion will eat straw that day. Also, if a man doesn't live to a hundred years old, he will be called accursed. That's interesting, isn't it? And we don't mind. We know that's coming, and if any man have not the spirit of Christ in him, he is a slave to bondage. I know you're all into bondage, so you need something just a little bit tough to hang on to. This song's called 'Hanging on to a Solid Rock Made Before the Foundation of the World.' And if you don't have that to hang on to, you better look into it. [1979]

The nights in Santa Monica were the culmination of eighteen increasingly impressive shows. The new songs had come into their own, and could now be perceived as heartfelt testaments of faith, a development on the more overtly sermonizing material on *Slow Train Coming*. However, it would be some time before he would play to such friendly crowds again. Next stop on the holy slow train: two shows in Tempe, Arizona, his first shows away from the coast, where he would be playing primarily to students at the local university, who were not at all tolerant of his new stance.

Dave Kelly: In Arizona he had to talk. I don't think they were walking out, but they were definitely heckling. They were insisting on the old songs . . . At the first one I thought he was going to put his guitar down and leave, but he stayed and talked to them.

And talk to them he most certainly did! The first night in Tempe, November 25, the audience refused to sit still, shouting between songs until Dylan asked his lighting crew to 'turn the light on them down there.' As the heckling continued, he began to sermonize, this time minus the gentle coaxing tone adopted in San Francisco and Santa Monica:

Bob Dylan: In San Francisco, we opened there about a month ago, about three or four people walked out because they didn't get the message. But we're still here. Don't you walk out before you hear the message through. Anyway, 'The lamb of God which taketh away the sins of the world'—I wonder how many of you people understand that? I'm curious to know how many of you *understand*?

The few believers in the audience were shouted down by the hecklers. As the second half progressed, the heckling started up again. If the college kids found his songs unpalatable, though, they liked what he had to say even less:

Bob Dylan: The world as we know it now is being destroyed. Sorry, but it's the truth. In a short time—I don't know, in three years, maybe five years, could be ten years, I don't know—there's gonna be a war. It's gonna be called the War of Armageddon . . . As sure as you're standing there, it's gonna happen. [1979]

However disconcerting his first night in Tempe had been, matters deteriorated the following evening. He was about to meet the most hostile audience of his entire career. One result was Dylan openly haranguing the crowd. Not waiting until 'Slow Train,' he gave his first sermon, five solid minutes of it, after the apposite 'I Believe in You.' Delivered against repeated shouts of 'Rock & roll!,' he finally spat words of damnation at the infidels.

Bob Dylan: Hmmm. Pretty rude bunch tonight, huh? You all know how to be real rude! You know about the spirit of the Anti-Christ? Does anyone here know about that? Ah, the spirit of the Anti-Christ is loose right now. Let me give you an example [*begins to tell story about a guru spraying his disciples with a fire extinguisher, at which point someone loudly shouts, 'Rock & roll!'*] . . . If you want rock & roll, you go down and rock & roll. You can go and see Kiss and you can rock & roll all the way down to the pit! [*continues story until, responding to further shouts of 'Rock & roll!'*] . . . You still wanna rock & roll? I'll tell you what the two kinds of people are. Don't matter how much money you got, there's only two kinds of people: there's saved people and there's lost people. Yeah. Remember that I told you that. You may never see me again. You may not see me, but sometime down the line you remember you heard it here, that Jesus is Lord. Every knee shall bow!! [1979]

Having hardly defused the situation, Dylan hurled himself into 'When You Gonna Wake Up?' His pre-'Solid Rock' rap occupied another five minutes, and again emphasized the imminence of the End. It concluded with a direct retelling of Hal Lindsey's Armageddon scenario:

Bob Dylan: Russia will come down and attack in the Middle East. China's got an army of two million people—they're gonna come down in the Middle East. There's gonna be a war called the Battle of Armageddon which is like something you never even dreamed about. And Christ will set up His Kingdom and He'll rule it from Jerusalem. I know far out as that may seem, this is what the Bible says. [*Somebody shouts, 'Everybody must get stoned!'*] . . . I'll tell you about getting stoned—what do you want to know about getting stoned? What you're gonna need is something strong to hang on to. You got drugs to hold on to now. You might have a job to hold on to now. But you're gonna need something very solid to hang on to when these days come. Let me tell you one more thing. When Jesus spoke His parables, He spoke them to people . . . everybody could hear the parables. Some people heard them and understood them, some didn't. He said the same thing to everybody. Do you understand? He didn't try to hide it. He just said it. Those that believed it, believed it and understood it. Those that didn't, didn't . . . You talk to your teachers about what I said. I'm sure you're paying a lot of money for your education, so you'd better get one. [1979]

The first night in Tempe, he had refrained from his usual second encore. Tonight, for the only time on the tour, he refused to play any encore. Instead, before the final song, 'In the Garden,' he preached one last time to those in the grip of Unbelief, asking them to 'remember what I said if you ever hear some other time that there is a truth, a life, and a way.' In Toronto the following April, he talked at length about the second Tempe show, and these shows in general. Though the Toronto audience was reasonably tolerant of Dylan's new set, he soon worked himself up into another frenzy:

Bob Dylan: Actually I wanna tell you a story. We were playin' about four months ago someplace that was a college or a campus. I forget exactly where. Arizona, I think it was. Anyway, I read the Bible a lot; it just happens I do. It says things in the Bible that I didn't really learn until recently, and I really mentioned these because there are higher learning people there, preaching their philosophy. So people can study all the different philosophies, of Plato and, uh, who else? Who? Well, I definitely recall reading Nietzsche and those people like that. Anyways, in the Bible it tells a specific thing in the Book of Revelations that just applies to these times . . . [*Dylan retells Lindsey's interpretation of Gog and Magog as Russia and Iran.*] So anyway, I was telling this story to these people. I shouldn't have been telling it to them. I just got carried away. I mentioned it to them and then I watched, and [I said] Russia was going to come down and attack in the Middle East. It says this in the Bible. And I been reading all kinds of books my whole life: magazines, books, whatever I could lay my hands on, and I never found any truth in any of it, if you wanna know the truth. But I said, This country is gonna come down and attack. And all these people—there must've been fifty thousand . . . [*looks at Drummond and laughs*]. Maybe it wasn't fifty thousand—five thousand maybe . . . they all booed. Everybody just booed; and it was the whole auditorium of people . . . And a month later Russia moved her troops into, I think, Afghanistan. And the whole situation changed, you know. I'm not saying this to tell you they were wrong and I was right, or anything like that. [But] these things that it mentions in the Bible I'm gonna

pay mighty close attention to . . . Been a lot of previews of what Anti-Christ
could be like . . . You need something strong to hang on to. It was manifested
in the flesh! Testified in the Spirit! Received by angels! Preached out in the
world! [1980]

On the video that exists of this Toronto show, the sweat is visibly
pouring off Dylan as he pushes himself to get the message across, proof
positive that each night's musical melodrama was aided and abetted by
the apocalyptic edge in his raps.

His initial response was to fight fire with hellfire, as confirmed a week
or two later, prior to two more shows in Arizona, on December 8 and
9, when for the only time on the tour he agreed to a telephone interview
on Tucson's local KMEX radio station, in response to a press release
from the Tucson chapter of the American Atheists Association, stating
that they planned to picket his two concerts. Throughout the brief
interview Dylan remains quite restrained, agreeing that religion may well
be 'just another form of bondage,' but there is no mistaking the doctrinal
chasm that separates him from the pickets:

*Bruce Heiman: I think basically what they are talking about is your stand in
the past and the type of music you played, with the message you tried to get
across, and the music you're playing today, [and] the different message you're
trying to get across.*
*Bob Dylan: Yeah, well, whatever the old message was, the Bible says, 'All
things become new, old things are passed away.' I guess this group doesn't
believe that. What is it exactly that they're protesting [about]?*
BH: Well, the atheists are against any sort of religion, be it Christianity . . .
*BD: Well, Christ is no religion. We're not talking about religion . . . Jesus
Christ is the way, the truth, and the life.*
*BH: There's another statement they made that maybe you could shed some
light on. They said they would like to remind Dylan fans and audiences that
one's right to say something does not per se lend any validity to that statement.
So, in essence, what they're saying is that you have followers who are going to
be at the concert and are going to listen to the message of your music.*
*BD: Right, I follow God, so if my followers are following me, indirectly they're
gonna be following God, too, because I don't sing any song which hasn't been
given to me by the Lord to sing.*
*BH: Okay. So I think that was one thing that they were concerned about. Do
you have any idea what they mean . . . see, they believe that all religion is
repressive and reactionary.*
BD: Well, religion is repressive to a certain degree. Religion is another form of

bondage, which man invents to get himself to God. But that's why Christ came. Christ didn't preach religion. He preached the truth, the way, and the life. He said He'd come to give life and life more abundantly. He is talking about life, not necessarily religion . . . My ideology now would be coming out of the Scriptures. You see, I didn't invent these things. These things have just been shown to me and I'll stand on that faith, that they are true. I believe they're true. I know they're true.
BH: Do you feel that the message of your music has changed over the years, from the music which talked about war to music that now talks about Christianity?
BD: No. There's gonna be a war. There's always war and rumors of war. And the Bible talks about a war coming up which will be a war to end all wars . . . [in which] the spirit of the atheist will not prevail. I can tell you that much.

The shows in Tucson signaled the end of the first stage of Dylan's mission, as he retired to his Minnesota farm for his first Christmas as a Christian in a family of Jews. But 'preaching the Gospel from place to place' was back on the agenda soon enough, commencing with shows the second week in January in Oregon. If the message remained the same, Dylan had shed the one force in the band close enough to coax him into a broader view of faith. Helena Springs had departed from the tour after a particularly uncomfortable confrontation.

Dave Kelly: [Dylan and Helena] had a big row and he told her to leave . . . I remember her throwing things around the room and Bob standing there. It [just] didn't work out.

A syndicated report suggested that while in Seattle, Washington, for three shows in the third week of January 1980, Dylan purchased a $25,000 engagement ring. The identity of the intended recipient remains unknown, though before the year was out he would be writing 'The Groom's Still Waiting at the Altar.' Meanwhile Carolyn Dennis took Springs's place in the band, and possibly his affections. By year's end, with Springs and Artes permanently fading from the picture, Dylan's most constant companion would become another midterm recruit on the road to Calvary, Clydie King.

For most of the month-long winter leg, Dylan was unusually restrained, refraining from preaching much between songs, though he couldn't resist making the odd brief aside about the muted reception he sometimes received. At one show he sarcastically observed, 'Well, the hits just keep a-comin',' while in the previously unfamiliar state of

Nebraska he suggested all potential hecklers better leave right away because they 'shan't be hearing any old songs tonight . . . [and there] might be somebody outside who wants the seat.' At the final two winter shows, in Charleston, South Carolina, a new song was introduced that seemed little more than an articulation of his between-song raps. 'Are You Ready?' was another catalog of preparatory questions about 'the day of the Lord.'

Five days later, Dylan was ensconced in Sheffield, Alabama, recording the song as the final cut for the successor to *Slow Train Coming*. Once again, he had decided to record an album live, in a matter of days, between bouts on the road. This time, though, the songs had already been realized as a live experience, and the band comprised the same soul drivers that had been running over the songs night after night, making for a set of sessions quite unlike the previous year's—from which Drummond and Dennis were the only survivors, save for Dylan and his producers.

Jerry Wexler: The arrangements were built in, because the band had been playing the songs live. Most of the licks are their own licks, which they perfected on the road, as opposed to the Dire Straits confections on the last album, which were all done in the studio. This one was like when Ray Charles used to call me up and say, 'Hey, pardner, I'm coming in in three weeks, let's do a record.'

Unfortunately, everyone in the band and the crew was fried from a month on the road. For once, Dylan's desire to catch the songs fast was matched by the band, who just wanted to get on a plane and go home. Wexler's strengths as an arranger were also largely absent from the process, making him little more than another of those well-paid engineers Dylan traditionally favored.

Arthur Rosato: We didn't go home. We went straight into the studio. [We thought,] 'We're never gonna get home.' 'Cause Muscle Shoals is as far away as you could possibly be from anything. It was tiring. And Wexler didn't really have a clue how to work with Bob, either . . . [Here] you have a real famous producer and a guy who's never been produced, and they just don't know how to work together.

Jim Keltner: I think that it's a pity those songs were recorded in the studio, instead of live. There was a show in Seattle when we got a standing ovation after 'Solid Rock' for almost five minutes. It was so extraordinarily powerful, and the people just flipped out and I'd never seen that before, ever. Now if you could get something like that on a recording of that song, instead of going into the studio and have a producer completely produce it to death, then you'd really have something . . . Jerry Wexler was one of my idols, [but] we got this sound that was so clean. I think that maybe they were trying to revisit the sound of *Slow Train*. And you can't do that with Bob . . . It didn't want to be anything like *Slow Train Coming*. It wanted to have a big, open, live, exciting sound to match the praise [in] the songs. And it didn't happen. It didn't come across on the tape. But it doesn't in any way diminish the power of [those] songs.

Keltner, in particular, suffered because of Wexler's determination 'to revisit the sound of *Slow Train*.' Gregg Hamm, the engineer, had taped all of Keltner's drums, presumably in an attempt to ensure that he did not overwhelm the other musicians. The result, though, was 'drums that sound like boxes,' until Arthur Rosato rescued him from his fate, a couple of days in, by pulling all the tape off. By then, though, the bulk of the album was already in the can, even if they 'went back and recorded some of that stuff again.'

According to Wexler, it was not until 'the fifth day . . . [that] we re-examined everything we'd done and wound up recutting "Covenant Woman" and "Saved." It was pretty much Bob's instinct to redo them' (the studio logs suggest the former *was* recut, though 'Saved' merely benefited from some overdubs). This was the final session. *Saved* ended up being completed in just five days, however labored the results sound. Of the album's nine cuts, only 'Are You Ready?,' 'Pressing On,' and 'Satisfied Mind' can really be said to work. In the case of 'Pressing On,' it was perhaps its stately new arrangement—replacing a simple concert arrangement that would never have worked on record—that prompted Dylan to reinvest the song with passion. Likewise, the snippet of 'Satisfied Mind' that opens the album sounds just like what it is, the most spontaneous moment of the whole damned session. Cut in a single take, one can well imagine Dylan just slipping into this old gospel standard between takes and the girls, recognizing a familiar refrain, picking up on it. 'Are You Ready?' remains an impassioned performance of a song stuck on a slow train, fast losing speed.

The remainder of the album was flawed beyond repair. In the cold isolation of the studio, the band seemed to be going through the motions, and Dylan's singing lacked that attention to detail brought to the live performances a week earlier. Evidence of lack of care lies strewn across the album. 'Solid Rock,' whose performance in Seattle had left such an indelible mark on Keltner a month earlier, was devoid of the insistent tension that its rumbling bass riff had previously given it. As Paul Williams recognized, in his *One Year Later* addendum to *What Happened?*, '*Saved* demonstrate[d] that the days have passed when divine grace would see to it that he always could capture a song in its prime by randomly running into the studio.' It was to be a highly significant fall from grace (at least as a recording artist), ushering in an era plagued by indecision in the studio and a series of albums inspirational in conception, debilitated by their execution. It also proved that Wexler was no nearer understanding Dylan's methodology than the likes of Bob Johnston and Don Devito.

Ironically, a mere eight days after the final *Saved* session, Dylan and the band delivered a definitive rendering of another song they had been nightly regurgitating in concert over the past three months. The song was 'Gotta Serve Somebody.' The occasion was the annual Grammy awards ceremony. Nominated for best male rock vocal performance, Dylan and the band proceeded to show what a week of rest, at home in LA, might have done for all parties concerned, even if the award was already in the bag (it was his first Grammy) and the next album in the can.

In fact, Dylan seems to have belatedly realized the error of his studio ways. Having turned in the new album to CBS, he apparently requested the opportunity to recut the songs live. Not for the first time, CBS failed to recognize that the best way to serve their shareholders was to serve the artist's needs, and though Dylan would, in fact, deliver a live album recorded in Toronto in April—an amalgam of songs from both albums— they would refrain from releasing it.

Dave Kelly: He wanted to redo [*Saved*] but there was no time . . . He was contemplating issuing a live record . . . It occurred to him to record the shows, but the record company were not interested. They wouldn't put any money into it.

By this point, CBS was hardly in the mood for a third album of Christian material in less than a year. The successor to the surprisingly successful *Slow Train Coming* had proven an even more uncompromising testament to the Lord. Nor did Dylan help matters by delivering an album cover that pictured Christ's extended forefinger picking out a believer's upraised hand from a sea of damned souls, making for an album that might have been more appositely renamed *Cut out*. Pick up thy bed and walk, yourself! It does not seem to have occurred to Dylan that such an Us and Them statement would rebound on him in the form of crateloads of returns. He was also about to forsake just about all the label support he had previously enjoyed, as the man who designed *that* cover was finding out.

Tony Wright: They were so rude, so nasty about Bob Dylan and said how they weren't going to promote this record, another gospel record . . . I was just astonished to hear these people, high-up people at CBS, talking about this man as if he were just *someone*. . . a 'fuck him' kind of attitude. They hated the sleeve, too.

Wright had first met Dylan shortly after the album was completed, in a back room of Rundown, in which, he recalls, there was 'a little writing table, a refrigerator . . . a big old bulldog . . . and [a] blackboard . . . covered with all these religious ideas.' Dylan told him that, during the *Slow Train* sessions, 'he had this vision of Jesus, of the hand coming down and these hands reaching up. And he said that at the same time he had this vision, he saw the whole album too.' Dylan later told Kurt Loder that he wanted 'to have [the image] posted up on Sunset Boulevard . . . [this] big bloody hand reaching down.'

In mid-April Dylan resumed touring activities in Canada, aiming to spend a month working his way across to, and down, the East Coast. Three new songs, written during this six-week respite from the road— 'Ain't Gonna Go to Hell (for Anybody),' 'Coverdown, Breakthrough,' and 'I Will Love Him'—hardly suggested any lessening of religious fervor, even if his fast souring relationship with CBS ensured that there would be no third religious installment in 1980.

If there were now fewer apocalyptic sermons, Dylan did not abandon his attempts to evangelize. The main subject matter of the raps at the East Coast shows was the same as Hal Lindsey's other book, *Satan Is Alive and Well on Planet Earth* (1972)—the 'prince of the power of the air,' and the ways he worketh on 'the children of disobedience.' The two shows in Hartford, Connecticut, in May, witnessed a more talkative Dylan than at any show since Tempe. On the first night he seemed to sense a degree of hostility and asked, before the fourth song:

Bob Dylan: Anybody left yet? They tell me everybody leaves at these shows. I don't know—it's kinda hard to see out there. Middle of the road, East Coast bondage! But God's waiting to set you free. I know you don't hear much about God these days. We're gonna talk about Him all night. We're not gonna be talking about no mysticism, no meditation, none of them Eastern religions. We're just gonna be talking about Jesus. Demons don't like that name. I'll tell you right now, if you got demons inside you, they're not gonna like it. [1980]

The following night the crowd was more evenly divided between testifiers and unbelievers, and though Dylan seemed in a considerably better mood, he still preached extensively to the crowd. Before 'Cover-down, Breakthrough' he tried out an alternative version of the demons rap.

Bob Dylan: I know the modern trend. It's not fashionable to think about heaven and hell. I know that. But God doesn't have to be in fashion because He's always fashionable. But it's hard not to go to hell, you know. There's so many distractions, so many influences; you start walking right and pretty soon there's somebody out there gonna drag you down. As soon as you get rid of the enemy outside, the enemy comes inside. He got all kinds of ways. The Bible says, 'Resist the Devil and the Devil will flee.' You got to stand to resist him. How we got to stand? Anybody know how to stand? How do we stand? Anybody know how? [*Dylan laughs at the muted response.*] We gotta stay here and play another night! [1980]

The last four shows of what proved to be the final leg of the gospel tour finally ventured into Middle America, taking in the more urban parts of Ohio. At both Akron shows, he was welcomed by a surprisingly friendly crowd, leading him to observe, in his introduction of singer Regina McCreary, 'Seems like I don't have to tell you about Jesus—seems like you know all about Him.' On both nights the fans were rewarded with a third encore. In Dayton, locale of the final gig, the audience were also suitably appreciative, even if Dylan talked little between songs.

With his third stint of public evangelizing at an end, Dylan gave his first major interview of 1980, to young Australian journalist Karen Hughes. Hughes had been introduced to the perils of journalism by a playful Dylan back in April 1978 in Sydney. Hooking up with him again at Hartford, she found him less interested in fetishwear and in considerably better physical shape, and more than willing to talk about his continuing faith in 'the resurrected Christ.'

Bob Dylan: Christianity is making Christ the Lord of your life. You're talking about your life now, you're not talking about just part of it, you're not talking about a certain hour every day. You're talking about making Christ the Lord and Master of your life, the King of your life. And you're

also talking about Christ, the resurrected Christ; you're not talking about
some dead man who had a bunch of good ideas and was nailed to a tree.
[1980]

Saved was finally released a month after the end of his gospel tour.
Dylan found that CBS did not share his conceptual vision, preferring to
ship the album to radio stations in a plain white sleeve, and using as the
promotional poster a pre-born-again Bob playing an acoustic guitar. The
subterfuge failed to convince consumers to take a second punt on a
Christian Dylan. *Saved* became the first Dylan studio album in sixteen
years to permanently reside outside the Top 20.

Six months playing the heart out of the songs live hadn't brought
Dylan the new audience he imagined might replace another set of
disenchanted souls. Though he was initially philosophical about *Saved*'s
failure—released, as it was, after he had come to the end of this particular
road—he hadn't as yet recognized a permanent divide opening up
between unregenerate adherents of the old Bob and the faithful few, for
whom his ongoing spiritual journey remained engaging. He would have
to wait another seventeen years before he would be welcomed back into
the upper echelons of the *Billboard* charts, when he had expelled all but
a handful of religious allusions from his released work.

1980–82: In the Summertime

29

You can't record every album and have it be a *Saved*-type album, because you just don't get that many kinda songs all in a row like that.

—Bob Dylan, 1980

If product was there to be had in the 1960s, record companies were geared up to putting out an album by their recording artists every six months. Between March 1965 and July 1966, Columbia released two single albums and a double album of Dylan studio recordings, plus two non-album singles. In the period from February 1980, when Dylan completed *Saved*, to August 1981, when *Shot of Love* was finally released, many of the words filling his head were falling to the floor because CBS were no longer interested in putting out two Dylan albums a year. Indeed, a clause in his 1978 contract specifically stated that 'no Album will be delivered earlier than six months . . . after the delivery of the preceding Album.' As a result, the body of work created in a yearlong, sustained jag of writing that sought to bridge his two great preoccupations would be represented by a single, barely realized collection of songs.

When Dylan concluded the spring 1980 leg of his gospel tour in Dayton, Ohio, he envisaged only a temporary hiatus, fully intending to return to the road that summer to promote the now-released *Saved* album. A major heat wave sweeping the North American continent curtailed his plans, leaving the album in the limbo of *Billboard*'s lower reaches and him with time on his hands and, perhaps, a quote from Ecclesiastes on his mind: 'Whatsoever thy hand findeth to do, do it with thy might, for there is no work, nor device, nor knowledge, nor wisdom, in the grave, whither thou goest.'

The songs Dylan wrote that summer may have abandoned the evangelism of *Slow Train Coming* and *Saved*—save for a 'Positively Fourth Street' for the religious era, 'Property of Jesus'—but his apocalyptic concerns remained. One of his recent songs dealing with depravity in the context of the Second Coming was given a makeover. On the new 'Ain't Gonna Go to Hell,' he introduced, into a previously straightforward Bible thumper, a Dylanesque Madonna, glistening like pure crude in a cold black dress, 'walking away with her legs spread apart.' He also transfused Ma Rainey's 'Yonder Comes the Blues' into his most extensive catalog of the 'total depravity of unregenerate human nature,' 'Yonder Comes Sin.' But neither of these suggested either a great advance in his theological position or a way to straddle the demands of Mammon and Maker.

The moment when 'the gates of heaven dissolve[d] into a universality' came shortly before Dylan reassembled his standing band at Rundown in mid-September, when almost the first recording made was an acoustic version of 'Every Grain of Sand' (the one on *The Bootleg Series*), perhaps his most sublime work to date. 'Every Grain of Sand' was the summation of a number of attempts to express what the promise of redemption meant to him personally. One of his most intensely personal songs, it also remains one of his most universal. Detailing 'the time of my confession/the hour of my deepest need,' the song marks the conclusion of his evangelical period as a songwriter, something its position at the conclusion of *Shot of Love* tacitly acknowledges.

Jim Keltner: I remember seeing a little lyric sheet just laying on the floor and people were walking on it. I picked up this little dirty piece of paper and I read the lyrics, and then I remember setting it aside. And then the next thing I heard was some little demo that he had done of it, and it was real pretty. [But] I don't think I remember playing it until we got to the studio.

Dylan *did* run down the song with the band the day he brought it into the studio, but there is no evidence he returned to the song again until the following April, when it was recorded, perfectly, as the closing track on *Shot of Love* (though he did *read* the lyrics to critic Paul Williams backstage at one of the November Warfield shows). Though several songs on *Shot of Love* would deal with men dead from the neck up, they would do so in a more worldly manner ('you've been captured, but by whom?'). The ethereal quality of 'Every Grain of Sand' would not be reached for again.

However, after eighteen months without an outlet for a more perennial preoccupation, the power of Women, the other two major songs written that summer—on his farm in Minnesota and sailing around the Caribbean—contrasted his troubled sexual relations with the demands of a higher calling. The two songs in question are clearly soul partners. If 'Caribbean Wind' and 'The Groom's Still Waiting at the Altar' do not deal with the same relationship, they address markedly similar ones. Both are set within an omnipresent soundscape of imminent apocalypse. In 'Caribbean Wind,' the backdrop is messengers 'bringing evil reports, of rioting armies and time that is short.' This time the 'distant ship of Liberty' doubles as the *Titanic*. But the song's central concern is a lady from Haiti, 'fair, brown and intense.'

Bob Dylan: I started it in St. Vincent, when I woke up from a strange dream in the hot sun . . . I was thinking about living with somebody for all the wrong reasons. [1985]

After two years of browbeating, 'Caribbean Wind' seemed a lot like the old Dylan, disaffected with love and on the run from the end times. 'Caribbean Wind' was the first of a number of songs he wrote while sailing the Caribbean in his newly constructed schooner, the *Water Pearl*, launched in November 1979. As some sense of the power of nature returned to his songwriting, the 'distant ships of liberty' became a recurring motif. 'Jokerman,' written two years later on the same schooner, has the self-same 'distant ships,' on this occasion 'sailing into the mist,' presumably never to return.

Bob Dylan: 'Jokerman' . . . came to me in the islands. It's very mystical. The shapes there, and shadows, seem to be so ancient. [1984]

In the final verse of 'Caribbean Wind,' the narrator asks himself whether he would have married the strange woman now preoccupying him. Just as he failed to get a handle on the woman, so he would fail to get a handle on the song, which underwent at least four major rewrites. Not for the first time, the rewritings took the song further and further from the place it needed to be, something Dylan himself admitted in the *Biograph* notes, recognizing that he had written 'something . . . very inspired' but hadn't 'quite finish[ed] it.' His 'Kubla Khan,' 'Caribbean Wind' was an example of 'go[ing] back and try[ing to] pick it up, [when] the inspiration is just gone.' He also recognized, this time speaking to *NME*'s Neil Spencer shortly after the *Shot of Love* sessions, that it was 'quite different to anything [else] I wrote [at this time].'

Jim Keltner: He struggled with ['Caribbean Wind'] and I could never figure out why. He could never figure out why. It was just one of those songs—it had great potential. The song was fantastic to play, but every time you'd hear it back there was something missing.

Clearly the original inspiration for 'Caribbean Wind' was personal, and the Dylanisms creeping into the song with each rewrite, as analyzed by Paul Williams in his *Performing Artist*, represented a deliberate attempt 'to try to obscure or even destroy its more personal elements.' Nor was it merely a question of dissipated inspiration that ultimately left 'Caribbean Wind' 'filled with the shadow of greatness to an intriguing [but] frustrating degree.' As with 'Idiot Wind,' Dylan was looking to deal with his life in code, and when the code was too easily broken he felt compelled to reconfigure it. In the case of 'Caribbean Wind,' he left little of the original matrix to strengthen the Dylanisms that remained. Not only would he drop the image of him proselytizing—'told her about Jesus, told her about the rain'—but do his best to dispel the original *ménage à trois* element, at the expense of one of his most evocative couplets ('Shadows moved closer as we touched on the floor, Prodigal son sitting next to the door/Preaching resistance, waiting for the night to arrive.') Evidently, 'thinking about living with somebody for all the wrong reasons' was back on the agenda. Only this time she apparently required him to put his faith on the line.

The companion piece to 'Caribbean Wind' carried the marriage motif into its title, 'The Groom's Still Waiting at the Altar.' Like 'Caribbean Wind,' it would be subject to a number of rewrites in the spring of 1981, before being recorded for, but omitted from, *Shot of Love* (only to be added on its 1985 reissue). In the rewritten version, Dylan again imagined a world on the brink—'cities on fire,' the killing of nuns, and 'fighting on the border.' Claudette, the lady in this song, finally leaves him for parts unknown.

In the original, he speculates that she might be found streetwalking the notorious Fanning Street immortalized by Lead Belly; in the rewrite she is given the benefit of the doubt, being possibly 'in the mountains or prairies.' In the original, he has to remind himself, each time chorus time comes around, to keep pressing on—'Set my affections on things above / Let nothing get in the way of that love'—recognizing witchy women like Claudette as distractions he must learn to walk away from. The *Shot of Love* chorus focuses instead on an imperiled world—a familiar motif overstated.

'Caribbean Wind' and 'The Groom's Still Waiting at the Altar' together represent a significant shift in Dylan's songwriting, and the lyrical bridge that leads to *Infidels*. That the songs reflected Dylan's own problems with women seems undeniable, particularly in the light of recent revelations. The implication in the original versions of both songs is of a theological schism having opened up between Dylan and

'Claudette' that had ultimately driven a wedge between them. He would write one more song to the same female apostate in the spring, though 'Angelina,' too, would be omitted from his third shot of salvation.

Mary Alice Artes wasn't in the mountains or the prairies. She had returned to the East Coast, to continue her career as an actress. Pastor Ken Gulliksen, in an interview at the end of 1980, while insisting that Artes and Dylan remained 'very good friends,' implied that the relationship had run its course. Dylan's most common companion that summer was the most recent recruit to his handpicked group of backing singers. Clydie King was a powerful singer straight out of the black gospel tradition, having been one of the most frequently used session singers of the seventies, appearing on albums by everyone from the Rolling Stones to Elton John via Tim Buckley, Lynyrd Skynyrd, and Steely Dan. She had even been given her own album (*Brown Sugar*) by Polygram in 1974. She seems to have quickly superseded all other female singers in Dylan's affections.

When Dylan called on Mark Knopfler at the Roxy in late October, and they adjourned to Knopfler's hotel room, Clydie was on his arm. When singing more religious material—whether the traditional 'Jesus Met a Woman at the Well' or Dylan's own 'No Man Righteous'—they would instinctively harmonize. However undemanding their relationship was intellectually, she was someone with a spiritual center when he needed it most, an uncomplicated, maternal figure who could glue together the grains of Dylan's vocal sand.

Ron Wood: He used to go to her for solace all the time. She was great with him, but they were like chalk and cheese. Two [more] different people you couldn't hope to meet—her a black, outrageous, hamburger-eating soul singer, and Bob all quiet and white, nibbling off the side of her hamburger. I always remember him trying to share her hamburger, and she was bossing him around and stuff. He needed it at the time.

It was probably his relationship with Clydie that prompted another song that came into its own at the handful of shows Dylan played that fall. 'Let's Keep It Between Us,' or as Dylan introduced it in concert, 'Baby, honey, let's keep it between us, things will work out just fine if we can just keep it between us,' with its references to moving to the back of the bus (deleted in *Lyrics*) and people meddling in their affairs, suggests a lack of acceptance for an interracial relationship. 'Let's Keep It Between Us' was played at all nineteen shows on the fall Northwest tour, starting with twelve more shows at the Warfield Theater in San

Francisco. The shows were billed as a retrospective, radio ads including rehearsal versions of 'Mr. Tambourine Man,' 'Blowin' in the Wind,' and 'Gotta Serve Somebody' in the background. Dylan even gave two radio interviews during the Warfield residency, during which he insisted, 'This is a stage show we're doing, it's not a salvation ceremony.' The sigh of relief from fans was audible.

However, on the first night at the Warfield, a year and a week on from the 1979 unveiling, the show opened with an identical six-song set from the girl singers before Dylan appeared on stage singing 'Gotta Serve Somebody' and 'I Believe in You'; and only five songs—'Like a Rolling Stone,' 'Girl from the North Country,' 'Just Like a Woman,' 'Señor,' and 'Blowin' in the Wind' predated the born-again albums. He also duetted with Clydie King on the old Dion classic 'Abraham, Martin and John.' Still, with only one encore and a Dylan set that clocked in at under ninety minutes, he had some very dissatisfied customers on opening night.

Dylan's exact intentions in embarking on this brief tour have never shone too clear. It promoted no new product, nor did it precede a major US or European tour. And yet the band had worked up at least nine new Dylan originals and a couple of dozen covers—everything from Neil Diamond's 'Sweet Caroline' to 'Somewhere over the Rainbow'— for these nineteen dates.

Fred Tackett: We'd rehearse all kinds of songs but we wouldn't rehearse the songs we were going to do. We'd rehearse them a little bit but he didn't want us to know them 'cause everybody'd get a little part, and everybody'd get an arrangement, and it'd be the same way every night. So he would like to go out and just surprise us, and just start playing something and we'd follow on and all kinds of interesting things would happen that way.

These dates really do seem to have come about as an alternative to cutting the album of new songs his label would not countenance. Predictably, the first night was lambasted by the same syndicated columnists who had attacked the previous year's shows. This time Dylan refrained from revoking licenses, though when he thanked Bill Graham, the promoter, at the final 1980 Warfield show, the scars again showed: 'Last year we came in here with the show, and the newspapers they distorted it, and slandered it, and lied about it . . . that's enough for most promoters in the business just to cancel out the rest of the shows.' Graham in 1980, as in 1979, kept faith with Dylan—though not without impressing on him the need for a finer blend of old and new—and was duly rewarded.

After he got rid of first-night nerves, the late 1980 tour became Dylan's most consistently inventive tour. The shows just got better and better. The arrangements of old chestnuts like 'To Ramona,' 'Señor,' and 'Girl from the North Country' were positively inspirational. The introduction of new songs like 'The Groom's Still Waiting at the Altar,' 'Caribbean Wind' (just once, sadly), 'City of Gold,' and 'Let's Keep It Between Us' provided a rare opportunity for fans to hear songs he had not even recorded for CBS. He even revisited his happy knack of rewriting songs that no longer held up; the new versions of 'Ain't Gonna Go to Hell' and 'Simple Twist of Fate' more than matched their originals. 'Simple Twist of Fate' now seemed to embrace more than one 4th Street affair, and a more capricious femme fatale: 'With the neon burning dim / He looked at her and she looked at him / With that look that can manipulate / Brought on by a simple twist of fate.'

He also introduced a number of surprising covers into the set, all of which carried his indelible brand: a contemporary Christian ballad called 'Rise Again' sung as a duet with Clydie; Shel Silverstein's 'Couple More Years,' Dave Mason's 'We Just Disagree,' the traditional English ballad 'Mary from the Wild Moor,' and an absolute knock-'em-dead version of Little Willie John's 'Fever' were all reincarnated by the grand interpreter. As 'Mary from the Wild Moor,' which he introduced as 'a real old song,' reminded fans of one unmarked path, he also brought out some musical partners from past vistas.

On the 15th Michael Bloomfield reproduced the ringing guitar riffs he'd immortalized on the original 'Like a Rolling Stone' (sadly, his last live performance), and then produced such a blistering lead retort to 'The Groom's Still Waiting at the Altar' that Jerry Garcia's attempt at replication the following night paled in comparison. The newly born-again Maria Muldaur contributed a song on the 19th; and finally, at the concluding Warfield show, Roger McGuinn joined Dylan for two eminently familiar excursions, 'Mr. Tambourine Man' (with Byrds-like intro) and 'Knockin' on Heaven's Door.' While Dylan's singing remained as impassioned as during the previous year's shows, the band found a superior blend of 'sensitivity and power,' guitarist Fred Tackett, in particular, coming into his own.

As the shows progressed, Dylan grew positively talkative, though he resisted the temptation to preach. On the 16th he prefaced 'Just Like a Woman' with a story about a beautiful transvestite approaching him as a woman, and then an hour later as a man; on the 18th he told a long story about being stranded in an underwater cave during one of his stays with Joan Baez in Carmel in the sixties; on the 22nd he told the audience an improbable tale about his first experience of live rhythm & blues, as a twelve-year-old in a bingo parlor in Detroit; on the 26th he related a story about a couple of newlyweds accidentally stumbling onto his hotel balcony the previous evening. Some raps became nightly occurrences, such as introducing 'Mary from the Wild Moor' with 'People always talk about old songs, this is a *real* old song.' He also dedicated songs to friends and other strangers, even one to an absent Greil Marcus. In Portland, on December 3, he dedicated 'Señor' to a lady called Victoria, someone he had met in 1972 in Durango—now 'happily married . . . I guess' (she would pop up again on the Never Ending Tour, no longer happily married). He even responded to a pre-show request by rock critic Paul Williams for 'Caribbean Wind,' prefacing it with a parable suggesting that not even the born-again can run away from themselves:

Bob Dylan: The first person I ever heard of play[ing] a twelve-string guitar was named Lead Belly . . . He was a prisoner in Texas State Prison . . . and he was recorded by a man named Alan Lomax . . . Anyway he got Lead Belly out and brought him up to New York and he made a lot of records there. At first he was just doing prison songs and stuff like that . . . until he'd been out of prison some time and decided to do children's songs. People said, 'Oh, what, has Lead Belly changed?' Some people liked the older ones, others liked the newer ones. But he didn't change—he was the same man. [1980]

The solitary live 'Caribbean Wind' may well be Dylan's finest single vocal performance to a paying audience. Propelled by a real sense of danger in the music, he rises to the occasion with an extraordinary verbal tour de force that hardly allows the listener to catch the story, a dramaturgy from Black Diamond Bay, just the whiff of lava in its distended lines. All the new songs came into their own at the Warfield, whether it was Dylan singing 'let's just move to the back of, back of the bus' with a venom last seen in Tempe, praying in the ghetto, or reasserting his refusal to go to hell for anybody.

Now was the time to book a week at Muscle Shoals. Hang the record company and their new romantics and funkmeisters! Dylan's contract was about to expire (*Shot of Love* would be the last album under his 1978 contract), and CBS seemed about as committed to its renewal as they had been back in 1973. And yet he proceeded to take time out to write a further set of songs. In the winter of 1981, while the band took another breather, he sketched out enough ideas to follow the Clash down to *Sandanista!* In March, he finally began thinking how he wanted his new

album to sound, and decided to road-test a few producers. As David
Mansfield puts it, 'When we did "Caribbean Wind", he was auditioning
producers the way he used to audition drummers back in '78.' It was
Jimmy Iovine's turn first.

Arthur Rosato: We did 'Caribbean Wind' at Studio 55. It was hell recording that particular song . . . He would call everybody he knows to come
down so we would have a band of like fifteen people . . . I had the original
recording that I did back at [Rundown]. I played that for all the musicians
. . . All the musicians loved the song. It had that 'Rolling Stone' feel to it.
So Bob finally shows up about three hours late, which was pretty much on
time for him . . . As soon as the musicians ran through it once he goes, 'Nah,
nah, nah, that's all wrong.' They could see it coming, because they had all
worked with him before: 'Oh, here we go.' And instead of that version, he
turned it into this country and western thing, like boom-chika kinda stuff . . .

Fred Tackett: At the time, the style of recording was to have everything
separated so you could control, so you could push the guitar up or you
could take it out . . . but in Bob's style, you couldn't take anything in or
out, it was just all in the room. It's the way they used to do it—old style. So
we get there early and Jimmy Iovine puts us all in little boxes . . . Bob comes
in and we cut the song and we go back and listen to the playback, which
sounds like a 1980s really slick pop record and, of course, Bob hates it. So
they said, 'Bob, this studio is where they cut the song "White Christmas,"
they want him to know this is an old-time studio . . . He goes, 'Yeah! Go
get me the music to "White Christmas" 'cause that's the only song we're
going to be able to cut in this studio. We're not going to be able to record
any of *my* music here.' In the middle of that session . . . we looked up and
Jimmy Iovine and Shelley Yucas just left. They just walked out of the studio
because they had no control over it, all control had gone . . . We had three
electric guitar players, a couple of drummers, and it was just chaos. And it
was great . . . studio is empty, there's only a second engineer in there, he's
doing all the recording.

'Caribbean Wind' was still seen as a starting point for 'the album after
Saved.' Just as the early *Blonde on Blonde* sessions had been occupied with
unlocking 'Visions of Johanna,' Dylan did not easily abandon this major
work. However, each time he rewrote the words—and he found another
set of 'clever phrases with no story to tell' between the attempt to record
the song at Studio 55 on March 31 and a further attempt to cut it at
Rundown a week later (the one on *Biograph*)—only further removed

him from the song. As he later said, 'Maybe I got it right. I don't know. I had to leave it.' Though he appears to have made one more attempt at the song at Clover studios at the end of April, he had already recorded another new song in March, written in kind, that he hoped might serve as a suitable substitute.

'Angelina,' clearly a close relative of Claudette—with perhaps as many twenty-four-carat lines as 'Caribbean Wind,' and more than enough to constitute another classic composition about a witchy woman manipulating the singer as 'marching men [are] trying to take heaven by force'— gave ammunition to those, like Clive James, who believe that 'no [Dylan] stanza will ever be as good as its best line, and no song will ever be as good as its best stanza.' Unlike its predecessors, 'Angelina' was a collection of lines bound together by a rhyming dictionary. Seductive as Dylan's singing is, the seven-minute 'Angelina' reads largely as a commentary on the final verses of 'Caribbean Wind' and 'The Groom's Still Waiting at the Altar.' Though it is hard to see how a segue from 'Every Grain of Sand' to 'Angelina' could ever have worked, in its original sequence Dylan envisaged closing *Shot of Love* with 'Angelina.'

The sessions at Rundown and Studio 55 convinced Dylan that Jimmy Iovine was not the man to whom he should loan the producer's chair. Having dispensed with one producer, Dylan booked sessions at Cream Studios and United Western Studios the first week in April, determined to find a studio in LA where making live music in a studio setting was still possible. Fred Tackett recalls a Dylan who was 'always looking for old microphones and old studios and guys who knew how to record old style.' According to Arthur Rosato, Dylan even tried to 'record in people's garage setups.'

Jim Keltner: We were going around looking for studios. He was looking for a vibe. He went to more length to find one than a lot of people. Some people will go to a studio and settle for it. He tried out quite a few different . . . producers. He didn't want to fall into that trap he got trapped into with *Saved*. So he was looking to do something more alive than that.

Though just two of the songs from this 'studio tour' would be mixed onto an 'Early Roughs' reel—both presumably covers, 'I Wish It Would Rain' and 'Let It Be Me'—the sessions gave him a chance to try out some riffing ideas ('all the way down / we're going all the way down,' etc.), and run down some new songs he had penned. 'You Changed My Life' compared and contrasted Christ with nonbelievers, 'Need a Woman' sounded like one of those lost '78 sound-check songs, and 'In the Summertime' seemed to hark back to one of those summers preceding 'the warning that was before the flood,' and to one of those soul partners Dylan talked about in the 1978 *Playboy* interview: 'you might see that person once . . . but you have the guarantee your lives are going to be in rhythm.' Once again, Dylan felt the need to return to Rundown, no nearer to finding an appropriate engine room.

Over the next couple of weeks, Dylan and the band worked through the stockpile of songs he had built up, arranging them, rewriting the words, recording some on the eight-track setup that had served Rundown since 1978, as the search for a co-producer and studio continued. Little Richard producer 'Bumps' Blackwell, one of those 'guys who knew how to record old style,' came to Rundown for a day, probably April 23. Dylan later enthused about the experience—feeling inspired enough to attempt a raucous remake of Junior Parker's 'Mystery Train' (not actually a Blackwell production)—and Blackwell seems to have managed to oversee the versions of 'Trouble,' 'Magic,' and 'Shot of Love' that made the original album sequence. However, working with Dylan was not an ideal vocation for a man with a dodgy ticker.

At Debbie Gold's suggestion, Dylan finally turned to Springsteen's co-producer, Chuck Plotkin, who immediately took the tapes accrued to date and gave them labels from Clover studio, where he planned to complete the album (thus making much of the studio information for these sessions unreliable). When sessions resumed at Clover at the end of April, many of the better songs recorded at the month of sessions to date were laid aside. None of the seven songs worked up successfully on the 23rd would be attempted at the five Clover sessions now scheduled. In keeping with prior practice, Dylan preferred to record songs on which the ink had barely dried—lightweight fillers like 'Watered-Down Love,' 'Heart of Mine,' and his peculiar tribute to 'Lenny Bruce'—to reworking the likes of 'The Groom's Still Waiting at the Altar' and 'Angelina.'

And yet, initially, the Dylan–Plotkin alliance seemed to achieve the improbable, producing a satisfactory sequence for *Shot of Love* from just five recording sessions and five mixing sessions. The sessions at Clover, from April 27 through to May 1, gave Dylan seven songs—'Heart of Mine,' 'Property of Jesus,' 'Lenny Bruce,' 'Watered-Down Love,' 'Dead Man, Dead Man,' 'In the Summertime,' and 'Every Grain of Sand'—to go with Rundown recordings of 'Magic,' 'Angelina,' 'Trouble,' and 'Shot of Love.' If 'Every Grain of Sand' seems to have been another remarkable first take, 'Dead Man, Dead Man' took its share of time at all five sessions, and still came out half-baked.

The sequence Dylan and Plotkin came up with on May 12 would

exactly replicate the running order of the released album, save for the additions of 'Magic' and 'Angelina' on side two. However, upon listening to the album the following day, Dylan chose to set about rerecording six of the eight songs he had just spent a week recording, as well as de-selecting 'Magic' and 'Angelina.' In the end, he favored rerecordings of 'Trouble,' 'Dead Man, Dead Man' and 'Heart of Mine,' recorded two to three days after the original sequence was approved. On 'Heart of Mine,' Fred Tackett remembers that 'Chuck Plotkin actually got behind Ringo Starr's drumset and was playing drums and Ringo's standing over next to me by the wall . . . and he can't believe this guy's playing . . . finally he went up and said, "Hey, mate, can I have my kit back?"' Even Dylan himself would later admit that this 'Heart of Mine,' in particular, was one of his poorer substitutions.

Bob Dylan: ['Heart of Mine'] was done a bunch of different ways . . . but I chose for some reason a particularly funky version of that—and it's really scattered. It's not as good as some of the other versions, but I chose it because Ringo and Ronnie Wood played on it, and we did it in like ten minutes. [1984]

Dylan's continuing determination to ensure 'my songs are done live in the studio,' and the fact that many of the songs he had already heard in rough-mix form (i.e., the studio monitor mix), meant that Plotkin's attempts to bring real production values to the mixing process, if not the recording process, soon brought him into conflict with his paymaster. Dylan also continued to embellish just about every song with a wailing chorus of girl singers, his fourth consecutive album to feature such a distraction. Not surprisingly, Clydie King, who was not only now Dylan's paramour but had a pair of lungs that could put out a forest fire, was particularly prominent.

Jim Keltner: Chuck [Plotkin] was wanting to get a nice mix at the end of each song, and Bob wouldn't have any of the nice mixes. Most everything you hear on that *Shot of Love* album turns out to be the monitor mixes.

Plotkin, having thought he had a sequence by May 12, found himself spending another month mixing and overdubbing the nine songs on *Shot of Love*. Each prototype mix was dubbed onto cassette, which would then have to be ferried over to Dylan at Rundown, only for him to disapprove any element that smoothed out the gritty monitor mixes, thus defeating the purpose of having Plotkin there in the first place. Not surprisingly, though some of the songs on *Shot of Love* contain a stick or two of aural gelignite, it lacked the accessibility of *Slow Train Coming*. If the May 12 sequence had been approved, then the album might have been ready for release during Dylan's scheduled tour of Europe that summer. Instead, mixing was not completed until June 7, overdubs not until June 16. As a result, there was no prospect of it being released in time for the tour.

Despite the tortuous recording and mixing process, Dylan himself has always had something of a soft spot for his 1981 album, describing it in 1983 as his personal favorite. As late as 1989 he was still performing 'Dead Man, Dead Man,' 'Trouble,' 'Heart of Mine,' 'Lenny Bruce,' and 'Every Grain of Sand' in his set, at a time when his other eighties albums received scant attention indeed. However, with songs like 'Property of Jesus,' 'Dead Man, Dead Man,' 'Watered-Down Love,' and 'Every Grain of Sand,' it was inevitable that the album would be viewed by the public as a third installment in a religious trilogy, and, though relatively successful in Europe in the wake of his tour, it fared even worse than *Saved* in the US.

Bob Dylan: The record had something that could have been made in the forties or maybe the fifties . . . there was a cross element of songs on it . . . The critics, [though] . . . all they talked about was Jesus this and Jesus that, like it was some kind of Methodist record. [1985]

This time he wasn't about to receive the usual benediction from *Rolling Stone*. A long-standing champion of his work, Paul Nelson, while recognizing that 'the man's past achievements . . . [mean] we tend to give his newest work the benefit of every doubt,' refused to look for excuses for 'the artist's churning mixture of ultimate love and ultimate hate . . . No more. For me, it stops right here.' Nick Kent, in *NME*, actually called *Shot of Love* 'Dylan's worst album to date.' Suffering from a backlash to *Saved*, *Shot of Love* became Dylan's most dismissed work so far. Despite the sublimity of 'Every Grain of Sand,' which even Nelson called 'the "Chimes of Freedom" and "Mr. Tambourine Man" of Bob Dylan's Christian period,' the powerhouse dynamics of the title track, and the wistful retrospection of the beguiling 'In the Summertime,' *Shot of Love* wasn't so much savaged as ignored.

Yet CBS could hardly accuse Dylan of failing to promote the album, as he undertook tours of both Europe and the US at which he played all but two of the *Shot of Love* songs (it would be another sixteen years before he would 'promote' another album so). He evidently believed in the album he had spent two months making. The two tours both ran to twenty-seven dates—the European leg in the summer, the Stateside jaunt in the fall. The European shows, prefaced by four warm-up gigs in the US, were almost universally impressive, with Dylan's voice still running on high octane and the choice of songs illustrating every musical sinew, from a powderkeg 'Ballad of a Thin Man' through the harmonica-driven 'Forever Young' to the only successful electric arrangement of 'Mr. Tambourine Man' Dylan has ever realized. The five *Shot of Love* songs also sounded fresh and alive, even if the album was again absent from store windows.

In Europe, though, Dylan again found himself on the receiving end of the Springsteen Effect. Playing with an incomparable rhythm section and displaying whole new sleights of vocal, he still found himself playing second fiddle to the sorcerer's apprentice, who was then embarking on his first-ever European tour. Springsteen had delayed his tour that spring, and ended up leaving England less than three weeks before the Dylan shows, thus making his much-hyped 1981 tour a fresh experience to compare and contrast with Dylan's considerably more demanding show. Springsteen benefited from European critics having no benchmark with which to compare his 1981 shows (it had been six years since a callow Springsteen had played two infamous shows in London). Thus an endless procession of critics lived out a new version of the Emperor's New Clothes.

The Old Pretender, though, refused to renounce his crown. He sprang surprises with every line, twisting words and phrases, wringing meaning from each tapestry of song he wove. That this was a conscious artist at work was brought home to guitarist Fred Tackett one night, when Dylan 'did back-phrasing, where he'll start to play a song and he won't start singing right away, he'll wait and start singing and playing catch-up before the next chord comes . . . After[wards] I said, 'Bob, you were really out on a ledge tonight. I didn't think you were going to make it.' . . . And the very next night we did the song, and he did the exact same thing again, and looked over at me and laughed.'

Though his new, highly mannered vocal delivery was initially dis-orienting—and certainly precluded any communal participation—repeated performances suggested he had found a voice which, in *NME* editor Neil Spencer's words, 'was quite astonishing, clearly superior to all his many past styles; from all of which he borrows for the present.' Though not required to defend his new show to Spencer, Dylan insisted, 'I feel very strongly about this show. I feel it has something to offer. No one else does this show—not Bruce Springsteen, [not] anyone.'

But perhaps even Dylan had stretched the most flexible vocal cords in rock & roll too far. At two shows in Birmingham, two days on from his six-night residency at London's cavernous Earls Court, he sounded in physical pain, and on the first night cut short his set. Though a respite before mainland Europe seemed to repair any damage, allowing Dylan to impress throughout the few remaining European shows, when he returned to the American stage three months later he sounded unwilling or unable to unveil the same vocal gymnastics, save on an occasional 'Simple Twist of Fate' or 'I Want You.'

The American shows in the fall were lackluster affairs, as if the reviews and sales figures for *Shot of Love* had already taken the wind out of Dylan's sails. His voice had also reacquired its high-pitched whine. With problems behind the scenes, and a most peculiar itinerary that excluded LA, New York, and Chicago, the tour remained one of the best-kept secrets of the season.

The three months off the road had clearly taken their toll on band spirit. Nor was Dylan any longer using his summers to pen a whole new set of religious broadsides or love songs for the endgame. An attempt to mix it up musically, forced on him by the premature departure of a sick Willie Smith, resulted in the recruitment of the versatile Al Kooper, who was given only a matter of days' notice and then all but restricted to providing that trademark organ sound. Dylan also decided to augment rock's only four-handed drummer, Jim Keltner, with a second set of drums, on which Arthur Rosato contrived to play along. Inevitably, the recruitment of Kooper was seen as a concession to 'greatest-hits'-loving fans.

Al Kooper: When it started it was almost totally Christian and when it was over it was almost totally greatest hits . . . The shows were long. We did like two-and-a-half, three-hour shows. It was brutal. One of the first nights we played 'Like a Rolling Stone' so slow it must have taken him twenty minutes to go through the whole song. So, after the show I put my arm around him and said, 'You can't play "Like a Rolling Stone" that slow, or if you do let's do it really slower and then we won't have to do any more songs.' . . . By the end of the tour the old Bob was back.

In fact, the set changed only marginally—'I Want You' received its first live outing in three years, alternating with 'The Lonesome Death of Hattie Carroll'; a lovely honky-tonk 'I'll Be Your Baby Tonight' was resurrected; and both 'A Hard Rain's A-Gonna Fall' and 'Señor' were also restored to favor. Otherwise it was the same mix of enthusiastic workouts for the *Slow Train Coming, Saved*, and *Shot of Love* songs and a begrudging smattering of golden oldies.

Barely five weeks on the road, the whole vibe of the fall tour was quite different from previous tours. For a band who had been together since the late summer of 1979, and had recorded two albums, neither of which had captured them at their best, the shows were becoming stale. Dylan was also audibly coming to the end of this particular road. Perhaps the occasional resurrection of some of his more unequivocal Bible thumpers—'Are You Ready?,' 'When He Returns,' even 'Jesus Is the One'—was his way of trying to restore the fervor in tired limbs, even as the communality of the touring band was giving way from within. Dylan, though, decided to memorialize the tour by bringing in a recording truck for two shows in New Orleans on November 10 and 11 and, at his behest, Keltner and Kooper asked their old buddy Bruce Gary to share the sticks.

Bruce Gary: I'd just left the Knack. Keltner and Kooper, on the same phone, called me up from New Orleans and said, 'Listen, we know you're depressed, we spoke to Bob and we asked him if it would be okay for you to come and play,' because there's two drum sets anyway. The drummer roadie was playing on the second drum set because Bob liked the idea of two drums at the time. So Kooper says, 'All you gotta do is get on a plane and get to New Orleans, and we'll take care of everything from there.' So I jumped on a plane and the following night I played at the Saenger Center two nights in a row . . . He was mixing his religious songs in with his hits but he was still very much into the Jesus thing. It opened my eyes. I remember joining in on a little session before a show. Every show anybody that was into it would get together in Bob's dressing room, and all put arms around each other and recite the Lord's Prayer. I thought what the hell, so I joined in. And I sensed a wonderful energy among everyone and it carried with us onto the stage, and it made those shows that much more special . . . I was invited to come down to Clearwater, but I decided to come home. I could see that everyone was crusty around the edges. The best thing that happened to me was the confirmation from Bob, he came up to me, wanted to thank me, [saying] that I'd breathed some new life into the shows.

The New Orleans shows were certainly special (though not as special as Paul Williams seeks to make them in the second volume of *Performing Artist*). Dylan even pulled out one of the most ambiguous songs of his so-called Christian era, 'Thief on the Cross.' Who was the thief on the cross? The 'malefactor' crucified alongside Jesus who said, 'If thou be

Christ, save thyself and us'? Or the other thief crucified, who asked Jesus
to remember him 'when thou comest into thy kingdom'? Or 'the thief
in the night' himself? Was Dylan looking for someone to reinforce a
decaying faith? He was hardly backsliding into apostasy at a show where
he played 'Gotta Serve Somebody,' 'I Believe in You,' 'Man Gave
Names,' 'Watered-Down Love,' 'Dead Man,' and 'In the Garden.' But
his faith no longer put fire in his fingertips, and it showed in the
performances.

Four days in New Orleans also afforded the opportunity to film
some more 'little scenes . . . [Howard Alk] had put together.' Dylan's
old filmmaking companion and sometime photographer had begun
shooting the sort of material that suggested a sequel to the spectacularly
unsuccessful *Renaldo and Clara*. Though it remained 'just a home movie'
to many, it was a lot more to Alk: it was a way back to the life he'd left
behind.

Bruce Gary: Most of the filming that I was involved with was done in
Houston, at the Astrodome. Howard took a film crew and a bunch of
costumes, and Bob was dressed in, like, a monkey suit running around the
bleachers, and being filmed like that, and Al was doing some kind of crazy
lunatic stuff, and I'm running around, and Howard's filming us jumping up
and down being silly.

Arthur Rosato: We had been on the road and we were shooting every
night. We'd play and then go out and shoot all night. We were doing skits,
and Bob was writing them after the fact. We'd go out and shoot things, and
he'd give some lines to somebody to say. There was a French guy [Roland
Grivelle], he became Bob in the film.

The motive for these escapades may have been, in part, simply to keep
everyone wrapped up in something separate from the shows. Rosato's
(likely reliable) take on it is that Dylan was involving himself 'more or
less as a favor to Howard. It was just a home movie. We were always out
shooting things, but it wasn't anything that involved. I think he was
trying to let Howard go.' Alk had been living in one of the houses on
Dylan's estate, with his second wife, for much of the year, attempting to
come to terms with a debilitating cocaine habit and a creative life that
had gone decidedly off the boil.

Whatever Dylan's input on the road, when the tour wound down in
the resort town of Lakeland, Florida, on November 21, at the very venue
where he had embarked on the 1976 leg of Rolling Thunder, he returned

to Rundown Studios in Santa Monica with Alk, apparently with a plan to move forward on another ill-defined film project. But on January 1, 1982, Howard Alk was found dead at Rundown Studios, having taken his own life. One story, surely indicative of Alk's state of mind, has it that he had been asked to attend a meeting about the film a couple of days earlier, and had stated that he would be unable to attend as he would be committing suicide.

Dylan was understandably devastated. Alk was one of his oldest and closest friends. They had been on a number of life's wilder roller-coaster rides together. That he had taken his own life was particularly painful to Dylan, for whom the reminders of mortality seemed relentless (recent months had seen the deaths of guitarist Michael Bloomfield and fellow Christian musician Keith Green). Alk's death also signaled the end of the Rundown era. Though the lease on 2501 Maine had another nine months to run, Dylan decided it was time to disband the band, indeed disassemble the whole setup (though he would use the eight-track equipment to demo some ideas with Bruce Gary in June 1982). It would be another thirty months before he felt the road call again, by which time his worldview would have taken another turn.

Arthur Rosato: [Alk's death] was the major reason we stopped . . . The last major conversation I had with Bob in that period, Bob said he was gonna close the studio down. He wasn't gonna go out on the road until 1984. That wasn't a history he wanted to be around. Even before that, he was trying to make [Rundown] into a commercial venture . . . When we got back to Santa Monica we had all this footage, we started editing and trying to figure out, What is the movie? . . . [but] Bob was pulling the plug on the project . . . We had no idea what we had, we had notes and pages of the script that they would type up, and then we'd try to figure out, what's the story here? . . . And then when the holidays came—it was just a tough time . . . I came right back down again, and talked to Bob. Bob realized it was the end of an era. We just all packed up and said goodbye.

1982–84: Songs of Experience

30

I don't really use all the technical studio stuff. My songs are done live in the studio; they always have been and they always will be done that way. That's why they're alive . . . A record is not that monumental for me to make. It's just a record of songs.

—*Bob Dylan, 1977*

Somehow, I figured I could always get away with just playing the songs live in the studio and leaving. It got to the point where I felt people expected that from me. But I decided [on *Infidels*] to take my time, like other people do.

—*Bob Dylan, 1983*

It wasn't just in the studio that Dylan now decided to take his time. There is a lovely story Leonard Cohen tells of Dylan asking him, in a café in Paris in January 1990, how long 'Halleluiah' had taken him to write—two years—and him asking, in return, how long 'I and I' took: fifteen minutes, apparently. In truth, 'I and I' is far too measured a lyric, each image weighed in the balance, for it to have been a quarter-hour flight of fancy.

Indeed, the songs that made up Dylan's first post-evangelist collection were all worked on wholesale, entire verses sacrificed as his shifting theology was allowed to beat against the sands of time in 1982, rather than mutate before unknowing eyes, as it had through three years of continuous touring. As in 1968 and 1972, he made no officially released recordings, nor did he play any shows, save for a single ten-minute guest appearance, joining Joan Baez at an anti-nuke concert at the Pasadena Rose Bowl in June, at which he sang Jimmy Buffett's apposite 'Pirate Looks at Forty.'

Unlike those two previous 'lost' years, though, 1982 was not without its recording activity. Dylan and Clydie King, who were now inseparable, recorded an album of duets, apparently at Gold Star Studios. However, his problems with CBS continued—even though he signed a new five-year, five-album contract in July—and the album remains unreleased, according to Dylan, because 'It doesn't fall into any category that the record company knows how to deal with.' Presumably the duets, to simple piano accompaniment, comprised the sort of standards they had rehearsed back in 1981, of which 'Let's Begin,' 'Let It Be Me,' and 'It's All in the Game' made it to the shows, and songs like 'Smoke Gets in Your Eyes,' 'Mansion Builder,' 'Vaya Con Dios,' and 'Your Cheatin' Heart' did not.

Dylan seems to have been working on this material with Clydie when he invited Bruce Gary down to Main and Ocean in mid-June to work on some original ideas. Gary recalls a number of riffs later cropping up on *Infidels,* though the purpose of the afternoon eluded him. The exercise was not repeated.

Bruce Gary: I got a call: Come down to Rundown. Somebody led me to where the drums were. He had a little makeshift studio setup, like an eight-track machine . . . He sat down at the piano and started playing, and then he moved over to the bass. This went on for about three and a half hours, just jamming along. He played guitar, keyboards, bass. It was all being recorded and the afternoon was climaxed by Clydie King showing up, and Bob sat at the piano and played a couple of songs . . . They ended up leaving together in a white Cadillac.

Rather than pushing himself to formalize these ideas prematurely, Dylan gave himself up to another summer in Minnesota, where he enjoyed the company of his eldest son, Jesse, with whom he took in a number of shows in Minneapolis, by the likes of the Clash, Elvis Costello and the Attractions, X, the Stray Cats, and Squeeze, all new-wave bands idolized by sixteen-year-old Jesse. In September, he returned to Jerusalem, in the company of his ex-wife, and again found himself back in the news, when he was photographed at the bar mitzvah of his son Samuel wearing a yarmulka. It was interpreted as considerably more than a sign of respect, and Dylan's next album would be recorded against a backdrop of religious crossfire from both sides of the messianic divide.

The media had begun to speculate about an element of backsliding in his much-vaunted Christian beliefs as far back as March, when a syndicated article alleged that 'a source close to' Dylan suggested he had reverted to the religion of his forefathers, and that, 'In a sense, he never left his Judaism. My interpretation is that the New Testament and Jesus were a message he thought he got, but that he was still testing.' Voices from the Vineyard, refuting such stories, were soon vying for the same column inches.

Paul Esmond: I don't think he ever left his Jewish roots. I think he is one of those fortunate ones who realized that Judaism and Christianity can work very well together, because Christ is just [Jesus the Messiah]. And so he doesn't have any problems about putting on a yarmulka and going to a bar mitzvah, because he can respect that.

Early in 1983, though, came reports that he had been spending time with an ultra-Orthodox Hasidic sect called the Lubavitchers. It was even alleged that he had recorded an album of Hasidic songs. While fans speculated upon how Dylan might go about settling the argument, an eminent Lubavitcher suggested that Abraham's son was about to bring it all back home.

Rabbi Kasriel Kastel: He's been going in and out of a lot of things, trying to find himself. And we've just been making ourselves available. As far as we're concerned, he was a confused Jew. We feel he's coming back.

That the author of 'Jesus Is the One' was not prepared to go on the record to support or refute the opposing theological camps in their war of words strongly suggests that he was distancing himself from the Vineyard Fellowship, if not the Lord. The songs he had been writing were not about to abate the speculation. Though there would be no songs on *Infidels* that do not contain allusions to the Good Book, only 'Jokerman,' 'I and I,' and 'Man of Peace' drew significantly from New Testament texts. 'Man of Peace'—based upon the dictum 'Even Satan disguises himself as an angel of Light' (2 Corinthians 11:14)—and 'Jokerman' continued his fascination with Revelation. In both, it was the battle to separate false messiahs assuming Christ-like attributes from the one true Messiah that began to preoccupy him. The closest to a public statement of his current position came in an interview published as he came to mix the successor to *Shot of Love*. To Martin Keller of the *Minneapolis City Pages*, he not only talked about Jewish roots and 'telling it right, like it is,' but made it clear he was not about to embrace a Judaic orthodoxy:

Bob Dylan: Roots, man—we're talking about Jewish roots, you want to know more? Check on Elijah the prophet. He could make rain. Isaiah the prophet, even Jeremiah, see if their brethren didn't want to bust their brains for telling it right like it is, yeah—these are my roots, I suppose. Am I looking for them? . . . I ain't looking for them in synagogues, with six-pointed Egyptian stars shining down from every window, I can tell you that much. [1983]

A Dylan returned to secular values, or even the faith of his father, was news. It provided reassurance to the majority of (ex-)fans who preferred a world operating as a series of accidents, without purpose or reason, to 'a perfect, finished plan.' Perhaps their singing spokesman again accepted chaos. Even the more questioning of his constituency preferred a confused Judaic humanist to an unequivocal evangelist.

The album that had occupied him for over a year as a songwriter continued to ask of these people hard, unyielding questions, but at least they were asked in elliptical, Dylanesque images: 'Freedom just around the corner for you / But with truth so far off, what good will it do?'; 'Wanna get married? Do it now / Tomorrow all activity will cease.' He had at least sixteen songs he wanted to record, some love songs for the end times, a couple of sacrilegious lullabies and a number of doomsday poems set to song.

As 1982 closed down, Dylan decided to approach a number of 'name' artists to offer them the producer's chair. Though he wanted to produce the album himself, as he had with *Blood on the Tracks,* he felt that technology had passed him by. He needed an artist at home in the modern recording studio. Hence, presumably, his approaches to David Bowie and Frank Zappa, who had at least produced their own records, and Elvis Costello, who had not (though he had produced others').

Though Dylan has hardly developed a reputation for deferring to others, each of these figures would have demanded an all-but-equal partnership in the studio. He perhaps presumed that his final choice, a guitarist still wet behind the ears last time they shared a studio, would prove more acquiescent, though equally au fait with a thirty-two-track digital zone. Since the recording of *Slow Train Coming,* though, Dire Straits had become one of the most successful acts in the rock pantheon, even as Mark Knopfler discarded most remnants of the original Straits, kith and kin included. However much using Knopfler would, in itself, attract sales and press coverage, Dylan seems to have always had in mind a technical assistant, not a partner in crime. He continued to enjoy Knopfler's not-so-unique guitar tone, and presumed that his ability to refrain from 'step[ing] all over [a song] with fancy licks' had survived stardom.

When Dylan entered New York's Power Station Studios on April 11, 1983, to begin recording his follow-up to *Shot of Love,* he knew the importance of these sessions. It had been two years since *Shot of Love,* which—in tandem with *Saved*—had all but dismantled two decades as a commercial artist. Since *Shot of Love,* the advent of MTV—a cable-TV station supplying a perennial diet of promotional videos, brief 'newsy' items on current pop stars, and the occasional half-hour 'in-concert' special—had placed a new onus on pop artists to conceive of an image for today's sound. It was into this alien landscape that CBS hoped to propel the father of social relevance in song.

It is all too easy to say that Dylan plows his own furrow, and if the world catches up, all well and good. Yet he, more than any contemporary, long ago realized the commercial benefits of the aural sweetener. *Bringing It All Back Home*'s second side had given the folkies some acoustic solace; he'd closed out *John Wesley Harding* with a little pedal-steel cornball; *Desire* gave social conscience and violins renewed relevance; on *Slow Train Coming* Knopfler's sinewy sounds and Wexler's superlative production gave fans his best-sounding album in years. He now put together one of his finest studio combos to mark his passage out of Christian orthodoxy, and into a faith based on responsibility and accountability.

Dylan had had no 'house band' since the closure of Rundown, and was required to construct a sound from scratch. Mark Knopfler's syrupy tone required a harder, bluesier second guitarist to provide some cutting edge. Bruce Gary had introduced Dylan to ex-Rolling Stone Mick Taylor the previous summer, at the Roxy, during a return stint with John Mayall. Taylor and Dylan had struck up a friendship that resulted in Taylor hearing the *Infidels* material first, in the months leading up to April 11. Taylor's presence at Record Plant seems to have unsettled Knopfler, who no longer deferred to those against whose pedigree his paled. The rhythm section also reflected musical ideas forming in Dylan's head. However, Dylan acceded to Knopfler when it came to engineer and keyboardist.

Mark Knopfler: I did suggest that Alan [Clark] be there . . . And I suggested the engineer, Neil Dorfsman . . . We were like a three-man team at that point. Sly Dunbar and Robbie Shakespeare were Bob's ideas, as well as Mick Taylor. I suggested Billy Gibbons, but I don't think Bob had heard of ZZ Top.

Whatever rethink he had undergone about studio technology, Dylan was not to be dissuaded from recording live with the band. As throughout his career, he planned on winging it, and the band was required to wing it too.

Alan Clark: We used to just sit at our instruments . . . and Bob would wander in, sit down, put his headphones on, and struggle with his guitar strap for a couple of minutes, light a cigarette and then stub the cigarette out, take his guitar off, take his headphones off, and walk across to the organ where I was sitting and write down about . . . half a dozen lines of the next tune in tiny, meticulous handwriting. It was quite interesting! And he'd sort of wander back over, maybe forget to put the headphones on, and start playing the track. Just like that! If you weren't sitting there—if you had to go to the bog or something—he just started, y'know. It was amazing. And that's the way the album went.

Mark Knopfler: With Bob, all I did was try and make sure that we were prepared. He would come around to my house and run down some songs on the guitar, and they would change dramatically by the time he left. I would try and make sure that we were in a going mode before we got to the studios . . . It was all done live. I learned that from doing *Slow Train Coming*. . . You try and get things run down before the thing is attempted, because after two or three times Bob would have moved on to something else.

It certainly seems, on the basis of the *Infidels* studio logs, that Dylan had a hard time keeping focused on the prime cuts. Rarely did a Record Plant session go by without him leading the guys through some wacky cover. One-time Sinatra signature 'This Was My Love,' Merle Travis's 'Sixteen Tons' and 'Dark as a Dungeon,' the traditional 'Jesus Met a Woman at the Well,' Stephen Foster's 'Oh Susannah!,' Booker T's 'Green Onions,' Ry Cooder's 'Across the Borderline,' Hank Williams's 'Cold, Cold Heart,' Hank Snow's 'I'm Movin' On,' Willie Nelson's 'Angel Flying Too Close to the Ground,' even that Tom Jones staple 'The Green Green Grass of Home,' contributed some of the lighter, more impromptu moments at these sessions. A number of instrumental jams, marked as 'Dadada Grateful Dead' or 'Dark Groove' or 'Don't Fly Unless It's Safe' or just 'Reggae Jam,' also ate up plenty of tape.

If the jams and covers occupied more than their fair share of the eighteen days of sessions, Dylan seems to have had a clear idea of which originals he most wanted to record. Not that a year of sustained songwriting had convinced him to forsake rewriting in the studio. The longer the sessions, the more he rewrote, perhaps in part to sustain his interest, but also because each song's endless evolution allowed him to put off the moment when it was definitively fixed. An all-consuming confidence that had previously provided surety when it came to capturing the moment was only in sporadic attendance this time around.

'License to Kill' was cut in a single take, but the other songs provisionally penciled in for the album took a good deal longer. For 'Foot of

Pride,' an unprecedented forty-three attempts left fourteen complete takes that alternated between reggae, rock, waltz, 'acoustic,' and bossa nova. 'Blind Willie McTell' took up most of the first and all of the last day in the studio—surely another example of Dylan kicking off the sessions with the song that opened up the album for him. 'Don't Fall Apart on Me Tonight' occupied the scrag end of the session on the 11th and all of the 12th. 'Neighborhood Bully' ate up all of the 19th, 'Tell Me' the 21st, 'Foot of Pride' all of the 23rd and sections of the 22nd, 25th, 26th, *and* 27th. 'Someone's Got a Hold of My Heart' was tried with Dylan's foot on the brakes on the 16th, and with his foot on the accelerator on the 25th and 26th. Evidently, he was serious about 'tak[ing] my time, like other people do,' giving the editor in him an unprecedented role in the process.

Evidence that these sessions had become extensions of Dylan's editing process exists in a remarkable running tape of Dylan and the band working on 'Sweetheart Like You,' presumably part of the April 18 session. They had had a couple of goes at the song four days earlier and it is clear, as the tape starts, that the arrangement is pretty much in place. But he has only a skeletal outline of words. As the second take of the day starts up, he cuts it dead after one line:

The boss ain't here, he gone north . . . he gone north' . . . No, wait a sec. That ain't right. [*Sings to himself.*] 'Well the boss ain't here.' Oh shit. [*Strums guitar while tapping his foot to the rhythm of the song.*] Okay. [*Count in.*] 'Well the boss ain't here, he gone north / I can't remember where / he caught the redeye, it left on time / he's starting a graveyard up there.

After more 'wild, obscure lines,' Dylan says, 'Let's try it again. I think it's getting closer. The bass part is getting right. It's got that feel, y'know.' The session continues until they get a satisfactory backing track, but by now Dylan has discovered the one great advantage of multitrack, the ability to redo a vocal, not because he didn't capture it live but because the song itself has moved on. At least two alternative sets of lyrics for 'Sweetheart Like You,' and a subtler, more acoustic arrangement, would be rejected in the selection process.

The rewriting option would become a major factor during both the recording sessions and the mixing process. Whole verses were dropped, rewritten, and resurrected. The original version of 'Union Sundown' featured a final verse that was a thinly veiled attack upon a man in the White House who, if 'he understands the shape of things to come,' will be allowed to remain there until he dies. 'Jokerman' would lose its hand-sewn shirt, and its soul, in the process. In the case of 'Someone's Got a Hold of My Heart'—Dylan's most successful reworking of the 'Caribbean Wind' motifs—the rewriting process did not finish until 1985, when it was recorded for *Empire Burlesque* as 'Tight Connection to My Heart.'

By the end of the April 26 session, Dylan had spent fourteen out of the last sixteen days in the studio, and he still did not feel he had captured 'Jokerman,' 'Blind Willie McTell,' or 'Foot of Pride'—the major songs of the sessions—nor given the album the necessary sweep. The following day Clydie joined him at the sessions, for the first time in an active role, and things began to go much more smoothly. Having gone back to 'Foot of Pride,' he nailed it in two takes. 'Union Sundown,' an ill-judged rant against the macro-economics of capitalism, also took just two takes, as did 'Julius and Ethel,' Dylan's account of how the Rosenbergs' misguided idealism had taken them to the electric chair in the 1950s.

Dylan had also brought another song to this session, a reggae-inflected confessional named 'I and I' that suggested just how great the oppressions of prophecy and fame had become. The problems facing the kingdoms of the world are making the narrator feel afraid, so he rises from his bed, leaving his lady love to dream her untroubled dreams. Worked up from scratch, the song took just three takes to become the most realized vision captured at these sessions. Clearly, Clydie's presence was a beneficent one. She returned with Dylan for the following two sessions, the second of which seemed to round off the album with a rerecorded (and rewritten) 'Union Sundown,' as well as the single-take dirge 'Death Is Not the End,' and the equally downbeat 'Lord Protect My Child,' and Willie Nelson's 'Angel Flying Too Close to the Ground.'

Dylan, though, still didn't feel he had quite got the song that set this wheel in motion, the immaculately conceived 'Blind Willie McTell.' Three days after the 'final' session, he decided to see if he couldn't just nail that one down, too—which he did, in just two takes. From his cough on the second line as his voice strains to hit the note, to the tap of what is surely Dylan's shoe counting the band in on the second verse, the way he sings 'can strut' like 'instruct,' the apposite harp fills, that trademark way he has of running the words in the first half of a line together just so he has time to bend the remainder of the line to the beat in his head—all work together to deliver the world's eulogy, sung by an old bluesman recast as St. John the Divine, forming those oh-so-familiar chords as he gazes out of the St. James Infirmary.

After a further four sessions of overdubs, Dylan and Knopfler set about sequencing. And sequence an album they did, nine tracks that made for Dylan's finest collection in eight years. Though it contained two all-but-meritless rants—'Neighborhood Bully' and 'License to Kill'—all seven remaining cuts had something going for them, notably four of his finest expositions on the end Times: 'I and I,' 'Jokerman,' 'Blind Willie McTell,' and 'Foot of Pride.' It was an album that would surely re-establish both his commercial standing and critical credibility. Despite the omission of a devastating 'Someone's Got a Hold of My Heart,' it was what all Dylan fans had been hoping for, an album that bridged his deepest preoccupations, wrapped in his most cogent sound in four years, and his best lyrics in eight. Sadly, it was not the album he chose to release.

Over the years, Knopfler has constructed a convenient story to cover his bruised ego and to explain away Dylan's decision to recast *Infidels,* without him.

Mark Knopfler: *Infidels* would have been a better record if I had mixed the thing, but I had to go on tour in Germany, and then Bob had a weird thing with CBS, where he had to deliver records to them at a certain time and I was away in Europe . . . Some of [*Infidels*] is like listening to roughs. Maybe Bob thought I'd rushed things because I was in a hurry to leave, but I offered to finish it after our tour. Instead, he got the engineer to do the final mix.

Dylan's disregard for the instincts of others, almost a *raison d'être* of the man's art, was coming into play. One night, early in May, he called on one of his few actual collaborators, Jacques Levy, at his New York home. He was clearly upset about the way that the sound had come out in the mixing process, telling Levy, 'If I knew it was going to sound like that, I would have sung it different.' In classic rock-star fashion, having decided that he didn't want Knopfler to help him finish the record, he arranged for somebody from his office to phone Knopfler's manager to tell him that his artist's services were no longer required. Knopfler later said, 'If anybody ever has the dubious fortune to end up in [Dylan's] producer's seat they'll find out for themselves that sometimes the best way to go forward is to respect others' feelings about things when they're directly opposed to your own.' One doesn't have to read between the lines to see that Knopfler had in mind a role that extended beyond sharing the load.

The first week in June, Dylan returned to the Power Station with engineer Ian Taylor. At this point, he decided to both remix and recon-struct the album, initially rerecording vocal tracks for three of the songs. The opportunity to rerecord vocal tracks proved too great a temptation, and, as with 'Idiot Wind,' 'Tangled Up in Blue,' and 'If You See Her,

Say Hello,' he took the opportunity to rewrite parts of both 'Jokerman' and 'Sweetheart Like You.' Talking to MTV's Martha Quinn, the following year, he divulged his reasons for the remakes.

Bob Dylan: We didn't really approach [*Infidels*] any differently than any other record. We put the tracks down and sang most of the stuff live. Only later when we had so much stuff, we recorded it over . . . I wanted to fill it up more. I've never wanted to do that with any other record . . . Did you ever listen to an Eagles record? . . . Their songs are good, but every note is predictable, you know exactly what's gonna be before it's even there. And I started to sense some of that on *Infidels,* and I didn't like it, so we decided to redo some of the vocals. [1984]

Ironically, though the rewrites on 'Jokerman' were an improvement, the finished version suffered from much the same plight as the released 'Idiot Wind'—the singer had become disconnected from the song's soul. The new lyrics to 'Jokerman' in no way sent the message awry; it remained the self-portrait of a gnostic. Unfortunately, if the original vocal performance was a blistering howl by the light of the moon, the new 'Jokerman' was simply less arresting, the vocals vying unsuccessfully with the band for the listener's attention. It wasn't just vocals, though, that Dylan 'decided to redo.' In a savage re-appraisal of the work to date, Dylan scrapped 'Foot of Pride' and 'Blind Willie McTell,' two songs that had preoccupied him throughout the sessions.

Despite having seven originals and at least two covers on his short list, he then chose to replace these two dense expositions on a troubled world with a four-minute 'state of the union' address, 'Union Sundown.' Seemingly, Dylan's perspective on his own work had gone haywire. Replacing the eighties equivalents of 'Visions of Johanna' and 'Stuck Inside of Mobile' with an eighties 'North Country Blues,' then substituting inferior reworks of the slight 'Don't Fall Apart on Me Tonight' and the heavyweight 'Jokerman,' was bound to tilt any album off its axis. The change made *Infidels* a pale reflection of its former self. Few would ever hear any of the outtakes until the 1991 release of *The Bootleg Series,* and even then compiler Jeff Rosen's second guesses excluded the original 'Jokerman,' the electric 'Blind Willie McTell,' and the best take of 'Someone's Got a Hold of My Heart,' irrefutable proof that Dylan's muse had been working overtime back in '83, even if his critical faculties were not.

A month of remixes and overdubs also meant that *Infidels* was not released until November 1983, a full six months after the sessions, when Dylan's mind had already moved onto something else. Yet if his perspective on his own songs had never been poorer, he was writing songs of real power, as he had been back in 1979–80, when *Saved* and *Shot of Love* gave equally minimal evidence of a renaissance. Ironically, *Infidels* was to be the final album from Dylan's second great songwriting era (1974–83), a renaissance that was to end as it began, with the scrapping of a true representation of his songwriting self for a counterfeit version.

To *NME*'s Graham Lock, and indeed much of the media, he remained 'culturally a spent force [who] may still toss off a good song now and then . . . [but is] a confused man trying to rekindle old fires.' The fact that Dylan issued a bastardized version of the album and then failed to promote it with a tour or even a spate of interviews—save for one with Robert Hilburn of the *LA Times* in which he barely mentioned the record—suggested that he no longer cared to set the record straight. As a result, he reversed neither his commercial nor critical decline.

And yet, despite its standing as one of Dylan's most unrealized works, *Infidels* was half a great album and all of a great-sounding one, and it required some promotion from a temporarily enthused CBS. Unfortunately, Dylan's ideas for his first promo video in eighteen years hardly suggested street cred. Not that the man behind *Renaldo and Clara* and *Eat the Document* was uninterested in the possibilities of the medium, it was just that a Zionist, 'David and Goliath' parable about the Battle of Armageddon might be fine hidden away on side two of the latest long-player, but not pumped into pubescents via cathodes and cables.

Bob Dylan: The market for video is new, but the form has always been there . . . [They view] 'Subterranean Homesick Blues' as a video. I don't know if it was a video. We didn't think of it as a video at the time, we just needed a piece of film to go at the beginning of a movie . . . We wanted to do 'Neighborhood Bully,' but [it's difficult] tryin' to explain to somebody what you see and drawin' up storyboards; I haven't really found anybody that really thinks a certain way that needs to be [done], like the German filmmakers, the English filmmakers. In the States there aren't people like that. They just don't exist . . . I visualized 'Neighborhood Bully' . . . there were certain segments which I just wrote down one night which I thought would look great on film, and it would be like a Fassbinder movie. [1984]

CBS felt 'Sweetheart Like You' might be a safer bet—even with that 'a woman like you should be at home' line—and duly arranged for the man who had sent up badly mimed pop videos way-back-when to lip-sync the song in a fake club setting. According to director Mark

Taylor, the original plan was 'to do a simple club scene where one woman's face was every woman's face, and we had thirty extras . . . lined up ready to shoot. But while we were setting up the club with upturned chairs on tabletops, there was someone sweeping up the cigarette butts . . . I went to Bob and suggested we take an old lady and have her sweeping up, with it all coming from her point of view.' The video may have got Dylan onto MTV, but it did nothing to persuade younger music fans to investigate the guy with the almost Islamic view of women and a pressing need for a new set of curlers.

Nevertheless, *Infidels* garnered its share of qualified but positive reviews on its release, and was a consistent seller in the run-up to Christmas. The album's modest success prompted CBS to provide a budget for a second promotional video to coincide with a February single release of 'Jokerman.' Having recruited two old friends from his Rolling Thunder days, Larry Sloman and George Lois, to co-direct the video, Dylan turned up at their initial meeting with his heart still set on making the 'Neighborhood Bully' film.

Larry Sloman: But Lois had each lyric from 'Jokerman' blown up and tacked to the wall in the conference room and underneath each line was the corresponding visual image we had selected. Now the big pitch . . . Lois began his lecture. 'Now when you say "You were born with a snake in both of your fists," that's the Minoan Snake Goddess from Crete, circa 1500 BC Case closed. That's what you meant, right Bob?' Dylan managed something between a shrug and a nod.

Though the 'Jokerman' video, with its clever use of Dylan's words beneath 'the corresponding visual image,' was an imaginative use of the medium, Dylan failed to see any relevance to what he did, and disliked the idea of fixing one meaning to his lyrics. He also resented the close-ups required of him for the chorus. He remained fiercely distrustful of the new medium and, sensing that he remained a man out of time, returned to his Malibu garage.

Beginning in the fall of 1983, Dylan had returned to the kind of music-making he loved best—informal. With Rundown no more, and the eight-track console moved to his Malibu house, he spent a happy few months recording demos and playing songs, a further installment of basement noise. Though he was again working on songs that would mostly fall by the wayside, Dylan as usual required the musicians to respond as best they could, refusing to provide guidance above and beyond the key. Among those who played on these sessions were fledgling songsmith Charlie Sexton and two of LA's more promising post-punk refugees, drummer Charlie Quintana and guitarist J. J. Holliday.

Charlie Sexton: He'd just pick up his guitar and start singing and playing without any introduction or explanation—no keys, no chords, nothing! And my job was to figure out all the charts and produce it on the spot . . . I'd keep asking him, 'Is this one yours?' and he'd just mumble in that gravelly voice, 'Nah, it's from the Civil War.'

Charlie Quintana: I got word that maybe I could come over and jam once in a while. Bob was really cool about it. Either he'd call or somebody else would, and they'd say, Come over! Or, bring another guitar player! So I would take other musicians down there . . . I'd just go down there, sit and wait, and he'd just come in and we'd start playing. He'd start tinkering, then I'd jump in, the other guitar player, and we'd go on for five minutes, or for forty-five minutes, and then he'd stop . . . I took a lot of local musicians from Los Angeles . . . My impression of what was going down there is that he was trying to get back into playing, that he just wanted some guys, low-key, to jam. And that's what we did. We didn't sit around and talk a lot. He came in, we played, we had some coffee, we played again. He'd say, All right, that's it, and he'd split, walk out.

J. J. Holliday: I remember saying things when we were playing together like, 'This is kinda like a Buddy Boy Hawkins thing'—Buddy Boy Hawkins is this old blues player from the twenties . . . and he goes, 'Yeah'—he knew exactly what I was talking about—and he goes, 'That, combined with some kind of Las Vegas striptease act.' That's how he would communicate—'Buddy Boy Hawkins combined with striptease act: that's the vibe we're looking for.' . . . We must have been there a month or six weeks or something, off and on. Then all of a sudden there was this break . . . and I thought, 'Well, that's it, we're not doing this anymore.' But then we got another call . . . It was January and we rehearsed again for a couple of months [more].

Though Holliday knew who Buddy Boy Hawkins was, he seemed to have only an imprecise idea of the credentials of the man he was working with. At one point on one of the later sessions, Dylan has to explain about *Shot of Love*, suggesting that perhaps he should check that one out. For Dylan, it was a return to music-making for its own sake, perhaps last savored on Fire Island. He had tapped into a whole generation of young firebrands for whom he was a name from their parents' record collections.

Just when it seemed as if Dylan wished to keep these earnest young musicians to himself, he agreed to a very public unveiling, on the popular *Late Night with David Letterman* TV show, on March 22. Letterman had been pestering the office for some time. Dylan finally said yes, on condition that he would not have to participate in the usual mutual backslapping that passed for a Letterman interview, and could supply his own band—it being usual to perform with Letterman's in-house band. Quintana and Holliday were to be joined by another young LA post-punk, Tony Marisco, on bass.

Charlie Quintana: Originally it was all very vague. There was talk of going to Hawaii and doing a show there for his label or something, and then it fell through. And then the Letterman show came out of nowhere, really. I think it was about a week's notice . . . It didn't really matter whether it was a week or a month because we didn't know what we were going to play until about a minute before we went on the air!

This was Dylan's first real dalliance with third-generation American rock & rollers. Flying to New York, they rehearsed for what they now knew to be a major national TV appearance the day before the show. The rehearsals followed a familiar Dylan pattern.

Charlie Quintana: We rehearsed at the TV sound-check and we'd rehearsed the night before, but the night before we went through fifty fuckin' songs we didn't know! At the sound-check they sealed off the studio and all the NBC brass was there, 'cause it's Bob, and we'd never start 1–2–3. He'd just start strumming and we'd just jump in and follow it. And it would end up the same way—he'd just stop playing. There was none of this Da-da-da-da, Boom Boom! to end a song, none of that! And it was five minutes before we were supposed to go on and I'm asking Bill Graham, saying, 'Jesus Christ, we're shitting bricks over here! Can you please go in and ask Bob what songs we're gonna do?' And he'd come back and say, 'He's not sure yet.'

Fortunately, the afternoon sound-check did form the basis for their three-song performance, Dylan and the band having run through 'License to Kill' and 'Jokerman' and a version of Roy Head's 'Treat Her Right.' The difference in performance between sound-check and TV appearance, though, was night and day. At the last minute Dylan decided he'd rather open with a cover of Sonny Boy Williamson's 'Don't Start Me Talking,' a song which Quintana does not think they even rehearsed.

Fortunately, a band of post-punks could hardly fail to know the song in its 1974 incarnation, by punk godfathers the New York Dolls. And it worked. The whole thing was Dylan's freshest and most vital perform-ance this side of a twenty-four-inch screen. 'License to Kill' was even more remarkable, with Dylan's wailing harmonica complementing a vocal that single-handedly proved the centrality of phrasing to his per-formance art. Reveling in the Marisco–Quintana rhythm section, 'Jokerman,' the final song, was abbreviated to three verses but still raged with an incandescent passion—until, that is, he picked up his harp for one final blow and realized it was in the wrong key. While technicians fumbled around looking for the correct harmonica, the band played on.

Charlie Quintana: Maybe if we had rehearsed a song from beginning to end, it would have fallen apart. But because we were used to not knowing what was happening, when he was fumbling around for the harmonica I was just able to keep on tapping it out—a couple of verses, a chorus. It seemed like ten years!

Dylan finally blew in with the harp finale his alter ego demanded, to a rousing reception from the stunned studio audience. Letterman asked if perhaps they could make it every Thursday, and Dylan finally cracked a grin. But he knew that he had delivered. Indeed, any viewer who ran out to buy *Infidels* on the strength of this set must have been mightily disappointed when they heard the leaden versions of 'Jokerman' and 'License to Kill' included on the album. Perhaps the pencil-thin, razor-sharp Dylan had found the lean sound he had been looking for. No question, these kids were hungry to fish the sea of possibilities, if only Dylan was prepared to make them his disciples. Second-guessing his initial instincts, though, had already begun to harden into a working methodology.

1984–85: Real Live Aid

31

If people can sit at home and see the person singing, why would they
go out to see him, you know? They're not gonna look as good . . .
They're gonna see him sweat and see him in different angles, they're
gonna see a lot of things they don't see on the video . . . It makes you
look real sanitized on the video. In reality, it's never that way.

—Bob Dylan, 1984

Between November 1981 and February 1986, Dylan took his second
(and, to date, last) sustained break from the rigors of the road. As a sign
of these synthetic times, he temporarily absented himself from the musical
melee, save for five weeks of stadium shows in Europe in June and July
of 1984. Little more than a curious footnote to a five-year period
that yielded just two studio albums—*Infidels* and *Empire Burlesque*—the
European tour yielded vinyl evidence, *Real Live*, of a Dylan seemingly
destined to endless replays of the past.

The Letterman appearance, in more dangerous times, would surely
have prompted Dylan to take that sound onto a world stage. He had
always wanted a band at his beck and call and, now, seemingly, he could
have one. However, he allowed himself to be guided by a businessman
first and last, promoter Bill Graham, who convinced him that occasionally
off-key kids who played with verve and resolve would not fit in with
the kind of moneymaking exercise he had in mind. Having steered Dylan
away from the notoriously unbusinesslike South Americans, to whom
he actually wished to play, Graham began to push him into a joint tour
with the sort of musical deadwood that punk was supposed to have
washed away. Beneficiaries of Latinized hits borrowed from Fleetwood
Mac and the Zombies, Santana hadn't had an inkling of a hit record in a
decade. That Dylan himself elected to use musicians whose best years
were also the realm of pop historians made for one of the sorrier alliances
of his career, and tied him to a nostalgia kick he had seemingly jettisoned
for good, back in 1978.

Despite the exhilaration written across his face at the Letterman performance, only drummer Quintana was ever a serious candidate for these

European gigs. Indeed, Quintana was kept waiting until the very last minute before being notified that he would not be a part of the summer tour. Ex-John Mayall timekeeper Colin Allen had been chosen instead. Allen was suggested by reluctant bandleader Mick Taylor, to whom Dylan seemed to be leaving most of the suggested slots for the requisite Stadium Rockers. Taylor also initially suggested Nicky Hopkins, whose keyboard playing had been almost de rigueur when singles sessions came around in the 1960s, and then, when Hopkins blew his chance, came up with Ian McLagen of Faces fame. If Dylan was looking for a belated pub-rock equivalent to LA's post-punk finest, minus the edge, he was going about it the right way.

Colin Allen: Nicky Hopkins . . . came up. But he was really . . . a piano player. He was saying to me on the phone, 'Get Bob to get a grand piano in to rehearse on.' . . . So he came up with this manager guy, and maybe it was all a bit too much for Bob . . . Then we got Ian McLagen . . . Ian finally got the word only a couple of days before we actually left Bob's estate and went to the Beverly Theater in Beverly Hills to rehearse in a theater situation for about five days.

Ironically, the only LA punkster to make the grade was bassist Greg Sutton, a sometime participant in recent Malibu jam sessions but hardly an upgrade on Tony Marisco, the Letterman powerhouse. Dylan's abnegation of the role of bandleader at the selection stage suggests an unprecedented detachment from the whole exercise. As soon as the South American option failed to materialize and Graham revealed Plan B, his level of interest experienced a serious pressure drop. As he put it at the time, 'At the last moment I had sort of set my mind mentally to do something. So I did this.' That he envisaged a less-than-transcendent return to the stage was perhaps indicated at the end of the first day of rehearsals with the newly constituted combo when, as he sat chatting at the kitchen table with Taylor, McLagen walked up to him and said, 'Thanks Bob, it's an honor and a privilege to work with you.' Dylan merely muttered, 'I hope you feel the same when the tour's over.'

Rehearsals only began in earnest at the Beverly Theater barely a week before the first show, in Verona, Italy. Previously, Dylan's commitment to his material had always been 100 percent. Arthur Rosato, who witnessed most rehearsals from 1974 through 1981, remembers a Dylan who, 'even if it's in rehearsal . . . sings his lyrics. He doesn't run through them; he *sings* them.' In 1984, he expressed no such commitment and as a result, whereas his previous bands had always responded to this man who brought fire to his kingdom, the 1984 band were denied any such spark. The rehearsals were frankly awful. Not only did the band sound as though they were playing under half a hundredweight of porridge, but Dylan's singing voice had lost its elasticity. The choice of material rehearsed was also defined by the kind of shows booked, almost exclusively stadiums, and the pretense that this was a stripped-down version of 1978. Without an album in the can, and playing venues where it would be unwise to premiere 'difficult' material, Dylan all but excluded his post-conversion canon. Only four songs from his latest album were even rehearsed, while the so-called religious trilogy yielded just 'Watered Down Love' (never actually performed), a garbled rewrite of 'When You Gonna Wake Up' and the innocuous 'Heart of Mine'. *Planet Waves*, *Desire*, and *Street-Legal* were treated with similar disdain, as Dylan set about constructing his first oldies show.

Four or five days of rehearsals was nowhere near enough time to get this particular band into shape. That Dylan was still somehow thinking of the rehearsals as an extension of the Malibu jam sessions was evidenced by the time he spent working on three new songs he had written. Though 'Dirty Lie' and 'Enough Is Enough' were strictly formulaic r&b, the third new song, 'Angel of Rain' (a.k.a. 'Almost Done') was an exquisite kindling of regret. McLagen, for one, was more than a little fazed by its sporadic reappearance in rehearsals.

Ian McLagen: There was one beautiful song he played occasionally that he'd never recorded and never [fully] rehearsed with us either. It was a tricky little number, we never knew the title, but he'd launch into it from time to time, leaving us totally in the dark.

On the rehearsal front, everything went from bad to worse as Dylan and the band flew into Italy for his first concerts to perhaps the world's most fanatical rock fans. The day before the opening show in the Arena di Verona, an open-air amphitheater replete with ancient footsteps, Dylan spent the afternoon rehearsing his new songs, a Willie Nelson cover, and an Ink Spots cover. Mamma mia! He was apparently operating under the illusion that Taylor had fully briefed the band about which oldies they were expected to shuffle through, and that song endings would be in the hands of God. Taylor, previously unaware of the weight of responsibility Dylan was looking to devolve to him, proceeded to get 'zonked out in his room' that night after matters had come to a head between them and he had been fired from the tour, presumably for using the word *unprofessional*.

Though Dylan had no option but to reinstate him the following morning, the tight bond previously established was no more, and Dylan's mood going into the first show couldn't have been darker. Although he finally ran through the basic set with his band on the afternoon of May 28, they still didn't know what their paymaster intended to play.

Ian McLagen: Bill [Graham] brought us a set list which consisted of five or six song titles in a box at the top of the page, some more in another box over to the right, and yet another box of maybe ten songs at the bottom. It wasn't very helpful.

Under-rehearsed and out of their depth, the band was visibly sinking as Dylan launched into 'Jokerman.' Without any obvious direction from Taylor, either, song after song spluttered to a conclusion. The opening nine-song electric set made the Letterman band sound like Muscle Shoals veterans, as the music flew off in any number of disparate directions. Though the band sounded a little more together during their second set, Taylor was no bandleader, and never had expected to be.

Perhaps it was Taylor calling Dylan's bluff, perhaps the lyrics of 'When You Gonna Wake Up?' hit home, but within a week of the Verona débâcle the band started to at least hold the songs together. Dylan, probably after an attendant Bill Graham had read him the economic riot act, seems to have realized that he had better stamp his authority on proceedings before the whole shebang collapsed around his ears. By the time they reached Rotterdam, seven days on from that first Verona show, he was at last singing with a little of the old fire and brimming with ideas, evidenced by an afternoon spent rewriting two of his greatest songs, 'Tangled Up in Blue' and 'Simple Twist of Fate.'

Bob Dylan: There's a version [of 'Tangled Up in Blue'] we used to do on stage with just electric guitar and a saxophone—keeping the same lyrics, thinking that maybe if I did that to it, it would bring it out in an emotional way. But it didn't hold up very well that way. So I changed the lyrics, to bring it up to date. But I didn't change it 'cause I was singing it one night and thought, 'Oh, I'm bored with the old words.' The old ones were never quite filled in. I rewrote it in a hotel room somewhere. I think it was in Amsterdam . . . When I sang it the next night I knew it was right. [1985]

Though the 1984 'Tangled Up in Blue' lyrics would not endure until its next incarnation, at the hands of the Dead, it rapidly became a nightly highlight for the fans. At the first few performances you could feel the crowd hanging on every word, just waiting to see what curves remained. The ending, in particular, was an audacious inversion of the original narrator's intent. In 1974, the singer was 'still on the road, heading for another joint,' for that is where he felt the subject of his quest lay. In 1984, the singer was 'still walking toward the sun [Son], /trying to stay out of the joints,' the joints having become distractions along the way, a subtle but crucial admission that he was still looking to set his affections on things above. The new 'Simple Twist of Fate,' though less revelatory, was an imaginative reworking, a little more surreal than the original, in which the hotel gains a name and a desk clerk: 'down to the Rio Grande Hotel / where the desk clerk dressed in white / with a face as black as night / he said, check out time's at eight.'

As the first set settled into a rigid seven-song pattern nightly, the band started to feel more at home, with both Sutton and Allen beginning to play with a certain familiarity that bordered on competency. Sutton was the first to realize Dylan enjoyed his little game of changing keys, to keep them on their toes.

Greg Sutton: He started 'Maggie's Farm' wrong [one night] and he asked me, 'What key are we in?' I said, 'Bob we're in G, the key you started it in.' And he says, 'Well, can you go back to the right key?' I said, 'Whatever you say, Bob.'

Allen also began to understand the boss a little better. In Rome, three weeks in, he finally summoned up the nerve to ask him about those song endings that collapsed from exhaustion. Dylan was his usual helpful self.

Colin Allen: One day we were sitting in this hotel in Rome, the Lord Byron Hotel ... We were sitting outside, and Bob was there, and I said, 'Hey Bob, you know when you look at me at the end of a song, what's the story? Do you want me to end the song[s] immediately, as soon as possible, or wait till the sequence goes?' He said, 'Well, I just figure we've done enough with the songs and that we should finish them when we feel comfortable.'

The 1984 tour in many ways became a template for subsequent Dylan tours. Succeeding tours would all rely heavily on his more famous sixties material, with collections of songs as impressive as *Planet Waves, Desire, Street-Legal,* and *Slow Train Coming* all but disregarded. On these tours, contemporary product, if it was to be had, became all but incidental to his performance art. From this point on, he would also favor a basic guitar/bass/drums, plus optional organ, setup. Though the girls would make a temporary comeback when touring with the Heartbreakers in 1986–87, Dylan had reverted to relying on his own voice just as his vocal range was audibly contracting.

He would also become increasingly intolerant of the rehearsal process, something Joan Baez delighted in ridiculing in her autobiography, *And a Voice to Sing With*. All but commercially washed up in the US, Baez retained a surprisingly staunch following in parts of Europe. With Santana failing to make audiences dizzy with expectation, particularly in Germany, Bill Graham decided to give the whiff of nostalgia a corrosive reek by adding Baez to a number of the bills. Graham assured Baez that she and Dylan would do something together, though without getting the nod from Dylan. When she turned up in Hamburg, to meet him and 'go over some stuff,' she discovered that he was not at the same hotel, and would not be in town until the next day. As she attempted to add a little Baez bonhomie to 'I Shall Be Released' at the Hamburg show, Dylan very visibly pulled away from her and Baez found herself as frozen out as she had been in 1965. This time, though, she packed her bags, leaving Graham to explain away her absence at later shows.

Evidently, there were still some things that Dylan would not do to sell tickets, and sharing the stage with Baez was one of them. Nevertheless, having committed himself to stadiums and large arenas at a time when his commercial standing was down on its knees, he was required to adopt some kind of public profile simply in order to sell tickets, even if all the press wanted to know was how he coped with living down the past. At press conferences in Verona and Hamburg he responded by being surly, uncommunicative, even downright rude. As the tour progressed, though, and he began to feel more confident about the worth of what he was peddling, he became more talkative. In France, Dylan actually agreed to his first televised interview in nineteen years, hoping to sell some more tickets for the Paris, Grenoble, and Nantes shows. In Spain, he talked at length to Mick Brown of the *Sunday Times*.

Bob Dylan: For me, none of the songs I've written has really dated. They capture something I've never been able to improve on, whatever their statement is . . . People say they're 'nostalgia,' but I don't know what that means really. *A Tale of Two Cities* was written a hundred years ago; is that nostalgic? This term 'nostalgic,' it's just another way people have of dealing with you, and putting you some place they think they understand. It's just another label. [1984]

Sparks from the ol' performing tinderbox began to ignite the shows in Germany, and carried over to three sold-out shows in Rome, at the last of which Dylan sang a word-perfect 'Desolation Row' in the acoustic set and debuted 'Enough Is Enough.' Finally getting up a head of steam, a month to the day after that disastrous first Verona show, Dylan arrived in Barcelona for his second-ever Spanish show. Singing like a bird, albeit one with a touch of laryngitis, he strained his way through the definitive 'Every Grain of Sand,' threw the band for a loop on the unrehearsed 'Señor' and 'Lay, Lady, Lay,' and, as the final song of a two-and-a-half-hour set, sang a 'Blowin' in the Wind' that expressed more sense of the song's meaning than any version he'd sung in twenty-two years. Actually cajoling the huge stadium crowd into chorus after chorus, he then delivered a reading of the last verse that suggested a whole new wind of change.

Continuing to feed audiences of between thirty and a hundred thousand a largely familiar diet, and the odd superstar guest—Van Morrison in Paris, Eric Clapton in London, Bono in Dublin—Dylan proceeded to weave his way through Nantes, Paris, Grenoble, Newcastle, and London, wrapping it up in Dublin on July 8. Though the last two shows, which constitute the bulk of the wretched album *Real Live*, were a little slick and lacking in passion, they were well received and Dylan completed his one and only stadium tour without discernibly diminishing his reputation as a powerful live presence. Considering the roofless barns he was playing, the wasted rehearsals, the problems with Taylor and Baez, and the uninspired rhythm section, this was certainly far more than any member of the May 29 Verona crowd had any right to imagine.

As in 1974, it would take time for him to get a handle on the 1984 tour. Only when he had reasserted himself as the quintessential interpreter of his own works would he recognize the trap he had fallen into.

Bob Dylan: You're either a player or you're not a player . . . If you just go out every three years or so, like I was doing for a while, that's when you lose touch. [1991]

That Dylan had some sense of himself as a performer, even in 1984, was evidenced by a conversation he had with a smitten French painter, Claude-Angèle Boni, in his bedroom after the Paris show. Boni had first been ushered into his presence by one of his French-speaking sidekicks, Roland Grivelle, a.k.a. Mr. P.

Claude-Angèle Boni: The first question I asked him was, 'When will you come to play in France again?' He answered straightaway, 'In three years.' I said, 'Three years is too long. I will be too old by then.' He asked me my age. I replied that I was thirty-eight . . . He said to me, 'I'm forty-three and I still do it. I want to play until I'm ninety.' . . . Dylan stood up, grabbed his little Martin and started to strum it walking around in circles in the room. Then he said it was time for him to go to bed. I don't remember all the details but I know I followed him.

However, the following day, when she attempted to reestablish contact with Dylan, Boni found that the scene changers had been at work. If Dylan remained the game master, pulling strings and playing games, he had several willing volunteers who enjoyed playing the tour version of Glissendorf.

Claude-Angèle Boni: [Back at my hotel] I was trying to sleep when the telephone rang. It was somebody who sounded like Dylan. I thought it was him. 'How are you?' said the voice. 'A little bit tired, I was trying to sleep for a little while,' I answered . . . Fortunately I realized in time it wasn't Dylan's voice . . . It belonged to one of the road managers. He was calling to tell me that Dylan wanted me to go with him to Grenoble, where he was giving his last concert before England . . . After that I received another call from Stan, Bob's bodyguard . . . He said that I was invited to a restaurant with the crew that night . . . Then Mr. P called me. He gave me a warning. 'Be careful,' he said. 'There is something weird going on.' . . . When I arrived at the Royal Montceau [Hotel], Mr. P had left. So I met Stan . . . I said that I was okay for Grenoble but that I wanted to travel . . . with Dylan in the same plane. He said that was impossible, that I could not travel with them and I had to take a train . . . Then he phoned somebody to say, 'She agrees to go to Grenoble incognito.' I asked him who was on the phone, if it was Bob, but he didn't want to tell me . . . He wanted to know what had happened in Dylan's room the night before, but I didn't tell him.

Dylan may well have viewed Claude-Angèle Boni as just another interlude to relieve the unremitting tedium of the road, but it suggested a worrying return to the kind of strangely impersonal liaisons that had punctuated the nights in 1978. He certainly had more pressing matters to attend to on his return to the States. The abortive rehearsals of new songs that had preoccupied him in Verona returned to his mind at tour's end, and he barely unpacked his bags in New York before entering the studio to lay down some of the songs he had been tinkering with during inevitable downtime on the road.

He had decided to revert to capturing moments of inspiration at sporadic sessions, as he had famously in the 1960s, rather than attempting to capture a collection of songs, and a new sound, by block-booking studio time, as he had since *Nashville Skyline*. If *Infidels* had occupied three solid months of recording and mixing, with *Empire Burlesque* the workload would be more evenly spread, but it would still represent an unprecedented expenditure of time on Dylan's part, sessions beginning in July 1984 and winding up in March 1985. When *Empire Burlesque* was finally released in June 1985, Dylan talked at length about this revivified approach to recording.

Bob Dylan: When I'm making a record I'll need some songs, and I'll start digging through my pockets and drawers trying to find these songs. Then I'll bring one out and I've never sung it before, sometimes I can't even remember the melody to it, and I'll get it in. Sometimes great things happen, sometimes not-so-great things happen. But regardless of what happens, when I do it in the studio it's the first time I've ever done it. I'm pretty much unfamiliar with it. In the past what's come out is what I've usually stuck with, whether it really knocked me out or not. For no apparent reason I've stuck with it, just from lack of commitment to taking the trouble to really get it right. I didn't want to record that way anymore . . . About two years ago I decided to get serious about it, and just record. [1985]

Empire Burlesque was another grand experiment, bound by what he hoped might represent common ground with his audience. Though production values would again taint the finished product, for the first time since *Planet Waves* it was the lack of an album's worth of quality songs that would most compromise its potential. Not that Dylan's yearlong respite from the studio had been an inactive one for the songwriter in him. Aside from the three songs penciled in for the European shows, he had worked up a number of melodic ideas in Malibu, of which one, 'Who Loves You More?' was among the first songs recorded for his new album.

One feature of these sessions, which began in New York, was Dylan choosing not to retain a nucleus of musicians. As August rear-ended July, he was working out of the Intergalactic, Delta, and Record Plant studios. After his disagreement with Knopfler, and with a few tricks acquired from the mixing of *Infidels,* he elected to produce the sessions himself. The first band he studio-tested came courtesy of soul singer Al Green, but the session at Intergalactic did not go well, as his idiosyncratic approach again tangled with a band used to refining their musical chops, take after take.

Ron Wood: All these guys from Memphis couldn't understand Bob's chord sequences. Every time he started off a new song, he'd start in a new key, or if we were doing the same song over and over, every time would be in a different key. Now I can go along with that with Bob, but the band were totally confused.

Sessions at Delta Sound studios were considerably more focused. Ron Wood again lent a helping hand, and New York veterans Anton Fig and John Paris provided a nicely loose rhythm section. Most of the half a dozen songs recorded, though, sounded like leftovers from Dylan's last two albums—as 'Clean Cut Kid' certainly was. The best song of the sessions, the funky 'Driftin' Too Far from Shore,' would be held over for the next album, awaiting a more fully formed set of lyrics. Strangely enough, having elected to dispense with a producer, Dylan failed to stamp his artistic authority on the finished sound. At the end of the sessions, Ron Wood looked on with astonishment as he allowed the engineer to mix the material according to some whim particular to him.

Ron Wood: When we'd go in at . . . Delta for a playback, every time he'd have the same attitude. The weak side of him would come out. They'd say, 'Hey Bob, we don't need this,' and he'd say, 'Oh, okay.' And they'd make a mix to their ears, and he'd just stand outside and let them do it. And I'd be saying, 'Hey! You can't let these guys . . . Look!! They've left off the background vocals!' or 'What about the drums?!' But there would be something going on in the back of his head which didn't allow him to interfere. And yet if he'd have gone into the control room with the dominance that he had while we were cutting the stuff, it could have been mind-bending.

At Delta he also demoed a song called 'Go 'Way Little Boy,' to donate to cowpunk contenders Lone Justice, a band his new girlfriend Carole Childs had signed to Geffen. Though Clydie King would continue to feature in the scheme of things, Dylan describing theirs as a love that 'surpasses even my understanding' in the fall of 1985, he was spending an increasing amount of downtime with Childs. Working in A&R (Artists & Repertoire) at Geffen Records, Childs had prevailed upon David Geffen to take her with him to the bar mitzvah of Dylan's son, Jakob, where she secured an introduction to the great man. One of Madonna's 'material girls' of the wisecrackin' New York variety, Childs seems to have quickly found a way into Dylan's affections at the expense of the more maternal King.

Childs' A&R responsibilities resulted in her signing several of LA's better post-punk combos, and keeping tabs on the sort of young hopefuls Dylan had previously been directing to Malibu. After some sustained nagging, she had persuaded Dylan to throw something into the melting pot that was Lone Justice's much-hyped debut platter. Lone Justice were trying to limit producer Jimmy Iovine's influence in the studio that summer. Childs regularly dropped in on proceedings. So it was no great surprise when Dylan turned up at Record Plant to give them the song in person, accompanied by Ron Wood.

Maria McKee: He came down to the studio when we were recording our first album and taught us the song. And he stayed around. He brought Ron Wood with him and they played on it . . . We ended up working on it a very long time because he didn't like the way I sang it . . . until I sang it like him! It got to the point where finally I just did my best Bob Dylan imitation—and he said, 'Ah, now you're doin' SOME REAL SINGING!'

McKee, though, recognized the song for what it was—an innocuous afternoon's diversion, strictly B-side fare—and stuck to her own stockpile for the album proper. Dylan also seems to have concluded that the summer season had yielded little that was usable. Returning to LA at the beginning of November, in time to catch young Maria on fire at the Palace during a TV filming, Dylan was set on resuming work in the studios of his adopted hometown. This time he had a couple of strong songs to record.

'Something's Burning, Baby,' an ominous tale set to a slow march beat, was a welcome reminder of his ongoing preoccupation with that dreadful day. Dylan rated the lyrics enough to rework them several times before settling on the final, released version. Though he continued to favor black backup vocalists, the shifting lyric and idiosyncratic delivery constantly tripped up his current favorite, Madelyn Quebec.

Ira Ingber: ['Something's Burning'] is a very weird song. And Maddy did not know the words when they did the vocal, 'cause I watched her trying to follow him. She was trying to sing harmonies with him live, which is tough because Bob doesn't necessarily know where he's going.

Even more impressive was a song Dylan had co-written that fall with Sam Shepard, who had abandoned rock & roll after the *Renaldo and Clara* odyssey to commit himself full time to acting and writing. A twelve-minute epic based on the Gregory Peck film *The Gunfighter,*

'New Danville Girl' (as opposed to Woody Guthrie's 'Danville Girl') began life as an attempt to write a reply to Lou Reed's 'Doin' the Things That We Want To.' (Reed's song, just released on *New Sensations,* had been inspired by attending one of Shepard's plays.) In 'New Danville Girl,' the narrator identifies with the murderer of Peck the gunfighter. The cinematic sweep of the song, as the narrator travels through Texas, with and without his Danville Girl, makes for travelogue cast within the same mythic western landscape as 'Lily, Rosemary and the Jack of Hearts.' Allowing each line to raise questions that lead the listener across the flatlands of Texas and time, Shepard contributes a conversational tone that hints at the very mundanity the song's characters are seeking to transcend. Like Dylan's other western epic, it lent itself naturally to a visualized form. Indeed, Shepard insists, it was written with such an intention in mind.

Sam Shepard: It has to do with a guy standing on line and waiting to see an old Gregory Peck movie that he can't quite remember—only pieces of it—and then this whole memory thing happens, unfolding before his very eyes. He starts speaking internally to a woman . . . reliving the whole journey they'd gone on . . . We spent two days writing the lyrics—Bob had previously composed the melody line, which was already down on tape . . . At one point he talked about making a video out of it.

Much of the song's drive was provided by Lone Justice drummer Don Heffington, who, finding himself recording at Cherokee with the great man, was determined to make the performance of 'New Danville Girl' more compelling than the tale of her two sisters, Lily and Rosemary. And yet 'New Danville Girl' would not make it onto *Empire Burlesque,* an album in dire need of such a lyrical linchpin.

If there had always been a certain deliberate perversity to Dylan's decisions in the studio (as one of his recent producers told me, 'If somebody likes something too much, he's bound to pull it. I'd sit there in the studio with him and, if I'd like something, I'd keep my mouth shut, because he'd literally take it away from me'), the case of 'New Danville Girl' serves to illustrate a man prepared to shoot himself in the foot, commercially and artistically, simply to prove to himself that he remained beholden to no opinion but his own.

Ira Ingber: When we first recorded ['New Danville Girl'], we . . . made a cassette. And he took it out and started playing it. He came back the next day we were working and said, 'Yeah, a lot of people like this thing.' And then he didn't do anything with it. It's like he was doing it to spite people who were all liking it, and he just held on to it.

After six months of earnest work on the follow-up to *Infidels*, Dylan had only two tracks destined to appear on *Empire Burlesque*. Talking about his new methodology at the time, he admitted that 'sometimes nothing comes out, and other times I get a lot of stuff that I keep . . . I just put down the songs that I felt as I wanted to put them down. Then I'd listen and decide if I liked them. And if I didn't like them I'd either rerecord them or change something about them.' The problem was that, as a rule, when he did this, he invariably ended up preferring the new version, however much it compromised his original vision. The two songs he decided to recast in a new image in the winter of 1985 were both all but destroyed in the process: 'When the Night Comes Falling from the Sky' and 'Tight Connection to My Heart,' his 1985 rewrite of the *Infidels* outtake 'Someone's Got a Hold of My Heart.'

'When the Night Comes Falling from the Sky' was one of the products of a session back in New York City, in February, at the Power Station, featuring two elements of the E Street Band sound, Roy Bittan's keyboards and Steve Van Zandt's guitar. In rough-mix form, the Van Zandt 'When the Night Comes Falling from the Sky', a seven-minute apocalyptic vision bristling with drama, sung without restraint, could have provided Dylan with another epic to counterbalance the mawkish filler he'd been recording since 'New Danville Girl.' Instead, Dylan again second-guessed some of his better lines ('I gave to you my heart like buried treasure / but suffering seems to fit you like a glove') and absolutely one of his best vocals from a fraught decade, rerecording the song *Infidels*-style, with a whomping synthesizer and horns track that only served to obscure a less than impressive new Dylan vocal.

If the younger 'When the Night' vocal fell short of its sibling, it was as nothing to the patricide committed on one of the trio of lost masterpieces from *Infidels*. The reinvention of 'Someone's Got a Hold of My Heart,' two years on, as 'Tight Connection' was a most un-Dylanesque act. In the process, he stripped just about every religious allusion from the original. Instead of a confession that he could never learn to 'drink that blood and call it wine,' resolving itself with a penitent Dylan unable 'to look at your face and call it mine,' it turned into a non sequitur: 'never could learn to hold you, love, and call you mine.' A song about being torn apart by irreconcilable demands became, in turn, little more than a cutup of stockpiled images, some Dylan's, many not. One of the best couplets—'I'll go along with the charade / Until I can think my way out'—actually comes verbatim from a *Star Trek* episode, 'Squire of Gothos.'

Another song on *Empire Burlesque*, 'Seeing the Real You at Last,' seemed to be merely a compendium of images half remembered from Hollywood movies. Allusions to Humphrey Bogart movies, *Shane*, even Clint Eastwood's *Bronco Billy*, confirm a deliberate conceit to write on remote—the TV remote, that is. Such was the suddenness with which Dylan descended into a lyrical landscape of secondhand images in the service of romantic platitudes ('Never Gonna Be the Same Again,' 'I'll Remember You,' 'Emotionally Yours') that the album all but keeled over from its deadweight of clichés. In an attempt to right the balance, Dylan decided to close out the album with an acoustic performance that, after forty minutes of insistent, whomping drums and reverberating bass, was bound to feel like the aural equivalent of cool, cool water.

Bob Dylan: [For] *Empire Burlesque*, there were nine songs I knew belonged on it, and I needed a tenth. I had about four songs, and one of those was going to be the tenth song. I finally figured out that the tenth song needed to be acoustic, so I just wrote it. I wrote it because none of the other songs fit that spot, that certain place. [1985]

If 'Dark Eyes,' affectingly sung, is occasionally lit up by a strikingly vivid line—'All I feel is heat and flame, and all I see are dark eyes'—it betrayed evidence of the same man who 'just wrote' 'Wedding Song' and failed to refine it. The folk melody proved beyond Dylan on the one occasion he attempted to play the song onstage himself, at Sydney in February 1986, and he was forced to abandon the attempt. In the studio, though, he managed to wrap it up, and with it his first album in two years, with seemingly minimal fuss.

What Dylan had accumulated by March was an innocuous collection of new songs—only 'Something's Burning, Baby' and 'When the Night Comes Falling from the Sky' had any real substance to them—but, still, an adequate holding exercise pending a time when he could again weld his critical faculties to his wanton creative spirit. Having produced the sessions himself, though, he decided he needed a helping hand to mix the sequenced album. Having initially hired one producer who proved too meticulous for his tastes, he eventually settled on the self-appointed Mixmeister of Pop, Arthur Baker.

Bob Dylan: [The other producer] listened to the songs too much. I could see him thinking too much, y'know . . . I saw him once and when he was mixing he would have rolls of paper, writing notes. I didn't want that. Arthur just listened to the stuff and said, 'Yeah.' And he fixed it up a lot. I listened to the sound of the previous record I made and the last one, and it does sound better. [1985]

Baker was the in-vogue producer. Work with Bruce Springsteen, New Order, and assorted funksters meant that Dylan caught the man just as the fifteen minutes assigned him in pop culture ran out. Unfortunately, Baker's idea of remixing was to place several extraneous layers of audio detritus over perfectly acceptable basic tracks, cluttering up the sound and hiding a conventional rock album behind a façade of processed drums and glistening synths.

Bob Dylan: I'm not too experienced at having records sound good. I don't know how to go about doing that. With Arthur Baker . . . I just went out and recorded a bunch of stuff all over the place, and then when it was time to put this record together, I brought it all to him and he made it sound like a record. [1985]

Though Baker gave the songs a unity of sound, it was not Dylan's sound. It really seemed as if Dylan himself lacked the will to complete the album. The last time he had washed his hands of an album at the rough-mix stage had been *Self Portrait*, which had proved an equally uncharacteristic listening experience. The rump that remained of his audience in 1985 were hardly about to start collecting New Order twelve-inch singles. Despite a full-page review in *Time*, announcing 'Rock's major magus brings it all back home again,' and portraying *Empire Burlesque* as 'full of turmoil and anger and mystery, an oblique diary of all this time just past . . . a record of survival and a tentative kind of triumph . . . hard evidence that he is ready to take the point again,' the bulk of the reviews again provided weary testimony to Dylan's increasing inconsequence. For the third time in five years, Dylan had spent a number of months working on an album, only to have it not so much unregarded as disregarded.

He also proved as unwilling to promote *Empire Burlesque* as he had *Infidels*, and though he belatedly came around to the importance of press coverage later in the year, it again devolved to the unfamiliar video medium to reach the audience denied him by the fragmentation of FM radio. The three *Empire Burlesque* videos would be his last serious attempt to embrace the MTV culture.

Having selected 'Tight Connection to My Heart' as the first single,

Dylan asked for film director Paul Schrader to shoot the video of the song. Schrader had just completed his Japanese epic *Mishima*, which had greatly impressed Dylan. He agreed to the assignment, but insisted it be filmed in Japan. Thus, in April, Dylan traveled to Tokyo to spend two days filming. The result, a vignette video of no fixed abode, Schrader dismissed as 'a little piece of eye candy I shot in Tokyo . . . [that] means as little as it looks like it means,' while at a press conference in Sydney the following February, Dylan also sought to isolate himself from the exercise.

Bob Dylan: I thought that I might be able to make a video with the man who made the movies and pull it off, but I was wrong. [1986]

Dylan did not abandon the idea of shooting a video that had something of the look of *Mishima*. Unfortunately, his reason for wanting to film two more videos in August in black and white was never relayed from 'executive producer' Dave Stewart of the Eurythmics to the actual video directors, Markus Innocenti and Eddie Arno.

Markus Innocenti and Eddie Arno: We were simply told by Dave that black and white was required. We weren't told why . . . We wished that Dylan had talked directly to us earlier, because we learned [later] that Dylan wanted it to look like an old Japanese movie. We could have filmed it differently. When we saw Paul Schrader's *Mishima* we understood why Dylan wanted it. If you ever watch that movie, look out for the black-and-white sequences. It would be interesting to put Dylan's music over the images—there would be something extraordinary, quite beyond what a music video can do. We could really understand why Dylan wanted Schrader for 'Tight Connection to My Heart,' but once the project had not lived up to his expectations it is reasonable to think that he wanted to try again [to] get the wonderful beauty and stillness that black and white can achieve.

The two videos, shot on 22 and 23 August in Los Angeles, comprised the A and B sides of a second *Empire Burlesque* single, 'When the Night Comes Falling from the Sky' and 'Emotionally Yours.' Reverting to the performance-style video attempted on 'Sweetheart Like You,' Dylan had a tenuous thread in mind to link the two sequences.

Markus Innocenti and Eddie Arno: Dylan is having an affair with a new girl. Dressed in buckskin, she goes with him to the gig where the band play 'When the Night Comes Falling.' Unknown to Dylan, a former lover—

also an attractive brunette dressed in buckskin—has seen Dylan on the way to the gig. She comes to watch the performance but the memories are too much and she has to leave, close to tears. She wanders off down Hollywood Boulevard, without approaching him again. This is where 'When the Night Comes Falling' ends and 'Emotionally Yours' begins. But Dylan has carried a torch for this buckskin-clad, dark-eyed beauty—why else would his new girlfriend be such a replica of the first? After the gig Dylan is left alone in the hall. Playing an acoustic guitar, his memories go back to his original Buckskin Girl. With regret, he remembers the moment when he told her the relationship was over.

Unfortunately, the results were once more disappointing, the video having none of that 'wonderful beauty and stillness that black and white can achieve.' Nor did the MTV format allow the two videos to appear side by side. Dylan, though, continued to have grander celluloid ambitions. He talked to Dave Stewart about an idea for his own film when shooting the two videos, perhaps the same movie he described to an interviewer in England in September 1986, when he was making a return to film, albeit someone else's.

Bob Dylan: I do have plans to make a movie . . . It's a complicated story about a piano player who gets into trouble because of a good buddy of his, and then he winds up doing some book work for a woman whose husband has disappeared, marries her, then falls in love with her daughter. And the other guy finally shows up again, and the movie comes to a screeching halt. [1986]

An unexpected by-product of the video shoot—or, more accurately, Dylan's insistence that the instruments in the shoot be 'live'—was that, in the words of the directors, he ended up, 'jam[ming] extensively with the band, mostly twelve-bar blues, though he didn't sing. He was more interested in riffing or taking solos on guitar.' He later told Mikal Gilmore of the *LA Herald-Examiner* that just that jam gave him a 'kind of direct connection,' jogging his memory as to how he might better promote his work.

Bob Dylan: [Dave Stewart] put together a great band for this lip-sync video and set us up with equipment on this little stage in a church somewhere in West LA. So between all the time they took setting up camera shots and lights and all that stuff, we could just play live for this little crowd that had gathered there. I can't even express how good that felt—in fact, I was trying to remember the last time I'd felt that kind of direct connection. [1985]

If the impromptu audience at the church in West LA was the smallest audience Dylan had played to in a while, he had five weeks earlier played to the largest audience of his career. Typically, it had been disastrous enough to permanently confine Dylan to a limbo of inconsequentiality in a billion minds.

Nineteen-eighty-five was the year in which American pop music decided to develop a conscience. The 'We Are the World' single, recorded in January 1985, and the huge Live Aid benefit shows in London and Philadelphia in July—designed to raise funds to aid starving Ethiopians—inevitably involved Dylan, whose image as the conscience of pop music was a tad more longstanding than those of Simple Minds and U2. Remaining unconvinced of the merits of 'We Are the World,' he nevertheless recognized a worthy cause.

Bob Dylan: People buying a song and the money going to starving people in Africa . . . is a worthwhile idea but I wasn't so convinced about the message of the song. To tell you the truth, I don't think people can save themselves. [1985]

Though many of the reasons behind Dylan's disastrous appearance at Live Aid, in front of an estimated two billion viewers, were beyond his command, it was perceived at the time as evidence that he could not even sing his old songs with any conviction, let alone write and perform new songs of quality. The decision not to play solo, but to perform accompanied by Ron Wood and Keith Richards, was certainly his. He had been unsure what to do at Live Aid, and mentioned his predicament when visiting Ron Wood's New York apartment.

Ron Wood: Bob says, 'I'm playing in Philadelphia the day after tomorrow . . . It's a big charity thing . . . Bill Graham's got a band for me, and I have to go along with it.' Then he says, 'Do you think that maybe you and me could play together sometime?' I said, 'Sure. Let's do the gig on Saturday.' He said, 'Really?' I said, 'Yeah. You don't necessarily have to go along with Bill Graham.' And I said, 'Keith would love to do it, too.' So I rang Keith up and I said, 'Get over here because Bob wants us to do Live Aid with him.' He said, 'You'd better not be lying, Woody.' . . . Some of the rehearsal tapes from my basement in New York are incredible. We were playing in there for a couple of days. We were playing in the upstairs dining room just before we left for Philadelphia, and it was brilliant. When we got to the stadium he was saying, 'I wonder what Bill Graham wants me to do?' We were going, 'Do what you want to do, Bob!' But he was saying, 'Bill might make me do this.' Very odd. He wanted to be bossed around again. Even going up the ramps—we'd decided what songs we were going to play— and he turns and says, 'Hey! Maybe I should do "All I Really Want To Do"!'

Only after he mounted the stage did Dylan discover that he would not be able to hear himself. The stage monitors had been switched off, as assorted would-be singers practiced how to wrestle the microphone from Patti Labelle in back of the curtain behind him. Of the three songs he sang, all from 1962–63, two were *very* strange choices. 'Ballad of Hollis Brown' dealt with a starving American farmer who chose not to save himself, while the vengeful 'When the Ship Comes In' seemed distinctly at odds with all this universal hand-holding.

Bob Dylan: They screwed around with us. We didn't even have any monitors out there. When they threw in the grand finale at the last moment they took all the settings off and set the stage up for the thirty people who were standing behind the curtain. We couldn't even hear our own voices, and when you can't hear, you can't play; you don't have any timing. It's like proceeding on radar. [1985]

Thankfully, Live Aid did have a single silver lining. After 'Ballad of Hollis Brown,' Dylan elected to strike a discordant note among the self-congratulatory back-patters by asking the billions watching to remember those in their own country struggling from economic events beyond their control. In particular, he chose to cite the plight of the American farmers. Missing the distinction between someone struggling and someone starving, Dylan's speech sparked Willie Nelson's attempt to organize a further event, solely to benefit American farmers. Farm Aid would signal Dylan's return to peak performing powers, and begin an association with Tom Petty's Heartbreakers that would ultimately re-establish 'that kind of direct connection' he had been looking for in his performance art.

1985–86: Junco and His Partners in Crime

32

He knows a million songs, old delta blues songs and stuff like that. Well, they sound like they may be delta blues songs. Sometimes I'm not sure if they're blues songs, or a new arrangement of 'It's Alright Ma.'

—Benmont Tench

Having unwittingly spawned this son of Live Aid, Dylan could hardly refuse organizer Willie Nelson when the request to appear at Farm Aid came. However far removed he had allowed himself to become from the contemporary flux, he knew he had a mountain to climb to re-establish his importance. Climbing aboard this particular benefit band-wagon might yet get him halfway there. Since the conclusion of the Farm Aid benefit was scheduled to be broadcast live on national prime-time TV, the September 22 gig gave him a real opportunity to remind the American public he still knew how to get their rocks off.

This time he decided to take Bill Graham's advice and ask a pre-assembled crew to lend him a hand. Graham had suggested grafting on Tom Petty and the Heartbreakers. They were an ideal choice. Organist Benmont Tench, guitarist Mike Campbell, and bassist Howie Epstein had all played on LA sessions for *Empire Burlesque*, and therefore had some sense of Dylan's working methods. Also, the Heartbreakers, though they'd initially sidestepped through cracks in the Punk/New Wave edifice, were essentially a roots-rock band, conversant with Dylan and aware of his importance. Scheduled to perform their own set at Farm Aid, they were unlikely to find backing such a key influence an imposition.

Determined to be prepared this time around, Dylan set aside a full week of rehearsals on a sound stage at Universal Studios in Hollywood. Inevitably, the rehearsals turned into a whole series of informal workshops on American song. As Petty put it, 'We played for *hours*, all week long.' Even Dylan was impressed by the Heartbreakers' broad knowledge of popular song, and their ability to fake their way through any gaps. They tried every genre, running down Hank Williams, Spector, Motown, blues, Tin Pan Alley, you name it.

On the final day of rehearsals, a film crew arrived to shoot some footage for a profile of Dylan, scheduled to be broadcast on the popular *20/20* TV program. He looked surprisingly comfortable, chatting between takes with the girl singers he had brought in to augment the Heartbreakers. Aside from witnessing Dylan improvise an organ–guitar arrangement of 'Forever Young' for their benefit, the cameras captured the guys slipping easily between a truly hammy 'Louie Louie' and a devastatingly understated 'That Lucky Old Sun.'

The night before Farm Aid, Dylan and the Heartbreakers sound-checked their entire set. There would be no repeat of Live Aid. Even here, they sounded revved up to play. The performance the following evening would be a revelation, contemporary in its reflections from a faithless country, timeless in its underlying message: 'if you want some-body you can trust, trust yourself.' All three *Empire Burlesque* songs— 'Clean Cut Kid,' 'I'll Remember You,' and 'Trust Yourself'—came into their own, even if Dylan left poor Madelyn Quebec hanging in the middle of the air, mouthing every other syllable at his mike. 'Trust Yourself' had him punching that air with the exhilaration of it all, before he made 'That Lucky Old Sun' sound as old as the hills and as wise as Solomon. Closing out with the appropriate 'Maggie's Farm,' his timing and intonation had never been more impressive.

Though only four of the six songs were broadcast on national TV, the joy of a man back where he belonged, fronting a great band, was evident for all to see. Not only was Farm Aid the perfect antidote to Live Aid, but it coincided with one of those strange sea changes when a man out of time is magically transformed by the media into a man for all seasons. With three videos receiving regular rotation on MTV; two live broadcasts in just over two months on national prime-time TV; a fifteen-minute profile on the popular *20/20* TV show; interviews syndicated that fall with the *Los Angeles Times* and the *Los Angeles Herald-Examiner*; the cover of the December issue of *Rolling Stone*'s new rival, *Spin;* plus interviews with *Rolling Stone* itself and *Time* magazine, he found himself for the first time adopting an elder-statesman-of-rock persona he felt comfortable with. In an unprecedented number of inter-views that fall, he began to confront his past as a way of clearing the decks, much as he had with *Writings & Drawings* back in 1973.

Indeed, one of the causes of the media's re-examination of Dylan's importance was the November 1985 publication of a revised edition of *Writings & Drawings*, entitled *Lyrics*. Dedicated to his newborn daughter, Narette, it was something of a disappointment, in that Dylan refrained from including many of the better songs left off his post-*Desire* albums—

songs like 'Blind Willie McTell,' 'New Danville Girl,' and 'Angelina'—
and it lacked the attention to detail of the original. However, the book
confirmed his status as rock's pre-eminent poet and, compact and nicely
produced as it was, sold well.

The best of the published interviews were by Mikal Gilmore in the
Herald-Examiner and a series of in-depth conversations by Scott Cohen
for the cover story in *Spin*. Cohen even managed to persuade Dylan to
answer his first questionnaire in twenty years. The categories included
Three Authors I'd Read Anything By (Tacitus, Chekhov, and Tolstoy)
and, pointedly, Questions You Can't Answer. Needless to say, four of
the questions were directed at journalists: 'How does it feel to be a
legend? How does it feel to have influenced a bunch of people? What
did you change your name from? Where's your music taking you?'

In November a five-album boxed-set retrospective, with a dozen or
so rare cuts to entice collectors, provided both a bewildering summary
of the most important canon in rock music and a template for a whole
slew of imitation sets, the size of which often reflected their subject's
ego more than their actual importance. Dylan himself was not unduly
impressed by the project, which was entitled *Biograph*. Compiled by Jeff
Rosen, an employee of his music publishing company, he saw through
all its flaws.

Bob Dylan: There's some stuff that hasn't been heard before, but most of
my stuff has already been bootlegged, so to anybody in the know, there's
nothing on it they haven't heard before . . . All it is, really, is repackaging,
and it'll just cost a lot of money. About the only thing that makes it special
is Cameron [Crowe]'s book. [1985]

Just so. Only one song—a demo of 'Forever Young'—was previously
unbootlegged. 'Cameron's book,' though, was a thirty-two-page,
twelve-by-twelve-inch résumé of Dylan's career, illustrated with a fine
cross section of unpublished photos, its accompanying essay freely
composed from a series of anecdotes given to Cameron Crowe, which
Dylan then corrected, allowing him an opportunity to comment on his
own history and talk about matters which he delighted in, or had upset
or angered him, outside the confines of the dreaded biography. In the
tradition of Neil Young's *Decade*, he also provided brief (and some
not-so-brief) commentaries on the songs chosen for the five-album set,
some of which proved quite illuminating.

The combination of Dylan's temporarily high profile, the impressive
look of the set, its motley assortment of favorites and unreleased gems,

and the novelty value, made for a surprisingly popular artifact in America, where *Biograph* became only the second boxed set to receive a gold disc for half a million sales (the other being the posthumous eight-album *Elvis Aron Presley* collection), and the first to reach the dizzy heights of thirty-three in the *Billboard* charts (ironically, the same position *Empire Burlesque* had stalled at). Though most of its initial sales were on vinyl, it was the three-CD version that convinced record companies that this was the way ahead. Lavishly packaged collections with just the right balance of the curious and the quintessential cost far less than three months of studio time, sales were assured, and promotion was a cool breeze.

After seeing most every journalist interested in beating a path to his door, Dylan returned to music-making in November 1985. Having resumed rehearsals with the Heartbreakers, with a view to establishing whether a long-term association was feasible, he decided to resume his policy of sporadic sessions. Stopping off to receive another award for work done and gone at the Whitney Museum in New York, he arrived in London around November 17 for his first English sessions in twenty years. At the behest of Dave Stewart, he had traveled there to record for four days at Stewart's own studio, a converted church in Crouch End. Indicative of a whole new attitude toward vocal overdubs, and an ongoing fit of forgetfulness in the lyric department, the sessions became a series of extended jam sessions. Given the two derivative blues jams excerpted on the BBC's *Whistle Test* TV program, permed from twenty-something basic tracks apparently recorded, whether he even had the 'vocal ideas' to salvage the instrumental tracks must be in doubt. When Waterboys frontman Mike Scott arrived to meet his hero, he joined the perplexed.

Mike Scott: Dylan was jamming around with a few ideas with Dave Stewart and he had, say, chord progressions, he had vocal ideas . . . [but] it was basically a free-for-all. Dylan turns around and says, 'Listen, you can play your heart out, just keep playing. It doesn't matter if you overplay, it doesn't matter what you do, just keep playing and we'll keep the best bits and we'll dump the other bits.' . . . He had a verse, a chorus, a middle eight, and that was the structure . . . Maybe he'd be humming along to himself, but he didn't actually stand at the mike and sing.

Perhaps the derivative nature of the jams was part of a process of reconnecting with his muse. The August jam session in a West LA church and the November jam session in a North London church—in both of which Dave Stewart and ex–Blondie drummer Clem Burke participated—were both informal ways to keep making music while waiting for lightning to strike. Likewise, Dylan's extended rehearsals with the Heartbreakers, which resumed on his return to LA and ran into the new year, may have been ostensibly conceived as tour rehearsals, but they were more about working his way back to the sources of popular song that had sparked his two great explosions of songwriting, in 1962 and 1967.

As in 1978, Dylan elected to road-test his new alliance in the Far East before bringing it back home. A month of shows in Japan and Australia gave the impetus to rehearsals, even as Dylan and the band again worked up a ream of covers, including several songs more associated with crooners than his croaky cords: 'This Was My Love,' 'All My Tomorrows' (both made famous by Sinatra), and The Ink Spots' 'We Three.' They also gave themselves up to the odd blues jam, some of which, like the song that had introduced them at Farm Aid, crossed the border between debt and theft. The Farm Aid opener, 'Shake,' had copped its riff from Roy Head's 'Treat Her Right,' but its semi-improvised lyrics had their share of Dylan, too.

In the shows in the Far East, they would also invariably open with a blues jam, which sometimes evolved into something recognizable, like 'Justine,' and sometimes remained a name on a set list ('Train of Pain'). Dylan also developed an encore, 'Cross On Over & Rock 'Em Dead,' that sounded so much like Warren Smith's 'Uranium Rock' that perhaps he could have comfortably bequeathed the copyright. This process would culminate in Dylan's reworking of Junior Parker's 'You Wanna Ramble' on *Knocked Out Loaded*.

Unlike similar exercises at Big Pink, though, no new 'Tears of Rage' came, and though the jams and covers helped maintain Dylan's interest in the extensive pre-tour rehearsals, these diversions again led him away from the matter at hand—to work up a professional set, of primarily original material, for a two-hour show to large crowds of mildly curious Antipodeans and Nipponese. When Dylan and the band arrived in Auckland on February 3, 1986, a further rehearsal was in order, the night before opening at the open-air Wellington Athletic Park. The volume of the three-and-a-quarter-hour sound-check/rehearsal, and the open-air stadium's proximity to local residences, nearly bequeathed an extra couple of days of rehearsals, when numerous complaints to the police put the opening concert under serious threat of cancellation.

In an immortal phrase coined by Tom Petty, their plan was to 'take the rehearsals on the stage.' Rather than adopting the spirit of the rehearsals, though, with their sense of the unexpected, the Heartbreakers found that what was loose at rehearsals was simply sloppy on stage.

Compounded by Dylan's inability to stick to agreed arrangements, the first shows in Wellington and Auckland were both scrappy affairs. The Heartbreakers, however, were enjoying the experience after the choreographed feel of their *Southern Accents* tour.

Mike Campbell: There's a lot of room for free playing in his songs, which makes everything pretty spontaneous. It's just never the same, that's the only way I can describe it. During one show in Australia we were supposed to do 'When the Night Comes Falling from the Sky,' and he didn't feel like doing it. He turned around to me and said, 'You know the chords for "All Along the Watchtower", don't you?' And we'd never rehearsed it. I said, 'There's only three, right?' And he said, 'Yeah, let's go!' You never know what's coming. There'll be different songs, or we'll do the same thing in different keys. It reminds me of a high-school dance band. It's more polished maybe, but it has that looseness, that freshness, that chaos.

If the results were considerably more hit-and-miss than Farm Aid, the Heartbreakers quickly came to an understanding of the rationale behind Dylan's devil-may-care approach.

Stan Lynch: There's nothing tentative about Dylan onstage. I've seen gigs where the songs have ended in all the wrong places, where it's fallen apart, and it's almost as if, in some perverse way, he gets energy from that chaos.

By the time they landed in Australia, they had begun to feed off the same energy field as Dylan, and the shows became a whole lot better. Dylan's looseness also seemed, for once, to carry over into his downtime. Indeed, his talkativeness, both on- and offstage, suggested someone glad to be back on the road. Dispensing TV and press interviews and even a mildly amusing press conference, he also re-established a musical bond with Mark Knopfler, whose Dire Straits tour was the other fare of the season, and fulfilled a minor ambition by getting drunk after hours with actress Lauren Bacall, who was in Sydney starring in a stage production of Tennessee Williams's *Sweet Bird of Youth*.

Tennessee Williams also came up during one of Dylan's more effective raps, as he engaged in a series of surprisingly frank exchanges with the curious audiences. He regularly prefaced 'Ballad of a Thin Man' with a story about refusing to answer questions at a press conference in England in 1965, insisting that a man's life speaks for itself; concluded 'Rainy Day Women' by admitting that, like a lot of his songs, it could be taken a couple of ways; and, one night in Sydney, introduced a one-off performance of 'License to Kill' as 'a song about the space program' ('man has invented his doom / first step was touching the moon'), which he was dedicating to the seven people who had been tragically killed in an American rocket days earlier, even if 'they had no business being up there in the first place . . . as if we haven't got enough problems down here on earth.' Meanwhile, he began to use a quote from Williams as a nightly prologue to 'Lenny Bruce':

Bob Dylan: Here's a song about recognition, or lack of recognition. Tennessee Williams . . . said: 'I don't ask for your pity, just your understanding. Not even that, but just your recognition of me in you, and Time, the enemy in us all.' Tennessee Williams led a pretty drastic life. He died all by himself in a New York hotel room without a friend in the world. Another man died like that . . . [1986]

The Dylan who gave this rap on March 8, in Nagoya, may already have been informed of the death of someone far dearer to him than Lenny Bruce; someone who had died alone, four days earlier, in a hotel room in Florida, feeling like he had run out of people he could talk to. The Band, minus Robbie Robertson, had returned to the circuit in 1983. They found themselves on March 2, 1986, in Winter Park, Florida, another pit-stop on the way to a dead end. Richard Manuel had phoned the home of Gary Shafner, Dylan's one-man personal organizer, in LA, insisting to Shafner's girlfriend that he needed to talk to Dylan right away. Shafner eventually gave him the number in Japan. Nobody save Dylan knows if he actually got hold of him that night, but a couple of mornings later Manuel was found hanging from the curtain rail in his motel room, having taken his own life, in much the same manner as Phil Ochs ten years before.

Dylan had only recently performed a rewritten version of 'I Shall Be Released,' the song he wrote for Manuel some nineteen years earlier, at a Martin Luther King tribute concert in January. In its new guise he advised his listeners, 'You're laughing now, you should be praying / This being the midnight hour of your life.' It was also the first Dylan song in a long time to directly refer to Jesus ('He will find you where you're staying'). Perhaps he felt the need to reinforce general awareness of his continuing faith in Christ. Even close friends had recently been openly talking about a Dylan looking to cross back to his former faith:

Allen Ginsberg: It might have been expected that he'd evolve out of [the born-again creed] as something closer to his natural Judaism. Which he has

. . . He hasn't been a born-again Christian for a long time now. People still think he is and five years ago he changed. In the conversation we had a couple of weeks ago there was a great deal of judgmental Jehovaic . . . a figure of judgmental hyper-rationality. There's this judgmental Jehovaic theism in his recent work.

Unsettling as the idea remained to the likes of Ginsberg, Dylan was still determined to place his faith not in some judgmental Jehovah but in Christ the Redeemer, something he did not leave in doubt at the shows in February and March 1986. Not only was the final song of each night's main set 'In the Garden,' hardly a song an apostate could have brought himself to sing, but he chose to preface the song with a rap that would also figure as the opening sequence in an hour-long concert special from Sydney, broadcast on HBO in June:

Bob Dylan: This last song now is all about my hero. Everybody's got a hero. Where I come from there's a lot of heroes . . . John Wayne, Clark Gable, Richard Nixon, Ronald Reagan, Michael Jackson, Bruce Springsteen. They're all heroes to some people. Anyway, I don't care nothing about those people. I have my own hero. I'm going to sing about him right now . . . 'When they came for Him in the garden, did they know?'

A month after the final show, on March 10, at Tokyo's Budokan Hall, it was announced that a joint American tour would run through June and July. It had always been each party's intention to take the Dylan/ Heartbreakers combination around the States that summer. They knew what a powerful combination it was. The Heartbreakers were a massively popular outfit in their own right, and the tour would be Dylan's first genuinely national tour in eight years. Coming on the back of his recently restored vogue, and the well-received Farm Aid appearance, the tour returned him to the very arenas he had forsaken as a result of his 1979 conversion. Not surprisingly, CBS saw a chance to sell a Dylan album that might do more than just recoup its advance, unaware that he had very little in his locker he might want to share with the great unwashed.

Nonetheless, having taken time out to get his head straight after the shock of Manuel's death, some time in mid-April Dylan convened with a few friends at Skyline studios, conveniently situated in the beautiful Topanga Canyon, between Malibu and LA, to begin recording his fifth album of the eighties. He was still hoping that he might make an album in much the same way he'd made them in the mid-sixties.

Ira Ingber: He said, 'Can we do it in a week?' I said, 'I don't think we can do it in a week.' He just wanted a band to play and to sing, but then we got into the recording world, which is a different mentality. He realized he was into this thing a little deeper than he initially thought.

Mikal Gilmore, engaged to write a cover story for *Rolling Stone*, was in attendance at several of the early sessions. He would later refer to hearing 'some twenty songs of R&B, Chicago-steeped blues, rambunctious gospel and raw-toned hillbilly forms,' none of which self-evidently feature on the finished album. The early sessions featured an extraordinary amalgam of musical elements, from the Tex-Mex of Los Lobos to the big brassy sax sound of Steve Douglas.

Mikal Gilmore: They were playing some really good stuff, and he was sort of tossing out vocals as he was going along. It wasn't always easy to hear what was being said, but the stuff that they were doing sounded really great, the stuff at Skyline . . . But they recorded a lot. I was there for at least twelve hours, over a two- or three-day period, and they were recording pretty much the whole time, and some of it was pretty wondrous. He had a nice, big rock & roll band but not like that band he had when he did that *Budokan* tour, and they were pretty fierce—he had someone from Los Lobos, James Jamerson, Jr., T-Bone Burnett, and Al Kooper—and they were really wailing . . . He was doing his own stuff but it was all pretty gut-bucket rock & roll, even though he said he never played rock & roll. Sitting there in a studio, it didn't sound to me like he was somebody with a studio problem—he was working very fast, moving from track to track, and really directing the sound.

From Gilmore's description—and recollections are about all that remain from these sessions—it sounds like Dylan, having refined the semi-improvised R&B ramble with the Heartbreakers, was hoping to make an album's worth of trains of pain. Nor is Gilmore the only eyewitness to speak of these early recording sessions with a certain sense of loss. Al Kooper, having last played with his buddy on the 'When the Night Comes Falling' session, found himself working with the same man who used to turn up at those pre-*Blonde on Blonde* sessions with a couple of riffs and a few scraps of verse. Kooper, though, rapidly became disenchanted with the whole vibe of the sessions and Dylan's approach to recording in the eighties, all the while insisting that much of real worth was recorded at these early sessions.

Al Kooper: There was enough stuff cut on *Knocked Out Loaded* to have put out a great album. There was some really wonderful things cut at those sessions, but I don't think we'll ever hear 'em . . . I was really frustrated because then I was involved, in a way that I get involved, and I made suggestions [that were ignored], and then I just sort of fucked off.

Dave Alvin, of the Blasters, one of the young bloods called up for these sessions, recalls his stint lasting around thirteen hours, and involving the likes of Kooper, James Jamerson, and Steve Douglas. He also recalls, when he got the call, being told that they would be working on *Self Portrait Volume Two*. They ended up recording nothing but covers, all 'gut-bucket rock & roll,' but with an assured Dylan pumping out ideas and 'directing the sound.'

Dave Alvin: We did everything from Elmore James's 'Look Over Yonder Wall' to 'Rollin' and Tumblin'.' Then it got pretty funny—Bob was playing acoustic, and I joined him on electric, and he said, 'You know this song?' and he started singing this old Warren Smith tune ['Red Cadillac & a Black Mustache']. Then we cut Johnny Carroll's 'Rock with Me Baby'—we cut it once with the core band, and then this girl choir came in with a horn section, and they tracked it again. Instantly, it was like changing the sound from Elvis Sun to Elvis RCA.

Once again, though, that unerring confidence began to fade in the studio, as Dylan began to 'fuck with the formula,' bringing in various incompatible elements in search of a musical lock. Charlie Quintana recalls being invited along one day:

Charlie Quintana: There was . . . a studio session, proper full-blown recording studio at Skyline in Topanga Canyon. I took these two guys, one an incredible bass player and an incredible guitar player, both extremely good technically. I said, 'When we get there and start playing, just follow me. Just follow me. Rule number one.' . . . I'd already played with Bob for three months, so I knew more or less the way the routine was. But when we got to the session, these guys both wanted to get the gig so desperately bad, and they were just so in awe of Bob, that they rushed the whole fucking thing.

Likewise, guitarist Ira Ingber, who had done such sterling work on 'Something's Burning, Baby' and 'New Danville Girl,' was asked to come up with an arrangement of a Ray Charles song that was quite beyond Dylan's own technical abilities.

Ira Ingber: He wanted me to do an arrangement for him of 'Come Rain or Come Shine.' It's a beautiful song and he gave me the record. We took down the chords, brought in the band, and tried playing it. It's a fairly complicated song and he wanted me to show him how to play it . . . I showed him, but there's some really weird chords because it's an orchestra arrangement, not piano or guitar. The chords more or less reflect the complexity, and Bob couldn't play those chords. They're not even guitar-player chords, they're orchestral chords, and he got kinda discouraged by that.

Slowly but surely, the sessions began to fall apart. Rather than assuming the pattern of successful Dylan albums, in which he would grow into the process, from initial torpor to positively brimming with ideas, the *Knocked Out Loaded* sessions never returned to an even keel after he began his daily experiments with different musicians. As his heart went out of the exercise, he became increasingly casual about turning up for work, often arriving at four in the morning for a midnight session, like as not with that night's lady friend on his arm.

Part of Dylan's disenchantment came about because the songs refused to come. It was one thing to create a musical collage out of twenty-five years' immersion in the folk-blues form, it was entirely another having to put some graft into his craft. Hoping for assistance, and looking for a different vibe, he joined Tom Petty and the Heartbreakers at their studio in Van Nuys, as they worked on their own collection of songs. Though Dylan traded an idea for a song called 'Jammin' Me' for one of Petty's discards, 'Got My Mind Made Up'—and then wrote a whole new set of verses to Petty's tune—the process was visibly beginning to defeat him. Gilmore caught up with him again in Van Nuys.

Mikal Gilmore: His mood was entirely different, the music wasn't as inspired. He still could hit it vocally at moments, but he was not in a good mood and he told me he'd thrown out all that other stuff, and now it was just gonna be an album of bits and pieces.

Staring failure in the face, Dylan didn't like what he saw, and when Gilmore began to question him about the political principles behind the songs of figures like Springsteen and John Cougar Mellencamp, he turned his face to Tempe, and out it came:

Bob Dylan: The only principles you can find are the principles in the Bible. I mean, Proverbs has got them all . . . There is no right and no left. There's truth and there's untruth, y'know? There's honesty and there's hypocrisy. Look in the Bible . . . I hate to keep beating people over the head with the Bible, but that's the only instrument I know, the only thing that stays true. [1986]

Mikal Gilmore: I talked to him several times over a period of roughly a year or so and he was always gracious and thoughtful, and every question was fair [game], but that one night with Petty . . . he seemed much more tense, and it was like pulling teeth . . . We got onto politics, and he got up and started to pace back and forth . . . he was pissed and there was a lot of people in the room. But he was also having fun with it. He was drinking a fair amount in those days. From what I saw, and having gone through my own phases, I think it was a bad period for him . . . Toward the end of the evening, after we had our argument and he did some more vocals on 'Got My Mind Made Up,' he loosened up and he said some stuff that I found quite interesting and genuine, but I didn't get back to what was wrong with these sessions, because that seemed stuff he was really tense [talking] around. So we talked about . . . his children.

In his report for *Rolling Stone,* Gilmore observed, 'Somewhere along the line [Dylan] . . . decided to assembl[e] the album from various sessions that have accrued over the last year. "It's all sorts of stuff," he says. "It doesn't really have a theme or a purpose." And so it came to pass, *Knocked Out Loaded* (which took its title from a line in the New Orleans classic 'Junco Partner') became Dylan's first 'concept album from the cutting-room floor' since *Self Portrait*, another album designed to cover up a dearth of inspiration.

Of the eight basic tracks on the released album, one came from the sessions with the Heartbreakers at Sound City, one from the November 1985 London sessions, and three from the *Empire Burlesque* sessions. The three cuts actually originating from the Topanga Canyon sessions were all covers. The final few sessions at Skyline were taken up reworking the *Empire Burlesque* outtakes. 'Maybe Someday' was given new words, as was 'Driftin' Too Far from Shore.' More importantly, Dylan decided to rework 'New Danville Girl,' now retitled 'Brownsville Girl,' thus saving the album from total disposability. To the November 1984 backing track, he added an impressive new vocal, a handful of new lines, an overzealous female chorus (courtesy of the omnipresent Queens of Rhythm), a trumpet, Steve Douglas's saxophone, and two new verses (the one in the French Quarter and 'they can talk about me plenty when I'm gone').

Dave Garfield: ['Brownsville Girl'] was one of the ones he would stop in the middle of things, sit down for fifteen minutes or so, right here in the lounge, and start penning some new lyrics.

Whatever his original conception, *Knocked Out Loaded* now lay somewhere between a second installment of *Empire Burlesque* and another helping of *Self Portrait*. Lapses of taste, like the use of a children's choir on the dreadful 'They Killed Him' and steel drums on 'Precious Memories,' combined with a total running time of thirty-five minutes, made for his most disposable collection since *Dylan*. That he had in mind the aural equivalent of pulp fiction was made ultra-clear when he selected as the album cover an image from a forties B-movie poster that a friend of Gary Shafner's girlfriend, Tony Goodstone, had brought over one afternoon. When Goodstone offered to check out the rights situation, Dylan just said, 'Let 'em sue us.'

As it is, the album might well have passed the copyright holder by, along with most of Dylan's fast-receding audience. *Knocked Out Loaded* continued his ten-year commercial decline, failing to even make the Top 50 at a time when he was making his most well received, not to mention lucrative, tour in eight years. Dylan himself seemed as unconvinced of the album's merits as the fans, refusing to play anything from it in the two months that separated the opening night's 'Got My Mind Made Up,' in San Diego, from a severely truncated 'Brownsville Girl' at the final show in Paso Robles, California.

If the recording studio now seemed to bring out the worst in Dylan, the rehearsal studio continued to bring out the best. The American tour rehearsals, at Zoetrope studios, followed the same pattern as for the Far East: 'inventive versions of wondrous songs [that] come and go and are never heard again.' When Gilmore asked Dylan about those moments, he ducked the underlying implication: 'I'm not sure if people really want to hear that sort of thing from me.'

Mikal Gilmore: One night, during a rehearsal, he did 'I Dreamed I Saw St. Augustine' and then, with his backing singers, 'White Christmas,' and it was great and everybody knew it. I talked to Benmont Tench about it and he said that was the stuff that would really blow his mind. That Dylan would pull some song that nobody had ever heard of, or that nobody ever expected Dylan to sing, and do a wonderful version of it. And yet they couldn't convince him to take that stuff to the stage . . . I saw great performances in rehearsals that were just of a very different tone and temperament [from] the live performances.

Dylan resolutely refused to bring that spirit to the shows, save perhaps for 'All My Tomorrows' and 'I Still Miss Someone' at shows in Pine Knob, Michigan, and 'House of the Rising Sun' in Saratoga and New York—he preferred to predetermine his audience's expectations. The American leg of the True Confessions Tour started impressively enough, with Dylan again responding to the plight of political prisoners, at an Amnesty International benefit show in LA, by getting truly trashed backstage. Unlike the long-ago Friends of Chile show, though, the three-song Amnesty performance was a delight.

Sadly, the 1986 US tour rapidly ran out of steam, spluttering to a conclusion after two months, back on the coast. Dylan certainly seemed to be coasting through most of his own songs, having once again adopted that declamatory arena voice previously in evidence in 1974, 1978, and 1984. Only the nightly covers—pick any three from 'We Had It All,' Lonesome Town,' 'So Long, Good Luck and Goodbye,' 'Unchain My Heart,' 'I'm Moving On,' 'Shake a Hand,' and 'Red Cadillac and a Black Mustache'—seemed to excite him. The same autopilot seemed to have also been fitted to the Heartbreakers, who, on their home patch, were given a larger part of the show and who quickly settled into familiar patterns, to predictable arena whoops.

Though a forty-five-year-old Dylan was clearly not able to give his all throughout the two-hour-plus sets, he seemed determined to defy the obvious, pushing himself through long shows rather than performing briefer, more cogent sets. A rethink was required. The Heartbreakers alliance might have been good for the wallet, but short of inviting his fans to rehearsals there seemed no way of bridging Dylan's delight in informal music-making with the demands of studio and stage.

1986–87: Imitators Steal Me Blind

33

That whole thing with Petty? He wants to be a rock & roll star. He doesn't know who he is—he's wearing the black leather, he's got the earring . . . He [really] doesn't know who he is in the rock pantheon.

—*Arthur Rosato:*

Reporter: You did the last tour with Petty for the money. Can we take that to be a new philosophy of yours?
Bob Dylan: I'm always doing tours for the money! What's so new about that?

—**Hearts of Fire** *press conference, August 18, 1986*

The man for whom money didn't so much talk as swear in 'It's Alright Ma,' who told the Emergency Civil Liberties Committee in December 1963 that 'money means very little t me,' and damned those for whom time was money in 'When You Gonna Wake Up?' spent the year that separates his American tour with the Heartbreakers from their European stint finding ways to fill the coffers. As the burden of being Bob Dylan again began to become oppressive; as his personal life became ever more convoluted; and as the songs of salvation all but dried up, Dylan turned the tables of the temple upright and began an audit.

As his royalty checks began to shrink, and the cost of quality backing bands threatened to become prohibitive, Dylan began to be concerned that he could not afford such a high-maintenance lifestyle. Down to his last hundred million, give or take, he found himself having to support not only a stable of willing and able new ponies, but his second family of the decade. Gospel singer Carolyn Dennis, having returned to singing duties in the four-piece Queens of Rhythm on the True Confessions Tour, and returned as well to his affections, was again with child, about to make Dylan a father for the sixth or seventh time. He had also convinced another African-American woman named Darlene, whom he had met in Texas on the Petty tour, to continue their occasional liaisons. Nor was Carole Childs out of the picture.

It was probably a relief, then, when he flew to England in mid–August, to shore up his bank accounts. He had never entirely abandoned his celluloid ambitions and, though his one experience of a *real* movie had been tortuous, he hoped the Peckinpah film might prove the exception. Before the summer leg of the Dylan/Petty association had kicked off, he found himself agreeing to star in a movie, to be directed by *Jagged Edge* director Richard Marquand, at the conclusion of the tour. It was to be called *Hearts of Fire*.

Richard Marquand: He's always been interested in film—I mean . . . his own film; it's always something that has intrigued him, and now at this stage of his life, forty-six, forty-seven, he's thinking, 'Well, let's really try it out, let's see if I'm any good.'

The storyline for *Hearts of Fire* was a surprisingly pat *ménage à trois* involving two rock stars, separated by a generation (or two), and one wanna-be. Dylan was to play Billy Parker, a disillusioned ex-rock & roll star, who takes an aspiring femme fatale with him to England. There she meets James Colt, a contemporary rock star played by Rupert Everett, who shares the same mystifying lust for the leading lady—played by Fiona Flanagan, the singer who went simply by the name of 'Fiona'—as the curmudgeonly Parker. Portraying the cynical old rock & roller as someone who threw his hand in at the height of fame to retire to the backwoods and raise chickens, probably suggests something written with Dylan in mind, playing as it did on a popular perception. The one element in the original screenplay that gave his character an added dimension had this 'rock & roll nigger' robbing tollbooths, Burger Kings, and even concert halls for kicks. This aspect was cut from the final shooting script.

Requiring its audience to not so much suspend disbelief as garrotte it, the tollbooth jailbait played by 'Fiona' had to exude enough sheer sexual presence to ensnare two very jaded rock & rollers. In fact, Flanagan generated as much sexual charge as a blow-up doll with a puncture, while exuding all the onscreen presence of an ex-parrot. Dylan himself had wanted his old friend Debra Winger to play the lead female role and, though she was hardly at the jailbait stage of her career, he gave her a copy of the script. When she dismissed it as garbage, asking rhetorically, 'Why would I want to do that?' Dylan righteously replied, 'Why, for the money!' When he arrived in London for an August 18 press conference, he found Winger's question being raised in a somewhat more pointed fashion. The attending journalists expressed no interest in his co-stars or director, doggedly pursuing him to answer the one question that burned in all their minds, finally articulated by Philip Norman: 'Why aren't you writing poetry and doing the things you're really best at?'

As it was, the large check Dylan was receiving for his efforts also required half a dozen examples of his poetry for the movie soundtrack. Caught off guard when asked about these songs at the press conference, he admitted he hadn't 'written those songs just yet,' but envisioned no problem rustling up the requisite Elvis-style soundtrack. Certainly the two efforts he came up with in the ten days before the soundtrack sessions, at London's Townhouse studios—'Had a Dream About You Baby' and 'Night After Night'—could have sat quite comfortably on the same album as 'He's Your Uncle, Not Your Dad,' 'Dominic the Impotent Bull,' or 'There's No Room to Rumba in a Sports Car.'

Linda Thompson: He expressed an interest in meeting me, so I went into the caravan and he's got like boxer-shorts on and I couldn't stop looking at his legs. They were like twigs. And all I could think of to say [was], 'Your legs are so thin.' He said, 'Oh yeah. I'm on a diet. I'm on the Fit For Life diet. You can only eat fruit before mid-day,' and this is like half past ten in the morning, and he's got a glass of brandy. I said, 'Is booze allowed on the Fit For Life Diet?' And he said, in that inimitable Dylan way, 'I think so' . . . His guitar was lying in the trailer and he handed it to me, 'D'you wanna play something?' I play the four chords I know, and we started to write a song. He gave me these two lines. I'll never forget them. They were absolute crap: 'I knew him when I was a little girl / His Daddy knew my Ma.'

When his established methodology—'digging through my pockets and drawers trying to find these *songs*'—refused to yield anything usable, he ended up recording three covers—Billy Joe Shaver's 'Old Five and Dimer,' Shel Silverstein's 'Couple More Years,' and John Hiatt's 'The Usual'—and one of his train jams, in the hope of supplementing the meager scraps left by his muse. 'Couple More Years' would unwittingly define the experience of making the movie, with its couplet, 'It ain't that I'm wiser / It's just that I spent more time with my back to the wall.' *Hearts of Fire* would be the effective end of Dylan's film career, even if he would continue to talk up five-minute ideas into ninety minutes of celluloid for the remainder of the decade.

Ironically, Dylan gave one of his more notable appearances on film while on the *Hearts of Fire* set. The highly respected BBC *Omnibus* team was intent on making a fifty-minute documentary, which as a result of his reclusiveness came to be entitled *Getting to Dylan*.

Richard Marquand: They knew that this was a chance to maybe find some sort of framework to do a film on Bob—the framework of the making of the movie.

Marquand, as a former *Omnibus* director himself, facilitated the process as much as he could, but as Dylan left England for Ontario at the beginning of October, they had still failed to ensnare their prey for the all-important interview. It would take a further fortnight of frustration in Hamilton, Ontario, before Dylan finally consented to an on-camera interview with *Omnibus* director Christopher Sykes. However, when he did, the twenty-five minute interview at the center of *Getting to Dylan* proved to be one of the most remarkable exchanges of Dylan's career. It may not have been Sykes's intention to update *Don't Look Back*, but in *Getting to Dylan*, we find out what happened to that man—and it is not a pretty sight. Before the interview even gets rolling, Dylan disappears from his Portakabin, returning with a case of the sniffles and the eyes of the wired.

Don't Look Back, the film of the 1965 English tour, perpetually froze him in monochrome hipness. In the first flush of fame he was the very prototype of supercool. The lines, whether scourging self-analysis— 'You're gonna die . . . you do your work in the face of that'—or half-whispered dismissals—'Oh, you're one of those. I understand now'—fixed him in a present tense where he could not grow old, a Dorian Gray Dylan.

Twenty-one years on, Dylan was again in England to make a movie, though without a tour to punctuate the nights. In *Getting to Dylan*, we again see him pursued by the press, a mystified film crew, and of course his fans. Just as the duel with Horace Judson in *Don't Look Back* represents the climactic point of the film, so does the one-to-one interview in *Getting to Dylan*. He insists, at the outset, that if Sykes is looking for revelation, 'it just ain't gonna come,' but then proceeds to show a man with few secrets to conceal:

Bob Dylan: Fame, everybody just kind of copes with it a different way. But nobody seems to think it's really what they were after . . . It's like, say, you're passing a little pub or an inn, and you look through the window and you see all the people eating and talking and carrying on. You can watch outside the window and you can see them all be very real with each other. As real as they're gonna be, because when you walk into the room it's over. You won't see them being real anymore. [1986]

In 1965 there had been precious few chinks in the armor. In 1986 the armor had become more of a weight than those it was designed to fend off. By his own admission, he saw only rare glimpses outside the castle walls constructed, back in the late sixties, to safeguard his privacy, and yet he remained unable, or unwilling, to dismantle them.

Bob Dylan: I don't know what people think of me. I only know about what record companies say . . . and managers and people like that—people who want you to do things . . . I only hear about that stuff. [1986]

Getting to Dylan, the essential filmed portrait of the post-conversion Dylan, remains an important adjunct to *Don't Look Back, Eat the Document*, and *Renaldo and Clara*, the three other films to confront the myth as it surrounds and, in *Getting to Dylan*, envelops the man. It signaled a return to an increasingly paranoiac worldview, evidenced by both a renewed use of the kind of cocktails that accentuate the negative, and an encroaching inability to recognize the importance of the good-news elements of the gospel he continued to avow. The final song of his next album would again portray him as a man adrift in the company of rank strangers, dreaming of the promised land.

In his self-imposed isolation, Dylan continued to look for solace in some sweet baby's arms. His relationship with Carole Childs had begun to wear on him, and though she made several attempts to convince him to let her join him in Ontario, he successfully dissuaded her. He had invited another brassy blonde, Susan Ross, up north, before persuading her to travel to Tucson to research Josephine Sarah Marcus Earp, Wyatt Earp's third wife, for one of the many screenplays he threatened to produce, but never did.

Dylan had first met Ross at the Whitney Museum bash in November 1985, when he was self-evidently in the company of Childs. However, when the self-styled former road manager for Jackson Browne, Fleetwood Mac, and ELO told him she was a budding playwright about to write her first effort, about the seven planes of consciousness, he did his best to look impressed before asking her where she was staying. As he continued to see Ross, he assured her that though he and Childs remained friends, they were no longer lovers. Having passed the credulity test with flying colors, Ross became one of Dylan's regular occasionals, at least until she began to demand a greater status.

Hearts of Fire would take a year to be released in England, where it lasted barely three weeks on general release before disappearing from the cinemas (a novelization equally promptly put the pulp into pulp fiction).

The film's financiers, Lorimar Pictures, decided to cut their losses and abandon a US theatrical release. The film had to wait until the spring of 1990 for its commercial video release in the States. Despite an ongoing struggle to memorize his lines and insistence that 'a hundred guys I know . . . could have played this role,' Dylan was one of the few highlights of the movie. He did at least exude a kind of stiff charisma:

Iain Smith: He's arguably the best thing in the film. It's not because he's a great actor, it's because Richard has worked very hard, by cutting and editing Bob's material, to bring out what is in the man, which is his natural charisma . . . He's funny and quirky and strange and you watch him on the screen and you think, 'Well, he's not acting . . . but, and it's a bit odd, he's very, very watchable.' You just want to watch him. And it's a totally undefinable quality.

In the long gap that separated the shooting from its limited release, Dylan seems to have given no real thought to the film, which died almost as quick a death as its director, who did not live to see even its English cinema release. When Mikal Gilmore found himself up in San Rafael, at the time Dylan was rehearsing with the Grateful Dead, they exchanged brief pleasantries, and when Gilmore asked him if he had finished the movie he was working on, Dylan initially professed ignorance and then, when prompted, replied, 'Oh yeah, that. That came out. It was called *Citizen Kane.*'

The one aspect of the ill-conceived project to suggest any potential had been the covers cut at Townhouse, filling the void his songwriting had left in the movie soundtrack. Though Dylan's faithful cover of the title track of Billy Joe Shaver's 1973 album, and his belting studio rendition of John Hiatt's 'The Usual,' were wasted as soundtrack filler (the former was supplanted in the movie by Silverstein's song), they were a reminder of the last time the songwriter in him suffered memory loss. He had mentioned the idea of recording another album of covers several times during the bout of interviews at the time of *Biograph*, even telling Cameron Crowe that he had set his mind on doing 'an album of standards,' that he'd 'like to do a concept album . . . or an album of cover songs, but I don't know if the people would let me get away with that . . . "A Million Miles from Nowhere," "I Who Have Nothing," "All My Tomorrows," "I'm in the Mood for Love," "More Than You Know," "It's a Sin to Tell a Lie."'

Though *Self Portrait* had become historically entrenched as the absolute low point of his record-making career, there was nothing intrinsically unsound about Dylan again attempting to redefine himself through the songs of others. Indeed, it was a technique he had sporadically adopted ever since coming to New York, as a spur to his next reinvention. His shows since 1975 usually permitted the odd cover to impinge. By 1986 these covers had come to occupy a quarter of the set. Perhaps he felt that by focusing on the master craftsmen who set the standards, he might yet learn new elements of the craft he himself had so dramatically reinvented. If the basement tape experiment had been largely folk-driven, and the *Self-Portrait* experiment betrayed his country influences, this time he hoped some torch ballads from the pre-rock & roll era might offer light out of the darkness. In his interview with Mikal Gilmore in late September 1985 he had expressed admiration for the great crooners of the forties and fifties:

Bob Dylan: Sinatra, Peggy Lee, yeah, I love all these people, but I tell you who I've really been listening to a lot lately—in fact, I'm thinking about recording one of his earlier songs—is Bing Crosby. I don't think you can find better phrasing anywhere.

He had recorded Sinatra's 'This Was My Love' for *Infidels*; and in rehearsals for the 1984 tour had worked up versions of the standards 'Always on My Mind' and 'To Each His Own.' In rehearsals for the 1986 tour he had returned to 'This Was My Love' again, along with 'All My Tomorrows' and the Ink Spots' 'We Three,' and as he prepared for sessions in LA in the spring of 1987, he performed an acoustic version of 'Soon,' a George Gershwin composition perhaps best known through Ella Fitzgerald, at a New York gala to commemorate the fiftieth anniversary of Gershwin's death.

Nevertheless, the musicians at an early April session at Sunset Sound in LA must have been a little taken aback when he insisted on recording the likes of 'Just When I Needed You Most,' 'Important Words,' and 'When Did You Leave Heaven?' If he had begun the April sessions with a specific theme to the album of covers, his resolve again proved fleeting. Rock & roll standards like 'Twist and Shout,' 'Willie and the Hand Jive,' 'Let's Stick Together,' and 'Got Love If You Want It' hardly shared a cell block with 'This Was My Love.' Nor did Dylan seem to have learned this lesson from *Knocked Out Loaded*, as he again interchanged musicians with each time-card shuffle.

Having made his version of a latter-day Elvis soundtrack for *Hearts of Fire*, it now appeared that he was using the Colonel's blueprint for the making of product—personal favorites like 'Rank Strangers to Me' and

'Shenandoah' vying with songs that suggested themselves on the spur of the moment (like 'Sally Sue Brown' or 'Got Love If You Want It'); even assigning a couple of numbers from the pen of a songwriter prepared to give him a share of the publishing for changing a couple of lines and copping a derivative riff.

The legacy of Elvis was certainly preying on Dylan's mind. Midway through the sessions, he had gone to Memphis to help Ringo Starr spend another record company's studio budget on some good time Chardonnay. While there, on April 14, his assistant Gary Shafner arranged for a private, VIP tour of Graceland, the mausoleum to the cult of personality that had ultimately convinced Elvis life wasn't worth living. Dylan couldn't believe just how gaudy the Memphis mansion was, nor how reverential the fans who came there were.

Bob Dylan: My first trip to Graceland was about six years ago . . . and it was very clear that Elvis was going to be a religion in a lot of different ways. [1993]

He also visited the site of Martin Luther King's shooting before returning to LA, hardly galvanized by the experience, and continuing to record an unconvincing hodgepodge of reference points from a series of incompatible genres. He excused the project in the following terms to a female journalist:

Bob Dylan: There's no rule that claims that anyone must write their own songs. And I do. I write a lot of songs. But so what, you know? You could take another song somebody else has written and you can make it yours. I'm not saying I made a definitive version of anything with this last record, but I liked the songs. Every so often you've gotta sing songs that're out there . . . Writing is such an isolated thing. You're in such an isolated frame of mind. You have to get into or be in that place. In the old days, I could get to it real quick. I can't get to it like that no more. [1988]

In fact, not only couldn't Dylan the songwriter 'get to it like that no more,' he couldn't even muster the enthusiasm to complete the album himself. When a couple of overdubs were required at the mixing stage, he left it to engineer Stephen Shelton to gussy up this lumpen mess. *Down in the Groove* confirmed that Dylan had become a man who was running out of ways of reinventing himself, and didn't even feel inclined to repeat himself convincingly. Not that he hadn't attempted to pen enough songs to make *Down in the Groove* a second installment in the sorry saga of collections with 'all sorts of stuff . . . [without] a theme or a purpose.' He had even allowed one of rock's more prolific magpies, U2's Bono, to remind him how easily a song might come if he could just shake the inclination to produce something original or inspired.

Bono: He's very hung up on actually being Bob Dylan. He feels he's trapped in his past and, in a way, he is. I mean, no one asks Smokey Robinson to write a new 'Tracks of My Tears' every album . . . Like, we were trading lines and verses off the top of our heads and Dylan comes out with this absolute classic: 'I was listenin' to the Neville Brothers, it was a quarter of eight / I had an appointment with destiny, but I knew she'd come late / She tricked me, she addicted me, she turned me on the head / Now I can't sleep with these secrets, that leave me cold and alone in my bed.' Then he goes, 'Nah, cancel that.' Can you believe it? He thought it was too close to what people expect of Bob Dylan.

Dylan's curiosity as to U2's recently acquired superstar status—definitively consolidated by their multimillion seller *The Joshua Tree*—prompted him to make an onstage endorsement at one of their LA Sports Arena shows that April, guesting on versions of 'I Shall Be Released' and 'All Along the Watchtower' that were debilitated by Bono's inability to defer to the songs' original lyrics. But Dylan was none the wiser as to the basis of U2's appeal, and after his effort at songwriting with Bono—which generated nothing but the trite 'Love Rescue Me' (on *Rattle & Hum*)—he turned to Grateful Dead lyricist Robert Hunter to help him provide the requisite filler to the slim collection he now had in mind. But, however cursory his treatment of the likes of Slim Harpo's 'Got Love If You Want It,' Hank Snow's 'Ninety Miles an Hour,' and the Stanley Brothers' 'Rank Strangers to Me' at these sessions, they surely did not deserve to share their grooves with the likes of 'Silvio' and 'Ugliest Girl in the World,' Robert Hunter lyrics even the Dead had passed on.

Such, though, was the dissolute state of Dylan's artistry that he seemed quite incapable of producing even the passable when inspiration passed him by. The polished rock he'd cast into the well with *Infidels* finally hit rock bottom with *Down in the Groove. Down in the Groove* also convinced CBS that any further investment in promoting their most long-standing rock artist was a waste of valuable resources. Their apathy, which held the album's release up for a whole year, convinced Dylan to reconfigure the album twice: at the mastering stage and after promotional copies had gone out (or, in Argentina's case, after the actual album had been pressed), replacing 1987 recordings with outtakes from 1983 ('Death Is Not the

End') and 1986 ('Had a Dream About You Baby')—but *Down in the Groove* remained a thirty-two-minute epitaph to a once-revolutionary career.

Dylan now seemed more concerned about ensuring he received his full due of revenue from past glories than generating any future money-spinning classics. Since 1981 he had been embroiled in an acrimonious legal dispute with his former manager, Albert Grossman. Essentially, some time around 1979 he had ceased to pay Grossman his share of the publishing royalties from Witmark, Dwarf, and Big Sky. When Grossman finally filed suit, Dylan responded by asserting eighteen counterclaims and sixteen 'affirmative defenses,' which alleged that 'he had been fraudulently induced into the various agreements by [Grossman] at a young age,' standard practice when it came to muddying the waters in a civil suit. He also made it quite plain to Grossman's legal representatives that any settlement would have to involve a complete buy-out of all rights Grossman had to future income under *all* previous agreements, including the Witmark contract.

Grossman had taught his pupil well. Quite simply, Dylan seemed to be relying on his ability to outspend his adversary and delay due process until the old man, and Grossman was now in his early sixties, gave up all the rights secured in the 1970 agreement. It took until April 1985 for the matter to come to court, at least for round one, after Dylan had twice failed to produce appropriate statements pertaining to the charges. The 1985 decision cut some of the ground away, and suggested that he might yet rue his decision to renege on the 1970 agreement. Judge McCoe dismissed three of Dylan's affirmative defenses and four of his counter-claims, which certainly materially enhanced Grossman's position. More importantly, Dylan was ordered 'to state with particularity a number of the factual predicates for the issues that had theretofore been couched in general and deliberately opaque terms.' One of the greatest living American wordsmiths was being ordered to cut the waffle, and actually answer some serious legal points, not evasively but directly, under oath. It meant another round of sworn depositions, not only for Dylan but for several of his agents and attorneys.

Only Dylan knows his motives for treating his father figure so, but as Grossman's lawyers advised their client at the beginning of 1986, 'the Songwriter's strategy was very clear . . . to delay and to prevent the case from coming to trial as long as possible.' Part of this strategy involved having two sets of lawyers, a prominent New York firm and Dylan's personal out-of-state counsel. As a result, with Dylan's counsel unavailable for extended periods, even the simplest legal matters could be spun out indefinitely. The strategy reaped unexpected dividends on January 25, 1986, when Grossman's weary heart gave up its struggle with the man's appetite on a plane to London. Dylan now had only to lock antlers with Sara's old friend, Sally Grossman.

The author of 'Dear Landlord,' though, continued to overestimate his ability to use the system for his own ends. As Sally resolved to continue the fight, counsel advised her that Dylan was clearly not bargaining in good faith and that no settlement was likely to occur before trial. In September 1986, though, Justice Stecher denied a motion to disqualify from the defense, and strongly castigated the tactics of Dylan's counsel. It was not going according to plan, and the chances of winning the case if it ever went to court began to look slim. Thankfully, in light of another setback in court, Dylan finally took heed of wiser counsel, his old friend David Braun, who had worked for both defendant and plaintiff, and who now attempted to instigate an out-of-court settlement with Grossman's estate.

At last, in May 1987, Dylan agreed to the estate retaining its rights in Witmark, paying a further $2 million 'to settle all plaintiffs' other claims, past and future.' The Witmark rights were valued at approximately another million dollars, making the size of the settlement—after six years of legal wranglings and enduring animosity between Dylan and the man most responsible for his initial success—effectively $3 million. Dylan, though, had finally obtained what he wanted, complete control of his music publishing. In another three years, the Witmark catalog would begin to be administered by him under the American 'twenty-eight-year rule' for renewal of copyright.

In fact, May 1987 was a good month for Dylan the businessman. After years of speculation, he finally agreed to play half a dozen shows with the Grateful Dead in July. It fulfilled one of Jerry Garcia's most ardent wishes, to share a stage with the great man, and the money was unimportant to Garcia, if not to the musical misfits who made up the numbers in his band. For Dylan, though, it was a payback for all the times they had dipped into his catalogue for ideas beyond their ken, and he was holding out for a 70–30 split of receipts for the tour to happen.

To place this in context, Dylan was committing himself to six stadium shows, to average audiences of seventy-five thousand, at a time when he would have struggled to sell out medium-sized arenas on his own. He would be backed by a band who, by 1987, could sell out multiple nights in stadiums at will, and who would be expected to play their own two-hour set in addition to their role as Bob's backing band. What was smart business, though, smacked of someone artistically bankrupt. It may have been just half a dozen shows, but Dylan was tying himself to a band who had all the ambition and conceit of one of the great Coltrane quartets but the technical ability of the Buzzcocks. The person who, under Grossman, had never been known to make a foolish move was now more interested in shekels than a strategy for rebuilding a career that came from nowhere and looked to be heading straight back there.

1987–88: Raised from the Dead

34

I was going on my name for a long time, name and reputation,
which was about all I had. I had sort of fallen into an amnesia spell
. . . I didn't feel I knew who I was on stage.

—*Bob Dylan, 1997*

Q: What did the Grateful Dead fan say when he ran out of drugs?
A: This band is shit.

—*Joke in popular currency, c. 1987*

That the Grateful Dead, by 1987, had become a cultural phenomenon is
undeniable. Renowned, if that's the right word, for playing without a
set list, they had become the rock equivalent of a Christian cult, a lifestyle
rock band whose original impetus had become a much mythologized set
of lost tablets. Though Dylan's rapport with Garcia was undeniable—
their mutual love of traditional music bound them like no others in their
chosen field—one listen to a 1986 live tape of this band should have
convinced him to steer a wide berth. Neither of the Dead's drummers
played the backbeat on which Dylan so heavily relied; they were as
sloppy in their beginnings as the man himself, rarely warming up from a
slow shuffle; they didn't listen to the singer, let alone respond to him;
and if they had ever been able to carry a tune in a bucket, their bucket
had now got a hole in it.

The idea of a Dylan–Dead tour had been in the percolator for a long
time—ever since Dylan attended one of their shows in New Jersey in
July 1972, which somehow sparked rumors of them making an album
together. At his Warfield residency in November 1980, he was joined
by Garcia the night after Bloomfield, and they had stayed in touch. Then,
in early July 1986, Dylan and the Heartbreakers had doubled up with the
Dead for three stadium shows, Dylan twice joining the Dead for a couple
of songs. The crude insensitivity of their playing on 'Desolation Row'
and 'It's All Over Now, Baby Blue,' the latter of which they had been
playing since 1966, should have provided ample evidence of the pall the

Dead could cast over any song. And yet the idea prevailed, essentially because Garcia and Dylan's accountant wanted it to happen.

Jerry Garcia: We always loved his music—we still do. It was one of those things we'd always thought, 'Wow, that'd be far out'—Bob Dylan and the Grateful Dead. So we hit on him later in [1986], and we talked about it and he said, Yeah. And he came around for two or three weeks, and we rehearsed stuff, and tried stuff out, and played through things and goofed around and hung around a lot.

The rehearsals provided fair warning of the shape of things to come. Dylan turned up at San Rafael at the beginning of June 1987, checking into the Stoufers Hotel with Carole Childs. Since this was the Dead, who had played a huge number of Dylan songs themselves over the years, fans were expecting varied sets and surprising selections. In this, they wouldn't be disappointed. One day Dylan suggested 'All I Really Wanna Do' after hearing the World Party version on his way to rehearsals. Putting their communal Deadheads together, the musicians suggested some equally overlooked gems, among which were 'Stuck Inside of Mobile,' 'Queen Jane Approximately,' 'Gonna Change My Way of Thinking,' 'The Ballad of Frankie Lee and Judas Priest,' 'Pledging My Time,' 'Watching the River Flow,' 'The Wicked Messenger,' 'If Not for You,' and even a couple of songs Dylan only ever demoed for Witmark, 'Walkin' Down the Line' and 'John Brown.'

When Dylan later defined his attitude to rehearsing a song as sometimes only 'knowing the title and what key to play it in,' he was perhaps thinking of these rehearsals. Songs were rarely finished, and the arrangements were nonexistent, save maybe in Deadspeak, where Garcia's doodling around the melody doubtless acquires whole layers of connotation. Certain members of the Dead were less than enthralled by having a vocalist as unfocused as the band.

Bob Weir: He was difficult to work with, inasmuch as he wouldn't want to rehearse a song more than two times, three at the most. And so we rehearsed maybe a hundred songs two or three times . . . This is sorta a standard critique of the way he works.

Dylan seemed to have reached a point in his life where he simply could not relate to his own songs, so detached had he become from prior experience. Hence, perhaps, his reluctance to work on them. However, as the 1986 tour had proved, the way to make things happen was to ease him into the process by playing the 'real old songs,' evocations of 'the only, true valid death' that would always retain their connection.

Jerry Garcia: He wasn't writing too much then, still isn't. I think he was looking for a new direction in which to take his songs . . . We talked about people like Elizabeth Cotten, Mississippi Sheiks, Earl Scruggs, Bill Monroe, Gus Cannon, Hank Williams. We tried a few of those things out at rehearsal. I showed Bob some of those songs: 'Two Soldiers,' 'Jack-A-Roe,' 'John Hardy,' and some others. Trouble was, Bob seemed to prefer to do these rather than to rehearse his own songs.

Sure enough, when the rest of the Dead permitted Dylan and Garcia to play a little bluegrass, on the likes of 'Stealin',' or revert to being folkies on traditional standards like 'John Hardy' and 'Roll in My Sweet Baby's Arms,' or country rockers on Hank Williams's 'I'm So Lonesome I Could Cry' and the Delmore Brothers' 'Blues Stay Away from Me,' or even try to twist the words out of Ian Tyson's 'The French Girl,' Dylan would begin to focus on the music. Though the Dead would continue to bastardize the likes of 'Minglewood Blues' in their own sets at the shows, it never seems to have occurred to them to let a singer thoroughly steeped in tradition share that road. They preferred to convene the night before each of the shows to confirm which dozen Dylan originals they intended to play the following day. Surprisingly, when they met up at the Red Lion Hotel, outside of Foxboro, on July 3, the night before the first show, it was Dylan who wanted to mix up the set, and the Dead who were angling for a more rigid repertoire—doubtless aware that they had just six shows to shape up in.

As it is, the results couldn't have been more ramshackle. Within two songs it was obvious, from the large video screens mounted either side of the stage, that Dylan wanted to be any place but where he was (when he figured out how close some of the video close-ups were, he sent very clear instructions for medium shots only at subsequent shows). The protracted tune-ups between songs he carried out with his back to the fans, and during the songs he either kept his head down, glanced up at Garcia (cue solo), or yelped his way through them. The voice sounded like it had incurred more wear and tear in the last year than it had in the eight years before the '74 Band tour, something his bedraggled appearance seemed to confirm. Nor could he figure out a way to bend the lines, as his backing band played straight through everything—middle eight, chorus, verse—as if it were all the same fodderstompf. One result was versions of 'John Brown,' 'Chimes of Freedom,' and 'Joey' almost akin to free verse, albeit with whole couplets falling by the wayside, as Dylan visibly blanked on unfamiliar words in an unfamiliar meter.

Though the shows simply had to get better, as Dylan's voice gained some range and the Dead recognized what passed for a cue, songs continued to stutter to an end and Dylan continued to mangle whole lines, one night killing off Joey Gallo in verse two. Though the final show in Anaheim verged on the semi-professional—Dylan pulling out 'Mr. Tambourine Man' for his ex-wife—the tour did nobody any favors. Still, perhaps Dylan could happily bank another coupla million and chalk it up to experience. After all, only the few thousand Dylan fans prepared to brave a sea of tie dye, and those Deadheads who stayed for the Dylan–Dead set, heard the fiasco—and, according to Jeff Tamarkin, in Deadzine *Relix*, 'before they came back with old Zimmy, *thousands* actually walked out.'

As it is, though, Dylan agreed to permit an official document of the tour, a *Dylan & The Dead* live album, and then, when the Dead provided a suggested sequence, pulled three of the best performances—'Wicked Messenger' at New Jersey's Meadowlands, 'Ballad of Frankie Lee and Judas Priest' at Eugene, Oregon, and 'Chimes of Freedom' at Anaheim—and replaced them with bland Anaheim run-throughs of 'Knockin' on Heaven's Door' and 'All Along the Watchtower,' songs already well represented on his live albums. He also insisted on the album being remixed after it failed to pass the ghetto-blaster test.

Jerry Garcia: We went over to his house in Malibu which is . . . out in the country somewhere . . . and he has these huge dogs which are like mastiffs, about seven of 'em. And so we drive up, and these dogs surround the car, and Dylan's kinda rattling around in the house, this rambling structure, and he takes us into this room that's kinda baronial—y'know, big fireplace and wooden paneling and steep roof. And on the table is about a thirty-nine-dollar ghetto blaster and he's got the cassette and he sticks it in there and he says, 'Don't you think the voice is mixed a little loud in that one?' So we just sat and listened to it on this funky little thing and he'd say, 'I think there ought to be a little more bass.'

In the years to come Dylan would talk about the Dylan–Dead tour as some kind of turning point, recognizing belatedly where he had taken a wrong turn. As he says, it took a tour like this to make him 'look inside these songs I was singing, [songs] that . . . at the time of that tour I couldn't even *sing*. . . The spirit of the songs . . . had been getting further and further away from me.' Deadheads have sought to take credit, on behalf of 'their' band, for the change that was about to come, even though the lessons Dylan took from the shows included how not to tour, what audiences to avoid, and who not to play with. To get to 'the spirit of the songs,' Dylan needed to return to a band who knew how to listen and learn.

What he needed most was to remember which songs he could still 'look inside.' One such song, which he had refrained from rehearsing with the Dead, was 'I Shall Be Released,' a song that promised 'any day now' to unchain the singer's melodies. He had not returned to the song since the death of Manuel—that is, until he decided to slip it between 'Masters of War' and 'Trust Yourself' at a show in Switzerland, three gigs into a tour of Europe in September 1987 with the Heartbreakers. The last time he had sung the song had been on a January 1986 telecast, during which the thief in the night reappeared as a lyrical preoccupation: 'He will find you where you're staying, even in the arms of somebody else's wife / You're laughing now, you should be praying, [this] being the midnight hour of your life.' If he was still reluctant to forsake 'the arms of somebody else's wife,' Dylan now chose to make that final couplet even more ominous: 'You're laughing now, you should be praying / Tomorrow might be your dying day.'

Like poor Richard, Dylan had generally preferred the traditional route to oblivion, a bottle of Jack Daniel's or its equivalent, to pills and powder. And, like Manuel, his alcoholic hazes invariably coincided with his darkest hours. By 1987, his drinking had again begun to get the better of him and when Kurt Loder arrived in Jerusalem on September 7 to interview him for a special twentieth-anniversary issue of *Rolling Stone*, he proceeded to sit through the interview drinking Kamikazes like they were Kool-Aid. Two days after he predicted tomorrow might be his dying day, an almost totally incoherent Dylan fell out of his chair after a hotel piano jam had found him hamming it up on 'You've Got a Friend' and 'I Left My Heart in San Francisco.' He was consuming up to four Kamikazes or, later on the tour, Kahlúa, cream, and cognac, before each show. That he could even stand some nights qualified as some kind of achievement. Journalists at the shows couldn't resist commenting on his shuffling demeanor, referring to his new image as the death-mask look.

And yet, however blasted he felt he needed to be to sing another set of blasts from the past, the Dylan that found himself singing 'I Shall Be Released' in Basel on September 10, 1987, suddenly found his performing muse had reconnected the cable. As he found himself stumbling between the old and new lyrics to 'I Shall Be Released', reaching for the feeling

that had not always been there, he suddenly began to hear her voice
again:

Bob Dylan: [In 1987] I'd kind of reached the end of the line. Whatever I'd
started out to do, it wasn't that. I was going to pack it in . . . I [couldn't]
remember what it means . . . is it just a bunch of words? . . . I had to go
through a lot of red tape in my mind to get back there . . . [In Switzerland,
though,] it's almost like I heard it as a voice. It wasn't like it was even me
thinking it: 'I'm determined to stand, whether God will deliver me or not.'
And all of a sudden everything just exploded. It exploded every which way.
And I noticed that all the people out there—I was used to them looking at
the girl singers . . . I had them up there so I wouldn't feel so bad. But when
that happened, nobody was looking at the girls anymore. They were looking
at the main mike . . . I sort of knew—I've got to go out and play these
songs. That's just what I must do. [1997]

Dylan himself located the epiphany to the second of two shows in
Switzerland, in Locarno on October 5, but on the evidence of the tapes
it seems clear that full service had been restored almost a month earlier,
at the first of twenty-eight shows in mainland Europe, after he had
opened the tour with two less-than-transcendent performances in Israel.

The shows in Tel Aviv and Jerusalem had come at the end of a nervous
couple of days for the band and crew. Dylan had decided to extend a
pre-tour, overnight trip to Egypt, staying at the Marriott Hotel in Cairo.
He had just been reunited with his old sidekick Victor Maymudes, on
whom the years in New Mexico had visibly taken their toll. Maymudes's
role, initially, was as understudy to Gary Shafner, whom Dylan had
informed the morning before the first show that he wished to take a bus
across the Gaza to Israel, rather than take the plane. The ten-hour journey
in a dust-filled bus, without air-conditioning, might have reminded
Dylan of how it used to be, but it also meant that there was no time to
rehearse for the opening show in Tel Aviv.

The two shows in Israel, his first ever, were not well received. Continuing the one principle worth acquiring from the Dead—an audacious
set list—Dylan had only served to confuse the Tel Aviv locals with the
likes of 'Señor,' 'I and I,' 'Dead Man, Dead Man,' 'In the Garden,' 'Joey,'
and, as an encore, the traditional spiritual 'Go Down Moses.' After
LA Times critic Robert Hilburn queried Dylan's choice of songs, the
following show in Jerusalem gave the Israelis more of what they wanted:
'The Times They Are A-Changin',' 'Like a Rolling Stone,' 'It's All Over
Now, Baby Blue,' 'Rainy Day Women' and 'Ballad of a Thin Man.'

Nevertheless, he continued to resent the media's attempts to place him in a time warp of their own choosing. In Basel, after reading a couple of negative reviews of the Israeli shows, he was heard to grumble, 'I don't think everything I've done since 1965 is irrelevant!' At that night's show, and for the remainder of the Temples in Flame tour, he would prove how disconnected the media had become from genuine performance art in the rock arena, combining audacious rearrangements of sixties classics with a thorough overview of his seventies and eighties albums.

Even with the set list ripped up, arrangements put through the shredder, and the Heartbreakers finally being put through their paces, the press response proved no better than on his two previous European tours. In the US, the only report (Hilburn's) came from his opening show in Tel Aviv, where circumstances—two shows commuted into one at the last minute, and a Saturday night crowd of young drunks, who heckled the support acts—hardly lent themselves to a transcendent occasion. But then, perhaps Dylan was right when he maintained, poolside at the Marriott in Cairo, that, 'the media is the devil and it won't be long before all it'll take is one charismatic leader to bring the whole world to its knees.' Hence, presumably, the restoration of such apocalyptic rants as 'Man of Peace,' 'When the Night Comes Falling from the Sky,' 'License to Kill', and 'Slow Train' to the set.

Most reviews to the contrary, this renewed association with the Heartbreakers was much more successful than the previous year's tours, primarily because Dylan began to approach the shows differently himself. Gone were the relatively uniform sets of the previous year, as were all uniform arrangements. The sets were astonishingly varied (fifty-six titles shared the fourteen- or fifteen-song sets) and duly abbreviated. Playing between seventy and seventy-five minutes most nights, Dylan was on the first encore of his third show before he repeated a single song from the two previous shows. Though most templates were in place from the two previous tours, the 1987 arrangements at last revealed the Heartbreakers' understanding of the artist at center stage, and his low boredom threshold, as they sought to reignite the flames of Farm Aid.

Benmont Tench: You can never let your mind drift. He'll give the most familiar song an odd twist; a change of rhythm or a peculiar delivery. Playing with Bob Dylan certainly gives you a good kick up the arse . . . One night he'll do something like he'll say—onstage—'Right, we'll begin with "Forever Young,"' and the Heartbreakers have maybe played the song once before. Then he'll say, 'And Benmont, you start it off.'

Unlike the shows with the Dead, the thirty-date Temples in Flame tour allowed Dylan time to put a little stretch back into his forty-six-year-old vocal cords, and though some shows started shakily, he was pushing himself vocally in a way he hadn't done consistently for six years or more. As the old confidence began to be revisited, he instructed Gary Shafner's girlfriend to make up the set list in Copenhagen on the 21st, which she duly did. Despite groaning that they hadn't rehearsed it, he agreed to do an electric 'Desolation Row,' Mike Campbell preserving its original melody line as Dylan weaved a vocal spell up, down, and around his lead. Four days later, in Gothenburg, he told the same lady that if he played 'Tomorrow Is a Long Time' that night 'everything will be all right.' And, sure nuff n yes I do, he devised a simple guitar–piano arrangement that could pierce the hardest heart. Indeed, this guitar–piano interlude would become a nightly highlight of the shows, later being expanded to two songs by the addition of a 'Don't Think Twice' alternating with 'The Lonesome Death of Hattie Carroll.'

The real highlights of the shows, though, as Dylan interspersed Germany with performances in Denmark, Sweden, and Finland, were nightly reinterpretations of a familiar trio of disaffected-love songs from 1974, 'Shelter from the Storm,' 'Simple Twist of Fate,' and 'Tangled Up in Blue.' Even if he refrained from rewriting the lyrics, each of these songs came alive as the voice, nicely sanded down by two weeks on the road, relived the price of infidelity.

No matter how much he poured himself into these songs from another lifetime, though, their lessons escaped him. His personal assistant, Gary Shafner, had been with him since the seventies, and a more loyal, reliable right-hand man would be hard to find. The death of his wife from cancer a couple of years earlier had devastated Shafner, but as of the winter of 1986, he had been seeing a vibrant, hands-on sometime realtor named Britta Lee Shain. The extent of her fan worship of his employer, Britta Lee wisely kept from her new suitor until she had successfully finagled her way into his setup. In September 1987, Britta Lee found herself accompanying her boyfriend on Dylan's third European tour of the eighties, and when Shafner was required to return to LA, two weeks into the tour, to attend to some business, she found herself on the receiving end of Dylan's charms full-time.

Even after eighteen months spent ferrying floozies, witnessing numerous examples of the unstable nature of the Dylan–Childs relationship, and seeing Dylan in both social and antisocial modes, Britta Lee remained entranced by the man. Dylan preferred to continue to keep his options open, though. Even if he and Britta Lee were now spending enough time together to co-author a song, ride a cycle in tandem, and succeed in finding Finland's only synagogue, the widow of one of his old session men had duly appeared and moved into Dylan's sleeping quarters. When, a week later, she returned home, Dylan proceeded to spend a night on the bus with the backing singers, perhaps on the run from some very personal demons.

As the shows maintained their newfound resilience into October, Dylan and Britta Lee seemed to have become inseparable. After the Rome show, October 3, they ended up celebrating Rosh Hashanah together at an Israeli dignitary's home, even if Dylan preferred to spend a romantic ride reading the Bible he invariably kept next to his journal on the bus. Afterwards, they returned to Dylan's room, where they were interrupted by Carole Childs calling, asking Bob to pay for some cosmetic surgery. Despite Ms. Shain's best endeavors, though, Dylan refused to make love on the grounds that it was still a high holy day and, anyway, it would be a sin against his 'best friend.' His resolve lasted barely twenty-four hours.

Whatever hijinks had kept Dylan, Neuwirth, and Maymudes amused in the sixties, Shafner was cut from a different cloth and had never adopted the amoral mind-set that made everything permissible when one was 'on the road.' Dylan proceeded to jeopardize a decade-long friendship, and one of the closest relationships of his working life, for a roll in metaphorical hay with a besotted girlfriend, something that cannot be said to reflect well on this particular Bible-reader.

That the lady had high hopes of the way the relationship might go was suggested one night in conversation with Maymudes when, after looking at some pictures Britta Lee had taken of Dylan, she said, 'I think we should use it as an album cover,' and Maymudes snapped back, 'We? I'm starting to get a bad feeling about all this.' Dylan had no such grand vision, as he duly confirmed the night before his English debut. Having flown in one of his new ponies, he casually suggested a little triad. Britta Lee passed.

The morning after, Dylan awoke to an all-too-stressful reminder that there are some women who will always haunt you, and who know exactly how to call you to account. It was Sara on the phone, and she had just found out about the baby Dylan had been buying clothes for all over Europe (presumably she was still unaware of his other young children). Not surprisingly, Sara was more than a little concerned about how their children might react to the news, and turned her slow-burn anger on her ex-husband for not telling them himself. Caught on the defensive, Dylan's only response until she hung up was to tell her to calm down, before teasing Britta Lee, 'A whole lotta women in this world have my babies.' Later, Maymudes would helpfully suggest to Britta Lee that she also might have one, as 'Bob always takes care of his kids.'

However, with Shafner due to fly in the morning after the first show in Birmingham, Dylan was already starting to remove himself from the scene of the crime. Though Britta Lee remains convinced that when Dylan sang, 'I'm pledging my time to you / hoping you'll come through, too,' that night at the NEC, he was singing it just for her, his actual intent, as always, was to play the Jack of Hearts. Unfortunately, he had not appraised Britta Lee of the rules of the road, and when Shafner joined her in her room, she told him she was in love with Dylan.

The fallout was almost immediate. Shafner flew back to LA, where he promptly took Carole Childs out for dinner and spilled the beans. Childs raced home to give Dylan his second long-distance berating of the week, informing him that she would be on a plane for London the following morning. As Childs was flying in, Shain was flying out, having been packed off by a worried man. When Shain told Dylan she couldn't get a flight out until morning, he just said, 'What're you crying to me for? [Tour manager] Elliott Roberts is the one who's holding your plane ticket.' Hasta la vista, baby.

If Dylan was ducking out from underneath the wreckage, yet again, he now threw himself into the final three shows of the Temples in Flame tour with a new urgency. The night before Shain's departure, he conjured up a marvelous harmonica-driven 'I'll Remember You,' while the night after, he sang, for the only time on the tour, a glorious 'To Ramona' in the piano–guitar slot, the most conciliatory of his 'I know better' songs, this one coming from the heart. The final show he was determined to make special. Apart from admonishing this ol' heart of mine, and musing about another simple twist of fate, he sang of salvation and damnation in fairly equal measures. In a fitting finale, he segued from 'Knockin' on Heaven's Door' to 'Chimes of Freedom' before bringing the tour full circle with a second and last performance of 'Go Down Moses.'

He knew it was time to let these people go. In particular, the Heart-breakers had their own careers to resume. Dylan would never again find such sympathetic musicality that never overplayed and always deferred to his better instincts. He had, however, rediscovered the drive to perform, and though his songwriting muse hadn't as yet rejoined her elder sister, he now knew he needed to find a standing band he could retain and refine. Saved from the more serious ramifications of Shafner's warranted enmity by Maymudes's return to the fold, Dylan returned to LA with Childs, after sharing a couple of days with George Harrison and his wife in Henley. Before resuming his search for a permanent band, he found time to turn on his TV set and tune in to NBC's ever-popular *Saturday Night Live*.

1988–90: Modern Work

Dylan was a revolutionary. Bob freed your mind the way Elvis freed your body. He showed us that just because the music was innately physical did not mean it was anti-intellectual. He had the vision and the talent to make a pop song that contained the whole world. He invented a new way a pop singer could sound, broke through the limitations of what a recording artist could achieve, and changed the face of rock & roll forever. Without Bob, the Beatles wouldn't have made *Sgt. Pepper,* the Beach Boys wouldn't have made *Pet Sounds,* the Sex Pistols wouldn't have made 'God Save the Queen,' U2 wouldn't have done 'Pride (In the Name of Love),' Marvin Gaye wouldn't have done *What's Goin' On?,* the Count Five wouldn't have done 'Psychotic Reaction,' Grandmaster Flash might not have done 'The Message,' and there never would have been a group named the Electric Prunes. To this day, wherever great rock music is being made, there is the shadow of Bob Dylan. Bob's own modern work has gone unjustly under-appreciated because it's had to stand in that shadow. If there was a young guy out there writing the *Empire Burlesque* album, writing 'Every Grain of Sand,' they'd be calling him the new Bob Dylan . . . So I'm just here tonight to say thanks, to say that I wouldn't be here without you, to say that there isn't a soul in this room who does not owe you his thanks.

—Bruce Springsteen, Rock & Roll Hall of Fame induction,
January 20, 1988

If the eighties had brought Dylan precious little recognition for his current work, it seemed he could not escape collecting awards for 'chang[ing] the face of rock & roll forever.' In March 1982, he had been inducted into the Songwriters Hall of Fame, despite not being able to read or write a single note of music. In November 1985, he was the subject of a tribute at the Whitney Museum in New York, attended by a veritable who's who of those who owed him their thanks. In March 1986, he had received a Founders Award from ASCAP (the American Society of Composers, Authors and Publishers). And now, the Rock &

Roll Hall of Fame. If Dylan seemed surprisingly touched by the plaudits of his peers, he insisted that what was 'more important was the recognition of Lead Belly and Woody, seeing them get the respect they deserve.' (Three years later, he would insist that if Johnny Cash is 'not in the Rock & Roll Hall of Fame, there shouldn't be a Rock & Roll Hall of Fame.')

Springsteen remained on a very lonely avenue, asserting that Dylan's modern work had 'gone unjustly under-appreciated.' His two most recent albums, *Knocked Out Loaded* and the still-unreleased *Down in the Groove*, hardly comprised 'songs that contained the whole world,' and a general re-evaluation of his latter-day work was still on the slow train. If Dylan's strategy for making people re-evaluate *Shot of Love* and *Infidels* was to make a series of albums that grew exponentially inferior, it was not going according to plan.

The remarkable surge that fired up the Never Ending Tour, birthed the Traveling Wilburys, and permitted a darker preoccupation to flower on *Oh Mercy* came from a recognition that, after three years staring at a creative brick wall, it was time to leap it. In fact, the walls that Dylan had begun to erect around not only his property, but his physical person, were denying many forms of beneficent input and stunting his creative soul. In this, he was not so unique. Many who owed him their thanks had similarly erected those walls as soon as royalties allowed, believing they could hide from all the inner fears that had initially prompted their all-consuming will to succeed. But Dylan had, for a long time, fiercely resented his detachment from humanity, even when the demands of others threatened to swallow him whole.

If a sense of isolation now indelibly marked his work, it had not as yet become the form of dread it would on *Time out of Mind*. In 1988, he still had the power to seize the moment, even if he had lost the power to be it. It was this sense of things slipping away that so oppressed certain critics and fans. Dylan's attempts to document the process made for some of his deepest, darkest work, even as it was illuminated by vestiges of that decade-old iridescent light.

(As I write, at the end of a decade when Dylan has contributed barely a dozen original songs to the canon, and not a single work of real stature, the creative block that body-checked the man's muse between 1985 and 1988 and the one that stretches from 1990 to the present certainly begins to seem like one great continuum, suggesting that the explosion of new songs in 1988–90 was but one last flare from the man's gun.)

Dylan's first recorded work of the year hardly permitted the darkness to impinge. But it served to remind him how, when it came to making music, informality invariably opened him up to a beckoning muse. Springsteen had had at least one ally that night at the Waldorf, when seeking to remind his audience of Dylan's ongoing creative struggle. George Harrison had witnessed Dylan's original bout of amnesia first-hand, and, though he had been witness to the rebirth of the Performer at Wembley in October, recognized the gait of a fellow amnesiac. When he appeared on a syndicated phone-in radio show, *Rockline*, in February 1988, Harrison insisted on reminding his audience of Dylan's credentials as a mature genius with an impromptu rendition of the song Springsteen had chosen to cite, 'Every Grain of Sand.'

The opportunity to push Dylan into writing songs again came unexpectedly, shortly after Harrison's on-air application for unpaid publicist. In early April, Harrison required a studio at short notice to record a bonus track for a European twelve-inch single, and wondered if he could use Dylan's garage setup at his home in Malibu.

George Harrison: Warners needed a third song to put on a twelve-inch single. I didn't have another song, I didn't have an extended version, so I just said to Jeff [Lynne]—I was in Los Angeles and he was producing Roy Orbison—'I'm just going to have to write a song tomorrow and just do it.' I was kind of thinking of 'Instant Karma'—that way. And I said, 'Where can we get a studio?' And he said, 'Well, maybe Bob, 'cause he's got this little studio in his garage.' . . . We just went back to his house, phoned up Bob; he said, 'Sure, come on over.' Tom Petty had my guitar, and I went to pick it up; he said, 'Oh, I was wondering what I was going to do tomorrow!' And Roy Orbison said, 'Give us a call tomorrow if you're going to do anything—I'd love to come along.'

If Harrison's memory serves him well, the Traveling Wilburys truly were the product of a series of simple twists. That Tom Petty, George Harrison, Jeff Lynne, and Roy Orbison assembled at Point Duma and, along with the homeowner, wrote and recorded a wholly impromptu single, 'Handle with Care,' was a chance happening. That they decided to proceed with the experiment, turning a one-off goof into an all-star long-player, was probably due as much to Warner Brothers' refusal to squander 'Handle with Care' on the back side of a twelve-inch 45 as to the refreshing informality of the initial arrangements.

Roy Orbison: George took the record to his record company and they said, 'This is much too good for a B side. We're not sure what to do with this.' And then we had the idea of putting together the album. We had all enjoyed it so much; it was so relaxed, there was no ego involved, and there was some sort of chemistry. So we'd go to Bob's house and we'd just sit outside, and there'd be a barbecue, and we'd all just bring guitars, and everyone would be throwing something in here and something in there, and then we'd just go to the garage studio, and put it down.

Tom Petty: We were a very self-contained group. We had one roadie and five Wilburys, and that was it . . . [Initially] we didn't [even] have a roadie . . . And you could see us all digging through boxes to find a cable and a cord: 'Well, there used to be one over there. Goddamn, I need new batteries for this.'

Once the decision had been made to replicate the process enough times to generate an album, it became a question of schedules, and it was Dylan's that proved the most problematic. He was planning a major American tour, kicking off in June, with his own band. The other Wilburys, though, were reluctant to proceed without their most note-worthy songwriter, and adapted accordingly.

George Harrison: He said, 'Well, I got a bit of time at the beginning of May,' so we just said okay, we had nine or ten days that we knew we could get Bob for, and everybody else was relatively free, so we just said, 'Let's do it! . . . We'll write a tune a day and do it that way.'

As a two-week crash course in the 'basement tape' aesthetic, the first Wilburys album perhaps shouldn't have come together as easily, nor have sounded half as engaging, as it did. If Orbison's almost operatic tenor, Harrison's Scouse whine, Dylan's jagged vocal edge, and Petty's southern accent blended surprisingly well, it was producer Jeff Lynne who articulated the album's real strength—'the [songs] hadn't been second-guessed and dissected and replaced—it's so tempting to add stuff to a song when you've got unlimited time.' Having spent the sixteen years since ELO's debut making records where time waited for him, nor was Lynne allowed any second guesses—unlike the next Wilburys installment.

Though each song had one or two major composers, each member contributed ideas to the melody, words, and arrangement. The first song they recorded at the bona fide Traveling Wilburys *Volume One* sessions was 'Dirty World,' a Dylanesque pastiche in the tradition of 'Leopard-Skin Pill-Box Hat' and 'Rita Mac.' According to Harrison, Dylan announced he wanted to 'do one like Prince . . . [and then] he just started banging away: "Love your sexy body . . ."' Ideas for songs that had been allowed to dissipate on *Knocked Out Loaded* and *Down in the Groove* were now being resolved in a communal process. Even if the resultant compositions were hardly 'Tears of Rage' or 'This Wheel's on Fire,' as he would tell a journalist the following year, 'Cooperation is great on something like that, because you never get stuck.'

The closest Dylan came to a serious statement on *Volume One* is the oft-overlooked 'Tweeter and the Monkey Man,' which, with its allusions to Springsteen song titles and its New Jersey setting, was taken at face value as another parody. In fact, 'Tweeter and the Monkey Man' had a less obvious model, Townes Van Zandt's 'Pancho and Lefty,' with which it shared its almost film noir sensibility, even down to the shootout at the 'riverside bridge, using Tweeter as a shield.'

George Harrison: 'Tweeter and the Monkey Man' was Tom Petty and Bob sitting in the kitchen, Jeff and I were there too, but they were talking about all this stuff which didn't make sense to me—Americana kind of stuff. And we got a tape cassette and put it on, and transcribed everything they were saying. And then Bob sort of changed it . . . He had one take warming himself up, and then he did it for real on take two; the rest of us had more time but Bob had to go on the road and we knew he couldn't do any more vocals again, so we had to get his vocals immediately. On take two he sang that 'Tweeter and the Monkey Man' right through.

That the song's narrator is intimately involved with events, yet stands one step removed at the fallout, links the song directly to the other epic ballads of Dylan's latter-day canon, 'Lily, Rosemary and the Jack of Hearts,' 'Joey,' and 'New Danville Girl.' 'Tweeter and the Monkey Man,' an aural Post-It sticker attached to a delightful confection, informed the more perceptive listener that there was more to come.

In the immediate present, the Wilburys sessions undoubtedly fired Dylan up for the road ahead. However, it seems unlikely that he gave the album a second thought when it appeared in the racks in October. He had, after all, just completed a five-month-long tour of the union, his most impressive and well-received American tour since the heyday of the Rolling Thunder Revue. Of course, the Wilburys' *Volume One,* with its exceptional cast of characters, was expected to sell well. But it did not seem an obvious candidate for Dylan's first platinum album of the eighties, and his first-ever double-platinum album. With over forty weeks in the charts, *Volume One* became one of the great commercial coups of the decade. Though there was precious little soul-searching going on, the album did feature some of Harrison's and Dylan's most accessible songs in years. It also opened up a potentially lucrative sideline for all five Wilburys.

Having seen the walls come down, Dylan now began to write a whole new type of song, attempting to do unselfconsciously what he used to do unconsciously. He would later describe them as 'stream-of-consciousness songs, the kind that come to you in the middle of the night, when you just want to go back to bed.' It had been a long, long time since the strands he returned to in the cold light of day had 'no sense of time.' After his attempts to replicate the craftsmanlike standards of Tin Pan Alley had yielded dross, Dylan was again looking to alchemize traditional forms of song.

It remains a guessing game which of the *Oh Mercy* songs came first, but two of the better candidates for the breakthrough that summer would have to be 'Series of Dreams' and 'Most of the Time,' two works revealing sunken depths, unfathomable in a single listen. 'Series of Dreams,' the more ambitious, is also the more lyrically self-conscious. Seeking to separate itself from linear time, it only achieved the necessary fluidity in tandem with an arhythmic atonality. 'Most of the Time' (and indeed 'Born in Time') flows down the same stream of consciousness without hitting any of the shallows that occasionally interfere with the progress of 'Series of Dreams.'

But Dylan's faith in his own faculties in the studio was all but shot, after a decade spent releasing a series of unrealized dreams. Nevertheless, he began to play some of his new songs to fellow musicians, as he tended to do when a breakthrough came. Harrison enthused about Dylan's new songs when promoting the Wilburys album in the fall, informing a skeptical world that the experience of recording the Wilburys had given him the urge to write again. Nor was Harrison the only songwriter privy to Dylan's new prototypes. A confidant more attuned to modern production values, at least when it came to giving songs with a familiar melodic quality the gleam of rain on a windowpane, proffered some advice.

Bob Dylan: Bono had heard a few of [my new] songs and suggested that Daniel [Lanois] could really record them right. Daniel came to see me when we were playing in New Orleans last year and . . . we hit it off. He had an understanding of what my music was all about. It's very hard to find a producer that can play . . . and [still] knows how to record with modern facilities. For me, that was lacking in the past. [1989]

Daniel Lanois's most high-profile work to date, U2 excepted, had been to give two important artists from the seventies, Peter Gabriel and Robbie Robertson, an ultra-contemporary sheen. Sadly, neither *So* nor *Robbie Robertson* repaid any skim beneath their Lanoisian surface. The role of the producer had changed out of all proportion since Dylan last mastered the process, and it was time for someone to 'push [him] around a little bit,' without assuming some consensual right to an equal say in the final product.

Bob Dylan: The recording studio itself is very foreign to me. The controls, the tape itself, the machinery is something that never really interested me enough to gain any control over [it] one way or another. It would seem to me you'd need somebody there who knew you, who could push you around a little bit. Daniel got me to do stuff that wouldn't have entered my mind. [1990]

The two of them first met in person when Dylan called in on a Neville Brothers session Lanois was producing in New Orleans, at the time of his September 1988 show there. The Neville Brothers planned to include two songs from *The Times They Are A-Changin'*—'Ballad of Hollis Brown' and 'With God on Our Side' (with a self-composed verse about Vietnam)—on their next album. Dylan enjoyed the informal nature of these recordings, made with a portable studio in an old colonial house in Louisiana, and dug the atmospheric sound Lanois had created for the well-received *Yellow Moon*. He also loved the idea of recording an album in this homestead of rock & roll.

Among the songs Dylan brought to New Orleans six months later was one catalog of troubles, 'Political World,' that was almost an update on 'With God on Our Side.' Though some of the other songs also trod familiar territory, with their portrayals of outlaws and saints struggling to remain true to themselves in a world on the brink, there were also songs of scourging self-analysis, notably 'What Good Am I?,' a surprisingly frank look at his own moral worth. His songs about personal relationships were now sad and resigned, hinting at the irreconcilable ('Most of the Time,' 'What Good Am I?,' 'What Was It You Wanted?'); while his songs on wider themes were once again suffused with the apocalyptic ('Ring Them Bells,' 'Everything Is Broken'). Each side of the album as released would end with the narrator stuck in a holocaust of terrifying proportions—'the water is high,' 'tree trunks uprooted,' 'the last fire truck from hell goes rollin' by.' By 1988, it required a conscious decision to confront the cacodemons of self-revelation.

Bob Dylan: Some people quit making records. They just don't care about it anymore. As long as they have their live stage show together, they don't need records. It was getting to that point for me. It was either come up with a bunch of songs that were original and pay attention to them, or get some other real good songwriters to write me some songs. [1989]

The *Oh Mercy* sessions first convened at a house in Emlah Court in New Orleans, at the beginning of March 1989, but something about the vibe, and possibly the musicians, wasn't quite right, and—with Lanois's portable Studio on the Move living up to its name—they relocated to 1305 Soniat Street, where they found something suitably surreal.

Daniel Lanois: We found an empty turn-of-the-century apartment building—a five-story building, a fantastic place . . . it had a bordelloish overtone. We essentially turned the control room into a swamp . . . we had moss all over the place and stuffed animals and alligator heads . . . On the record there's not really the obvious presence of synthesizers, just straight-ahead drums and bass and guitars, yet there's this blazing strangeness around it.

Reflective of the after-hours feel of many of the lyrics, the sessions were usually held late at night, and the composition of musicians seems to have been as casual as who was on hand and willing to play. Lanois himself contributed to all but one of the album's songs, providing dobro, lap steel, guitar, and even omnichord. Engineer Malcolm Burn was also required to turn his hand to tambourine, keyboards, and bass, and was rewarded, like Barry Beckett on *Slow Train Coming*, with a co-production credit. But it was the ease with which talented players could be rustled up late at night that delighted Dylan, who had grown tired of the punch-the-clock mentality of many an LA session.

Bob Dylan: Daniel just allowed the record to take place any old time, day or night. You don't have to walk through secretaries, pinball machines and managers and hangers-on in the lobby and parking lots and elevators and arctic temperatures . . . Some people expect me to bring in a Bob Dylan song, sing it, and then they record it. Other people don't work that way—there's more feedback. [1989]

Besides the band of willing cohorts a call away—notably guitarists Mason Ruffner and Brian Stoltz, bassist Tony Hall, and drummer Willie Green—Lanois's Studio on the Move came complete with its own set of textures. And that sound lent itself naturally to Dylan's music at this point, just because of the fluidity of his new song structures. Lanois knew the Dylan methodology well, and was more than happy to push the musicians to cut much of the finished record live. With only fourteen or fifteen songs he planned to record, Dylan was looking to make the album with his usual minimum of fuss, and the track sheets suggest he succeeded, cutting all the basic tracks in a matter of hours. However, the live vocals, almost without exception, were to be superseded by vocal overdubs, themselves subject to later lyrical tinkerings.

Daniel Lanois: Bob likes to get something quickly, if possible, in the name of spontaneity. On this record . . . some things came quick and we grabbed them that way. And then we spent a lot of time on detail. Some of the vocals we worked on quite a bit and the lyrics were changed and we chipped away at them.

As with *Infidels,* Dylan took a break from proceedings after the basic track sessions, hoping that these ten days might shine some clear light on the tracks already recorded. It seems to have worked. He returned revitalized, and in many cases with new sets of lyrics he wished to impose on the basic tracks. In the case of a song listed as 'Broken Days/Three of Us' on the track sheets, he had come to what appears to be the first overdub session, April 3, with a whole new song. Unfortunately, 'Everything Is Broken' stripped the original song of its evocation of a fragmented relationship (or two), becoming the Sears catalog version of 'Times Ain't What They Used to Be.' Other rewrites were considerably more successful. 'Shooting Star' in its original form had the motif and that apocalyptic middle eight full of fire trucks from hell, but none of the tight circularity of the finished version.

Almost all of the multitracks to the *Oh Mercy* songs contain multiple vocal tracks which Lanois, if he so chose, could punch between. On 'Dignity,' there was a live vocal from the March session and three vocals from the overdub sessions, two of them a week apart. The last of these vocals is identified on the track sheet as 'woman lyrics,' suggesting that in the interim Dylan had indeed been 'chipp[ing] away at them.' How much each vocal track contributed to the finished version, only these multitracks are ever going to reveal.

Though many a critic who had despaired at the sound of Dylan's more recent albums enthused about the sound on *Oh Mercy,* it was evident that rock music's foremost lyric writer had also rediscovered his previous flair with words. His powerful reinterpretation of the 'Daemon Lover' motif, 'Man in the Long Black Coat,' the convincingly resigned

'Most of the Time,' and the portentous but wistful 'Shooting Star' revealed lyric writing as incisive and acutely human as the best of his daunting canon.

Daniel Lanois: Bob Dylan is a very committed lyricist. He would walk into the studio and put his head into the pages of words that he had, and not let up until it was done. It was quite fascinating to see the transformation that some of the songs made. They would begin as one story and at the end of the night they would be something else. One of my favorites is 'Man in the Long Black Coat,' which was written in the studio, and recorded in one take.

'Man in the Long Black Coat' and 'Ring Them Bells' appear to have been the only 'live' vocals to survive the second set of sessions intact, as Dylan finally sought to embrace the possibilities of the technology to hand. Not surprisingly, much as he reveled in the opportunity to rework his lyrics after the fact, his natural antipathy for the environment began to get the better of him some way through these sessions. With just a producer and an engineer to interact with, the doubting self that had repeatedly snuck into the process at the death to deal a mortal blow sought to do so again. Lanois, though, now knew the right incantation— No!—and the sessions were permitted to arrive at a resolution.

Daniel Lanois: With all records there comes a time when people get a little bit lazy, because it's a tiring and unnatural process. At that lull it's very important to take command and turn that . . . valley into a mountain; whatever it takes to reach that mountain is what you have to do at that point to turn the record into a great record. There came a time with Bob Dylan when I felt he fell into old habits—'Get somebody else to play on it,' he'd say, or 'just hire somebody,' when really he should have been playing the parts. And I made it clear to him that we weren't going to fly anybody in, and we weren't going to have session players play these parts. The parts would be played by the people in the room, by himself, by myself, by the engineer Malcolm Burn, by the neighborhood guys that we'd chosen to be on the record. It was not going to be a studio record. He was going to play the parts, and if they were a little sloppy they would be accepted that way.

The release of *Oh Mercy* capped a year when several of rock's soul survivors had come back with their best work of the eighties: Neil Young, with *Freedom,* and Lou Reed, with *New York,* being other outstanding examples. Sharing *Infidels'* sense of fraying mortality, and its patchy but occasionally dazzling brilliance, *Oh Mercy* suggested there was considerably more life in this sixties survivor than other renegades from that decade, like the Stones, the Who, and Paul McCartney, all of whom made the circuit of American arenas and stadiums that summer, playing to huge numbers of fans, old and new, all searching for a time machine.

And yet, even after enthusiastic reviews, on the back of the Wilburys' success and fifteen months of sustained touring, *Oh Mercy* didn't achieve re-entry into the Top 20. But at least it proved to be Dylan's most consistent seller since *Infidels,* the album with which—in its lengthy gestation, methodology, and thematic preoccupations—it had the closest links. And, at year's end, it was his only appearance (the Wilburys album notwithstanding) in *Rolling Stone*'s Hundred Best Albums of the Eighties (at number forty-four). Reflective of a new positivity about his ongoing importance, the magazine even suggested that

While it would be unfair to compare *Oh Mercy* to Dylan's landmark Sixties recordings, it sits well alongside his impressive body of work. It is also an encouraging sign that Dylan's creativity will continue to flourish in the coming decade.

In fact, as with his only other credible candidate for inclusion in this chart, 1983's *Infidels,* Dylan had had the songs to make an album that could more than rub dubs with those 'landmark Sixties recordings.' He had even realized those songs under Lanois's steady gaze. *Oh Mercy* was yet another collection where he had, after all the thrust and parry of the recording process, failed to finish the job. The perversity that had increasingly displaced sounder instincts had led Dylan to find slots for 'Political World,' 'Where Teardrops Fall,' and 'Disease of Conceit,' songs that limped from lyrical lapse to lyrical lapse, rather than permitting songs like 'Dignity' and 'Series of Dreams' to display his desperately bleak worldview in all its warped glory.

This time, though, he did not intend to wholly abandon these children of the night. In the case of 'Series of Dreams,' Lanois pushed Dylan as far as he felt he could to include it on the album, but finally accepted the artist's right to call the shots—even if he substituted them with blanks. If the songs did not come as easily as before, and time spent honing lines was perpetually invaded by past references, he could no longer afford to discard the songs that didn't fit onto the current collection. Though, in the end, Dylan would not return to the approach adopted on 'Series of Dreams' for another eight years, another *Oh Mercy* outtake became the starting point for his next foray.

As in 1989, the early months of 1990 were primarily taken up with writing and recording not one, but two new albums, as the songs continued to come. Unlike *Oh Mercy*, though, Dylan was determined to sandwich sessions between shows, so that the follow-up was the product of considerably less studio time than its predecessor. The basic tracks to *Under the Red Sky* came from just half a dozen sessions in January and March, produced by the Was brothers, whose production duties sometimes took a backseat to their own band, Was (Not Was). Originally from Detroit, Don and David Was were recommended by Debbie Gold, a long-standing confidante whose credentials also included services rendered to Springsteen and Garcia.

Dylan originally played the Was brothers a demo of 'God Knows,' a song he had attempted at the *Oh Mercy* sessions without giving it enough of an identity to lift it out of Lanois's swampy soundscape. On or about January 6, 1990, the Was brothers attempted to give the outtake the Was touch, assembling an entirely different sound from anything Lanois dreamed of in his philosophy. The musicians who arrived at Oceanway studio that day had all been summoned at David and Don's behest, so that Dylan was initially nonplussed by the identity of the personnel, even as a fan of the Vaughan brothers since the Double Trouble days.

Don Was: The personnel for the first session was Stevie Ray and Jimmy Vaughan, David Lindley, our keyboard player from Was (Not Was), Jaimie Muhoberac, Kenny Aronoff. I played bass and Bob was set up at the piano. And he walked in and Stevie walked up to him. I don't think they'd ever met before and he said, 'Hi, Stevie Ray Vaughan.' But Stevie didn't have his hat on and Bob [was] just like, 'Yeah, sure,' and kept going . . . and then he saw Jimmy and he flipped . . . And then he saw Lindley. Then he realized it was Stevie Ray, and he went back and he was very warm and very excited about having Stevie Ray on the record.

Whatever demo version of 'God Knows' Dylan had played to the Was boys—and it was probably not the *Oh Mercy* outtake—as soon as it came time to record his vocal live, Don immediately felt that something wasn't quite right.

Don Was: When he sang his first vocal I thought, 'Aw, man, he sounds real nasal and it doesn't have that full rich tone that I was hoping for.' Fortunately, before asking him to sing again, I tried stripping the track down to the rhythm guitar and his vocal. And, *voilà*! It sounded like the same voice that was singing on *Another Side*. It wasn't that he hadn't sung well, it was that the snare drum and the guitar were playing in the same tonal range where the warmth in his voice was. I thought: *That's* what's been going on in these records.

Even if Dylan hadn't intended to do a great deal more than see if he could un-Lanois-ize 'God Knows,' the Was / Vaughan brother combinations seem to have pushed him into consolidating the sound on a couple of other songs sketched out in his pocket. And if 'God Knows' was 'one that we had difficulty with,' Don Was recalls the other three songs cut that day being 'much smoother.' In fact, '10,000 Men' seems to have started, and ended, life as a one-take jam over which Dylan pulled a number of images from half-remembered nightlines. What sounds like the dynamo being cranked up at the beginning of the song is actually the multitrack whirring into life as somebody behind the glass realizes this ain't just Dylan riffing in the studio. 'Cat's in the Well' also jump-starts, in waltz time, as Dylan dances out the world's destruction.

'Handy Dandy,' on which Stevie Ray was finally allowed to slide into trouble, was no such off-the-cuff exercise. Even though it would be subject to some lyrical recrafting at the overdub stage, 'Handy Dandy' portrayed someone still hounded by the moonlight in his soul. As with 'Cat's in the Well,' the song seemed, at least for its duration, to release its author from a sea of troubles. '10,000 Men' excepted, the songs from the January session suggested a vague empathy with the darkness settling in the man's cranium. Dylan certainly seemed to have another album of real quality within his grasp, barely nine months after the completion of *Oh Mercy*.

But the second installment would have to wait for him to return from the briefest, and best, of all the jumping-off points for the Never Ending Tour, ten dates in Paris and London in February. The energy of these shows sustained Dylan through to the final night at Hammersmith Odeon and, on its internal lyrical evidence, prompted one of his stranger tirades against the media juggernaut, 'TV Talkin' Song.'

On his return to LA, he was keen to see if the second stage of the process could come as easily as the first. Offered the opportunity for a dry run at his new sound, Dylan assembled Lindley, Aronoff, and bassist Randy Jackson at a rehearsal studio in Culver City to film a live perform-ance video of 'Most of the Time.' Ostensibly promoting *Oh Mercy*, the new 'Most of the Time' had none of the subterranean sonority of Lanois's sound, instead giving a very public intimation of the sound Dylan was now reaching for, a thudding presentiment of *Under the Red Sky*.

The most disturbing use of this sound, though, Dylan refrained from making public at all (though the bootleggers obliged, on *Genuine Bootleg Series Vol. 3*). The original 'TV Talkin' Song' remains one of the most scary songs in his post-evangelist canon, though there is nothing in this tirade against TV dads and TV moms living under bombs that one couldn't have suspected from reading all those mid-1980s interviews in which he pooh-poohed all accoutrements of 'progress and the doom machine.' Crossing the preacher of 'Black Cross' with Frankie Lee, over a spraypaint of lead instruments rooted to an ever-present slapback bass, he intones a story of a crazed mob hanging an orator from a lamppost at London's Speakers' Corner for suggesting that TV rots the brain.

Perhaps the sentiment scared even its author, as Dylan turned back from the more disturbing aspects of this vision, overdubbing a more innocuous set of lyrics—in which the orator survives, as does the post-nuclear family—over a more anodyne backing track. Thus were the Was boys introduced to creeping second-guessing, a studio-only ailment that Dylan had become increasingly prone to.

David Was: I didn't think he was improving upon ['TV Talkin' Song'] after a certain point . . . [When] it underwent the revisions at mix time, I think it lost something.

Another of the stronger songs at the March sessions was, itself, a second guess. The *Oh Mercy* outtake of 'Born in Time' was one of those Dylan performances that so surrendered itself to the moment that to decry the lyrical slips would be to mock sincerity itself. Revisiting the song, Dylan ended up recording three vocal takes and picking the most self-conscious—and, therefore, the least convincing—though none of the trio held a candle to the shining star of a performance at 1305 Soniat. By this time, Dylan was also revisiting other bad habits, burying true sentiments beneath clever phrases, turning the original self-reproach of 'I took you close, I got what I deserved,' into something as simplistically sappy as 'You won't get anything you don't deserve.'

David Was: I started to develop this unified field theory, that if something was too beautiful, if it looked like it was trying to please, then it was against his purposes . . . It's not necessarily out of a lack of generosity of spirit . . . It says more about . . . his inability to yield to audience-pleasing.

One song that suffered no such second-guessing, indeed seems to have not even been permitted more than two takes, became the title track for Dylan's second collection in a year, the much-underrated 'Under the

Red Sky.' Using images culled from children's songs and the folklore of the nursery, the song was dismissed as some kind of joke. In fact, it is the only song from the album to feature regularly in concert a decade later; the only nineties selection chosen by Dylan for his third greatest-hits collection, in 1994; and the one song that he was prepared to discuss with one of his producers:

Don Was: That's the only time I really ever asked him about a lyric and he told me about it. He said, 'It's about my hometown.' . . . It's such a great little fable. These people who have all this opportunity and everything, and they choose to be led around by a blind horse, and they squander it. It's beautiful and it was so simple, and he just sang it one time through, and it was perfect.

If the second set of sessions had not gone as smoothly as the January session, by the end of March he had another set of songs he could turn into a strong album. Or not. As co-producer David Was later said of the experience, 'Bedside manner I think is 90 percent of a job . . . Can you get someone in the mood to work? Especially a reluctant dance partner like Bob who . . . I think . . . fights every minute of his day between the necessity of doing what he does and the contingency of it.' Thankfully, Dylan wasn't about to abandon these songs to the nether regions of vaultdom, even if the Was brothers ended up reaching for the hair glue at the end of the process.

David Was: The first song we were mixing, he breaks out his papers again and says he's gonna redo the vocal. Now, if you say you're gonna redo the vocal at the mixing session, the producer starts to lose his mind! . . . Well, in fact, it happened on every song. He redid the vocal . . . At the moment before he sings it, he's still writing, and after he's recorded it, he's still writing, and then at the mixing session, he's still writing . . . [But] somewhere in there is the most formidable trove of fragments, both in terms of language and blues phrases, and . . . when the time comes to have to record some songs, he runs a kind of random program and this phrase or image winds up with this one.

In at least two cases—'Two by Two' and 'Unbelievable'—Dylan completely rewrote the lyrics at the overdub sessions, though even the rewrites failed to salvage 'Two by Two,' an incantation best left to Sunday school singers. 'Unbelievable,' on the other hand, had one of the nastiest Dylan riffs since 'Band of the Hand,' and attitude to spare.

The overdubbing process also involved some curious cameo appearances, reminders from his past. Al Kooper dolloped organ all over the Vaughan boys on 'Handy Dandy,' George Harrison sidled in to lead his guitar around on the title track, and David Crosby added backing vocals to 'Born in Time.' All three were impressed by Dylan's dedication to the task.

Al Kooper: On some record I think he learned what the pros were [of overdubbing] and now, Don tells me, he works for hours on vocals, getting it just the way he wants it . . . I think that's positive, not negative.

Under the Red Sky was completed and delivered before Dylan resumed life on the road, in Montreal on May 29. It was an album with a unity of sound and a sense of purpose. The rough edges had not been honed. It had that 'gutbucket rock & roll' feel that he had been searching for on *Knocked Out Loaded,* and parts of *Down in the Groove,* but had been unable to find since the title track to *Shot of Love.* However, the album received nothing like the plaudits for *Oh Mercy.* Indeed, *Rolling Stone* reviewer Paul Evans suggested that after the 'evolving, fully chromatic splendor' of *Oh Mercy,* Dylan 'had made us hope for so much more.' Once again, Dylan was being made a prisoner of past achievements. The most perceptive reviewer was Allan Jones, in England's *Melody Maker,* who placed the album in context, and set himself apart from a hastily conceived critical consensus:

There are people who will find *Under the Red Sky* well nigh unlistenable . . . [It] has already come in for a fair amount of ridicule. And for sure, it will seem to many a sharp disappointment after *Oh Mercy,* whose brooding introspection and melancholy reflections it puckishly refuses to echo or pursue . . . But when the dust settles, and the listener stops looking pointlessly for something as obviously magisterial as 'Most of the Time' or as noble as 'Ring Them Bells,' the LP quickly becomes approachable and the Was production begins to make more sense.

Harrison's presence at one of the last *Red Sky* sessions came as Dylan prepared to re-embrace the Wilburys' more devil-may-care attitude to record-making. The death of Roy Orbison, in December 1988, had temporarily put the kibosh on a reunion, but the demand for a second album remained far greater than for new product by its constituent parts (Petty excepted), and paydays like the one at Coldwater Canyon came rarely these days. The vitality of the experience, though, could never come close to *Volume One.*

Jim Keltner: They wanted to do [*Volume Three*], they knew they sorta had to do it, but, no, it wasn't the same at all. From my point of view I enjoyed the second album more than the first one musically, because we played virtually all the stuff live. [It was] recorded at this big old estate at the top of Coldwater Canyon and this big old room, and I was facing the guys . . . [but] Roy wasn't there. It was a good effort but the tremendous spirit from the first one wasn't there.

Tom Petty: There was no Roy Orbison. And it was done under different circumstances . . . Everyone was looking at you pretty hard this time. Whereas the first one was just sort of a party, this was more serious work, and yet done in a hurry . . . I like the songs we did, I just don't think it was a commercial record, and I don't think it was intended to be.

Without the Orbison baritone, and with all parties deferring to a newly galvanized Dylan, the jokingly titled *Volume Three* could have easily ended up as a Lynne-produced addendum to *Under the Red Sky*, particularly as it was released six weeks after Dylan's own collection. Of the thirteen originals recorded for the album, Dylan was vocalist and main songwriter on six, and chipped in on a further three. Unlike *Volume One*, where there was little need to distort the nature of each party's input, on *Volume Three* there seems to have been a concerted effort on the part of Lynne and Harrison, after the tapes were conveyed to Henley for post-production, to present a more egalitarian model than the sessions supported. As such, one of Dylan's better solo contributions, 'Like A Ship (On the Sea),' was dropped altogether, while 'She's My Baby' and 'Where Were You Last Night?,' aside from being given the full Jeff Lynne treatment, substituted secondary Wilburys for sections of Dylan vocals. The result was an album that lived down to Petty's billing, an intentionally uncommercial collection that successfully quelled any demand for a genuine third volume.

In the seven years that separated *Volume Three* and *Under the Red Sky* from Dylan's next collection of original songs, the suggestion would gain ground that these albums were little more than afterthoughts to the more fully realized *Oh Mercy*. In fact, though some of the decisions at the overdub and mixing stage on both projects remain questionable, *Volume Three* was a bravely traditionalist album of which Orbison would have approved, while *Under the Red Sky*—an audacious attempt to make an album quite unlike its predecessor—fully succeeded in having an identity all its own.

Previous chapters have detailed Dylan's struggle to come to terms with modern technology, with the new limits age has imposed on his singing voice, and with his second great creative drought. With the Wilburys' *Volume One* and *Oh Mercy,* he had seemingly banished the doubts and, in the latter's case, wrapped the songs in an alluringly subterranean sound. Both albums garnered good sales, as well as positive reviews. If the Dylan on *Under the Red Sky* once again confounded his critics, he showed wiser souls he still had the ability to conjure up profoundly disturbing images and wrap them in a cogent sound spanning the entire era of rock & roll. The album's stripped-down, guitars-blazing ambience also tipped a hat to the sound he and his band had been touting around the world the previous three years. But the commercial and critical failure of *Under the Red Sky*, compounded by the general apathy that greeted the second Wilburys collection, seems to have prompted him to abandon making albums on the run. Since this was the only way he knew how to make albums, the result was silence. Dumping his muse by the roadside, he again lit out for parts unknown.

1988–90: The Never Ending Tour

36

This guy happens to be far and away the seekingest troubadour of his era but, in the end, five hundred years ago, he'd have pulled his wagon up to the fair in the village, and pulled the curtains open in the back. That simple and that honest.

—*David Was*

When I [have been] touring, it [has been] my line of work, to go out there and deliver those songs. You must accept that in some way. There's very little you can do about it. The only other thing to do is not to do it.

—*Bob Dylan, 1968*

Since 1975 the primary arena for Dylan's art has unquestionably been the stage, if it was ever the studio. After his halfhearted return to live performance in 1974, the Rolling Thunder Revue represented a triumphant return to form. It affirmed, not only to the press and the punters, but to Dylan himself, that he could still cut it up there, where it mattered. Nineteen-seventy-five was also the year when he seems to have realized that technology had passed him by. No longer did he feel comfortable in the studio. No one among his contemporaries went into the studio and recorded an album in a matter of days. No one except Dylan, who recorded the bulk of *Planet Waves* at two sessions, the original *Blood on the Tracks* at three, and two-thirds of *Desire* in a single session.

From there on in, though, Dylan would increasingly struggle to get his vision onto vinyl (and/or CD). Though at the onset of the Never Ending Tour anyone else would have been proud of a post-*Blood* legacy that included *Desire, Street-Legal, Slow Train Coming,* and *Infidels,* he would have been the first to admit that the results had only been sporadically satisfying. Most of the time, he committed his artistic energies to something far more spontaneous.

Bob Dylan: What I do is more of an immediate thing: you stand up on stage and sing—you get it back immediately. It's not like writing a book, or even making a record . . . What I do is so immediate it changes the nature, the concept, of art to me. [1981]

However much he had been responsible for expanding the parameters of popular song, Dylan continued to prefer to portray himself in terms of more traditional troubadours. In interviews, his points of reference remained Doc Watson, the Stanley Brothers, Cisco Houston, Sonny Terry, 'and Lead Belly, too.' Like poor Cisco, he pictured himself staying on the road until the doctor finally read him the last riot act. The struggle to reconcile the desire to perform with the inspiration to write had never been easy. Since February 1986, when he had recommitted himself to the road, it had become an increasingly uneven contest. Two extended tours in 1986, and two further tours the following year, reinstilled the bug to perform.

The Heartbreakers, though, could never commit themselves to the type of relentless touring Dylan now had in mind. Indeed, a touring band remained an intractable problem for him. In 1975, he had assembled the first of his rolling revues—a tour that would never end, a free-rolling express through the heartland of America. It was not to be. In 1979 Dylan assembled another kind of medicine show. Preaching the gospel from place to place, only months after completing an 115-date world tour, he again committed himself to the road, this time the one that 'leads to Calvary.'

When the fervour went out of that particular roadshow, and his Rundown touring group was disbanded, Dylan seemed, for the first time in six years, weary of the road and reluctant to live the life. Save for a twenty-seven-date tour of Europe in the summer of 1984, his four-and-a-half-year respite endured until the Heartbreakers came to his aid in the fall of 1985.

But Dylan knew his time with the Heartbreakers was up at the end of the 1987 European tour, even if the live epiphany in the Alps restored a resolve to create his own traveling band. Barely a month after that alliance had burnt down its last temple, he was in New York rehearsing at Montana Studios with a band led by guitar maestro G. E. Smith, the bandleader for the in-house *Saturday Night Live* combo, augmented by Danny Kortchmar, guitarist on *Shot of Love*; bassist Randy Jackson; and Expensive Wino Steve Jordan on drums. How long they rehearsed, and what mission statement they were given, has not been documented, but on the basis of a single rehearsal tape, from November 22, the combination proved less than inspirational.

As with the 1983–84 Malibu jams, Dylan wanted to play through some ideas and, if a genuine interplay became its natural by-product, so much the better. A couple of the songs, 'She's So Easy' and 'Carrying My Cross,' may even have been prototypical originals. But the choice of covers—Screamin' Jay Hawkins's 'Susie Q,' Glen Glenn's 'Everybody's Movin',' Johnny Cash's 'Folsom Prison Blues'—was largely formulaic. Only a dramatic cover of 'Trail of the Buffalo,' with a delightful accordion wash, suggested a purpose redefined.

The absence of backup singers probably already foretold an intent to strip things down. Though Jordan, Jackson, and Kortchmar were also deemed surplus to requirements by the time Dylan felt ready to resume the process, six months further down the line, he seems to have always envisaged constructing a sound around bandleader G. E. Smith. As rehearsals resumed in May 1988, G.E. brought in a young drummer named Christopher Parker, as well as guitarist and songsmith Marshall Crenshaw. Crenshaw was initially asked to play a six-string bass, an instrument favored by country pickers but hardly appropriate for a powerhouse trio.

Kenny Aaronson: Six-string bass and Marshall Crenshaw means to me . . . one of those old Danelectro six-string basses that they used to double the upright with in Nashville for more distinction. The six-string bassist would play with a pick . . . Now, that's not really the kind of a bass that's gonna give you real low end. It's more of a midrange instrument . . . Apparently he wasn't really playing as a bass player, more like he was just floating . . . [though] they would try different amps to get him to be louder.

Should Dylan have been planning a semi-acoustic format—backdrop drums, acoustic guitars with pickups—then the six-string bass might have worked. But all the evidence suggests he had a more guttural sound in mind. When he ventured down to rehearsals himself, having left G.E. to fend for himself for a few days, he was less than impressed with the combination, as he confided to new guitar tech Cesar Diaz.

Cesar Diaz: Bob went by the studio that first day of rehearsals and comes over to me. He goes, 'Who's that guy?' I go, 'That's Marshall Crenshaw.' He goes, 'Does he have any records out?' I go, 'Yeah, man, he's been around for a while.' He goes, 'Uh, I don't know, he should be paying us to give him guitar lessons.'

In fact, it was Dylan who was sorely in need of guitar lessons. He had always been able to hide that 'scrub-board style that grates through everything,'—having had the likes of Robertson, Ronson, Tackett, Taylor, or Campbell there to cover up the glitches—but with such a basic setup, electric rhythm duties devolved to him and, after twenty-five years in gentle stasis as a guitar player, he was now having to force himself to fit in behind the lead. Thankfully, fate conferred another stalwart rhythm section, allying Parker with another New York perennial, bassist Kenny Aaronson.

Aaronson's introduction was predictably sink or swim. Without keyboards or singers to work into the arrangements, Dylan was looking to work up a huge repertoire, something like seventy songs—though 'worked up' might be something of a euphemism. Like others before him, Aaronson was given less than a week to master not only the songs, but the method.

Kenny Aaronson: I got this call from someone who represented him saying, Can you come down to rehearsal tomorrow? . . . Bob didn't show up that day. I just played with the band . . . So I came down a second day and Bob showed up for that day, and then we started playing. They didn't even tell me if I had the gig. They just had me playing for days, and I was learning fifteen to twenty tunes a day. A couple of days before the tour starts, they finally say, 'Oh yeah, you got the gig.'

Cesar Diaz: The music sounded the best when Kenny was there, because he just dictated what he wanted to do. He didn't follow anyone . . . G.E. had pretty much no control of Kenny.

The format Dylan had in mind followed on from the more compact sets on the Temple in Flames tour, even if the sound was a million miles removed. Playing sets of, on average, fourteen or fifteen songs, he assembled a repertoire of over ninety songs in the first two months of touring. If Aaronson's cramming had had a purpose, as Dylan abandoned set lists for the second year running, he was at least spared the need to learn some of the more unexpected choices for the season, those introduced into the three- or four-song acoustic interludes that intersected the two electric sets. In these, a harmonica-less Dylan showed G.E. that, whatever his deficiencies with a Fender, he was no slouch when it came to an acoustic Martin.

Perhaps predictably, Dylan reserved his best vocal performances each night for the one or two traditional covers included in these acoustic sets. Giving his audiences an insight into his musical roots, with gorgeous renderings of folk classics like 'Barbara Allen,' 'Trail of the Buffalo,'

'Wagoner's Lad,' 'Lakes of Pontchartrain,' 'The Two Brothers,' 'Eileen Aroon,' and 'Man of Constant Sorrow,' as well as country standards like 'Rank Strangers to Me' and 'Give My Love to Rose,' the contrast sat surprisingly well with two sets of flat-out, bust-a-gut rock & roll, spat out à la '74.

Surprises were by no means confined to the acoustic portion of the shows. Indeed, the first short, sharp shock at each and every show was an amphetamine blast of 'Subterranean Homesick Blues.' This opening volley revealed the shape of things to come, as Dylan stuck fairly doggedly to his sixties repertoire. He did, however, feel confident enough in himself and his fellow musicians to drop songs into the set as the fancy took him. In some cases, like his latest single, 'Silvio,' the song lent itself to live performance so well that it remained in the set. Most, though, did not reappear, except on rare occasions. If large tracts of his work in the seventies and eighties were laid aside, regular workouts were given to the three obvious candidates from *Blood on the Tracks*—'Shelter from the Storm,' 'Tangled Up in Blue,' and 'You're a Big Girl Now'; a fairly consistent 'In the Garden'; and the soon-statutory 'Silvio.' Other diamonds from the mine—'Forever Young,' 'One More Cup of Coffee,' 'Gotta Serve Somebody,' 'Every Grain of Sand,' and 'I'll Remember You'—were rare but welcome excavations.

Kenny Aaronson: On the road, every so often, before the show G.E. [Smith] would come back and go, 'Fellows, Bob wants us to do this tune and here's how it goes.' And G.E. would show it to me and Chris Parker right before the show.

Among the one-off covers that cropped up in the electric sets were a couple of songs performed in the hometowns of the original songwriter: 'Nadine' in Chuck Berry's St. Louis and 'Hallelujah' in Leonard Cohen's Montreal. Dylan also occasionally felt compelled to try the occasional folk-rock arrangement. Though the stolidly traditional 'Wild Mountain Thyme' never made it past a single introduction, an impressive electric 'Pretty Peggy-O' became a Never Ending Tour perennial.

Cesar Diaz: Wasn't it dramatic back [in 1988]? I think that they handed me a guy who was wild . . . He was definitely like a wild horse when I got him. He was a bronco. You couldn't ride him, that's for sure. You could hardly communicate. He couldn't tell me what strings he used, what guitar, what gauge, what brand. There were no road cases. Here's a guy that's been on the road for thirty years—what happened to all his equipment?

Unfortunately, the less beneficial side of that wildness was in evidence at the first two shows of the summer. Dylan's sixty-five-minute opening show was not well received. The picnickers were merely perplexed by an audacious set that included two biblical belters and one *Knocked Out Loaded* debut. Far worse was the second show, two days later in Sacramento, when, after twelve songs and less than an hour on stage, he departed, refusing even an encore. Most fans assumed it was simply the end of the first set. After being informed that the show was over, they audibly made their feelings known.

The press barbs the following day seem to have sunk in, as Dylan was made to recognize his perilous commercial standing. Though it was his second major tour of the States in two years, the unchristened 1988 tour was very different from the True Confessions tour. An arena tour on the scale of 1986 had always been out of the question. Dylan's commercial stock was at an all-time low. *Down in the Groove*, released on May 31, 1988, coming two years after *Knocked Out Loaded*, suggested a man doomed to a never-ending decline in musical powers. Thankfully, as the band kicked into gear, Dylan rode his moods each evening until his energy began to prove contagious. That double hiccup was consigned to the history books, and the vast majority of reviewers began to spread the gospel of the Never Ending Tour.

Attendees at the third and fourth shows in California—whose most recent parameters of live Dylan were the final shows of 1986 and the last three DylanDead débâcles—must have been stunned by his rediscovery of purpose, reflected in a newly toughened voice that could still contain the most unexpected vocal twists. He had rediscovered something about the relationship between the singer and the song. As he embarked on the Never Ending Tour, he found himself observing:

my songs are different & i don't expect others to make attempts to sing them because you have to get somewhat inside & behind them & its hard enough for me to do it sometimes . . . nobody breathes like me so they couldn't be expected to portray the meaning of a certain phrase in the correct way without bumping into other phrases & altering the mood, changing the understanding . . . so that they then become only verses strung together for no apparent reason, patter for a performer to kill time.

No longer killing time himself, Dylan may have been the only party who envisaged his summer '88 tour stretching into the next millennium. As it is, the summer stint ended up crisscrossing the North American continent twice, starting in California in June, working across the Midwest to the East Coast, then across Canada, back down to California, up through the Northwest states, then back down the East Coast, before reaching Florida and Louisiana in late September. As if this were not enough, after a three-week break, Dylan slotted in two 'warm-up' shows in Philadelphia, finishing the performing year proper with four shows at New York's Radio City Music Hall. Seventy-one shows in four and a half months showed commendable stamina for a forty-seven-year-old man. He was committing himself totally to his performance art again, as the 1988 tour began to evolve into what Dylan himself would christen the Never Ending Tour.

Bob Dylan: It's all the same tour—the Never Ending Tour—it works out better for me that way. You can pick and choose better when you're just out there all the time, and your show is already set up. You know, you just don't have to start it up and end it. It's better just to keep it out there with breaks . . . extended breaks. [1989]

In fact, the 'extended break' between the last performance of 1988 and the first in 1989 was to be the longest on the whole Never Ending Tour, occupied as it was by the demands of a new, all-original album. The ninety-nine shows in 1989 retained the same format and, initially at least, the same set of musicians. He had already put the band through its paces, and knew just how flexible a tool they had become. Smith, in particular, had more than taken up the challenge of telegraphing Dylan's intentions to the rhythm section, introducing his own set of subtleties to the singer's gravelled road. The rehearsals, then, for the first European shows with his new sound, were not about working up a set, but figuring out which elements of the sound to preserve, and which to add. On the basis of the list of songs rehearsed, Dylan had decided to introduce a whole set of electric covers into an already eclectic mix.

Chris Parker: Among the stranger things we did [at rehearsals] were 'I Can See for Miles,' the Who tune; 'You Keep Me Hangin' On,' the Vanilla Fudge song, slow version; 'Where or When' by Rodgers and Hart; 'Mystery Train'—that's Junior Parker; something called '12 Volt Waltz'—that was pretty neat; 'Sweet Dreams of You'—Patsy Cline; 'Walking After Midnight'; 'Little Queen of Spades,' I think that's Robert Johnson; 'Poison Ivy'; 'The Blue Ridge Mountains'; 'High School Hop' [sic]—Jerry Lee Lewis; 'Mountain of Love'—Johnny Rivers; 'Ring of Fire'; 'Give My Love to Rose'; 'Love's Made a Fool of You'—Buddy Holly; 'God Only Knows'—the Beach Boys.

In fact, he sometimes had to be pushed into doing his own material. And yet, being pushed into focusing on his songs could be a rewarding experience.

Chris Parker: I requested 'When I Paint My Masterpiece' and he got out the lyric book and sang the lyrics, and to watch him singing, it was like rediscovering the song for himself.

Though the fans only heard a few of these songs, Dylan performed something like forty covers in the next six months on the road, the majority of these electric. The diversity of source material made for a crash course in popular song that bassist Kenny Aaronson, for one, found a little tough going.

Kenny Aaronson: The second time around . . . he was pulling out tunes that I'd never heard, and I was having a hard time there for a while. I was making notes constantly, and writing out charts, and going home with tapes that the sound man would give me.

The covers were one way Dylan endeavored to keep from getting bored with the regime he had committed himself to. Another was to rustle up a few more spare parts. At the initial rehearsals, the boys were augmented by a woman named Mindy, who had apparently been part of Billy Joel's band, and who was expected to contribute some acoustic guitar, fiddle, and backing vocals. At the rehearsals, she even warbled through her own versions of 'Both Sides Now' and 'Too Far Gone' before she was recognized as redundant. It was left to Dylan to restore a more traditional texture, ordering a brace of new harmonicas. As the songs he had just recorded down in Louisiana proved, he had spent the past six months looking deep into his soul, and the darkness unleashed in those songs—if not the songs themselves—was about to be carried abroad. The musicians who had previously found him reasonably outgoing—at least for someone so intensely private—saw another side return from the swamps.

Kenny Aaronson: He was a lot more distant . . . He seemed a bit more distracted. I'm sure that's one of the many moods of Bob Dylan . . . I found rehearsals with him the second time around very, very vague . . . Like he'll just play something and you kinda don't know what he wants you to do; and then you mess around and he'll never really tell you much . . . He hardly said a word or even hardly looked at me at all for [the] two, three weeks I rehearsed with him in '89.

Nor did Dylan prove unduly sympathetic when Aaronson informed him, just before flying to Europe, that he would be unable to complete the European leg, as he had been diagnosed with skin cancer. An immediate operation would probably be successful, but it meant finding a replacement in the interim.

Though the European sortie was a mere twenty-one shows, scarcely touching base with many centres of support, Dylan planned to return to the lucrative North American 'picnic circuit' immediately on his return. What he needed to shake by then was the almost uninterested state of mind with which he approached the opening shows in Scandinavia. He also needed to lose 'the hood.' In an extraordinary gesture of contempt for his audience, he had performed at the shows in Malmö, Stockholm, and Helsinki with an anorak hood over his head.

At the fourth show, the first of two consecutive gigs in Dublin, though still hooded, he at least began to approach his songs with a degree of commitment, as the set crept over the ninety-minute mark for the first time. He also conjured up a seemingly impromptu electric version of 'The Water Is Wide,' presumably a conscious tip of the hat to the Irish folksong canon. The tide had turned. The following night the hood was gone, and Dylan brought out U2's Bono for a rabble-rousing encore. On to Scotland and England, where the shows were full of pugnacious energy and Dylan's voice was restored to its previous strength, before resuming the European mainland campaign—just as Kenny Aaronson was saying au revoir.

Aaronson's replacement was Tony Garnier, who had played in one of G. E. Smith's earlier bands. His recruitment returned full control of the band to its leader. However, Garnier was a journeyman of a musician. Unobtrusive to the point of indifference, Garnier was a stand-in looking for a standing gig. Having flown into Dublin on June 3, and rehearsed with the band the following day, he found himself playing the first Dublin gig in the evening, as his paymaster introduced the most challenging set of the tour.

Unperturbed by Garnier's lack of rehearsal time, Dylan now began to pepper the shows with previously unperformed covers, including Sonny Knight's 'Confidential to Me,' Eddy Arnold's 'You Don't Know Me,' Townes Van Zandt's 'Poncho and Lefty,' and a compelling electric arrangement of 'Trail of the Buffalo.' As he began to enjoy himself again onstage, Dylan discovered another notch to his phrasing on songs of redemption like Hank Williams's 'House of Gold' and Thomas A. Dorsey's '(There'll Be) Peace in the Valley.' He even restored two songs from *Slow Train Coming* to prominence, 'Gotta Serve Somebody' and

'I Believe in You,' and, one night in Greece, sang a one-off acoustic version of 'Every Grain of Sand.' The holy slow train was back on the tracks.

If Garnier felt he was in at the deep end in Europe, Dylan's homeland debut failed to reveal shallower waters. The first half-dozen shows featured Never Ending Tour debuts for Van Morrison's 'One Irish Rover' and 'And It Stoned Me,' Gordon Lightfoot's 'Early Morning Rain,' and Lead Belly's 'In the Pines.' Dylan also mined the likes of 'Pledging My Time,' 'Driftin' Too Far from Shore,' 'I Dreamed I Saw St. Augustine,' 'Tomorrow Is a Long Time,' and 'Just Like Tom Thumb's Blues' from the back catalog. Equally impressive were versions of Don Gibson's 'I'd Be a Legend in My Time,' Steve Earle's 'Nothing but You,' Jesse Fuller's 'San Francisco Bay Blues' and Jimmy Cliff's 'The Harder They Come.' If he was reluctant to play any of his own new songs, Dylan was more than happy to honor a few favored contemporaries.

Unfortunately, the odd unexpected cover was not the only trend now introduced into the NET modus operandi. Dylan also began to show himself to be a less than honorable employer. Kenny Aaronson had headed up to Jones Beach, Long Island, on July 23, to inform him that the operation had been a great success and he was ready to return to the field. Though Garnier had stuck to his task, his bass playing lacked the rib-thudding resonance of Aaronson, who was also a far more colorful contributor to the band. Nor can there be any doubt that Aaronson had been led to believe that Garnier was only subbing until he proved himself fit to fiddle.

Cesar Diaz: I was there [when Bob told him,] 'If you ever get better, if you ever get cured, you can come back and get your gig. This is your gig, this is your home.' . . . So, boom, miracle happens, he gets better and they don't answer his calls, [so] he shows up at Jones Beach, and Bob wouldn't even come out and see him . . . I just didn't know that was the way Bob got rid of people.

Kenny Aaronson: That was a weird day for me, man . . . I got there and every guy in the crew came up to me and hugged me and in my ear whispered, 'When you comin' back, man? We miss you.' And I said, 'Well, I came to talk to Bob.' About half an hour, forty minutes before the show Bob's manager came up to me and said, 'Bob wants to know if you wanna come up and play some tunes.' I said, 'Sure.' Then, about five minutes before the show, Bob called me into the dressing room just to have a chat. He just wanted to talk, I guess, and see how I was doing. I was all focused on wanting to come back to work. So we talked for a little while and then I said, 'Well, do I look like I'm a sick guy? I'm ready to come back to work.' And he started giving me this beating around the bush kinda thing. 'Well, I wanna get out of this area and get up back out there and think about it, and I'm not sure if I wanna change the band right now.' Just gave me all this shit. Basically I got the vibe, y'know . . . He actually said to me, 'I don't give a shit who plays bass.'

Though the best NET shows were six months further down the road, the Smith-Aaronson-Parker trio would never be matched for sheer onstage dynamics. As Dylan did his best to make the summer shows sound fresh, introducing slow, taunting arrangements of three of his 1965 classics—'Positively Fourth Street,' 'Queen Jane Approximately,' and 'It Takes a Lot to Laugh'—he also began to embellish more and more songs with the piping whine of his (occasionally off-key) harmonica. As the shows began to stretch beyond ninety minutes night after night, the song endings began to deconstruct until the electric sets became almost a series of segues.

The plethora of covers, though, to which Dylan was bringing that extra degree of vocal commitment, seemed to be there at the expense of new songs. At one of the earlier rehearsals at Montana studio, in New York, he had stood outside the midtown high-rise, clutching his copy of *Lyrics,* and told Susan Ross, 'You know, no matter what anyone says, I have written my share. If I never write another song, no one will ever fault me.'

But it wasn't true. Fans wanted to hear the songs he had recorded only six months earlier. And when rehearsals resumed at Montana, on October 8, 1989, it was with the specific intent of revamping a now lagging sound with some contemporary observations revisited. The landmark residency at New York's Beacon Theater, October 10 through 13, turned the Never Ending Tour about, and returned it to the present. It also gave Dylan a renewed impetus that would sustain him through to the following summer, enabling a set of new songs and the finest days of the NET to neatly coincide.

Dylan again reinvented the band's role, pushing them to embrace the sea of possibilities. At the opening night at the Beacon, one of the most bewildering nights of the NET, he was again challenging audience preconceptions. Opening with a trio of songs that spanned a troubled decade, Dylan was almost fusing their components together. 'Seeing the Real You at Last' segued into a heartfelt 'What Good Am I?,' and on into a rambling 'Dead Man, Dead Man.' The third night also saw the welcome introduction of 'Man of Peace' into the set; the fourth, a powerhouse 'Precious Memories.' Though just two additional cuts from *Oh Mercy* initially entered the set, the second set was soon torn down, to be replaced by a five-song suite from *Oh Mercy*: 'Everything Is Broken,' 'What Good Am I?,' 'Most of the Time,' 'Man in the Long Black Coat,' and—with Dylan at the piano for the first time since 1966—a surprisingly impressive 'Disease of Conceit.'

The spirit of adventure carried over into some more tarnished gems at these fall 1989 shows. A startling, extemporized 'Queen Jane Approximately' at the third Beacon show proved that even a *Highway 61 Revisited* cut could have hidden depths waiting to be mined. The electric 'My Back Pages' was now treated to the vocal it had always deserved. 'Positively Fourth Street,' tinged by an underlying sorrow, was revealed as the long-lost brother of 'I Believe in You.' Dylan the sometimes erratic harmonica player was now challenging the band to push the envelope of each song. He was also starting to visibly loosen up. When a woman jumped onstage at a show in Sunrise, Florida, in November, and proceeded to strip to 'Tangled Up in Blue,' he carried on regardless, though a grin rarely left his face.

Having found the spirit in those Beacon nights, Dylan wasn't about to let it go. The traditional Christmas respite in Minnesota was cut short as he returned to LA to record some songs the first week in January. Six days later, he crossed the continent to play the most unexpected performance in a thirty-year career. On January 12, as a warm-up for two stadium shows in Brazil and ten further dates in Paris and London, he played his first club gig in over twenty-five years, at Toad's Place in New Haven. The seven hundred lucky witnesses saw this forty-eight-year-old man play for a total of four and a half hours.

Starting at a quarter to nine, with a cover of Joe South's 'Walk a Mile in My Shoes' ('before you accuse, criticize, or abuse / walk a mile in my shoes'), Dylan finally left the Toad's stage at twenty minutes past two in the morning, after four sets, interspersed by three breaks of just twenty-five minutes each, having played fifty songs in total, only eight of which derived from his supposed halcyon days of 1963–66. The majority of the songs were either previously unaired eighties originals like 'Tight Connection to My Heart,' 'Political World,' and 'What Was It You Wanted?'; some eighteen covers, embracing everything from Springsteen's 'Dancing in the Dark' to Muddy Waters's 'Trouble No More' via Kris Kristofferson's 'Help Me Make It Through the Night'; and several quite outlandish requests (after 'Joey,' he informed one fan that he had already played five of his requests).

Having shown off this coat of many colors, he just as quickly reverted to dressing subsequent sets in familiar favorites. The *Oh Mercy* songs, though, survived, as did an arrangement of 'Tight Connection to My Heart' that at least hinted at the greatness of its original archetype. If most of the Toad's covers fell by the wayside, they fell alongside uniform set lists, as Dylan re-established his credentials as the finest interpreter of his own works at ten shows in Paris and London, at which he performed some seventy-eight songs.

From *Oh Mercy*, only 'Shooting Star' and 'Ring Them Bells' remained unperformed during that February fortnight, while lovers of tradition were treated to acoustic versions of 'Barbara Allen,' 'Man of Constant Sorrow,' and 'Dark as a Dungeon' and electrifying reworkings of 'Pretty Peggy-O' and 'Hang Me Oh Hang Me,' the latter last performed for the BBC production of *Madhouse on Castle Street* twenty-seven years earlier. Though the European fans still welcomed the inevitable hits, the greatest cheers seemed to be reserved for the *Oh Mercy* songs. The English press for once shared the fans' fervor, responding with their best concert reviews in twelve years. The new catch-all music/lifestyle monthly, *Q*, captured the mood with a full-page review by an enthusiastic Adrian Deevoy:

On the opening night, he speaks, laughs and persistently performs a peculiar hip-swinging trouser manoeuvre that owes as much to Elvis Presley as Shakin' Stevens . . . It's one of many surprises—some verging on treatable shock—that Dylan springs during his triumphant six-night residency at the punter-friendly 3,500 capacity theatre . . . Of course, as is always the case with Dylan, anything could happen next.

As Deevoy suggests, the most unexpected aspect of Dylan's fully fledged renaissance was his demeanor. Having astonished fans at certain shows in the fall by diving into the audience during the last encore (the first time, at the Beacon, so confounding the uninformed band that they had to jam out on 'Leopard-Skin Pill-Box Hat' for three full minutes before being told to wind it up), at the Hammersmith shows he actually mumbled the occasional one-liner to the audience, at one point informing them that 'Watching the River Flow' was in fact a new arrangement of 'Subterranean Homesick Blues.'

By the North American shows in early June, he was being positively garrulous. When a reviewer, after bemoaning the lack of backup singers at the first show in Ottawa, suggested that 'as his mass popularity dwindles . . . he would do well to think about reaching out to his audience a little more,' Dylan decided to preface 'Boots of Spanish Leather' at the second Ottawa gig with a little market research:

Bob Dylan: There used to be a bunch of girls that sang with me . . . but they decided to let me try and play the harmonica for a while and they'd stay home. Anyway, it seems like there was an article in the paper about me The girls should come back and the harmonica should go . . . Anyway, the girls might be back next time. But it's okay to play harmonica on this one, right? [*Much cheering.*] Phew, what a relief! [1990]

Three nights later, in the middle of a guitar introduction to 'It's All Over Now, Baby Blue,' a request for 'Tomorrow Is a Long Time' caused him to stop and observe, 'It sure is. Awfully long,' before reverting to the requested tune, which he then embellished with some uncharacteristic flamenco flourishes. By now, the acoustic sets had evolved into a communal exercise, with Garnier taking to stand-up bass and Parker adding the lightest of brushstrokes.

Whether Dylan genuinely sought the interplay or just felt he wasn't getting value for money from his musical backers, this format would remain standard for the remainder of the decade. Meanwhile, money was again beginning to rear its presidential head as a third consecutive summer of Stateside gigs began to affect receipts—and spirits. When the second leg of the 1990 tour wound down in Switzerland on July 9, Dylan summoned up the nerve to ask G. E. Smith to take a pay cut from the ten thousand dollars a week he was apparently commanding. Recognizing the thin end of a very large wedge of cash (Dylan, after all, was still grossing a cool coupla million for each month spent on the road), and assured of his ongoing *Saturday Night Live* gig, Smith just said, Nein.

Dylan would later dub the first post-Smith leg the Money Never Runs Out tour. But the economics of maintaining a standing band were still bound as much by consumer demand as the logistics of the road, and he was now faced with a pressing decision—to subsidize a crack band out of ever-diminishing returns, as he had in 1979–80; to simply take some time out until there was a resurgence of demand; or recruit more musicians who would do what they were told, attend sound-checks and rehearsals (even when Dylan didn't), and generally put up with a decidedly offhand employer no longer interested in establishing a rapport with his musicians. Smith agreed to stay on board long enough to find a replacement, as several guitarists flung themselves onstage to prove their worth under his detached gaze.

Cesar Diaz: There were like seven people [auditioning for Smith's place]. We were out in somewhere like Tulsa, or Texas, and that's where we were having the auditions, and then they went on the road with us. Every once in a while a new guy would come in. One of the guys . . . asked Bob for an autograph right after he auditioned for Bob . . . He blew it. Only one of them came back, [John Staehely]. I saw him drink a pint of Jack Daniel's backstage before a gig, 'cause he was so nervous . . . Steve Bruton flew in his wife, thinking he was starting the shows at the Beacon Theater, and Bob just blew him off.

Even as they returned to the plush interior of New York's Beacon Theater for five shows in October 1990, having worked through onstage auditions for John Staehely, Steve Bruton, Miles Joseph, Steve Ripley, and even guitar tech Cesar Diaz, Dylan remained no closer to a definitive replacement for his versatile erstwhile bandleader than in August. And these shows were most assuredly G.E.'s final stand. At the couple of warm-up shows prior to New York, it seemed that Dylan had settled on Diaz and Bruton, but then Diaz found himself out on his own for the first three songs on opening night in New York, and was audibly sinking in the sound. Smith's belated appearance at his right side rescued Diaz, as he showed just how the newly debuted material from *Under the Red Sky* ought to be played. The lesson was not entirely lost on Dylan. He immediately reinforced the sound with second guitarist Staehely, who by default was temporarily assured of Smith's slot. With a further twenty-two shows booked through November, Diaz, Dylan, and Staehely attempted to beef up a sound that had previously been amply endowed by Smith's single ringing tone. It would take a long time for Dylan to take heed of this lesson in false economies.

It would be no exaggeration to say that, between June 1988 and October 1990, Dylan and G. E. Smith redefined the performance form of rock in an era when the pomp of the spectacle had increasingly drawn attention away from the essence of the rock & roll experience—live music played and sung with a commitment to the genre. Though Dylan would only begrudgingly admit the significance of Smith's departure—recognizing in his 1993 *World Gone Wrong* notes that 'there was a Never Ending Tour but it ended . . . with the departure of guitarist G. E. Smith'—he remained fully committed to the road as it stretched out of sight. However, the experience was no longer filling him with the necessary *joie de vivre*. As he stuck his head in Mississippi at the end of October, crew members were witness to Dylan's re-immersion in the moonshine blues again.

1990–91: A Man So Defiled

37

Bob went through what I would call [his] Picasso period, he actually took his art so low that all he had to do, to come back, was just to throw out a signal that he was still alive.

—Cesar Diaz

Happiness is *not* on my list of priorities. I just deal with day-to-day things . . . You know, these are yuppie words, happiness and unhappiness. It's not happiness or unhappiness, it's either blessed or unblessed. As the Bible says, 'Blessed is the man who walketh not in the counsel of the ungodly.'

—Bob Dylan, 1986

For some reason, I am attracted to self-destruction. I know that personal sacrifice has a great deal to do with how we live or don't live our lives.

—Bob Dylan, 1997

Writing in the fall of 1990, my conclusion to *Behind the Shades* (Take One) was that 'for the man born Robert Zimmerman, who is only Bob Dylan when he has to be, the future seems less [than] rosy.' The oppressiveness of the lyrics and his onstage demeanor reminded me of that sad quote from Suze Rotolo about the twenty-five-year-old Dylan:

Suze Rotolo: People live with hope for green trees and beautiful flowers, but Dylan seems to lack that sort of simple hope, at least he did from 1964 to 1966. This darkness wasn't new to me. [But] it became stronger as the years passed by.

My view, then as now, was that Sara had temporarily rescued him from that darkness, and his faith initially seemed to provide renewed light, but as the eighties progressed his faith seemed only to reinforce him in his view of a world gone mad, or just plain wrong. 'The most pressing question as Dylan approaches fifty,' I mused, was whether the darkness would continue to grow, and how the artist in him would deal with it if it did . . .

The darkness can be most beguiling. Dylan had twice before surrendered to the night, and the results had been devastating (def. 1: 'to lay waste') personally, and devastating (def. 2: 'overpoweringly effective') artistically. In 1966, it was drugs that had pushed him to the brink. The easy loquaciousness and freedom from inhibitions that alcohol induced had a readier appeal when the darkness returned in 1978. Now, twelve more years down the road, the darkness was again threatening to overwhelm him and, this time around, to lay his art to waste, too.

The first onstage evidence since 1987 that the man who liked a drink was fast approaching a time when he'd prefer to just be a drunk came in August 1990, at the last of five shows where G. E. Smith was sharing guitar duties with John Staehely. At an open-air theater adjacent to a winery in George, Washington, he looked for all the world as if sound-checking had given way to some serious sampling. In particular, a Dylan who seemed to have a problem locating the mike also had trouble finding the melody for a one-off rendering of the Otis Redding classic 'Sitting on the Dock of the Bay.' Nine days later, in Merrillville, Indiana, he had returned to the straight and narrow, when he attempted an even more outlandish choice of cover, 'Moon River,' a song of friendship dedicated to Stevie Ray Vaughan, 'wherever you are,' who had been tragically killed in a helicopter leaving Alpine Valley in treacherous weather the previous evening. Though they had only recently formalized their professional respect into a knowing acquaintance, the death of Stevie Ray hit him hard.

Cesar Diaz: When Stevie Ray died, he called me in and asked what happened . . . That's a beautiful version of 'Moon River,' and he never did it before and he never did it since. That was the only time, and it was all rehearsed with G.E. and stuff. He was all teary-eyed. He was really highly affected by friends that die, it was like tearing [out] a chunk of his heart.

The following night's show in Merrillville featured a Dylan again teetering on the brink. This time he sang a song not for Stevie Ray, who was past caring, but for himself. Another song from Thomas Dorsey's gospel canon, it was a plea to the Lord to 'Stand by Me' in this hour of darkness. And it seemed to work. With two weeks left before a month-long respite, and then the Beacon, he threw himself into the remaining shows with renewed fire, even as the second guitarist continued to chop and change. A week further on, he professed himself, in the words of Lowell George, 'to be willin' / to be movin'.' But when he found himself, five weeks later, moving on without G. E. Smith in tow, he was no longer so convinced. Come November, he was opening a show in East Lansing with Bobby Bare's 'Detroit City,' best known for its memorable refrain, 'I wanna go home, I wanna go home / Oh, how I wanna go home.'

The grand experiment with three rhythm guitarists—Diaz, Dylan, and Staehely—had not gone well. Though the fall assault on Middle America had its entertaining moments, they were invariably examples of Dylan pouring water on a drowning band, or Garnier, Parker, and Dylan coming up for air in the acoustic set and wrestling with 'Visions of Johanna' or 'Desolation Row,' songs that demanded 20/20 artistic vision. For the second time, he had lumbered himself with a set of musicians who seemed incapable of responding to his idea of cues, and his initial answer—now as then—was to augment them with Jack Daniels. Christmas in Minnesota doesn't seem to have greatly cleared his head, for his first plan on his return to rehearsals in January 1991 was to fire the one member of the band who could play with the necessary dynamics—drummer Chris Parker.

Cesar Diaz: This guy comes in and starts like playing with us, and I show up and I go, 'What are you doing here?' 'Oh, I used to play with Bob. He asked me to come by.' He comes in, and starts telling us about the days when they had nothing but Learjets, and I'm like, 'Oh, this definitely ain't now! We don't do that anymore.' So then Chris [Parker] walks in and sees somebody else sitting on his kit and [it] was, like, wow, somebody else is fucking my wife. Chris pretty much just went out of the room, and Bob went out there and talked to him. And we never saw him again . . . [I'd] never seen anyone get fired by calling somebody and making sure that the other person gets there, and when the person shows up there will be somebody else playing.

Parker's replacement was the man once described by his rhythm-section partner as having 'a beat like a cop,' Bury-born Ian Wallace. Whatever Wallace's strengths, he seemed incapable of propelling a band of novices to play tag. And a band of novices they were shaping up to be. Though Diaz held on to his gig, he was expected to defer lead duties to Staehely's much-needed replacement, a young, wholly unknown picker from Tennessee, whose only previous noteworthy association had been as guitarist in Cajun rocker Joel Sonnier's band. J. J. Jackson, who came complete with a permanent Cheshire Cat grin, was so far out of his depth that air-sea rescue would have had trouble locating him. He had also queered the pitch, moneywise, for all subsequent comers, having agreed to an initial weekly retainer of just five hundred dollars. The lack of notice and the terms of recruitment had turned the hottest gig in town, twelve years earlier, into a no-no for any musician with a mortgage and maintenance payments to make.

Cesar Diaz: At the end [of those January rehearsals], when Bob couldn't get anybody—he went through everybody—he goes, 'Jesus Christ. They suck, don't they?'

That's right, they sucked. But, with a dozen UK shows and warm-up gigs in Zurich, Brussels, and Utrecht booked, Dylan seems to have somehow convinced himself that he had it in him to institute another 1984 turnaround. In fact, the fifteen European shows became progressively worse as his pickup partners floundered, and he hid inside a bottle. With eight sellout shows booked at the scene of last year's triumph, London's Hammersmith Odeon, the ship sailed into Glasgow on February 2, 1991, the first sighting of the year for Dylan's fanatical British fans. Allan Jones, that voice in the wilderness when it came to the virtues of *Under the Red Sky*, caught the band in the act of musical mutilation at the first of two shows at the Scottish Exhibition Centre. The shock to the system was palpable:

Dylan now resembles nothing so much as an alcoholic lumberjack on a Saturday night out in some Saskatchewan backwater, staggering around the stage here in a huge plaid jacket and odd little hat. The band, meanwhile, have all the charisma of a death squad in some bandit republic . . . These people aren't so much under-rehearsed as almost complete strangers to each other, and Dylan's music specifically. Dylan, hilariously, doesn't give a fuck . . . [Diaz] starts strumming the intro to 'Mr. Tambourine Man.' After a couple of minutes he pauses, waiting for Dylan's vocal entry. He turns to look for Dylan, but Bob's not at his microphone. He's somewhere at the back of the stage wrestling with his harmonica holder which has come loose and now appears to be attempting to strangle him . . . [Diaz] looks vaguely panic-stricken, still waiting for Dylan. But Dylan doesn't seem to be in any hurry to bail him out . . . The inclusion of ['In the Garden'] takes everybody by surprise. The song seems to be winding down when, at Dylan's insistence, the group smash into a protracted, cacophonous coda. It goes on forever, an excruciating, hellish din.

Though Diaz does not deny that Dylan was slowly but surely working his way through the malt reserves of a few Highland distilleries on the winter 1991 jaunt, he also insists that Dylan was seriously ill and, by refusing to rely on doctors, only made the situation worse.

Cesar Diaz: He was very sick right before we got [back] to the States [in February 1991]. Bob was sick from the beginning [of the tour] . . . He came down with a cold, and he doesn't like to take regular medicines. He's really very holistic about it, herbs and teas, and crap like that. I blame Suze [Pullen, his dresser] for that. At night, I'd go, 'You should go see a doctor,' but you'd have to do it to him all day long before he'd go, 'Oh, okay, let's go.' . . . But even in the early years [of the NET] I was always giving him a cup of something, tea and some kinda booze. I saw a couple of real funny things. One night he turns around and goes to the [drum] riser, and grabs this bottle and starts squirting it on his hair. I thought he's got . . . some kind of tonic for his hair. The concert ends and I take the bottle and I throw it away. The next night we're sitting up and he goes, 'What happened to my bottle?' I go, 'What bottle?' 'The bottle of Sambuca.' 'You gotta be kidding me, you're putting that shit on your hair?' and he goes, 'Didn't it look good?'

With Dylan entering the twilight zone, the brunt of responsibility for presenting a holograph of competency at these shows devolved to Garnier and Diaz, but, even with their combined experience of five-hundred-plus shows, they found their boss taking an almost childish delight in making the band look as bad as possible, as if, somehow, he might succeed in shifting the blame by humiliating the likes of Jackson. At least Diaz knew enough to sit back and let him make his move first.

Cesar Diaz: Some of the other guys would try to make their moves before Bob, and then Bob would just go the other way out of spite! He would just fuck with them to prove a point . . . 'You never really know what I'm going to do, and that's the way I like it!'

At the second Glasgow show, which, thankfully, Jones did not catch, Dylan's perversity reached new heights, albeit at the expense of any pretense at artistry. Having placed himself deep in the mire, he had so far refrained from mixing the set up, fearful of the consequences. But on February 3, the set list was abandoned and the panic buttons removed. After throwing his audience for a loop by opening with an instrumental version of 'The Mountains of Mourne,' he led the band through increasingly unfamiliar back streets from a thirty-year repertoire until he came to 'Positively Fourth Street,' a song they did not seem to have even rehearsed, at which point he decided to depart the stage, leaving Diaz, Garnier, Jackson, and Wallace to their own devices for a fair few minutes. The experience only served to instill more fear in the constituents, and confusion among the fans.

Five days later, Dylan began his second London Hammersmith residency. The man onstage singing 'God Knows,' during the coldest winter in many a year, for a whole week in London, was visibly 'hanging himself every night.' Even in the gloomy backlit shadows of the Hammersmith stage, it was clear that the singer was sweating out a number of poisons from his system, night after night, only to self-administer further poisons the following day. A stumbling, bumbling Dylan, backed by a band of bungling incompetents, lost large sections of the audiences that week as they left in their droves, muttering their disgust. Scalpers, who had been asking (and getting) three figures for good tickets twelve months earlier, quite literally could not give tickets away, arctic temperatures outside being as nothing to the chill of death inside. Having been skirting the edge for some time, Dylan was in no fit state to walk any line, let alone *the* line.

The European tour took place against the backdrop of the Gulf War, amid ill-conceived fears of Iraqi reprisals on civilian airlines. Indeed, on the plane over, Dylan and Diaz had talked 'about Armageddon and biblical things,' and Dylan had told Diaz that he did not think it was yet Time. That he still believed in the end Times, though, he made abundantly plain to New York journalist Joe Queenan a month or so later, even as he was disavowing those, like Hal Lindsey, who had brought him to Jesus:

JQ: *What do you think about the Apocalypse?*
BD: *It will not be by water, but by fire next time. It's what is written.*
JQ: *Which edition of the Bible do you read?*
BD: *King James's version.*
JQ: *That's not really a fundamentalist version of the Bible, is it?*
BD: *I've never been a fundamentalist. I've never been born-again. Those are just labels that people hang on you. [1991]*

Curiously enough, the man who asserted to Queenan that he had 'never been born-again' was still closing the main set at his shows with the same uplifting finale as he had back in 1979. And, when he came to 'In the Garden,' he was still singing about a Nicodemus who 'came at night, so he wouldn't be seen by men / Saying, Master, tell me why a man must be born again?' These were hardly the sort of words that an ex-believer might want to reinvoke, however much Dylan's view of Christ had moved on from the Vineyard Fellowship's. As it was, though he was still holding the torch of faith, it was now failing to shine the necessary light on what was evidently a very personal despair.

Whatever oppressions were threatening to push him six feet under, in double-quick time, they were about to get worse. If the Hammersmith '91 shows, and the attendant reviews, had done untold damage to his standing in the UK, a single four-minute reprise, based on its worse moments, was about to do the same in the US. Barely forty-eight hours after his return to his own shores, Dylan was expected to perform and receive a Lifetime Achievement Award at the 33rd annual Grammy Awards ceremony, at Radio City Music Hall in New York. He would tell a couple of female fans, the day after, that it was like going to your own funeral; and Queenan, a month later, that 'the flu greeted me that morning in a big way. All my drainpipes were stopped up. Those kinds of things just happen to me . . . the night I'm going to be on a big TV show . . . The inside of my head was feeling like the Grand Canyon . . . It was not a good night for me . . . We just did that one [song] . . . You know, war going on and all that.'

Though the war against Saddam Hussein had the blessing of the majority of Americans polled, Dylan had elected to sing 'Masters of War' at the ceremony, an ambiguous selection at best from the author of 'Neighborhood Bully' ('Then he destroyed the bomb factory, nobody was glad'). The performance itself rendered all ambiguity moot by its sheer indecipherability. As New York journalist David Hinckley noted, 'Someone in the press room asked if he were singing in Hebrew.' But the evening was not yet over for this lifetime achiever. As he shuffled up to the rostrum to collect his award from an effusive Jack Nicholson, he looked around anxiously for some way outta here.

Cesar Diaz: He didn't want to do that Grammy because he felt so ill, but he had to do it because it was a Lifetime Achievement Award . . . They're giving you a medal so you don't come around anymore. I was convinced the way he was holding the award just like a plate that he was just gonna smash it in front of everybody. 'Cause he wanted to come right out, just take it, Thank you very much, but they closed the partitions and he's trapped over there—that wasn't supposed to be—he wanted to leave, but the two chicks came over and blocked him, and he realized what was going on: 'Well, they got me trapped, I better say something. What the hell do I say?'

Whether it was off the top of his head, or already conceived, Dylan's Grammy Award speech was perhaps the most honest speech he had given since the ECLC dinner. It was also a first-person cry for help from a man peering through the eyes of a self-loathing alcoholic:

Bob Dylan: My daddy once said to me, he said, 'Son, it is possible for you to become so defiled in this world that your own Mother and Father will abandon you. If that happens, God will believe in your own ability to mend your own ways.' [1991]

If he needed a further incentive to reflect on his ways, it came a matter of days later, when another long-standing African-American ex-girlfriend, who had settled in Los Angeles in the eighties and organized exhibitions of Australian aboriginal art, took her own life. Carol Lopez, one of the many Carols in his life, had apparently named Dylan among others in her suicide note. Whatever the cause-and-effect element of their relationship on her despair, and ultimate suicide, at her home in Sydney, Australia, it managed to remain a private matter between Dylan and his Maker. But for a man 'really highly affected by friends that die,' it was a particularly personal ghost that now haunted him.

Though Dylan never made any public reference to Lopez's suicide, one night in April 1992, when playing in Carol's adopted hometown of Sydney, he performed a rare acoustic performance of 'Desolation Row' and, most uncharacteristically, when he came to the verse about Ophelia—for whom 'death is quite romantic'—visibly became moved to tears, stumbled over the melody, and dropped the verse, indeed could barely carry on. Perhaps it wasn't simply the empty jeroboams of whiskey that were making Dylan feel 'so defiled.'

Certainly, the signs were few and far between that he was mending his ways. A resumption of the Never Ending Tour in April 1991 committed him to fifty-two shows in America and Europe before the end of July. Though Diaz had again been sidelined to tech duties, the response from Jackson was more that of an overanxious puppy than a man unleashed. Though Dylan tried to inject something of himself into the sets, it was only when he decided to wholly dispense with those on retainer for a nightly solo slot that he sounded like a man ready 'to throw out a signal that he was still alive.' On June 12, in Budapest, his one-off acoustic 'When First unto the Country' certainly came with a vocal for the ages.

But then, four days later, he proceeded to deliver what would get many fans' vote for the worst Dylan concert ever, in Stuttgart's Leiederhalle. An eight-minute 'New Morning' where he failed to articulate a single line from the 1970 composition opened a show that, for its first half hour, was excruciating in its ineptitude. Dylan's manhandling of an electric piano had been a feature of the shows since February, but in Stuttgart he was once again a callow teenager, in the back of his father's store, clanking his way toward a melody, any melody. Though such melodic fumbling was also a feature of some of his harmonica playing that summer, occasionally he managed to strip away the years, yearning for the same unquestioning, journeylike quality to his harp playing that he had in 1966.

The ability to endure, just that, may have denied Dylan a career with the necessary neatness to make the academic syllabus in his lifetime, but it once again seems to have saved his life in the summer of 1991. This time there would be no basement tape or *Slow Train Coming* to afford his fans a rear view out of the darkness that began to recede, as summer turned slowly to autumn. And yet when he resumed music-making in October 1991, another epiphany—one that returned him, in the words of Susan Ross, from a mean-spirited alcoholic into a considerate, generous soul—seems to have occurred. Ross, who had been with Dylan at the Grammys, had been staying at one of his town houses that summer, traveling to work in his limo, and, between tours, saw at first hand the effects of his alcoholism.

The fifty-year-old ex-poet evidently decided he'd like to make sixty and, between shows in Brazil in August and a Guitarists' Festival in Seville, Spain, in October, he not only stopped pouring himself another double of trouble, but rethought his whole purpose, having come to terms with the fact that 'a person gets to the point where they have written enough songs', as Dylan informed Robert Hilburn of the *LA Times* a week into his fall '91 Midwest tour. He also hinted at the process by which he had returned to his performance art with 'a sense of vocation':

Bob Dylan: It was important for me to come to the bottom of this legend thing, which has no reality at all. What's important isn't the legend, but the art, the work. A person has to do whatever they are called on to do. [1991]

What Dylan was required to do, in late October and early November of 1991, was give the Never Ending Tour a new impetus to replace the one G. E. Smith had taken with him—one that would sustain 'the art, the work,' while its solitary focus was performing. With the same three journeymen who had barely propped up the sound in the summer for the final stint of 1991, he significantly reinvented his performance art, for the last time.

In the finest analysis to date of Dylan's performance art, *Performing Artist*, Paul Williams has written that 'the power of Dylan's personality, his ability to create musical excitement, and his casual confidence in the ability of the musicians, whoever they are, to keep up with and contribute to the program . . . when it does [work], works phenomenally well.' The fall 1991 tour was just such an instance. Though it was less than a month of shows, off the record save for the ubiquitous tapers from the Secret Sennheiser Society, and without the hoopla of a new album to lend it import, the tour confirmed an unlikely resurrection. After a year of being left to sink or swim, Garnier, Jackson, and Wallace had found the right rafts and, after a full two weeks of rehearsals in LA in September— indicative of a seriousness sadly lacking at the start of the year—began to reward Dylan's 'casual confidence.'

Jackson, in particular, found himself freed from rhythm duties by Dylan's renewed willingness to underline his own voice on the Fender, his guitar fills at last suggesting a real talent freed from inappropriate responsibilities. Jackson's soloing on songs like 'Across the Borderline,' 'One Irish Rover,' and 'Simple Twist of Fate' even gave Smith a run for his money. Dylan also began to master his devolved duties as bandleader, leading his simple trio through a number of extended workouts with his strident rhythm work and subtle harmonica codas. The *Oh Mercy* songs, in particular, became seven- or eight-minute guitar/harmonica inter-changes that only served to extend their innate mysteries. But, once again, it was Dylan's singing commanding the songs, 'play[ing] the musicians with his voice,' as Eddy Arnold's 'You Don't Know Me' was remade into a crooner's dream; the traditional ballads—including an absolutely gripping rendition of the first Child ballad he ever sang, 'The Golden Vanity'—held the audiences viselike in the drama of their centuries-old moment; and the originals again became spontaneous exercises in tonal breath control.

Coming to terms with the limitations of fifty-year-old vocal cords, Dylan stripped his repertoire of songs beyond his range, and gave those he wished to retain a thorough revamping that again enabled the singer and his songs to interact on an equitable basis. The rumbling resonance that his voice had acquired on *Oh Mercy* was retained for the duration, and the vocal gymnastics were reined in, to be dispensed when they stood to gain maximum effect (say, on a heartfelt 'Answer Me My Love' at the first half-dozen shows; or a '20/20 Vision' in Austin).

One particular moment, at the tenth show that fall, in Madison,

Wisconsin, on November 5, showed that he was also coming to terms with this world of toil and trouble, even as he continued to yearn for release. Ironically, Dylan himself would dismiss what was one of his finest performances in ten years as 'useless . . . it just wasn't there.' Confiding in Robert Hilburn, temporarily along for the ride, with a sincerity borne of recent missed opportunities, he asserted, 'If you are going to be a performer, you've got to give it your all.' One song he certainly gave his all that night was an acoustic version of 'That Lucky Old Sun,' one of a number of acoustic, or semi-acoustic, performances he'd given on the Never Ending Tour, which contrasted this life of strife, implicitly or explicitly, with a better place. One of that decreasing number of songs he could place himself in, 'That Lucky Old Sun' yearns for the Lord Above to 'show me that river, take me across, wash all my troubles away'; just as, in Frejus in 1989, he sought a place 'where the lion will lie down with the lamb' ('Peace in the Valley'); or, on the occasional 'Rank Strangers to Me,' for 'a beautiful home by the bright crystal sea . . . where no one will be a rank stranger to me.'

Paul Williams, in a piece he wrote on 'Bob Dylan and Death' in 1988, recounts Dylan handing him Howard Alk's phone number backstage at the Warfield in 1980. Alk was a fan of Williams's heartfelt, of-the-moment monograph on Dylan's conversion, the self-published *What Happened*? When Williams finally visited Alk, a couple of months later, he found a surprisingly earnest Alk had something on his mind:

Paul Williams: He said some nice things about my book, but what he really wanted to talk about . . . was the fact that I had overlooked, in his opinion, a major possible factor in Dylan's conversion to Christianity: awareness of and fear of death.

That 'awareness of and fear of death' had increasingly drained the color from Dylan's work in the decade now gone. By the end of 1991, though, he was no longer seeking to obliterate a disturbed sense of his own mortality by whatever means were available. Even as he continued to envy that lucky old sun, with 'nothing to do but roll around heaven all day,' the man of constant sorrow knew he was 'bound to ride that open highway' for a while yet.

1992–96: Traditional Troubadour

38

After making thirty or forty records, the impetus to make 'em starts to disintegrate.

—Bob Dylan, 1993

My influences have not changed—and any time they have done, the music goes off to a wrong place. That's why I recorded two LPs of old songs, so I could personally get back to the music that's true for me.

—Bob Dylan, 1997

In his famous 'Letter to Dave Glover,' in the 1963 Newport Folk Festival program, Dylan had written 'i can't sing "Little Maggie" with a clear head, i gotta sing "Seven Curses."' Well, resurrected as it had been on 1991's *Bootleg Series* boxed set, 'Seven Curses' had been a long time gone. Yet here he was singing 'Little Maggie' onstage in Perth, Australia, at the start of another year on the never-ending road. And in an electric guise. In fact, the Antipodean tour, his first in six years, yielded a number of similar nuggets, mined from his pre-songwriting repertoire. 'The Lady of Carlisle,' 'Little Moses,' 'Trail of the Buffalo,' and 'The Golden Vanity' were all excavated in the acoustic sets, while Blind Willie McTell's version of the Bahamian ballad 'Delia' was recast with a powerful electric current.

Nor did Dylan's re-immersion in the black muddy river of tradition end there. The British ballad tradition, in particular, was energizing the Never Ending Tour. Most nights he was twinning 'Little Moses' with an ultra-obscure British broadside ballad, 'Female Ramblin' Sailor,' as, for two precious songs, he reverted to a genuinely solo acoustic guise and, in turn, rediscovered how good an acoustic player he could still be, even if the Fender continued in its ill-gotten role.

Arthur Rosato: He is really a great acoustic guitar player, but you listen to something from '65, you listen to his electric guitar playing, and you listen to it now, it's exactly the same. There is no improvement . . . The only time he would work out whatever the lead was, was when the lead came around.

This return to his, indeed modern popular song's, real roots was an admission that the songwriter in him needed another swim in the stream of tradition. Having tapped into the same wellspring in 1967, 1970, and (to a lesser extent) 1986–87, he had found *The Basement Tapes, New Morning*, and *Oh Mercy* on the banks of the river, where the willows hang down. But this time, his second great drought (1985–88) had barely subsided when the third drought had come on, and he had begun to convince himself that perhaps he had written enough. Talking to Paul Zollo about the craft of songwriting, as it passed from his mind, in April 1991, he confessed:

Bob Dylan: There was a time when the songs would come three or four at the same time, but those days are long gone . . . Once in a while, the odd song will come to me like a bulldog at the garden gate and demand to be written. But most of them are rejected out of my mind right away. You get caught up in wondering if anyone really needs to hear it. Maybe a person gets to the point where they have written enough songs. Let someone else write them. [1991]

Traditional covers had been a regular feature of the NET, though almost always in the acoustic sets. The one electric arrangement of a traditional song to have lasted the distance was 'Pretty Peggy-O,' a song that now had a more traditional flavor than in 1961 ('what would your mama think / If she could hear my guineas clink'), though it had been clearly modeled on its gang rape by the Grateful Dead in recent years. Indeed, Dylan seems to have become surprisingly smitten by the attempts of Garcia and lyricist Robert Hunter to write in a traditional style, interchanging 'Black Muddy River,' 'Deal,' and 'Friend of the Devil' with genuine articles like 'Delia' and 'Pretty Peggy-O.' Not that these Garcia–Hunter efforts were the only stylistic stabs at a traditional style to now occupy the stage, or preoccupy its master. He was also playing Paul Simon's 'Hazy Shade of Winter' and, at studio sessions in June, Tim Hardin's exquisite 'The Lady Came from Baltimore' ('I was there to steal her money / To take her rings and run / But then I fell in love with a lady / Got away with none'), songs that had also taken traditional modes as their springboard.

Bob Dylan: If you can sing those [folk] songs, if you can understand those songs and can perform them well, then there's nowhere you *can't* go. [1997]

Despite the ill regard in which *Self Portrait, Dylan,* and *Down in the Groove* were held, Dylan seems to have decided to produce a curious mélange of genuinely traditional ballads like 'Polly Vaughn' and 'Duncan and Brady' as well as modern productions modeled along traditional lines on his new album, but still with the sort of grandiose instrumentation that had interfered with the songs' natural simplicity on previous covers collections. If sometime girlfriend Susan Ross is to be believed, his initial intent was simply to produce another contractual filler. The sessions were scheduled to last two weeks, at Chicago's Acme Recording Studio, and were to be produced by David Bromberg, whose association with Dylan ran deep. Initially, the frisson of Dylan's sheer presence in this funky Midwest studio seems to have sparked one of those remarkably productive evenings.

Dan White: We worked with the Bromberg band for about three days, wondering if Dylan would show up. Then when he did, there was electricity in the air and they laid down tracks for seven songs in one night.

Unfortunately, the choice of Bromberg as producer put paid to any low-key 'return to roots' record, as their long-standing friendship convinced Bromberg that he could successfully interpret Dylan's own thoughts and feelings. When he suggested a children's choir on the contemporary Christian ballad 'Rise Again,' already nailed by Dylan and Clydie back in 1980, warning lights were doubtless flashing. Dylan initially fought his corner, then became difficult, and finally left Bromberg to it, all the while doing his best to make sure his producer was denied the full allocation of clear moments.

Dan White: One thing I do remember. At times we would get what would sound like the recording of the year. It would be one of those magical musical moments. Then Dylan would say, erase it. I had to record over more than one golden track. At first, I thought he was just teasing us.

Blaise Barton: You have to stay on your toes when you work with Dylan . . . I literally sat there the whole day every day with my finger on 'record,' watching for him to start playing. The first couple of days he'd be in there looking like he wasn't doing anything, so I'd adjust a compressor or something, and then he'd just start playing.

Failing to read the writing on the Acme walls, Bromberg persevered with mixing an album's worth of songs from the sessions while Dylan replenished the coffers with just eleven summer shows in mainland Europe, at which the set list was again up for grabs. The tapes awaited

Dylan on his return to Malibu in mid-July and, initially, he hoped he might yet salvage something from them. Apparently, his original plan was to record a couple of solo acoustic tunes at his garage studio to break up the album, but, soon enough, the acoustic songs began to stack up—unlike the Acme songs, that is.

Neither Dylan nor Bromberg have ever sought to explain the exact problem with the Chicago tapes, which remain uncirculated. But there seems little doubt that, when Dylan spoke the following year about how 'Modern recording technology never endeared itself to me; my kind of sound is very simple, with a little bit of echo, and . . . I'm most disappointed when producers overlook the strength of my music,' he was still musing about his most recent studio experience. The songs he was now recording needed very little, save that 'little bit of echo,' because they had already stood up to the onslaughts of time.

Bob Dylan: Those songs worked their way into my own songs, I guess, but never in a conscious way . . . It's like nobody really wrote those songs. They just get passed down. [1993]

Save for 'Little Maggie,' nothing that he had performed in the six months of shows, or is known to have recorded with Bromberg, made the finished *Good As I Been To You*. Instead, Dylan astounded producer and engineer by coming down to the Malibu sessions sans notes or lyrics, ransacking British and Irish tradition, for 'Froggy Went A-Courtin',' 'Blackjack Davey,' and 'Arthur McBride,' African-American blues-makers for the likes of 'Frankie and Albert' and 'Sittin' on Top of the World,' and his fellow folk revivalists for 'Little Maggie' and 'Diamond Joe.' However, as with the original Bromberg sessions, he did not confine himself to the authentically traditional, recording an affecting rendition of Lonnie Johnson's 1947 hit, 'Tomorrow Night,' The Duprees' 'You Belong to Me'—which producer Debbie Gold begged him to include on *Good As I Been to You*, but had to await its incongruous inclusion on the *Natural Born Killers* soundtrack—and Stephen Foster's world-weary 'Hard Times.'

The shocking simplicity of the sound, and the stark intensity of Dylan's fifty-one-year-old voice, brought a series of unexpectedly enthusiastic reviews on the all-acoustic album's release. *Rolling Stone*'s David Wild, for one, recognized its apposite nature:

In its stripped-down intensity, *Good As I Been to You* recalls the midshow acoustic segments that in recent years have been a consistent highlight of

Dylan's Never Ending Tour. Even more than that, the album's intimate, almost offhand approach suggests what it would be like to sit backstage with his Bobness while he runs through a set of some of his favorite old songs. This is a passionate, at times almost ragged piece of work that seems to have been recorded rather than produced in any conventional sense.

Though almost all the reviewers concluded that Dylan-as-songwriter was a spent force, there was a welcoming tone to many of the reviews, as if they too had come to terms with the fact that the guy had written his share. His voice, in particular, came in for much praise, albeit in sarcastic tones. The *Sunday Telegraph*'s David Sexton, who called the voice 'pretty broken—although his unique tone and phrasing remain,' recognized the intent at work: 'Dylan sounds now, in comparison to his younger self, like one of those ghosts. But a powerful ghost. The effect is not so much nostalgia . . . as deeply inward.' For Dylan, though, the figures conjured up on and by these songs were hardly otherworldly.

Bob Dylan: When my songwriting started, all that [music] was kind of left to one side . . . But it was necessary for me to get back to the stuff that meant so much to me at one time. These people who originated this music, they're all Shakespeares, you know? . . . There was a bunch of us, me included, who got to see all these people close up, people like Son House, Reverend Gary Davis, or Sleepy John Estes . . . Those vibes will carry into you forever, really, so it's like those people, they're still here to me. They're not ghosts of the past or anything. They're continually here. [1993]

The most curious aspect of *Good As I Been to You* was that Dylan's gifts as an interpreter seemed to have found the same locker, marked Abeyance, as his songwriting self. Perhaps his reverence for all these Shakespeares had, for once, got the better of him. Perhaps the extent of his artistic ambition in 1992 was to *be* Mississippi John Hurt or Cisco Houston. Yet here was a man who had, in the last six months, performed original interpretations of songs like 'Delia,' 'Little Maggie,' 'Pretty Peggy-O,' and 'Newlyn Town' who was producing identikit 'arrangements' of Paul Brady's 'Arthur McBride,' Mick Slocum's 'Jim Jones,' and Nic Jones's 'Canadee-I-O,' to name but three. Of the thirteen cuts on *Good As I Been to You*, only the transposed-to-acoustic 'Tomorrow Night'— which someone had the impertinence to credit as Public Domain on the CD—had the stamp of originality. At least one reviewer, Ian Andersen, editor of *Folk Roots*, was incensed by Dylan's disregard for his sources:

Mississippi John Hurt's version of 'Frankie and Albert' . . . he delivers with a tiny residue of the storytelling flair epitomized by 'Lily, Rosemary and the Jack of Hearts' . . . [but] the thing that really irritates [is] it's *definitely* from Mississippi John, no shadow of a doubt. Just like there is *absolutely no question* that 'Canadee-I-O' comes from Nic Jones and 'Arthur McBride' from Paul Brady, and very little doubt that Stephen Foster's 'Hard Times' comes from De Dannan. So why has the rich old has-been copyrighted every damn track as 'Traditional arranged Dylan'? . . . Somebody should sue . . .

As it happens, someone threatened as much. Australian folksinger Mick Slocum's unique rearrangement of the traditional 'Jim Jones' had been recorded by his band, the Original Bushwhackers, back in 1975 and Dylan's music publisher was obliged to cry *mea culpa*. Dylan's much professed reverence for the folk tradition, and those who propagate it in adversity, had once again not been reflected in song credits.

Though the process was repeated the following year, media flak and sleepless nights may have caused Dylan to pause. When he decided to again 'compose' an album of public-domain songs, in his garage with just him and his guitar, he did at least provide a glossary of sources— that is, if they could be gleaned from the paranoid, word-association free-for-all that passed for sleeve notes to his 1993 collection, *World Gone Wrong*. The sleeve notes also showed why there had been no Dylan songs in three years. Not only had that economy of phrasing gone out of his art, but the words themselves had lost all meaning. Maybe the lone pilgrim knows what 'hegemony takes a breathing spell' means; maybe Dylan knows what a 'de facto group' is; and to Dylan (and maybe Nick Cave) perhaps the Henry in 'Love Henry' is indeed 'an infantile sensualist—white teeth, wide smile, lotza money, kowtows to fairy queen exploiters & corrupt religious establishments, career minded, limousine double parked, imposing his will & dishonest garbage in popular magazines,' but such views are also incidental to the song, as are most of the shards of 'wisdom' that fly off from their original reference (the songs) in these notes. It may be revealing, biographically, to know that Dylan honors a time 'before the celestial grunge, before the insane world of entertainment exploded in our faces,' but as song commentary it is less than useful. And yet, the notes drew as much comment as the album they accompanied. Andy Gill wrote in *The Independent*:

It's the liner notes that offer the most interesting aspect of the album . . . [With] the songs steeped in deceit, treachery, venality and despair—not to mention his sometimes slightly berserk annotations—the picture builds up of the Blues as Bible Study, a series of lessons to be interpreted.

If *Good As I Been to You* had begun life as a contractual filler, *World Gone Wrong* never departed from this path, fulfilling the terms of Dylan's January 18, 1988 contract and leaving him temporarily a free agent. Whereas the 1992 acoustic sessions had occupied a couple of weeks, and a whole song-selection process, Dylan's 1993 offering was recorded in a matter of days, just fourteen songs being taped, without a single change of strings. The recording quality was shockingly primitive, the process of miking having evidently occupied as much time as tuning Mr. Dylan's guitar, something London *Times* reviewer David Sinclair did not stint from observing:

It is hard to excuse the wilful incompetence of the performances. His flat, croaky singing is accompanied by some shockingly duff guitar playing, and while a Dylan album without the fluffed notes would hardly be authentic, it is astounding, given the sophistication of modern studio technology, that a single acoustic guitar can be so badly recorded that it *distorts*.

Stories of Dylan mastering the album from cassettes abound. Certainly, when it came to sequencing *World Gone Wrong*, he persevered with a technique he had refined in the Rundown era:

Arthur Rosato: We would record, we'd put it on a cassette, and he'd go sit out in his car and listen to it and then say, Okay, that was a take. Or in the pool room [at Rundown], he'd put it on a tiny little boom box and listen to it there. We'd never listen to it on playback through the studio speakers.

After his previous fifty-eight-minute offering, though, Dylan still sacrificed four songs from the sessions, including a version of Robert Johnson's '32.20 Blues,' ensuring the maximum publishing revenue.

The focus, this time around, was more roundly on the bluesmakers, songs from the Mississippi Sheiks (two), Blind Willie McTell (two), Willie Brown, and Frank Hutchinson taking preference over those of Tom Paley and Doc Watson, not only numerically but emotionally. 'The Two Soldiers,' a song Dylan had been playing since 1988, he unintentionally invested with that classic impersonality the true tradition-alist seeks, while 'Jack-a-Roe' carried none of the momentum of his earlier live performances of another broadside from the same template, 'Female Ramblin' Sailor.' And yet, the reviews in the US were almost universal in their praise, *Rolling Stone* calling him "a genius blues singer, oracular and timeless,' Ira Robbins insisting in *Newsday* that 'the record expresses as much about Bob Dylan's art as any collection of originals,' while Bill Flanagan, in *Musician,* gave the album an unwarranted endorsement that belittled braver attempts to reinforce his pioneering work:

Bob Dylan is probably the greatest talent to have come out of rock & roll . . . However, it has been a long time since Dylan has made the best records or done the best work in rock & roll. It seems that, like a great painter, he can only give us what he is feeling at the moment his work is captured. If the tape recorder is running on a good day, we get *Blood on the Tracks*. If it's a bad day we get *Under the Red Sky*. . . Dylan may tell tall tales until every last journalist gives up and goes home, but he seems to be incapable of lying in his music . . . In the last decade much of Dylan's recorded work has been for True Believers only. But *World Gone Wrong* is for anyone with ears to listen and a heart to feel.

After years as a curmudgeon, his worldview was being bought hook, line, and melody by those who, with a little reading, might have known better. The usually perceptive Albert Lloyd wrote in *LA Weekly* of Dylan 'revisit[ing] that early territory like a man who's earned the ticket. This is just where he lives now. It's no act. He walks the walk. He sings like a man who can't sleep at night. He pours himself out of himself into songs that were old ages before he took the name Dylan.' In fact, all but three of the songs on *World Gone Wrong* date from the twentieth century, and it was most assuredly an act for a middle-class white boy from Hibbing to walk a mile in the shoes of Blind Willie McTell, a man who, by Dylan's own admission, could sing the blues like nobody else, and then deliberately downgrade the results to make it sound 'like a record.'

At least he took the opportunity, in a couple of interviews ostensibly promoting a Dylan—Santana tour in the fall, to send people back to the sources, even as he hung on to all those royalties:

Bob Dylan: Singers in the fifties and sixties were [still] just one step removed from the early ones, and you could hear that. But you can't hear it anymore, it's so polluted and unclean . . . Even *World Gone Wrong* is a step or two removed. People should go to those old records and find out what the real thing is, because mine is still second generation. [1993]

However much this type of song had provided the foundation for the man's art, the songs on *World Gone Wrong* seem not to have been ones

Dylan was content to explore in performance. Though half a dozen songs from *Good As I Been to You* had gradually worked their way into the NET sets, the only live performances bestowed on the *World Gone Wrong* songs came at four club shows he gave in November 1993, at Manhattan's ultra-intimate Supper Club, with the specific intent of recording an *Unplugged*-style TV special, without conferring any points on MTV for their brand name.

He had become convinced of the benefits of such an exercise after the receipts had come in from a jacket-and-tie jamboree laid on for his benefit the previous October, at Madison Square Garden. Billed as 'A Tribute to Bob Dylan,' the affair was organized by his record label to celebrate thirty-one-and-a-half years helping to fill their coffers. Charging between $80 and $150 to the lucky attendees, and $19.99 to those for whom pay-per-view sufficed, Sony assembled a bill that included figures of the stature of Sophie B. Hawkins, Tracy Chapman, Sinéad O'Connor, and Mary Chapin Carpenter before they remembered that the man had actually influenced the genuinely important, like Lou Reed, Eric Clapton, George Harrison, and Neil Young, and had in turn been influenced by the likes of Carolyn Hester, John Hammond, Jr., and the Clancy Brothers.

When Sinéad O'Connor turned the whole Bobfest into her own one-woman primal-scream session, even the idea of celebrating rock's finest songwriter was sacrificed to a teen tantrum. But with Dylan receiving the lion's share of a gross that topped $10 million, for a three-song acoustic set more perfunctory than anything he'd sung in a two-hour set in Poughkeepsie six nights earlier, he was happy to let TV do the talking. *Billboard* reported at the time, 'Columbia is [already] considering an acoustic television special for Dylan.'

For the Supper Club special, he was even prepared to rehearse a number of songs from the last two Sony collections. Indeed, he managed to invest 'Jack-A-Roe,' 'Delia,' and Blind Boy Fuller's 'Weeping Willow' with a power and passion that had been missing from a whole year of lackluster performances. If the sets in 1993 had settled into stagnancy, save for the occasional night in Vienna, Dylan had set aside several days of rehearsals before the filming began and then, with the cameras rolling, spent a couple of days at the Supper Club itself running through songs he actually had a yen to perform.

Winston Watson: He said he liked the bit where we were rehearsing [at the Supper Club] and the cameras were rolling . . . He said that was the magic, 'cause everyone had their street clothes on, there's people milling around doing stuff, and we were just playing for the sake of sheer playing, and it was really great.

If the rehearsals were 'really great,' the shows themselves were exceptional. The Supper Club shows were everything the NET shows for the past two years should have been—low key, understated, diverse, unexpected—and, best of all, Dylan found his voice audibly acquiring range and depth over the four shows, the 'last supper' representing perhaps his finest performance of the nineties. Having given his influences air and grace, he transcended them with versions of 'Ring Them Bells' and 'Queen Jane Approximately' that spoke with all the hurt that inner voice felt when left crying to be heard. And yet, he refused to perform sets like these at the seventy-six shows he had played in 1993, or the 105 shows he would play in 1994. And herein lies an essential contradiction.

Winston Watson: [At rehearsals] we used to do all this obscure stuff. A lot of times he would just start this riff, and Tony and I would come in behind him, and he'd sing lyrics to a song I thought I knew . . . We would do a lot of really cool stuff and then it would be back to business as usual, or [occasionally] one of the cool things would sneak into the set, like 'Minglewood Blues.'

Corroborative evidence for drummer Winston Watson's assessment came as late as September 1995, when Dylan played another warm-up show à la Toad's, at a discothèque in Fort Lauderdale, Florida, called The Edge, at which he played a fourteen-song set that included eight covers, including Van Morrison's 1980 composition 'Real, Real Gone,' Lowell George's 'Willing,' and Big Bill Broonzy's 'Key to the Highway,' as well as a stately new arrangement of 'With God on Our Side.' However, when asked by a local journalist about the Edge version of 'Confidential to Me,' prior to a seven-date tour of Florida, Dylan replied, 'You won't hear that again.' He had developed a fixed view of his audience that he no longer seemed prepared to challenge.

Bob Dylan: People don't think they can respond to a song that they haven't heard on a record. It didn't used to be that way. [1997]

So how has Dylan come to have such little faith in the willingness of his audiences to hear lesser known or more challenging material? Or has it always been that way? There is a story that Paul Simon once complained to him that his fans always seemed to want to hear 'Homeward Bound,' 'The Sound of Silence,' and so on. Dylan's supposed reply was that if he went to a Paul Simon concert those would be the songs he'd like to hear. Yet he himself has not always seen fit to dish out the hits. In 1975, the Rolling Thunder set concentrated on the as-yet-unreleased *Desire* songs. In 1976, song selection was deliberately perverse. In 1979–80, 'old songs' were wholly excluded, and even when reintroduced in late 1980 were outnumbered by covers and as-yet-unreleased originals.

Arthur Rosato: He wants to do something new all the time, but sometimes the momentum of other things carries over and forces him to do [more obvious] stuff.

Since 1984, Dylan has not been quite so tenacious in resisting audience preconceptions. Though on all of his mid-eighties tours (1984, 1986, 1987) he began with reasonably audacious sets, within two or three shows he had revised them at the expense of more recent songs. In 1984 the shambolic first show in Verona featured versions of 'When You Gonna Wake Up?,' 'Heart of Mine,' and 'Man of Peace,' all of which became rare events at later shows. In 1986 an equally ramshackle opening show in Wellington featured 'Gotta Serve Somebody,' 'Shot of Love,' and 'Heart of Mine,' all quickly dropped. In 1987, at his first show in Tel Aviv, five of the seventeen songs were from the seventies, four from the eighties, and one was a traditional cover. The response was such that Dylan was required to defend himself in print, insisting to Robert Hilburn, of the *Los Angeles Times*, before the next show:

Bob Dylan: You don't want to just get up there and start guessing with the people what they want. For one thing, no one agrees on that. The songs a few people want to hear may not mean anything to a whole lot of others, and you can't let the audience start controlling the show or you're going to end up on a sinking ship. You've got to stay in control, or you might as well go hole up in Las Vegas . . . because you're not being true to the music anymore . . . You're being true to something else that doesn't really mean anything except some applause. [1987]

And yet the show in Jerusalem, two days later, restored much that was irksomely familiar. Indeed, since the late seventies Dylan has constantly had to balance the wishes of the members of the audiences there for a night out, who know him mainly by reputation and inferior cover versions—and perhaps the odd compilation album left behind at an all-night party—with some sense of artistic integrity. With his low commercial stock in the nineties, and the sheer need to put derrières on seats in annual summer gigs with the same outfit, Dylan no longer trusted himself and his band to take the paying customers somewhere other than on a sentimental journey.

This concern may have also played its part in the aborting of the Supper Club CD/TV extravaganza. Despite the costs of a film crew and multitrack digital audio, which came from his own pocket, and the genuine excitement in serious fan circles for these shows, come January 1994, Dylan had decided to scrap the TV special of his best filmed performances since Toronto in 1980. He also decided that he would give MTV its due, permitting them to market the results of a second set of intimate shows, the following November, at Sony Studios in New York. Dylan's level of detachment from the exercise was perhaps exemplified by the fact that, at both shows, he played the entire set wearing a set of shades that successfully obscured his tired orbs. He also, again, spoke of the resultant album and TV special as if he were but a helpless vessel swaying in the sea of commerce.

Bob Dylan: I would have liked to do old folk songs with acoustic instruments, but there was a lot of input from other sources as to what would be right for the [MTV] audience . . . At one time, I would have argued, but there's no point . . . I felt like I had to deliver, and I delivered something that was preconceived for me . . . It wasn't necessarily what I wanted to do. [1995]

For much of the nineties, Dylan has sought to paint himself as someone made to do things that were not 'what I wanted to do.' And yet, as Dave Sinclair noted about *World Gone Wrong*, 'only an old dog like Dylan could make an album so genuinely unheeding of market conditions.' Indeed, after *Good As I Been to You* had been delivered, Columbia president Don Ienner was quoted as saying, 'We never question his creativity, ever. What he gives us, he gives us.' As an article of faith, Ienner even agreed to a new ten-album contract with Dylan at the end of 1993. And yet *Unplugged*, as released, was another live collection of tired retreads of 'All Along the Watchtower,' 'Like a Rolling Stone,' and 'Knockin' on Heaven's Door'—three rare examples of songs Dylan perfected in the studio, and has never surpassed live—while a seductively paced 'I Want You,' a powerful 'Absolutely Sweet Marie,' and a unique live 'Hazel' would all be consigned to the bootleg equivalent, a double CD of both shows (direct from Sony promotional cassettes). And still,

Dylan continued to push himself to tour, performing the mostly old, rarely new, sometimes borrowed, often blue, for an ill-defined demographic of would-be fans, ex-fans, the curious, and the inquisitive, most of whom wondered, Why?

Bob Dylan: A lot of people don't like the road, but it's as natural to me as breathing. I do it because I'm driven to do it . . . It's the only place you can be who you want to be . . . I don't want to put on the mask of celebrity. I'd rather just do my work and see it as a trade . . . I don't make a record every three years, then go and tour so that audiences will buy it as a souvenir. I'm not that kind of artist and never wanted to be; I don't approach music so dispassionately . . . Having to grasp my kind of stage show in a competitive nature isn't really the correct way to do it because there's nothing to compare it to out there. The influences are completely different [to] whatever the popular music trends are . . . [it's] just American folk music and maybe rockabilly. [1997]

Without new product to keep his audience interested through the nineties, and without feeling a need to maintain the same sense of perpetual change that had made the Never Ending Tour so compelling between 1988 and 1992, Dylan was making music on a nightly basis that, by and large, passed large sections of that would-be audience by. By 1994, it was clear that those attending the shows for a night out were taking far more from the performances than the so-called Bobcats, each of whose NET scores ran to three figures.

Bob Dylan: There's always new things to discover when you're playing live. No two shows are the same. It might be the same song, but you find different things to do within that song which you didn't think about the night before. It depends on how your brain is hooked up to your hand and how your mind is hooked up to your mouth . . . [People say,] 'Doesn't it ever get tiring singing the same song over and over again?' No, it doesn't. That's the thing about music, it's not on the page. It's got a life of its own. [1989]

Bob Dylan: Once the architecture is in place, a song can be done in an endless amount of ways. That's what keeps my current live shows unadulterated. [1999]

In popular perception, Dylan's Never Ending Tour only now impinged for the biannual moment that the circus was in town, at least until 1994, when two TV broadcasts provided compelling evidence that the man still had something to say. A pay-per-view contract gave Dylan another useful payday in August when Neil Young pulled out of a scheduled twenty-fifth-anniversary Woodstock II. Hearing of the $600,000 fee Young had been offered, Dylan intimated his willingness to redeem his omission from the original 1969 bill with a statutory NET set. As drummer Winston Watson notes, 'It took us longer to get there than to play—I had to get dressed on the bus—he comes off his bus, we talk about the set, we go out and play, and it's over with . . . [But] he came there to rock.' And rock he did, on a storming 'Just Like a Woman,' a highly focused 'God Knows,' and a blistering 'Highway 61 Revisited,' highlights of an impressive seventy-eight-minute set.

His other TV appearance of the year was of a higher caliber still, even if it was yet another frustrating example, barely six months after the Supper Club shows, of someone whose career had become one big If Only. Between May 20 and 22, 1994, Dylan had agreed to perform three songs, nightly, in the stunning visual setting of the Todaiji Temple in Japan's Nara City, as part of 'The Great Music Experience,' an ambitious collision of orchestral arrangements by celebrated conductor Michael Kamen, utilizing the percussive talents of Jim Keltner and Ray Cooper and a couple of Western songwriters whose work might warrant such attention to detail: Dylan and Joni Mitchell.

In Dylan's case, he had been persuaded to perform the full 'A Hard Rain's A-Gonna Fall,' plus 'I Shall Be Released' and 'Ring Them Bells,' all augmented by an orchestra. The challenge, for a man used to disregarding the niceties of scored arrangements, was considerable, but by the time he came to the final show, to be filmed for a worldwide telecast, he had once again shown that 'the strength of his music' could sustain the most ambitious of arrangements as long as the singer in him retained his commitment to the material. Q journalist Danny Kelly, paid to witness proceedings, concluded:

Perhaps moved by the wondrous surrounds, maybe hemmed in by the discipline of having 60-odd musicians dependent on him, Dylan sings, really opens his lungs and heart and sings, like he's not done for many a year. Kamen's arrangements keep pushing him gently along; it's like watching a creaking old galleon, long becalmed, suddenly setting full sail again, propelled by an irresistible breeze. The only word for it is majestic.

Though 'A Hard Rain's A-Gonna Fall' was perhaps the song that lent itself most to the orchestral scale, it was for 'Ring Them Bells' that Dylan saved his vocal *coup de grâce*. Even though he proved that he could withstand even the most baroque of backings, he would show no discernible desire to repeat what had been an art-affirming experiment. Six weeks later, it would be back to the Parisian Periphérique, and a thirteen-song set, of which 'All Along the Watchtower,' 'Just Like a Woman,' Tangled Up in Blue,' 'Don't Think Twice,' 'Highway 61 Revisited,' 'Masters of War,' 'Maggie's Farm,' and 'It Ain't Me Babe' were all nudging 250-plus NET performances. His distaste for this less-than-great musical experience was expressed by looks withering enough to finally, and definitively, wipe the smile from his long-suffering guitarist, J. J. Jackson.

By 1994, Jackson was second only to Garnier in the NET survivor stakes. The year 1992 had seen the band go through its last significant changes, as pedal-steel/mandolin player Bucky Baxter was recruited from Steve Earle's band to add some new textures. Dylan also decided to resume his experiment with two drummers, adding the no-longer-inexperienced Charlie Quintana in April, to play the beats Ian Wallace tended to leave standing at the gate. Presumably enamored of the sound achieved by the Grateful Dead and the Allman Brothers, he persevered with the experiment even when Quintana bailed out in early September for a more secure job offer. Quintana suggested the young but willing Winston Watson as a potential replacement.

Winston Watson: Well, [Charlie Quintana] called me as I was burning dinner. I thought [he] needed a tech to come out, and then he said, 'No, you're gonna play with Dylan.' I go, 'Ha ha ha, not the dead Welsh poet.' He goes, 'Yeah.' I go, 'When do rehearsals start?' He goes, 'No, no, no, you're flying out to Kansas City tomorrow to play with the guy.' And I said, 'An audition?' He said, 'No, you're gonna do a show with him.' It still didn't soak in . . . We land and nobody's there, and the airport's in the middle of nowhere. I got my bags and went to the hotel, and the first person I saw was Victor [Maymudes] and he was no help whatsoever. Everyone was being really, really cryptic . . . I'd seen Ian [Wallace] work before, wasn't necessarily a fan of his playing, but I had a lot of respect for the guy. I knew he was left-handed and his feel was really, really different. I thought, 'What am I gonna do up there?' I talked to Ian for a bit but he was no help [either], because there were no rules . . . It was very humid that night. The whole time we're playing [Dylan's], like, looking at me, but not in a bad way . . . After the show, there was some commotion and it was [Dylan] making his way through this crowd of people, and he came up to me, and he looked me up and down, and he shook my hand and gave me a hug, and he said, 'Hey, you play really great, I'll see you tomorrow.'

In October 1992, Watson found himself playing a couple of gigs on his own, as Wallace attended to a family commitment and, as the first show in Poughkeepsie progressed, Dylan began to wander offstage to talk to Cesar Diaz. After the show, a nervous Watson collared Diaz to ask what that was all about. Diaz reassured him that all the boss had said was, 'It sounds better, right, it sounds really good, huh?' After another Gulf Coast tour said farewell to that year's gold, rehearsals resumed in January 1993, at which point Wallace found himself on the receiving end of the Parker treatment.

Winston Watson: At one point Ian had gotten pretty irritated with the whole thing, pulled [tour manager] Jeff Kramer aside, and said, 'What's the deal here?' . . . Ian didn't want Charlie there, he certainly didn't want me there, but then when Ireland came about they told him [he was out], the day before he was leaving.

The four-piece Garnier/Jackson/Baxter/Watson combo would last from February 1993 through August 1996, playing some 357 shows, the longest-standing of Dylan's bands. Even though Watson was prone to playing until his cymbals runneth over; Jackson had been cowed into giving Dylan's guitar rein; and Baxter went on the nod on occasions, all three were capable of a degree of instrumental intuition. The level of intimidation Dylan's presence alone could induce should not be under-estimated.

Bucky Baxter: He's in a lot of different moods [onstage]. He'll be looking at you like you're king of the world. Two songs later, he's shrinking you with his eyes: 'You suck so bad.' At the end of a show you almost forget about the good parts, because you're uptight about the parts he isn't digging . . . My friends say, 'What's it like?' And I always say, 'It's not that much fun. But it's incredibly interesting.'

And yet, save for a couple of tribute-CD sessions, for Jimmie Rodgers and Elvis Presley respectively, in 1994, his touring band would never participate in an official Dylan session; and, but for the Supper Club shows, where Dylan held some of Watson's overplaying in check, their first two years together would be spent playing strangely nondescript shows, halfway between the occasionally shambolic approach of 1976, 1987, and 1988–90 and the 'putting on a show' aspect of 1966, 1975, and 1979–80. Quite simply, the 1993–94 shows failed to satisfy the demands of the most faithful sections of his audience.

In part, this was because Dylan would neither define himself as band-leader nor assign the duties elsewhere. He had become overly enamored of playing electric lead, and expected the band to play follow the leader. Unfortunately, as David Mansfield observes, '[Though] he now knows how to play a lead solo in the key that the band is playing in, I think what he's doing is improvising solos on the guitar the way he did on the harmonica. But it doesn't work on a guitar. He'll take two or three notes, get like a little motif, vary the rhythm, vary the expression and play with it, but not having the breath control you have on harmonica, it has none of the interest.' Joel Bernstein concurs: 'He has very good ideas about what it is he thinks he wants to play . . . but he *so* doesn't practice.' Though certain born-again critics have sought to convince all comers that this is a brilliantly intuitive way of playing free-form guitar, this closet Deadhead mentality only holds its appeal to those who prefer width to quality. The crew certainly had no such illusions.

Cesar Diaz: G.E. and I had this very affectionate name for him, we used to call him Grandmaster Scanner because we would be playing in A and there would be Bob starting on an E chord, which is the first chord on the fretboard, then he would bar down with an F, an F sharp, a G, and an A, and sometimes he would go past the key and come back, and then sync into the key. He was scanning for the chord we were playing on. Okay, he's trying to reinvent himself, but [sometimes] he gets caught up in his own turmoil.

His intuitive approach, which stood him in such good stead when harnessed to a little tonal breath control, simply could not replace a little rehearsing, either with the band or alone. Increasingly unaware of a clock ticking when it came to playing solos, he had become like an autistic child with a blade of grass, playing the same riff until the neck snapped or the audience keeled over.

Winston Watson: I think a lot of the time it's like, 'Okay, we've done 148 bars of this, is anybody gonna open the door so we can walk through?' . . . You had to really watch the guy, and the guy has really obvious body English . . . When he would nod to me, that basically meant take it to the moon . . . If you watched him enough, [you'd know] when he was gonna do something—but you had to be a little clairvoyant at times too.

To give the man his due, he was merely displaying the same fearless attitude that had prompted his greatest work, albeit without the same direction home.

Cesar Diaz: I never saw Bob, at any of those shows, where he had any kind of stage fright, or any hesitation. I always thought that was the sharpest thing . . . he never showed any fear . . . [The band members] try to play like everybody [in rock] is trained to play, and they expected Bob to play by those rules. So they would go ahead and then Bob would go, 'Oh, gotcha! Now I'm gonna stay here for another three minutes.'

Perhaps the most painful examples of this came on the summer 1993 European tour, when many of the songs began to assume quite absurd proportions. Determined to out-Garcia Jerry, 'Tangled Up in Blue' and 'Shelter from the Storm' in Marseilles both clocked in at over twelve minutes, while 'Stuck Inside of Mobile,' 'Highway 61 Revisited,' and 'It's All Over Now, Baby Blue' all nudged ten.

What this man who 'never showed any fear' needed was a format that played to his strengths, as well as a band sufficiently versed in his wicked ways to be unfazed by anything.

It had taken him two years, but by the winter of 1995, he had blooded his band. And Dylan himself began to sense a change in his audiences. He had told Hilburn in 1991, 'It's hard for me to know . . . why people come out and what they are looking for, or listening for . . . Maybe the same things I was looking for when I wrote the [songs].' As the NET entered its eighth year, the people who 'were coming out to see the Legend' had been satiated, and he felt that perhaps he could now 'just get on stage and play music.' Scheduled to begin another European tour in Prague, on March 10, 1995, he found Lufthansa had given him a first-class dose of the flu. The show was put back twenty-four hours, giving the man some necessary pause. When he took to the stage the following night, still sick, he had no guitar strap across his chest, just a harmonica in his hand. The band, just as nonplussed as the punters, played on, Watson pounding out only the second-ever 'Down in the Flood,' introducing the year's opening statement: 'crash on the levee / water gonna overflow.'

Winston Watson: I guess that threw everybody for a loop—including us. I had no idea that that's what was going to happen . . . plus we were both as sick as dogs. I still had a temperature of 102.

If the electric guitar had never suited Dylan's of-the-moment approach to improvisation, his harmonica refrains had always acted as extensions from his vocal gymnastics, able to express something through breath and tone that turned words into worthless foam. When he forsook the guitar entirely, performing an entire hundred-minute set in Prague with just his voice and harmonica, not only was the consummate performer unleashed, but so was the band. The acoustic set of 'Mr. Tambourine Man,' 'Boots of Spanish Leather,' and 'It's All Over Now, Baby Blue' wouldn't have shamed any 1966 stage, as Dylan slipped in an oft-forgotten verse, seguing harmonica breaks into verses and, on 'Baby Blue' in particular, expressing a sorrow for the human condition in a simple harmonica fugue that even its finely wrought lines could not match.

Though his strange shadow-boxer moves and an odd interlude on the drum rise, scrunched up in pain, suggested just how much Dylan was forcing himself to the brink, once he had gotten there he seemed content to stay for the remainder of the European leg. The momentum was maintained into early summer. Gradually adopting the guitar for more and more of the set, he still worked up a head of steam as the electric sets were renewed by some unexpected NET debuts, notably those precursors to grunge, 'Tombstone Blues,' 'Pledging My Time,' and 'Obviously Five Believers.'

He also got to share the bill on five shows with the Dead, though this time he played with his band and Garcia stuck to his. If Dylan was no longer waiting for the man, Garcia was about to wait on God. Less than two months after they shared the stage of the RFK Stadium in Washington for the last time, Garcia was found dead at a rehab clinic in California, his great hulking body having given up its uneven contest with a previously sharp mind that had shown as little self-discipline in its personal habits as in its music-making. Dylan, though, felt the loss keenly, reflected in a heart-rending statement he gave to the press:

Bob Dylan: There's no way to measure his greatness or magnitude as a person or as a player. I don't think eulogizing will do him justice. He was that great, much more than a superb musician with an uncanny ear and dexterity. He is the very spirit personified of whatever is Muddy River Country at its core and screams up into the spheres. He really had no equal. To me he wasn't only a musician and friend, he was more like a big brother who taught and showed me more than he'll ever know. There's a lot of spaces and advances between the Carter Family and, say, Ornette Coleman, a lot of universes, but he filled them all without being a member of any school. His playing was moody, awesome, sophisticated, hypnotic, and subtle. There's no way to convey the loss. It just digs down really deep. [1995]

If he had never had a real chance to pay testimony to his old friend in life, Dylan was there at the funeral. He was more fortunate in November

1995, becoming one of the more surprising members of a cast of thousands assembled at the Shrine Auditorium in Los Angeles to celebrate the eightieth birthday of the original Blue Eyes. At Sinatra's own request, he even dug up a song he had not sung in thirty-one years, his own parting glass, 'Restless Farewell,' and then, augmented by a string quartet, delivered a performance as understated as anything the don of all crooners could have conjured up in his younger days.

Preoccupied as he was by those for whom time had slipped away, Dylan learned that another old friend who had seen too many close friends slip away was preparing her return to the public arena she'd abandoned sixteen years earlier. Though it was unknown for him to tour in December—interfering as it did with time on the farm—on his instructions, his 'people' began to prod his old admirer, Patti Smith, into a joint tour of the East Coast. Back in 1979, Smith had done a Dylan, married her sweetheart, Fred 'Sonic' Smith, and moved to Detroit to start a family. A series of personal catastrophes, which first claimed photographer Robert Mapplethorpe and pianist Richard Sohl at the turn of the decade, culminated in the deaths of her husband, Fred, and her brother, Todd, in the second half of 1994. A pressing financial need now pushed Smith into beginning her first album in a decade and playing some acoustic shows, at which she sang a quite bewitching version of 'Dark Eyes,' usually prefaced by a reading of her poem 'Dylan's Dog.' If she wasn't sure whether she was quite ready to descend again into the rock maelstrom, Dylan leaned on her until she shoved back. With the onus on someone else to sustain the bulk of the program, Smith took this unique opportunity to ease herself back into the limelight.

With the ten-date Paradise Lost tour, as it was billed, rolling off the tracks, Dylan took Smith aside, at a 4 P.M. sound-check on the first night in Boston, and told her, 'Patti, I was worried about you. You gave your soul away to somebody else. Don't ever do that again.' It was both a surprisingly acute insight into the relationship between Patti and Fred, and an admission that he knew all too well what it was to give 'your soul away to somebody else.' That he was no longer prepared to do anything of the sort had prompted a life of dislocation, but, fleetingly, he now had someone with whom he could share the sentiments of 'Dark Eyes,' their one-song duet in the Dylan set and the most affecting, if not the most musical, moment of the evening.

Though the Patti Smith sets could barely contain that sense of discovery so lacking in the majority of Dylan shows since 1992, the Paradise Lost shows provided the opportunity for a reconditioned headliner to flash his credentials occasionally, even if he was usually content to just see that night's journey through. The eight-verse 'Desolation Row' in Bethlehem, Pennsylvania, on December 13, the 'One Too Many Mornings' at the Beacon the following night, and the 'Forever Young' at the penultimate Philly show, were the first moments in six months to hark back to those Never Ending Tour nights—from Mountain View to Prague—when in Dylan's words, 'the moon is conducting the show almost.' And now, back in Philadelphia, playing out his 118th show of 1995, Patti Smith lent her rekindled voice to a strident 'Knockin' on Heaven's Door'. As she had back in '75, at the beginning of her great adventure, Patti's example seems to have reminded her mentor that it was time again for him to slide.

1997–98: Almost Meeting Elvis

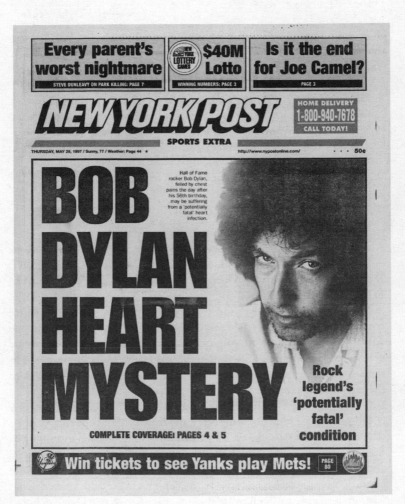

39

Everybody works in the shadow of what they've previously done.
But you have to overcome that.

—*Bob Dylan, 1989*

I hate recording, man. It's so unreal.

—*Bob Dylan, 1994*

I lose my inspiration in the studio real easy, and it's very difficult for
me to think that I'm going to eclipse anything I've ever done before.
I get bored easily, and my mission, which starts out wide, becomes
very dim after a few failed takes.

—*Bob Dylan, 1999*

A year more of spinning his wheels at shows, trying to get the band out
of its rut, had yielded a single clue as to the likely landscape another Bob
Dylan album could inhabit. The song in question was a Fred Neil rewrite
of an old Elizabeth Cotton spiritual. 'I've Got a Secret (Didn't We Shake
Sugaree)' was played barely half a dozen times, its last performance
coming at the first of two farewell shows for Winston Watson at the
Atlanta House of Blues in August. According to Watson, 'I knew he
wanted to do something different and I was really, really homesick.' His
replacement was an ominous choice, David Kemper, the drummer from
the Jerry Garcia Band.

'I've Got a Secret' managed the difficult trick of making the seemingly
traditional appear both contemporary and timeless. The opening verse—
'I've got a secret I shouldn't tell / I'm going to go to heaven in a split-pea
shell / Lordy me, didn't we shake up sugaree / Everything I had is done
and pawned'—had all the resonance of many a true, valid death but little
of the commonplace imagery. However much Neil had taken from
Cotton, he had very much made the song his own. When Dylan debuted
the song in Germany in June 1996, it was obvious that he was investing
its performance with a whole locker of expression he'd been hiding from

his own songs all year. Whether he could turn this trick himself, and whether an album of Dylanesque departures would result, were questions he now began to ask himself. It had been a frustrating few years for the erstwhile songsmith. The previous year he had admitted in an interview:

Bob Dylan: In the past few years, events have affected me and I've addressed them. But unless a song flows out naturally and doesn't have to be chaperoned, it just dissipates . . . I'll write a verse down and never complete it. It's hard to be vigilant over the whole thing . . . As you get older, you get smarter, and that can hinder you because you try to gain control over the creative impulse . . . In my case, a lot of these songs, they lay around imperfectly. [1995]

Garcia's death in August 1995 had prompted a few days in Marin County in the company of Robert Hunter, with whom Dylan attempted to write some lyrics, but he again felt hamstrung by the need to reinvent himself. As he told Edna Gundersen of *USA Today* in 1997, 'I was constantly thinking, will these songs stand up to what I'm playing night after night?' If what Dylan told guitarist Jim Dickinson is to be believed, it was only when he found himself snowed in on his farm in Minnesota, in the chill winter of 1996, that he phoned his tour manager, Jeff Kramer, and told him, 'Well, I'm snowed in, so I'm writing songs. But I'm not going to record them.' The songs in question were apparently of a type.

Bob Dylan: [These songs] just naturally hung together, because they share a certain skepticism. They're more concerned with the dread realities of life than the bright and rosy idealism popular today. [1997]

Having carried the songs with him on his travels in 1996, Dylan intended to spend January 1997 recording the album at Criteria in Miami, making *Time out of Mind* 'the first album I've done in a while where I've protected the songs for a long time.' Many of the songs took Neil's template, binding stray lines and couplets from tradition with some disembodied phrases of his own until they formed a cohesive whole. Here was a man who, whenever he went out one morning, had previously turned sideways into a Dylanism; who might 'step lightly . . . near the wall,' but always pulled back into originality. However, 'Trying to Get to Heaven,' the most successful of these attempts to wrap traditional lines in contemporary binding, still reads as the folk equivalent of the TV movie song 'Seeing the Real You at Last.' Dylan insists he was uninterested in making, in his own words, 'a poetic literary type of thing.'

Bob Dylan: Some people, when it comes to me, extrapolate only the lyrics from the music. But in this case, the music itself has just as far-reaching an effect, and it was meant to be that way. [*Time out of Mind*] is definitely a performance record instead of a poetic literary type of thing. You can feel it, rather than think about it. [1997]

He was as serious about the performance aspect of this new record as the shows he would give that winter and spring, his most experimental format in two years. He said he was tired of making records the old way, he wanted to make a 'record [that] is not a blueprint . . . but goes through that . . . labyrinth of fire that it takes to perfect the arrangement and structure.' Though he had been known to play friends and other strangers home demos of new songs in the past, he had never made it a practice to cut a demo version of an album he was about to record (save as the album itself). This time, though, he demoed a number of the songs under studio conditions. Indeed, one of the demos would provide the basic track for the pukka recording. According to Winston Watson, elements of the touring band 'did some work down in Miami, but . . . it was[n't] the sessions that Jim [Keltner] and Brian [Blade] played.' Presumably this was while Watson was in the touring band, in the summer of 1996. Watson recalls the music-making as very loose, clearly a formulating of ideas, rather than a resolution. At one point, Dylan just began playing a country-blues riff of indeterminate origin.

Winston Watson: He had intrigued me so much with this really primitive porch music, 'cause it was just like stomping your foot to [that kinda music], and I started messing around with just bass drum, brushes, snare drum, and my foot on the hi-hat.

The result was the incongruous 'Dirt Road Blues,' a song that had such a peculiar groove that producer Daniel Lanois remembers 'pull[ing] out the original [demo] cassette, sampl[ing] sixteen bars, and we played over that.' Watson also recalls working on 'Can't Wait,' though just 'a groove as such,' while Lanois recalls the demo of 'Not Dark Yet' as having 'a radically different feel . . . in the studio, he changed it into a Civil War ballad.'

Despite the lengthy gestation period, Dylan was still working on the lyrics when the sessions proper began, in January 1997. For the seventeen-minute album closer, 'Highlands'—which took its central motif, 'My heart's in the highlands,' from a chorus Robert Burns had purloined from a stall ballad, 'The Strong Walls of Derry'—Dylan didn't so much improvise as take 'a lot of different thoughts [and] connect [them] in a lot of different ways.' Guitarist Jim Dickinson—the man Dylan called his brother at the 1998 Grammy ceremony—recalls him 'leaning over the equipment case working on the lyrics . . . with a pencil.' And yet, despite his professed determination to make an album not of blueprints, but of finished articles, 'Highlands' was just one instance where, in the end, Dylan chose the initial run through, rather than 'when it settled down into a groove.'

If Dylan wanted lyrics that took the listener back to a time 'before the celestial grunge . . . before all the ancient & honorable artillery had been taken out of the city,' he required a sound that would maintain the effect—a sound neither retro nor contemporary. As he put it himself, 'Technology is not really my friend. It just takes it and trivializes my particular style of music.' His solution was to recruit the man who had made his last quantum leap a safe landing: Daniel Lanois.

Since *Oh Mercy*, Lanois had established a certain reputation for making records that sounded like Daniel Lanois records, irrespective of the artist on the spine. He had recently taken his wrecking ball to the songbird Emmylou Harris, and then made a film (*The Making of 'Wrecking Ball'*) that documented the destruction. Yet Dylan was convinced by an assured Lanois that he could help 'to make a record that sounds like a record played on a record player.' Lanois even humored Dylan to the extent of sampling certain sounds from scratchy old records, to get a sense of their 'natural depth of field.'

Daniel Lanois: What we . . . did this time was make reference to some old records from the 1950s that Bob really likes because they had a natural depth of field which was not the result of a mixing technique. You get the sense that somebody is in the front singing, a couple of other people are further behind and somebody else is way in the back of the room. So we set up the studio like that.

Dylan might have remained enough of a Luddite to be unaware of the impossibility of replicating the analogue warmth of a room-miked two-track in the icy realms of digital multitracks, but Lanois must have known all along that there was no possibility of making *Time out of Mind* sound like—let alone as good as—one of the Stanley Brothers' King recordings. Lanois also liked to have his own troops in his subterranean camp, even though he knew Dylan had his own ideas about who he wanted to play on his new album. Of those Lanois brought to the party, it would appear only drummer Brian Blade and slide guitarist Cindy Cashdollar were left in the final mixes.

Jim Dickinson: Of the drummers that were there when I was playing, Keltner was clearly there at Dylan's request . . . Bob Britt, the guitar player from Nashville, a world-class session player, was called specifically by Dylan, as I was. And Duke Robillard, and Augie Meyers. I kind of got the impression we were Dylan's band, and there was another band that was more or less Lanois's band.

Rather than removing Lanois's chosen few from the studio at the onset, Dylan seems to have thrived on the clash of elements. He was not about to change the deliberately chaotic methods he had used in the past to keep musicians jumping, and electricity in the air. Though a handful of songs on the record might have gone 'through that . . . labyrinth of fire,' much of the time they were settling for the best Dylan vocal and leaving it at that.

Jim Keltner: [When there was] consternation, [it] would be the band [who] would [be] playing this configuration that wouldn't quite work. Maybe the tempo was not right, maybe too many people playing at this time, various things like that, there were things about the style of the song, shall we do it like this—the normal things that happen at a session when you're trying to figure out how to break the code. Each time you got great performances from the artist, and I think in the end that was the final consideration—let's get the best performance from Bob . . . Whoever happened to be on the songs that had the best performance from Bob, those are the names that were gonna appear on the record.

Dylan had always found the idea of two drummers appealing, and, though he had only attempted it in the studio on the disastrous *Desire* big-band session, he seems to have enjoyed the contest between his chosen drummer, the hugely experienced Jim Keltner, and Lanois's choice, Brian Blade—not that there was a great deal of point supplementing the most dextrous hands in drumming. Keltner also had unparalleled experience of Dylan's methods, which had not changed unduly in the twenty-six years since they first met, in Blue Rock on March 16, 1971. Those changes of tempo were all part of the flow.

Daniel Lanois: There's always going to be a sense of discovery with Bob because, at the last second, without warning and as the 'record' button is pressed, he'll change the key and time signature! Then musicians will just look at themselves and dribble in and often Bob will say, 'That's it.'

Jim Dickinson: Even with the twelve people playing, it would be, like, an hour to an hour and a half of chaos, and then like eight or ten minutes of just clarity and beauty. During that ten minutes we'd nail it to the wall. [But] he doesn't want it nailed down too tight. He definitely wants it loose . . . If we got too close to 'arrangements,' he would change the tempo and the key radically.

So much for perfecting the arrangement and structure! Quite how Lanois intended to replicate the close-miking of an earlier era and, at the same time, retain all the options that multitracked instruments afforded, was a mystery he reserved for the mixing. The sessions themselves, at Criteria, had taken just a couple of weeks, and in that time, it had been Dylan who had held the helm. As Lanois himself observed, after the sessions, 'He doesn't like too much democracy.' Lanois seems to have relied on a degree of subterfuge to get the sound *he* wanted.

Duke Robillard: [Lanois] asked me to not play like me . . . not play anything related to blues, which was kind of interesting because Bob Dylan obviously wanted me there to be who I am and add that to the music . . . I wasn't really sure what to do to please either one of them . . . Just the fact that Dylan asked me to be there means that he liked what I played, but I think Daniel wants things to be combinations of elements that haven't been heard before.

Jim Dickinson, a producer in his own right, was left wondering at times what 'Dylan really wants from a producer . . . because this is obviously a muralistic, a panoramic vision this guy has got. Not just of the words but of the sounds that must be in his head . . . There is something going on everywhere you look.' Should Dylan have wanted an engineer with a title, Lanois was an expensive choice, and an acquired taste, even if his six weeks in New Orleans eight years earlier had taught him when to keep his mouth shut and when to prod.

Jim Keltner: Nowadays you have producers who are as important as the artist—or seemingly so—as much a star in their own right . . . But Bob will always deliver the songs. It's always going to be a big dynamic when the producer is well known in his own right and strong, but it can be difficult for a producer to try to produce somebody like Bob who is very strong in his own ideas. I saw Dan struggle a bit. But to his credit, I think he didn't push Bob too hard, [which] would have been disastrous.

At the end of the sessions, Dylan had recorded thirteen original songs, in a live studio situation, and though the quotient of clunkers to classics was higher than it had been on *Oh Mercy,* the length of the songs—some were six minutes long, some were seven, one, believe it or not, was seventeen—suggested an eight-song collection at most. And he had four songs that justified a level of expectation, if not necessarily the one that had grown exponentially in the years between albums. The best of these, indeed 'the best song there was from the session' according to Jim Dickinson, was called 'Girl from the Red River Shore,' an allusion to 'Girl from the Green Briar Shore,' a song Dylan had performed in concert back in 1992. Once again, it didn't make the final cut, even though the album that Dylan elected to release was an unprecedented (for him) seventy-two minutes long.

Rather than building an album around 'Standing in the Doorway,' 'Trying to Get to Heaven,' 'Not Dark Yet,' and 'Girl from the Red River Shore,' and editing 'Highlands' down to a pleasant six-verse closer, Dylan (and Lanois) had a grander statement in mind. As the mixing began of what Dickinson portrayed as 'the muck and the mire of this syrupy mix, [where] you can't tell what's playing what, or who is doing what,' Lanois came into his element. Like a good film editor, a technically competent mixing engineer or producer can make any number of records from a set number of songs and takes, particularly from sessions at which its dozen or so participants have been instructed to let it stay loose. And, though the actual melodies and lyrics were down to Dylan, the submerging of the melodies and the full frontal vocals were down to Lanois. Dickinson, for one, was unimpressed by the finished artifact.

Jim Dickinson: What Lanois has done in the mix is he's turned some instruments off, and there is not a multiple drum kit anywhere . . . Some of the mixes are playbacks from the tracking [i.e., monitor mixes] . . . The mixes are strange to me, what can I say? . . . It's just the frustration of having been there and having heard another thing in my head. There is a ghost of another record . . . in my head . . . Because I have secret knowledge of the moment of creation, there is no way I could validly judge the product, the art shell, because that's all it is.

Having promised Dylan a 'record that sounds like a record,' Jack Frost Productions delivered a Dylan CD that sounded like a Lanois CV. After all the search for authenticity, Lanois produced perhaps the most artificial-sounding album in the man's canon. As Dylan again took to the road in February, rumors circulated that he was still uncertain whether he wanted the results released. Though it may have been a classic Dylan subterfuge, designed to deflate unnaturally high expectations, the fact that he was still sequencing the album when he was forced to put it out of mind, late in May, suggests that he was not quite convinced he'd pulled off the Great Comeback. Indeed, he would suggest, at the 1997 Grammys, that it had taken Columbia chairman Don Ienner to convince him to put it out.

Bob Dylan: Up until I was sick, I was putting songs on, taking songs off. I didn't know what picture it was forming. When I got sick, I had to let it go. [1998]

Once portrayed as the Comeback Kid, it had been a long time since there had been a Dylan album that had sustained a convincing consensus among critics, beyond the initial relief that he hadn't released another *Down in the Groove* or *Dylan and the Dead*. And yet models assembled by contemporaries like Paul Simon, Neil Young, and Lou Reed in the last decade had achieved the necessary consensus, and if these examples were anything to go by, the longer the gap between albums and the more disappointing the previous platters, the better the chances of turning pre-release hype into gold, or even platinum, discs. Such seemed to be the extent of Dylan's ambition in 1997, when he crafted an album whose sense of dislocation and contemporaneous sound convinced a happy band of commentators that he had spent the past seven years honing his songwriting skills until he could do justice to the profound insight that he was gonna die, and should do his work in the face of that.

When *Time out of Mind* was released in September 1997, many critics would enthuse—if that is the right word—about the way the songs dealt with their author's mortality. Coming from a man who had sung songs betraying 'what it's like to every moment face his death' on each and every album he had made in the past eighteen years, it suggested they had hardly been paying attention. In truth, it was the critics, and dilettantes from the fan base in general, who had awoken to the man's mortality in the interim, after a health scare had put Dylan in hospital and on the front pages of the daily news at the end of May 1997. On May 29, 1997, the front page of the *New York Post* was emblazoned with the 72-point headline DYLAN COULD BE IN FIGHT FOR LIFE! and a two-page report, the leading paragraph of which ran:

Legendary folk and rock singer Bob Dylan is in the hospital after suffering chest pains the day after his 56th birthday, and may be fighting for his life. A source close to the singer said last night that one of the tests being conducted would determine whether the problem is a potentially fatal fungal infection called histoplasmosis.

Whether he had caught it in a bat cave, or down by 'one of the rivers . . . where I live,' or driving through the Midwest in his tour bus, with the air-conditioning off and the windows wide open, the 'potentially fatal fungal infection' wasn't about to kill him. However, the histoplasmosis, as it expanded, began to put pressure on the heart—hence the kind of pain that can fry the mind, and a spell in a hospital in LA (even if the press release said he was in New York).

Bob Dylan: It was something . . . that came from just accidentally inhaling a bunch of stuff that was out on one of the rivers by where I live. Maybe one month, or two to three days out of the year, the banks around the river get all mucky, and then the wind blows and a bunch of swirling mess is in the air. I happened to inhale a bunch of that. That's what made me sick . . . I was down for about six weeks, but I don't remember particularly having any kind of great illuminations at that time. [1999]

Bob Dylan: The pain stopped me in my tracks and fried my mind. I was so sick, my mind just blanked out. [1997]

One immediate result was the canceling of a joint tour of Europe with the equally curmudgeonly Van Morrison, due to start a week later. Another all-but-immediate result was a complete re-evaluation of the man's importance by the media itself. If he himself 'didn't have any philosophical, profound thoughts,' those who criticize with their laptops most certainly did.

A renewed desire to treat the man's art seriously had begun its roll the previous September, when the story broke that Dylan had been nominated, by a professor at the Virginia Military Institute, for the Nobel Prize for Literature. The professor in question, Gordon Ball, asserted that Dylan 'has restored the oral tradition with his minstrelsy. His work qualifies as both poetry and music.' Perhaps surprisingly, he found support from a number of eminent doyens of academia, notably Christopher

Ricks at Boston University, though the award itself went to an obscure Polish poet of the page. It mattered not, as other respected writers, like Bryan Appleyard, in a cover story in the London *Sunday Times* in September, began to come clean as to Dylan's importance:

If we must have lists of the greatest ever rock albums then the highest anybody else can come is 42nd. At his worst Dylan is more interesting, more intense, more fecund not only than the Springsteens . . . of this world, but also than fine artists such as Tim Buckley, Gram Parsons or Kurt Cobain . . . But more than that, he is also greater than older pop idols such as Frank Sinatra and Cole Porter. In fact, he is the one true genius of popular music, the only pop artist who can stand comparison with the very greatest. I am, at last, unafraid to place him alongside Beckett and Stravinsky, Eliot and Matisse.

After a decade of touring without respite, six weeks in the hospital seems to have done more for Dylan's profile than five-hundred-plus Never Ending Tour shows. Even his son Jakob was getting in on the act with his band, the Wallflowers, whose second album, *Bringing Down the Horse*, thanks to a number one spin-off single ('One Headlight'), had achieved something that Daddy himself had yet to do—a triple-platinum disc. The association alone seems to have encouraged a younger audience to check Papa out. Suddenly Sony was remembering all those Dylan albums that had repaid the hype and more, and, as *Time out of Mind* was scheduled for late September release, began to orchestrate a campaign of sorts.

Mikal Gilmore: For years Columbia has not cared that much about Dylan's albums, they just stick 'em on cassette and send 'em out . . . [But] Larry Jenkins, he'd take [*Time out of Mind*] around the country and play it for various people. At that point I thought I was working on a story about Dylan for *Rolling Stone* and had spoken with Larry Jenkins . . . he [had] played it in New York at the *Rolling Stone* office . . . They had the album here for one day at Sony's offices in Santa Monica and they scheduled very carefully who could come and hear it. I went over with Edna Gundersen from *USA Today*. . . I had heard it was a really good record, but people were hedging a little. I was there at the appointed time, listened to the album, and then when it was over, there was a car waiting downstairs for [the cassette]. There is something, of course, ludicrous about [that], but I also thought it was heartening that Columbia were taking Dylan seriously.

Even though no one had even gotten their hands on a copy of the album—just a promo of the first four tracks—the word was already disseminating outward. Greil Marcus—whose own new book, *Invisible Republic*, was heavily tied to the idea of Dylan's continuing relevance and his wholly conscious debt to totems of Americana like Harry Smith's *Anthology of American Folk Music*—was, not surprisingly, an enthusiastic advocate. As he touted his own book around the world, fans began to ask, What is the new album like? Well, yea, heavy:

When *Time out of Mind* plays, another country comes into view. It's less the island of one man's broken heart than a sort of half-world, a devastated, abandoned landscape where anyone might end up at any time, so long as that time is now . . . Though crafted out of fragments and phrases and riffs far older than anyone living, bits of folk languages that joke and snarl as if for the first time, this is a picture of a country that has used itself up, and the peculiar thrill of *Time out of Mind* is in its completeness, its absolute refusal to doubt itself.

Dylan himself grew cautious. He was keen to ensure that the album's presumed strengths were not overly beholden to 'fragments and phrases and riffs far older than anyone living.' After seven years' wait, another collection of other anonymous souls' words was hardly the order of the day. In the past, whenever he had opened the door on tradition, it had been to step on through. Now he was standing in the doorway or, as he put it to Gundersen, 'These songs are not allegorical. I have given that up.' As he began to give interviews, promoting what was fast perceived as his first major collection in almost a decade, he seemed almost dismissive of the lyrical content.

Bob Dylan: I don't think it eclipses anything from my earlier period. But I think it might be shocking in its bluntness. There isn't any waste. There's no line that has to be there to get to another line. [1997]

As he had with *Oh Mercy*, to which it was lyrically beholden, he chose to describe the new songs as 'stream of consciousness thing[s] . . . the riff . . . just going repeatedly, hypnotically in my head, then the words eventually come along.' In fact, it was quite clear that he had worked long and hard at giving the lyrics the pretense that they had all been randomly collected by his id from some close approximation of a concordance of folk songs. Having mourned for a world where 'there won't be songs like these anymore,' in the *World Gone Wrong* notes, he was now credited with a brilliant collage of the original and timeless by those who knew not the landscape he'd ravaged with his strip mining.

Though reviewers were finally recognizing Dylan's extraordinary capacity for making the most mundane of sentiments resonate with import, they were also attributing a powerful poetical sensibility to a man who could no longer see that nerves cannot be both 'vacant *and* numb'; who would use a folk cliché like 'she wrote it so fine' simply to get the rhyme with 'what was on her mind'; whose own links between the lines of others were, as 'the darns in a silk stocking,' quite manifest. To Damien Love of the *Sunday Times*, though,

Dylan has continued cutting away at the words—a process instigated with *John Wesley Harding*—and [on *Time out of Mind*] pared his language right down to the bone; beyond, in fact, into the suckable marrow, the elemental, almost formless stuff that life and strength and movement rely upon. That no one else could have made this record seems obvious: it reeks of time and lessons learned. Everything is plainly stated yet nothing is made exactly clear. And right there, echoing at the centre of the noise, is the voice, a holy ruin of sound, shredded, broken, grated, lost.

At least Love also responded to a long-overdue impetus to re-evaluate the work of a man whose post-accident albums, save *John Wesley Harding* and *Blood on the Tracks,* had 'fallen subject to some strange, unspoken Orwellian conspiracy, almost written out of history as non-albums.' Surprisingly few picked up on the hollowness of Dylan's desolation. If any Dylan album of the past twenty years smacked of a man for whom the oppressions of the world had pushed him into apostasy, *Time out of Mind* was it. Even 'Trying to Get to Heaven,' with its superbly constructed vocal lifting the whole song heavenward, suggested that the door, it might be closed. R. J. Smith, in the *Village Voice*, recognized the unremitting nature of the message, even as others were celebrating Dylan's return:

Dylan sings about a kind of broken heart he can never get over, about a love he can't forget. It provokes just enough hostility to women that he'll probably never play a Promise Keepers rally, but in the end you wonder how real the lover he's missing is. These are songs written by a man who for an entire decade has lived on the road. They are steeped in drift, in the inertia that wipes features off the horizon and off any particular face. Nobody seems that real to him.

Mr. Smith was a lone voice. The *Village Voice* poll, at year's end, perhaps the most thorough compendium of American rock-criticdom, voted *Time out of Mind* their album of the year, and, though the *Voice*'s own Robert Christgau tried to temper some of the more unseasonal praise, he had to admit:

In 1997, [Dylan] not only got it right but scored his greatest PR coup since he fell off that motorcycle. I don't mean to belittle an illness we're blessed he survived, but I'm convinced that *Time out of Mind* is in no intrinsic way 'about death.' Its subject is the end of a love affair, plain as the skin on your face, and at times its bleakness is overstated . . . The mortality admirers hear in it is their own, mirrored in a vocal mask half sage and half codger, in the nakedness of the one-syllable words the artist affects and the weary music that backs them. The timelessness people hear in it, on the other hand, is what Dylan has long aimed for—simple songs inhabited with an assurance that makes them seem classic rather than received.

It had been an extraordinary six months since Dylan had returned to the road on August 3rd. Though, on medical advice, he was steering clear of the harmonica-driven arrangements that had enlivened some extraordinary renditions of 'Born in Time,' 'Love Minus Zero/No Limit,' and 'You're a Big Girl Now' in the spring, Dylan and his reconstituted band—Larry Campbell having replaced J. J. Jackson on guitar in March—seemed to sense that the time was back in joint, as they worked up a rollicking live arrangement of 'Tough Mama,' aired 'One of Us Must Know' for the first time in twenty years, gave 'Cocaine' a sprightly semi-acoustic workout, and, best of all, gave 'Blind Willie McTell' an arrangement that had been gestating in all the years that lay between, enabling Dylan to pour out one of his vintage vocals.

Starting in October, the *Time out of Mind* songs also began to fill in the cracks until, by January 1998, seven of the eleven tracks had received live debuts. Though he managed to leave two of the best three songs standing in the doorway, 'Cold Irons Bound' and 'Till I Fell in Love with You' suggested some underlying qualities that had been previously buried by Lanois, 'Million Miles' and 'Can't Wait' still hankered after tunes, and 'Not Dark Yet' never entirely cracked the code (at least not until June 1999). The shows themselves were very well received, even as the sets slipped effortlessly into knees-up mode in the second half.

Dylan now found himself playing to the pope (a hundred thousand Italians and a European TV audience of millions) at an event in Bologna, at the end of September, as part of the World Eucharistic Congress.

Whether the honor took precedence over the $350,000 he was reportedly paid for his three-song set, he was not about to say. For the $200,000 he received as part of the Dorothy and Lillian Gish Award, two weeks later, at the Lotus Club in New York, he had only to say thanks and that he 'wish[ed] Lillian Gish was still alive—I wish I'd made a movie with her.' The final plaudit of an eventful year came the first week in December, when he received the Kennedy Center Honor and, at a White House reception, was heralded by President Clinton as the man who 'probably had more impact on people of my generation than any other artist.'

For the eighteen years that separate his conversion from his illness, it seemed Dylan could do no right. Now he could do no wrong. On February 25, 1998, the day after the *Village Voice* declared *Time out of Mind* the top album of 1997, Dylan stood up to perform its opening song, 'Love Sick,' at the Grammy Awards. He had been nominated for no less than three Grammys, all of which he won. Aside from making a Best Contemporary Folk Album so eclectic that it had on it the year's Best Hard Rock Vocal, Male ('Cold Irons Bound'), he was also in line for the Grammys' Album of the Year. As he stepped up to collect the award, Dylan recollected what a long strange trip it'd been.

This time he spoke not in parables, nor did he feel so defiled, but thanked his label chairman, Don Ienner, for 'convinc[ing] me to put it out—although his favorite songs aren't on it'; his producer and engineer for getting 'a particular type of sound that you don't get every day'; and the musicians, who 'didn't know what we had when we did it, but . . . did it anyway.' And then, suddenly, he placed himself back where it had all started, one night in late January 1959, when he had come face-to-face with rock's original singer-songwriter for the first and last time, at the Duluth Armory, just in time to catch the baton:

I just wanted to say, one time when I was about sixteen or seventeen years old I went to see Buddy Holly play at the Duluth National Guard Armory . . . I was three feet away from him . . . and he *looked* at me.

The Finishing End:
Trying to Get to Heaven?

i

I think he has this pattern of not being able to forge permanent
relationships. I don't even know if it's serial monogamy. He's had a
lot of relationships with a lot of women, but there seem to have been
some that have [stuck] around through other [relationships] . . . For
him there's always been a struggle to reconcile who he is personally
with who he is creatively.

—*Ellen Bernstein*

The downside of Dylan's newly restored media profile did not take long
to manifest itself. If the Grammy awards were the culmination of a
decade's worth of re-evaluating the man's role in contemporary culture,
then the story that broke worldwide a couple of weeks later opened up
a number of cracks in his personal life, beneath which much had been
bubbling. The story itself, which first ran in the *New York Post* two days
after the Grammys, came about because one of Dylan's (many) girlfriends
had finally decided to break cover. The lady in question, Susan Ross,
had spent the previous six months trying to generate interest in a proposal
for a book, to be called *Oh Mercy—The Private Life of Bob Dylan*. Claiming
to be known throughout the entertainment industry as Dylan's girlfriend,
Ross also asserted in her proposal that the notoriously private Dylan had
read the first three chapters and given her leave to continue decon-
structing the legend.

Though her writing style had editors scampering for the hills, and the proposal told them a lot more about Ross than Dylan, the portrait of the man she had known since 1985 was hardly a flattering one. Portraying a man who knew that his greatest work was behind him, she alleged that his constant touring was designed simply to occupy a raging mind. Accusing him of self-absorption and vanity, she became the first to speak 'publicly' of the way he assigns his acquaintances and employees to carefully sectioned-off enclosures in his many lives. Writing about the many female 'cousins' who would sneak into his hotel room, his obsession with secrecy, his alcoholism, alleged secret marriages and resultant children with African-American women, she even related a late night call in which Dylan told her about an Elvis sighting he had had at a small diner out west in the summer of 1992. Strange but true?

But, however much she portrayed herself as the great love of his life—and as the entire subject matter for 1989's *Oh Mercy*—Ross was merely one of a number of occasional female witnesses to the man's mysterious ways. Her association also spanned a period of Dylan's career—the late eighties and early nineties—that held little allure for the general reader. Her visions of six-figure sums, either from Dylan to keep mum or from editors to depict one of many private lives, were soon all that remained. When she misled Dylan into believing that she had been offered a huge advance to write the book, he told her, 'I can't give you that kind of money.'

Even when certain choice revelations from the proposal somehow found their way into the hands of the press, it brought Ross no closer to a book deal. Worldwide headlines like BOB DYLAN'S 'SECRET WIVES' ARE REVEALED, though, could almost have been designed to cause maximum embarrassment. Though Ross would not 'disclose the identity of his third wife or the mothers of Dylan's other two children,' the story proceeded to claim that 'Dylan is currently reading a manuscript of the biography before it is handed to publishers.' A ubiquitous 'inside source' insisted that the unsold manuscript was 'not a nasty kiss-and-tell book [though] it doesn't shy away from the truth.' Perhaps not, but a proposal graphically depicting Dylan prematurely ejaculating onto Ross's leg during lovemaking certainly wasn't about to win any prizes for taste or decorum.

Not that Ross's 'revelations' were by any means the first media mutterings to delve into Dylan's prodigious sex drive. In 1986, a story in the *Melbourne Truth* alleged that an Australian actress named Gypsy Fire had been his sex slave on his recent Australian tour. Gypsy Fire herself was less than amused by the story and sued the paper for 'obscene and blasphemous libel,' a case she went on to win the following year, despite

admitting that they had indeed made love, even if the act 'was beyond
sexuality,' and that she hadn't had sex with anyone else for six weeks
before Dylan came to Australia because she 'didn't want other men's
vibrations on her soul.'

The New Age vernacular employed by Gypsy Fire suggests a classic
Dylan type. As one journalist delving into his private life wrote in 1990,
'There are a lot of different women he sees, from all different walks of
life. But they all tend to have one thing in common. They're invariably
all very weird or very intense.' They have also tended to have something
else in common: the pretense, at least, of creativity. There is no evidence
that Dylan has ever knowingly entered into a relationship with a woman
who could challenge him artistically, but it has been from the creative
media that he has liked to draw his companions.

No less weird or intense than Gypsy Fire was Claude-Angèle Boni, a
French painter of sorts (who once wrote to me asking for certain unreleased Dylan lyrics in the hope of finding lyrical references to their 'all
too brief affair'). Her eventual response to a series of rebuffs, after their
brief assignation in 1984, was a little monograph in 1993 entitled *Stuck
Inside of Mobile (with a Rhapsody for Bob Dylan),* which unwittingly
depicted both the sort of women who pursued Dylan and the detachment
that such pursuit engendered.

A preternatural intensity afforded more regular admission to the Dylan
clan, as has been the case with a number of Hollywood types who, in
Ellen Bernstein's words, 'have [stuck] around through other [relation-
ships].' Actress Sally Kirkland had first known Dylan, in the biblical
sense, in 1976, but had been supplanted in his affections by her roommate,
Mary Alice Artes. In the eighties they resumed their friendship until, in
1989, Kirkland began to talk openly about their relationship, claiming
that 'we keep in touch through his songs and my poems.' She, too, laid
claim to sections of *Oh Mercy,* alleging that certain specific lines in
'Everything Is Broken' were directed at her. It seems Dylan still had no
answer to that fifth question—'Did you write that song for me?' Kirkland
exemplified the kind of fierce loyalty and protective streak that Dylan
seemed to command from his women friends, even when he was guilty
of extraordinary insensitivity or duplicity.

Ross and Kirkland were apparently not the only girlfriends to imagine
a greater status than was the case. On Wednesday, November 2, 1994,
the jigsaw puzzle Dylan constructed from his private life in the eighties
yielded its first serious splinters. On that day, Ruth Tyrangiel, who
(somewhat ironically) had played the Girlfriend in *Renaldo and Clara,*
filed a palimony suit against Dylan for $5 million in respect of property,

and an unspecified additional sum in respect of royalties. The suit asserted that Tyrangiel and Dylan had lived together for seventeen years, during which time she had acted as 'nurse, confidante, companion, homemaker, cook, social hostess and adviser,' before breaking up in 1993.

According to Tyrangiel, they had agreed early in their relationship to 'hold themselves out to the general public as husband and wife.' The serious financial aspect of the suit, in a system in which nuisance suits had become a way of life, was contained in the statement that the 'plaintiff and defendant enjoyed and maintained, during the course of their relationship, a certain standard of living, which standard of living the defendant promised to maintain for the plaintiff for the rest of her life.' Having endeavored to make her way backstage at the Woodstock concert in August 1994, presumably with the intention of confronting Dylan, Tyrangiel's summary ejection seems to have prompted her legal action, if simply to embarrass her former suitor. Though, on the face of it, there was a certain lack of credibility about Tyrangiel's suit, the veil of secrecy surrounding Dylan's private life was bound to work against him, and a fear of publicity about his lifestyle may have paid its part in the settlement that ensued, albeit for a fraction of Tyrangiel's original claim.

If Tyrangiel had indeed been one of a number of women whose lifestyle had been (partially) maintained by Dylan through the eighties and nineties, and whose phone calls for funds were a daily feature of life at his New York office, it was only the mothers of his children who were assured of receiving regular maintenance. In the case of his 'secret wives,' he had been singularly successful in keeping such relationships outside the media gaze. However, in June 1995, he confided to Kirkland in Washington that some kind of previously private matter was going to break real soon.

The subject of marriage, which had never entirely left Dylan's life (or art), was about to rear its head again. Here was the man who had asked, in 1980's 'Caribbean Wind,' 'Would I have married her? I don't know. I suppose'; who had sung an extraordinary plea to the Lord to protect an unspecified child at the *Infidels* sessions; and who had seriously considered remarrying Sara in 1983, when their relationship had returned to an even keel after a traumatic five years (it was Sara's photo of Dylan on the hills of Jerusalem in September 1982 that had graced the inner sleeve of *Infidels*). Even though he and Sara ultimately decided to preserve the status quo (though not before such a story ran in the *Sun*), he continued to muddy the waters when it came to his marital status. In one of the stranger interviews he gave at the time of *Biograph*, to Charles Kaiser of the *Boston Review*, he seemed on the brink of providing Kaiser with a major scoop:

When I asked him if he had been married again after his brutal divorce from his first wife, Sara, he said, 'Yes, in a manner of speaking.' A few minutes later he reconsidered and made that 'Yes, as a matter of fact.' Asked if he was still married to the woman who became his second wife in 'about '80,' he said, 'I'm not sure.'

The idea of marriage continued to appeal to Dylan, even if monogamy did not. According to country singer turned novelist Kinky Friedman, 'Bob is always on about getting married . . . He [once] said to me that everyone should have a wife somewhere in the world.' As such, the 'revelations' of Ross need not have proved earth shattering. Nor should it have seemed so surprising, that this devout Bible reader should want children of his born in wedlock, however skewered his moral code might appear viewed from the suburbs of Normality.

As the current incumbent at the White House could have told the man from Duluth, at their meeting in December 1997, it was the cumulative impact of revelation upon revelation that did the damage. Though Ross's colorful prose looked set to sink her particular ship, at least two other former girlfriends had decided to follow in her wake, detailing their liaisons with the great folk poet. Stephanie Buffington and the now-married Britta Lee Shain had not only shared his bed but experienced firsthand the collapse of Dylan's relationships with his wife Sara and Carole Childs respectively. Both also benefited from a degree of emotional distance entirely absent from Ross's proposed tome.

Fortunately for Dylan, his paramour from 1976, Stephanie Buffington, was persuaded by her editor to write an entirely different book. And, though Britta Lee Shain's 280-page manuscript, entitled *Bob Dylan: Seeing the Real You, At Last*—about her triangular love affairs with Gary Shafner and Bob Dylan during 1986 and 1987—was refreshingly well informed and engagingly written, it again only dealt with the man's 'lost' years, and was held to have little appeal in the mainstream publishing world. Come the end of 1998, the lid on an increasingly strange world had been rattled a couple of times, but it continued to hold, and with it the pressure cooker of paranoia that kept every employee, confidant, and lover in line.

ii

I think that Dylan's relations with people are poor. I think that he has integrity about his art, and I respect him for that, [but] Dylan and I never hung out and got drunk or high together.

—*Bruce Langhorne*

Like most famous people, I just want to be left alone.

—*Bob Dylan, 1997*

The picture of Dylan built up by Ross and Shain may not fit any of the idealized portraits composed by psychologically myopic fans, but it amply accords with many of the relationship songs he has composed since 1981. The author of 'Love Minus Zero,' 'I Want You,' and 'Simple Twist of Fate' has, in that period, composed a series of monologues in song that suggest a man for whom, as relationships have become little more than a series of transitory assignations with strange women, has developed a vocabulary of intimacy that may have worked on a personal level (just because), but remain hard to credit in song. Songs like 'Don't Fall Apart on Me Tonight,' 'I'll Remember You,' 'Emotionally Yours,' 'Never Gonna Be the Same Again,' 'Under Your Spell,' 'What Was It You Wanted?,' and 'Make You Feel My Love' could have easily accommo-dated the kinds of conversations that Ross and Shain depicted in their manuscripts, indeed the types of conversation enacted in a number of scenes in *Renaldo and Clara*.

His latter-day love songs lack an enduring faith in womankind. In this he is not so alone, sharing this particular trait with many a middle-aged lyric poet. Nor has his disenchantment been absolute, just as his fascin-ation for the weird and intense has hardly been a new phenomenon. Those who are convinced that they are Dylan's sister, or lover from a previous lifetime, or simply destined to be a star-crossed lover in this lifetime 'and into eternity,' seem to have always held as great a fascination for him as he does for them. Though most celebrities would rather entomb themselves in San Simeon than come face-to-face with such personages, Dylan himself is genuinely attracted to the cod-mysticism of many a suitress.

Thus, when Ross confessed, almost on first meeting, that their souls had known each other on an intimate level 'in another lifetime,' she was met by a willing credulity on Dylan's part. Indeed, he informed her that a few months before their first meeting a soothsayer had told him he would meet a tall, blonde, Jewish woman who would play an important role in his life (since he had been attracted to such types since his youth, this was hardly the psychic equivalent of going out on a limb). Sara's fascination with astrology and the occult was undoubtedly part of her attraction to him. Ditto Faridi McFree.

In my preface, I accused the latter-day Dylan of 'romantic attachments to women unworthy of the moniker Muse,' but there is a crucial difference between Sara and some of his post-divorce relationships— they come on opposite sides of the divide provided by his religious conversion, one that seems to have come about in large measure because of the divorce. (Dylan once told a latterday lover, 'I knew [the divorce] was my fault . . . I knew I'd done wrong. You see, there's just women you have to fuck because they demand it.') His comment may be a poor excuse for infidelity, but it suggests that he has always felt himself to be in the grip of what Paul Williams, in attempting to nail the 'true' cause of Dylan's Christian conversion in *What Happened?,* called 'the power of Woman':

Dylan has always believed, not unreasonably, in the power of Woman. When he finally lost faith in the ability of women to save him (and he seems to have explored the matter very thoroughly, in and out of marriage, in the years 1974 through '78), his need for an alternative grew very great indeed, and he found what people in our culture most often find in the same circumstances: the uncritical hospitality of Jesus Christ.

One book Dylan had surely read by the time of his confession was Robert Graves's historical novelization of *The White Goddess* ethos, *King Jesus,* in which Jesus proclaims, 'I have come to destroy the works of the Female . . . who delays the hour of perfection.' It was this version of Christ to which he perhaps hoped to cling, along with his 'God-fearing woman.' It was not to be. The reappearance of the Earth Mother, with her 'bells in her braids / [that] hung to her toes,' in 'Caribbean Wind,' was reaffirmed in 'Need a Woman,' in which he again asked for 'a woman / just to be my queen.' Though there are plenty of candidates in Dylan's 1995 collection of drawings, *Drawn Blank,* and though there has been no shortage of love songs on the albums from *Infidels* to *Time out of Mind,* the narrator seems almost invariably disaffected, a permanent apologist for another all-too-brief love affair, until finally, on *Time out of Mind,* he announces: 'I'm sick of love / but I'm in the thick of it.'

Just as Dylan's romantic attachment to women unworthy of the moniker Muse has a direct bearing on the dissolution of his worldview, so the failure of his artistic resolve has denied him relief. As his resolve failed him—turning him only fleetingly from an invoker of the muse to a religious advocate—Dylan not only allowed himself to become detached from his muse, but failed to find a place in his enduring faith where he 'would always be renewed.' For much of the last decade, he has seemed as much at a loss in the company of his fellow men as in the company of women. Having previously relied on the intellectual stimulation of men of ideas, he has increasingly removed himself from the kind of confidant who can challenge him intellectually or artistically. Having become used to getting his own way—as people in five-star goldfish bowls tend to do—he has denied himself the friction that friendship on an equal footing brings (when a friend of Britta Lee Shain's asked Gary Shafner what he did for Dylan, he replied, 'Paid friend, I guess').

Cesar Diaz: I didn't ask to be his personal friggin' valet . . . he would just unload all his frustrations on me and I was just supposed to react and say, 'Okay, Bob, this is what we're gonna do about it.' But so many people wanted to get so close to him . . . People don't understand that they cannot throw themselves on Bob, he's not that kinda guy. He's not that warm a person . . . There's all this philosophy that goes behind the whole Dylan thing that a lot of people don't understand, 'cause they've never had the opportunity to say, 'Wow, he's totally different in real life than I would ever have imagined.' You only see it by being there day after day after day. When it's a beautiful day and you say, 'Bob, it's a beautiful day, it's great, let's go out for a walk.' [*Dylan accent*] 'No, it's not a nice day. It sucks.' . . . You go, 'Okay. The sky's purple, it's not blue. See you later. I'm going for a walk.' 'Er, no wait for me.' 'Okay, Pops, let's go.' Of course, you go for a walk and then everybody harasses you. You're having a great conversation and some-body will, like, shove a piece of paper between the two faces. Whatever thoughts we were having, they go out the door . . . Must be a drag to be like that. How could anyone live like that, and remain in true form and be the same? . . . [But] I'd been searching for the same guy for years and years. I'd get a glimpse of the guy once in a while . . . He actually put his cards down a couple of times . . . You would have to be with him, and be there at that right moment when he just opens up and says, 'Okay, I'm just Bob, and Bob has no last name.'

Perhaps this is the only way he can deal with the myth, to detach himself from his own iconic status. As Stephanie Buffington informed me, '[Even] he speaks of himself in the third person.' Such psychological armor is undoubtedly necessary when making work as uncompromising as Dylan's in a medium where compromise is usually the main message. That mental toughness has always been there. As Suze Rotolo put it, 'He just won't accept anybody's point of view about himself . . . It's somehow all too negative, too pessimistic.' And yet, in his younger days, it was possible to pierce the armor, and when that happened, some chemical change was prone to produce the next artistic rebirth, the reinvention of self that presupposed an ongoing evolutionary state.

As Diaz says, 'you have to be there at that right moment,' a moment like the one painter David Oppenheim caught in the spring of 1975, when 'I got him to understand that he was completely mad, [and] he would grow pale in the face, and that made me feel good because I identified with the person that I thought he was in those moments of inner understanding.' That person was someone more than Just Bob, he was someone capable of 'that righteous thought.' But who is there now who can make a fifty-something rock star understand that he is 'completely mad'?

The contrast between Dylan, I Bob, and Just Bob has inspired its fair share of pithy aphorisms, of which perhaps Woodstock café-owner Bernard Paturel's 'There's so many sides to Bob Dylan, he's round' comes closest to its mark. Dylan himself has said, about the endeavors of my kind, 'They usually interview people who know me or think they know me or barely know me, but . . . it's [still] like reading about somebody else that never existed.' But then he has always enjoyed playing with the myth, confident that the last layer will never be stripped away. When he wisecracked to his secretary, 'Tell Scaduto as long as he's talked to everybody who knows everything about me, he doesn't need me to tell him about me,' it was both a brilliant debunking of the idea itself of 'an intimate biography' (Scaduto's chosen subtitle) and a necessary defense mechanism. But then, there are probably a lot more layers to Dylan than those of his contemporaries who have invested all their personalities in their fame.

Mel Howard: There are many people whom you spend time with, and the more time you spend with them the less enigmatic, charismatic, and powerful they seem, but with Dylan one's respect and even awe, if anything, increased. I've worked with some of the biggest—Redford, Streisand—and Dylan's genius and charisma transcends that of any of them.

And Dylan would like to keep the mystery going, something he let slip in an interview with Scott Cohen of *Spin* in 1985, when asked who he would like to interview himself. The list he came up with was a fascinating one—Hank Williams, Apollinaire, Joseph of Arimathea, Marilyn Monroe, John F. Kennedy, Mohammed, Paul the Apostle— but even more fascinating was the general comment that came after:

Bob Dylan: I'd like to interview people who died leaving a great unsolved mess behind, who left people for ages to do nothing but speculate. [1985]

In Dylan's case, few would disagree that his post-accident career has become one 'great unsolved mess,' containing as it does both his greatest writing (*The Basement Tapes, John Wesley Harding,* and *Blood on the Tracks*), and work unregenerate in its abjectness (*Self Portrait, Dylan,* and *Down in the Groove*). But, however much the mass media (and therefore the biography industry) seek to fix an artist's character in the moment of the last full stop, it is something no real artist can accept.

Cesar Diaz: They try to pin him down with this aren't you like an icon, the voice of your generation? See, if he accepted that title then he would lock himself into a certain time and period and he could never get himself out of it because . . . that was the best that he could ever do and he will never do anything else. But by denying it he can go on and keep reinventing himself. There's always the hope that there will be something else better than that. But people try to give you titles all the time. Aren't you so and so that did so and so? . . . They always talk about the past because of course it's all they know about you. But they don't realize that they are trapping you in a certain time and period that already happened.

Of course, it is one thing to twist in the idiot wind, asserting that much of worth yet remains, but in Dylan's case he has instilled a 'who is not for me is against me' credo that has become institutionalized in Camp Dylan. Though the game has been refined over the years, as new variants spring to mind, Dylan still enjoys the role of game master, and in order to participate in the proceedings, insiders must first interpret whether a request is a request, an order, or a test.

Arthur Rosato: He's laying on his bed in the studio down in Santa Monica and he's talking about the sound company that I picked. It was the one that Neil Diamond used. I knew Neil Diamond's production manager and he said, 'Well, [if] you wanna check out his system, come on up to Seattle.' So I flew up with Neil and his band in his private plane and [the system] was really nice . . . Bob goes, 'You just picked them because they flew you up in their plane.' I just went off. I'm looking down, I'm pointing at him . . . He's falling back further into the pillow, [going,] 'Okay, okay.' I could see he was just being a brat. But he tests people to see what they'll do . . . We didn't play that game too often . . . [But] he'll do that to a lot of people. He'll say something just to see where they go with it. On many occasions people will just run out and do it.

Such is the price of fame. At one point, sometime shortly after the accident, Dylan even seems to have convinced himself that he could somehow walk away from his past. By the time he entered his fifties, he realized that no number of *Self Portraits*, no ramshackle tour, no display of petulance was going to ultimately detonate his iconic status, they would only further inter his reputation in a mythical past of others' choosing. On one of the last occasions they met, he told Allen Ginsberg that fame was something that had no redeeming features. By then, he had been living the life for nigh on thirty years. What that life is like, on a daily basis, no outsider can ever imagine. As Diaz recognized: 'How can anyone live like that, and remain in true form and be the same?' When he delivered his pub parable on the permanent outsider, in the 1986 *Getting to Dylan* documentary, Dylan was probably alluding to an actual event. Possibly he had in mind an incident from 1971, when he was attempting to live a normal family life in the West Village:

David Amram: One time we went to the Village, [me,] Sara and him and we were looking through the window and I said, 'Man, I'm glad to be with you guys, this looks like a pretty weird scene.' It was mostly middle-aged . . . they were older people, very well dressed, beautiful Village town house, everybody drinking cocktails, and I was sorta trying to read everybody's body language, and [they] looked like a bunch of really tense people . . . not what you call going-to-the-Village hanging out, just relaxing, sitting on the floor, drinking a glass of wine and rapping, the usual scenes we enjoyed. And Bob said, 'I don't know what kind of a scene it is, but after I've been there it's gonna change.' And he laughed. So we walked in there and all these successful, established people—when they suddenly saw Bob Dylan walk in—completely freaked out and became like gawking high-school stu-

dents. They didn't mob him, everybody got silent. It was like the pope had
arrived, it was amazing, it blew my mind. Bob was just really quiet and then
after a while he'd just act so natural everyone cooled out a little bit. I said, 'My
God, man, what it must be like to have to deal with that all the time.'

Dylan's ultimate choice, made little more than a year later, was to
settle for the uniquely Californian version of fame, something that has
perhaps wreaked more damage on his art than anyone may ever know.
And yet his choice, back in 1973, to place himself within the secure
confines of the Malibu colony of stargazers, was oh so understandable.
As his attorney told the judge in his divorce case, as a preamble to his
request to have the records of the case sealed:

David Braun: When people know where he is, his garbage is sifted and
examined regularly; groups appear in front of his house on his birthday.
Fans constantly try to reach him to talk to him, to touch him, and to see
him. Recently, the sheriff had to be called to remove a girl from the driveway
of his home; afterwards she sprayed black paint all over his windows. A
disturbed person has been trying to reach Mr. Dylan through me and is
threatening to harm himself if he is unsuccessful. As a result of this and
much, much more, Mr. Dylan has been required to engage twenty-four-
hour guards about his property to prevent trespassers and protect the privacy
of himself and his family . . . In my twenty-two years' experience of representing famous personages no other personality has attracted such attention, nor created such a demand for information about his personal affairs.

It is not surprising, then, that he has developed and extended a veil of
secrecy over all aspects of his life and art, even as he seeks to surround
himself with those he can contain with glares and threats. Sad to say, the
results have been (must be?), if not the absolute atrophy of one's art, then
the production of an art form as isolated and self-absorbed as the island
the artist has become.

In 1980–81 it seemed that Dylan was reaching for a universality in his
music (and his faith) that was reflected in songs of real communion, like
'Every Grain of Sand,' 'City of Gold' and 'In the Summertime.' But it
now looks like he can no longer get back to that point as a songwriter,
and that he senses as much—even if a performance like the 'Every
Grain of Sand' in Binghampton in February 1999 still suggests that he
remembers the *meaning* of these songs. By 1983, when he attempted to
make 'Death Is Not the End' a simple offer of salvation, he had allowed
himself to become overwhelmed by 'cities on fire with the burning flesh

of men.' By 1989 he'd heard the tongues of angels and the tongues of men, and could no longer discern the difference. As of 1997, he had apparently detached himself from his fellow man entirely, sick of love and longing for some mythical 'Highlands,' where his Burnsian homilies need never be sidetracked.

As his last recording of the old millennium, Dylan wrote an original song for the soundtrack to another mainstream movie, *Wonder Boys*, and the gloves truly came off. On 'Things Have Changed' the central character is 'locked in tight [and] out of range/ I used to care, but things have changed;' with a view of the opposite sex—'I'm in love with a woman who don't even appeal to me'—that would qualify as misogynistic, if it wasn't just part of an all-pervading misanthropy—'People are crazy and times are strange;' and a view of the world damning in the extreme—'All the truth in the world adds up to one big lie.' As to the fate of mankind, the narrator seems in little doubt: 'If the Bible is right, the world will explode.'

As the apocalyptic strain in his work became fused with a very personal sense of imminent mortality—affirmed by covers of 'This World Can't Stand Long' and 'It's Too Late' in the last year—a number of doubts have nagged away at Dylan's faith. And yet his recent performances suggest someone who longs to return to the simple embrace of his original Born Again faith. Of the dozen or so covers added to the repertoire in 1999, the likes of 'Halleluiah, I'm Ready To Go,' 'Somebody Touched Me,' 'Pass Me Not, O Gentle Savior,' 'I Am the Man Thomas' and 'Rock of Ages' testify to both a world-weary yearning for release and an abiding faith in Christ's promise of redemption. They are also each drawn from the Stanley Brothers' repertoire—as if Dylan's last reinvention, after aspiring to be Hank Williams, Woody Guthrie, Jack Kerouac, Arthur Rimbaud, Joseph Conrad and John the Baptist, is now Ralph Stanley (indeed, when Dylan sang with the living legend himself, for a 1998 double-CD of duets, he considered it the proudest moment of his career).

If the extent of Dylan's ambition is now the Country Music Hall of Fame, he also evidently no longer subscribes to the view that songs can change the world. No longer, it seems, does he even believe he can convince people to have faith in something bigger. Only his very personal quest remains, and he is in little doubt as to where best he might find the necessary faith, hope and charity:

Bob Dylan: I find the religiosity and philosophy in the music. I don't find it anywhere else. Songs like 'Let Me Rest on a Peaceful Mountain' or 'I Saw the Light'—that's my religion. I don't adhere to rabbis, preachers, evangelists . . . I've learned more from the songs than I've learned from any of this kind of entity. The songs are my lexicon. I believe the songs. [1997]

The way that Dylan's fifty-nine-year-old vocal cords can still communicate the meaning of a song like 'Rock of Ages' suggests he continues to set his affections on things above, even if he has let other things get in the way of that love. It seems, indeed, that he has come full circle from the twenty-one-year-old for whom 'there came a certain point where . . . I had to write what I wanted to sing.' As he has intimated, he pretty much feels that he has written his share. And yet, as he says, 'It's all that ever remained true for me.' If for no other reason then, he continues to invest his sense of identity in the songs, and to find his earthly reward in performing them. And, even if he has genuinely written his share, long may he endeavour to repaint his masterpieces.

Dramatis Personae

This is a brief checklist of the individuals quoted verbatim in the main text, and a quick summary of their involvement with Dylan. It does not aim to provide any résumé of the individual's own pedigree, however distinguished.

KENNY AARONSON: Bassist on the 1988 shows, and for six of the first seven 1989 shows.

HARVEY ABRAMS: Fellow student at the University of Minnesota, drinking companion and fellow folksinger.

HOWARD ALK: Cameraman on the 1965 and 1966 tours; co-editor of *Eat the Document* and *Renaldo and Clara*; toured with Dylan in 1981; committed suicide in January 1982.

COLIN ALLEN: Drummer on 1984 European tour.

DAVE ALVIN: Guitarist in The Blasters and X; played at *Knocked Out Loaded* session.

DAVE AMRAM: Classically trained musician; shared music-making with Dylan on Fire Island, 1969; played on Dylan/Ginsberg sessions in 1971; accompanied Dylan to Songwriters Hall of Fame, 1982.

EDDIE ARNO: Co-director of two Dylan promo videos, 1985.

AL ARONOWITZ: New York journalist; introduced Dylan to Ginsberg and Beatles; remained confidant through Woodstock years; accompanied Dylan to Isle of Wight, 1969.

BILL AVIS: Roadie for the Band.

JOAN BAEZ: The Queen of Folk, she began an affair with Dylan in 1963, which lasted until 1965; reunited on the 1975–76 Rolling Thunder Revue; last sung with Dylan in 1984.

ELLEN BAKER: Girlfriend from Minneapolis, 1960.

STEVE BARD: A fraternity brother at Sigma Alpha Mu.

BLAISE BARTON: Engineer at sessions at Acme Studio, Chicago, in 1992.

BUCKY BAXTER: Pedal-steel player on the Never-Ending Tour 1992–98.

BONNIE BEECHER: The 'real' 'Girl from the North Country.'

DAVE BERGER: Driver on Dylan's first trip to New York.

ELLEN BERNSTEIN: Columbia A&R rep. whose affair with Dylan inspired *Blood on the Tracks*.

JOEL BERNSTEIN: Guitar technician on the 1976 tour, and assistant on rehearsals and on the first leg of the 1978 tour.

BOB BLACKMAR: Interviewed Dylan in December 1964.

NORMAN BLAKE: Guitarist on sessions for *Nashville Skyline* and *Self Portrait*.

RONEE BLAKELY: Singer/actress on the 1975 Rolling Thunder Revue and in *Renaldo and Clara*.

PETER BLANKFIELD: Village folkie in the early sixties.

MICHAEL BLOOMFIELD: Guitarist on *Highway 61 Revisited* and at the Newport '65 performance, Bloomfield first met Dylan in 1963 and last played with him in November 1980, barely three months before his own death.

CLAUDE-ANGÈLE BONI: French painter with whom Dylan shared a bed in 1984.

BONO: Interviewed Dylan in 1984 and subsequently collaborated on a couple of songs in 1987.

JOE BOYD: One of the organizers of the 1965 Newport Folk Festival.

MARLON BRANDO: Met Dylan after the Hollywood Bowl show in 1965, and again in December 1965 and at the SNACK benefit in March 1975.

EVE BRANDSTEIN: Member of the Kibbutz Givat Haim.

DAVID BRAUN: Dylan's personal attorney.

MARSHALL BRICKMAN: At school in Madison when Dylan passed through on way to New York in January 1961.

HARVEY BROOKS: Bassist on *Highway 61 Revisited* and *New Morning*, and at Forest Hills and Hollywood Bowl in 1965.

CHARLIE BROWN: Played on the New York *Blood on the Tracks* sessions.

JOHN BUCKLEN: Schoolfriend.

STEPHANIE BUFFINGTON: Girlfriend on the 1976 tour.

ERIC BURDON: Singer in the Animals, who met Dylan in New York in the winter of 1965.

KEN BUTTREY: Drummer on *Blonde on Blonde*, *John Wesley Harding*, *Nashville Skyline* and *Self Portrait*.

JOHNNY BYRNE: English poet.

MIKE CAMPBELL: Lead guitarist with Tom Petty and the Heartbreakers. As well as touring with Dylan through 1986 and 1987, he played on *Empire Burlesque* and *Knocked Out Loaded*.

RUBIN 'HURRICANE' CARTER: Unjustly imprisoned middleweight boxer whose cause Dylan championed in 1975.

MARTIN CARTHY: Respected English folksinger who befriended Dylan on his first trip to London in December 1962.

JOHNNY CASH: An early champion of Dylan, they first met at Newport in 1964, and again in England in 1966, before recording an unreleased album of duets in February 1969.

LIAM CLANCY: Member of the Clancy Brothers and regular habitué of the early sixties Village scene.

ERIC CLAPTON: First played with Dylan as a member of John Mayall's Bluesbreakers in May 1965. Has subsequently worked in the studio with him in 1975, 1976 and 1986, and they have shared the stage in 1978, 1984, 1992 and 1999.

ALAN CLARK: Dire Straits keyboard-player, who worked on *Infidels* and *Empire Burlesque*.

JAMES COBURN: Portrayed Pat Garrett in the film, *Pat Garrett and Billy the Kid*.

JOHN COHEN: Photographer and member of the New Lost City Rambler folk group, also interviewed Dylan in 1968.

RICH COHEN: Fraternity brother at Sigma Alpha Mu.

MEL COLLINS: Saxophonist for Kokomo, played on 'big band' *Desire* sessions.

JOHN COOKE: Photo-chronicler of the early sixties Boston scene.

RON CORNELIUS: Guitarist at the *New Morning* sessions.

DAVE CROSBY: Formerly of the Byrds, and Crosby, Stills, Nash and Young; sang harmony on *Under the Red Sky*.

ETHEL CRYSTAL: Friend of Dylan's mother, Beatty Zimmerman.

RICK DANKO: Bassist in the Band.

PAUL DAVIES: A Minneapolis folkie/student.

CLIVE DAVIS: President of the CBS record division between 1967 and 1973.

GORDON DAWSON: Associate producer of *Pat Garrett and Billy the Kid*.

CESAR DIAZ: Dylan's guitar tech. in the years 1988–93 and second guitarist in the NET band from October 1990 to March 1991.

JIM DICKINSON: Guitarist on the *Time out of Mind* sessions.

TIM DRUMMOND: Bassist on *Slow Train Coming, Saved* and *Shot of Love* and a member of Dylan's touring band from 1979–81.

SARA DYLAN: Married to Dylan from November 1965 to March 1977, and mother to four of his children.

RAMBLIN' JACK ELLIOTT: Important influence on the young Dylan, as the previous generation's link to Woody Guthrie.

TERRY ELLIS: Interviewed Dylan backstage in Newcastle; memorialized in *Don't Look Back* as the Science Student.

PAUL ESMOND: A pastor at the Vineyard Fellowship who counselled Dylan in his Born Again period.

MIKE EVANS: Road manager on the 1976 Rolling Thunder Revue.

LARRY FABBRO: Guitarist in the Shadow Blasters.

MARIANNE FAITHFULL: English chanteuse who frequented Dylan's hotel room on the two UK tours of 1965 and 1966.

BOB FASS: WBAI disk-jockey and early champion of Dylan's work.

JERRY FIELDING: Supervised the scoring of the music in *Pat Garrett and Billy the Kid*.

HUGHIE FLINT: Drummer in John Mayall's Bluesbreakers; played a session with Dylan in May 1965.

RAY FOULK: Co-organizer of the 1969 Isle of Wight festival.

KIM FOWLEY: Notorious Los Angeles scene-shaker.

ROB FRABONI: Producer/engineer on *Planet Waves, Before the Flood* and *The Basement Tapes*.

KINKY FRIEDMAN: A member of the 1976 Rolling Thunder Revue.

STEVE FRIEDMAN: Teenage friend.

BARRY FURLONG: Childhood friend in Hibbing.

JERRY GARCIA: Grateful Dead guitarist who played with Dylan in 1980, 1986, 1987, 1992 and 1995. Died August 1995.

DAVE GARFIELD: Assistant engineer on *Knocked Out Loaded*.

BRUCE GARY: Drummer who rehearsed with band in 1978, second drummer on three shows in 1981, and recorded some demo material with Dylan in June 1982.

ROSEMARY GERRETTE: Australian actress/journalist befriended by Dylan on 1966 Australian tour.

DANA GILLESPIE: English model/singer and companion on the 1965 UK tour.

MIKAL GILMORE: LA journalist who interviewed Dylan in the fall of 1985 and was an eye-witness to the *Knocked Out Loaded* sessions in May 1986.

ALLEN GINSBERG: Beat poet who first met Dylan in 1963, recorded with Dylan in 1971 and 1982, and toured as part of the Rolling Thunder Revue in 1975–76. Died in 1997.

TONY GLOVER: Minneapolis blues musician who taped Dylan on occasions in 1960, 1961, 1962 and 1963. Eye-witness to the *Highway 61 Revisited* sessions.

J.R. GODDARD: *Village Voice* journalist.

BARRY GOLDBERG: Pianist at Newport 1965; self-titled debut album produced by Dylan in 1973.

CYNTHIA GOODING: Folk revivalist of some reputation, who first met Dylan in the fall of 1959 and made a number of home recordings of him in New York, as well as putting him on two of her radio shows.

ROBERT GOTTLIEB: Chief editor at Alfred Knopf, publisher of *Writings & Drawings*.

STANLEY GOTTLIEB: A member of the Dinkytown folk scene in 1960.

RON GOULD: English folksinger, habitué of the London folk scene in winter of 1962–63.

SUSAN GREEN: Herbalist on the 1976 Rolling Thunder Revue.

SALLY GROSSMAN: Wife of Albert Grossman; old friend of Sara Dylan and the lady langorously draped across cover of *Bringing It All Back Home*.

KEN GULLIKSEN: Pastor at the Vineyard Fellowship.

GEORGE HABEN: Hibbing High School classmate.

JOHN HAMMOND JNR.: Folk-blues musician, befriended Dylan in 1961.

JOHN HAMMOND SNR.: Legendary Columbia producer who signed Dylan to the label.

EMMYLOU HARRIS: Sang harmony on the *Desire* sessions.

GEORGE HARRISON: The Beatle who has maintained the most regular contact with Dylan, and with whom he co-founded the Traveling Wilburys in 1988.

MICKEY HART: Drummer for the Grateful Dead.

LEVON HELM: Drummer in the Band.

ECHO HELSTROM: Hibbing girlfriend in the years 1957–58.

NAT HENTOFF: Respected jazz/folk critic who conducted several important interviews with Dylan between 1962 and 1966.

CAROLYN HESTER: Befriended Dylan in August 1961; invited him to play on her Columbia debut record the following month.

GRETEL HOFFMAN: Minneapolis 'girlfriend,' who subsequently married Dave Whitaker.

LEROY HOIKKALA: Drummer in the Golden Chords.

J. J. HOLLIDAY: Guitarist in the 1984 'Letterman' band.

JAC HOLZMAN: Head honcho at Elektra Records.

MEL HOWARD: Associate producer of *Renaldo and Clara*.

NEIL HUBBARD: Kokomo guitarist, who played on the 'big band' *Desire* sessions.

GARTH HUDSON: Organist in the Band.

IRA INGBER: Guitarist on sessions for *Empire Burlesque* and *Knocked Out Loaded*.

MARKUS INNOCENTI: Co-director, with Eddie Arno, of *Empire Burlesque* promotional videos.

BILLY JAMES: Dylan's Columbia publicist between November 1961 and October 1963, when the *Newsweek* story created a rift between them.

LARRY JOHNSON: Filmmaker responsible for shooting much of *Renaldo and Clara*.

MICKEY JONES: Drummer on the fabled 1966 world tour.

ANTHEA JOSEPH: Co-organizer at the London Troubadour club who stayed friendly with Dylan through his many subsequent visits to the UK. Died in 1997.

DANNY KALB: First met Dylan in Madison in January 1961 and subsequently followed him to New York to share in the Village folk revival.

RABBI KASRIEL KASTEL: A member of the Lubavitchers sect in Brooklyn, New York, at which Dylan was allegedly studying in 1983.

LARRY KEENAN: One of a number of photographers at the City Lights bookstore in December 1965, where Dylan, Ginsberg, Ferlinghetti, McClure and others were photographed together.

NEVILLE KELLETT: TV go-fer who attended Dylan on his 1964 UK TV appearance on *Halleluiah*.

DAVE KELLY: Personal assistant from the summer of 1979 through the winter of 1980.

JIM KELTNER: Legendary drummer who has played with Dylan in the studio in 1971, 1973, 1980, 1981, 1988, 1990 and 1997, and was part of his touring band 1979–81.

LOU KEMP: Friend from Camp Herzl who subsequently organized the 1975 Rolling Thunder Revue.

TOM KEYLOCK: Dylan's chauffeur/bodyguard on the 1966 UK tour.

MARK KNOPFLER: Dire Straits' guitarist who played on *Slow Train Coming* and co-produced *Infidels*.

SPIDER JOHN KOERNER: Minneapolis folksinger who was occasionally part of a duo with the young Dylan, and was responsible for teaching him several songs in his early repertoire.

AL KOOPER: Organist/guitarist on *Highway 61 Revisited, Blonde on Blonde, New Morning, Empire Burlesque, Knocked Out Loaded* and *Under the Red Sky*, has also played with Dylan in concert in 1965, 1981, 1986 and 1996.

BARRY KORNFELD: Folksinger on the Village folk scene.

DANIEL KRAMER: Photographer who documented Dylan on many occasions in 1964–65, and was an eye-witness to the BIABH sessions.

ARTHUR KRETCHMER: Magazine editor who was part of the Village folk scene.

KRIS KRISTOFFERSON: Singer and actor who played the role of Billy the Kid in *Pat Garrett and Billy the Kid*.

KEVIN KROWN: Met Dylan in Denver in 1960 and was perhaps Dylan's closest friend in his first year in New York. Died in 1991.

ELLIOTT LANDY: Photographer who documented Dylan's Woodstock years and took the famous cover of *Nashville Skyline*.

BRUCE LANGHORNE: Guitarist on *Freewheelin', Bringing It All Back Home* and *Pat Garrett and Billy the Kid*.

DANIEL LANOIS: Producer of *Oh Mercy* and *Time out of Mind*.

C. P. LEE: Eyewitness at the Free Trade Hall, Manchester concert in May 1966.

JOHN LENNON: Spent time with Dylan on both of his mid-sixties UK tours; they recorded together after the Isle of Wight concert in 1969. Assassinated in December 1980.

MURRAY LERNER: Director of the Newport documentary film, *Festival*.

HAROLD LEVENTHAL: Woody Guthrie's manager and organizer of the 1968 tribute concert.

JACQUES LEVY: Lyrical collaborator on the *Desire* album.

STAN LYNCH: Tom Petty and the Heartbreakers' drummer.

JEFF LYNNE: Member of the Traveling Wilburys.

PAUL MCCARTNEY: Visited Dylan on various occasions in his hotel suite on the 1965 and 1966 UK tours.

CHARLIE MCCOY: Guitarist on *Highway 61 Revisited, Blonde on Blonde, John Wesley Harding, Nashville Skyline* and *Self Portrait*.

FARIDI MCFREE: Art-teacher to Dylan's children, who had a heated affair with him against the backdrop of the 1977 custody battle with Sara.

ROGER MCGUINN: New York folkie who reinvented himself as lead-singer in the Byrds. Played on the *Pat Garrett and Billy the Kid* soundtrack album, and guested at shows in 1980 and 1987.

MARIA MCKEE: Singer in Lone Justice, to whom Dylan donated one of his leftover songs in 1984.

IAN MCLAGEN: Keyboardist on the 1984 tour.

JIM MCLEAN: Folksinger on the London folk scene during Dylan's winter 1962 visit.

EVE MACKENZIE: Dylan's unofficial landlady in his first year in New York.

PETER MACKENZIE: Son of Eve MacKenzie.

DAVE MANSFIELD: Multi-instrumentalist who was a regular feature of Dylan's touring bands between 1975 and 1978; he also played on *Street-Legal* and a single session in 1981.

RICHARD MANUEL: Singer-pianist in the Band. Committed suicide in March 1986.

BILL MARINAC: Guitarist in the Golden Chords.

BOB MARKEL: Editor of *Tarantula*.

RICHARD MARQUAND: Director of *Hearts of Fire*.

GERARD MELANGA: Photographer/filmmaker and member of Warhol's Factory clique, who made a brief celluloid study of Dylan in 1965.

PAT MESTEK: A Hibbing contemporary.

PAUL MORRISSEY: Another member of Warhol's Factory clique.

ROLAND MOUSSA: American Indian musician who first met Dylan at the Dylan–Ginsberg sessions in 1971; was subsequently invited on the Rolling Thunder Revue but turned Dylan's offer down.

MARIA MULDAUR: With her then husband Geoff, was a member of the early sixties Village folk scene; guested at a 1980 concert.

PAUL NELSON: Co-editor of the *Little Sandy Review*, who clashed with Dylan in 1963 over his review of *Freewheelin'*, but subsequently championed his transition to electric as then-editor of *Sing Out*.

BOB NEUWIRTH: First met Dylan in May 1961 at the Indian Neck Festival and became his regular sidekick when touring in the 1960s, and again on the Rolling Thunder Revue in 1975–76.

NICO: European chanteuse who met Dylan in Paris in May 1964 and subsequently accompanied him to Greece. In May 1965, they met up again in London when Nico was recording her first single for Immediate.

JACK NISSENSON: An early fan, who recorded Dylan at the Finjan Club in Montreal in July 1962.

PHIL OCHS: Prolific topical songwriter on the early Sixties Village scene who subsequently fell out with Dylan in November 1965, but later cajoled Dylan into appearing at his Friends of Chile benefit in 1974. Committed suicide in April 1976.

DAVID OPPENHEIM: After painting a mural for the rear-cover of *Blood on the Tracks*, Dylan stayed at his home in the south of France for six weeks in the spring of 1975.

ROY ORBISON: A Traveling Wilbury who died shortly after the release of their first album.

JON PANKAKE: Co-editor of the *Little Sandy Review*.

CHRIS PARKER: Drummer in the first Never Ending Tour band (1988–90).

TOM PAXTON: Singer-songwriter on the Village folk scene.

D. A. PENNEBAKER: Documentary filmmaker who orchestrated the two documentaries of Dylan's mid-sixties UK tours, *Don't Look Back* and *Eat the Document*.

RICHARD PENNIMAN: a.k.a. Little Richard, author and performer of 'Tutti Frutti.'

VAL PETERSEN: Music teacher at Hibbing High School.

TOM PETTY: Leader of Dylan's touring band in the years 1986–87, and fellow Traveling Wilbury.

KENNETH PITT: Publicist on Dylan's UK visits between 1964 and 1966.

JOHN PRINE: Chicago singer-songwriter, whose debut New York performance was graced by an impromptu appearance by Dylan.

CHARLIE QUINTANA: Drummer at various jam sessions in 1983–84 and on the Letterman TV appearance in 1984, he subsequently toured as Dylan's second drummer between April and September 1992.

ADRIAN RAWLINS: Australian poet-writer who gained temporary entry to Dylan's coterie in 1966 on the basis of a favourable article written prior to the visit.

SCARLET RIVERA: Violinist on *Desire* and the Rolling Thunder Revue.

DUKE ROBILLARD: Guitarist on *Time out of Mind*.

ROBBIE ROBERTSON: Guitarist in the Band.

MARK ROBINSON: Director of 'Sweetheart Like You' promo video.

MICK RONSON: Guitarist on Rolling Thunder Revue.

ARTHUR ROSATO: Assistant and engineer (and occasional second drummer) throughout the Rundown Era (1977–82); first worked with Dylan on the 1974 tour.

SUSAN ROSS: Erstwhile girlfriend from 1985 to the early nineties.

PAUL ROTHCHILD: Record producer for Elektra, who witnessed a number of Dylan sessions and shows in the years 1963–66.

CARLA ROTOLO: Sister to Dylan's girlfriend, Suze, and early supporter, before cruel portrayal in Dylan's 'Ballad in Plain D.'

MARY ROTOLO: Mother of Suze and Carla Rotolo.

SUZE ROTOLO: Dylan's girlfriend in the formative years in New York; first met in July 1961; their break-up in March 1964 prompted a number of songs of remorse.

PETE ROWAN: Bluegrass musician who witnessed at least one of the *Blonde on Blonde* sessions, and was subsequently privy to a home preview of the *Blood on the Tracks* songs.

JUDY RUBIN: Early girlfriend from summer camp, whose rejection of Dylan in the winter of 1960 prompted a number of later poems.

KATEY SAGAL: Girl singer in the formative 1978 tour band; replaced prior to the actual tour by Helena Springs.

RICK SAUNDERS: Eye-witness to the Free Trade Hall, Manchester concert in May 1966.

PAUL SCHRADER: Film-director who shot the 'Tight Connection to My Heart' video in 1985.

MIKE SCOTT: Waterboys frontman who played on a Dylan session at The Church, in London in November 1985.

PETE SEEGER: Renowned topical folksinger whose early championing of Dylan played its part in his acceptance by wider folk circles, but who renounced him after his performance at Newport in 1965.

CHARLIE SEXTON: Guitarist at a number of jam sessions in Malibu in 1983; in 1999 joined Dylan's touring band.

ROBERT SHELTON: The journalist whose *New York Times* rave in September 1961 was Dylan's first big break. They maintained regular contact in the early years and, after 1964, sporadic contact which culminated in Shelton's long-awaited 1986 biography, *No Direction Home*.

SAM SHEPARD: Playwright ostensibly employed on the 1975 Rolling Thunder Revue to write a screenplay for *Renaldo and Clara*, but ended up appearing in the largely improvised film as an actor and writing a book about the experience, *Rolling Thunder Logbook*. Subsequently collaborated on the 1984 epic song 'New Danville Girl' and wrote a 1987 one-act play based on conversations with Dylan the previous year.

JULES SIEGEL: Journalist who wrote an extensive feature on Dylan for the *Saturday Evening Post* in 1966.

LARRY SLOMAN: Chronicler of the 1975 Rolling Thunder Revue, in his definitive *On the Road with Bob Dylan*, and co-director of a 1984 promo video of 'Jokerman.'

IAIN SMITH: Line producer of *Hearts of Fire*.

PATTI SMITH: New York-based rock & roll poet championed by Dylan in 1975; cajoled back into live performing by Dylan in 1995.

STEPHEN SOLES: Once house-sat for Dylan back in 1969, before becoming a multi-instrumentalist in Dylan's various touring bands in the years 1975 to 1978.

PHIL SPECTOR: Renowned producer who worked on the Concert for Bangladesh project.

MARK SPOELSTRA: Folksinger and sidekick in Dylan's early days in New York.

HELENA SPRINGS: Backing singer on the 1978 and 1979 tours, who wrote a number of songs with Dylan during their time together.

BRUCE SPRINGSTEEN: Inducted Dylan into the Rock & Roll Hall of Fame. They finally played together at a Tom Petty and the Heartbreakers gig in March 1990.

PETE STAMPFEL: Folksinger on the early sixties scene, prior to forming the Holy Modal Rounders in 1964.

ROB STONER: Bassist and musical director on the Rolling Thunder Revues and the first leg of the 1978 tour, and on the *Desire* album.

GREG SUTTON: Bassist on the 1984 European tour.

FRED TALKETT: Guitarist in Dylan's touring band between 1979 and 1981, and on the *Saved* and *Shot of Love* albums.

JONATHAN TAPLIN: Road manager in 1965–66; subsequently tried to produce a film based upon 'Lily, Rosemary and the Jack of Hearts.'

BENMONT TENCH: Keyboard player in Tom Petty and the Heartbreakers.

TERRI THAL: Girlfriend of Dave Van Ronk, and Dylan's first (part-time) manager.

LINDA THOMPSON: Met Dylan on the *Hearts of Fire* film set.

HAPPY TRAUM: Folk musician who recorded with Dylan in 1963, 1970 and 1971, and also interviewed Dylan as editor of *Sing Out* in 1968.

DAVE VAN RONK: An important influence on the early Dylan, and a still active folk-blues singer/guitarist on the folk revival scene.

BOBBY VEE: Rock & roll singer from Fargo, North Dakota, who recruited a young Bob Zimmerman as a piano player in the summer of 1959.

ERIC VON SCHMIDT: Cambridge folksinger, who befriended Dylan in June 1961 and whose arrangement of 'Baby Let Me Follow You Down' he appropriated.

JERRY WALDMAN: A friend from Camp Herzl, and frat brother at Sigma Alpha Mu.

TERRI WALLACE: A fan from Minneapolis, whose sister Karen made the first extant recording of Dylan.

DAVID WAS: Co-producer of *Under the Red Sky*.

DON WAS: Co-producer of *Under the Red Sky*; who has subsequently produced Dylan recording sessions in 1992 and 1994.

WINSTON WATSON: Drummer in the Never Ending Tour band from September 1992 to August 1996.

A.J. WEBERMAN: Self-proclaimed Dylanologist; finally met Dylan in January 1971.

BOB WEIR: Guitarist/vocalist in the Grateful Dead.

ERIC WEISSBERG: Bluegrass musician who first met Dylan in 1961; invited to play on *Blood on the Tracks* in September 1974.

JERRY WEXLER: Legendary Atlantic producer who co-produced Barry Goldberg's solo album with Dylan in 1973, and co-produced *Slow Train Coming* and *Saved* with Barry Beckett.

DAVE WHITAKER: A mentor of sorts during Dylan's time in Minneapolis. Married Gretel Hoffman, much to Dylan's initial chagrin.

DAN WHITE: Assistant engineer on Chicago sessions in June 1992.

TOM WILSON: Dylan's record producer from April 1963 to June 1965, when he produced 'Like a Rolling Stone.' Died in 1980.

RONNIE WOOD: First worked with Dylan on Eric Clapton's *No Reason to Cry* in March 1976. Subsequently worked together on *Empire Burlesque* and *Hearts of Fire*. Has also guested at a number of Dylan shows since 1985.

TONY WRIGHT: Artist/designer for the *Saved* album sleeve.

RUDY WURLITZER: Screenplay-writer for *Pat Garrett and Billy the Kid.*

HOWIE WYETH: Drummer on the Rolling Thunder Revue and *Desire*. Also rehearsed for the 1978 tour. Died in 1994.

PETE YARROW: The Peter in Peter, Paul and Mary.

IZZY YOUNG: Owner of the Folklore Center in New York in the early sixties; arranged Dylan's first concert proper, at the Carnegie Recital Hall in November 1961.

FRANK ZAPPA: Avant-garde rock artist; was approached by Dylan with a view to producing *Infidels*. Died in 1993.

ABRAHAM ZIMMERMAN: Dylan's father. Died in 1968.

BEATTY ZIMMERMAN: Dylan's mother. Died in 1999.

DAVID ZIMMERMAN: Dylan's brother.

MAURICE ZIMMERMAN: Dylan's uncle.

Song Discography

Copyrighted Dylan Songs

Code for Albums

I: Known studio recordings and the album they appear on (where no known studio or live recording exists, a copyright date is included)
II: First known live performance (where applicable)

BD = *Bob Dylan*
FR = *Freewheelin'*
TIM = *The Times They Are A-Changin'*
AS = *Another Side*
BIABH = *Bringing it all Back Home*
H61 = *Highway 61 Revisited*
BOB = *Blonde on Blonde*
BT = *The Basement Tapes*
JWH = *John Wesley Harding*
NS = *Nashville Skyline*
SP = *Self Portrait*
NM = *New Morning*
MGH = *More Greatest Hits*
PG = *Pat Garrett and Billy the Kid*
PW = *Planet Waves*
BOTT = *Blood on the Tracks*
DES = *Desire*
SL = *Street-Legal*
STC = *Slow Train Coming*
SAV = *Saved*
SOL = *Shot of Love*
INF = *Infidels*
EB = *Empire Burlesque*
BIO = *Biograph*
KOL = *Knocked Out Loaded*
DITG = *Down in the Groove*
TW1 = *Traveling Wilburys, vol. 1*
OM = *Oh Mercy*
URS = *Under the Red Sky*
TW3 = *Traveling Wilburys, vol. 3.*
TBS = *The Bootleg Series, vols 1–3*

TOOM = *Time Out of Mind*
BOBD2 = *Best of Bob Dylan*, vol. 2
45 = single release only
TAFR = Third Annual Folk Reunion
BR = *Broadside Reunion*
BB = *Broadside Ballads*, vol. 1
ATB = *Across the Borderline*

Abandoned Love
I: Studio E 31/7/75 [BIO]
II: Other End, NY 3/7/75

Absolutely Sweet Marie
I: CBS Nashville 8/3/66 [BOB]
II: Concord 7/6/88

Ah Ah Ah
I: United Western 2/4/81

Ain't Gonna Go to Hell for Anybody
I: no known studio recording
II: Toronto 17/4/80

Ain't Gonna Grieve
I: Witmark demo 8/63

Ain't No Man Righteous (No Not One)
I: Muscle Shoals 1+3/5/79
II: Warfield, SF 16/11/79

All Along the Watchtower
I: CBS Nashville 6/11/67 [JWH]
II: Chicago 3/1/74

All I Really Want to Do
I: Studio A 9/6/64 [AS]
II: Newport 26/7/64

All Over You
I: Witmark demo 1–3/63
II: NY Town Hall 12/4/63

All the Tired Horses
I: Studio B 5/3/70 [SP]

All the Way
I: LA Cream 1/4/81

All the Way Down
I: Rundown 24/4/81

Almost Persuaded
I: LA Cream 1/4/81

And He's Killed Me Too—Billy
I: CBS Mexico City 20/1/73

Angelina
I: Rundown 26/3/81 [TBS]

Apple Suckling Tree
I: Big Pink 9–10/67 [BT]

Are You Ready?
I: Muscle Shoals 14/2/80 [SAV]
II: Charleston 8/2/80

As I Went Out One Morning
I: CBS Nashville 6/11/67 [JWH]
II: Toronto 10/1/74

Baby, Give It Up w/ Helena Springs
I: no known studio recording, © 1979

Baby, I'm in the Mood for You
I: Studio A 9/7/62 [BIO]; Witmark
demo 12/62

Baby Let Me Follow Me Down
I: Witmark demo 1/64
II: Burlington 23/10/65

Baby, Stop Crying
I: Rundown 28/4/78 [SL]
II: LA Universal 1/6/78

Ballad for a Friend
I: Leeds Music demo 1/62

Ballad in Plain D
I: Studio A 9/6/64 [AS]
II: Ann Arbor 7/64

Ballad of a Thin Man
I: Studio A 2/8/65 [H61]
II: Forest Hills, NY 28/8/65

Ballad of Donald White
I: WBAI 5/62 [BR]

Ballad of Easy Rider w/ Roger
McGuinn
I: no known studio recording, © 1969

Ballad of Frankie Lee and Judas Priest
I: CBS Nashville 17/10/67 [JWH]
II: JWH, Philadelphia 10/7/87

Ballad of Hollis Brown
I: Studio A 14/11/62; Witmark demo
12/62; Studio A 6/8/63 + 7/8/63
[TIM]; 19/5/93 [TAFR]
II: Carnegie Hall 22/9/62

Band of the Hand (It's Hell Time Man)
I: Festival 8–9/2/86 [45]
II: LA Forum 6/6/86

Billy
I: CBS Mexico City 20/1/73; Burbank
2/73 [PG]

Billy 1
I: Burbank 2/73 [PG]

Billy 4
I: CBS Mexico City 20/1/73
[PG]

Billy 7
I: Burbank 2/73 [PG]

Billy's Surrender
I: CBS Mexico City 20/1/73

Black Crow Blues
I: Studio A 9/6/64 [AS]

Black Diamond Bay
I: Studio E 29/7/75 + 30/7/75
[DES]

Blessed Is the Name
I: no known studio recording
II: Warfield, SF 1/11/79

Blind Willie McTell
I: Power Station 11/4/83; 18/4/83;
5/5/83 [TBS]
II: 5/8/97

Blowin' in the Wind
I: WBAI 5/62 [BR]; Studio A 9/7/62
[FR]; Witmark demo 7/62; Studio B
30/6/70
II: Gerde's 16/4/62

Bob Dylan's Blues
I: Studio A 9/7/62 [FR]; Witmark
demo 4/63

Bob Dylan's Dream
I: Studio A 23/4/63 [FR]; Witmark
demo 4/63
II: NY Town Hall 12/4/63

Bob Dylan's New Orleans Rag
I: Studio A 6+7/8/64; 12/8/63; 24/10/
63
II: NY Town Hall 12/4/63

Bob Dylan's 115th Dream
I: Studio A 13/1/65; 14/1/65
[BIABH]; 14/1/65 II
II: Philadelphia 13/10/88

Boots of Spanish Leather
I: Witmark demo 4/63; Studio A 6/8/
63; 7/8/63 [TIM]
II: Carnegie Hall, NY 26/10/63

Born in Time
I: Soniat 3/89; Complex 3/90 [URS]
II: Belfast 25/2/93

Borrowed Time
I: LA Cream 1/4/81

Bourbon Street
I: Big Pink 6–8/67

Bowling Alley Blues
I: no known studio recording

Broken
I: Soniat 14/3/89

Brown Skin Girl w/ Helena Springs,
© 1980
I: no known studio recording

Brownsville Girl w/ Sam Shepard
I: Skyline 5/86 [KOL]
II: Paso Robles 6/8/86

Buckets of Rain
I: A&R 17/9/74; 18/9/74; 19/9/74
[BOTT]
II: Detroit 18/11/90

Bunkhouse Theme
I: Burbank 2/73 [PG]

California
I: Studio A 13/1/65

Call Letter Blues
I: A&R 16/9/74 [TBS]

Can You Please Crawl Out Your
Window
I: Studio A 30/7/65; 5/10/65; 6/10/65
[BIO]

Can't Wait
I: Criteria 1/97 [TOOM]
II: 24/10/97

Cantina Theme
I: Burbank 2/73 [PG]

Caribbean Wind
I: Rundown 10/80; Studio 55 31/3/81
[BIO]; Clover 30/4/81
II: Warfield, SF 12/11/80

Catfish w/ Jacques Levy
I: Studio E 28/7/75 [TBS]; 29/7/75

Cat's in the Well
I: Oceanway 6/1/90 [URS]
II: Perth 18/3/92

Champaign, Illinois w/ Carl Perkins
I: no known studio recording, © 1969

Changing of the Guards

I: Rundown 25+27/4/78 [SL]
II: Paris 5/7/78

Child to Me
I: Rundown 24/4/81

Chimes of Freedom
I: Studio A 9/6/64 [AS]
II: Denver 15/2/64

City of Gold
I: no known studio recording
II: Warfield, SF 10/11/80

Clean Cut Kid
I: Power Station 14+15/4/83; Delta 7/84 [EB]
II: Farm Aid 22/9/85

Clothesline Saga
I: Big Pink 9–10/67 [BT]

Cold Irons Bound
I: Criteria 1/97 [TOOM]
II: 25/10/97

Coming from the Heart
I: Rundown 1/6/78
II: St. Paul 31/10/78

Congratulations w/ Traveling Wilburys
I: Stewart Home 7–16/5/88 [TW1]
II: Glasgow 6/6/89

Cool, Dry Place w/ Traveling Wilburys
I: Wilbury Home 4/90 [TW3]

Country Pie
I: CBS Nashville 14/2/69 [NS]
II: Anaheim 10/3/00

Covenant Woman
I: Muscle Shoals 11/2/80; 15/2/80 [SAV]
II: Warfield, SF 1/11/79

Cover Down, Break Through
I: no known studio recording
II: Toronto 17/4/80

Crash on the Levee (Down in the Flood).

I: Big Pink 6–8/67 [BT]; Studio B 24/9/71 [MGH]
II: NY Academy of Music 1/1/72

Crosswind Jamboree
I: Village 2/11/73

Cuban Missile Crisis
I: Broadside 11/62

Dark Eyes
I: Power Station 2/85 [EB]
II: Sydney 25/2/86

Dark Groove
I: Power Station 16/4/83

Day of the Locusts
I: Studio E 12/8/70 [NM]

Dead Man, Dead Man
I: Rundown 23/4/81; Clover 27?, 28, 29, 30/4/81; 14/5/81 [SOL]
II: Poplar Creek 10/6/81

Dear Landlord
I: CBS Nashville 29/11/67 [JWH]
II: Providence 25/10/92

Death is not the End
I: Power Station 2/5/83 [DITG]

Death of Emmett Till, The
I: Studio A 24/4/62; WBAI 5/62 [BR]; Witmark demo 12/63
II: Finjan, Montreal 2/7/62

Denise
I: Studio A 9/6/64

Desolation Row
I: Studio A 30/7/65; 2/8/65; 4/8/65 [H61]
II: Forest Hills, NY 28/8/65

Devil's Been Busy, The w/ Traveling Wilburys
I: Wilbury Home 4/90 [TW3]

Dignity
I: Soniat 13/3/89; (vcl 11/4/89) [GH3]
II: Sony Studios, NY 17/11/94

Dirge
I: Village 14/11/73 [PW]

Dirt Road Blues
I: Criteria 1/97 [TOOM]

Dirty World w/ Traveling Wilburys
I: Stewart Home 7–16/5/88 [TW1]

Disease of Conceit
I: Soniat 3/89 [OM]
II: Albany 27/10/89

Do Right to Me, Baby (Do unto Others)
I: Muscle Shoals 4/5/79 [STC]
II: Miami 16/12/78

Don't Ever Take Yourself Away
I: Rundown 23/4/81

Don't Fall Apart on Me Tonight
I: Power Station 11+12/4/83; (vcl 6/83) [INF]

Don't Fly Unless It's Safe
I: Power Station 15/4/83

Don't Think Twice, It's All Right
I: Studio A 14/11/62 [FR]; Witmark demo 3/63; CBS Nashville 17/2/69; Studio B 1/5/70
II: Gaslight Cafe, NY 10/62

Don't Ya Tell Henry
I: Big Pink 10–11/67

Down Along the Cove
I: CBS Nashville 29/11/67 [JWH]
II: 6/99

Down the Highway
I: Studio A 9/7/62 [FR]

Drifter's Escape
I: CBS Nashville 17/10/67 [JWH]
II: Eugene 30/4/92

Driftin' Too Far from Shore
I: Delta 7/84; (vcl Skyline 5/86) [KOL]
II: Concord 7/6/88

Dusty Old Fairgrounds
I: no known studio recording

II: NY Town Hall 12/4/63

Emotionally Yours
I: Cherokee 1/85 [EB]
II: Sydney 11/2/86

End of the Line w/ Traveling Wilburys
I: Stewart Home 7–16/5/88 [TW1]

Enough is Enough
I: no known studio recording
II: Rome 21/6/84

Eternal Circle
I: Studio A 7/8/63; 12/8/63; 24/10/63 [TBS]
II: Carnegie Hall 26/10/63

Every Grain of Sand
I: Rundown 23/9/80 [TBS]; Rundown 3/81; Clover 29/4/81 [SOL]
II: Lakeland 21/11/81

Everything is Broken
I: Soniat 3/4/89 [OM]
II: Beacon, NY 10/10/89

Farewell
I: Broadside 19/1/63; Studio A 6/8/63; Witmark demo 12/63

Farewell Angelina
I: Studio A 13/1/65 [TBS]

Father of Night
I: Studio E 5/6/70 [NM]

Field Mouse from Nebraska
I: no known studio recording, © 1973

Final Theme
I: Burbank 2/73 [PG]

Firebird
I: Delta 7/84

Foot of Pride
I: Power Station 22–29/4/83 [TBS]

Forever Young
I: New York demo 6/73 [BIO]; Village 2, 5, 8, 9, 14/11/73 [PW×2]
II: Chicago 3/1/74

Fourth Time Around
I: CBS Nashville 14/2/66 [BOB]
II: Hempstead 26/2/66

From a Buick Six
I: Studio A 30/7/65 [H61]
II: Forest Hills 28/8/65

Fur Slippers
I: United Western 2/4/81

Gates of Eden
I: Studio A 15/1/65 [BIABH]; Studio
B 1/5/70
II: NY Philharmonic 31/10/64

George Jackson
I: Studio B 4/11/71 [45×2]

Get Your Rocks Off
I: Big Pink 9–10/67

Girl of the North Country
I: Studio A 23/4/63 [FR]; Witmark
demo 5/63; CBS Nashville 18/2/69
[NS]
II: Philadelphia 9/64

Go 'Way Little Boy
I: Delta 7/84

God Knows
I: Soniat 9+16/3/89; 10/4/89;
Oceanway 6/1/90 [URS]
II: Zurich 28/1/91

Goin' to Acapulco
I: Big Pink 10–11/67 [BT]

Going, Going, Gone
I: Village 5+8/11/73 [PW]
II: Lakeland 18/4/76

Golden Loom
I: Studio E 30/7/75 [TBS]

Gonna Change My Way of Thinking
I: Muscle Shoals 2/5/79 [STC]
II: Warfield, SF 1/11/79

Gonna Love Her Anyway
I: LA Cream 1/4/81

Goodbye Holly
I: CBS Mexico City 20/1/73

Got My Mind Made Up w/ Tom Petty
I: Sound City 5/86 [KOL]
II: San Diego 9/6/86

Gotta Serve Somebody
I: Muscle Shoals 4/5/79 [STC]
II: Warfield, SF 1/11/79

Groom's Still Waiting at the Altar
I: Rundown 10/80; 27/3/81; 23/4/81
[SOL]
II: Warfield, SF 13/11/80

Guess I'm Doing Fine
I: Witmark demo 1/64

Gypsy Lou
I: Witmark demo 8/63

Had a Dream About You Baby
I: Townhouse 27–28/8/86 [DITG]
II: Sacramento 9/6/88

Handle with Care w/ Traveling
Wilburys
I: Home Studio 4/88 [TW1]

Handy Dandy
I: Oceanway 6/1/90 [URS]

Hard Rain's A-Gonna Fall, A
I: Studio A 6/12/62 [FR]; Witmark
demo 12/62
II: Carnegie Hall 22/9/62

Hard Times in New York Town
I: Beecher Apt. 22/12/61 [TBS]; Leeds
demo 1/62

Hazel
I: Village 5+6/11/73 [PW]
II: Winterland, SF 25/11/76

Heading for the Light w/ Traveling
Wilburys
I: Stewart Home 7–16/5/88 [TW1]

Heart of Mine
I: Clover 28+29/4/81; 15/5/81 [SOL]
II: Earls Court, London 1/7/81

Heartland w/ Willie Nelson
I: Power Station 19/10/92 [ATB]
II: 13/1/93

Her Memory w/ Helena Springs
I: no known studio recording, © 1980

Hero Blues
I: Studio A 6/12/62; Witmark demo 5/
63; Studio A 12/8/63
II: NY Town Hall 12/4/63

Highway 61 Revisited
I: Studio A 2/8/65 [H61]
II: MSG, NY 31/1/74 I

Hurricane w/ Jacques Levy
I: Studio E 28, 29 + 30/7/75; 24/10/75
[DES]
II: WTTW, Chicago 10/9/75

I Am a Lonesome Hobo
I: CBS Nashville 6/11/67 [JWH]

I and I
I: Power Station 27/4/83 [INF]
II: Verona 28/5/84

I Believe in You
I: Muscle Shoals 3/5/79 (vcl 11/5/79)
[STC]
II: Warfield, SF 1/11/79

I Can't Leave Her Behind
I: Glasgow Hotel 19/5/66

I Don't Believe You
I: Studio A 9/6/64 [AS]; Studio B 1/5/
70
II: NY Philharmonic 31/10/64

I Don't Want to Do It
I: no known studio recording, © 1985
[composition date: 1968]

I Dreamed I Saw St. Augustine
I: CBS Nashville 17/10/67 [JWH]
II: Isle of Wight 31/8/69

I Must Love You Too Much w/
Helena Springs
I: no known studio recording
II: Binghampton, NY 24/9/78

I Need a Woman
I: LA Cream 1/4/81; Clover 27/4/81
[TBS]

I Pity the Poor Immigrant
I: CBS Nashville 6/11/67 [JWH]
II: Isle of Wight 31/8/69

I Shall Be Free
I: Broadside 11/62; Studio A 6/12/62
[FR]; Witmark 4/63

I Shall Be Free No. 10
I: Studio A 9/6/64 [AS]

I Shall Be Released
I: Big Pink 6–8/67 [TBS]; Studio B
24/9/71 [MGH]
II: Plymouth 30/11/75

I Threw It All Away
I: CBS Nashville 13/2/69 [NS]; Studio
B 1/5/70
II: Isle of Wight 31/8/69

I Wanna Be Your Lover
I: Studio A 5/10/65; 6/10/65 [BIO]

I Want You
I: CBS Nashville 10/3/66 [BOB]
II: San Antonio 11/5/76

I Want You to Know I Love You
I: LA Cream 1/4/81

I Will Love Him
I: no known studio recording
II: Toronto 19/4/80

I'd Hate to Be You on That Dreadful
Day
I: Broadside 11/62; Witmark 1–3/63

I'd Have You Anytime w/ George
Harrison
I: no known studio recording, © 1970
[composition date: 1968]

Idiot Wind
I: A&R 16/9/74; 19/9/74 [TBS];
Sound 80 27/12/74 [BOTT]
II: Clearwater 17/4/76

If Dogs Run Free
I: Studio E 5/6/70 [NM]

If I Don't Be There by Morning w/
Helena Springs
I: no known studio recording, © 1978

If Not for You
I: Studio B 5/3/70; 1/5/70 [TBS]; 2/
6/70; 12/8/70 [NM]
II: Sydney 14/4/92

If You Belonged to Me
I: Wilbury Home 4/90 [TW3]

If You Gotta Go, Go Now
I: Studio A 13/1/65; 15/1/65 [TBS]
II: NY Philharmonic 31/10/64

If You See Her, Say Hello
I: A&R 16/9/74; 19/9/74 [TBS];
Sound 80 [BOTT]
II: Lakeland 18/4/76

I'll Be Your Baby Tonight
I: CBS Nashville 29/11/67 [JWH]
II: Isle of Wight 31/8/69

I'll Keep It with Mine
I: Studio A 13/1/65 [BIO]; 14/1/65 II;
Witmark ?5/65; 27/1/66 [TBS]; CBS
Nashville 15–16/2/66

I'll Remember You
I: Cherokee 1/85 [EB]
II: Farm Aid 22/9/85

I'm Not There (1956)
I: Big Pink 6–8/67

In the Garden
I: Muscle Shoals 13 + 14/2/80 [SAV]
II: Warfield, SF 1/11/79

In the Summertime
I: Clover 27/4/81 [SOL]; 14/5/81
II: Earls Court, London 28/6/81

Inside Out w/ Traveling Wilburys
I: Wilbury Home 4/90 [TW3]

Instrumental Calypso
I: LA Cream 1/4/81

Is It Worth It?
I: LA Cream 1/4/81; United Western
2/4/81

Is Your Love in Vain?
I: Rundown 26+28/4/78 [SL]
II: Budokan, Tokyo 28/2/78

Isis
I: Studio E 30/7/75; 31/7/75 [DES]
II: Plymouth 30/10/75

It Ain't Me Babe
I: Studio A 9/6/64 [AS]; Studio B 1/5/
70
II: Royal Festival Hall, London 17/5/
64

It Takes a Lot to Laugh, It Takes a
Train to Cry
I: Studio A 15/6/65 [TBS]; 29/7/65
[H61]
II: Newport 25/7/65

It's All Dangerous to Me
I: LA Cream 1/4/81

It's All Over Now, Baby Blue
I: Studio A 13/1/65; 14/1/65 II; 15/1/
65 [BIABH]
II: Santa Monica Civic 27/3/65

It's Alright Ma (I'm Only Bleeding)
I: Studio A 15/1/65 [BIABH]
II: NY Philharmonic 31/10/64

Jammin' Me w/ Tom Petty & Mike
Campbell
I: no known studio recording, © 1986

Jesus is the One
I: no known studio recording
II: Oslo 9/7/81

Jet Pilot
I: Studio A 5/10/65 [BIO]

Joey w/ Jacques Levy
I: Studio E 14/7/75; 30/7/75 [DES]
II: Foxboro 4/7/87 [D+D]

John Brown

I: Broadside 2/63 [BB]; Witmark 8/63
II: Gaslight Cafe, NY 10/62

John Wesley Harding
I: CBS Nashville 6/11/67 [JWH]

Jokerman
I: Power Station 13+14/4/83 (vcl 6/83)
[INF]
II: Verona 28/5/84

Julius and Ethel
I: Power Station 27/4/83

Just Allow Me One More Chance w/
Henry Thomas
I: Studio A 9/7/62 [FR]; Studio B 1/5/
70
II: Gerde's 16/4/62

Just Like a Woman
I: CBS Nashville 8/3/66 [BOB]
II: Vancouver 26/3/66

Just Like Tom Thumb's Blues
I: Studio A 2/8/65 [H61]; Studio B 1/
5/70
II: Forest Hills 28/8/65

Kingsport Town
I: Studio A 14/11/62 [TBS]

Knockin' on Heaven's Door
I: Burbank 2/73 [PG]
II: Chicago 3/1/74

Last Night w/ the Traveling Wilburys
I: Stewart Home 7–16/5/88 [TW1]

Last Thoughts on Woody
Guthrie
I: no known studio recording
II: NY Town Hall 12/4/63
[TBS]

Lay Down Your Weary Tune
I: Studio A 24/10/63 [BIO]
II: Carnegie Hall 26/10/63

Lay, Lady, Lay
I: CBS Nashville 13/2/69; 14/2/69
[NS]
II: Isle of Wight 31/8/69

Legionnaire's Disease
I: no known studio recording, © 1980
[composition date: 1978]

Lenny Bruce
I: Clover 29/4/81; 30/4/81 [SOL]; 14/
5/81
II: Poplar Creek 10/6/81

Leopard-Skin Pill-Box Hat
I: Studio A 25+27/1/66; CBS Nash-
ville 14/2/66 [BOB]; 10/3/66
II: Westchester, NY 5/2/66

Let Me Die in My Footsteps
I: Studio A 25/4/62 [TBS]; Witmark
12/62
II: Finjan, Montreal 2/7/62

Let Me See
I: – date unknown

Let's Keep It Between Us
I: Rundown 10/80
II: Warfield, SF 9/11/80

License to Kill
I: Power Station 13/4/83 [INF]
II: Late Night with David Letterman,
NY 22/3/84

Like a Rolling Stone
I: Studio A 15/6/65 [TBS]; 16/6/65
[H61]
II: Newport 25/7/65

Lily, Rosemary and the Jack of Hearts
I: A&R 16/9/74; Sound 80 30/12/74
[BOTT]
II: Salt Lake City 25/5/76

Living the Blues
I: CBS Nashville 24/4/69 [SP]

Lo and Behold!
I: Big Pink 6–8/67 [BT]

Lonesome Death of Hattie Carroll
I: Studio A 23/10/63 [TIM]
II: Carnegie Hall 26/10/63

Long Ago, Far Away

I: Witmark demo 11/62

Long-Distance Operator
I: no known studio recording
II: Berkeley 3/12/65

Long Time Gone
I: Witmark demo 3/63

Lord Protect My Child
I: Power Station 2/5/83 [TBS]

Love is Just a Four-Letter Word
I: no known studio recording, © 1967
[composition date: 1965]

Love Minus Zero/No Limit
I: Studio A 13/1/65; 14/1/65
[BIABH]; 14/1/65 II
II: Santa Monica Civic 27/3/65

Love Rescue Me
I: no known studio recording, © 1989
[composition date: 1987]

Love Sick
I: Criteria 1/97 [TOOM]
II: Bournemouth 1/10/97

Maggie's Farm
I: Studio A 15/1/65 [BIABH]
II: Newport 25/7/65

Magic
I: Rundown 23+24/4/81

Main Title Theme (Billy)
I: Burbank 2/73 [PG]

Make You Feel My Love
I: Criteria 1/97 [TOOM]
II: 12/97

Mama, You Been on My Mind
I: Witmark demo 6/64; Studio A 9/6/
64 [TBS]; Studio B 1/5/70
II: Forest Hills 8/8/64

Man Gave Name to All the Animals
I: Muscle Shoals 4/5/79 [STC]
II: Warfield, SF 1/11/79
V: 79–80; F80; 81; 87; NET

Man in Me, The
I: Studio E 5/6/70 [NM]
II: Budokan, Tokyo 20/2/78

Man in the Long Black Coat
I: Soniat 3/89 [OM]
II: Beacon, NY 13/10/89

Man of Peace
I: Power Station 14/4/83 [INF]
II: Verona 28/5/84

Man on the Street
I: Studio A 22/11/61 [TBS]; Leeds
demo 1/62
II: Gaslight Cafe, NY 6/9/61

Margarita w/ the Traveling Wilburys
I: Stewart Home 7–16/5/88 [TW1]

Masters of War
I: Broadside 24/1/63; Witmark 3/63;
Studio A 23/4/63 [FR]
II: NY Town Hall 12/4/63

Maybe Someday
I: Cherokee 1/85 (vcl Skyline 5/86)
[KOL]

Meet Me in the Morning
I: A&R 16/9/74 (vcl 19/9/74)
[BOTT]

Mighty Quinn (Quinn the Eskimo)
I: Big Pink 9–10/67 [BIO]
II: Isle of Wight 31/8/69 [SP]

Million Dollar Bash
I: Big Pink 6–8/67 [BT]

Million Miles
I: Criteria 1/97 [TOOM]
II: 1/98

Minstrel Boy
I: no known studio recording
II: Isle of Wight 31/8/69 [SP]

Mississippi
I: Criteria 1/97

Mr. Tambourine Man
I: Witmark demo 6/64; Studio A 9/6/

64; 14/1/65 II; 15/1/65 [BIABH]
II: Royal Festival Hall, London 17/5/
64

Mixed Up Confusion
I: Studio A 26/10/62; 1/11/62; 14/11/
62 [BIO/45]

Money Blues w/ Jacques Levy
I: Studio E 28,29 + 31/7/75
II: no known live recording

More Than Flesh and Blood w/ Helena
Springs
I: no known studio recording, © 1979
[composition date: 1978]

More to This Than Meets the Eye
I: LA Cream 1/4/81

Most Likely You Go Your Way
I: CBS Nashville 9/3/66 [BOB]
II: Chicago 3/1/74

Most of the Time
I: Soniat 3/89 [OM]
II: Beacon, NY 10/10/89

Motorpsycho Nitemare
I: Studio A 9/6/64 [AS]

Mozambique w/ Jacques Levy
I: Studio E 29/7/75; 30/7/75 [DES]
II: Clearwater 17/4/76

My Back Pages
I: Studio A 9/6/64 [AS]
II: Mountain View 11/6/88

My Oriental Home
I: LA Cream 1/4/81

Nashville Skyline Rag
I: CBS Nashville 17/2/69 [NS]

Neighborhood Bully
I: Power Station 19/4/83 [INF]

Never Gonna Be the Same
Again
I: Power Station 2/85 [EB]
II: Melbourne 21/2/86

Never Say Goodbye
I: New York demo 6/73; Village 2/11/
73 [PW]

New, Blue Moon w/ Traveling
Wilburys
I: Wilbury Home 4/90 [TW3]

New Danville Girl w/ Sam Shepard
I: Cherokee 12/84

New Morning
I: Studio E 4/6/70 [NM]
II: New Orleans 19/4/91

New Pony
I: Rundown 26/4/78; 28/4/78; 1/5/78
[SL]

Night After Night
I: Townhouse 27+28/8/86 [HOF]

No Time to Think
I: Rundown 27/4/78 [SL]

Nobody 'Cept You
I: New York demo 6/73; Village 2/11/
73 [TBS]; 5/11/73

North Country Blues
I: Studio A 6/8/63 [TIM]
II: Carnegie Hall, NY 26/10/63

Not Alone Anymore w/ Traveling
Wilburys
I: Stewart Home 7–16/5/88 [TW1]

Nothing Was Delivered
I: Big Pink 9–10/67 [BT]

Number One
I: Studio A 5+6/10/65

Obviously Five Believers
I: CBS Nashville 10/3/66 [BOB]
II: Palm Springs 15/5/95

Oh Sister w/ Jacques Levy
I: Studio E 28/7/75; 29/7/75; 30/7/75
[DES]
II: Plymouth 30/10/75

On a Night Like This
I: Village 6+8/11/73 [PW]

On a Rainy Afternoon
I: Glasgow Hotel 19/5/66

On the Road Again
I: Studio A 13/1/65; 14/1/65; 15/1/65
[BIABH]

One More Cup of Coffee
I: Studio E 28/7/75; 30/7/75 [DES]
II: Plymouth 30/10/75

One More Night
I: CBS Nashville 13/2/69 [NS]
II: Sunrise, FL 29/9/95

One More Weekend
I: Studio E 3/6/70 [NM]

One of Us Must Know (Sooner or
Later)
I: Studio A 25/1/66 [BOB]
II: Corpus Christi 10/5/76

One Too Many Mornings
I: Studio A 24/10/63 [TIM]; CBS
Nashville 17+18/2/69; Studio B 1/5/
70
II: Carnegie Hall 26/10/63

Only a Hobo
I: Broadside 2/63 [BB]; Witmark demo
8/63; Studio A 12/8/63 [TBS]; Studio
B 24/9/71

Only a Pawn in Their Game
I: Studio A 6/8/63; 7/8/63 [TIM]
II: Greenwood rally 6/7/63

Open the Door Homer
I: Big Pink 9–10/67 [BT]

Outlaw Blues
I: Studio A 14/1/65 [BIABH]

Oxford Town
I: Broadside 11/62; Studio A 6/12/62
[FR]; Witmark demo 3/63
II: Oxford, MS 25/10/90

Paths of Victory
I: Broadside 11/62; Studio A 12/8/63
[TBS]; Witmark demo 12/63

Patty's Gone to Laredo
I: ?SIR 10/75

Peco's Blues
I: CBS Mexico City 20/1/73

Peggy Day
I: CBS Nashville 14/2/69 [NS]

Percy's Song
I: Studio A 23/10/63; 24/10/63 [BIO]
II: Carnegie Hall 26/10/63

Playboys and Playgirls
I: Broadside 11/62.
II: Newport 27/7/63 [NB]

Please Mrs. Henry
I: Big Pink 6–8/67 [BT]

Pledging My Time
I: CBS Nashville 8/3/66 [BOB]
II: Modena 12/9/87

Political World
I: Soniat 3/89 [OM]
II: Toad's, New Haven 12/1/90

Poor Boy Blues
I: Leeds demo 1/62

Poor House
I: Wilbury Home 4/90 [TW3]

Positively Fourth Street
I: Studio A 29/7/65 [H61]
II: Berkeley 3/12/65

Precious Angel
I: Muscle Shoals 1/5/79 [STC]
II: Warfield, SF 1/11/79

Pressing On
I: Muscle Shoals 13/2/80 [SAV]
II: Warfield, SF 1/11/79

Property of Jesus
I: Rundown 10/80; Clover 28/4/81
[SOL]

Queen Jane Approximately
I: Studio A 2/8/65 [H61]
II: Foxboro 4/7/87

Quit Your Lowdown Ways
I: Studio A 9/7/62 [TBS]; Witmark
demo 12/62
II: Finjan, Montreal 2/7/62

Rainy Day Women Nos. 12 & 35
I: CBS Nashville 10/3/66 [BOB];
Studio B 1/5/70
II: Isle of Wight 31/8/69

Ramblin' Down Thru the World
I: no known studio recording
II: NY Town Hall 12/4/63

Rambling Willie
I: Leeds demo 1/62; Studio A 24/4/62
[TBS]

Rattled w/ Traveling Wilburys
I: Stewart Home 7–16/5/88 [TW1]

Responsibility w/ Helena Springs
I: no known studio recording, © 1979

Restless Farewell
I: Studio A 31/10/63 [TIM]
II: Berkeley 22/2/64

Ring Them Bells
I: Soniat 3/89 (vcl 6/4/89) [OM]
II: Poughkeepsie 20/10/89

Rita May w/ Jacques Levy
I: Studio E 14/7/75; 30/7/75 [DES]
II: New Orleans 3/5/76

River Theme
I: Burbank 2/73 [PG]

Rockin' Boat
I: LA Cream 1/4/81

Rocks and Gravel
I: Studio A 25/4/62; 1/11/62
II: Finjan, Montreal 2/7/62

Romance in Durango w/ Jacques Levy
I: Studio E 28/7/75 [DES]
II: Plymouth 30/10/75

Sad–Eyed Lady of the Lowlands
I: CBS Nashville 16/2/66 [BOB]

Sally Gal
I: Studio A 24+25/4/62
II: Carnegie Hall 22/9/62

Santa Fe
I: Big Pink 6–8/67 [TBS]

Sara
I: Studio E 31/7/75 [DES]
II: Plymouth 30/10/75

Saved w/ Tim Drummond
I: Muscle Shoals 12/2/80; 15/2/80
[SAV]
II: Warfield, SF 1/11/79

Saving Grace
I: Muscle Shoals 13/2/80 [SAV]
II: Warfield, SF 1/11/79

Seeing the Real You at Last
I: Cherokee 1/85 [EB]
II: Wellington 5/2/86

Señor (Tales of Yankee Power)
I: Rundown 26/4/78; 28/4/78 [SL]
II: LA Universal 1/6/78

Series of Dreams
I: Soniat 24/3/89 [TBS]
II: Vienna, VA 8/9/93

Seven Curses
I: Witmark demo 5/63; Studio A 6/8/
63 [TBS]
II: Carnegie Hall 26/10/63

Seven Days
I: no known studio recording
II: Clearwater 17/4/76

Seven Deadly Sins w/ Traveling
Wilburys
I: Wilbury Home 4/90 [TW3]

She Belongs to Me
I: Studio A 13/1/65; 14/1/65
[BIABH]; 14/1/65 II
II: Santa Monica 27/3/65

Shelter from the Storm
I: A&R 17/9/74 [BOTT/JM]
II: Clearwater 17/4/76

She's My Baby w/ Traveling Wilburys
I: Wilbury Home 4/90 [TW3]

She's Your Lover Now
I: Studio A 21/1/66 [TBS]

Shooting Star
I: Soniat 3/89 [OM]
II: Alpine Valley 9/6/89

Shot of Love
I: Rundown 11/3/81; 6/4/81; 23/4/81
[SOL]
II: Earls Court, London 1/7/81

Sign Language
I: Shangri-La 3/76 [NRTC]

Sign on the Cross
I: Big Pink 6–8/67

Sign on the Window
I: Studio B 1/5/70; Studio E 5/6/70
[NM]

Silent Weekend
I: Big Pink 6–8/67

Silvio w/ Robert Hunter
I: Sunset 4/87 [DITG]
II: Cuyahoga Falls 21/6/88

Simple Twist of Fate
I: A&R 16/9/74; 19/9/74 [BOTT]
II: WTTW Chicago 10/9/75

Sitting on a Barbed Wire Fence
I: Studio A 15/6/65 [TBS]

Slow Train
I: Muscle Shoals 3/5/79 [STC]
II: Warfield, SF 1/11/79

Solid Rock
I: Muscle Shoals 12/2/80 [SAV]
II: Warfield, SF 1/11/79

Someone Else's Arms w/ Helena Springs
I: no known studio recording, © 1979

Someone's Got a Hold of My Heart
I: Power Station 16+26/4/83 [TBS]

Something There is About You
I: Village 5+6/11/73 [PW]
II: Chicago 3/1/74

Something's Burning, Baby
I: Cherokee 12/84 [EB]

Song to Woody
I: Studio A 20/11/61 [BD]; Studio B
1/5/70
II: Gaslight Cafe, NY 6/9/61

Spanish Harlem Incident
I: Studio A 9/6/64 [AS]
II: NY Philharmonic 31/10/64

Stand by Faith
I: Rundown 10/79
II: no known live recording

Standing in the Doorway
I: Criteria 1/97 [TOOM]

Standing on the Highway
I: Leeds demo 1/62

Steel Bars w/ Michael Bolton
I: no known studio recording, © 1991

Stepchild
I: no known studio recording
II: Augusta, ME 15/9/78

Stop Now w/ Helena Springs
I: Rundown 1/6/78

Straight A's in Love
I: Power Station 2/85

Straw Hat
I: LA Cream 1/4/81

Stuck Inside of Mobile
I: CBS Nashville 16–17/2/66 [BOB]
II: Pensacola 28/4/76

Subterranean Homesick Blues
I: Studio A 13/1/65 [TBS]; 14/1/65
[BIABH]; 14/1/65 II
II: Concord 7/6/88

Suzy (the Cough Song)
I: Studio A 24/10/63 [TBS]

Sweetheart Like You
I: Power Station 14+18/4/83 [INF]

Talkin' Devil
I: Broadside 19/1/63 [BR]

Talkin' Hava Negeilah Blues
I: Studio A 25/4/62 [TBS]

Talkin' John Birch Paranoid Blues
I: Studio A 24/4/62; Witmark 1–3/63
II: Carnegie Hall 22/9/62

Talkin' World War III Blues
I: Studio A 23/4/63 [FR]
II: The Bear, Chicago 25/4/63

Talking Bear Mountain Picnic Mass-
acre Blues
I: Leeds demo 1/62; Studio A 25/4/62
[TBS]
II: Gaslight Cafe, NY 6/9/61

Talking New York
I: Studio A 20/11/61 [BD]
II: Gerde's 16/4/62

Tangled Up in Blue
I: A&R 16/9/74; 17/9/74 [TBS]; 19/
9/74; Sound 80 30/12/74 [BOTT]
II: New Haven 13/11/75 I

Tears of Rage w/ Richard Manuel
I: Big Pink 9–10/67 [BT]
II: Patras, Greece 26/6/89

Tell Me
I: Power Station 21/4/83 [TBS]

Tell Me Momma
I: no known studio recording
II: Westchester, NY 5/2/66

Tell Me That It Isn't True
I: CBS Nashville 14/2/69 [NS]
II: Anaheim 10/3/00

Tell Me the Truth One Time w/
Helena Springs
I: no known studio recording, © 1979

Temporary Like Achilles
I: CBS Nashville 9/3/66 [BOB]

Ten Thousand Men
I: Oceanway 6/1/90 [URS]

That's Alright Mama
I: Studio A 26/10/62; 1/11/62; 23/10/
63

Thief on the Cross
I: no known studio recording
II: New Orleans 10/11/81

Things Have Changed
I: studio session 1999 [BOBD2]
II: Anaheim 10/3/00

This Wheel's on Fire w/ Rick Dando
I: Big Pink 6–8/67 [BT]
II: Madison, WI 13/4/96

Three Angels
I: Studio E 4/6/70 [NM]

Tight Connection to My Heart
I: Power Station 2/85 [EB]
II: Toad's, New Haven 12/1/90

Till I Fell in Love with You
I: Criteria 1/97 [TOOM]
II: 12/97

Time Passes Slowly
I: Studio B 4/3/70; 1/5/70; Studio E 2/
6/70; 12/8/70 [NM]
II: no known live recording

Time to End the Masquerade w/ Gerry
Goffin
I: no known studio recording, © 1995

Times They Are A-Changin', The
I: Witmark demo 10/63 [TBS]; Studio
A 23/10/63; 24/10/63 [TIM]
II: Carnegie Hall 26/10/63

Tiny Montgomery
I: Big Pink 6–8/67 [BT]

To Be Alone with You
I: CBS Nashville 13/2/69 [NS]
II: Tower, Philadelphia 15/10/89

To Ramona
I: Studio A 9/6/64 [AS]
II: Newport 26/7/64

Tombsone Blues
I: Studio A 29/7/65 [H61]
II: Forest Hills 28/8/65

Tomorrow is a Long Time
I: Witmark 12/62; Studio E 4/6/70
II: NY Town Hall 12/4/63 [MGH]

Tonight I'll Be Staying Here with You
I: CBS Nashville 17/2/69 [NS]
II: Waltham, MA 22/11/75

Too Much of Nothing
I: Big Pink 6–8/67 [BT]

Tough Mama
I: Village 5+6/11/73 [PW]
II: 3/1/74

Tragedy of the Trade w/ Gerry Goffin
I: no known studio recording, © 1995

Train A-Travellin'
I: Broadside 11/62 [BR]

Trouble
I: Rundown 23/4/81; 14/5/81 [SOL]
II: Holmdel, NJ 21/7/89

Trouble in Mind
I: Muscle Shoals 30/4/79 [STC]

Troubled and I Don't Know Why
I: no known studio recording
II: Forest Hills 17/8/63 [RLC]

True Love Tends to Forget
I: Rundown 26+29/4/78 [SL]
II: Dortmund 27/6/78

Trust Yourself
I: Cherokee 1/85 [EB]
II: Farm Aid 22/9/85

Tune After Almost
I: LA Cream 1/4/81

Turkey Chase
I: Burbank 2/73 [PG]

TV Talkin' Song
I: Complex 3/90 [URS]
II: C. W. Post, NY 11/10/90

Tweeter and the Monkey Man w/
Traveling Wilburys
I: Stewart Home 7–16/5/88 [TW1]

Two By Two
I: Complex 3/90 [URS]
II: Correggio, Italy 5/7/92

Ugliest Girl in the World w/ Robert
Hunter
I: Sunset 4/87 [DITG]

Unbelievable
I: Complex 3/90 [URS]
II: Ottawa 22/8/92

Under the Red Sky
I: Complex 3/90 [URS]
II: CW Post 11/10/90

Under Turkey
I: CBS Mexico City 20/1/73

Under Your Spell w/ Carole
Bayer-Sage
I: The Church 19–22/11/85 (vcl Sky-
line 5/86) [KOL]

Union Sundown
I: Power Station 27/4/83; 2/5/83 (vcl
6/83) [INF]
II: Saratoga Springs 13/7/86

Up to Me
I: A&R 16/9/74; 19/9/74 [BIO]

Very Thought of You, The
I: Power Station 2/85

Visions of Johanna
I: Studio A 30/11/65; 21/1/66; CBS
Nashville 14/2/66 [BOB]
II: Berkeley 4/12/65

Wait and See
I: LA Cream 1/4/81

Waiting to Get Beat
I: Power Station 2/85

Walk Out in the Rain
I: Rundown 1/6/78

Walkin' Down the Line
I: Broadside 11/62; Witmark 3/63
[TBS]

Walking on Eggs
I: LA Cream 1/4/81

Wallflower
I: Studio B 4/11/71 [TBS]

Walls of Redwing
I: Studio A 23/4/63; 7/8/63 [TBS]
II: NY Town Hall 12/4/63

Wandering Kind, The w/ Helena
Springs
I: no known studio recording © 1979

Wanted Man
I: CBS Nashville 18/2/69 (inc.)

Watching the River Flow
I: Blue Rock 16–18/3/71 [MGH]
II: El Paso 21/11/78

Watered-Down Love
I: Clover 27+28/4/81 [SOL]; 15/5/81
II: Poplar Creek 10/6/81

We Better Talk This Over
I: Rundown 26/4/78 [SL]
II: Paris 4/7/78

Wedding Song
I: Village 9/11/73 [PW]
II: Philadelphia 7/1/74

Well Water
I: LA Cream 1/4/81

Went to See the Gypsy
I: Studio B 3/3/70; 4/3/70; 5/3/70; 1/
5/70; 5/6/70 [NM]

What Can I Do for You?
I: Muscle Shoals 12/2/80 [SAV]
II: Warfield, SF 1/11/79

What Good Am I?
I: Soniat 3/89 [OM]

II: Beacon, NY 10/10/89

What Kind of Friend is This?
I: Glasgow Hotel 19/5/66

What Was It You Wanted?
I: Soniat 3/89 [OM]
II: Toad's, New Haven 12/1/90

What Will You Do When Jesus
Comes?
I: ?SIR 10/75

Whatcha Gonna Do?
I: Studio A 14/11/62; 6/12/62; Witmark 8/63

What's the Matter? w/ Helena Springs
I: no known studio recording

When He Returns
I: Muscle Shoals 4/5/79 [STC]
II: Warfield, SF 1/11/79

When I Paint My Masterpiece
I: Blue Rock 16–18/3/71 [MGH]
II: Plymouth 30/10/75

When the Night Comes Falling
I: Power Station 19/2/85 [TBS]; 2/85
[EB]
II: Wellington 5/2/86

When the Ship Comes In
I: Witmark demo 9/63 [TBS]; Studio
A 23/10/63 [TIM]
II: Carnegie Hall 26/10/63

When You Gonna Wake Up?
I: Muscle Shoals 2/5/79 (vcl 11/5/79)
[STC]
II: Warfield, SF 1/11/79

Where Are You Tonight (Journey
Thru Dark Heat)?
I: Rundown 26+27/4/78 [SL]
II: Blackbushe 15/7/78

Where Teardrops Fall
I: Soniat 3/89 [OM]
II: Toad's, New Haven 12/1/90

Where Were You Last Night? w/
Traveling Wilburys
I: Stewart Home 4/90 [TW3]

Who Killed Davey Moore?
I: no known studio recording
II: NY Town Hall 12/4/63

Who Loves You?
I: Delta 7/84

Wicked Messenger, The
I: Nashville 29/11/67 [JWH]
II: Giants Stadium, NJ 12/7/87

Wiggle Wiggle
I: Complex 3/90 [URS]
II: Toad's, New Haven 12/1/90

Wigwam
I: Studio B 4/3/70 [SP]

Wilbury Twist w/ Traveling Wilburys
I: Wilbury Home 4/90 [TW3]

Wild Wolf
I: Big Pink 6-8/67

Wind Blowin' on the Water
I: Rundown 24/4/81

Winterlude
I: Studio E 5/6/70

With God on Our Side
I: Studio A 6/8/63; 7/8/63 [TIM]
II: NY Town Hall 12/4/63

Without You
I: no known studio recording, © 1980

Wolf
I: Delta 7/84

Woogie-Boogie
I: Studio B 3/3/70 [SP]

Working on a Guru

I: Studio B 1/5/70

Ye Shall Be Changed
I: Muscle Shoals 2/5/79 [TBS]

Yea! Heavy and a Bottle of Bread
I: Big Pink 6-8/67 [BT]

Yes Sir, No Sir
I: United Western 2/4/81

Yonder Comes Sin
I: Rundown 10/80

You Ain't Goin' Nowhere
I: Big Pink 6-8/67 [BT]; Studio B 24/
9/71 [MGH]
II: 4/97

You, Angel, You
I: Village 5/11/73 [PW]
II: Penn State 14/1/90

You Changed My Life
I: Rundown 11/3/81; LA Cream 1/4/
81; United Western 2/4/81; Rundown
23/4/81 [TBS]

You Don't Have to Do That
I: Studio A 13/1/65

You Took My Breath Away w/
Traveling Wilburys
I: Wilbury Home 4/90 [TW3]

You're a Big Girl Now
I: A&R 16/9/74; 17/9/74 [BIO]; 19/
9/74; Sound 80 27/12/74 [BOTT]
II: Hattiesburg 1/5/76

You're Gonna Make Me Lonesome
When You Go
I: A&R 16/9/74; 17/9/74 [BOTT]
II: Clearwater 22/4/76

You've Been Hiding Too Long
I: no known studio recording
II: NY Town Hall 12/4/63

Uncopyrighted Dylan Songs

(Asterisked items are known to have been recorded in some form)

Ahoooah: Studio instrumental 5/6/70.★
Ain't It Funny: *Blood on the Tracks* notebook.
All You Have to Do Is Dream: Basement Tapes (2 takes).★
Almost Done: Rehearsed for 1984 tour.★
Almost Persuaded: Cream studio 1/4/81.★
Baby Don't You Go: Sydney 11/2/86.★
Baby Won't You Be My Baby: Basement Tapes.★
Back to the Wall: Power Station, NY 13/4/83.★
Ballad of the Ox-Bow Incident: Mentioned to Robert Shelton 12/61.
Be Careful: Rundown Studio 23/4/81.★
Belltower Blues (Climbed Up the Bell Tower): *Blood on the Tracks* notebook.
Big City Blues: MacKenzie mss.
Bonnie, Why'd You Cut My Hair?: Minneapolis 'Party' Tape 5/61.★
Bound to Lose: Discarded Witmark demo c. 3/63.★
California Brown-Eyed Baby: MacKenzie mss.
Colorado Blues: MacKenzie mss.
Columbus Georgia: Power Station, NY 13/4/83.★
Come a Little Bit Closer: Studio B 5/370.★
Cross On Over & Rock 'Em Dead: True Confessions Tour 1986.★
Dead for a Dollar: MacKenzie mss.
Death of Robert Johnson: Mentioned to Izzy Young 2/62.
Dirty Lie: Rehearsed for 1984 tour.★
Don't Drink No Chevy: Power Station, NY 29/4/83.★
Don't Tell Him: Denver Hotel Room tape 13/3/66.★
Don't Want No Married Woman: *Blood on the Tracks* notebook.
Don't You Try Me Now: Basement Tapes.
Dope Fiend Robber: MacKenzies mss.
Down at Washington Square: MacKenzies mss.
East Orange, New Jersey: Minneapolis Hotel Tape 22/12/61.★
First to Say Goodbye: Rundown Studio 26/12/77.★
Gates of Hate: Mentioned to Gil Turner 9/62.
Girl on the Red River Shore: *Time Out of Mind* outtake.★
Going Back to Rome: 'The Banjo Tape' 21/1/63.★
Gonna Get You Now: Basement Tapes.
Greyhound Blues: Rumored 1960 composition.
'Headful of Gasoline': Incomplete track rec. Studio A, NY 16/6/65.
I Can't Come in with a Broken Heart: Basement Tapes.
I Was Young When I Left Home: Minneapolis Hotel Tape 22/12/61.★
I Wish It Would Rain: Cream studio 1/4/81.★
I'll Get Where I'm Going Someday: MacKenzie mss.
I'm a Fool for You: Basement Tapes.
I'm Your Teenage Prayer: Basement Tapes.
If You Want My Love: Denver hotel room tape 13/3/66.★

It's Breakin' Me Up: *Blood on the Tracks* notebook.
It's Just Another Tomato in the Glass: Rumored Basement Tape track.
Justine: True Confessions Tour 1986.
King Is on the Throne, The: Rundown Studio 4/81.★
King of France: Basement Tapes.
Las Vegas Blues(?)
Like a Ship: Traveling Wilburys Vol. 3 outtake.★
Little Bit of Rain: *Blood on the Tracks* notebook.
Liverpool Gal: Tony Glover home-tape 17/7/63.★
Lock Your Door: Basement Tapes.★
Makin' a Liar: Rehearsed for fall 1980 tour.
March around the Dinner Table(?)
Medicine Sunday: Studio A, NY 5/10/65.★
Movin': United Western 2/4/81.★
No Shoes on My Feet: Basement Tapes.★
Oklahoma Kansas: Power Station 13/4/83.★
On a Rainy Afternoon: Basement Tapes.★
One Eyed Jacks: Karen Moynihan home-tape 5/60.★
One for the Road: Basement Tapes.★
One More Ride: Soundchecked at 1978 US shows.★
Over the Road: MacKenzie mss.
Positively Van Gogh: Denver hotel room tape 13/3/66.★
Preacher's Folly, The: MacKenzie mss.
Prison Station Blues: Power Station, NY 26/4/83.★
Reach Out: United Western 2/4/81.★
Red Travelin' Shoes: MacKenzie mss.
Repossession Blues: Rundown Studio 1/2/78.★
Ride This Train: Townhouse Studios 27–28/8/86.★
Rocking Chair: MacKenzie mss.
Round and Round: Beverly Theatre, LA rehearsal 23/5/84.★
See You Later Allen Ginsberg: Basement Tapes.
Shake: Farm Aid 22/9/85 + True Confessions Tour 1986.★
She's Not For You: Rehearsed for fall 1980 tour.★
Shirley Temple Don't Live Here Anymore: *Under the Red Sky* outtake.★
Singing This Song for You: United Western 2/4/81.★
Slow Try Baby: Power Station 13/4/83.★
Song to Bonny: Ms. in Bonnie Beecher's possession.
Spanish Song, The: Basement Tapes.
Strange Rain: Mentioned to Izzy Young as a song he composed 12/61.
Take It or Leave It: Soundchecked at 1978 US shows.★
Talkin' Hugh Brown: 1st Minneapolis Tape 9/60.★
Talkin' Hypocrite: Tony Glover home-tape 11/8/62.★
That California Side: Unassigned ms. published in Isis fanzine, c.1962.
There Ain't Gonna Be Any Next Time: *Blood on the Tracks* notebook.
This Way, That Way: Soundchecked at 1978 US shows.★
To Fall in Love with You: Townhouse Studios 27–28/8/86.★
Train of Pain: True Confessions Tour 1986.★
Try Me Little Girl: Basement Tapes.★

Under Control: Basement Tapes.★
V. D. Seaman's Last Letter: MacKenzie mss.
Where Do You Turn (Turning Point)?: *Blood on the Tracks* notebook.
Wiretappin': Rumored outtake from *Desire* 7/75.
You Can't Make It on Your Own (?)
You'd Love Me to Go: New Haven soundcheck 17/9/78.★

Bibliography

This is a bibliography of all the written source material, published and unpublished, that has been useful in the composition of this book. Because of the sheer size of the book already, and because exact notation of sources is of interest only to a small number of readers, I have chosen to make the full notes available on my website (www.andrew. homer.btinternet.co.uk/clinton) rather than fill up yet more pages herein. Alternatively, readers can write to me via my publishers for a hard-copy of the full notes. The bibliography is divided in six sections:

(i) Reference sources
(ii) Primary source material – published
(iii) Secondary source material – published
(iv) Unpublished and privately disseminated material
(v) Interviews with Dylan ultilized in *Behind the Shades*
(vi Interviews drawn from published periodicals

(i)

Dundas, Glen, *Tangled Up in Tapes* (SMA Services, 1999)
Heylin, Clinton, *Bob Dylan: The Recording Sessions* (St Martin's, 1995)
Heylin, Clinton, *Bob Dylan: A Life in Stolen Moments – Day By Day 1941–45* (Schirmer, 1996)
Krogsgaard, Michael, *A Dylan Sessionography* in *The Telegraph* 52–56; *The Bridge* 1

(ii)

Baez, Joan, *And a Voice to Sing With* (Summit Books, 1987)
Balfour, Victoria – *Rock Wives* (Beech Tree, 1986)
Boni, Claude-Angele, *Stuck Inside of Mobile (with a rhapsody for Bob Dylan)* (privately published)
Dylan, Bob, *Writings & Drawings* (Alfred Knopf, 1973)
Dylan, Bob, *Lyrics* (Alfred Knopf, 1985)
Engel, Dave, *Just Like Bob Zimmerman's Blues: Dylan in Minnesota* (Amherst Press, 1997)
Faithfull, Marianne, with Dalton, David, *Faithfull* (Michael Joseph, 1994)
Farina, Richard, *Long Time Coming and a Long Time Gone* (Random House, 1969)
Flannagan, Bill, *Written in My Soul* (Contemporary, 1986)

Fong-Torres, Ben, *Knockin' on Dylan's Door* (Straight Arrow, 1974)

Ginsberg, Allen, *First Blues* (Full Court Press, 1975)

Gross, Michael, *Bob Dylan: An Illustrated History* (Elm Tree, 1978)

Guralnick, Peter, *Careless Love: The Unmaking of Elvis Presley* (Little Brown, 1999)

Helm, Levon, with Davis, Stephen, *This Wheel's on Fire: Levon Helm and the Story of The Band* (Morrow, 1993)

Heylin, Clinton (ed.), *Saved! The Gospel Speeches* (Hanuman, 1990)

Kramer, Daniel, *Bob Dylan* (Castle Books, 1967)

Lawlan, Val, *Steppin' Out* (privately published)

Lee, C. P., *Like the Night: Bob Dylan and the Road to the Manchester Free Trade Hall* (Helter-Skelter, 1998)

Marcus, Greil, *Invisible Republic: Bob Dylan's Basement Tapes* (Picador, 1997)

McCartney, Paul with Miles, *Many Years from Now* (Secker & Warburg, 1997)

McLagen, Ian, *All the Rage* (Watson-Guptill, 2000)

Miles, Barry, *Ginsberg: A Biography* (Simon & Schuster, 1989)

Rawlins, Adrian, *Dylan Through the Looking Glass: A Collection of Writings on Bob Dylan* (privately published)

Rooney, Jim, and Von Schmidt, Eric, *Baby Let Me Follow You Down* (Anchor Books, 1979)

Scaduto, Anthony, *Bob Dylan* (Grosset & Dunlap, 1971)

Seay, Davin, and Neely, Mary, *Stairway to Heaven* (Ballantine, 1986)

Seeger, Pete, Introduction to *California to the New York Island* by Woody Guthrie (Oak Publications, 1960)

Simmons, Garner, *Peckinpah: A Portrait in Montage* (University of Texas Press, 1982)

Sloman, Larry, *On the Road with Bob Dylan* (Bantam Books, 1978)

Spitz, Bob, *Dylan: A Biography* (McGraw-Hill, 1988)

Thompson, Toby, *Positively Main Street* (Coward-McCann, 1971)

Webster, Patrick, *Friends & Other Strangers* (private publication)

Wexler, Jerry and Ritz, David, *Rhythm and the Blues: A Life in American Music* (Alfred Knopf, 1993)

Witts, Richard, *Nico: The Life and Lies of an Icon* (Virgin, 1993)

Woliver, Robbie, *Bringing It All Back Home* (Pantheon, 1986)

Worrell, Denise, *Icons* (Atlantic Monthly Press, 1989)

Zollo, Paul, *Songwriters on Songwriting* (Da Capo, 1997)

(iii)

Bauldie, John, *The Ghost of Electricity* (privately published)

Bauldie, John, and Gray, Michael (eds), *All Across the Telegraph* (Sidgwick & Jackson, 1987)

Bauldie, John (ed.), *Wanted Man: In Search of Bob Dylan* (Black Spring Press, 1990)

The Bible (King James version, 1611)

Bicknell, Alf, and Mars, Garry, *Baby, You Can Drive My Car* (privately published)

Bockris, Victor, *Patti Smith: An Unauthorized Biography* (Simon & Schuster, 1999)

Bowden, Betsy, *Performed Literature: Words and Music by Bob Dylan* (Indiana University Press, 1982)

Brady, Frank, *Citizen Welles* (Charles Scribner, 1989)

Bronson, Bertrand Harris, *The Ballad as Song* (University of California Press, 1969)

Burroughs, William, *Naked Lunch* (Flamingo, 1993)

Cable, Paul, *Bob Dylan: The Unreleased Recordings* (Dark Star, 1978)

Cantwell, Robert, *When We Were Good: The Folk Revival* (Harvard University Press, 1996)

Carroll, Jim, *Forced Entries* (Penguin, 1989)

Cartwright, Bert, *The Bible in the Lyrics of Bob Dylan* (Wanted Man Study Series, 1985)

Child, Francis, *English & Scottish Popular Ballads* (Houghton Mifflin, 1904)

Cohn, Nik, *Pop from the Beginning* (Weidenfeld and Nicolson, 1969)

Cooper, Chris, and Marsh, Keith *The Circus is in Town* (privately published)

Dallas, Karl *et al.*, *The Electric Muse: The Story of Folk into Rock* (Methuen, 1975)

Davis, Clive, *Clive: Inside the Record Business* (William Morrow, 1974)

Dawson, Jim, and Propes, Steve, *What was the First Rock 'n' Roll Record* (Faber and Faber, 1992)

Day, Aidan, *Jokerman: Reading the Lyrics of Bob Dylan* (Blackwell, 1988)

Dylan, Bob, *Tarantula* (Macmillan, 1970)

Dylan, Bob, *Drawn Blank* (Random House, 1994)

Garret, Pat F., *The Authentic Life of Billy, the Kid* (New Mexico Publishing Co., 1882)

Gilmore, Mikal, *Night Beat: A Shadow History of Rock & Roll* (Doubleday, 1998)

Goddard, Donald, *Joey: A Biography* (Harper & Row, 1974)

Goodman, Fred, *The Mansion on the Hill: Dylan, Young, Geffen, Springsteen, and the Head-on Collision of Rock and Commerce* (Random House, 1997)

Graham, Bill, with Robert Greenfield, *My Life Inside Rock and Out* (Dell, 1993)

Gray, Michael, Introduction to UK ed. of *Tarantula* (MacGibbon & Kee, 1971)

Green, Jonathon, *Days in the Life: Voices from the English Underground 1961–71* (William Heinemann, 1988)

Graves, Robert, *King Jesus* (Cassell, 1946)

Graves, Robert, *The White Goddess* (Faber, 1948)

Guthrie, Woody, *Bound For Glory* (E. P. Dutton, 1943)

Harris, Sheldon, *Blues Who's Who* (Da Capo, 1994)

Heylin, Clinton, *Bootleg! The Secret History of the Other Recording Industry* (St Martin's, 1995)

Heylin, Clinton, *Dylan's Daemon Lover: The Tangled Tale of a 450-year-old Pop Ballad* (Helter-Skelter, 1999)

Heylin, Clinton (ed.), *The Penguin Book of Rock & Roll Writing* (Viking, 1992)

Hinton, Brian, *Nights in Wight Satin: An Illustrated History of the Isle of Wight Pop Festivals* (Isle of Wight Cultural Services, 1990)

Holzman, Jac, with Gavan Daws, *Follow the Music: The Life and Times of Elektra Records in the Great Years of American Pop Culture* (First Media, 1998)

Kerouac, Jack, *On the Road* (Viking Press, 1957)

Kooper, Al, *Backstage Passes* (Stein & Day, 1971)

Ledeen, Jenny, *Prophecy in the Christian Era* (privately published)

Lindley, John, *Seven Days* (privately published)

Lindsey, Hal, *The Late Great Planet Earth* (Zondervan, 1970)

Lindsey, Hal, *Satan is Alive and Well on Planet Earth* (Zondervan, 1972)

Lomax, Alan, *Folk Songs of North America* (Doubleday, 1960)

Lomax, John and Alan, *Folksong USA* (Signet, 1966)

Mabey, Richard, *The Pop Process* (Hutchinson, 1969)

754 BIBLIOGRAPHY

Manso, Peter, *Brando* (Weidenfeld & Nicolson, 1994)

McGregor, Craig, *Bob Dylan: A Retrospective* (William Morrow, 1972)

Milne, Larry, *Hearts of Fire* (New English Library, 1987)

Nietzsche, Friedrich, *The Portable Nietzsche* (Viking, 1954)

Remnick, David, *King of the World* (Vintage Books, 1998)

Ribakov, Sy and Barbara, *Folk-Rock: The Bob Dylan Story* (Dell, 1966)

Rice, Anne, *The Vampire Lestat* (Alfred Knopf, 1985)

Rimbaud, Arthur, *Complete Works* (ed. Paul Schmidt) (Harper Colophon, 1976)

Williams, Paul, *Performing Artist* (Underwood-Miller, 1990)

Williams, Paul, *Performing Artist Vol. 2* (Underwood-Miller, 1992)

Williams, Paul, *Watching the River Flow* (Omnibus Press, 1996) [incorporates *What Happened?* and *One Year Later*]

Wurlitzer, Rudy, *Pat Garrett & Billy the Kid* (Signet, 1973)

(iv)

Anon., Shooting schedule for Hearts of Fire

Columbia Records (later CBS and Sony Records), Recording contracts pertaining to Bob Dylan 1961–93

Dylan, Bob, Song to Bonny (published in *Telegraph* 46), 1960

Dylan, Bob, Misc. lyrics written at the MacKenzies, *c.* 1961 (privately published in *In His Own Write – Personal Sketches Vol. 3*); as well as setlists and misc. published material, annotated

Dylan, Bob, Misc. MSS and typescript material, *c.* 1963, sold by Margolis & Moss auctioneers in 1988

Dylan, Bob, Letter to Lawrence Ferlinghetti, April 28, 1964

Dylan, Bob, Letters to Tami Dean, *c.* 1964 (published in *Telegraph* 16)

Dylan, Bob, Misc. MSS and typescript material, *c.* 1964, pertaining to the *Another Side of Bob Dylan* album

Dylan, Bob, A single page typescript with handwritten verse from 'Absolutely Sweet Marie', *c.* 1966

Dylan, Bob, A single page typescript with handwritten lyrics to 'Most Likely You Go Your Way', *c.* 1966 (published in *Lyle Price Guide: Film & Rock'n'Roll Collectibles*)

Dylan, Bob, Typescript for 'I'm Not There' (published in *Telegraph*)

Dylan, Bob, Handwritten MS for 'Tonight I'll Be Staying Here With You', 1969

Dylan, Bob, Lease on 21336 Pacific Coast Highway (signed), 1973

Dylan, Bob, *A Book of Dreams* (inc. *Planet Waves* sleeve-notes), 1974

Dylan, Bob, Notebook of seventeen songs intended for *Blood on the Tracks*, 1974

Dylan, Bob, Production notes for *Renaldo and Clara* film, circulated with press pack, 1978

Dylan, Bob, Tribute to Jimi Hendrix intended for public exhibition, 1988 (privately published in monograph titled *Writings*)

Dylan, Bob, Press release on death of Jerry Garcia, August 1995

Dylan, Bob, and Lennon, John, Conversation in limousine, May 1966 (transcribed in *Mojo* 1)

Dylan, Sara, Press release on instigating divorce proceedings, March 1977

Ginsberg, Allen, Journal *Rolling Thunder*, Oct. 28 to Nov. 15, 1975

Grossman, Albert, Estate papers, filed at county court offices, Kingston, NY

Hentoff, Nat, Original galleys to *Freewheelin'* sleeve-notes, 1963 (published in *Telegraph* 8)

Rosato, Arthur, Misc. papers pertaining to Dylan tours 1978–81

Ross, Susan, Proposal for *Oh Mercy – The Private Lives of Bob Dylan*, 1997

Shain, Britta Lee, MS of memoir on Dylan entitled *Seeing the Real You, At Last*, 1998

Shelton, Robert, Transcripts of interviews undertaken for bio with John Koerner, Jon Pankake, Paul Nelson, Beattie and Abraham Zimmerman (due to be serialized in *Isis*)

Wurlitzer, Rudy, *Pat Garrett & Billy the Kid* (actual shooting script)

Young Izzy, Diary entries for 1961–2 ref. *Dylan* (published in *Other Scenes*, December 1968)

Zimmerman, Robert, 'The Drunkard's Son' (published in *Isis* 44)

(v)

Anon., *Gargoyle*, February 1964

Anon., *New York Post*, 12/1/65

Anon., *Photoplay*, 1978

Anon., *El Diario Vasco*, 18/6/89

Adler, Philippe, *L'Expresse*, 3/7/78

Allen, Lynne, *Trouser Press*, June 1979

Aschenmacher, Bob, *Duluth News Tribune and Herald*, 29/6/86

Austin, John, Source unknown

Baker, Kathryn, *The Stars and Stripes*, 7/9/88

Bowles, Jennifer, *New York Post*, 1993

Bronstein, Martin, Canadian Broadcasting Company, 20/2/66

Brown, Bob, *20/20* TV show, 20/10/85

Brown, Mick, *Sunday Times*, 1/7/84

Bueno, Eduardo, *Telegraph*, 12/6/91

Burling, Klas, Swedish public radio, 29/4/66

Campbell, Mary, *Houston Post*, 12/2/78

Chase, Donald, *San Francisco Chronicle*, 23/11/86

Coburn, Bob, *Rockline* radio show, 17/6/85

Cohen, John, and Traum, Happy, *Sing Out*, October 1968

Cohen, Scott, *Spin*, December 1985

Cohen, Scott, Interviews, February 1986

Cott, Jonathan, *Rolling Stone*, 26/1/78

Cott, Jonathan, *Rolling Stone*, 16/11/78

Crane, Les, Transcript of TV show, 17/2/65

Creswell, Toby, *Australian Rolling Stone*, 16/1/86

Crowe, Cameron, *Biograph*, 1985

Damsker, Matt, *Circus Weekly*, 19/12/78

Deevoy, Adrian, *Q*, December 1989

De Yong, Jenny, and Roche, Peter, *Darts*, May 1965

Dolen, John, *Fort Lauderdale Sun-Sentinel*, 28/9/95

Ephron, Nora, and Edmiston, Susan, *A Restrospective*, ed. McGregor (see above, section iii)

Engleheart, Murray, *Guitar World*, March 1999

Flannagan, Bill, *Written in My Soul* (see above, section ii)

Flippo, Chet, *Rolling Stone*, 15/3/73

Fong-Torres, Ben, *Knockin' on Dylan's Door* (see above, section ii)

Gates, David, *Newsweek*, 6/10/97

Gilmore, Mikal, *Los Angeles Herald-Examiner*, 13/10/85

Ginsberg, Allen, *Telegraph* 33

Gooding, Cynthia, *Folksinger's Choice*, February 1962

Gundersen, Edna, *USA Today*, 21/9/89

Gundersen, Edna, *USA Today*, 14/9/90

Gundersen, Edna, *USA Today*, 5/5/95

Gundersen, Edna, *USA Today*, 29/9/97

Heiman, Bruce, KMEX radio, 7/12/79

Hentoff, Nat, *New Yorker*, 24/10/64

Hentoff, Nat, Original *Playboy* interview, 10/65 (privately published as the booklet *Whaaat!*)

Hentoff, Nat, *Playboy*, March 1966

Herman, Dave, *The London Interview* promo album, 1981

Hickey, Neil, *TV Guide*, 11/9/76

Hilburn, Robert, *Los Angeles Times*, 28/5/78

Hilburn, Robert, *Los Angeles Times*, 12/11/78

Hilburn, Robert, *Los Angeles Times*, 23/11/80

Hilburn, Robert, *Los Angeles Times*, 30/10/83

Hilburn, Robert, *Los Angeles Times*, 17/11/85

Hilburn, Robert, *Los Angeles Times*, 7/9/87

Hilburn, Robert, *Los Angeles Times* magazine, 9/2/92

Hilburn, Robert, *Los Angeles Times*, 14/12/97

Hill, Gary, Syndicated interview, 3/10/93

Hughes, Karen, *Rock Express* 1

Hughes, Karen, *Dominion*, 2/8/80

Iachetta, Michael, *New York Daily News*, 8/5/67

Jackson, Alan, *The Times* magazine, 15/11/97

James, Billy, Transcipt of Columbia promotional interview, December 1961

Jones, Max, *Melody Maker*, 23/5/64

Kaganski, Serge, *Mojo*, February 1998

Keller, Martin, *New Musical Express*, 6/8/83

Kerr, Barbara, *Toronto Sun*, 26–29/3/78

Kleinman, Bert, and Mogull, Artie, *Westwood One* broadcast, 25/11/84

Kot, Greg, *Chicago Tribune*, 1993

Loeder, Kurt, *Rolling Stone*, 26/6/84

McGregor, Craig, *Sydney Morning Herald*, 18/3/78

Mankiewicz, John, *Sound*, 12/11/78

Meer, Dan, *Close Up* radio show, 30/10/89

Merryfield, Mary, *Chicago Tribune*, 21/11/65

Oppel, Pete, *Dallas Morning News*, 18–23/11/78

Pareles, Jon, *New York Times*, 28/9/97

Queenan, Joe, *Spy*, August 1991

Quinn, Martha, MTV, 7/7/84

Robbins, Paul J., *Los Angeles Free Press*, 17 & 24/9/65
Rockwell, John, *New York Times*, 8/1/78
Rosenbaum, Ron, *Playboy*, January 1978
Rowland, Marc, US radio, 23/9/78
Saal, Hubert, *Newsweek*, 4/4/69
Scaduto, Anthony, *Bob Dylan* (see above, section ii)
Seeger, Pete, transcript of unbroadcast May 1962 WBAI radio show
Shelton, Robert, *Melody Maker*, 24/6/78
Shepard, Sam, *Esquire*, July 1987
Siegal, Jules, *Saturday Evening Post*, 30/7/66
Sloman, Larry, *On the Road with Bob Dylan* (see above, section ii)
Smith, Jack, *National Guardian*, 22/8/63
Spencer, Neil, *New Musical Express*, 15/8/81
Steen, Margaret, *Toronto Weekly*, 29/1/66
Stone, Allen, WDTM radio, 24/10/65
Sykes, Christopher, *Getting to Dylan*, BBC-TV, 18/9/87
Sykes, Christopher, Tour program, 1989
Terkel, Studs, *Wax Museum* radio show, 26/4/63
Turner, Gil, *Sing Out*, October 1962
Varadarajan, Tunku, *The Times*, 28/10/97
Various, Beverly Hills Hotel press conference, 4/9/65 (transcript)
Various, San Francisco press conference, 3/12/65 (transcript)
Various, Adelaide press conference, 21/4/66 (transcript)
Various, Travemunde press conference, 13/7/81 (transcipt)
Various, Sydney press conference, 10/2/86 (transcript)
Vincent, Paul, *Endless Road* 2
Vox, Bono, *Hot Press*, 24/8/84
Welles, Chris, *Life*, 10/4/64
Wenner, Jann, *Rolling Stone*, 29/11/69
Worrell, Denise, *Icons* (see above, section ii)
Yamamoto, Akihiko, *Crossbeat*, February 1994
Yurchenco, Henrietta, *Sound and Fury*, April 1966
Zollo, Paul, *Songtalk*, winter 1991 (reprinted in *Songwriters on Songwriting*, see above,
section ii)

(vi)

Dylan Fanzines:
The *Telegraph* (issues 1–56; now defunct): Colin Allen (28); Bonnie Beecher (36); Dave
Berger (43); Joel Bernstein (35); Ronee Blakely (41); Joe Boyd (31); Harvey Brooks
(47); Mike Campbell (25); Martin Carthy (42); Liam Clancy (18); Eric Clapton (36);
Dave Crosby (45); Ramblin' Jack Elliott (50); Terry Ellis (31); Mike Evans (46); Kinky
Friedman (42); Allen Ginsberg (20); John Hammond Jr. (44); Carolyn Hester (43); J. J.
Holliday (44); Mel Howard (46); Mickey Jones (55); Danny Kalb (47); Elliott Landy
(56); Daniel Lanois (34); Stan Lewis (45); Stan Lynch (25); Eve MacKenzie (56); Bob
Markel (52); Richard Marquand (28); Maria McKee (27); Chris Parker (33); D. A.
Pennebaker (16/26); Tom Petty (56); Ken Pitt (46); Charlie Quintana (37); Adrian

Rawlins (55); Mark Robinson (16); Pete Rowan (44); Iain Smith (28); Greg Sutton (27); David Was (44); Don Was (37); Dave Whitaker (26); Ronnie Wood (33); Tony Wright (43) and Izzy Young (56)
On The Tracks (issues 1–18): Ronee Blakely; John Bucklen (8); John Cohen (7); Rick Danko (10); Jim Dickinson (12); Bob Fass (13); John Hammond Jr. (9); Larry Keenan (14); Daniel Lanois (13); Jacques Levy (4); Bill Marinac (8); Charlie McCoy (8); Pat Mestek (8); D. A. Pennebaker (2); Katy Segal (5); Larry Sloman (2); Steven Soles (2), Eric Von Schmidt (4); Dave Whitaker (12)
Isis (issues 1–90): Duke Robillard (73); Jules Siegel and Cesar Diaz (83–85)
The Bridge (issues 1–4): Fred Tackett (3)
Zimmerman Blues (issues 1–10; now defunct): Nat Hentoff (6)
Endless Road (issues 1–7; now defunct): Helena Springs (7) and Eric Burdon (5)
Fourth Time Around (issues 1–4; now defunct): Ray Foulk (3) and David Oppenheim (2)
Occasionally (issues 1–5; now defunct): Emmylou Harris (5)

Other Periodicals

Alk, Howard, *Take One*, March 1978

Aronowitz, Al, *Village Voice*

Barton, Blaise, *Mix*, November 992

Baxter, Bucky, *Rolling Stone*

Bono, *New Musical Express*, 19 & 26/12/87

Brown, Charlie, *Rolling Stone*, 21/11/74

Cash, Johnny, *Musician*, May 1988

Clapton, Eric, *Rolling Stone*, 20/11/75

Coburn, James, London *Evening Standard*, 31/9/89

Collins, Mel, *Liquorice*, 1975

Cornelius, Ron, undated *Melody Maker*, 1971

Danko, Rick, *Woodstock Times*, March 1985

Dawson, Gordon, London *Evening Standard*, 31/9/89

Drummond, Tim, *Rolling Stone*, 29/8/74

Esmond, Paul, *Christianity Today*, 1983

Faithfull, Marianne, *Record Mirror*, 22/5/65

Fraboni, Rob, *Recording Engineer-Producer*, March–April 1974

Friedman, Steve, *Duluth Tribune*, 29/6/86

Garcia, Jerry, *Melody Maker*, 13/5/89

Gerrette, Rosemary, *Canberra Times*, 7/5/66

Gillespie, Dana, *News of the World*, 31/8/80

Gillespie, Dana, *British Blues Review*, February 1990

Ginsberg, Allen, *Ramparts*, March 1966

Ginsberg, Allen, *Melody Maker*, 18/3/72

Ginsberg, Allen, *Rolling Stone*, 15/1/76

Goddard, J. R., *Village Voice*, 26/4/62

Goldberg, Barry, *Crawdaddy*, July 1974

Gottlieb, Robert, *Crawdaddy*, September 1973

Green, Susan, *Burlington Review*, Fall 1998

Grossman, Sally, *Musician*, July 1987

Gulliksen, Ken, *Buzz*, November 1980

Haben, George, *Duluth Tribune*, 29/6/86

Hammond, John Sr., *Fusion*, 31/10/69

Hammond, John Sr., *Rolling Stone*, 21/11/74

Hart, Mickey, *Melody Maker*, 13/5/89

Helm, Levon, *Modern Drummer*, August 1984

Hester, Carolyn, *Goldmine*, 26/1/90

Hubbard, Neil, *Liquorice*, 1975

Hudson, Garth, *Musician*, July 1987

Kastel, Rabbi Kasriel, *Christianity Today*, 1983

Kristofferson, Kris, *Rolling Stone*, 15/3/73

Kristofferson, Kris, *Rolling Stone*, 23/2/78

Lanois, Daniel, *New Musical Express*, 7/10/89

Lanois, Daniel, *Request*, October 1989

Lennon, John, *Playboy*, 1980

Levy, Jacques, *Rolling Stone*, 7/4/77

Marinac, Bill, *Duluth Tribune*, 29/6/86

McCartney, Paul, *Mojo* 1

McCoy, Charlie, *Hit Parader*, October 1966

Nissenson, Jack, *Montreal Saturday Gazette*, 12/1/74

Petersen, Val, *Duluth Tribune*, 29/6/86

Petty, Tom, *The Leeds* magazine, November 1988

Prine, John, *Illinois Entertainer*, November 1981

Robertson, Robbie, *Hit Parader*, January 1967

Robertson, Robbie, *New Musical Express*, 17/6/78

Robertson, Robbie, *Crawdaddy*, March 1976

Ronson, Mick, *New Musical Express*, 15/12/79

Shelton, Robert, *Record Mirror*, May 1966

Shepard, Sam, *Rolling Stone*, December 1985

Sloman, Larry, *Music Video*, 1984

Soles, Steven, *New Musical Express*, 8/9/79

Spector, Phil, *Rolling Stone*, 2/3/72

Tench, Benmont, *Chicago Sun-Times*, 26/1/86

Vee, Bobby, *Duluth Tribune*, 29/6/86

Weissberg, Eric, *Rolling Stone*, 21/11/74

Wexler, Jerry, *Rolling Stone*, 27/11/80

Wilson, Tom, *Melody Maker*, 31/1/76

Wilson, Tom, *Fusion*, 31/10/69

Wurlitzer, Rudy, *Melody Maker*, 3/2/73

Wurlitzer, Rudy, *Rolling Stone*, 15/3/73

Yarrow, Pete, *Musician*, July 1987

Acknowledgments

This book is the culmination of some two decades writing about Dylan, initially as part of Wanted Man, the Bob Dylan Information Office, and for the last ten years as a biographer and chronicler, over a series of three books. With *Behind the Shades – Take Two* I return to the starting point, and so my thanks firstly go out to my fellow Wanted Man founders, the late John Bauldie, Dave Dingle and John Lindley.

The original edition of this book was written within the framework of Wanted Man, and utilized many of its resources. This new version relies far more heavily upon original interviews, and I wish to thank especially the following, for sharing their thoughts and memories: Kenny Aaronson, Dave Amram, Eddie Arno, Al Aronowitz, Ivan Augenblink, Bonnie Beecher, Joel Bernstein, Rich Bruyner, Stephanie Buffington, T-Bone Burnett, Ken Buttrey, Cesar Diaz, Barry Feinstein, Kim Fowley, Rob Fraboni, Dave Garfield, Bruce Gary, Ellen Gilbert, Mikal Gilmore, Allen Ginsberg, Tony Glover, Ira Ingber, Markus Innocenti, Billy James, Larry Johnson, Anthea Joseph, Jim Keltner, Tom Keylock, Sally Kirkland, Spider John Koerner, Al Kooper, Russ Kunkel, Bruce Langhorne, C. P. Lee, Murray Lerner, Peter MacKenzie, Dave Mansfield, Elliott Mazer, Faridi McFree, Roland Moussa, Paul Nelon, Adrian Rawlins, Jean Ritchie, Scarlet Rivera, Arthur Rosato, Pete Seeger, Joel Selvin, Rob Stoner, Mick Taylor, Anne Waldman, Winston Watson, Howie Wyeth.

I would also like to thank all the various friends and subscribers who have carried out interviews on my behalf, for *The Telegraph*, *On the Tracks*, *Isis* and/or other Dylan fanzines. It is they who have laid the groundwork for any kind of serious Dylan biography. Hope I've caught you all: Graham Barrett, John Bauldie, Andy Bell, Chris Cooper, Adrian Deevoy, Peter Doggett, Dave Engel, Roger Gibbons, Arne Hartelius, John Hinchey, Chris Hockenhull, Patrick Humphries, Joe Jackson, Larry Jaffe, Ake Johnson, Jon Kanis, Masato Kato, Reid Kopel, John Lattanzio, Val Lawlan, Spencer Leigh, Jorgen Lindstrom, Shelly Livson, Laurie McCuiston, Barry Miles, Jonathan Morley, Tony Norman, Stephen Pickering, Stephen Scobie, Wes Stace, Brian Stibal, Jacques Van Son, Brian Wells, Marcus Wittman.

I'd also like to extend *mucho gratias* for general help in my various attempts to document Dylan, for sharing thoughts and theories, for generosity with their archives and sheer hospitality to the following – deep breath!: Bill Allison, Rod Anstee, Graham Ashton, George Bailey, Bob Bettendorf, Victor Bockris, Dave Brazier, Bert Cartwright, Carlos Colon, Stuart Cope, Mike Decapite, Dalton Deilan, Norbert Dierks, Dave Dingle, Glen Dundas, Tim Dunn, Dave Engel, Susan Fino, Erik Flannigan, Roger Ford, Geoff Gans, Terry Gans, Sandy Gant, Fred Gardner, Simon Gee, Roger Gibbons, Joel Gilbert, Andy Goldstein, Fred Goodman, John Green, Dennis Grice, George H.,

Larry Hansen, John Hinchey, Nick Hill, Chris Hockenhull, Pete Howard, Rick Howell, Steve Keene, Ken Kieran, Robby King, Glen Korman, Harvey Kornhaber, Michael Krogsgaard, Val Lawlan, Mick Lawson, Tony Legge, Spencer Leigh, Richard Lewis, Denis Liff, John Lindley, Rod MacBeath, Greil Marcus, Blair Miller, Colin Moore, Harald Muller, Philipp Nicolet, Bill Pagel, Freddie Patterson, Rani Singh, Bob Strano, Dave Tulsky, Robert Van Estrick, Jacques Van Son, John Way, George Webber, Brian Wells, Rob and Lynne Whitehouse, Paul Williams, Ian Woodward, Shane Youl.

An especial thanks to five old friends who really pulled out the stops to help me access folks and files this time around: Joel Bernstein, Mitch Blank, Susie Decapite, Michelle Engert and Raymond Foye. Finally, thanks to David Bristow, Andy Muir, Peter Vincent, and Roy Whittaker for listening to all my Dylan-oriented rants, later toned down for print; to my long-suffering editor at Penguin, Tony Lacey, for duties above and beyond . . .; and to Ben Schafer at Morrow, who helped in so many ways to make this second take a reality (still hate the cover, though).

One and all, take that metaphorical bow!

Clinton Heylin, May 2000

Permissions

The publishers are grateful for permission to reprint the following copyright material:

Chapters 1–38

Inset

Index

refresh yourself at penguin.co.uk

Visit penguin.co.uk for exclusive information and interviews with
bestselling authors, fantastic give-aways and the
inside track on all our books, from the Penguin Classics
to the latest bestsellers.

BE FIRST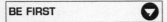

first chapters, first editions, first novels

EXCLUSIVES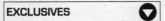

author chats, video interviews, biographies, special features

EVERYONE'S A WINNER

give-aways, competitions, quizzes, ecards

READERS GROUPS

exciting features to support existing groups and create new ones

NEWS

author events, bestsellers, awards, what's new

EBOOKS

books that click – download an ePenguin today

BROWSE AND BUY

thousands of books to investigate – search, try and buy the perfect gift online – or treat yourself!

ABOUT US

job vacancies, advice for writers and company history

Get Closer To Penguin . . . www.penguin.co.uk